M

28 DAY BOOK

DALTON TRUMBO

DALTON TRUMBO

Blacklisted Hollywood Radical

Larry Ceplair

and

Christopher Trumbo

 UNIVERSITY PRESS OF KENTUCKY

Scholarly publisher for the Commonwealth,
serving Bellarmine University, Berea College, Centre College of
Kentucky, Eastern Kentucky University, The Filson Historical Society,
Georgetown College, Kentucky Historical Society, Kentucky State
University, Morehead State University, Murray State University,
Northern Kentucky University, Transylvania University, University of
Kentucky, University of Louisville, and Western Kentucky University.
All rights reserved.

Frontispiece: Dalton Trumbo, 1959. Photograph by Cleo Trumbo.

Editorial and Sales Offices: The University Press of Kentucky
663 South Limestone Street, Lexington, Kentucky 40508-4008
www.kentuckypress.com

Cataloging-in-Publication data is available from the Library of
Congress.

ISBN 978-0-8131-4680-5 (hardcover : alk. paper)
ISBN 978-0-8131-4681-2 (epub)
ISBN 978-0-8131-4682-9 (pdf)

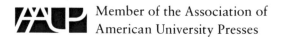

To Mitzi Trumbo and Nancy Escher,
for their unstinting support;
and to Christine Holmgren,
for her unwavering love.

Contents

Introduction

For the only thing
That makes sense in life
Is Struggle!
        —Dalton Trumbo

This was supposed to be Christopher Trumbo's book. He (and his two sisters, Nikola and Mitzi) knew Dalton Trumbo best. They experienced the blacklist period—their father's inquisition by the Committee on Un-American Activities, his imprisonment, the family's sojourn in Mexico, and fourteen years of aliases and fronts. Christopher had studied and thought about the subject for many years and had amassed a prodigious amount of research data, but the fates did not allow him the time he needed to complete the project. In December 2010, knowing he did not have much longer to live, he asked me to finish the book for him. He died a few weeks later, on January 8, 2011.[1] Thus, this has become my book, and he has become a reader over my shoulder.[2]

Christopher had been the subject of many interviews; in addition, he had recorded many of his ideas and thoughts, made copious notes, and composed a series of extended commentaries. He is quoted extensively throughout this book, and for the sake of clarity, his words are presented as quotations. What follows is an approximation of what he might have written by way of an introduction:

> For a long time, I stayed on the sidelines of the history of the blacklist. But in 1995 I decided I had better start taking charge of this, mostly because there was a lot that I knew that other people didn't, and I knew that my experience of the blacklist period was unique. My ideas first took shape in the form of a play I wrote to help raise money for a First Amendment–blacklist sculpture.[3] [That play, *Trumbo: Red, White and Blacklisted*, was first performed on November 24, 1997. Six years later it opened in New York City, directed by Peter Askin.

1

Askin then adapted it for his documentary film titled *Trumbo*. Christopher worked closely with him on both projects.][4]

The play succeeded in telling a particular kind of story, or the story in a particular way and had a particular kind of effect. The documentary film, though it covered the same time period, had a very different effect. You can do things with a documentary film that you can't do with a play. The same is true of a book, and I think a book about my father will finish off a lot of what I think is worthwhile knowing about him.[5] The book I have in mind will answer the questions people have about Trumbo, tell the story of his life, clear up the misconceptions, distortions, and lies that have accumulated over the years, and place him in proper context. It will straighten out the historical record, and it will include insights that can only be provided by somebody who knew him well. It will tell the story of a man who won a major book award [for *Johnny Got His Gun*], stood up to the House Committee on Un-American Activities, sacrificed a career for principle, gave to his foes as good as he got from them (and maybe then some), spent a year in prison for refusing to change his opinions, wrote the script [*Roman Holiday*] that would make Audrey Hepburn forever a princess in our minds, won two Academy Awards [*Roman Holiday* and *The Brave One*], and engineered the destruction of the Hollywood blacklist.

As he had done for the play, Christopher intended to use letters as the backbone of his book. The letters he used in the play were carefully selected "to balance the defeats Trumbo suffered. That he was writing humorous and graceful letters at the same time as he was handling all that other stuff gave the audience a larger picture of what he was like." Dalton Trumbo loved letters, and he wrote thousands of them. They were, in effect, Trumbo's journal, a means of keeping track of the important events and people in his life and the battles he fought. He kept copies of almost all those letters, and collectively, they provide the reader with an indelible image of Trumbo's place in the world he lived in.

Letters were also, for Trumbo, a form of amusement, a way to acknowledge the absurdities he saw all around him. He said: "If you can write an amusing letter, you know someone is going to laugh at it. And I like absurdity. And absurdity is rarely spontaneous. It takes constructing. Absurdity takes careful thought. My sense of the absurd is well developed."[6] It is clear that everything Trumbo wrote was carefully thought out; his archive is filled with notes, drafts, and multiple rephrasings of his ideas. According to Mitzi, "he never dashed off a letter, or even something as simple as a shopping list." Letters were for him an art form, a sort of haiku and performance. Indeed, from an early age, Trumbo consciously practiced language as performance.

The letters also provided him with a stage for his humor. "He was," Christopher recalled, "a very funny guy, and his was regularly the loudest voice in the room. People learned not to duel with him verbally, because he always put them away. His saving grace was that he was also very humorous about himself and his personal predicaments." (In an undated, handwritten note, Trumbo scribbled: "God put me in a position to make a fool of myself, but no one expected me to take such glorious advantage of it.")[7] Michael Wilson said at Trumbo's memorial, "One cannot understand the man unless one appreciates his mordant sense of humor."[8]

An understanding of Trumbo also requires an appreciation of the leitmotif of his adult life, which he identified in the cover letter that accompanied several dozen boxes of his papers he sent to the Wisconsin Center for Film and Theater Research in 1962:

> I've always thought of my life as a sequence of conflicts, each a separate battle, segregated in my mind under the heading, "My fight with these guys" or "My fight with those guys." In thinking back I now realize I have regarded each fight as distinct and unrelated to the other, and have sometimes marveled how one man could have so many of them. I now realize it was all one fight; that the relation of each to the other was very close; and I am really no more combative than any other man. It just happened in my case that the original fight once undertaken, expanded marvelously into what seemed like many fights and the most recent in a sequence of fights is actually no more than the current phase of the primary engagement.[9]

This "one fight" was stoked by Trumbo's radical definition of liberty. He probably would have agreed with James Harrington, writing three centuries earlier, when he explained why a commonwealth cannot invade the liberty of conscience of its citizens: "For the power that can invade the liberty of conscience can usurp civil liberty, and where there is a power that can usurp civil liberty, there is no commonwealth. To think otherwise is to measure a commonwealth by the overflowing and boundless passion of a multitude not by those laws or orders without which a free people can not otherwise have a course than a free river without the proper channel."[10]

Trumbo signified his fighting spirit in the epigraph he chose for his greatest political pamphlet, *The Time of the Toad* (1949): "The battle for one's legal rights is the poetry of character." He borrowed this phrase from Rudolph von Jhering, a nineteenth-century German legal theorist.[11] This phrase eloquently captured the nature of Trumbo's struggle against the Committee on Un-American Activities, and the book in its entirety reflected Trumbo's understanding of the meaning of rights and the concept of dignity. According to Jhering, a nation's legal system ultimately derives its strength from "the courageous and constant exercise of the feeling of right." When a person feels that his or her rights have been violated, or when a person feels slighted and morally pained, that person should experience a valid urge to resist. A person who chooses to defend his or her legal rights is participating in the work of strengthening the nation by contributing his or her "mite towards the realization of the idea of law on earth." This idea—that the source of all valid struggle is a visceral moral feeling—is one of Jhering's main themes: "The pain which a person experiences when his legal rights are violated is the spontaneous instinctive admission, wrung from him by force, of what the law is to him as an individual, in the first place, and then of what it is to human society." If that pain is transformed, in the individual's mind, into a universal principle of moral behavior, it lays the basis for a valid urge to resist and to act. If this feeling of pain at being wronged, of having one's moral principle transgressed, does not lead to an act of resistance, one's conscience will languish, become blunted, and become almost insensible to pain. According to Jhering, "irritability and action" are "the two criteria of a healthy feeling of legal right."[12] For most of his adult life, Trumbo was an exemplar of irritability in action.

Trumbo was a polarizing, unpredictable, unclassifiable person. Few who knew Trumbo were neutral about him. His barbed tongue and slashing pen drew blood from foe and friend alike. And once he became enraged and engaged, he proved to be a relentless adversary. "My father," Mitzi recalled, "could be so dominant, irascible and tenacious. He enjoyed confrontation; he never hesitated to jump into a dispute full throttle, and he rarely let anyone else win." He was not "a peaceful man, not at all agreeable, not one to step back from a fight." Charles White, a painter who lived next door to Trumbo for a number of years, said of Trumbo's humor: "Sometimes it is sardonic and biting and at other times light. He has a way of using it as a weapon that can be quite devastating. . . . He doesn't use sarcasm in a malicious way. . . . It's just there as a weapon to be used, so don't cross him."[13] Blacklisted director John Berry, who directed the short film made by the Hollywood Ten just before they went to prison as well as one of Trumbo's black-market scripts (*He Ran All the Way*), told biographer Bruce Cook: "He's a mean fuckin' mother to have on the other side."[14] Stephen Fritchmann, minister of the First Unitarian Church in Los Angeles, said at Trumbo's memorial: "He could with a sentence pin an apostate to human dignity to the wall."[15] And Donald Sutherland, who worked with Trumbo in the anti–Vietnam War movement and acted under his direction in *Johnny Got His Gun*, said: "Dalton was a contrarian; he had fights. I'm just glad he never had fights with me."[16]

"My father," Mitzi told me, "enjoyed antagonizing people, hunting for a debate, an argument, something new and different. He was restless, mentally and physically; he was not at ease with or interested in peace and quiet. He constantly challenged people. He filled up every room he was in. He was bigger than everyone else, and if someone tried to be bigger than he, that person usually failed. He was both an extremely difficult and extremely good man. He had enormous personal charm and was extraordinarily loyal to his family and his friends." Ring Lardner Jr.'s son, Joe, told me: "Trumbo tended to see the world in an agonistic way. He seemed to see everything personally, emotionally, even those worldly situations that others would try to be detached about. He invested himself personally in whatever he did."[17] And yet, during the domestic cold war, when friendships and families were shattering and meanness stalked the land, Trumbo proved to be both generous and compassionate.

Trumbo's combativeness was a late development. Endowed by nature with a powerful libido, and driven to succeed by his family's circumstances, the teenaged Trumbo was tightly wound, rebellious, and prone to outbursts of temper, yet desirous of pleasing adults. Possessed of a quick mind and a quicker tongue, he developed a distinctive voice and an extensive vocabulary as a way to vault himself above the mundane aspects of his home and school lives and forge his own way forward. In the articles he wrote in the 1930s, language was a powerful weapon in his hands. When he became a reader and a screenwriter and a guild organizer, he came into contact with many other rapier-like talkers and began to joust with them. By the early 1940s, verbal combativeness had become an integral part of his identity. This was intensified by thirteen years of blacklisting, imprisonment, foreign living, and black-market writing. Several years into his life on the blacklist, Trumbo's notion of dignity widened beyond that discussed by Jhering to include his personal, professional, and political reputation. He ceased to make qualitative distinctions between large and small affronts and reacted strongly to both types.

Though screenwriting was his vocation, and though he is far better known for his movie screenplays than for most of his other writings (the one exception being the novel *Johnny Got His Gun*), his scripts do not define him; they do not exhibit the full extent of his writing skills or reflect his qualities as a radical political thinker. Trumbo possessed a formidable intelligence that is not necessarily reflected in his movie work. That is why this book focuses on his life, his struggles, and his ideas. It reveals how his writing skills developed, and it notes the problems certain scripts presented to him. But, with the exception of *Spartacus* and *Johnny Got His Gun*, no extensive analysis of the plots, characters, and dialogue of his work is attempted.[18] Essentially, the thesis of this book is that Trumbo was, at heart, a political person who also happened to write movie scripts.

This book, then, is the story of a radical who was, for much of his life, a writer. Dalton Trumbo was not born a radical, nor did he undergo a sudden conversion. During his youth and early adulthood, he was exposed to a variety of radicalizing and reactionary events and ideas, from which he developed a particular mode of radical thinking and a reservoir of radical thoughts. That reservoir fed a political credo that coincided, at certain times, with communism.[19] But when he marched alongside Communists, it was never as an apparatchik, an automaton, or a robotic follower of dogma. According to Paul Jarrico, who met him at RKO in the late 1930s, "Trumbo was certainly the most original, the most flamboyant, the most unique [of the leftists I have known]. . . . He chose the unpopular side; he was a renegade, a maverick."[20]

This "maverick" does not, of course, fit the stereotypical image created by anti-Communists, for whom Trumbo was and remains a bête noire. As is their wont, anti-Communists have not examined the reasons behind or the context of Trumbo's decisions to join (twice) and leave (twice) the Communist Party. Rather, they assume that Trumbo's membership in the party tells them all they need to know about his politics. They filter the man through his party membership, rather than his party membership through the man; they stereotype and characterize party members as people who think and respond robotically; and they cram Trumbo into that mold. These critics have methodically perused the writings of his pre– and post–party membership years, looking for clues to the "Communist Trumbo," and they cherry-pick his scripts for "Communist" material. They refuse to accept the possibility that Trumbo's political ideas continually evolved and that a non-Communist leitmotif underlay his political thinking and acting. They fail to understand that the "redness" of Trumbo's ideas, at any particular time, must be carefully analyzed and that Trumbo's Communist Party membership was only a small part of a much larger life. In sum, they refuse to acknowledge that Trumbo's Communist affiliation reflected only one aspect of the man and only one episode in his life, and that party membership is an inexact guide to the entirety of any person's beliefs, thoughts, or behavior.

In his entirety, Trumbo was paradoxical: predictably unpredictable. One of his closest friends, Ring Lardner Jr., probably offered the best overall description when he spoke at Trumbo's memorial:

> At rare intervals there appears among us a person whose virtues are so manifest to all, who has such a capacity for relation to every sort of human being, who so subordinates his own ego drives to the concerns of others, who lives his whole life in such harmony with the prevailing standards of the community, that he is revered and loved by everyone with whom he comes in contact. Such a man Dalton Trumbo was not. . . . I think it's quite possible he antagonized as many people as he attracted. . . . No one I've known can more aptly be described by the word "fascinating," but a word of almost opposite meaning— "abrasive"—belongs in the description, too. So do a good many other adjectives, including wise, funny, greedy, generous, vain, biting, solicitous, ruthless, tender hearted, devious, contentious, altruistic, superbly rational, prophetic, shortsighted and absolutely indefatigable. . . . He lived at least three normal lives—a sheer outpouring of energy so disproportionate to the intake of fuel as to transcend the laws of physics.[21]

His energy was clearly the most defining aspect of his presence. According to Mitzi, he projected a powerful "personal magnetism. People were absolutely drawn to him, especially young people. I remember people sitting on the floor surrounding his chair to talk to him." And yet, physically, he was rather ordinary. He stood five feet nine inches tall and weighed about 150 pounds. Mitzi described him as being "neither heavy nor slim, of average build and weight. His legs were extremely strong. He was pale, freckled on his arms and legs. He developed a slight paunch in his sixties, but he was never flabby." (An FBI report, circa 1940, noted that Trumbo had brown eyes, brown hair, and a light complexion.)[22]

He almost always wore a mustache. (On two occasions—during his trip to the Pacific war zone and for a short period in the mid-1960s—he wore a beard. He was clean-shaven in 1950 when he went to prison.) He periodically changed the shape and style of his mustache, going from a pencil-thin one in the 1930s to one that was bushier, carefully shaped, and, of course, whiter. He was very fastidious about his mustache. "He shaved every morning," Mitzi said, "and he had a little comb for his mustache. Once, he became annoyed that nobody had noticed a change he had made in his facial hair."

In terms of his dress, Mitzi told me: "He was quite dapper—he ordered expensive suits and dress shirts from London and always wore a stylish red or white silk handkerchief in the jacket pocket. But around the house, especially during the last decade of his life, he loved wearing one-piece zippered jumpsuits in all materials. He had over a dozen of them, including a red velvet one for Christmas. His ever-present cigarette was usually in a black cigarette holder. He wore the same dark-rimmed glasses until the last two or three years of his life."

Trumbo had a distinctive voice, which he once described as having a "fruity quality."[23] It was slightly higher-pitched than most, and he spoke in a cultivated, thoughtful manner, enunciating his words precisely. In both his private correspondence and his public appearances, his sentences and paragraphs were carefully constructed.

Perhaps the most interesting aspect of Trumbo's life was his ability to live comfortably with his contradictions, like Albert Camus's "absurd man," who preferred "his courage and his reasoning" to nostalgia for a unified, noncontradictory, comprehensible world.[24] Though Trumbo remained faithful to certain ideals (liberty, justice, fairness, untrammeled free speech), he did not boast of being a consistent thinker about them. He abhorred orthodoxy in himself and others. He once said: "I do not think there have been more than ten minutes of consistency in my life, because it is so hard to be consistent, which means unchanging."[25] And yet he was, in the opinion of blacklisted screenwriter John Bright, "the most unhypocritical man I have known in a town of hypocrites. A strictly no-bullshit character in a town of bullshitters."[26] Though Trumbo occasionally regretted this or that decision, he was neither a torn nor a divided soul. He did not, that is, go through life haunted by Marley's ghost, but rather spurred by three spirits from ancient Greece: Agon (contest), Thrasos (boldness), and Dikē (moral order and fair judgment).

Larry Ceplair

1

Under Western Skies

Until he was twenty, he was centered in Colorado. His sensibility is western. His politics were local, based on ideas of land, independence, and individualism. He had an idea of the West as an open place, where people can reach agreements.

—Christopher Trumbo

Dalton Trumbo was an authentic American of a special breed. Only a country predominantly free but scarred by episodic periods of ugly repression could have produced so extraordinary a figure.

—Phil Kerby

No region of the United States is more American than the West. It is no accident that one of the most enduring movie genres in history is the western. Thus, for someone like Dalton Trumbo, who was born and raised in the West, to be labeled "un-American" was noteworthy. Indeed, in terms of family lineage and history, no family was more American than the Trumbos, or, as Trumbo described himself: "Native-born. One hundred percent. True blue." His father's family came from Switzerland, where they called themselves the Von Trummelbachs, after a local waterfall. But when their name was recorded by Swiss officials, it became Trumbach. Forced to flee Switzerland owing to a false accusation, the family moved to Alsace-Lorraine, where their name was recorded as Trumbeau. In 1730, again on the run, they immigrated to Virginia, where it became Trumbo.[1]

In a biographical sketch he wrote for Lippincott, publisher of the first edition of *Johnny Got His Gun*, Trumbo stated: "My first American ancestor of whom I have any knowledge was one Jacob Trumbo, a mixture of Swiss and French, who arrived in 1730 and settled in Virginia."[2] H. Jacob Trumbo married a woman named Mary, and they had seven children; he died sometime around 1783, in Virginia. One of his sons, John, was born in 1745, eventually moved to Pennsylvania, and had eleven children. John Jr. was born in 1770. He married Rebecca Dye, and they had at least ten children; they moved to Ohio at some point. One of their sons, John, was born in 1816 and later married Jane Prouty. They moved to Noble County, Indiana, where he was a justice of the peace for twenty-one years. One of their sons, John James, was born in 1851; he was Trumbo's paternal grandfather.[3] The maternal branch of his family—the Tillerys—emigrated from Scotland, settled in Virginia, then moved to Kentucky and later to Missouri. During the Civil War, the Trumbos fought with the Northern armies and the Tillerys with the Confederacy.

The Tillerys were a close-knit family, and Trumbo was, according to Mitzi, more a Tillery than a Trumbo. "We children never knew any Trumbos, but the Tillerys were very much in our lives," Mitzi recalled. "My father adored his aunts, Elsie and Myrtle, and hired his uncle Tom to work at the ranch. The Tillery women were funny, rowdy, and strong, and my father grew up in their boisterous midst" in Montrose and Grand Junction, Colorado. Montrose is a small city located in the Uncompahgre Valley, between the Gunnison River and the Black Canyon of the Gunnison National Monument, sixty-seven miles south of Grand Junction. It was founded in 1882, along the newly laid tracks of the Denver and Rio Grande Railroad; its name came from Sir Walter Scott's novel *The Legend of Montrose*.

Grand Junction, sometimes referred to as the jewel of the Grand Valley, is situated on the western slope of the Rocky Mountains, at the confluence of the Gunnison and Upper Colorado Rivers. It lies 4,856 feet above sea level and is surrounded by beautiful geological formations: the majestic Bookcliff mountains in the north, the colorful Mesa range of the Colorado National Monument to the west, and the San Juan mountains to the south. Those mountains, wrote David Sundal, "are sheltering and beautiful. The Monument has its majestic cliffs of red and ochre. The Bookcliffs can be lit by the westering sun with deep roses and dusky blues. The Grand Mesa is a broad azure silhouette, mantled with snow in winter. On our horizons, sunrise and sunset can be flaming with color."[4] Trumbo described the city's vistas in a different but equally vivid manner:

The Colorado River meandered through the valley, a treacher-
ous sluggard intent upon its rendezvous with the Green beyond
the state border. In August it was yellow oil fringed with pale
cottonwoods, willows, sweet clover—all its majesty turned
sickly from the spending of turbulent spring passions. North of
it lay green fields and pleasant orchards laved with ditch water,
fading fifty or sixty miles beyond into lofty mountain pastures.
But to the south of the river stretched an empty desolation con-
tested only by hard-bitten squatters, serried with canyons and
fantastic horrors in rock, tinted with red from decayed sand-
stone, thirsting for moisture which never came.[5]

Originally part of the Spanish Empire, western Colorado became
part of Mexico in 1821 and was ceded to the United States in 1848 by
the Treaty of Guadalupe-Hidalgo. At that point, it was the homeland
of the Ute tribe, but the end of the Civil War and the completion of the
transcontinental railroad brought land-hungry settlers to the region,
and in 1881 Congress legitimized the area for settlement by Anglos.
The first settlers mainly grew crops and raised livestock to feed the mining towns in the surrounding mountains. Later, farmers planted peach
trees and sugar beets, and in 1899 a group of Grand Junction entrepreneurs built Colorado's first sugar factory. But the most significant economic move made by the town leaders was to convince the Denver and
Rio Grande Railway to build a line connecting Grand Junction with
the silver towns of Glenwood Springs, Red Cliff, and Aspen and, later,
to build its maintenance shops and roundhouse in Grand Junction. As
a result, Grand Junction became an entrepôt, providing goods and services for the entire valley.[6]
    The region was also fertile ground for political dissent, and a vari-
ety of reform and third-party movements sprang up there, including
the Greenback-Labor Party, Prohibition Party, Union-Labor Party, and
Independent Party; various farmers' groups; the Women's Christian
Temperance Union; and a suffrage organization (women were given the
right to vote in Colorado in 1893). In Grand Junction, two labor unions
were established in 1886: the Knights of Labor and the International
Brotherhood of Locomotive Engineers. But the most significant political movement arose during the economic depression of the 1890s, when
Coloradans organized the People's Party to fight the tyranny of eastern bankers and the government corruption that threatened to destroy
democracy in the United States. In the 1892 election, the People's Party

candidate for president, James Weaver, won 57 percent of the vote in Colorado; in 1896, William Jennings Bryan, the candidate of the fused Democratic and People's Parties, won 85 percent of the vote; and in 1900, Bryan, now simply the Democratic candidate, won 56 percent of the Colorado vote.[7] When Trumbo was a boy, his father took him to hear Bryan speak. But by then, the more moderate Progressive movement had won control of Colorado politics and inaugurated a series of municipal reforms.

There were four people who played important roles in Trumbo's formative years. One was his maternal grandfather, Millard Fillmore Tillery, who impressed the young Trumbo with his bravery, independence, westernness, and kindness. Also influential were his parents—his father for his integrity and honesty, and his mother for her courage, tough-mindedness, ambition, and fearlessness. The fourth was Walter Walker, publisher of the *Grand Junction Daily Sentinel* newspaper, who encouraged, inspired, and supported Trumbo's ambition to become a writer.

Tillery was born in Clinton County, Missouri, on May 12, 1857. His father, who rode with John Hunt Morgan's Confederate raiders, died from wounds in February 1863. Young Millard grew up and worked in northwestern Missouri until about 1880, when he decided to head west. He arrived in Gunnison, Colorado, the following year and took a job as a track layer on the Denver and Rio Grande Railroad. By the time the tracks and Tillery reached Montrose, he owned four horses and decided to buy land and raise cattle there.[8] He returned to Missouri in 1884 and married Huldah Catherine Beck, who was three years older and of Irish descent. They lived in Gower for three years, and Huldah gave birth to two children (Maud in 1885 and Thomas in 1887). The family then moved to Colorado, where three more children (Myrtle, Harry, and Elsie) were born. In the ensuing years, Tillery was elected sheriff and appointed town marshal; he also helped organize the Montrose County Cattle and Horse Growers Association.[9]

Trumbo's admiration for his maternal grandfather, whom he regarded as the quintessential westerner, percolated throughout his life. Trumbo described Tillery as "a grand old man who cleared the land, fought in the cattle-sheep wars, put in twelve years as a sheriff when fast shooting and hard riding were essential, and is still hale enough to enjoy any slight triumph his grandson might render him." He wanted the dedication to *Eclipse*, his first published novel, to read: "To my pioneer grandparents, Millard and Huldah Tillery" (for reasons unknown, the publisher did not include it.)[10]

Dalton Trumbo, age three, with his mother (Maud) and his maternal
grandparents (Millard and Huldah Tillery), 1908. Courtesy of Trumbo family.

Trumbo's paternal grandfather, John James Trumbo, was a very
different sort of man. Born in Richland County, Ohio, on December
16, 1851, he was, Trumbo wrote, an "old-line hard-shell-Baptist American." He married Sarah Martha Bonham on August 5, 1873, and their
only child, Orus, was born in 1874 in Albion, Indiana. "My father,"
Trumbo recounted, "went to 'Normal School' after high school, got
his teacher's certificate along with the wanderlust, and came to Montrose, Colorado, where he was determined to make his fortune as a bee-
keeper. The bees didn't do well, so [in 1903] he became a grocery clerk
and married my mother." According to Grand Junction historian Dave
Fishell: "Orus had no clear ambition, spent lots of time reading books,
and took whatever job came along. Maud, in contrast, grew up used to
hard work on her father's Cimarron ranch, used to having handcuffed
[?] outlaws spend the night in the ranch house before her father hauled
them off to jail. She was tough and durable, and had a definite idea of
what the future should bring." After they married, Orus and Maud
lived in a small apartment above the Montrose Public Library. Maud
suffered a miscarriage but subsequently, after a difficult delivery, gave
birth to James Dalton on December 9, 1905.[11]

In 1908 the family moved to Grand Junction, where Orus hoped
to find a better-paying job. Four years later, Orus and Maud bought
a house at 1124 Gunnison Avenue with a living room, a kitchen (one
faucet for cold water), a canvassed-in sleeping porch (where Trumbo
slept for the next twelve years), and an outdoor privy.[12] Their house was
considered out of town, and it was surrounded by empty dirt lots. Two
other children, Catherine (1912) and Elizabeth (1916), were born there.

In Trumbo's semiautobiographical novel *Johnny Got His Gun*, Joe
Bonham's parents are, to a significant degree, modeled on Orus and
Maud Trumbo:

> [They] never had much money but they seemed to get along all
> right. They had a little house set far back on a long wide lot
> near the edge of town. In front of the house there was a space
> of lawn and between the lawn and the sidewalk his father had
> a lot of room for gardening. People would come from all over
> town to admire his father's garden. His father would get up
> at five or five-thirty in the mornings to go out and irrigate the
> garden. He would come home from work in the evenings eager
> to return to it. The garden in a way was his father's escape
> from bills and success stories and the job at the store. It was his
> father's way of creating something. It was his father's way of
> being an artist.
>
> At first they had lettuce and beans and peas and carrots and
> beets and radishes. Then his father got permission from the
> man who owned the vacant lot next door to use it for garden-
> ing space also. . . . So on the vacant lot his father raised sweet
> corn and summer squash and cantaloupes and watermelons
> and cucumbers. He had a great hedge of sunflowers around it.[13]

On one side of the vacant lot Orus had six stands of bees, and in the
backyard of their house he kept chickens and rabbits.

Orus Trumbo was an intelligent, educated, sensitive, informed, and
hardworking man. All the young men of Grand Junction liked Orus,
probably because he liked them. He was not, however, ambitious, and
he was not successful in the conventional, material sense. In Grand
Junction he worked at several different jobs before becoming a shoe
salesman at Benge's Shoe Store.[14] He also oversaw the Mesa County
Credit Association and served as a town constable. In *Johnny*, Joe's
father (based on Orus) "always ran unopposed, on both tickets, and

received only fees for particular jobs. He owned an Excelsior single cylinder motorcycle, with a belt drive. He used it to fulfill his constable duties. That he was a bad collector seemed pretty obvious because he was so easy on those who were presumed by law to be his victims. He had an American flag, which he always displayed on national holidays, and he helped raise money for the Chautauqua lecture circuit."[15]

"My father," Trumbo later wrote, "was a much braver man than I, in that, with very little money, he cheerfully assumed the responsibilities of parenthood; while I assumed those same responsibilities with what would have been to him a princely income. . . . [But] he was predestined from the start to have a much more difficult time than I." In *Johnny Got His Gun*, Trumbo refers to Joe's father as a failure. Christopher, however, noted: "Orus was not a failure; he just was not a smashing success. The family's life was not easy, and they were always close to the edge financially, but he managed to provide for his family, buy a house for them to live in, and send his son to college for one year. Though Trumbo admired successful men, he also respected and admired his father, because Orus had principles and he thought about things." As a result of that respect, Trumbo was determined not to displease his father, and when he did something wrong, he inevitably tried to deny responsibility for it: "I was not afraid because of any physical punishment he might inflict—but because I dreaded to see him—or rather the expression on his face—when he was hurt by anything I had done."

Orus was probably most disappointed by his son's lack of interest in sports. Dalton remembered that his father was always late coming home because he had stopped to play baseball or volleyball. Orus encouraged his son to be an athlete, and finally, in his senior year of high school, Dalton joined the football team. But, he recalled, "I was a very bad player, and I would only tackle someone from behind. They gave me a letter, but I returned it. Both my father and grandfather wanted me to be a very masculine athletic kind of boy. They even conferred special nicknames upon me—nicknames which really made no sense aside from the fact that they sounded masculine—in order to encourage me along this course."

Trumbo did, however, take after his father in three key respects. Orus had a passion for reading and language, and he was a precise and articulate speaker. He read the *Saturday Evening Post*, *Physical Culture Magazine*, the novels of Harold Bell Wright, and Finley Peter Dunne's "Mr. Dooley" columns.[16] In addition, he had read all of Charles Dickens's novels and all of Shakespeare's plays. On the day of his marriage, he had bought a complete set of Shakespeare's works (something he thought every house should have), from which he regularly quoted. Orus also told his son that every household should contain a copy of the Bible. Both Christopher and Mitzi commented on their father's love of the stories and poetry in the Bible. "His great love," Mitzi told me, "was the Song of Solomon; he loved the rich sensuousness of the verses."

Orus was also a very proud man, and pride made a deep impression on the young Dalton. After being called a sissy in the fifth grade, Trumbo became, in his words, "a very wild boy." He put sawdust in the school fountain and in girls' pockets, hurled books through windows, and tied cans of rocks to window shades. He did not tell his parents the reason for his misbehavior because he was too ashamed, or too full of pride. In this, he was like his father, whose pride was "so great that he could never accept defeat. He considered anything of that sort a disgrace. My pride was equally great."

Finally, Orus insisted that all people be treated equally and courteously. Although there were only a few black people in Grand Junction, and no racial segregation, Trumbo recalled:

In our house the word *nigger* was never spoken, and whoever used it, guest, employee, friend or relative, was sternly corrected.[17] The word *girl* and *boy* for Negroes was never corrected because it was never used, and, I suspect, not even known in that context. There were *hired girls* who, at about forty, became *hired women*. There were *hired men*. But all the hired girls, hired women and hired men were whites. In the very rare instance when a well-to-do white family employed a female Negro, she was never called girl or hired girl or hired woman. Whether she was cook, nurse or laundress, she was always called *the maid*. It was considered ritzier that way. So I did not grow up with the burden of the words *boy* and *girl* as terms of opprobrium for Negroes upon the consciousness, and I have never been aware of them.

When I was in the second grade I became the friend of a Negro classmate. I asked him home to dinner. It did not occur to me to ask my mother in advance if I could bring a Negro. Actually, I presume I was not educated to the point where I considered him a Negro or anything else other than a boy. When we arrived home he was very shy. He was greeted as pleasantly as any other of my friends by my mother and father, but still he was shy. He wanted to go home. He wouldn't say why. Finally my mother solved the problem. She put a special card table in the living room and served dinner there to him and me, while she and my father and my baby sister ate together in the dining room. My friend was content and we ate together happily. I remember our table was decorated with special paper doilies. The meaning of this scene I shall not speculate upon. He did not remain my friend long, because his parents moved away from town a few weeks later. *This was not considered an historic event in our family.*

One afternoon when I was about fourteen, I was running down the sidewalk on Main Street trying to catch up with three friends who were half a block ahead. Coming toward me was a Negro woman whom I knew named Mrs. Lennox. As I ran past her I said, "Hello Mrs. Lennox" without stopping, and ran on. About two hundred yards farther on I felt a hand on my shoulder. It came down on my shoulder hard. I stopped and looked up into the angry face of my father, who had been standing in the recessed entrance to the shoe store in which he was a clerk, and had seen my encounter with Mrs. Lennox. He said: "You passed Mrs. Lennox and spoke to her and you didn't tip your cap. Don't ever let me see you do that again. Now start around the block, running just as fast as you can, and you'll be able to meet Mrs. Lennox again before she reaches the end of the block. Say 'hello' to her and tip your cap! If you can't meet her in this block, then run two blocks and meet her in the next." Which I did.[18]

For whatever reason, in *Johnny Got His Gun* (both the book and the movie), Trumbo's portrayals of Maud are significantly shorter than those of Orus and lack the same depth of feeling. Perhaps that was because Maud was still alive, or perhaps Trumbo simply did not know how to describe her. Joe's mother (based on Maud) is depicted mainly as working in the kitchen: "Every autumn, his mother worked from day to day and from week to week scarcely ever getting out of the kitchen. She canned peaches, cherries, raspberries, blackberries, plums, and apricots, and she made jams, jellies, preserves, and chili sauces. And while she worked she sang the same hymn, over and over, in an absent voice, without words, as if she were thinking of something else all the while."[19]

According to Mitzi, "Maud was not at all the passive figure of [Mrs.

Bonham in] *Johnny.* She was the power in the family, the driving force. She believed her son was destined for greatness, and she pushed and pushed him as a child and as an adult. He felt as strong a need to live up to her expectations as he felt to live up to his father's." And though he later referred to her as "indomitable" and told her, "I have had rather phenomenal luck in being born of you," there was often enormous friction between them.[20] He regularly flouted her rules and prohibitions, especially those regarding drinking and smoking.[21]

When Dalton was about ten years old, Maud attended a Christian Science lecture and became a devotee. The Church of the Christ, Scientist, was one of several new Christian movements (premillenarianism, social gospel, ethical culture, mind cure) vying to replace the steadily weakening old-line Protestant churches. It attracted most of its members from the educated middle class, those who were "civic-minded and moderately progressive in their politics."[22] Its central doctrines were physical healing, redemption from sickness, and salvation of the body and soul.[23]

Orus did not join the church, but he and the children attended services with Maud every Sunday. Trumbo later told Bruce Cook that for him, Christian Science "was fact. I was never touched by a doctor until well into my twenties. . . . [I]t was an excellent religion in which to be raised, because you were taught that fear was the cause of human ills. . . . It's really lack of a sense of fear that Christian Science gives many people. And this is a very healthy thing to have." Whereas Trumbo approved of his mother's battles against school vaccinations, his sister Catherine was embarrassed. She told Cook: "That was humiliating as a child—not to be able to stand in line and get vaccinated with the rest of the kids in your class."[24]

There is no indication that Trumbo read any of the works of Mary Baker Eddy, the founder of the Church of the Christ, Scientist, nor that he took seriously the theology, metaphysics, or methodology of the religion. But he clearly imbibed Eddy's injunction: "'Be not afraid!' . . . To succeed in healing, you must conquer your own fears."[25] And, like most of the church's adherents, Trumbo fervently believed in the First Amendment's guarantee of free exercise of religion and challenged the so-called overriding interests of the state to regulate that exercise.

Trumbo did not remember Grand Junction as a politically radical city or himself as harboring radical thoughts. The city seemed rather conservative to him, "geared as naturally to patriotism, to success, to education, to marriage, to family, and a decent funeral as any town can be."[26] Neither of Trumbo's parents belonged to any political organization. When they met, Orus voted Republican and Maud Democratic. But in 1916 Orus voted for Democrat Woodrow Wilson because he pledged to keep the United States out of the war. Maud started to vote Republican in 1920.

Trumbo later described his early years in Grand Junction:

> [They] gave me so many pleasures and privileges. . . . To see a cow and perhaps even to milk it; to see chickens and pigs and sheep and not find them strange; to swim naked in an irrigation canal; to fish in Kannah Creek or on Grand Mesa; to pick strawberries and cherries and apples in season; to see plowed fields and growing crops; to raise vegetables in one's own back yard; to have cats and a dog; to walk barefoot on dirt roads; to have a paper route; to know practically everyone in the community and be known by them; to go crazy each autumn over football and each winter over basketball and each spring over the Western Slope track meet in Montrose, hating Gunnison High School all the time and fearing it every step of the way; to fall in love with the girl next door and not get her; to sleep on a porch on warm summer nights; to clean snow from winter sidewalks; to smell the burning of autumn leaves.[27]

Like his father, the young Trumbo was a reader; like his mother, he was a hard worker. His parents never had to push him to find ways to earn money. As a young boy, he sold gunny sacks, old bottles, other things he picked up around town, and his father's homegrown vegetables. While attending Hawthorne Grammar School, he launched a four-page, mimeographed newspaper titled *Fax*. He sold six-month subscriptions for fifteen cents, but for undisclosed reasons, he suspended publication after just one issue.[28] He also had a newspaper route, and one day he volunteered to fill in and do another boy's route as well as his own. "It began to snow," he remembered. "I had to abandon my bicycle and carry the papers on foot. I used a flashlight, I recall, to seek out the addresses and the houses. I remember people taking me in and giving me hot coffee and pie and cake and so forth." Later, he added three more routes, so he was delivering two morning papers and two evening papers. He was earning more money than his father, but he became ill from the effort and had to quit two of the routes.

The First World War (referred to as the Great War) commenced in

Trumbo (holding fish) and Orus (directly behind his son), 1914. Courtesy of Trumbo family.

July 1914 and made an indelible imprint on the people of Grand Junction, including the young Trumbo. Four decades later, he said: "God, but we were crazy about the first World War. The enthusiasm . . . I remember young boys going to Canada to volunteer in the Canadian Air Force. They just couldn't wait for the United States to get into the war."[29] According to a state historian, "Colorado went to war in 1917 before the rest of the nation," and Congressman Edward Keating, who had voted against the declaration of war, was defeated for reelection.[30] Many of the townspeople became chauvinistic nationalists. Indeed, the "barbarity" of the Germans, grossly exaggerated in US newspapers, made Trumbo "whole-heartedly against the Hun." He was outraged when he learned in March 1917 that German foreign minister Arthur Zimmermann had sent a telegram to the German ambassador in Mexico City, suggesting that if Mexico joined the Triple Alliance, it could regain the territories it had lost to the United States in 1848. Trumbo "robbed" his savings bank of all it contained—$2.70—"and sunk the roll in a Red Cross button. For weeks I felt good about the action."

He felt differently when he learned about the Loyalty League, a secret organization formed by a group of businessmen in Grand Junction. He recalled:

> [Some nights my father] would be summoned by a mysterious telephone call, hasten out of bed and into his pantaloons, and disappear into the night. I received no answer but the deepest silence when I questioned him about those forays. At last I found the explanation. While going through his desk drawers for scratch paper, I came across an intriguing little book which contained the minutes of the Loyalty League. My father was secretary. The preamble to its declaration of purposes was a panegyric worthy of comparison with that immortal document signed by the patriots of 1776. From the minutes of the various meetings, I kept well in touch with the strange activities of the league which had taken unto itself the protection of our town from the enemy. Later my father detected me in the act of reading the sacred book, and appeared slightly ashamed as he bound me to secrecy. I have always felt that he did not take the august body of which he was secretary quite seriously enough. Upon one or two occasions he actually laughed as he described their exploits to me.

In fact, many of the deeds of the Loyalty League were far from funny. Its members investigated and warned citizens of German ancestry against expressing any pro-German sentiments, and they also accosted any citizen who was deemed laggardly in Red Cross and Liberty Bond subscriptions. One night a mob ransacked a German photographer's shop; on another occasion, a group tarred and feathered a high school teacher. (Attacks like these occurred in many other cities and towns, and in St. Louis, a German man was lynched.) Orus resigned from the Loyalty League after the latter incident, even though he knew its members were not responsible. Still, he felt that they had created the climate for it. From this experience, Trumbo learned his first lesson in the dangers of nationalism.

In the spring of 1918 Dalton learned another lesson from his father—this one about propaganda in films. When *The Kaiser, the Beast of Berlin*—one of the most extreme anti-German films made during the war, and one of the most popular—came to Grand Junction, Orus reluctantly acceded to his son's petulant demand for the price of admission. But he made his displeasure so clear that, in the end, Dalton did not go.[31]

According to Trumbo, after the war ended, "the more responsible of [the Loyalty League's] members withdrew into a more secret organization, the name or membership of which I have never been able to learn." But he was "certain that the nucleus of the Loyalty League were the first to gather under the shadow of the fiery cross" of the Ku Klux Klan.[32] Trumbo later recalled that the Klan "was a movement everyone was terribly interested in joining," including him. "I wanted, for what fool's reason I can't imagine, to join. I asked my father for the $20 initiation fee. After a heroic struggle with his temper, he finally managed to say: 'All right, I'll give you the money. But I'll not give you a dime toward your college. If you're willing to join the Klan you won't need an education and wouldn't know how to use it if you had it.'" An abashed Dalton decided not to join.[33]

Aside from the Klan, the citizens of Grand Junction were spared the worst excesses of the postwar period. They did not experience large, violent labor strikes or race riots. The "red scare" and the influenza epidemic spared the area. And they already had four years' experience with a state prohibition law. Perhaps that is why Trumbo left behind so few contemporary observations or recollections of that period. Or perhaps his vision was narrowed by his economic circumstances, and he focused his energies on climbing out of his situation rather than analyzing it.

His burning ambition was to be a writer. One of his contemporaries said: "Dalton was the only kid we knew who knew what he wanted to be—he always wanted to be and always knew he would be a writer."[34] A movie studio publicist, obviously echoing what Trumbo had told him, wrote: "Dalton Trumbo has been writing stories ever since the time he wrote an excuse to his fourth grade teacher, asking her to permit him to leave school for the day so he might have a tooth pulled. He signed his mother's name. Instead of having a tooth pulled, he walked out into the Grand Junction hills of Colorado and wrote a play. It was about Indians."[35]

During his high school years, 1920–1924, Trumbo was hired by Walter Walker, publisher of the *Grand Junction Daily Sentinel*, as a cub reporter. Walker has been described as "a transplanted Kentucky gentleman with a deep love of the arts, an affection for formal dress, and a fresh rose in his lapel"; he "brought with him from Kentucky a slight, soft-spoken Southern drawl and a near-religious allegiance to the Democratic Party." He was a God-like presence in the newsroom, and to outsiders, he represented the *Sentinel*, Grand Junction, Mesa County, and the entire western slope.[36] Trumbo covered the courts, the mortuary, the high school, and various civic organizations, and Trumbo's scrapbooks contain several letters from Walker congratulating the young man for stories he had written. In one of them, Walker promised to pay Trumbo an extra $30 "in recognition of the splendid work" he had done and for his "exceptionally good" stories about football, murder trials, and the Teachers' Association. Walker also lauded Trumbo's coverage of the Rotary Club and his automobile-page stories. At one point, Walker advised Trumbo to go to law school and return to western Colorado to practice law and become a politician.[37]

In addition to his reporting job, Trumbo was very active at Grand Junction High School. One classmate remembered him as a man in a hurry, "churning along with that thin trench coat he wore flapping in the breeze behind him." Another referred to him as "a busy-assed guy, wound up like an eight-day clock," noisy, talkative, and generous.[38] Though he had more than 120 classmates, Trumbo stood out. As a freshman, he was selected to write the class history for the yearbook. Trying for a witty conclusion, he wrote: "We really imagined that we were pretty well up on the various phases of high school life and were extremely conscious of our superiority over our fellow students. Alas! he murmured a precious truth who said 'Ignorance is bliss.' The Freshman today is a typical example of the ruin that can be made by tireless A-expecting teachers."[39]

The following year, Trumbo began to display his public-speaking skills. He won the Western Slope Rhetorical Contest for best original oration, declaiming enthusiastically about "Service," which he defined as seeking "the common good of the greater number." One should forget petty jealousies, sacrifice private interests, and serve God, country, and fellow men, he said. While lauding people's service during the recent world war, he expressed this interpretation of it (significantly different from his later feelings): "America went into the war without a single, selfish motive, other than to protect her people and the world from an imperial mad man [Kaiser Wilhelm II], who sought to dominate with the policy of the 'mailed fist.'" Trumbo later wrote on his copy of the oration: "I think, God forgive me, I won!"[40] Walker wrote to him: "It was indeed a creditable manner in which you delivered your oration yesterday. I was very proud of you. You have much real ability along this line."[41] Trumbo practiced what he preached about service and joined the school's Junior Rotary Club, whose motto was "to serve our high school in a worthy manner and by worthy means, to aid in keeping our athletics clean, our school life worthwhile, to foster high ideals, preserve worthy traditions and co-operate in every progress and betterment of our high school." Trumbo was elected class president, and he served as athletics editor of the *Orange and Black*, the school newspaper.[42]

In his junior year, the Grand Junction High School debate team won the Western Slope Rhetorical Contest championship. The team argued the negative side of this resolution: "that the United States should adopt a law entirely prohibiting all immigration in the country for a period of four years." In addition to being a member of the winning team, Trumbo was awarded first place in the original oration contest, delivering a speech on "Idealism." His point total was the highest among the competitors.[43] Debating was, he later told his children, the most important part of his formal education. According to Mitzi, as a result of those debates, "he learned how to study both sides of an issue and to argue either one and to speak confidently in front of an audience. He came to love public speaking, and he urged all of us to join speech and debate clubs, but none of us did."

The 1924 edition of the *Tiger* summed up Trumbo's very successful high school career: in addition to the achievements already mentioned, he was president of the Boosters Club, a member of the Scholastic Team (junior year), and a participant in the school's operettas and minstrel shows. As a senior, he was again on the championship team in the Western Slope Rhetorical Contest. In his original oration, "The Unknown Soldier," he reiterated his earlier theme of service and added a new one: "We, as Americans, must re-dedicate ourselves to the lofty ideals of eternal peace—the cause for which the Unknown Soldier died." He earned 85 out of a possible 100 points—a new record—and won his third consecutive C. E. Adams Award for best original oration. A news-

Trumbo (first row, left) with Grand Junction High School Debate Team, 1923. Courtesy of Trumbo family.

paper account of the contest stated: "Dalton is one of Western Colorado's brightest young men."[44] Not surprisingly, he was awarded the school's A. E. Templeton Leadership Cup, "for having been the best, outstanding and all-around leader in the four-year term of high school."

The caption under Trumbo's senior picture reads: "A follower of Bacchus." He may have chosen that phrase simply to annoy his mother, or perhaps he had already developed a fondness for alcohol. Or it is possible that both reasons were valid.

On June 9, 1924, a *Daily Sentinel* story lauded Trumbo for being "one of the most popular and active of the high school students of the class of 1924" and for his numerous school activities. "Through his work on *The Sentinel* he developed into a news writer of exceptional ability and has done excellent work as a member of *The Sentinel* staff." W. G. Hines, chairman of the Colorado Educational Association, which sponsored the high school debate contests, wrote to Trumbo: "I know that you can make more than good & I know you will."[45]

Trumbo wrote very little about his romantic yearnings. However, he told Cook that during his high school years he had a girlfriend named Sylvia, who was one year younger. Her father owned an ice cream factory, and according to several of Trumbo's contemporaries,

Sylvia was "a beautiful girl who was immensely talented as a dancer." After Trumbo left Grand Junction for college, she moved to Los Angeles to pursue a dancing career. When Trumbo moved to Los Angeles the following year, they continued to see each other, but at some point Sylvia broke up with him, and he pined for her for several years.[46] Between his breakup with Sylvia and his marriage, Trumbo apparently had no serious romantic relationship, nor is there any indication that he was a serial womanizer.

Trumbo's one year at the University of Colorado was difficult for him, in terms of both finances and his sense of identity. His letters to his parents were filled with details of job searches, pleas for additional money, and budgetary concerns. In his first letter, he wrote that he had resolved to study, get through all his classes, and become a member of the debate team. He noted that among people he knew, he could be "as gay as the rest, but among strangers I draw up within myself, and am content to watch." He felt he had "reached a crisis, or turning point" in his life but could not say precisely what it was. He also stated: "I am no angel . . . but at the same time I have a definite set of ideals and ambitions, from which I refuse to retrench."[47] He took a job sweeping the floor of a newspaper office and another stoking the furnace at the Delta Tau Delta house, where he lived. He began to write for *Silver and Gold* (the student newspaper) and *Dodo* (the campus humor magazine). He also earned money by writing papers for Delta Tau Delta members and serving meals at the fraternity house.

He proudly told his parents that the English-placement essay he had written "was judged by the faculty to be the very best ever handed in in the history of the Freshman and Sophomore English classes, and as such was read to [those] . . . classes."[48] There was little political commentary in his letters, save his remarks that he had attended a talk by William Jennings Bryan and favored that year's Democratic presidential candidate, John W. Davis.[49] He also noted that he had made a stand of sorts against anti-Semitism: He had invited a high school friend to dinner at the fraternity house, and after the friend left, Trumbo had been advised of the fraternity's policy against enrolling or inviting Jews. Trumbo claimed he moved out of the fraternity house that night but was later persuaded to return.[50]

Among those who knew him, Trumbo's outward lack of worry about his problems was notable. When asked how he had acquired this trait, he ascribed it to his Christian Science upbringing: "They don't exactly figure me out here, but they respect me nevertheless. It's all due

Trumbo (center) with Delta Tau Delta "Kitchen Squad," 1924. Courtesy of Trumbo family.

to the wonderful faculty [Christian] Science has given me to refrain from worry and plainting." He noted that he was called the "Sleepless Wonder" and "[Edgar Allan] Poe the second."[51] But Trumbo did worry, particularly about his finances and his low grades in French. As for his other courses, he bragged to his parents: "You bet your boots there will be a lot of disappointed instructors in Grand Junction High School. Those who predicted that although I bluffed my way through high school, I would find myself unable to study in college, and would return like the rest, will have to take a back seat because I'M MAKING GOOD."[52] In December he reported that although he did not have time to work up a speech for the debating team, he had decided to enter an oratorical contest—"You know how I eat original orations."[53]

His main recreation seemed to be drinking. He told an interviewer, many years later:

When we couldn't steal alcohol from the lab or extort wine from the cook or dig up two dollars for a half pint of potato whisky, we invested eight cents with the campus pharmacist for patented stomach-sweetener called Jamaica Ginger, which was made of alcohol, white gunpowder and a dash of ginger extract. The only way you could make it potable was to pour it into a Mason jar already filled with lemon sherbet, and shake well. It hissed a little on its way down and seemed to have a shriveling effect on one's vital center, but after two gulps of the stuff you began to prophesy, and from there on out the Book of Revelations was kid stuff.[54]

During his second quarter at the university, Trumbo fell into a malaise. His courses did not interest him, and he was still scrambling to earn money. In mid-February he wrote: "I seem to be busy all the time, and yet have a dead sort of feeling that I'm not getting anywhere. There is a lot of disgusting artificiality about college life, and college people."[55] He later told his children that to fulfill his physical education requirement, he had chosen swimming, thinking it would be the easiest. However, because he missed so many sessions, he was told he would fail the course unless he spent the requisite number of hours in the pool. Since there were only two days left in the term, he had to float in the pool for fourteen hours one day and ten the next.

Unbeknownst to Trumbo, his parents had much deeper worries than he did. His father had been fired from his job at Benge's Shoe

Store. According to Dave Fishell, Orus had not been a very good sales-man, so when business declined, he was the first to be let go.[56] He could not find another job, but a cousin in Los Angeles wrote and offered him a job at a Harley-Davidson dealership there. So, in the spring of 1925, Orus moved the family to California. Many years later, Trumbo wrote himself a note, reminding him to ask his mother about "some of the expedients that were used . . . to raise money to send back to me while I was in college. I never had any idea how tough things really were and [I] was very demanding."[57]

At the end of his first year in college, Trumbo wrote to his parents: "This last quarter has been pure misery for me, it seems. I just seem tired, tired, tired."[58] That theme appeared in one of his earliest attempts at a novel, in which David, the main character, concludes at the end of his freshman year that he "was living as the rest of them were living, from one class to the next, from one week to the next, and from one quarter to the next." He was struck by a "bitter realization . . . that he had wasted one precious year of his life."[59]

In June 1925 Trumbo returned to Grand Junction because he did not have the money for train fare to Los Angeles. A sympathetic official of the Grand Valley National Bank loaned him $50. He never returned to Grand Junction, and he never explained why. He did, however, con-tinue to read the *Sentinel*, use his memories of the city in his writing endeavors, and make sure its residents knew about his later success as a writer. And he probably intended to return in triumph as a famous writer, but the palpable hostility aroused by his first novel (see chapter 3) likely dissuaded him.

2

Baking Bread and Writing in Los Angeles

I need to write about the shock of Los Angeles, and the shock of his family's cramped living quarters, his father's deteriorating health, his mother's job outside the home, and Trumbo becoming the first family member to work in a factory. I want to capture his sense of desperation. Of being trapped with his mother and his sisters and how much he wanted to be free of them. He sensed another world, knew it was there, if only he could get there.

—Christopher Trumbo

According to the 1920 census, Los Angeles had become the tenth largest city in the United States (population 576,623). (In stark contrast, the population of Grand Junction was 8,665, and the population of Boulder was 11,066.) Ten years later, Los Angeles would be the fifth-largest city in the country. It was predominantly white (almost 92 percent), but the Mexican American population was growing rapidly. This population explosion was accompanied by economic growth: oil was being discovered in many places, the movie industry was moving west from New York, the aviation industry was expanding rapidly, there were more automobiles per capita in Los Angeles than in any other US city, and construction was booming. Indeed, almost all types of industry flourished. Prohibition, which had been instituted in California in 1916, had made bootlegging a profitable business, and three years later, following ratification of the Eighteenth Amendment, it became a thriving enterprise. With rival companies vying for control of the liquor market, bribes and municipal corruption also multiplied.

When Trumbo arrived in Los Angeles, he discovered that his father was both ill and unemployed, and his mother was working as a book-

First Trumbo home in Los Angeles, at 1116 West Fifty-Fifth Street.
Photograph by Mitzi Trumbo.

keeper at an automobile agency. The family lived at 1116 West Fifty-Fifth Street, in a place Trumbo described in *Johnny Got His Gun* as being "on the alley above a garage behind a two story house. To get to it he walked down a narrow driveway which was between two houses close together."[1] (Forty years later, while filming the movie version, Trumbo used that same apartment for Joe's father's deathbed scene.)

The various unpublished novels he wrote over the next decade contained numerous reflections on Trumbo's lack of purpose and direction when he arrived in Los Angeles. In one fragment he described the thoughts of his protagonist Ezra Pilgom, who (like Trumbo) had been born in late 1905 in Shale City (Trumbo's frequently used pseudonym for Grand Junction), Colorado, and had journeyed to Los Angeles in the summer of 1925:

> This much Ezra knew very clearly about himself. When he asked questions of himself about himself, he went solemnly over these facts, embellished them with personal memories, and tried to discover what had made him the man he was.

But he never went any farther. He never considered the world which has ushered him through adolescence onto the verge of adulthood. It never occurred to him that events were occurring all over the globe which had their direct reflection in the life of his native town, which were to shape his thoughts and his growth in ways he had never suspected.[2]

In these manuscripts, Trumbo also emphasized how his father's deteriorating health affected him. In a later draft titled "The Gelding of the Unicorns," Trumbo described Ezra's reaction when he got off the train and greeted his father: "His father's Colorado rupture—& the motorcycle job—My god, he realized with a little shock—they're hammering him to pieces! He noticed as he got off the train his father looked older."[3] In the draft of another novel, Trumbo wrote:

The old happy times [of his family] were gone. The little apartment was small for five people. There were little economies, small sacrifices of which he had been totally unaware in the past. . . .

[His mother] was brave. . . . She planned and stinted and saved to make the family budget cover the multitude of things for which it had to provide. Each Saturday night [his father] brought his pay check home with an ashamed air. . . .

[Later that year, his father's] face grew thinner. His face became more pallid. His shoulders developed a more pronounced stoop. . . . The specter of worry had settled down upon his life and was exacting its deadly toll. He did not complain. Instead, his gay bantering smile appeared more often. But it was strained and hopeless—a mask to throw at the world.[4]

Upon arriving in Los Angeles, Trumbo's first task was to find a job, and with the assistance of an alumnus of Grand Junction High School, he was hired to operate an automatic bread-wrapping machine at Davis Perfection Bakery, at a salary of $27.50 a week. Davis Standard Bread Company had originally started in 1904, when it employed individuals to carry baked goods in small baskets and sell them directly to homes. In 1917 it renamed its product Davis Perfection Bread, and by 1922, it had 182 home-delivery trucks. At some point, the business became Davis Perfection Bakery, and it claimed to be the largest bakery on the Pacific Coast. The factory was located in downtown Los Angeles, at the corner of Beaudry Avenue and Mignonette Street (now the site of several upscale condominiums). Trumbo probably traveled to work on the Red Cars of the Pacific Electric Railway or the Yellow Cars of the Los Angeles Railway.

Trumbo described the bakery as a "red brick redoubt" that "occupied half a square block in the industrial section. . . . Twenty-seven horse-drawn carts had given way to a hundred and sixty-eight Model T delivery trucks. The Werner and Pffleiderer ovens had been torn from their masonry foundations and replaced with the most modern rotaries. The employees numbered six hundred. It was reckoned the largest bakery west of the Mississippi" by its three owners.[5] Since Los Angeles was a strictly open-shop city, there was no union.

"For some idiotic reason," Trumbo later remarked, "I felt the job was only a temporary one against my return to college in the autumn. As matters turned out, however, I worked a nine-hour night shift at that bakery for eight straight years at a salary which declined to $22 per week in 1929 . . . and stood at $18 when I quit the job in the summer of 1933."[6] The bakery was a very noisy place. In *Johnny Got His Gun*, Trumbo evoked "the click-click-click of the Battle Creek wrappers and the rattle of the belt conveyors and the howl of the rotary ovens upstairs and the rumble of steel route bins being hauled into place and the sputter of motors in the garage being tuned up against the morning's work and the scream of dollies that needed oil."[7] He then described his (Joe's) job:

> At the bakery he walked all night long. He walked eleven miles every night. He walked with his legs on the cement floor and his arms in the air swinging free. He hardly ever got tired. When you got to thinking about it it wasn't bad. Walking all night long and working hard and getting eighteen dollars at the end of the week for your trouble. Not bad. Friday nights were always the heaviest in the night shipping department because on Saturday morning the drivers would take out enough bread and pies and cakes and rolls to last their customers over Sunday. That made a hell of a lot of work and a hell of a lot of walking on Friday nights. But it wasn't bad.[8]

What was bad, however, was Orus's rapidly deteriorating health. After spending about a year working in the bakery, Trumbo wrote in a novel manuscript that his father had been "brought home from his work in the middle of the day, trembling and delirious, a complete nervous wreck," and the family commenced "a grim desperate battle" to keep him alive.[9] Maud called in a Christian Science practitioner, and each morning Trumbo followed his directions, bathing and dusting Orus with powder and giving him milk to drink. These efforts proved fruitless, and one night while Trumbo was working at the bakery, his mother called to say that his father had died. In *Johnny Got His Gun*, Trumbo described what he (Joe) found when he arrived home:

> Everything was very quiet. . . . In the living room his father lay dead with a sheet pulled over his face. He had been sick a long while and they had kept him in the living room because the glassed-in porch which was the bedroom for his mother and father and sisters was too drafty. . . . He looked down at a tired face that was only fifty-one years old. He looked down and thought dad I feel lots older than you. I was sorry for you dad. Things weren't going well for you and it's just as good you're dead. People've got to be quicker and harder these days than you were dad. Goodnight and good-dreams. I won't forget you and I'm not as sorry for you today as I was yesterday. I loved you dad goodnight.[10]

Although Orus's official cause of death was pernicious anemia, for which there was no cure at the time, Trumbo decided he had died because of "shame at his inability to get a job."[11] Trumbo dedicated his first completed novel, *American Sonata*, to his father's memory, "as the first fruit of his hopes."[12]

His father's death and the increased responsibility he felt to provide for the family angered and frustrated him. In Mitzi's words: "He was twenty-two years old; his big dreams probably seemed dashed; he lived in a tiny three-room apartment above a garage; he supported his mother and two younger sisters." Both his work ethic and his fixation on money became embedded in his psyche during these years. In his unpublished novel "Genius from Kingsley," Trumbo wrote: "Everywhere a wall was raised against escape—a black wall. Instruments with which to demolish the wall were unavailable. One had to use one's fingernails, if anything." He wrote about "the grimness of the bakery and its hostages," and his alter ego David had dire thoughts: "There were times when he thought he would go mad . . . commit murder . . . do anything to pull himself from the rut in which he had mired himself. . . . What he needed was money, money, money." David "rented a typewriter and spent every moment of his spare time in a frenzied attempt to write . . . short stories, essays, novels—anything that would bring them [his family] sudden dazzling wealth." The novel proved especially frustrating: "Night and day he pored over its contents, rejecting, revising, and substituting. It was a wearisome task. There were days when he saw nothing in it that was good. He grew to despise the sight of it, yet he never lagged in his determination to improve it."[13]

"The years in the bakery," Nikola Trumbo wrote, "changed my father. In Grand Junction and in Boulder he was an energetic, talented, brash, determined young man. He believed that with hard work and his natural talent he would succeed. Just a few years later, fortunate enough to be employed at all in the midst of the Great Depression, he found himself in a job he hated, fearing that he was trapped. His determination to succeed took on a driven edge."[14] Many years later, when Trumbo was still developing ideas for his novel about the bakery, and perhaps reflecting his inner thoughts at the time, he decided to begin the novel with the protagonist running out on his mother and his two young sisters and never seeing them again.[15]

And yet, the bakery became a school for Trumbo. Each night he worked there "added to his fund of human knowledge. The bakery, with its worries, new experiences, ambitions, disappointments, tenderness, and hatred fascinated him."[16] According to Nikola, he also "became keenly aware of social class differences. . . . In Grand Junction his family had struggled, but there was always food on the table, and if other distinctions of class existed, they didn't seem to be particularly noticeable or troubling to him. In Los Angeles he saw the differences and experienced hardship first-hand."[17]

When he spoke about his bakery experience, Trumbo always emphasized that although it had altered his outlook, it had not radicalized him. He told J. Marks, for example: "That face-to-face experience of my own impotence as part of the work-force changed me."[18] But, he told Victor Navasky, he "never considered the working class anything other than something to get out of."[19] He led a wildcat strike, consisting of four men, that lasted a few hours and won them a pay raise, but that was the extent of his labor activity. Trumbo later said he saw no radical tendencies at all in the bakery:

We all hated the boss, but that's pure American, but we didn't do much about it. I wasn't even interested in the Sacco-Vanzetti

case. Somebody came into the bakery and said they've executed
them. I said who. They said Sacco and Vanzetti. I said, well,
it's about time. It's been going on six or seven years, hasn't
it? I hadn't paid any attention. I worked nine to ten hours a
night, six days a week. I didn't have time [for politics]. I didn't
meet anybody. I wasn't terribly conscious politically. During the Depression I had my job. I was hanging on to it. My
only friends were those at work, and none of them were Left.
I had no contacts with the Left. My mentor of the period was
H. L. Mencken. . . . Then the election of 1932 swept everybody
up into politics and I went along—when you see hundreds of
able-bodied people begging for bread, you know something is
wrong. . . . You begin to have some doubts, so I was fairly radicalized, but not in any ideological way.[20]

Trumbo did, however, become radicalized in a quasi-criminal way. He
drank heavily, he stole bread and cakes, he bribed policemen, he sold
bootlegged alcohol, and he kited checks.

In the midst of all this activity, Trumbo—or at least the autobiographical characters in his manuscripts—fretted about the meaning of
his existence and his need to have a "philosophy of life." David, one
of his protagonists, decided to create his own credo in which God was
rejected and replaced "with some supreme virtue. The virtue would be
honesty. It would embody for him all the virtues. The honest man would
recognize the right of each man to happiness, and hence he would be
generous. To be honest would require courage, hence he would be brave.
Justice was an attribute of honesty, and to be honest he would necessarily be just." Honesty also required intelligence and temperance. Finally,
David's new religion would be factually based, and free will would be
its "supreme dictator."[21] Trumbo tried to live by these tenets for the rest
of his life, failing only completely at temperance.

Trumbo developed an "ardent belief in democracy" after reading
the Democratic Party platform of 1924, which contained the following
phrase: "In the event of war, in which the manpower of the nation is
drafted, all other resources should likewise be drafted. This will tend
to discourage war by depriving it of its profits." Trumbo was, he said,
"totally swept away" by those words, which were "quite close to socialism," and he copied them on a piece of paper he always carried with
him. Four years later, when he was eligible to vote, he cast his first presidential ballot for Al Smith, the Democratic candidate and a Catholic,

Dalton Trumbo with his Aunt Elsie, 1926. Courtesy of Trumbo family.

"not because of the man himself, but as an act of sheer political rage against the oceans of religious filth that destroyed his career. Thus my first conscious political act was a protest against bigotry."[22]

Trumbo displayed a prodigious work ethic during the years following his father's death. He worked at the bakery at night, attended college during the day, and devoted every free moment to writing. He managed to complete eighty-eight short stories and six novels, all of which were rejected by the editors he sent them to. He had received his first story rejection in September 1925 from *Pictorial Review*. Two months later, *Liberty* rejected "Jasper Green Goes to College." He sent several of his stories to Robert Thomas Hardy, a literary agent, who replied that he could not find "a likely home" for any of them.[23] Another agent, F. M. Holly, told Trumbo at the end of 1927 that the story he had sent Holly lacked "magazine value." The plot was contrived, the ending was cheap, and the whole story lacked "human appeal." Holly asked Trumbo to send him "a story nearer the verities of life."[24]

Perhaps the most interesting of his rejected stories was "The Return." Its basic plot is unremarkable: Jim Norton returns to his hometown a failure, and no one is willing to help him make a fresh start. But the ending—Jim's suicide—is evocative. It contains some of Trumbo's best early writing and clearly reveals Trumbo's ability (at least in some situations) to think himself into his protagonist's mind. Using an interior monologue, Trumbo has Jim say to himself, as he prepares for his suicide: "That was the coward's way. It was an easy thing to do. But was it? His mind darted about for some way. He thought with feverish activity. He must do it before his mind cracked. He had a gnawing fear he was going insane." Jim made "a desperate attempt to keep his reason until—the end." Thereafter, Trumbo effectively and concisely depicts Norton carrying out his self-appointed task—purchasing handcuffs and a quart of gasoline, making his way to a deserted area outside the city limits, gathering logs and brush, and stacking them into a pyre:

> Then he deliberately and carefully saturated his clothes with the gasoline, and stepped into the center of the pile, working his way down by moving his feet, and twisting his body. [Trumbo failed to include a sentence to the effect that Jim had placed kindling around a pole.] He then lighted a match, and with the same careful deliberation which had marked his other movements since arriving at the spot, he dropped it at the outer base of the pole, on the side from which the wind was blowing. He

then placed the handcuffs on his wrists, snapped them shut, and threw the key away.

He waited calmly while the brush at the base of the pile crackled cheerfully. Then the flames, caught by the wind, were fanned until they reached the man, huddled in the midst of the pile. With a smothering, triumphant puff, they greedily ignited the gasoline-soaked clothes.

Jim Norton laughed. It was a hollow, horrible laugh, and his face, lit up luridly by the flames, presented a fearful study in hate, mockery, sorrow, and fear. So only a coward committed suicide, eh? Well, he'd show 'em! God, how it burned! He moved his feet in a vain endeavor to extricate himself. They were caught! The logs beneath were holding him in his improvised furnace! With the final realization, he laughed again. The handcuffs on his wrist burned like the chains of Hell. He couldn't breathe! He screamed, the scream of a human being in mortal agony—a scream which died into a moan, only to be followed by a series of hideous laughs. A coward, eh? Ha, ha, ha! He'd show 'em! The heat. . . . that old swing. . . .

A hoot owl in the distance ceased its greeting to the night. A rabbit slunk into its burrow. The fire slowly burned out, leaving only glowing embers as mute evidence of the tragedy. A star, high in the heaven fell, and the night wore on.[25]

Trumbo had no better luck with what he called his realistic novels. "The task of the realist," he wrote in the preface to one of them, "is peculiarly sacred, because he first must plant his feet solidly in the mire of truth, and then must build his superstructure with utter fidelity to the deadly laws of cause and effect."[26] Some of his characters were based on people he knew; some he invented. Some of the incidents were true; some were imaginary. Part of the setting or context was faithful to the original; part was supplied by his own imagination. Whatever the mix, he could not find a publisher. In July 1928, the autobiographical "Genius from Kingsley" was rejected by Harcourt, Brace; sixteen months later, it also declined to publish "Thine the Victory." But the editor who read the latter noted: "There are flashes of real power in it. It is difficult to venture a detailed criticism of your story, or to describe the specific causes for rejection. But at least we can say that, among the large number of manuscripts that come in day after day, yours was outstanding and impressive." Instead of try-

ing to revise it, the editor recommended that Trumbo start work on a
new novel.[27] Three months later, Harper and Brothers rejected "Bleak
Street," writing to him:

> It is an impressive book both for its length and high serious-
> ness. We do not find, however, that it is sufficiently convincing
> to make us feel that we should be able to publish it success-
> fully. There are passages of unusual power and vividness in the
> story, but, equally, there are pages which do not hold the inter-
> est of the reader, and, in our judgment, fall below the level you
> have set for yourself of serious and important work. This swing
> of the pendulum between excellence and mediocrity, assurance
> and uncertainty, weakens the effect of the book to a marked
> degree.[28]

He fared no better with his screenplays, although the first one,
which he sent to author and critic Laurence D'Orsay, received a partially encouraging response: "I have read your story, 'Beloved,' with a
good deal of interest because of its literary quality. And because I am
impressed with your talent, I am going to be quite candid with you in
this letter, for only by perfect frankness can I hope to help you, and
show you how to put your very real ability to proper use." D'Orsay
praised the story for its "human interest" and some of the dramatic
scenes, and he complimented Trumbo's characterizations, dialogue,
and action. But, he concluded, Trumbo had fared poorly in the "paramount" aspect of scriptwriting: plot selection. There is, D'Orsay wrote,
"far too much that is essentially hackneyed."[29] Sixteen months later,
"Street Gammon," a story about the adventures and misadventures of
two street urchins, was rejected by Universal Pictures.

Understandably, after this wave of rejections, Trumbo despaired of
ever learning how to write. He later told Cook: "It seemed two or three
years before I had any confidence in myself. The problem of plot . . .
troubled me greatly."[30] Trumbo correctly assessed his main limitation,
both as a short story writer and as a novelist. He overflowed with ideas,
but only occasionally did those ideas translate into a satisfactory tale,
and only rarely did his novels contain a clear, consistent narrative. The
"big" novels he wanted to write, about the bakery and World War II,
were structurally complicated by their autobiographical elements and
by the "big" themes (the social history of the United States, the resil-
iency of human beings) he wanted them to encompass. Most of the nov-

els he envisaged or completed during these years were really a series of
vignettes and character studies, tenuously linked.

During the spring of 1929 Trumbo decided to complete his college
degree work and enrolled in some courses at the University of Southern
California. In a review of Carl Sandburg's *Good Morning America* for
an English class, Trumbo, in what might have been his first semiradi-
cal commentary, lamented that Sandburg, like all writers in the United
States, neglected "the gigantic struggle between capital and labor."[31]
He also began reading novels about social issues, most notably those by
Mark Twain, Sinclair Lewis, and Theodore Dreiser.

The stock market crash of 1929 and the resulting economic depression did not markedly affect the arc of Trumbo's life. Though his wages
were cut, he continued as before, working at the bakery and writing
prodigiously. The long-awaited breakthrough came in December 1930
when Welford Beaton, editor of *Film Spectator*, responded positively
to a submitted manuscript: "Your article is excellent. You are a graceful, witty and intelligent writer." Though Beaton could not pay him for
the article, he promised Trumbo a writing job as soon as the magazine
became large enough to support a staff.[32] Beaton published the article in the January 31, 1931, issue of the magazine, marking the debut
of a witty and sarcastic Trumbo who defended, with sharp ripostes,
West Coast culture from pretentious eastern attacks. In it, he took on
the condescending attitude of New York's most celebrated drama critic,
George Jean Nathan. Trumbo invited Nathan to come to Hollywood so
that he could "appreciate the immense amount of good" his criticism
had accomplished. Trumbo promised that Nathan would find westerners "in the convolutions of higher education—the higher the better. We
never miss an opportunity to acquire culture. We take the humanities in
ponderous gulps. We attend lectures. We become linguists. . . . Practically all of us own a book, and most of us, if necessary, can read it also."
From sarcasm about the West, Trumbo moved to a frontal assault on
the East, writing that westerners "have been so engaged in self-defense
that we have never thought to look into the back yards of our attack-
ers. The graveyard of rotten novels, over-rated poetry, and intolerable
stage plays is filled as amply as the crypt reserved for miserable films:
and the number of our artistic successes will stack up rather well beside
yours."[33]

A few months later, Trumbo received a letter from an editor at *Vanity Fair*, informing him that both the editor and the publisher of the
magazine had been "amused by his 'Appeal to George Jean.'" If, the

editor wrote, Trumbo had "other axes to grind" or "future pulveriza-
tions" to undertake, he should submit them to *Vanity Fair*.[34] Trumbo
immediately took up the challenge, using his experience as a bootlegger to compose a witty satire titled "Bootlegging for Junior: A Brand
New Field of Business Opportunity Is Now Available to This Season's
Crop of Ambitious University Graduates." In it, Trumbo compared
the skills necessary for success in legal business ventures with those
needed by entrepreneurs in the illegal trades. This gibe at big business
and the Hoover administration began: "When an impartial history of
the Great Depression is written, it will be set down therein that while
bankers squealed hideously for a place at the public trough, their closest competitors for our national income—the bootleggers—asked no
favors. On the contrary (the account will continue), they went hopefully forward, conducting their comings, and goings and killings with
regularity worthy of Hooverian applause. Nor will anyone gainsay the
historian's comment that in no instance did a good liquor merchant
trade his rugged individualism for a place in the breadline." Trumbo's
"liquor merchants" also displayed "an adaptability woefully lacking
among other bigwigs." Once the Depression began, they quickly realized that their former clientele could no longer afford expensive liquor,
so they began brewing beer, a product that can be manufactured "from
last night's garbage and [then] sold for a better price than tomorrow's
milk." This huge growth in volume—from the thousands who formerly
bought expensive liquor by the case to the million who were now buying
beer by the pint—allowed the "new era bootlegger" to advance to the
more profitable arenas of racketeering, extortion, and political graft.
"There is no better candidate for the positions now available in this
industry than the college man who finds his pathway to legitimate success swarming with Masters of Arts and Doctors of Philosophy." This
university-trained bootlegger will have learned from his undergraduate
experience that "a law which does not receive public support morally is
no law at all," and he also will have imbibed a "Messianic enthusiasm"
for the product. "But above all, he will be honorable—a gentleman in
the finest sense—for a business in which a contract is illegal and a law
suit out of the question requires personal honesty to a degree not com-
prehended in legitimate undertakings."[35]

    In June 1931, just before Trumbo received the invitation to write
for *Vanity Fair*, Beaton hired him as a full-time writer-reviewer for the
renamed magazine the *Hollywood Spectator*, which was now a compendium of articles, opinions, and reviews. Trumbo continued to work

at the bakery, write for other magazines, and sleep only a few hours a night. But he clearly enjoyed working for Beaton. In one of his lighter articles, Trumbo wrote:

> I come in to the office each morning around ten o'clock, read the publicity with which the studios so kindly furnish me, chat with two charming young ladies who run the business, and leave about noon. Sometimes, Mr. Beaton thoughtfully informs me that my copy is rotten, and other times he assures me it is quite good. Occasionally I run down to his beach home where we gravely discuss dogs, the surf, and recently the time it will take to read Sigrid Undset's twelve hundred page *Kristin Lavransdatter*. Once in a while we talk about motion pictures also, but never about what we are going to write of motion pictures.[36]

In addition to his long articles on the movie industry, Trumbo usually reviewed five or six movies for each issue. In the introduction to his first set of reviews, he stated that he would be expressing the opinions "of a middling intelligent person who probably represents a number of millions of middling intelligent persons with box-office money in their pockets."[37] A few weeks later he wrote: "I attend a showing not as a critic, but as a spectator seeking amusement."[38] He clearly wanted to amuse his readers as well. He wrote of *East of Borneo* (Universal, 1931): it "furnished me with more thrills than I was prepared to withstand, in consequence of which I wrestled in my sleep with the identical python that slid over a sleeping native in the picture. I was not so shrewd as the native, who awakened, stiffened quietly, and waited for the serpent to complete its crossing. I wrestled with the snake, was nearly strangled, and awakened in a very trying position with covers badly disarranged."[39]

The movie reviews were usually two paragraphs long. Trumbo never mentioned the screenwriter, and he only occasionally commented on the quality of the direction. He focused mainly on the actors and the story being told. Among the actors, Trumbo clearly admired Charlie Chaplin. In his first review, of Chaplin's *City Lights*, Trumbo called him "the screen's finest tragedian," who "has the courage to retain delicacy and subtlety."[40]

During Trumbo's first year of writing movie reviews, three films in particular earned strong praise. He said of F. W. Murnau's last film, *Taboo: A Story of the South Seas* (Murnau-Flaherty Productions, 1931),

"For sheer loveliness of conception and beauty of execution, I can think of nothing finer in recent pictures. . . . Here is screen art, but it is more than that. It is a promise of what may be done with silent pictures and a sympathetically synchronized musical score."[41] He also extolled two films of the social realism genre: *An American Tragedy* (Paramount, 1931) and *Street Scene* (Samuel Goldwyn, 1931). The former he called "genuine art and a credit to Hollywood"; the latter he described as "one of the finest motion pictures I have seen; perhaps it is the finest. . . . [It] is dominated by an almost serene intelligence."[42]

Five themes pervaded the articles Trumbo wrote for the *Hollywood Spectator*: (1) his western, down-to-earth attitude toward art and the media; (2) his disdain for eastern literary pretentiousness; (3) his belief that movies did not have to take second place to any other art form; (4) his conviction that the movie studios were producing too many shoddy films; and (5) his populist political ideas. The fourth theme was most prevalent. He frequently chastised moviemakers for their failure to use sound effectively, their lack of imagination, their blindness to the possibilities of fantasy and romance, and the general mediocrity of their films' dialogue. Even though he believed that screenwriting was more important to the quality of a film than directing, Trumbo was far from complimentary about screenwriters. In his estimation, probably 50 percent of them "are hopeless incompetents even as half of the directors are incompetent. Many of them are big names imported at three figures to loll in the sunshine and impart box-office to any production that bears their names. But there must be a few—say five percent—who know motion pictures, and who are capable of turning out a script that could be directed by a nitwit, and still be a fairly entertaining picture." And yet, the work of those 5 percent did not survive the studio process: "Nobody knows how many first rate scripts have been murdered in the endless rounds of conferences. Nobody knows how many writers' souls have writhed after everyone from script girl to director has made revisions. Nobody knows how many times that which was blue in the script turned out to be a sickly purple on the screen. And nobody knows how great a percentage of the success of really fine pictures should be attributed directly to the script." The ideal situation, he thought, would be for writers to become directors, but even then, great results would probably be infrequent, because "literary imagination and executive energy rarely are infused in the same man." Nevertheless, he hoped that one day writers would rise to the top and be "in full command" of the movie product.[43]

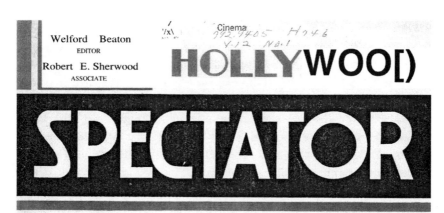

Welford Beaton
EDITOR
Robert E. Sherwood
ASSOCIATE

Cinema

HOLLYWOO[)

SPECTATOR

JIJNE 20, 1931

Introducing a new Associate Editor
in the p~rson of
ROBERT E. SHERWOOD

Film Firms Are Going Broke
Is Irving Thalberg Really A Genius?
We Call on an Aristocratic Cow
-*By* the Editor

Breaking Into A Picture Studio
Only God Can Make A Blonde
They Can't Fool Howard Hughes
-*By* Sherwood

Names and Some Hollywood Vanities
Walter Wanger and Ben Schulberg
--*By* Daugherty

Babel and Sound Effects
-*By* Trumbo

Reviewed in This Number

KICK IN	SVENGALI
LADIES' MAN	DUDE RANCH
MAD PARADE	SWEEPSTAKES
STEPPING OUT	FINGER POINTS
PARTY HUSBAND	SUBWAY EXPRESS
THE MILLIONAIRE	MEN CALL IT LOVE
DADDY LONG LEGS	TRANSPORT OF FIRE
UP POPS THE DEVIL	WOMEN OF ALL NATIONS

PRICE **15** CENTS

Hollywood Spectator. Courtesy of Ned Comstock.

As the Depression deepened, an anti–Wall Street, pro-populist theme dominated the articles Trumbo wrote for the *Hollywood Spectator* and a variety of nationally circulated magazines. In one, published in *Forum* in March 1932, Trumbo depicted the industry as "a forlorn creature," torn between the desire to please eastern critics and the necessity of making money. Despite its abasement to please eastern critics, Hollywood films were not making money. Filmmakers did not seem to realize that eastern critics were contemptuous of the cinema, ignorant of moviemaking, and unaware that the cinema is "a distinctive art form." He advised the studio executives to ignore the eastern critics and make "carefully aimed class entertainment." (He was not referring to Marxist-type classes—the bourgeoisie, petit bourgeoisie, and proletariat—but rather the "popular" and "quality" classes.) He called for a "popular" cinema that was "untinctured with philosophical considerations or thought-provoking problems . . . and sold to an audience at popular prices." He recommended that the executives make "pictures uncontaminated by the emotional pap which hitherto had been added for the sake of popular appeal." Such films could be aimed at "quality audiences at quality prices."[44]

A few months later, Trumbo's populist attitude toward the movies resurfaced when he remarked, "The greatest curse of show people is their contempt for audience intelligence." He complained that, for the most part, they ignored the fact that "great art has been popular art. Art for art's sake is a decadent and horrible affair; but art for public entertainment—and all great art by its very nature is just that—will follow its ageless practice and make money."[45]

The following year, in a draft of an unpublished article, Trumbo chided industry leaders for their unwillingness to admit that their "vast manufacturing plants" had "grown into Frankensteins [actually, Frankenstein was the name of the doctor who created the nameless monster], steadily devouring more money than can be raised to sink into them." As a result, the studios had become "automatic producers of standardized public entertainment," and the industry had become "an enterprise for gamblers" whose own money was not at risk.[46] In a lengthy article for *Forum*, Trumbo blamed Wall Street's control of the studios for the poor quality of movie scripts and direction.[47]

The western studio bosses did not escape his criticism either. He called them "power-drunk megalomaniacs" who systematically pillaged the industry.[48] Likewise, he condemned what he called the "steady, remorseless drain of [their] nepotism" on moviemaking. Under the reign of the studio czars, rather than being efficient industrial institutions, the studios had become "consanguineous societies chartered to fry the fat out of the stockholder." Trumbo unfairly accused the studio bosses of being unconcerned with making good movies; he charged that they were chiefly concerned with securing salaries for themselves, their in-laws, and their friends, thereby turning the studios into their "personal poaching ground."[49]

Trumbo's growing political consciousness was also evident in some of the articles he wrote for other periodicals. But his review of a new radical publication titled *Experimental Cinema* clearly demonstrated that he had not become a proponent of proletarian culture or Communist dogma. "I was suspicious," he wrote, "when I read that the magazine would 'succeed in establishing the ideological and organizational foundations of an American working-class cinema.' And I was surfeited when I read comments on the 'American imperialist policy,' 'capitalist propaganda,' and 'working-class audiences.' I do not recall ever having met a man who considered himself permanently a member of the working class." He also flatly debunked as spurious the art-versus-propaganda debate. "All art is propaganda," he wrote, and Hollywood movies are propaganda for capitalism only in the sense that they reflect "the foremost interest"—"money and its accumulation"—of 120 million people. Finally, he rejected the concept of "mass impulse in art," as championed by *Experimental Cinema*, characterizing it as "stultifying and priggish irrespective of what righteous cause it involves." Nevertheless, he recommended the magazine as a "sincere and sometimes brilliant" undertaking that could be read most profitably not by the "working class it seeks to unshackle" but by "the best minds in Hollywood."[50]

It is noteworthy that Trumbo reviewed only one Russian movie, *The Patriots* (*Okraina*). Like all Russian films, he wrote, it "must be approached with a perspective entirely apart from the American. For the Russian cinema cannot adequately be judged by the degree of entertainment it places upon the screen, but by the degree of effectiveness with which the original conception is presented to the audience. Characters of the Russian screen play are not persons in a story: they are protagonists in a struggle. In the abstract, they are impersonal robots, playing before the camera the composite character of millions of their countrymen." Unlike *Storm over Asia* (a 1928 film directed by Pudovkin), with its brilliant "climax in the struggle of revolution itself, . . . *The Patriots* makes the fatal mistake of ending with a parade, which fails somewhat to typify the supreme end of Soviet philosophy."[51] Trumbo did not denote what that "supreme end" was supposed to be, but based on the context of the piece, he seemed to be referring to a workers' society.

In one of his "Reports on Babylon" columns that appeared periodically in the *Hollywood Spectator*, Trumbo addressed international events and made his first extended commentary about war hysteria and US foreign policy. The occasion was the Japanese army's invasion of

Manchuria (northern China) in 1931 and the announcement by the government of Japan on February 18, 1932, that it had established the "independent" state of Manchukuo there. Some Americans began to discuss war as a means of halting Japanese expansion, and Trumbo, using the epistolary form (also a feature in several of his short stories), composed a letter to Emperor Hirohito, assuring him: "All this war talk is exaggerated. Don't pay any attention to it. Our newspapers are so hard put for news in these days of [economic] depression that Manchukuo and Jehol [the chief city of Eastern Inner Mongolia] and those longer names are gifts from heaven." Trumbo used the letter to take a swipe at US imperialism, comparing Japan's annexation of Manchuria to previous annexations by the United States and telling Hirohito: "You have invested heavily in the province, and you need the land. We had the same idea when we wanted a little strip of land upon which to build our Panama Canal. So we went out and fomented a revolution, recognized the insurgent government with indecent haste, signed a contract, moved in—and that was that. The revolution gag is fairly ancient; and you weren't doing a thing out of the ordinary when sprang that new nation of Manchukuo."[52]

In October 1933 Trumbo enjoyed two successes. First, he was appointed managing editor of the *Hollywood Spectator*, allowing him to quit the bakery at last. Beaton had promised to pay him $50 a week, but Trumbo's checks amounted to only $35.[53] Second, another of his stories, "Kidnaped," was published in *International Detective Magazine*. In it, Trumbo spun a flimsy tale about the kidnapping of the grandchild of a wealthy businessman. To deal with this latest event in a storm of lawlessness affecting the community, the businessman convenes a meeting of his peers to unveil his plan to root out the perpetrators. They must act, he says, because the government and the people cannot. "In a capitalist country," he tells them, "we are the leaders. We must justify our wealth by organizing it in such a manner that the forces of good are upheld." They agree to organize a volunteer force of 72,000 men, sweep the city, and round up criminals in a "courteous but firm" fashion. At the end, the gang leader is captured and tries to make a deal, but he is told: "You can't be fool enough to think you can compromise with the American people, can you? When they're aroused, they're pure hell!" Trumbo later dismissed this story as a piece of "Fascist crap."[54]

Although Trumbo's *Hollywood Spectator* salary and his earnings from other magazines were less regular than his bakery wages, he managed to move the family to a duplex in the Hollywood Hills. His mother worked as a seamstress for various Hollywood dressmakers and some-times did special jobs for movie actresses, but Trumbo was the family's major financial support. His sister Elizabeth recalled: "Money was such a problem for a long, long while. We were dependent on him and must have been an awful burden. But he did take care of us all. He took his responsibilities very seriously." Once, when his other sister, Catherine, told him she needed $10 to buy a new dress for a dance, Trumbo left the house and returned an hour later with the money. When she asked where he got it, he said he had won it in a crap game.[55]

According to Elizabeth, "There was no doubt when I was growing up that he was the dominant force in the family—not by giving orders or giving us advice or any of that—but just because it was always assumed he was going to be somebody important." Catherine concurred: "He never ordered us around," and "he tried to open up our minds" by talk-ing about ideas. They both remembered that Maud and Dalton fought constantly over his politics, his lifestyle, and his drinking. Catherine recalled a night when they were still living on Fifty-Fifth Street: "Dalton came weaving and stumbling up the stairs, and I ran out to him to keep mother away from him. I got him into his room, but mother was in hot pursuit, and she was there before I could shut the door. 'There's nothing wrong with him,' I told her. And just to prove it was so, Dalton stood up to pull off a sock and fell flat on his face."[56]

In the spring of 1934 the *Hollywood Spectator* temporarily shut down, forcing Trumbo to seek another means of earning a living. Fortu-itously, he ran into a man named Frank Daugherty, an occasional con-tributor to the *Spectator* who worked in the story department at Warner Bros. When Trumbo mentioned that he needed a job, Daugherty offered to put in a good word for him at the studio. That summer Trumbo was hired as a reader in Warner's story department.

Coincidentally, several months earlier, Trumbo had extolled the brothers Warner as, "beyond all doubt, the most astonishing produc-ers in Western America. There is no way to gauge them, no way to curb them, and no way to anticipate them. . . . Bad taste they have displayed time and again—and bad manners, and oh Lord! bad pictures. . . . Their career is simply a magnificent crazy quilt; but in its design one detects a certain elemental vitality, a rude energy such, for example, as never could be expected from Fox and Paramount."[57]

He began his new occupation with a political credo that was still unformed. His populist propensity was evident, but it had not yet been refined into an ideology. He later recalled, disingenuously, that only after escaping from the bakery did he realize "that the country—and, indeed, the whole world—was in the throes of a social, economic and political crisis in which, for me, at least, it was impossible not to take sides." He also saw "that in most of the great struggles of the period . . . the Communists were among the most effective forces in these struggles—note the word *among*—and incontestably the hardest working and best organized. . . . All in all, feeling as I did, it's rather significant that I waited until the winter of 1943–44 to join a party with which I had been in almost complete sympathy since 1935 or 1936."[58]

3

Playing the Studio Game and Organizing Guilds

In the story department he was different from everybody else. There was a quickness and a drive to him, and he had such an original turn of mind. He was the most industrious person I ever knew.

—Alice Hunter

On June 1, 1934, Trumbo was hired by Warner Bros. to read and analyze novels, plays, and stories, at a salary of $27.50 a week. At that time, the Warners "ran the most economical and efficient studio in Hollywood." Not only did the studio's profits climb steadily during the decade, but it had political cachet: it was the only major studio that refused to conduct business with Germany, and the only one whose "production program most enthusiastically reflected the New Deal."[1]

Clearly, Trumbo intended this job to be only a way station. He was counting on a rapid promotion to the far more lucrative and challenging job of writing directly for the screen, which would sustain him and his family until he achieved success as a writer of novels and stories. But his progress was slow. One year later, still a reader, he received a raise to $35 a week. On the back of his time card, his supervisor had written: "One of the best men in the department. Since we call on him to do a great amount of special work it is only fair that he be paid the wage our best readers receive. Mr. [Walter] MacEwan [executive assistant to the head of production] promised this raise last October, but for various reasons could never put it through."[2] Trumbo later told a radio interviewer: "A reader is a man who is paid to synopsize a story which he usually could write much better than the original author."[3] Although he was technically a member of the story department, Trumbo admitted, "That is sheer vanity. I am simply a reader, which means that my personal dignity and prestige is almost equal to that of an alert messenger boy. I am informed by those who have had bitter experiences, that the studio not only demands that a reader [who wants to graduate to screenwriting] submit his stuff to them first, but that, if it likes the story, insists upon paying its own price, which never in history has gone higher than $300."[4] John Bright, one of the top screenwriters at Warner, recalled that Trumbo wasn't happy: "He thought he should be further along than he was. He was too talented to be just a reader. . . . Most readers played it safe and said no to everything. But not him." Few other readers would have recommended *Lady Chatterley's Lover*, *Candide*, *Ulysses*, and *Gargantua and Pantagruel*.[5]

Trumbo was also working on his seventh novel. This one, which he titled *Eclipse*, was based on his memories of Grand Junction. He had been thinking about the dramatic aspects of the story for ten years, but he lacked an idea for what he called "a fitting climax. . . . The bank holiday of March, 1933, struck me as the most logical crisis, and I started the story at that time, doing it completely three times in twenty-four days. I then laid it on ice, partly to gain perspective on it, partly because I had the idea I would not submit it until the real-life character upon whom it is admittedly founded passed away."[6] A year later, however, his pride in his accomplishment overcame his reservations, and he began to send the manuscript to literary agents in New York. In his letter to one of those agents, written on a Warner Bros. letterhead and dated September 12, 1934, Trumbo reviewed what he termed his "unimpressive" publishing record thus far and stated: "Since I am not yet thirty, I feel that if I can find someone to play ball with me, I can produce sound commercial stuff—perhaps, in time, better."[7] And he was very confident about the quality of *Eclipse*. He obviously wrote the same letter to several agents, and he received a positive response from Elsie McKeogh dated September 19; a couple of weeks later, she wrote that she was "extremely enthusiastic" about the manuscript.[8] But sixteen other US publishers did not share her enthusiasm. The novel was finally accepted, in December of that year, by Lovat Dickson and Thompson, a small British publisher.

The novel takes place in "Shale City," and all the main characters are based on people Trumbo had known in Grand Junction. It depicts the rise and fall of John Abbott, a seemingly honest man who harbors a debilitating secret—he is impotent—and a crippling inability to reveal his thoughts to the women in his life. It is, Trumbo later wrote, the story of what a "good, imperfect" man gave to a town "and how the town, in his time of financial failure and emotional despair, gave him nothing but ingratitude and betrayal in return."[9] Trumbo based Abbott on a living individual, William J. Moyer, who had been treated badly by the citizens of Grand Junction. Moyer had opened a very successful department store in town, and in 1890 he had helped found the Grand Valley National Bank. Along the way, he also supported a number of civic improvement projects, but when the Depression ruined him, many of the people he had once assisted refused to help him. Trumbo followed the decline of Moyer's fortunes in the *Sentinel* and saw parallels to his father's treatment by Benge: "It was in essence the same thing, a man destroyed. And that possibly accounted for some of my passion against the town itself, which actually had been quite good to me."[10]

In Book I of *Eclipse*, Trumbo provides an excellent portrayal of the city, its inhabitants, and the lives and thoughts of the Abbotts, an unhappily married couple. He later wrote: "I had all the basic material well in hand before I left Grand Junction in 1925, since I knew all of the principals, and needed only a few incidents occurring after my departure to round out the story."[11] Trumbo depicted his own young self in the character of Freddy Kilner, a cub reporter for the *Monitor*. "He covered the high school news, and on Saturdays, when there were no classes, he scouted around the town for local items. He was laying the foundations for what he confidently expected to be a brilliant literary career. His ability was widely recognized in high school English classes, although *The Monitor* work offered little outlet for his talents."[12]

In Book II, the follies of John Abbott, a self-anointed business prophet, are vividly conveyed; in Book III, Trumbo provides a compelling account of the effects of the Depression. Trumbo's message is crystal clear: With the exception of Abbott, the business and political leaders of Shale City are generous only when they can afford to be. When economic circumstances change for the worse, most of the townspeople behave selfishly and meanly. Ironically, the only person who remembers Abbott's good deeds and comes forward to help him in his hour of need is the town's madam.

The citizens of Grand Junction were kept informed of Trumbo's writing career by occasional articles in the *Daily Sentinel*, and they eagerly anticipated the publication of *Eclipse*.[13] Trumbo, however, had some trepidations about the novel's reception in Grand Junction. Shortly after the book appeared, he wrote to Walter Walker: "I hope you will not be angry if you find characters whom you recognize in it. I am convinced that all novels are based in fact, and distorted for fiction purposes to suit the author's particular talent. I do not pretend that any of the portraits in 'Eclipse' are real, yet you will, I am sure, see at least some characteristics of their counterparts in real life. I have no apologies, although I do confess to some qualms. But the job is done, and it took a long time in the doing." Walker replied:

> It goes without saying that "Eclipse" has caused a great deal of local comment. . . . I have no feeling of anger toward you concerning the book. After all, it is your privilege to utilize your old home town in demonstrating your talents as a writer if you wanted to do so. . . . Frankly, however, with the personal regard and affection I have for you and the admiration I hold for your talent, I do regret that you saw fit to release this story at this time. The only personality in the book that actuates me in saying this is that of W. J. Moyer. Had not misfortune piled up on him quite so heavily and so frequently, and if he were not alive, this regret of mine would be considerably reduced in volume.[14]

The vast majority of Grand Junction residents who read the book were not as understanding or forgiving as Walker. Some thirty-seven years later, in 1972, Alice Wright wrote in the *Sentinel*'s Sunday magazine: "*Eclipse* . . . created a tidal wave of resentment in Trumbo's hometown, and it's still a fighting word in some circles. . . . [T]here was a general feeling that the author had taken more liberties with facts than literary license warranted, even if the book was labeled fiction. They felt then, and still feel, that a lot of images were unjustly marred. . . . Which is why a copy of *Eclipse* is hard to come by now. The few that weren't wrathfully destroyed are held under lock and key."[15]

It is clear from Trumbo's efforts to get *Eclipse* published that he had grander aspirations than screenwriting. Morton Grant, Trumbo's office mate in the writers' building at Warner, sent a copy of the manuscript to someone named Denny and observed: "The novel is a good, solid piece of work. . . . I want to assure you that the author and his later work is a much more valuable piece of publishing property. I have seen the prospectus of his new novel, and it will eclipse *Eclipse* in about the same manner that [Sinclair Lewis's] *Main Street* overshadowed *Free Air* [Lewis's previous book]."[16]

In early 1935 Trumbo sent literary agent Elsie McKeogh three completed magazine stories and two parts of a projected magazine series about adolescents. One of the stories, "Darling Bill," was written expressly for the *Saturday Evening Post*. "It seems to me," Trumbo noted in the accompanying letter, "that the time is ripe for a little anti–New Deal satire. . . . Though I've carefully avoided specific party references in it." Since, he continued, "I've sold only one short story, my lack of success has made me none too sure of my ability in the medium. I have purposely tried to make this stuff as diverse as possible, and you may be able to give me an idea as to what type of thing I should concentrate on." He was not, he remarked, at all sensitive to criticism, and he urged Elsie to "fire away."[17] She did so, telling him that two of the stories were "a bit confusing," and the two parts of the proposed series were "pretty thin." She did, however, like "Darling Bill" very much, as did the editors of the *Saturday Evening Post*, who published it in the April 20 edition.[18]

"Darling Bill" was the first in a series of tales about political corruption that Trumbo wrote for magazines and for the screen. It is clear that he was not writing from the point of view of a "Communist," accusing New Deal programs of fooling the proletariat and diverting them from the path of revolution. Rather, he was a populist, distrustful of all politicians and government programs. In this first example of the genre, Trumbo tells the tale of a secretary to a congressman who, while writing a letter to her fiancé, Bill, is instructed to type a press release about her boss's opposition to the Sparling bill. She makes an obvious error in the press release, referring to the legislation as the Darling bill. Although no such bill exists, journalists, politicians, and Bill pretend that it does and attempt to exploit it to their own advantage.[19] Soon thereafter, Trumbo wrote a follow-up titled "Trouble in Horsefly." That story did not sell, and, as Trumbo later wrote, "it shouldn't have."[20]

Trumbo used the publication of "Darling Bill" to gain publicity for himself. Indeed, during this period, he was actively honing the public relations skills he would wield so effectively in the late 1950s to get himself off the blacklist. He arranged (or he had the studio arrange) for the *Los Angeles Examiner* to photograph him with Warner's biggest female star, Bette Davis, as she held a copy of the *Saturday Evening Post*. According to the accompanying story, Davis was known for encouraging young writers, and "when she learned of Mr. Trumbo's aspirations to become a writer she promised to treat him to a luncheon the first time his name appeared as an author." Trumbo was identified as being "on the story department staff of Warner Bros.–First National Studios."[21]

Trumbo with Bette Davis, 1935. Courtesy of *Los Angeles Examiner*.

When Trumbo showed a copy of "Darling Bill" to a story editor at the studio, the editor suggested that Trumbo write a treatment on his own time, "cutting politics out of it and substituting big business with stockholders instead of voters." The editor promised to show it to studio head Jack Warner if it was any good. But Trumbo did not want to submit anything to the studio until he had a movie agent to represent him. Elsie had suggested that he hire H. N. Swanson, one of the elite agents in Hollywood. Taking her advice, Trumbo replied:

> [Swanson] might be able to rescue me from my slave pit and land me in a writer's job. A close study of the habits and routine of writers has convinced me that they work very little, whereas I, as a reader, am not only read out but written out at the close of a day. Thus my own writing suffers considerably. But if I were occupying a writer's office—I'm sure I could turn out twice as much of my own stuff, and that it would be considerably better. At present I am boiling over with another novel, but hesitate to start it until I can see more free time in the evenings to do it justice.[22]

Trumbo was convinced that if he sold enough magazine and screen stories, he could turn his little writing room at home "into a first-class fiction factory." But Trumbo became convinced that Swanson either did not know how to handle new writers or did not care about them,[23] and in a gutsy move, he dropped Swanson and began to search for a new agent. He later explained to Elsie that he had, "by virtue of [his] own political skullduggery," made himself into a salable commodity:

> Half a dozen [agents] made my office their chief port of call.
> . . . Of the whole bunch, [Arthur] Landau was the only one who
> displayed either enthusiasm or initiative. He was the lad who
> scared up a job elsewhere which could be used to cudgel War-
> ners into giving me at least a living wage. For six weeks I had
> been writing a script at thirty-five dollars a week—six weeks
> during which any agent could have snatched me. Naturally,
> I went with Landau. My contract is a very modest one. Lan-
> dau himself was furious when I signed, since my contract with
> him calls for no commission until I receive $250 a week—eigh-
> teen months hence. But I wanted a place in which to hibernate,
> safe from the ballyhoo and the pressure to which a highly paid
> movie writer invariably succumbs. In a word, I want the mov-
> ies to subsidize me for a while, until I establish myself firmly as
> a legitimate writer.

Of course, he noted that Landau, like all agents, "is a robber—but he is an efficient and a fearless one, which is exactly what a writer needs in a town filled with robbers."[24]

With Landau's assistance, Trumbo signed a writer's contract with Warner on September 16, at a beginning salary of $100 a week. Every twenty-six weeks, the studio had the option of continuing or terminating the contract. Each time the studio exercised its option to continue, Trumbo's weekly salary increased by $50. The contract also specified that he would be allowed to write three novels. He was assigned to the B unit, located on Sunset Boulevard in the area of Hollywood known as "Poverty Row." It was studio policy that all the plots of its A pictures could be remade by the B unit, as long as the cost of production did not exceed $100,000. "It was our job," Trumbo later said, "to watch a successful 'A' picture, steal it, transform it to another background, use the plot, and go right ahead. That was the way I learned."[25]

Trumbo did not expect to remain at Warner Bros. for the entire seven years of the contract; he was confident that he and Elsie would, "in the not too distant future sell a lot of stories together, perhaps make a lot of money together, and at least cement a dignified and pleasant business relationship such as is totally unknown in this western land of long knives and sharp deals."[26] So Trumbo kept writing magazine stories, and later that year, Elsie was able to place another one with the *Saturday Evening Post*. It was a much slighter story than "Darling Bill," about a group of Damon Runyonesque characters, one of whom concocts a scheme that backfires on him.[27] Trumbo also wrote a number of original stories for the screen.

In the early days of his screenwriting career, he was hyperconfident about his scriptwriting capability, noting: "I can do any sort of screen work, original or adaptation. I've studied the thing rather closely, and I think I'm ready for a try at it."[28] Many years later, however, he acknowledged that screenwriting was a craft with a long learning curve: "I liked writing [scripts], but it was the cultivation of a very small talent which is not stupefyingly exalted to this day."[29] Although Trumbo cultivated that talent, he was never fully satisfied, even as a well-paid screenwriter; he always aspired to become a writer of novels and stage plays. And for six years he managed to be both a highly paid screenwriter and a published novelist (four books). But as inevitably happened to many screenwriters with lofty literary ambitions, unexpected events and centripetal forces kept him bound to the studios. In Trumbo's case, it was a combination of the salary, his fascination with the medium, the size of the audience he could reach, and the craft of screenwriting. He never denigrated screenwriting, which he came to see as a unique craft that could not be mastered by every accomplished writer. Only rarely, when he was deeply discouraged with his assignments, did he consider himself a hack or a sell-out. Yet he rarely bragged about any of his scripts, and he took pride in only a few.

His first screen credit was for *Road Gang*, a municipal corruption–prison farm tale that was clearly modeled on Warner's hugely successful *I Am a Fugitive from a Chain Gang* (1932). Trumbo was given an original story that had been written and revised by two other studio writers. The story was about an honest newspaper reporter who exposes a corrupt political boss, is framed by the boss, and is imprisoned and sent to a slave-labor mine. With the help of his fiancée and editor, along with a conveniently timed prisoner uprising, the jailed reporter exposes the corruption ring. Many of the words spoken by the reporter reflect Trumbo's ideas about integrity. For example, when the reporter is offered a better-paying job if he will abandon his exposé, he replies: "I may sell out when I'm so old I can't make a living any other way. But for the present, I've at least got to keep clean enough to live with myself." And at the end of the script, when his fiancée tells the reporter that he has won, he replies: "No, I haven't, honey. Not yet. As long as there are men like Metcalfe [the corrupt boss]—there'll be fights. You put one in jail and a dozen others are ready to take his place. . . . They want so *much* these Metcalfes. It's not just money, it's *power*—power such as no man should ever have. That's why they're dangerous. That's why we've got to keep right on fighting." The final script is dated October 10, 1935.[30]

Trumbo's name was mentioned in only a few reviews of the movie. *Welford Beaton's Hollywood Spectator* credited "Dalton Trumbo with some superb screen writing" and expressed the hope that "there should be more Dalton Trumbos discovered."[31] The reviewer for the *Los Angeles Times* noted that Trumbo had written a "good" but "contrived" script.[32] Another reviewer suggested that the screenwriters should have forgone "the obvious theatrical tricks" they resorted to and "allowed their story . . . to tell itself."[33] Most reviewers called *Road Gang* a grim melodrama.

Five months later, Trumbo received cowriting credit for *Love Begins at Twenty*, a domestic comedy about a bank robbery. The film received light praise from the trade papers: *Daily Variety* called it "a sprightly constructed screenplay," and the *Hollywood Reporter* referred to it as a "moderate entertainment."[34]

We have very little evidence of Trumbo's political, social, and cultural activities between the time he left the bakery in 1934 and his marriage in 1938. He was still living with and supporting his mother and sisters, but as a result of his screenwriting success, they had substantially improved their living quarters. Trumbo had moved them to a duplex in the Hollywood Hills (3115 Hollycrest Drive), not far from the Hollywood Bowl, and then to an even better neighborhood a little farther northeast (2416 Hollyridge Drive). Trumbo gambled and drank, and he carefully cultivated a rags-to-riches image of himself by planting stories in various gossip columns. For example, one story in the *Hollywood Citizen-News*, titled "Film Writer Hits Top via Bakery," stated: "Dalton was so broke in 1935 that he actually walked from Hollywood to Burbank to see about getting a job as a script reader at Warner Bros." In later press stories, Trumbo was referred to as "the Horatio Alger of American letters," and his success was likened to "an Alger tale."[35]

Although Hollywood boasted a very active political and cultural
life, Trumbo apparently did not participate in it. For example, there
was a John Reed Club as well as numerous salons, patronized mainly by
emigrés; political types could meet at Stanley Rose's bookstore, Musso
and Frank Grill, or Lucey's restaurant. Trumbo's letters written during
this time do not refer to any of these venues, nor does Cook's biography mention them. Likewise, there is no comment about the guberna-
torial election of 1934, one of the most contentious and vicious in the
state's history. Conservatives, reactionaries, and Republicans—including most of the studio heads—had done everything in their power to
defeat socialist Upton Sinclair, who had secured the Democratic Party's
nomination and was running on a platform to End Poverty in California (EPIC). The studio bosses even forced their employees to contribute
money to Sinclair's opponent, Frank Merriam. Warner Bros. executives
deducted $100 from the salary of each employee, and MGM dunned its
employees one day's pay.[36] Many of Trumbo's future colleagues in the
Screen Writers Guild and the Communist Party were active supporters
of Sinclair. The Communist Party itself, however, was strongly opposed
to Sinclair, referring to him as a social-fascist.

We do not know how Trumbo voted in that election, but two years
later he caricatured Sinclair, his running mate Sheridan Downey, and
the EPIC program in his second published novel, *Washington Jitters*.
"Downie Sincere" is running for governor on his MILLENNIUM Plan,
an acronym for "Make Interest, Loans, Legacies, Equities, Navies, 'N'
Armies Illegal Under Me." Trumbo describes Sincere as a "Marxian
Lucifer hurled from red heavens" who concocts "slogans that were
the despair of competent advertising specialists."[37] Contrary to fact,
Trumbo allies Sincere with two right-wing demagogues: Dr. Burghlimit
(Dr. Francis Townsend) and the Reverend Dr. Laughlin (Father Charles
Coughlin).

Trumbo's first strong, public political statement concerned censorship, which in turn generated his first open conflict with the establishment. The strict new Production Code that had just been promulgated
by the Motion Picture Association of America had captured Trumbo's
attention. He accused the Catholic Church, the code's main supporter,
of "saddling the motion picture industry with the most appalling set
of rules ever devised for the emasculation of free expression," and he
accused the leaders of every other religious denomination of making
"Hollywood a scapegoat to cover their own immeasurable incapacity
to face contemporary problems." In words he would apply to the House

Committee on Un-American Activities ten years later, Trumbo accused the church of taking on the movie industry because "they are afraid of a real fight, and they understand the timidity of Hollywood." But it was not movie censorship that really bothered him: "Like any ordinary idiot, I know that moral censorship is, and always has been, simply the opening wedge for political censorship."[38]

When he was criticized by the Catholic *Motion Picture Herald* editor Terry Ramsaye, Trumbo replied, again foreshadowing his later eloquence on the subject:

> In a democracy the vast movie public is the best censor and . . . the box office is its logical polling place. For self-appointed meddlers and meretricious clergymen arbitrarily to assume the job is a studied and officious insult. Once started, nothing but complete power will appease them, and since smut is the first object of their attack it must, willy-nilly, become the first line of our defense. . . . [I]t is the focal point through which the camel of professional reform thrust its snout into the creative tent. And I hate the camel so deeply that smut, by comparison, seems clean. In it I can occasionally smell the robustiousness of life; but from the priests of moral reform I catch only the stench of putrescence and death—that intellectual death which is the beginning of tyranny and the handmaiden of censorship in any form.[39]

Though there is nothing in his correspondence about the Depression and its effects, nor about his financial success in the midst of so much unemployment, there is clear evidence that Trumbo still considered himself an exploited worker. Shortly after he joined the readers' department at Warner Bros., he became involved in efforts to organize a readers' guild. At first, the organizers worked in secret. When they decided to surface (around late 1934 or early 1935), they held a cocktail party at Trumbo's house on Hollyridge Drive, featuring Dashiell Hammett. Once he became a screenwriter, Trumbo joined the Screen Writers Guild (SWG), just as it became involved in a highly contentious dispute with the studio bosses. Nikola Trumbo recalled that her father often talked to her about his organizing work: "The labor movement was important to him and he explained to me why workers needed to organize, how difficult it was to organize because of the opposition of the owners who didn't want to pay higher wages."

In fact, in the 1930s, reluctance to pay higher wages was not the reason why the studio bosses hated the idea of an independent writers' organization. They were opposed to it because they were afraid of losing control over story material. Indeed, two of the new SWG's actions seemed to confirm that possibility. Guild organizers planned to amalgamate with the eastern writers' organizations (the Authors League, Dramatists Guild, American Newspaper Guild, and Radio Writers Guild) to form a national writers' bloc. They also prepared for a possible strike in the summer of 1938 by adding Article XII to the guild's bylaws, which required all screenwriters to refuse to sign contracts that extended beyond May 2, 1938. The attitude of industry leaders was aptly expressed by a headline in the *Motion Picture Herald*: "Writer Dictatorship Looms on Coast with Strike Weapon." The reporter accused the SWG of planning to establish "a closed shop for all writing talent in the United States" and to get "an iron grip on the production of motion pictures."[40]

The Association of Motion Picture Producers responded with a four-page statement, the gist of which was that these worrisome tactics were the work of "a few radical-minded and power-seeking . . . malcontents and disturbers" who did not represent the majority of screenwriters, who "are constructive in their attitude toward the industry."[41] The producers were clearly sending a message to the older, more conservative writers who cherished their relationships with the producers and preferred that writers' organizations resemble gentlemen's clubs. A group of writers at MGM who were disturbed by what they called the "trade-unionism" and class-divisiveness of the SWG announcement met with the head of production, Irving Thalberg, and proposed that he help them organize a producer-friendly ("sweetheart") writers' organization. With Thalberg's assistance, they organized the Screen Playwrights (SP), and the studio heads immediately began to pressure their writers to leave the SWG and join the SP. The person who had recruited Trumbo for the SWG urged him to resign from that organization and join the SP, but he refused.[42] Hundreds of other writers did resign from the SWG, however, although most did not join the SP.

Trumbo's decision caused him problems at Warner Bros. His script work had clearly satisfied his bosses, because in February 1936 his supervisor had exercised the studio's first option and extended Trumbo's writing contract for another twenty-six weeks, thereby raising his salary to $150. Shortly thereafter, studio head Jack Warner called his writers together and, according to Trumbo, told them the following:

The producers absolutely would not tolerate the passage of Article XII. He said our leaders were communists, radical bastards, and soap-box sons of bitches. . . . He added that as a matter of fact, many of the leaders of the SWG were even then under investigation by the Department of Justice and that a lot of them were cooked geese. He said that he, personally, didn't care because he had five million dollars in cold cash and that the studio could close up tomorrow, as far as he was concerned. He said repeatedly, "There are a lot of writers in the business who are active in the SWG now who will find themselves out of the business for good," and it wouldn't be a blacklist because it would all be done over the telephone.[43]

In April, Trumbo was called into the office of Walter McEwan, who suggested that Trumbo get in touch with screenwriter Howard Emmett Rogers, one of the founders of SP. "I asked him," said Trumbo, "if he was asking me to resign from the Guild, and he said, 'Not exactly.' I said, 'Because if you are, my signature to an SWG contract is worth exactly as much as my signature to a Warner Bros. contract and since it exists in both contracts, it would be impossible for me to violate both.'" The next day William Friedberg, assistant to B unit head Bryan Foy, told Trumbo that he was being laid off for six weeks, and if he did not accept the furlough, Foy would tear up his contract. Trumbo refused the furlough.[44]

According to Trumbo, he was blacklisted for three months during the SWG-SP tangle. He later told a panel of National Labor Relations Board examiners that when he asked Harry Cohn (head of Columbia Pictures) for a job, Cohn agreed, but only on the condition that Trumbo accept the same salary he had received at Warner Bros. When Trumbo protested that he had two screen credits and therefore deserved a higher salary, Cohn told him: "There *is* a blacklist [in this town] and you are definitely on it, and you have your choice of signing or staying out of the business." Years later, Trumbo recalled that Cohn "didn't give a damn" about the blacklist.[45]

In July 1936 Cohn hired Trumbo to revise the script for *Tugboat Princess*. Cohn was sufficiently pleased with Trumbo's work to offer him a contract for $250 a week. In addition, the studio purchased Trumbo's caper story "Double in Diamonds" (which Trumbo had also sold to a British publisher). Trumbo signed the contract on August 20, and he was immediately assigned the job of adapting Ring Lardner's story "Golden Honeymoon," but shortly thereafter he was reassigned to revise the script for *The Devil's Playground*. When the latter film was released in early 1937, the reviewer for the *Hollywood Reporter* wrote: "There is nothing new about this comedy-melodrama of the U.S. Navy and the submarine service, but it builds to a thrilling climax that has a hefty wallop and will put it over for fair box office success as a program leader." The *Los Angeles Times* reviewer called it "well scripted" but did not mention any of the three credited writers. The reviewer for *Daily Variety* noted that Trumbo had written "a sufficiently absorbing melodrama."[46]

Meanwhile, Trumbo had completed his second novel. In January 1936 Moss Hart agreed to dramatize it, and one month later, Alfred Knopf contracted to publish the novel as soon as the play opened.[47] When Hart encountered difficulty with the adaptation and moved on to another project, Trumbo, worried that Knopf might refuse to publish the book, decided to write the play himself. He wrote to Elsie: "I have never done a play, but on the other hand there was a time not too distant when I hadn't done a short story or a novel. . . . I am spending tomorrow afternoon with Hart and [George S.] Kauffman, at which time I plan to chisel whatever actual work they have done out of them. This should give me some idea of structure as conceived by experts, and I shall rely on what ability I have to supply the rest."[48] However, his new contract with Columbia left him little time to work on the play, and he was relieved when another producer, Walter Hart, purchased an option on it. Hart, who had staged other political plays, including *Merry-Go-Round* and *Bury the Dead*, for the left-wing theater group Theatre Union, agreed to complete the dramatized version in three months.[49] It actually took him four.

Knopf published the novel, now titled *Washington Jitters*, that summer. It was a different take on Trumbo's political corruption theme: An honest but hapless amateur, after some missteps, summons the strength to turn the tables on the professional (and corrupt) politicians in the nation's capital. His path is made clear by a good woman who has fallen in love with him.[50] In the novel, Trumbo makes fun of all political parties and ideologies and calls one of the corrupt politicians "an architect of souls," perhaps a mocking reference to a 1935 statement by Andrei Zhdanov, who told a writers' congress in the Soviet Union that Soviet writers should be the "engineers of human souls." Trumbo also clarifies that, at this point in his political evolution, he sees no significant difference between what the Communist Party demands and what "decent people" want. At one point, Henry Hogg, the main character, states: "Oh no, . . . I'm not Communistic in any sense of the word. . . . I just feel that everyone should have jobs, and that the money should be divided up more equally so that everybody can go to school and have enough to eat and all that, and so that the poor man won't always be going to war to fight for the rich man's investment. But then I guess all decent people feel that way."[51] However, in the book's "big" speech, which is a staple of Trumbo's political novels and some of his screenplays, Hogg delivers a populist message, telling his listeners that they do not have to be told how to think or how to make political decisions. Just read about current political issues, he urges them; ignore what others are saying; "just sit down and think" and decide for yourselves what to do.[52]

Washington Jitters received just a few short reviews. Beatrice Sherman wrote in the *New York Times Book Review*: "His picture of the timid sign-painter's meteoric ride on the Washington merry-go-round is funny and fantastic." Another reviewer said: "Dalton Trumbo is a good shot. He has peppered Pennsylvania Avenue from end to end with poisoned arrows of satire." And H. P. Berger compared Trumbo to P. G. Wodehouse, but "Wodehouse with a bludgeon." Berger also commented on Trumbo's talent for mixing slapstick with "the damning, ridiculous, but very vital truth." The *Los Angeles Times* reviewer observed that the novel "makes shrewd fun" of Roosevelt's brain-trusters.[53] Reading it today, it seems very much a product of its time, in terms of both its political statements and its humor. Trumbo himself saw its shortcomings. He told Elsie: "Nobody knows better than I that 'Jitters' has absolutely no literary merit. . . . But the book came out of the headlines, and it can only be sold through the headlines."[54]

Even though *Jitters* had been published by a major firm, its appearance in print did little to resolve what Trumbo called his "literary quandary." He still wanted to complete his bakery novel, but he was also harboring an idea for another political novel "satirizing the conflict between left and right through the problems of a Henry Hoggish sort of liberal who eventually encompasses his complete destruction by reason of the fact that he can't decide on which side of the fence to jump." He was unhappy with his short story skills and discouraged by the demands of the genre: "I grind out very conventional formula stuff [for the studio] all day long, and see no reason why I should do it at night as well. When the sun sets and I'm giving up a riotous evening for the typewriter, I want to enjoy myself, and I don't think I could do it writing for the [*Saturday Evening*] *Post*."[55] Nevertheless, he continued to grind them out, and Elsie managed to place one, "The World and All," in *McCall's*. It is an inventive story about the Depression in which one event leads to another, which leads to another, and so on, each producing a more dire outcome than the previous one.[56]

Trumbo was also unhappy at Columbia. He broke his contract with the studio in October 1937 and signed a one-year deal with MGM, to which he sold a romance story, "Caprice," and a script he had written on his own time.[57] He worked on a variety of scripts for MGM, but either they were never made into movies or his contributions did not merit credit. He did a script polish on *Thoroughbreds Don't Cry*, a Judy Garland–Mickey Rooney vehicle; contributed dialogue to *Everybody Cheer*, a Garland musical comedy; and worked on *Paradise for Three*, a comedy set in Vienna. During the years 1936–1938, Trumbo also wrote several unproduced scripts, one of which, "Three Men in the Snow," was an adaptation of a German comedic novel by Erich Kästner, a pacifist and anti-Nazi. On March 3, 1938, *Daily Variety* reported that Trumbo had "washed up his contract with MGM and left the lot."[58]

He kept busy helping to resuscitate the SWG. One year earlier, on April 12, 1937, the US Supreme Court had announced its decision upholding the constitutionality of the National Labor Relations Act.[59] Trumbo and other SWG loyalists had immediately called an open meeting for writers. Some 400 showed up and approved the decision to file a representation petition with the suddenly empowered National Labor Relations Board (NLRB). The board scheduled a hearing on the matter, and Trumbo was one of the star witnesses for the SWG. During his testimony, one of the producers' lawyers asked him if he was a member of the Communist Party. "No, I am not," Trumbo replied. "Have you ever been?" the questioner persisted. "I have never been," Trumbo said.[60] In June 1938 the NLRB ordered a representation election, and the SWG soundly trounced the SP, winning by a substantial majority in every studio, including MGM.[61] Trumbo told Nancy Schwartz that writers began leaving the SP "like shits leaving a sinking rat."[62] Several months later, the studios agreed to recognize five other guilds, the Screen Readers Guild among them.

Trumbo was not lying when he told the NLRB examiners he was not a member of the Communist Party. Nor had he joined any of the Hollywood Popular Front organizations. These mainly antifascist groups (the Hollywood Anti-Nazi League and Motion Picture Artists Committee to Aid Republican Spain, among others) began to appear in the spring of 1936, and they attracted a large number of non-Communists.[63]

Trumbo with his fancy Chrysler, 1937. Courtesy of Trumbo family.

But there is nothing in Trumbo's papers or in his comments to Cook that indicates he joined any of them. The explanation that he was preoccupied with establishing himself as a screenwriter seems insufficient, given that many other young, struggling writers were actively engaged in the Popular Front. He probably kept his distance because of his anti-war feelings, choosing not to be involved in organizations that supported war (as in Spain) or openly advocated war as a means of halting the advance of Germany, Italy, and Japan. Trumbo's organized political activity likely began in the spring or summer of 1938, when he helped create, probably at the behest of Dashiell Hammett, the Motion Picture Democratic Committee. This group was formed to work within the Democratic Party to bring New Deal reforms to California.

Meanwhile, desperately needing money, Trumbo agreed to undertake what seemed to be an unlikely ghostwriting project. He had met Baron Friedrich de Reichenberg, an Austrian nobleman who was writing a book on Prince Klemens von Metternich (1773–1859), chancellor of the Austrian Empire and one of the architects of the Congress of Vienna system. The author planned to write "an impartial study" based on rigorous research and to demonstrate that, contrary to conventional wisdom, Metternich was not "a veritable embodiment of guile and chicanery." According to the baron, Metternich was "a man possessed of magnetic personal charm, keenly penetrating discernment, a unique grasp of contemporary military and political strategy, and an incredible interest in the welfare of the human family in general." When Reichen-berg decided that his vision would best be presented as a thoroughly documented "historical romance," he hired Trumbo.[64]

It is possible that Trumbo knew very little about Metternich, who was notorious for his successful suppression of the liberal forces of national liberation unleashed by the Napoleonic Wars. Even more intriguing, Trumbo found himself in "a real nest of Nazis. . . . The Baron himself didn't like Hitler too much. . . . But his friends *loved* Hitler—anti-Semites all."[65] Nevertheless, Trumbo complied with the baron's wishes to present Metternich in a positive light, and the final product reads like a good piece of historical fiction. In his preface to the book, Reichenberg wrote: "I appreciate particularly the co-operation of my young friend, Mr. Dalton Trumbo."[66] Trumbo later said that he had been paid $100 and given permission to "forage" at the baron's table.[67]

Nearly broke, still living with his mother, drinking too much, and without a screen credit since *The Devil's Playground* premiered in January 1937, a deeply unhappy Trumbo wanted to get married and start a family. In 1938 everything changed for him, emotionally and creatively. It was his annus mirabilis.

4

Marriage and *Johnny Got His Gun*

Cleo was a force in his life that caused him to redefine himself
in some ways. It changed his attitude about himself. It is as if he
decided to become a grown-up.

—Christopher Trumbo

Trumbo later said that 1938 "was probably the best year of my life."[1]
He could just as easily have added 1939 and called it the best two years,
because it was during that time that he married Cleo Fincher; they con-
ceived their first child, Nikola; his play *Washington Jitters* was staged in
Washington, DC, and New York City; he wrote his best novel, *Johnny
Got His Gun*, for which he won an American Booksellers Association
award; and he received eight screen credits, including for *A Man to
Remember*, one of his favorites.

But it was the first event (the marriage) that made the rest possible.
Earl Felton, a fellow screenwriter and one of Trumbo's closest friends,
introduced Trumbo to Cleo.[2] In his notes, Christopher reminded himself to treat his parents' meeting not as some sort of fairy tale or love-
at-first-sight moment but as a process, moving from definite interest
to flirtation to infatuation. Aside from Cleo's beauty, Trumbo was
undoubtedly attracted by what Christopher called her "air of integrity.
There was no duplicity in her; the character she presented to the world
was genuine." Mitzi described her as "natural, without artifice. She
never saw herself as others saw her; she never thought she was pretty.
She was eloquent in her simplicity, her clarity, and the depth of her
understanding of human nature. She was a private person, rarely complaining or talking about her own difficult childhood with an absent
father and a fierce and unloving mother. How she overcame the adversity of her own childhood remains a mystery to me. She spoke very little

about her early years, but over time we children were able to piece her past together from snapshots of her childhood."[3]

Cleo Beth Fincher came into the world on July 17, 1916, the youngest of the three children of Orville Day and Elizabeth (Bessie) Fincher. She was born at home in Fresno, California, unwanted, premature, and not breathing. She was resuscitated by her quick-thinking grandmother, who put her in the oven. Bessie was a vain and ambitious woman who had theatrical aspirations for her three children, hoping they would make her fortune. The older two, Richard and Georgia, were trained in violin and ballet, respectively. Cleo, a natural athlete, taught herself to do acrobatics and contortions. When she was four or five, she and her siblings began to perform before audiences. A few years later, their mother enrolled Cleo and Georgia at the Severance Dance Academy, created a vaudeville routine for them, and started to book them into as many venues as she could. They performed at Rotary Clubs, Lions Clubs, and other groups' meetings in and around Fresno. In May 1924, at the school's Springtime Fantasy and Ballet Classique, Cleo was a dew fairy in "Birdland," danced a solo to "Something Different," and teamed with Georgia in "Joy of the Rose." That December, at a production staged by the Winchell Elementary School PTA, the sisters performed novelty acrobatics, executing a series of cartwheels and closing the show with a handstand pirouette. The following year, the three siblings performed a song, dance, and musical act for the Nutritional Home Benefit, sponsored by the labor unions of Fresno. In 1926 they appeared together at the Fresno Stage Talent Review and danced "The Joy of the White Rose," in conjunction with a showing of D. W. Griffith's *The White Rose* at the Liberty Theater. Cleo later performed a colonial pantomime and toe-dance minuet to a work by Luigi Boccherini. She enjoyed performing, especially the applause afterward. And although the schedule was rigorous, it was the only life she knew and her one source of happiness.

Cleo's parents separated when she was ten years old, and Bessie and the children moved to Pasadena. A trial reconciliation in Santa Barbara failed, and mother and children moved to Los Angeles, where they rented a one-bedroom apartment on Olympic Boulevard, near downtown. Ten years passed before Cleo saw her father again. (He had remarried and fathered four other children.) She was, Mitzi said, "devastated by the divorce, as she had been close to her father, and she was ignored and mistreated by her mother." The three siblings were close, however; they looked after one another and tried to get their mother to remarry.

TWO LOCAL STAR ENTERTAINERS WHO WILL TAKE PART IN NUTRITIONAL HOME BENEFIT

This is one of the 18 acts that will appear at the Civic Auditorium Tuesday evening, April 28, when a performance will be given for the benefit of the Nutritional Home by the labor organizations of Fresno. The entire proceeds will be used for the building of this home for undernourished children.

The youthful performers whose picture appears opposite are Cleo and Beth Fincher, children of Mr. and Mrs. O. D. Fincher. Master Richard Fincher will also be on the program, and is considered one of the leading juvenile violin artists of Fresno.

Georgia and Cleo Beth Fincher, ca. 1922. Courtesy of Trumbo family.

At Sentous Junior High School, Cleo realized she was good at athletics. Baseball, basketball, and volleyball all came easily to her, and she enjoyed playing them. When the two sisters were in high school, Georgia, who was tired of dealing with their mother, dropped out and became a professional dancer, but Cleo stayed in school and continued to perform in various school programs; her goal was to become a gym teacher.

When she was sixteen, during an ocean swim, Cleo was thrown by
a wave and inhaled a large amount of salt water. She developed empy-
ema, an infection of the pleural space, and her right lung burst; the doctors did not think she would survive. She spent six months in the public
ward of Los Angeles County Hospital. She later said about that experience: "The sisters from the church came to visit me. My uncle came to
visit. My gym teacher came to visit me. My mother never came to visit."
When Cleo was well enough to go back to school, she found that she
no longer fit in with her classmates, so she began to spend a lot of time
on the tennis court. "Being in the hospital had aged me," she said. For
the remainder of her life, Cleo suffered from chronic health problems.

After high school, Cleo had to go to work. She became a carhop
at a Hollywood drive-in restaurant, delivering orders on roller skates.
She left home, rented a room in a boardinghouse, and bought a car. It
was the happiest moment in her life—she felt "free," and she wanted to
maintain that freedom. Cleo told Nancy Escher, Christopher's wife: "I
had no prospects. I just wanted to enjoy myself. At the drive-in restaurant, I could have had screen test after screen test, casting couch after
casting couch, but I wasn't interested. I knew how to keep advances in
check, without being harsh." Cleo was twenty when Felton first brought
Trumbo to the drive-in in late 1936, telling him: "I know the girl you're
going to marry." The story of their courtship could have come from a
B-movie plot or a pulp-fiction magazine. Trumbo was instantly smitten
with Cleo and arrived at the drive-in every night in a chauffeur-driven
Chrysler. He parked in her serving area and gave her lavish tips (which
she saved and gave back to him a year later). Trumbo also urged her
to go to secretarial school, and he gave her the tuition ($100) to do so.
Although she enrolled, the combination of work and school exhausted
her, so she stopped going to classes after two weeks and repaid Trumbo
the money. Finally, Trumbo asked her out on a date.

Two years after he met Cleo, Trumbo, filling in for a movie gossip
columnist, attacked the working conditions at drive-in restaurants and
encouraged patrons to tip the waitresses generously. But, he hastened
to add, "even if you tip generously, you must not expect her to accept
your invitation to drive her home when she's through work. She won't
go. I know. I tried for 14½ months to get a date with her. By that I mean
I tried at least once a day of every week of every month. If I had been
more persistent and come in twice each day, it is possible that I would
have succeeded sooner."[4]

Unbeknownst to Trumbo, Cleo had a boyfriend, and when she told him about Trumbo's interest in her, the boyfriend persuaded Cleo to elope. That marriage did not dissuade Trumbo. "It was," Christopher remarked, "simply another problem to solve, another obstacle to overcome." When one of Cleo's friends told Trumbo that she suspected the husband had another wife, Trumbo hired a private detective, who inveigled his way into the husband's confidence and learned that he was married to two women. When Cleo learned about the bigamy, she left her new husband. Trumbo then mounted his final offensive and won the day. To Cleo, his major appeal was that he was not a phony; he would not exploit her or try to change her. In addition, he was well-spoken, came from a close-knit family, and seemed to be successful. On the downside, Cleo told Christopher, "he was just not doing anything at the time that I thought was commendable. He was drinking, playing around, and wasting his talent."[5] In the final analysis, it was Trumbo's energy that tipped the balance in his favor. Cleo later said of her husband:

> He is just *not* an ordinary man. He goes at everything like a sort of dynamo. Imagine how he seemed to a kid like me. He'd be there, night after night, maybe he would be drinking and maybe not. It didn't matter. Either way he was so intense, so single-minded in his courting—if you want to call it that. He goes at anything in this way. He'll do anything to get what he wants. That was how he was; he acted *crazy*. Eventually, of course, this crazy quality of his—and I do mean slightly nuts—which had frightened me at first actually began to attract me. He just isn't like other men.[6]

"My father," Mitzi said, "was the complete opposite of my mother. She was athletic and fun-loving—she had a lot of good spirit to her—and my father was not athletic at all. He sat at a typewriter and read books all day. I think she brought a lot of joy into his life." Cleo was, according to Christopher, "the only person that my father truly cared about in terms of what she thought of him. She gave him a moral compass. She was the one he tried out ideas on [with the major exception, as we shall see, of financial ventures and places of residence]. She was a kind of conscience for him. They were incredibly loyal to each other."

Initially, Maud Trumbo objected to Cleo. Christopher liked to tell the story of Maud's reaction to a photograph of Cleo in her drive-in uniform: "Maud referred to her as a 'Chinese whore,' though I have no idea

Cleo, 1938. Photograph by Harry Baskerville; courtesy of Trumbo family.

what Maud thought a 'Chinese whore' looked like. But as Maud came to know and understand Cleo, she realized that of all the possible people Trumbo might marry, Cleo might be the only one who might tether him, be a center of strength and solidity. Maud then became her champion and adviser. She taught her what to wear and what fork to use."

Their engagement came during one of Trumbo's financial troughs. He had been fired by MGM, leaving him with about $1,200 in savings.

He did, however, sell an original story, "Broadway Cavalier," to Warner Bros., which released it as *The Kid from Kokomo*. Just before he married Cleo on March 13, 1938, Trumbo was signed by RKO, the smallest of the major studios, on a week-to-week basis, at a salary of $350 a week. In monetary terms, their years together resembled a roller coaster, with regular ascents and descents. But whether the roller coaster was on the incline or decline, Trumbo spent money lavishly. "Being broke," Christopher recalled, "never stopped my father from spending money." For example, in May 1938, still without a permanent job, Trumbo bought a ranch and 320 acres of land in Kern County, a few hours' drive from Los Angeles. He told Elsie McKeogh he would finally be able to do some "serious writing" there.[7] But Cleo told Christopher: "I think Trumbo wanted me up at the ranch so I'd be hidden from view. He was always afraid I'd leave him."[8]

Whatever the motivation, Trumbo named the ranch the Lazy-T, and he immediately began to pour money into it. "The ranch was in a way my father's toy," Christopher recalled. "It became a constant source of tinkering. Earthmoving machinery and men were summoned to build a dam and divert a stream to create a pond, which Trumbo characteristically insisted on calling a lake." He began to dig this "lake" in February 1939, and the following month, he decided he wanted to use authentic adobe bricks to build an addition onto the ranch house. He hired a crew to fashion the bricks, but the men must have used too much water, because after six months of lying in the sun to dry, the bricks were still wet.[9] Meanwhile, Trumbo filed for bankruptcy, listing assets worth $3,387 and liabilities worth $10,593. He did so, he claimed, so that he could work without having to fend off bill collectors. At the end of eight months, he paid all his bills and was discharged from bankruptcy.[10]

Trumbo described the ranch as "the nearest thing to Colorado we have been able to find, with its 320 acres, mountain stream, four horses, two cows, two pigs, three dogs and a cat named Homer." He hired his uncle, Tom Tillery, to make it a working ranch, and he intended to live there permanently.[11] It would be difficult to overestimate the importance of the ranch to Trumbo. He was hoping that its isolation—there was no telephone, and the nearest neighbor was six miles away—would allow him to become a writer of novels.

Jean Butler and her husband, Hugo, were very close friends of the Trumbos, and they spent many weeks at the Lazy-T. In her memoir, Jean describes the ranch and its transformation:

The Lazy-T, a rambling Xanadu of a place, had started life as a scraggly little farmhouse on property worked by a cantankerous Trumbo uncle. The acreage, a few thousand feet above sea level, was covered with brush and scrub pine, with a brook running through it. It was land no crop could grow on, and any horse put there to forage would surely starve. . . . [D]uring Trumbo's half-dozen prosperous years before the congressional hearings, they [the family] had remodeled, expanded, and refurbished till the house was transformed, with picture windows, marble fireplaces, oil paintings, and more silver bric-a-brac than I'd ever seen—all out in the middle of nowhere.[12]

Trumbo, however, did not see it as an extravagance. In his notes to Cook, circa 1973–1974, Trumbo wrote: "The gaudy high-living which the Lazy T seems to represent to some really wasn't that at all. It represented an extremely sound investment, converted by the blacklist from a probable $320,000 gain over the years to an immediate 1951 loss of $35,000." As he explained, he had purchased it for $80,000 but had to sell it for $45,000. (In the early 1970s it sold for $400,000.)[13]

However, his investment of time and energy in the play *Washington Jitters* did not pan out. As previously noted, the novel had been optioned by Walter Hart, who cowrote the script with John Boruff and coproduced it with Worthington Miner.[14] It was performed twenty-four times in Washington, DC, in March 1938 and was scheduled to open in New York City on April 18 as a Theatre Guild–Actor's Repertory production. When the opening was postponed, Hart and Boruff revised the script. It finally opened on May 2, after three weeks of previews for guild subscribers. *New York Times* drama critic Brooks Atkinson called it "a mildly amusing satiric fantasy" that was "written with high good humor" but "without much inner coherence" or political bite.[15] Wolcott Gibbs described it as "dull, heavy-handed and without perceptible value either as comment or entertainment."[16] It closed on May 21. Trumbo did not attend the New York opening, and he claimed he saw none of the performances.

While his playwriting career seemed to die aborning, his screenwriting career was finally taking off. In late September RKO released *Fugitives for a Night*, a mystery-comedy for which Trumbo received sole credit. It was his first screen credit in twenty-one months. Three weeks later the studio released another Trumbo-scripted film, *A Man to Remember*. The plot of this medical drama, set in a small town, is

Trumbo and Cleo at the ranch, 1939. Courtesy of Trumbo family.

remarkably similar to that of *Eclipse*; Trumbo even named the movie's protagonist Dr. John Abbott.[17] While the script was in progress, Trumbo discussed it with Garson Kanin, who occupied an adjoining office in the RKO writers' building. "We talked and we talked," Kanin recalled, "and, as people do when they talk, I sparked some ideas from him, and he from me, and at the end of that process, he said to me, 'How would you like to direct this picture?' I said, 'I'd like to if they let me.'" Since it was a B movie, the studio bosses agreed to allow Kanin (who was new and low-paid) to direct Trumbo's script. During the film's fourteen-day production period, Kanin said: "I worked with [Trumbo] daily, I made a lot of suggestions and cuts, I had a lot of ideas, and we had a lot of quarrels, but they were professional quarrels, not personal ones."[18] The final script is a model of tight plotting and dialogue, and it is a wonderful movie. Perhaps that is because Dr. Abbott is the personification of Orus Trumbo—an intelligent, moral, kind, community-minded, and unappreciated man.

The movie opens with Abbott's funeral parade, which is intercut with scenes of the town's three richest men, who are grumbling about Abbott and the money he owed them. Then the movie flashes back to

Abbott's return to his hometown, with his motherless son, to establish a medical practice. (They lived at 1124 Gunnison Avenue, the Trumbo family's address in Grand Junction.) His former high school classmates, now very successful, look down on him as a ne'er-do-well. Abbott makes little money, mainly because he treats poor and working-class people, but he constantly works to make the town a better place for its citizens. He shames the town supervisors into building a sewer in the poor section of the community, and he blackmails the banker into building a hospital. He manages to send his son to medical school, but when the son returns, he chooses to practice with the wealthiest doctor in town, rather than his father.

The film's dramatic high point occurs when Dr. Abbott diagnoses an outbreak of infantile paralysis and warns the town supervisors to cancel the upcoming county fair. When the supervisors, the other doctors, and Abbott's son reject his advice, Dr. Abbott has circulars printed and distributed at his own expense, warning the townspeople about the epidemic and offering to vaccinate their children free of charge. The parents heed his warning, have their children vaccinated, and keep them home. As a result, their town is the only one in the region spared from the epidemic. After the scare has passed, a minister organizes a letter of thanks to Dr. Abbott, signed by nearly 9,000 people. The members of the county medical association apologize and elect Abbott a member, and his son joins his practice. After the funeral procession has moved past their offices, the three grumblers find an envelope containing the money Abbott owed them, fully repaying his outstanding debts. The banker remarks: "He paid every cent he owed. He was a good man."[19]

Reviewers loved the movie. Edwin Schallert deemed it "one of the outstanding small-budgeted features of recent months."[20] Frank S. Nugent termed it "a distinguished and unusual film" and congratulated Trumbo and Kanin for their work.[21] But Bosley Crowther, commenting on the movie several months later, gave most of the credit to Kanin, mentioning Trumbo's script only at the end of his article.[22] When the picture opened in the United Kingdom in April 1939, the reviewer for the *Manchester Guardian* called it "one of those happy accidents that we all wish could happen much more often in the film industry. . . . [T]he characters live, the script and direction have wit, hardness, and hardly a touch of . . . the inevitable transatlantic sentimentality."[23] Ironically, considering what was to come, an RKO press release listed several organizations that had given the movie their seals of approval, including the American Legion Auxiliary, Daughters of the American Revolution, and National Board of Review.[24]

Film historian Lea Jacobs cites *A Man to Remember* as an example of a B film that, during production, attained sufficient "quality" to be deemed good enough to distribute as an A feature.[25] And it was profitable, earning $145,000 for the studio. For Trumbo, it was the one screenplay he had written "of which I am heartily proud. . . . I got as much satisfaction out of doing it as a man can get. The way in which the story came out on the screen greatly increased my enthusiasm for motion pictures as a medium of expression."[26]

As noted earlier, Kanin indicated that most of Trumbo's work hours at RKO consisted of conversation. According to Paul Jarrico, who also worked on B movies at RKO:

> You had to turn in five pages every day and have the script finished in six weeks. I found this very difficult, so I put in long hours. But Trumbo never seemed to work. He'd come in with word games, or some political news, or he was drinking, or working on some fantastic thing. And I'd start to worry about him, playing around for five weeks. But then, the sixth week, the typewriter would go nonstop, and he'd have a brilliant, first-rate script. He did his work in his head, and at the end of five weeks he'd be ready to write.[27]

In December 1938 Trumbo signed a yearlong contract with RKO, at $450 a week.[28] One month later the Trumbos' first child, Nikola, was born. In her syndicated gossip column, Louella Parsons wrote: "The new daughter of Mr. and Mrs. Dalton Trumbo will be named Nikola for a very good reason. Just the day the young lady was born the author parent sold Twentieth Century–Fox 'Heaven over a Barbed Wire Fence' [*sic*] for the pleasant sum of $10,000. The heroine's name was Nikola."[29] (The heroine's name was later changed to Anita.) For the occasion of his daughter's birth, Trumbo wrote a poem about his feet (which were very odd looking—a feature Nikola did not inherit): "Feet are to walk on / Not to entice . . . / If Trumbo won love in spite of his feet / Nikola oughter."[30]

Trumbo's first credit under his new contract was *The Flying Irishman* (released April 7, 1939). This film was based on *That's My Story*, the autobiography of Douglas Corrigan, who had been labeled "Wrong-Way Corrigan" by newspaper reporters after he flew from New York to

Ireland instead of from New York to Long Beach, California. Trumbo's next assignment, *Five Came Back*, offered him the opportunity to insert a small dose of his political thinking into a script. The original script, written by Nathanael West and revised by Jerry Cady, told the story of an airplane crash in the jungles of Panama. The nine survivors manage to repair the plane, but it can carry only five of them. The final decision as to who goes and who stays is made by a criminal named Vasquez. In Trumbo's revision, Vasquez is an anarchist, and he makes the decision "fairly, honestly, without regard to personal feelings."[31] This B film, ably directed by John Farrow, did much better than expected at the box office. Critics complimented the writers for their "sharp" dialogue, and Frank S. Nugent called the film "a rousing salute to melodrama, suspenseful . . . , exciting . . . , spectacularly explosive."[32] Trumbo also received credit for *Sorority House* (May 1939), a college drama, and *Career* (July 1939), a rural drama. The latter, based on a novel by Philip Duffield Strong, bears a striking resemblance to *Eclipse*. Twentieth Century–Fox released *Heaven with a Barbed Wire Fence* in November. It tells the story of an unemployed man in New York City who inherits land in California and rides the rails to get there. Along the way, he meets a variety of characters and finds true love. Trumbo's story radiates an optimistic view of the United States, with lines extolling the freedoms enjoyed by its citizens and the many opportunities available to them. Trumbo's script was rewritten by Leonard Hoffman and Ben G. Kohn, and the three writers shared screen credit.[33] The reviewer for *Hollywood Reporter* called it "a fine example of a well-made low-budget picture. Its story is wholesome and leaves one with the kind of feeling you have after a cold shower bath on a hot day."[34]

But those successes paled in the face of what Trumbo was writing on his own time—a novel he had provisionally titled "Christ Came up from Tucson." Trumbo had first begun to think about this book in 1933, when he read a story from the *London Times*:

> It was about a British major who had been wounded in 1918, and who had been reported to his family as missing in action, though, in fact, he was hospitalized. After years of treatment, the major died and the British army admitted that it had withheld information about the identity of the soldier because his condition had been so *absolutely terrible* . . . yes, so absolutely terrible, they said, that it would have been quite impossible for the family to see him. Well, that arouses one's imagination, now

doesn't it! I mean, after all, what condition was this man in that they didn't even dare tell his own family that he was still alive. About a year later, in 1934 it was, the Prince of Wales—later the Duke of Windsor [Edward VIII]—was visiting a Canadian military hospital. At the end of the corridor was a door marked "No Admittance." When the Prince asked to be admitted, the officials said that they wished he would not make that request. He insisted, and of course they opened the door and let him pass. When he came out, according to the press, he was weeping. Yes . . . weeping. They asked him why he was upset and he told the reporters that he had seen . . . a man who was so frightfully mutilated by war the only way he could possibly communicate with him was to kiss him on the forehead. So, these two very tragic stories worked in my mind for about five years. Like recurrent nightmares they came and went, prodding me as if they somehow meant something beyond themselves, as if they were apocryphal in some way I could not yet comprehend . . . a decree about things to come. These feelings resulted in the book *Johnny Got His Gun*.[35]

He told another interviewer: "Well, in brooding about these two items, I was slowly bringing a character to life, and I think the conclusion to the existence of such a character had to be in the nature of a book. And so, as to why do you write it—this sort of thing gets at you and you get so interested in it that you bloody well do it."[36]

Another motivating factor was his memory of and reflection about the First World War. He later wrote that his alter ego Joe Bonham, like Trumbo's entire generation, had been "bewitched by World War I and the promise of making the world 'safe for democracy.'" But they had also wondered, given the "many, many prayers for victory" printed in every belligerent country, "how the deity was able to deal justly with so many prayers for victory from so many faithful but warring supplicants."[37]

Finally, the novel satisfied Trumbo's long-standing desire to depict the depth of his feelings for Grand Junction and the whole western slope of Colorado. "The central character," he later said, "I imagined to be myself, and those portrayed as boyhood friends were based on my own boyhood friends."[38] He told another interviewer that *Johnny Got His Gun* "is about the adolescence of a western American," a typical boy in a western town.[39] Joe is, in Trumbo's imagination, an almost perfect reflection of the values of the prewar United States: "He is the simple believing, honest and quite unremarkable child of his time whose only distinction is what happens to him and how he reacts to it." He accepts every aspect of the "'system' (a word he would not have recognized) into which he was born. . . . He has few political thoughts, and the idea of social revolution never enters his mind."[40]

Trumbo worked on this novel for fourteen months, writing on weekends and in the evening. "It was," he later said, "the most painful job I have ever done,"[41] because "I had to imagine myself in Johnny's [Joe's] initial condition, and from that time forward seek to discover the extent of my injuries, find something to occupy my mind with (obviously memory), search out the physical definitions of the exterior world, and finally to come into communication with it."[42] Trumbo concluded that Joe—blind, deaf, and without limbs or a tongue—could perceive his environment only by feeling, and distinguishing between, the vibrations made by the footsteps of those coming into his room. He could "tell" time only by feeling the sun on his body when the windows were opened.[43]

Johnny is unlike any previous work of fiction about the First World War, and it was the last significant one to be published before the Second World War. Most of the previous novels were set either on the battlefield or behind the front lines (John Dos Passos's *One Man's Intentions*, 1917); some recounted the disappointments of postwar existence (Laurence Stallings's *Plumes*, 1924), and a few were love stories (Ernest Hemingway's *A Farewell to Arms*, 1929).[44] Thus, Trumbo was not alone in his negative depiction of the war, but no other writer so effectively individualized the terrible human consequences of war or so graphically portrayed the pointlessness of the soldiers' sacrifice. Nor did any other writer place the commentary inside the mind of a horribly maimed protagonist, hidden away in a locked hospital room. Trumbo heightened the effect by his decision to forgo an ironic or detached tone. *Johnny* is an in-your-face narrative.

After the book appeared in print, Trumbo told gossip columnist Hedda Hopper: "Everything in it is a product of my imagination. . . . The first half of the story was easy to write. Once I got into it I was practically living the part and it was written under the most peculiar circumstances. I looked upon Joe as a man who was telling the story of his life after death and thereby it was a book of pleasant reminiscences between recollections of horror. . . . I considered it a beautiful thing and not revolting and I particularly resented editorial remarks inferring that the story was even more terrible than anything Edgar Allan Poe ever wrote."[45]

Cleo recalled: "Trumbo spent the early years of our marriage revealing the ultimate pain of the *victim* [of a senseless war]. . . . His purpose was to tell a story that might challenge the concept of the glories of war. The story said: *This happens*. The story said: *This happens because of us*."[46] Christopher thought *Johnny* gave the reader "the best sense of Trumbo, the best indication of what he thinks and what he believes."[47]

When Trumbo finished the manuscript in January, he wrote to Elsie: "Granting the fact that I'm usually wrong, I have very definite ideas about this book. I think it is damned good. I think it is a cinch to be a best seller. I think it will do me more good than anything or everything I have ever written. I think it's probably the best thing I'll ever do. I probably won't write many or any good books in my life. But in this one I've got my best chance."[48] Elsie submitted the manuscript to Knopf, and an impatient Trumbo wrote to her again in February, concerned that the publisher had not yet responded. He expressed the same concern he had had about *Washington Jitters*: it was a topical novel whose sales would suffer if publication were delayed. He told Elsie:

> One of the things that disturbs me is the fact that there is growing up in this country among liberals and intellectuals a strong pro-war sentiment. They appear to view war as the only salvation for democracy, when I see it as a sure destruction for the kind of democracy we know at present. These perfectly sincere war-mongers are becoming louder, more influential and even more dangerous. . . . If the book is any good at all it is good as an argument against war; and it will be utterly valueless if the country is either in war or in favor of war by the time it is published.[49]

One week later, Elsie informed Trumbo that Knopf had rejected the manuscript because "it would be difficult to merchandize."[50]

In March, however, Elsie made a deal with Lippincott, which paid Trumbo a $500 advance and royalties of 10 percent on the first 2,500 copies sold. The manuscript included a foreword, but Bertram Lippincott advised Trumbo to omit it because it "would be detrimental to the novel. It gives, we think, the impression of propaganda and, at the same time, an apology for the book. The text will speak for itself on all counts."[51] Elsie also contacted several periodicals about serializing it, but only the *Daily Worker* responded favorably.[52] An editor at the *Atlantic Monthly* wrote: "It seems to me brutal and sickening and beau-

Trumbo and Cleo at American Booksellers Association award ceremony,
1939. Courtesy of Trumbo family.

tifully done, but it would be impossible for serialization with all those
parts which are almost unreadable in their horror. But as a passionate
anti-war statement it seems to me one of the best jobs I have ever seen."[53]

Johnny Got His Gun was published on September 3. It sold more
than 18,000 copies, was voted most original book of 1939 by the American Booksellers Association, and has been reprinted many times.[54]
Trumbo told Hopper that actress Carole Lombard had purchased
ninety-seven copies and personally autographed each of them, as did
her husband Clark Gable. They intended to give a copy to each US senator and to the president, as Lombard considered it the best book ever
written against war. But she did not follow through "because the studios felt it was unwise of Gable and Carole to put themselves on record
as being against war—that the subject was controversial and therefore
out of keeping with the policy of any performer." Trumbo also told
Hopper that William Holden had tried to convince Paramount to adapt

the novel for the screen, and when the studio declined, Holden vowed to raise enough money to make the film himself. Trumbo, however, did not think his novel could ever be made into a movie: "There is a great difference between writing stories for the screen and writing stories for magazines or books. The treatment and the type of story are miles apart and since I refuse to compromise it looks at least in this case that never the twain shall meet."[55] He thought briefly about turning the novel into a play and then selling the script to a studio.

Johnny Got His Gun was widely praised. The phrase "tour de force" was used by several reviewers. A short review in the *Atlantic* stated: "A literary *tour de force* of the first order, is the voice of a dead man crying for life, beautifully done, philosophically not quite fair, since the dead man is presented as willingly taking up a hard destiny he later regrets."[56] In a much longer review in the *New York Times*, Harold Strauss also called the book a *"tour de force*, which derives its intense but morbid interest not from any of the common allurement of fiction, but from the unraveling of an unusual physical and psychological puzzle. The solution is one of considerable brilliance and probability, and it holds the reader engrossed."[57]

All the reviewers remarked on the book's gruesomeness. One wrote: "*Johnny Got His Gun* is strong meat for a queasy stomach. Gruesome physical details are copiously supplied, but one feels not for mere effect. The whole thing seems to be a sincere attempt to describe with fiendish clarity the effect on body and soul of subjection to war. . . . It stands as a fierce and infinitely pitiful diatribe on the senseless futility of war."[58] The reviewer for the *New Republic* described it as "a gruesome, shocking, original book."[59] A very short review in the *New Yorker* labeled it "a gruesome affair that should probably be kept away from old ladies and little children. Has a macabre interest, however, and is well told."[60]

Trumbo also received three laudatory responses from within the film community. Novelist James Hilton, then working at Warner Bros., wrote to Trumbo: "Apart from being an intensely moving and successful handling of an almost impossibly difficult theme, it is a terrifically timely answer just now to the censored and senseless nonsense that is coming over from Europe."[61] Ultraconservative gossip columnist Hedda Hopper wrote that *Johnny Got His Gun* "is a book everyone should read—at least everyone who wants to keep America out of war."[62] And actor John Garfield, during an April 1940 speech in Washington, DC, urged his audience to read the "powerful anti-war novel, *Johnny Got His Gun*."[63]

The book was read twice on radio broadcasts. The first, dramatized by Arch Oboler and read by James Cagney, aired on January 13, 1940. A few months later, Lester Pine wrote a radio adaptation for the Chicago Repertory Group. In March 1941 a member of the American Youth Congress in Chicago wrote to Trumbo: "[We], as well as all anti-war people, [have] been completely carried away by the powerful appeal of 'Johnny Got His Gun.' We really feel that it is one of the most important novels written in the 20th century, and we have conceived the idea of making a sound film adaptation to be done in connection with Peace Week." The group's members intended to use Pine's radio script, and they were seeking Trumbo's permission to do so. "We feel that this movie should be distributed rapidly and shown as often as possible before censorship makes it impossible."[64] Although Trumbo gave his permission, the movie was never made.

Thirty years later, Trumbo said about *Johnny*: "It is *not* a great novel. It is, rather, an extraordinarily successful *tour de force* which has outlived most of its contemporaries of the 1930s—a good novel, and that is enough, although some would call it only fairly good."[65] *Johnny* is very good. It continues to attract a significant number of readers not simply because of its statements about war but also because of its imaginative construction. The novel is a meditation on five themes: war, memory, the human mind, the nature of time, and religious symbolism. The bulk of the book consists of the interior monologues of Joe Bonham, a young man who has been badly mutilated while serving in France during the First World War. Joe's memories are based mainly on Trumbo's youth in Grand Junction and his work at the Davis Perfection Bakery.

Joe is, in effect, a variation on the classic brain-in-a-vat philosophical thought experiment and an exemplar of René Descartes' apothegm: I think, therefore I am. The novel opens with Joe coming to consciousness: "He was dreaming. He wasn't dreaming. He was awake even though he couldn't see. He was awake even though he couldn't hear a thing except a telephone that really wasn't ringing" (9). During the next fifty pages, Joe discovers the reality of his condition: He has no ears, no arms, no legs, no mouth, no jaws, no nose, and no eyes. What he does have, however, is a mind. As he rationally evaluates his situation, Joe concludes: If you perceive that you no longer have all those body parts and are able to think about that lack, then "you must be alive because dead men don't think. Dead men aren't curious and he was sick with curiosity so he must not be dead yet" (63). All he has, then, is a mind, and he has to discover a way to think clearly with it.

It occurs to Joe that measuring the passage of time is the best way to think clearly about his present identity: "The important thing is time. . . . If you can keep track of time you can get a hold on yourself and keep yourself in the world but if you lose it then you are lost too" (129–30). Joe understands that time exists only for those who are conscious. And he soon discovers that he can keep track of time by noting temperature changes on his skin. Once he learns how to keep track of the intervals between feeling the sun beating on his skin and not feeling it, he is triumphant: "He had recaptured time" (144). He felt like he was in control of "a little world of his own" (146). A few pages later, Joe realizes that "he had made a new universe he had organized it to his liking and he was living in it" (148).

In terms of its war message, Trumbo intended the novel to be a specific warning against US involvement in a World War I–type situation, where the national leaders mouth empty slogans to manipulate young men into enlisting. The book contains several long interior monologues explaining Joe's thoughts about war. Early in the novel, as Joe awakens to his condition, he thinks to himself: "This was no war for you. This thing wasn't any of your business. What do you care about making the world safe for democracy? All you wanted to do Joe was live. . . . Oh why the hell did you ever get into this mess anyhow: Because it wasn't your fight Joe. You never really knew what the fight was all about" (25). In the scene depicting Joe's embarkation, Trumbo juxtaposes the good-byes with all the patriotic slogans that were used in 1917 (37–39). Later, Joe berates himself for not being more skeptical about those slogans, particularly the one that proclaimed he was fighting for liberty. He now asks the questions he should have asked then: "What kind of liberty were they fighting for anyway? How much liberty and whose idea of liberty?" And what's so noble about dying for words? (114, 118). In perhaps the most powerful sentences in the novel, Joe thinks:

> Nobody but the dead knows whether all these things people talk about are worth dying for or not. And the dead can't talk. . . . If a man says death before dishonor he is either a fool or a liar because he doesn't know what death is. He isn't able to judge. He only knows about living. He doesn't know anything about dying. . . . There's nothing noble about dying. Not even if you die for honor. . . . The most important thing is your life little guy. You're worth nothing dead except for speeches. Don't let them kid you anymore. Pay no attention when they tap you

on the shoulder and say come along we've got to fight for liberty or whatever their word is there's always a word. (119–23)

Having discovered a means of communicating with the outside
world by tapping out Morse code messages with his head, Joe requests
that he be put on public display to educate people about war:

That would be a great thing to concentrate war in one stump
of a body and to show it to people so they could see the difference between a war that's in newspaper headlines and liberty
loan drives and a war that is fought out lonesomely in the mud
somewhere a war between a man and a high explosive shell. . . .
He would show himself to the little guys and to their mothers
and fathers and brothers and sisters and wives and sweethearts
and grandmothers and grandfathers and he would have a sign
over himself and the sign would say here is war and he would
concentrate the whole war into such a small piece of meat and
bone and hair that they would never forget it as long as they
lived. (232–33)

Joe's tragedy is that the outside world does not want him to deliver this
message.[66] When he has finished tapping out his idea, he is told: "What
you want is against regulations." Frustrated, Joe taps his head again,
more and more desperately. The doctor in charge decides that Joe must
be silenced. Joe feels "a sudden wet coolness. The man who had tapped
his answer was applying an alcoholic swab. Oh god he thought I know
what that means don't do it please don't. Then he felt the sharp deadly
prick of the needle. They were giving him dope again. . . . His taps came
slower and slower. . . . But still he tapped. He was tapping why? why?
why?" (242, 246–47). As he fades into unconsciousness, Joe proclaims
the great truth Trumbo discovered while writing the book: wars will
cease to be fought only when people are no longer willing to die for a
symbol, be it God, country, tribe, or whatever. Joe finally realized:

He was the future he was a perfect picture of the future and
they were afraid to let anyone see what the future was like.
Already they were looking ahead they were figuring the future
and somewhere in the future they saw war. To fight that war
they would need men and if men saw the future they wouldn't
fight. So they were masking the future they were keeping the

future a soft quiet deadly secret. They knew that if all the little people all the little guys were the future they would begin to ask questions. They would ask questions and they would find answers and they would say to the guys who wanted them to fight they would say you lying sons-of-bitches we won't fight we won't be dead we will live we are the world we are the future and we will not let you butcher us no matter what you say no matter what speeches you make no matter what slogans you write. (249)

Probably the weakest portions of the book are those in which a Jesus figure appears. Here, Trumbo seems to be reaching for a symbolic effect, but it does not fit comfortably with the book's naturalistic tone. During a hallucination, Joe hears the voice of a mother calling for her son: "The voice faded away but he knew the whole thing now. That boy was Christ and he had come up from Tucson and now his mother was hunting and crying for him. He could see Christ coming up from Tucson trembling out of the desert heat waves with purple robes flowing from him like in a mirage" (199). The Jesus figure is a herald of death, but it is powerless to prevent it. At the end, Joe "had a vision of himself as a new kind of Christ as a man who carries within himself all the seeds of a new order of things. He was the new messiah of the battle-fields saying to people as I am so shall you be." But unlike the historical Jesus, he was going to be prevented from letting others see what he saw (248–49).

Although _Johnny_ is clearly antiwar, was it the work of a pacifist? Pacifist is an inexact and frequently misleading label, regularly used to identify any person who opposes war because he or she believes that killing is wrong. But Trumbo never advocated pacifism per se. At the time he wrote _Johnny_, he was an antiwar advocate of a specific type—an antijingoist opposed to nationalistically inspired wars that lacked a "just cause" and a "right intent." He did not, however, maintain a clear distinction between pacifism and antijingoism. In an interview with two FBI agents in January 1944, Trumbo told them _Johnny_ had given him the reputation of being a pacifist, which was not true. In their report of the conversation, the agents wrote: "Trumbo explained that his own theory was that all war should be opposed 'unless it is a people's war where the people have a chance to benefit.'" Trumbo told the agents that "he had not changed his views regarding war immediately, but that the change had been gradual over a period of months and that he had

retained this pacifist view until June 22, 1941."[67] But in the introduction Trumbo wrote for the 1959 reprint of *Johnny*, he intimated that
the novel is pacifist in the sense that it warns against First World War–
type wars, which he characterized as "the last of the romantic wars."
And, he added, *Johnny* was probably the last American novel written
about that war before an entirely different, nonromantic war began.[68]
Later that year, in the closing scene he wrote for *Exodus* (see chapter
19), Trumbo pointedly explicated the complex nature of modern, nonromantic wars.

Trumbo's comments in the 1970s further reflected his ambivalence
toward these nonromantic wars. In one letter he wrote: "Although not
strictly a pacifist I think that World War I was a great folly in which
the U.S. should not have participated."[69] One year later he stated that
"both the novel and its protagonist are profoundly anti-military, which
is to say pacifistic," and the novel advocates "resistance to military service."[70] But two years after that, in a set of handwritten notes, he wrote:
"I was not a pacifist when I wrote *Johnny Got His Gun*. I was not a
pacifist when I wrote *A Guy Named Joe* (MGM, 1943). I am not a pacifist today, although the changing nature of war and the imminence of
a world holocaust causes me to believe that it may be the only possible
moral position for the future."[71] In another letter written that same
month, he stated: "[*Johnny*] is anti-war. . . . I am and was anti-war, as
any intelligent man is bound to be; but to be anti-war does not mean
that one is willing to let the world be turned into a concentration camp
manned by book-burners and Jew-gassers."[72] At one point in 1972 he
freely admitted how difficult it had become to subscribe to a pure pacifism: "If I were a North Vietnamese do you think I would be a pacifist?
How could one be? It's tough."[73]

In the biography he wrote for Lippincott in early 1939, Trumbo insisted
that he was an uncommitted libertarian who wished to live under a form
of government that permitted an individual more freedom "to think, to
talk, to act and to earn a livelihood" than is currently allowed in the
United States.[74] But as massive tremors rattled international affairs in
1939, Trumbo began to reassess his position on commitment to a cause.
In the spring, Spanish rebel forces captured Madrid, the United States
recognized the new government led by Francisco Franco, and Spain
joined Germany, Italy, and Japan in the Anti-Comintern Pact. Germany
seized the remainder of Czechoslovakia and threatened Poland, and
British prime minister Neville Chamberlain guaranteed the sanctity of

the Polish borders. In late August, German foreign minister Joachim von Ribbentrop flew to Moscow to sign a nonaggression treaty with his Soviet counterpart Vyacheslav Molotov. News of this accord stunned the world's Communists, leaders and rank and file alike. The two statesmen also signed a Secret Additional Protocol, outlining the "territorial and political rearrangement" of Poland and the Baltic states.[75]

On September 1, 1939, German armed forces invaded Poland, and on September 3 the United Kingdom and France declared war against Germany. That same day, leaders of the Communist Party of the United States of America (CPUSA), who had gathered for a special conference in Chicago, composed an open letter to President Roosevelt, expressing their "firm accord" with his decision not to involve the United States in the war and placing blame for the war on the "imperialist ambitions and interests" of the warring countries. The word "fascism" was conspicuously absent. Following the Soviet invasion of Poland on September 17, the CPUSA issued a manifesto titled "Keep America Out of Imperialist War!"[76] Over the next few weeks, the Soviets pressured Latvia and Lithuania into signing agreements that would allow the Red Army to occupy those countries. On September 28 a joint Soviet-German communiqué announced that lasting peace had been established in eastern Europe and accused the British and French of warmongering.[77]

Since Trumbo was not a member of the Communist Party, he did not have to defend or rationalize this abrupt change in the party line because, ironically, it brought the party closer to Trumbo's nonintervention-in-this-type-of-war position. He was hardly in the minority. A Gallup poll taken in October indicated that 95 percent of respondents thought the United States should not declare war against Germany. In a November poll, 68 percent agreed that it had been a mistake for the United States to join the First World War. And in December, 47 percent of those polled cited staying out of the current war as the most important problem facing the United States (twice the number who chose unemployment as the most pressing issue).[78]

In October 1939 Trumbo delivered a speech to the Southern California Youth Rally for Peace, which brought him to the attention of the Federal Bureau of Investigation. The special agent in charge of the FBI's Los Angeles office labeled Trumbo a fellow traveler of the Communist Party and opened a dossier on him. Several months later, an FBI informer fingered Trumbo as an active supporter of the "Communist-dominated" United Studio Technicians Guild, a member of the Hollywood chapter of the League of American Writers, and an instructor or lecturer at the league's School for Writers.[79] In November Trumbo spoke to another Youth Rally at Pasadena Junior College, and the following month he helped organize the Hollywood League for Democratic Action (as a replacement for the Hollywood Anti-Nazi League).[80]

In January 1940 Trumbo chaired a debate arranged by the Hollywood Peace Forum titled "Public Controversy No. 1—Is Roosevelt Leading Us towards War?" That same month, *Hollywood Now: A Journal in Defense of American Democracy* (published by the Hollywood League for Democratic Action) printed one of Trumbo's antiwar speeches. In it, Trumbo identified and criticized "the many powerful forces . . . attempting to draw this country into war." In what many considered its most controversial section, he stated: "I do not accept the thesis that this is a war between black and white—between evil and righteousness. To me and to humanity the blood of a German soldier is just as precious as the blood of a Finn, a Russian, a Frenchman, an Englishman or a Pole." A few paragraphs later, he upped the rhetoric by stating that, so far, England and France "are doing very well and Germany is slowly [being] forced toward starvation." In addition, he asked why people were so exercised about Finland, given their previous indifference to China, Spain, Ethiopia, Austria, Albania, and Czechoslovakia. He warned that the current and "deliberately inspired war hysteria" had only just begun, and he predicted that the coming war would not preserve democracy because there could be no such thing as democracy in this type of war. "It is a lie, a deliberate deception to lead us to our own destruction. We will not die in order that our children may inherit a military dictatorship!"[81]

Trumbo's antiwar position would undergo a seismic change on June 22, 1941, when German armed forces invaded the Soviet Union. CPUSA leaders immediately proclaimed that the Soviet Union was "waging a struggle for the cause of freedom of all nations and peoples,"[82] and Trumbo heartily concurred with that statement. And since the war in Europe had now become, in Trumbo's view, an antifascist people's war, he did not object when Lippincott chose not to reprint *Johnny*. This juxtaposition of Trumbo's support of World War II and the Lippincott decision has led some of Trumbo's critics to accuse him of inconsistency, hypocrisy, and "Stalinism." In a rejoinder to these anti-Communist authors, Christopher wrote, "They want Trumbo to be a party member in the 1930s because it will fit him neatly into their rendering of the history of left-wing politics and bolster the various cases they wish to make against him. If they can place Trumbo in the party on the date

Dalton Trumbo, 1940. Photograph by Harry Baskerville.

Johnny was published, they think they can connect *Johnny* to the Non-Aggression Treaty."

As explained in chapter 7, Trumbo joined the CPUSA four years after *Johnny* was published. He did not write the book on orders from party bosses or to ingratiate himself with them. Neither he nor any-one else had any inkling that the Soviet Union would sign a nonaggression treaty with Germany. Trumbo was as opposed to war after the publication of *Johnny* as he was before it. He always believed that the Second World War was "a mad, unnecessary war" that could have been avoided if the Western democracies had reacted earlier and more strongly to Hitlerian Germany. By 1941, however, Hitler had become a menace to the whole world, and when the United States entered the war against Germany in December of that year, Trumbo saw "no other way than to support it." Given that position and the fact that *Johnny* had become fodder for pro-Hitler, peace-now groups, he was not sorry that Lippincott decided not to reprint it.[83]

5

From B Films to A Films

A discernible pattern has become apparent in Trumbo's life, which will continue to the end of his life: He will spend money to the point that he is often seriously in debt. That crisis then becomes the motivation for him to work, which also ties him to the movie business, for nowhere else is so much money available to a writer.

—Christopher Trumbo

Happily married, busy renovating the ranch, awaiting the birth of a second child (Christopher, born in 1940), and the recipient of a prestigious literary prize, Trumbo became exceedingly prolific and successful as a screenwriter. Although he seemed to be doing nothing but writing scripts, much of what he wrote in these years did not resonate strongly with him. He was still under contract to RKO and had to write on whatever subject the studio assigned him, and he was becoming increasingly restive under those constraints. When he freelanced, however, he gravitated toward stories he thought would be immediately salable— *The Lone Wolf Strikes* (Columbia, January 1940), about a reformed jewel thief who helps an heiress recover a stolen necklace, and *Half a Sinner* (Universal, April 1940), about a straitlaced schoolteacher who decides to have fun and winds up in a cops-and-robbers scenario.

In August 1939, however, he came up with a story that closely reflected his sociopolitical concerns, titled "To Own the World." Although the twelve-page summary his agent submitted to various studios contained no political commentary, this simple tale of a young married couple struggling to survive the Depression had strong socioeconomic overtones.[1] A reader at MGM described it as "a moving simple story of young love. . . . [I]t is so beautifully done that it is sure to have a wide audience appeal. . . . Even if the studio is not interested in this story, I am sure that they would find the author an invaluable asset to the writing staff."[2] The studio bought the story, Trumbo submitted a complete script on December 29, and RKO loaned him to MGM to make revisions. Studio executives titled the film *We Who Are Young*.

Trumbo's script exemplified a persistent theme in left-wing, Depression-era writing: people cannot maintain their dignity as human beings and citizens unless they have jobs. In Trumbo's script, Bill and Margy, who work at the same company, marry. Margy is summarily fired because of the company's policy against employing married women. She is told that a married woman, who has a husband to support her, would be depriving an unemployed man of a job. Margy becomes pregnant, the couple runs short of money, and Bill takes a loan, violating another company rule. When he cannot repay the loan, his salary is garnished, and he is fired. One theme that runs through the script is that authority figures constantly cite "rules" to justify their inhuman decisions. At one point, Bill shouts: "I'm *sick* of your rules: They only work one way! I want a rule that works for *me* once in a while!" A second theme is the shame of being unable to find a job and having to go on relief. After being rejected for a job at a construction site, Bill simply picks up a shovel and starts digging. When the foreman tells him that no amount of digging will earn him a job, Bill replies: "I don't care. . . . What I want to do is shovel dirt—feel that I'm *doing* something. . . . [T]he important thing is for me to work." He is arrested for trespassing, and the owner of the construction site visits Bill in jail and asks him why he picked up the shovel. Bill replies: "I've been getting a relief check for the last three months. Understand? *A relief check!* When you get money without working for it, it does something to you. . . . It makes you sick inside. It makes you hate yourself. Makes you hate everybody else, too. Till finally you say—I've *got* to work!" The owner, who was once hungry himself, empathizes with Bill's plight, gets him out of jail, and gives him a job.[3]

The Production Code Administration (PCA) advised the studio that the basic story met the requirements of the Production Code, but it demanded changes in the scenes depicting the marriage ceremony, the couple in bed, and the wife's pregnancy.[4] Nothing was said about the movie's ideology or politics.[5] *Daily Variety*'s reviewer disliked *We Who Are Young*, describing it as "drab, slow moving, and at times even draggy" and criticizing Trumbo for overemphasizing the cruel aspects of life.[6] But the *Hollywood Reporter* reviewer called it "a gem of motion picture making" and congratulated Trumbo for writing "a rarely [*sic*] moving work" and depicting "a slice of real life in America that has never been more effectively presented."[7]

Trumbo unhappily returned to RKO in early January 1940. He had been feuding with RKO executives for some time, complaining that he was confined to writing B films at what he considered B wages and claiming that he was entitled to a better grade of assignments and a much higher salary (even though RKO had raised his pay to $550 a week).[8] After completing two other screenplays, *Curtain Call* (released in April 1940) and *Bill of Divorcement* (released May 31, 1940), he took a leave of absence at the end of January 1940, which RKO extended into a three-month layoff. Trumbo changed agents in March, signing with H. N. Swanson; sixteen months later he switched again, to Berg-Allenberg.

During the layoff he sold an original story, "The General Came to Stay," to Paramount for $20,000 down; he would receive an additional $7,500 if, before the script was written, it was published as a novel and an additional $2,500 if it was published as a magazine story. He notified Elsie McKeogh that he was trying to extend his layoff from RKO so he could devote his full attention to turning "The General" into a novel. "It will be the first time I have ever had a chance to work uninterruptedly on a single job and I am going to do my absolute best to try to make 'The General' as good a book in its fluffy way as 'Johnny' was. . . . I daily receive offers of work in other studios at twice my present salary, and you can imagine how frantic I get at the thought of so much gold slipping by me without being able to clutch so much as a farthing of it."[9]

At the end of April, Trumbo achieved the breakthrough into A films he had been seeking, as well as the leverage he needed to break his contract with RKO. The studio recalled him from his layoff to revise a script written by Donald Ogden Stewart, adapting Christopher Morley's best-selling novel *Kitty Foyle*.[10] Trumbo agreed to take the assignment only if the studio promised to cancel his contract when the script was finished.[11] *Kitty Foyle* became the first of two movies about working-class women Trumbo wrote during the early 1940s, both of which starred Ginger Rogers. Although Rogers and Trumbo liked each other, and she won an Academy Award for her performance in *Kitty Foyle*, her mother would later accuse Trumbo of putting subversive dialogue into her daughter's mouth.

Morley's novel tells the story of Kitty, a working-class woman from Philadelphia who is strong enough to find her own way in the world. Kitty is conscious of social and class differences and their effect, so when she falls in love with Wyn, a Main Line man, she refuses to marry him because she does not want to be "improved" by his family. Kitty discovers she is pregnant and decides to have an abortion. At the end of the novel, she meets and marries Mark, a Jewish doctor. One of the studio's readers thought the book could be made into a movie that depicts "a modern girl's struggle for romantic and financial existence during the chaotic 1920's and '30's; the story of White Collar girls in the business world, fighting for survival and recognition as desperately as the early American pioneers and the dust bowl victims."[12]

The reader did not, however, address the main problem facing any screenwriter assigned to adapt this novel: *Kitty Foyle* violated key sections of the Production Code. Indeed, after reading the RKO reader's synopsis of the novel, Joseph I. Breen, head of the PCA, informed the studio that "the material, in its present form, is definitely unacceptable, because it is a clear-cut violation of the Production Code." Breen cited three problems: "the suggestion of frequent illicit sex affairs between your two leads," Kitty's pregnancy, and her abortion. Either these offensive elements had to be omitted from the script, or the writer must "inject into the story the necessary compensating moral values of punishment." In other words, the movie had to clearly and firmly show that "illicit sex" was "wrong"; it could neither be "condoned nor justified, nor made to appear right and acceptable," and the "sinners must be punished."[13]

In Trumbo's first draft, dated June 1, the movie opens with words that replicate the theme proposed by the studio's reader: "This is the story of a white-collar girl."[14] Trumbo retained Morley's flashback structure, but he eliminated those parts of the story covering Kitty's early life. To placate Breen, Trumbo contrived a short-lived marriage between Kitty and Wyn, which ends when Kitty meets Wyn's family and they insist the newlyweds live in Philadelphia. If they did, Kitty tells them, "I'd always be Kitty Foyle from Griscom Street and he'd always be Wyn Strafford from the Main Line."[15] When Wyn sides with his parents, Kitty leaves him, goes to New York, gets a job, and learns she is pregnant. Again, to placate Breen, the baby is stillborn.

Breen, however, was not satisfied. He rated the script "unacceptable" and described it as being "hardly more than a story of illicit sex without sufficient compensating moral values." Unless the "illicit sex relationship" was completely removed, the annulment scene clarified, and the child shown to be the product of a post-annulment marriage, the script would not be approved.[16] Although the final script (dated August 13) retained the couple's "illicit" night together in the Poconos, it met the rest of Breen's demands,[17] and he finally approved the script

Trumbo and Cleo at Academy Awards ceremony, 1941. Courtesy of Trumbo family.

on September 19. Two months later, after viewing the final cut, the PCA issued a certificate of approval.

According to a researcher for the American Film Institute, Trumbo retained much of Stewart's dialogue, and another writer, Robert Ardrey, made a "significant" contribution to the continuity.[18] Nevertheless, Trumbo received sole credit for the screenplay, while Stewart received an "additional dialogue" credit. When the movie was released in December 1940, most of the reviewers praised the film, but only a few specifically congratulated Trumbo. The review in *Motion Picture Herald* noted that Trumbo's script had eliminated "a measure of sinning with gain rather than loss of power," while *Motion Picture Daily* congratulated Trumbo for keeping "intact the basic thread" of Morley's novel, spinning it "a bit tighter," and maintaining all "the shadings of significance."[19] Ginger Rogers later lauded Stewart and Trumbo for their expert writing, saying, "It was the best dramatic part that ever came my way."[20] Rogers, Trumbo, and director Sam Wood were nominated for Academy Awards. It was the first and only Academy Award nomination Trumbo received in his own name. Rogers won the Oscar for best performance by an actress in a leading role. And the movie was RKO's biggest hit that year. (Five years later, Wood and Trumbo would be exchanging vitriolic, politically tinged comments. See chapter 8.)

In the autumn of 1940, after finishing his work on *Kitty Foyle* and transforming "The General" into a novel, Trumbo wrote another story that reflected his social concerns, titled "Man with a Shovel." He sold the story to Twentieth Century–Fox, which released it the following summer as *Accent on Love*. It tells the story of a married man who has gone to work for his father-in-law, a slum landlord. The son-in-law becomes disgusted with his father-in-law's treatment of his tenants and quits his job. He then joins a Works Progress Administration project, where he helps organize workers who happen to live in his father-in-law's slums. After the requisite misunderstandings and recriminations, the father-in-law repents.

Lippincott published *The Remarkable Andrew: Being the Chronicle of a Literal Man* in January 1941. It is not a great novel, by any means, but it faithfully represents Trumbo's political thinking at the time. It is another tale of municipal political corruption (set in Shale City again) exposed by an honest citizen, Andrew Long. Although Long has good instincts and is a devoted student of US history, he requires instruction from the ghosts of Andrew Jackson, George Washington, Thomas Jefferson, Benjamin Franklin, and James Madison on how to be a good citizen. The first shade to appear is that of Andrew Jackson, one of the heroes of the War of 1812 and the seventh president of the United States. The two longest chapters are devoted to a debate between the two Andrews about the growing naval bond between the United States and Great Britain. Long defends it, intoning the same slogans Trumbo derides in *Johnny Got His Gun*—that is, the United States is fighting "to make the world safe for democracy," and "if the Germans win this war it will be the end of civilization as we know it." When Jackson states that America's only concern should be America, an astonished Long accuses him of being "a nationalist." Jackson agrees and rejects the notion that the United States has a moral responsibility to the rest of the world. He then asks Long, does the United States *always* intervene in wars where civilians are being slaughtered? When Long admits that the United States did not participate in the recent wars in Spain and China, Jackson replies:

> You've been talking about the moral responsibility of one nation to another. Yet a moment later you tell me that these

frightful things have been going on practically continuously, and no nation—not even America—has seen fit to assume the moral responsibility you now insist upon. Either morals are consistent, or they cease to be morals. And moral responsibility—unless the phrase is simply a hypocritical catchword—must apply to all rather than to one. . . . If the United States admits a moral obligation to crush aggression in one instance, then—morals being what they are—it must necessarily assume the same obligation in all instances. If not, then our morals are perverted and our logic is even worse.[21]

Long insists that the United States must ally with Great Britain because the two countries share the same language, customs, laws, and blood. Jackson pitilessly replies that those leaders who speak about war, who contemplate the death of millions, must base their decisions on something more logical than emotional nonsense. Between nations there are no ideals, nor have there ever been. . . . [W]ars are not fought unselfishly for moral or emotional reasons. They are waged either because a nation wants something, or is having something taken away from it. Nations make alliances for expediency, not for love. . . . Between nations there are no morals" (135–36).

These two chapters were not well received at Lippincott. One of the editors wrote to Trumbo: "All of us who have read [*The Remarkable Andrew*] feel strongly that the conversation between Andrew Long and General Jackson on the subject of American aid to Britain in the present war is a red herring in the story. . . . [I]t looks like a passage that was inserted as an afterthought." In effect, the editors saw no clear link between these chapters and the story of political corruption in Shale City; they believed these chapters would stick out like a sore thumb to reviewers and might cause the story to be outdated by the time the book went to press. Reviews pointing out those problems would, the editor stated, have an adverse effect on sales.[22]

Trumbo agreed that the passage might harm sales, but he responded: "I must, therefore, reconcile my natural desire to sell books with that personal philosophy which impelled me to write this particular kind of book." He did not want his children, twenty years from now, "to be preparing themselves for slaughter at the orders of some jingo politician," and the only way to prevent that from happening was "to write as furiously as I know how against the things which ultimately may cost them their lives." Trumbo referred to an age of "hideous compromise" and noted that if he were to omit those chapters, he would have taken "the first—which is always the fatal—step toward compromise." The present war, he continued, is "the great motivating fact of our age," and failing to include a discussion about it would be "to cheat my reader, to dodge my question, to distort truth. It would, in my view, constitute very bad novel writing, since I am dealing with contemporary happenings." Someone, Trumbo concluded, must write for those who are opposed to war; "if the people are to choose for themselves, they must have all sides of a controversy presented to them." As for those who might object to the inclusion of those chapters, Trumbo stated: "I actually relish the prospect of reading those critics who praised *Johnny Got His Gun* for its anti-war content, now reversing themselves when they read *Andrew*. For it is they, not I, who have changed."[23] (A few years later, Trumbo admitted that the Lippincott editor had been right. Those two chapters were, he wrote, "a disgrace to me as a novelist, and a worse disgrace to me as a man who thinks logically or pretends to. But then the whole damned book was a fake anyhow."[24])

Trumbo's antiwar attitude even permeates the chapters on municipal corruption. When Long is unjustly accused of being an embezzler by the real culprits and is brought to trial, one of the prosecution's witnesses, a businessman, spouts the standard pro-war, anti-Communist line: Every businessman is behaving patriotically, and labor must do the same. But the workers, instead of making concessions, "have fallen entirely under the sway of gangsters and murderers. Most of them reds and Communists. . . . We must revive in Shale City the patriotic fervor of the frontier. We must band ourselves together, to strike down reds, pacifists, racketeering union leaders. . . . Honest workmen will report to their foremen any subversive union statement designed to sabotage national defense. We must organize ourselves into a Christian group prepared to defend our liberties to the last" (281–87).

Another prosecution witness presents a variant of the current jingoism: "Now there *is* danger. This is no time for dissent. Either we must silence those who dissent, or face destruction at the hands of brutal dictatorships. . . . The place for agitators and fifth columnists is prison. . . . We must shove Americanism down their dirty throats. There is no other way for this great democracy to survive" (303). But Long (speaking for Trumbo) states:

> I know that whether they like it or not, people sometimes have
> to fight. . . . I suppose if this country went to war, I would go

to war too—even if it was a *bad* war—because once you're in it there doesn't seem anything to do but fight your way out of it. But I also think that it is my right, if I want to, to oppose this country going to war, even if the war is a *good* one. Because the people of a country should have something to say about whom they will fight, and when, and where, and how. I don't think it's pacifism to be against war. I just think it's being decent. (313, 317)[25]

Most of the reviews of *The Remarkable Andrew* were positive, but the reviewer for the British *Times Literary Supplement* was put off by "the lengthy couple of chapters in the middle," which left "a nasty taste" in his mouth because they fed into the "suicidal" isolationist tendencies in the United States.[26] Reviewers in the United States were not so concerned about that section. Beatrice Sherman concluded that the "book makes some trenchant points and offers some stimulating comment, but its blending of the didactic and fantastic, the romantic and practical, is more remarkable than felicitous."[27] Holmes Alexander found it to be a "facile satire on American politics," and he approved of Trumbo's "ghostly patriots" doing "some fiery sounding-off for the author."[28] Only two reviewers mentioned Trumbo's other antiwar book. The liberal *Nation* noted: "The author of that memento mori called 'Johnny Got His Gun' has tied one hand behind his back and tossed out a jaunty little fantasy. . . . [I]t gets in some easy and not very telling cracks at political corruption and at our present foreign policy. It all adds up to nothing more than an entertaining little scherzo."[29] The other reviewer who made the comparison was, in all likelihood, Whittaker Chambers, a former Communist Party member who would later become a famous witness. That review in *Time* compared *Andrew* to Theodore Dreiser's *America Is Worth Saving*, characterizing the latter as "a wretchedly written tract" and the former as a novelistic version of it, not at all like *Johnny*, which was "as sharp as bloodied barbed wire, retchsome as the smell of gas gangrene." This reviewer also noted that Andrew Jackson's statements about isolationism almost paralleled those made by Dreiser, which should "surprise no one who has observed George Washington and Abraham Lincoln zealously following the Communist Party Line in recent years." As for the trial of Andrew Long, this reviewer characterized it as "devoted to the remarkable Dalton's attempt to outwit charges of Communism and pacifism with tedious parodies of Red-baiting."[30]

During this period, Trumbo also sold "The Doctor's Husband" to

Columbia (released as *You Belong to Me* in October 1941) and "The Widow Wouldn't Weep" to Warner Bros. In March 1941 he was back at RKO, working on "They Married for Money." The next month he was at Paramount, writing a script titled "War Boom." Shortly thereafter, Paramount decided to shelve "The General," apparently "because the studio assumed its somewhat anti-British flavor would offend the English market and would be unpopular in many sections of their country, as well."[31] But studio executives changed their minds in May, and Trumbo finished the first draft of *The Remarkable Andrew* script on June 5, 1941. Over the next two weeks, he revised it twice. In the June 5 draft, there is no discussion of the war; in the June 19 draft, which was finished two days before the Germans invaded the Soviet Union, Trumbo added a scene from the book in which the two Andrews discuss the war between England and Germany. But in the third revision, completed three weeks after the invasion, Long proudly names all the countries fighting Germany. The following witty exchange then occurs:

> Jackson: By Jupiter, it's our opportunity, sir.
> Long: Opportunity for what?
> Jackson: While the rest of them are at each other's throats—we'll move an Army west and capture California.
> Long: We have California already.
> Jackson: Then we'll move in and civilize 'em!
> Long: But California is *already* civilized.
> Jackson: You're talking like a lunatic.[32]

The PCA censors were much more concerned that the focus on corruption would put "democracy in an unfavorable light" than they were that the foreign policy comments might affect US diplomacy.[33] After several rewrites of the courtroom scenes, the final script was approved by the PCA on July 19, and the finished picture was approved on September 26. It was released in January 1942.

The quirky Long, well played by William Holden, and the ghosts work better on film than on the printed page. All the war comments have been eliminated, except for the exchange between Long and Jackson noted above, and the film retains only one lengthy speech on democracy and patriotism. Long tells the jury that democracy is "not like a Sunday suit to be brought out and worn only for parades. It's the kind of life a decent man leads. It's something to live for and to die for." He is

Trumbo with William Holden on the Paramount lot, 1941. Courtesy of Paramount Pictures.

not "flag-waving," because he has always believed that "flag-waving is something sacred and quiet and not to be done for any selfish motive."

The reviewer for *Film Daily* wrote: "Every so often, but not often enough, a picture emerges from the lesser budget brackets with true, dramatic distinction. *The Remarkable Andrew* attains such status, because of the sincere and eloquent manner in which it combines entertainment and a reaffirmation of the fundamental truths of our democracy." The reviewer, who had also read the novel, called it "a fine literary achievement" and congratulated Trumbo for his skillful adaptation.[34] The *New Yorker*'s film critic wrote: "The comedy is not too reverent about the great dead, and it will divert well-fed, good-natured, easygoing citizens of small demands."[35]

Almost three decades later, Trumbo told an interviewer:

> I do not like this film very much. I did not like the book. I had the habit of writing histories for the movies which were not destined to be published. This was a sort of racket: you would write in a manner that would capture the attention, not of the studios, but of editors, to give them a desire to purchase your idea. That keeps you from subsequent responsibility when a poor screenwriter likes the history and finds it impossible to adapt it into a film. It is in this vein that I wrote the original version of *The Remarkable Andrew*. When my agent sent it to an editor, the editor said he was prepared to pay an advance if I could draw from it a short story. Oh well, that is the worst way in the world to write a short story. When I finished, I truly regretted having begun that way.

Trumbo also said that on the third day of shooting, Brian Donlevy (playing Jackson) and William Holden demanded that Trumbo replace Stuart Heisler as director, but he refused.[36]

While the censors were haggling with Paramount over the *Andrew* script, Trumbo was having a string of bad luck. Paramount had assigned him to rewrite a script for Bob Hope titled "Murder Farm," but after handing in sixty-three pages, he was taken off the project (the film was not made). He was then assigned to "I Married a Witch" but was again removed (the film was released the following year, but Trumbo did not receive screen credit). Nor did he receive credit for *True to Life* (Paramount), *Tales of Manhattan* (Twentieth Century–Fox), or *Somewhere I'll Find You* (MGM). The last film, a vehicle for Clark Gable and Lana Turner, was one of two antifascist scripts Trumbo worked on (for the second one, see chapter 6). It is the story of three foreign correspondents, two brothers and a woman, and their romantic triangle. They are in Berlin in March 1938, waiting to hear the outcome of the Munich conference that has been convened to decide the fate of Czechoslovakia. They are watching an (allegorical) poker game involving four players from the United Kingdom, France, Germany, and Italy (the countries meeting at Munich). Even though the French and British players have better hands, the German wins the pot by skillfully bluffing. When the correspondents learn that the Munich conferees have given one-third of Czechoslovakia to Germany, one of them says: "I suppose we'll all go home." A young man listening to him says, with "sheer horror in his eyes": "Home? Home? (Shakes his head, dazedly.) My home is in . . . Czechoslovakia." The script was subsequently rewritten by two other writers, and the film was released in 1942.[37] By then, the United States had entered the war, and Trumbo had become a supporter of the war effort.

6

Money, Politics, and War

People have tended to view him [Trumbo] in terms of his politics. So, one's opinion of him tends to depend on one's own political opinions.

—Christopher Trumbo

By the spring of 1940, Trumbo had become very active politically. On April 6 he spoke at a Peace Crusade meeting at the Olympic Auditorium, where he accused the current administration of following the same path as its predecessor in 1916–1917, using loans and material aid to friendly countries to prepare for US entry into a world war. "What assurances have we," Trumbo asked, "that the American dead of 1919 will not be multiplied vastly by the American dead of 1940?" In the past three years, the US government had done nothing while six nations (China, Spain, Ethiopia, Austria, Albania, and Czechoslovakia) "fell before brute force and dictatorship." Why, he asked, was this government now providing a variety of loans to aid Finland, which had been invaded by the Soviet Union in November 1939? There could be only one answer: the government was deliberately moving the country toward war. Trumbo saw no reason for what he labeled an "imperialist war." To his way of thinking, the Soviet Union's invasion of Finland was not an act of aggression or aggrandizement but a legitimate act to ensure its national security. He urged the people of the United States to say: "'War will *not* come.' Let us insist upon it to our fellow-workers, to our families, to our children, to ourselves. Let us organize. Let us picket. Let us, if necessary, threaten! . . . If they say to us, 'we must fight this war to preserve democracy,' let us say to them, 'there is no such thing as democracy in time of war. It is a lie, a deliberate deception to lead us to our own destruction. We will not die in order that our children may inherit a permanent military dictatorship.'"[1]

Trumbo delivering a political speech, n.d. Courtesy of Trumbo family.

When he finished speaking, a peace pledge he had written was read aloud to the audience, who then recited it in unison: "We are Americans. We are not the humble subjects of an all-powerful government. We are the people. We are the sovereign citizens of the United States of America. We are the government. We do not beg for peace like slaves. We do not plead for it like serfs. We command it!"[2]

A few months later, on July 28, Trumbo joined Theodore Dreiser and Carey McWilliams at a forum sponsored by the Hollywood chapter of the League of American Writers, titled "Should American Writers Support Our Participation in War?" After the three speakers had responded "no" and denounced the perfidy of Britain, France, and Poland, ultraconservative writer Howard Emmett Rogers asked why they had failed to mention the perfidy of Adolf Hitler.[3]

In August Trumbo gave a speech titled "The Writer's Position in the Present War" at a dinner sponsored by the Exiled Writers Committee of the League of American Writers. He urged the US government to stay out of the war and warned Americans not to succumb to the "hysterical fear of invasion" or to heed fifth columnists. These people were also waging war at home, Trumbo claimed, via the Alien Registration Act, which was aimed not at the real traitors—fascists—but at workers and labor leaders—that is, those who resist tyranny. If these warmongers succeeded in using the mere threat of war to "stifle the voice of Americans, what better proof do we need that war itself will mean the total destruction of all our liberties?" The only sure way to strengthen the United States against its enemies, Trumbo concluded, was by ending unemployment, hunger, disease, economic insecurity, and intellectual corruption.[4]

In February 1941 Trumbo spoke at an American Peace Mobilization meeting at the Shrine Auditorium to protest Lend-Lease and aid to Great Britain. Writer John Charles Moffitt, who was collaborating with Trumbo on a script, noted that Trumbo's political activity kept him away from his office at Paramount during this period. He was "very apologetic" about his absences and told Moffitt: "I am rather dogging this but I am extremely busy at this time because I am endeavoring to block lend-lease," which, he said, was an example of President Roosevelt's "warmongering in assisting Britain and France in a capitalistic war."[5] Trumbo made similar remarks in May to an American Peace Mobilization meeting. The following month, at the initial meeting of the National Federation for Civil Liberties of Southern California, he "drew an analogy between the events and conditions that ultimately led to dictatorship in Germany" and current events and conditions in the United States. For example, Trumbo "likened the Nazi anti-labor drive to the United States government's use of troops against the North American [Aviation] strikers." Likewise, Trumbo "denounced companies, such as North American, who made millions in profits and yet paid their workers low wages."[6]

Trumbo also spoke at a banquet for Harry Bridges, radical leader of the International Longshoremen's and Warehousemen's Union. In 1934 Bridges had led a waterfront strike on the West Coast, and as a result, he became the target of anti-Communists who insisted he was a secret member of the Communist Party and relentlessly tried to have the Australian-born labor leader deported. The US Department of Justice spent many years and significant resources investigating Bridges. Trumbo came to his defense on two of those occasions. In 1941, during the government's second effort to deport Bridges, Trumbo wrote *Harry Bridges: A Discussion of the Latest Effort to Deport Civil Liberties and the Rights of American Labor*. The Hollywood chapter of the League of American Writers printed 100,000 copies of the pamphlet, which used as its epigraph a quotation from former Supreme Court justice Louis D. Brandeis: "The greatest dangers to liberty lurk in insidious encroachment by men of zeal, well meaning, but without understanding." In several ways, this pamphlet was a rehearsal for Trumbo's most notable pamphlet, *The Time of the Toad*, written in 1949 during the next red scare (see chapter 11), when Trumbo was blacklisted and imprisoned. Trumbo opened the *Harry Bridges* pamphlet with a statement of his own credo: "I believe that the forthcoming deportation hearings . . . constitute a grave and dangerous challenge to the civil rights of the American people. I believe it is the duty of patriotic persons to expose and resist such a challenge. I believe that the great virtue of the democratic system is contained in the right—even the obligation—of Americans freely to criticize the actions of their government. I believe that such criticism can and should be made without either the actual or implied advocacy of any other form of government." Foreshadowing what he would write eight years later about the defense of the Hollywood Ten, Trumbo stated that the principles of the Constitution and the traditions of the American people "can best be defended by defending Harry Bridges."[7] He also restated his antiwar message. And yet more than a year passed before the special agent in charge of the Los Angeles office sent an eight-page report to FBI headquarters, detailing

Trumbo with Harry Bridges, William Gettings (ILWU organizer), and Bartley Crum (future attorney for the Hollywood Ten), 1943. Photograph by Otto Rothschild.

Trumbo's alleged political connections and noting that he was being considered for "Custodial Detention."[8]

Everything changed on June 22, 1941, the day German armed forces invaded the Soviet Union. Overnight, the Communist Party's position flip-flopped, and Communists became fervent supporters of the war and the Lend-Lease program. Communist Party leaders even changed the name of the American Peace Mobilization to the American People's Mobilization. According to party executive William Z. Foster, the involvement of the Soviet Union "drastically changed the character, scope, and perspectives of the war in a democratic direction," and of course, it allowed Communists to rejoin the battle against fascism.[9] But Trumbo claimed he did not become a proponent of US involvement until December 7, when the Japanese air force and navy attacked Pearl Harbor. Ring Lardner Jr. supported Trumbo's claim, noting that in June 1941 Trumbo still "found it very difficult to support the war." However, over the next few months he "became increasingly less pacifist in his approach," and when the Japanese attacked Pearl Harbor in December, Trumbo "changed his mind."[10]

In a rough draft of a letter Trumbo wrote to the FBI, probably in early 1944, he stated that his opposition to US entry into the European war had been based on the lack of clarity regarding who was fighting whom and why. He had not wanted to entrust the lives of American soldiers to the leaders of the British and French governments, who had acted so suspiciously in responding to the Russo-Finnish War. "It almost looked as if the French and British governments couldn't make up their minds whether they were going to fight the Germans or the Russians. . . . [It seemed to me] that before the United States jumped into the struggle, we should first find out *which* one." He also thought the United States should "come to some understanding with the Russians about the war and about the peace." In sum, he saw no reason why the United States should "leap into the fray at the earliest possible moment."[11]

Trumbo's statements in this letter to the FBI (which was never sent) echo the ideas expressed in *Johnny Got His Gun* and *The Remarkable Andrew*: he would not support a war based on sloganeering about democracy and freedom, nor one that was fought on behalf of the suspect policies of democratic governments, nor one whose underlying purpose might be the destruction of the Soviet Union. As Lardner noted, Pearl Harbor was the turning point for Trumbo. By that time, Trumbo later said, "All the conditions which had seemed to me to make for an honest and effective and successful war against the Axis had been fulfilled. And when the Vice-President [Henry A. Wallace] began his brilliant series of interpretations of the war and its aims, I was delighted to note that it was precisely the kind of war which the maimed hero of *Johnny Got His Gun* had declared to be a good and worthy battle—a war for the liberation of people, a war to make the slogans into realities. And the Atlantic Charter, as a slogan, is good enough for me."[12]

After December, Trumbo delivered frequent speeches advocating aid to the Soviet Union. He had concluded that a strong, enduring alliance between the United States and the USSR was the cornerstone of a democratic peace. His first major effort in this regard was the composition of "An Open Letter to the American People: On the Imperative Necessity of Opening a Second Front in Europe." This speech paralleled Communists' efforts to convince the Roosevelt administration to launch an invasion of western Europe and force the Germans to shift a significant number of troops from the eastern European (first) front, thereby relieving the pressure on the Soviet Union.[13] Trumbo carefully framed his argument for the second front to avoid criticizing the presi-

dent. He assumed that Roosevelt was caught between the "well organized [fascistic] opposition" to a second front and "the mass pressure"
of the people who supported it. This "democratic war," he concluded,
"cannot be won with fascist theory." The president must therefore listen
to the demands of the people and immediately open a second front, providing "the moral impetus and the mass support" for "the overthrow of
fascism throughout the world."[14]

In April 1942 Trumbo spoke at a meeting of the Russian-American
Society for Medical Aid to Russia. In August he urged those attending a meeting of the Screen Office Employees Guild to pass a resolution in support of a second front. In October he was listed as one of the
promoters of a performance of Dmitri Shostakovich's Seventh (War)
Symphony, sponsored by the Hollywood Writers' Mobilization. And
in December Trumbo gave a speech at a United Nations War Relief
meeting titled "Old Lies Blasted." After reviewing what he called the
Allies' bloody history toward the Soviet Union, he said: "There can be
no victory in the present and no enduring peace in the future unless
we set ourselves right in our relationship with Russia. It is the duty of
fascists to cultivate dissension, mistrust, fear and hatred between the
United States and Russia; it is the duty of patriotic Americans to resist
such propaganda with the most powerful of all weapons which is truth.
For if we fall victim to the old lies, we will repeat the old pattern, and
twenty-five years hence our children will pay for your criminal stupidity with their lives."[15]

However, the bulk of Trumbo's political activity during the war
centered on electoral politics and racial issues. In the summer of 1942
he joined with former left-wing members of the Motion Picture Democratic Committee (one of the many victims of the liberal-Communist
division resulting from the Nonaggression Treaty) to promote the
reelection of Governor Culbert Olson and the election of Will Rogers
Jr. to Congress. Buoyed by their success in the latter race, they created
the Hollywood Democratic Committee the following January, with the
goal of electing progressive candidates in 1944 and promoting a "democratic" peace.

This vision of a democratic peace dominated Trumbo's thinking about the war. He believed a democratic peace would guarantee
civil rights, civil liberties, and national liberation for all peoples of
the world. He began his campaign on behalf of racial minorities with
the Mexican American youths who had been indicted in the Sleepy
Lagoon case (August 1942). A Mexican American youth had been

murdered at Sleepy Lagoon, a reservoir in Bell, California, and more than a hundred Chicanos had been arrested; eventually, twenty-four were indicted. In response to the lurid and racist media accounts of the case, the Communist Party and several of its front groups organized the Sleepy Lagoon Defense Committee. Despite the wide-ranging publicity and educational efforts, twelve of the defendants were convicted of murder, and five were convicted of assault. In his pamphlet, Trumbo wrote:

> We are at war not only with the armies of the Axis powers, but with the poison gas of their doctrine, with the "biological basis" of Hitler and with his theories of race supremacy. The unity of all races has been sealed in blood, in the blood of our heroes [on battlefields all over the world]. Our coming victory on the continent of Europe will be won by "men of the same stamp" though different races. . . . And with it will go the last vestiges of discrimination in the United States, the Jim-Crow wars in the south, the signs in Los Angeles that still say "Mexicans and Negroes not allowed." This is not only the faith for which we fight, it is our armor and our sword, our weapon and our battle cry. We are at war with the premises on which seventeen boys were tried and convicted in Los Angeles. . . . And because this global war is everywhere a people's war, all of us are in it together, all of us take up together the challenge of Sleepy Lagoon.[16]

In October 1944 all the convictions were overturned by the California Court of Appeals.[17]

Trumbo continued his civil rights theme in a paper titled "Minorities and the Screen," which he presented to the 1943 Writers' Congress organized by the Hollywood Writers' Mobilization and the University of California. (The Hollywood Writers' Mobilization had been established in early 1942 by the writers' guilds and unions in Los Angeles, enrolling more than 3,000 members. As the largest wartime Popular Front organization on the West Coast, it became the constant target of anti-Communist accusers.) The conference included dozens of panel discussions of every conceivable political, social, and cultural subject. Trumbo sat on the minority groups panel (with, among others, Carey McWilliams and John Collier) and used the occasion to discuss the many tribulations faced by the "American Negro," who, in addition to the heavy cross of racial prejudice, must bear the cruel slanders "we as writers in the press and radio, in magazines and the novel, on the stage and screen" have piled on him. White writers not only avoided "Negro" themes in their work but also failed to promote the employment of "Negro" writers. In his peroration, he made a powerful appeal for writers to mobilize against racism. It was not enough for them to simply swear an oath never to write material that was insulting to racial minorities: "simply to forswear evil is a peculiarly supine and negative contribution to human progress." Instead, writers' organizations must "form an army with an invincible singleness of purpose." This would help win the war, assure a democratic peace, and gain self-respect for participants in the march of history.[18]

When the conference proceedings were published, Trumbo wrote an "announcement" of it for *Arts and Architecture*. This book, he predicted, "will *not* be read by millions. It is neither pure entertainment nor escapist literature. . . . This book will make you think. After reading, you'll keep it on a conspicuous shelf because its 800 pages of ideas, processes, methods and reports will help you understand this war of steel and ideas, and the peace that can come out of it—the peace that has a purpose—or the peace that will mean only one untroubled generation before the nations are at war again."[19]

Many years later, in response to an accusation that Communist screenwriters had done nothing to advance the cause of black people, Trumbo protested. He had written an extensive film adaptation of the biography of Toussaint-Louverture (leader of the eighteenth-century Haitian revolt against the French), another about a black GI who had been lynched in Louisiana during the war, and a third about a love affair and marriage between a black man and a white woman, but none were purchased. Additionally, he had urged MGM executives to retain the black publicist it had hired for *Cabin in the Sky* (1943), an all-black movie. "I made every possible effort to convince studio executives that it was in their own best interest to keep him on as a permanent liaison with the black press for all Metro films. My arguments did not prolong his employment for so much as an hour." Nor was he singular in this regard: other left-wing writers had made similar efforts.[20] Indeed, the only discernible blot on Trumbo's record of racial tolerance during the war was his failure (to his subsequent shame) to protest the incarceration of West Coast Japanese Americans in concentration camps.[21] It should be noted that, at the time, only a handful of people objected.

Unsurprisingly, in an FBI report dated October 19, 1942, the agent concluded: "Subject [Trumbo] is a Communist fellow traveler, member of the League of American Writers and movie writer. . . . Subject has been active in affairs adhering strictly to the Communist party line." The agent then listed all of Trumbo's political activities since publication of the Bridges pamphlet and noted, in particular, his "frequent" association with Herbert Biberman, who was characterized as a "suspected agent of the U.S.S.R."[22] Nine months later, FBI headquarters notified its Los Angeles office that "a custodial detention card had been prepared at the Bureau, for Trumbo, Dalton, with alias James Dalton Trumbo: native-born Communist."[23]

In late 1943 a peculiar situation arose involving Trumbo and the FBI. The revelation of the incident in *Additional Dialogue* led some critics to accuse him of inconsistency as well as hypocrisy. The year before, Trumbo began to be "showered . . . with fiercely sympathetic letters denouncing Jews, Communists, New Dealers and International bankers" who, the writers claimed, had suppressed *Johnny Got His Gun*. These letter writers believed that circulation of his novel would advance their campaign for an immediate peace between the United States and Germany. Based on the return addresses on the envelopes, Trumbo concluded that a nationwide network of antiwar anti-Semites was distributing pamphlets and corresponding with interned pro-Nazis. "They proposed a national rally for peace-now, with me as cheer leader; they promised (and delivered) a letter campaign to pressure the publisher [of *Johnny*] for a fresh edition."[24] Trumbo, in a note he attached to two of these letters, wrote: "These are the letters my friend, Everett Riskin [who produced *A Guy Named Joe*] urged me to turn over to the FBI, as a matter of patriotic duty. Much against my better judgment, I did." The FBI, however, reported a different story: "On December 30, 1943 [blacked-out name] advised that Dalton Trumbo had received letters from several pacifist organizations . . . and that Trumbo had intimated to him he would like to talk to a representative of the F.B.I. regarding these anti-war groups."[25] In any event, on January 8, 1944, two agents from the Bureau appeared at Trumbo's house, and he apparently enjoyed the verbal joust that ensued: "I had an excellent two hours with the young gentlemen who were extremely interested in the books I read, the magazines to which I subscribed, and the extent of my travels abroad, specifically [whether I had traveled] to the USSR. As they left (having forgotten all about the letters, on which they took no notes), they suggested that I get in touch with them 'whenever I changed my opinions.' I told them that would involve almost weekly conferences, since my opinions change as swiftly as the events which gave rise to them."[26]

After the agents left, Trumbo began to compose a letter to the FBI, parts of which have already been discussed. In it, he extolled his own patriotism: He bought war bonds, subscribed to war charities, and contributed "whatever talent I have to enterprises approved by the government for the furtherance of the war." More to the point, he continued: "I share with men of your organization a sincere desire to see an end to all such seditious propaganda as criminal slander of the Commander in Chief, defeatism, pacifism, anti-Semitism and all similar deceits and stratagems designed to assist the German cause. Which, of course, was why I called on you when I possessed evidence of such activity."[27]

The first critic to use this letter to impugn Trumbo's veracity and reputation was film historian Richard Corliss. In 1971 he asserted that Trumbo, in "a respectful letter written to some FBI agents around 1944," denied that "'Johnny Got His Gun' was pacifist (which it certainly is) and, implicitly, that he was a Communist (which at the time he was)."[28] In his reply, Trumbo challenged Corliss's characterization of the letter: "The letter was not respectful; it was ironical: the appeal of an earnest, simple-minded citizen who is eager to explain himself to his masters. . . . You don't write to the FBI like that, Mr. Corliss, unless you are putting them on. Communists, incidentally, do not write letters to the FBI, respectful or otherwise; neither do they allow FBI agents into their homes."[29] (For their dispute over the date Trumbo joined the party, see chapter 7.)

Many years later, two anti-Communists used the letter to challenge Trumbo's post-blacklist reputation as a defender of the First Amendment. In a 2004 review of a book by two anti-Communist scholars, Glenn Garvin accused Trumbo of naming names and "secretly pointing the FBI to Hollywood figures he believed were suspiciously anti-war." Christopher wrote a letter to the editor, correctly pointing out that his father had not pointed the FBI toward any "Hollywood figures," but he did not explain why Trumbo had pointed the FBI toward Ms. Wheelwright and Ms. Hale. In his reply, Garvin loosed a few more untrue epithets, calling Trumbo "one of Stalin's loudest apologists" and "one of J. Edgar Hoover's pet rats."[30] One year later, Art Eckstein picked up this baton in his rant against the dedication of a free-speech fountain in Trumbo's name at the University of Colorado (see chapter 27). Once again, Trumbo was labeled a "Stalinist, who faithfully followed every twist and turn of the Party line."[31]

By the spring of 1942, Trumbo was being paid $1,250 a week by Paramount, but he pleaded with his new agents, Phil Berg and Bert Allenberg, to try to break the contract. They were successful, and Trumbo signed a one-picture deal with MGM to write the script for *A Guy Named Joe* ("Joe" was the generic term used for combat aviators). He turned in a ninety-three-page treatment on May 18. The gist of the plot is that a hot-shot pilot dies in a suicide mission to destroy a Japanese ship, goes to pilot heaven, and is sent back to earth to help other fliers. Like many war stories written by leftists, Trumbo's treatment featured a united-nations cast. Pete, the dead hero, is met in heaven by a British pilot. Others include Livotsky, a member of the Red Air Force, who "put on a splendid show outside of Kharkov"; a German who "went down in one of the early Hurricanes at Dunkirk"; and Captain Wong of the Chinese air force. The multinational theme is repeated at the end of the movie when Pete's lover, Dorinda, dies in a suicide dive to destroy a Japanese ammunition dump. As they enter heaven together: "Suddenly silence falls upon them. The air is filled with a voice from General Headquarters. It comes over some sort of celestial loud-speaker system, and seems to echo hollowly from world to world. . . . 'Attention!' calls the voice. 'Attention!' [The names of twenty-four nationalities follow, including Spanish Republicans.] 'All out—all out—all out for the Battle of Tokyo! All out for the Battle of Berlin!'"[32] In the final script, however, Dorinda survives her mission. The PCA censors objected to Dorinda's death as Trumbo had written it because it suggested she had deliberately committed suicide.[33]

The script also had to pass muster with the War Department if the studio wanted access to military bases, personnel, and technical advisers. But after reading the script, Falkner Heard, head of the review branch of the War Department's Bureau of Public Relations, wrote: "No degree of supervision could make this picture a contribution to the war effort. . . . It is suggested that Hollywood be told that the War Department recommends it not be produced." A revised version was not approved either. The head of the department's Information Branch, Edward L. Munson, wrote: "The production of this script in its present form would be unwise because of the psychological effect it would have on potential fledgling and experienced pilots as well as their parents. The presence of hovering ghosts of deceased pilots, and the unreal, fantastic, and slightly schizophrenic character of the scenario hardly combine to produce a sensible war-time film diet." Another revised script was eventually approved.[34]

Joe is an unusual war movie, in that it contains only a few minutes of action. Basically, it is the sentimental story of two love affairs. There is no chauvinism in it, and it is not overtly patriotic. Also unique is the fact that a female is the combat hero. The reviews were mainly positive. *Life* magazine selected *A Guy Named Joe* as its "movie of the week." *Life*'s reviewer stated that it "manages to remain strong and exciting despite such weaknesses as verbosity and a climax that is almost pure 'Perils of Pauline.'"[35] The *New Yorker*'s reviewer called it "a real weird number," but he went on to say that the "dialogue is fine and well handled," and overall, it had "a little more solid tucked away in the thing than many movies have." He credited the filmmakers with making "a sane effort to interpret the purpose of the men, or at least the fliers, who are fighting the war on our side."[36] Philip K. Scheuer called it "one of the season's more distinctive films."[37] The reviewer for the *Hollywood Reporter* wrote: "The story is utterly right, may even be termed an inspiring conjecture for our times."[38] And *Daily Variety* raved: "Imaginative speculation as to the nature of survival after death, stated in finest artistry, coupled with matters of deepest concern to virtually every family in America, gives this picture outstanding importance and audience value."[39]

In September MGM executives offered Trumbo a lucrative contract ($1,250 per week), but he had become discouraged with screenwriting and wanted to retire to the ranch to do some serious writing. He informed Elsie McKeogh that he had been reading the short stories of Edna O'Brien and O. Henry and noted, to his surprise, "how feeble most of them are." He was convinced he could write just as well, and he had about twenty story ideas. But, he said, these stories were not intended for the *Saturday Evening Post*: "To hell with the *Post*. I'm hungry for a little prestige, and the prestige stuff looks easier to me than the *Post* anyhow. Besides, I do my duty to the mass mind in pictures, and wouldn't dislike thumbing my nose at it for a while."[40] He planned an ambitious writing program for 1943: two novels, a biography, and a book of short stories. He admitted this might sound "like nonsense," but he listed several reasons why it was not:

> First, I have never devoted myself exclusively to writing. Second,
> I would have the most important asset for such a job, which is

enthusiasm. Third, I have really limitless energy, and work better and faster from work itself—in other words real work builds
up a desire and a creative energy for more work. Fourth, I am
very fast: witness, all except the last sixty pages of "Andrew"
in two weeks: witness, the last fifty pages of "Jitters" in one
night. Granted I don't write my best at such speed—still, to do
the above year's job, I wouldn't need to write at nearly such a
spell. It's the starting that's tough with me—but I'll either have
to start or starve, since in the past there was no real financial
compulsion. "Andrew" was spoiled for me by getting all that
dough in advance and losing the fun. Fifth, I think I am maturing, and there is no reason why I shouldn't be prolific, since I've
done most of the distracting things I promised myself ten years
ago, and now want a solid reputation. . . .

I can hear you saying you're not going out and make a fool
promise for July delivery of a manuscript, and have one of those
"Andrew" situations pile up at the last moment, with me wiring
and renouncing everything for an extra week's time. Believe me
it won't. From now on I am your little dynamo.[41]

But, as we have seen before and shall see again, Trumbo's literary
intentions withered when confronted by monetary factors. In January
1943 he informed Elsie that his plans had changed. He had intended
to support his family by selling a script he had coauthored with Ring
Lardner Jr., but that did not work out. Initially, they had hoped one of
the studios would pay $100,000 for "The Fishermen of Beaudrais." So
when MGM offered them $25,000, they rejected that offer and placed
the screenplay on the open market. "The open market," he told Elsie,
"threw it right back on us."[42]

As a result, Trumbo accepted MGM's offer, and the studio assigned
him the task of adapting *Thirty Seconds over Tokyo*, Captain Ted Lawson's firsthand account of his role in the April 1942 air strike on Tokyo.
The studio sent Trumbo to Washington, DC, to talk with Lawson and
various government officials. During the course of his research, Trumbo
learned that "there was really no sound military purpose for the raid,"
which had inflicted very little damage on Tokyo and cost the US Air
Force every bomber it had and a good many lives. "It was," he discovered, "a public relations raid and admittedly so. Its purpose was to lift
morale when our Eastern European Theater of Operations was a sham-
bles. There were also some political implications involved."[43]

The movie, as Trumbo saw it, had to dramatize two political issues: first, it must demonstrate "the value of the Tokyo raid in terms of Chinese-American relations," raising American morale and lowering Japan's; second, it must "make a genuine contribution to relations between the American people and their courageous Chinese allies." With respect to the latter, Trumbo wanted to "establish the falsity and danger" of claims by the Hearst newspapers that "the War in the Pacific is the World War, the war of Oriental races against Occidental races for the domination of the world." Trumbo hoped that when American parents saw that Chinese guerrillas had carried their sons on their backs to save them from the Japanese, "they will not readily subscribe to the theory of Oriental-Occidental war to the death."[44] One political problem Trumbo had to finesse was Lawson's statement that it had been *Communist* Chinese guerrillas who carried the airmen to safety.

The studio received the full cooperation of the US Navy and US Army Air Forces. Trumbo was permitted to study the briefing papers from the training sessions; he was permitted to fly on a B-25 and examine every aspect of the plane, as well as every crewman's job on it. He also worked closely with Lawson to make his characters and the details of their training as accurate as possible. Trumbo wanted to show the public that despite the careful training of pilots and planning of missions, mishaps are unavoidable. He knew he was writing propaganda, and he had no problem doing so. In the preface to his treatment, Trumbo wrote:

> The motion picture resulting from [this book] must contribute constructively and dynamically to the public morale. The best propaganda, of course, is the truth; and in Captain Lawson's book the truth is presented so decently and so dramatically that the liberties usually required for screen dramatization become not only unnecessary, but actually undesirable. We wish to make a picture in which there are no heroes because all are heroes; a picture in which the leading characters are the living symbols of millions of service men and their wives who quietly and gallantly offer to the American people the greatest sacrifice within their power to give. We wish to make a picture which every service man will recognize as authentic—which every service man will find reassuring, even comforting—and which every American will view with a sense of pride and heightened determination.[45]

Trumbo (far left) with Captain Ted Lawson (with cane), 1943. Courtesy of
MGM Studios.

Years later, Trumbo told an interviewer: "I happen to believe that the
war could have been averted by compassionate and intelligent leadership in this world. But, once it was engaged in, it had to be won. Had
to be won! Therefore, any propaganda means, effective ones, were justified. I was perfectly frankly and openly writing propaganda films.
Whether they were good or not is beside the point."[46]

Trumbo's script was very faithful to Lawson's book. He finished
it in mid-June, and it was sent to the PCA and the Office of War
Information. The PCA gave its generic approval,[47] and the Office of
War Information was pleased with Trumbo's depiction of the "genuine cooperation and friendship" between the American flyers and the
Chinese and recommended the film for "special distribution in liber-
ated areas."[48] The War Department, for its part, generally approved of
the script but expressed its desire that "this picture will result not in
the glorification of one officer, but of the heroic exploits of the Army
Air Force as a whole." It also warned about the possible "damaging repercussions" if the film emphasized that China as a nation was
assisting fliers out of enemy-occupied territory. "That angle should
be reduced to a minimum."[49] In other words, the War Department

wanted to ensure that the Chinese rescuers were nonpartisan, human-itarian-inspired individuals.

The movie was directed by Victor Fleming, a conservative and a staunch anti-Communist. But Trumbo later described him as "a good guy" and said they "got on well."[50] The finished film is more about teamwork than war. The first half is a procedural, devoted to the fliers' training in takeoff and landing procedures. The second half depicts the crash landing of Lawson's airplane in China and the crew's escape. Unlike most of the movies written by left-wingers, it does not feature a multiethnic cast. And, unlike most World War II films, it contains no racial slurs against the Japanese. Conversely, like many war movies, it depicts the strong emotional bond between the wives at home and the fighting men overseas.

New York Times critic Bosley Crowther termed *Thirty Seconds* "a worthy example" of the blending of the real and the imag-ined in a war film—an explicit and clean telling of a true story and "a warm romance."[51] It was selected as *Life*'s "movie of the week."[52] The reviewer for the *Hollywood Reporter* raved, calling it "more than one of the greatest war pictures ever made. . . . [I]t is an all time winner. It has everything." He did not, however, mention Trumbo's script.[53] The *Daily Variety* reviewer was almost as effusive, describing the film as "first and last an honest, valid and completely absorbing account. . . . Dalton Trumbo's script is a craftsmanly arrangement [of the book]."[54]

None of these accolades were applied to Trumbo's third war script, "Tender Comrade." The title was taken from a phrase in Robert Louis Stevenson's poem "My Wife": "Teacher, tender comrade, wife, / A fel-low-farer true through life / Heart whole and soul free."[55] In early 1943 Trumbo wrote an original film story about women on the home front, and he instructed his agent to place it on the open market for $60,000. Two studios met his price: Columbia wanted it for Jean Arthur; RKO wanted it for Ginger Rogers. Trumbo chose RKO because he "liked Ginger."[56] The RKO reader's report on the story idea was enthusiastic: "This can hardly fail to be a successful picture. It is a well-knit, moving account of a good marriage combined with dramatizations of almost every topic affecting the lives of service men's wives. The things said here need to be said."[57]

MGM agreed to lend Trumbo to RKO to write the script. He com-pleted a first draft on June 25 and the final draft on September 4. The two central figures, Jo and Chris (the latter named after the coauthor of this book), are from Shale City. When the movie opens, Chris has just been drafted, and Jo is working in an ammunition factory. Trumbo endows Jo with a feminist attitude about work, but he gives her too many preachy speeches. In one of the flashbacks to their early married life, Jo tells Chris that when the war is over she will not quit her job. "I'm a rotten housekeeper. But I'm a darned good hand on an assembly line. . . . I can make a hundred a month in *any* man's world." She plans to put the children in a nursery school, where they can be raised by experts, which she knows she is not.[58] In another flashback, she tells Chris: "Women don't lie down and starve to death if something happens to their husbands. They get out and find a job and take care of *themselves*. And that's what *I'll* do, too" (90). (These speeches were cut from the final script. Instead, in the film, Jo delivers a diatribe against housekeeping.) After Chris is shipped overseas, Jo and three of her workmates decide it would be cheaper if they all lived together. Helen wonders how they are going to resolve the inevitable disputes. Jo replies: "That's simple—we can take a vote. We'll run the joint like a democracy! Anything comes up, we'll just call a meeting" (25). A few scenes later, when they have to make a decision about taking in a fifth woman to help pay the bills, Jo says: "OK. Democratic vote!" (49). When Manya, the new roommate, asks about the financial arrangements, Jo tells her: "We're going to pay the rent and the expenses of the house and then what's left over we'll share equally. We'll run this joint like a democracy."[59] Manya replies: "Oh, yah, that is good. We had in Austria [changed to Germany in the film] a democracy once. . . . We did not lose it. We let it be murdered. Like a little child" (57). When one of the other roommates complains about rationing and the inconveniences of the war, Jo tells her that kind of talk "comes straight from Berlin! . . . You're the kind of people Hitler counted on when he started this war—and that's where *he* made the biggest mistake a guy ever thought of! Because there aren't enough of *you*, and there are too many of *us*" (73–74).

Trumbo's effort to depict strong women is overwhelmed by the mawkish sentimentality of Jo's speech to her baby after she learns that Chris has been killed. That long, sappy speech is the antithesis of Joe's words at the end of *Johnny Got His Gun*. In *Tender Comrade*, Jo tells her son: "Don't let anybody ever say he [your father] died for nothing! Because if you let them say it, you let them call your dad a fool. You let them say he died without knowing what it was all about." He died to make "the best world a boy could ever grow up in," so don't ever betray that value, don't let it slip away or let anyone talk you out of it or swindle you out of it or fight you out of it. If you do, "you might as well be dead, too" (152–53).

As the years passed, Trumbo's dislike of this film grew, mainly because of that speech, which he characterized as "one of the most maudlin effusions in screen history—was unfairly cited as characteristic of my later work and, indeed, of my whole work."[60] And yet, variations of that speech are found in each of the six drafts Trumbo wrote. He probably did not realize how sappy it was until he heard Rogers deliver it. When he saw the rough cut, he told David Hempstead, the producer: "Oh my god, it's pretty bad . . . we must get rid of that last long speech of Ginger's." But Hempstead replied: "'There's no way to cut it.' I said, 'why not?' 'Well, A, because she did it in one take, the camera's on her all the time. You have no place to cut to. B, she loves it because she had memorized it so much and said it so perfectly.' So there was nothing to do. That was a case where they were true to the script in a way that was almost fanatical."[61]

The reviewers at the Office of War Information loved *Tender Comrade*. One gave it "all cheers and hosannas," while another called it "the most effective and moving screen portrayal" of women's role in the war and praised its presentation of the issues.[62] But Bosley Crowther, in his provocatively titled "Comrade Ginger," scorched the movie, calling it "a hot bath of sentiment. . . . [A]n overboard attempt to wring the heart with the anguish of separation and the gallantry of girls who lose their men. [Trumbo] was apparently more intent on being cute and wistful than he was on cutting close to life. And the consequence is that his female is a thoroughly incredible lot. . . . But worst of all, from the standpoint of writing, is the scene at the end of the film, when the lady reacts to the blunt news of her husband's death by giving a lecture to the infant child." Crowther had no kind words for either Ginger Rogers or the film's director Edward Dmytryk.[63] Most of the New York critics disliked the film, terming it overly sentimental, banal, cutesy, clichéd, and trapped in "embarrassing monologues."[64] The trade papers were much kinder: "Dalton Trumbo's story . . . is deftly contrived to mix strong human drama with light and romantic comedy."[65] Trumbo has written "an immensely human screenplay," and the movie is "an honest, dramatic tribute to the service widows of America."[66] Film historian Jeff Smith recently noted that the film's "egalitarian and communitarian spirit . . . is unique among home-front films."[67]

When Trumbo returned to MGM, he planned to take a four-month leave of absence, from September 1943 to January 1944, and follow through on his oft-delayed plan to do the sort of writing his "fancy dictated." When Robert Sisk asked him to adapt George Victor Martin's novel *Our Vines Have Tender Grapes*, Trumbo told the producer that he "greatly felt the need of a space of time" when he would be under obligation to no one. However, he was "tempted away from this resolve" by his liking for Sisk and the assignment. So he told Sisk he would agree to do the adaptation only if he could write it at the ranch, at his own pace, and without having to participate in any story conferences. His only obligation would be to deliver a completed script at the beginning of the new year.[68] Sisk agreed.

Trumbo saw this assignment as an opportunity to leave the war behind and to reflect on the coming peace and traditional American values, as seen through the experiences of honest, hardworking farmers (Thomas Jefferson's yeomen). As good as these farmers are, they sometimes need to be reminded that community feeling and sharing are more important than increasing the size of their farms. Toward the end of the story, a newspaper editor who is trying to raise money for a needy family reads from an editorial his father had written for the paper's first edition:

> We are all children by adoption of the land in which we live. The earth is here, and the water and the sunlight, and the labor to make it yield. The only thing that can make a land evil is the people who inhabit it. ~~Today we are testing whether this place we love is truly good or truly evil~~ [crossed out in pencil]. If we have in ourselves the nobility to share our own abundance with those who—through no fault of their own—are destitute, then we can raise our heads with dignity among the princes of the earth. Then we can say with verity: "This is a good land, and the man who live in it have no fear."[69]

Years later, Trumbo told Bruce Cook: "It turned out to be a lovely picture, I thought. . . . [I]t was a very sweet, honest, decent picture of farm life, and that's because it came from a lovely novel."[70]

When it was released the following year, Howard Barnes found it to be "a gentle bucolic story" with its "full share of sentimental overtones," but he was disappointed that the director "did not make a tighter shooting script out of Dalton Trumbo's screen play."[71] The reviewer for *Daily Variety* thought it was a "quiet drama with warm, human appeal."[72] The *Hollywood Reporter* reviewer called it "one of the most charming, delightful and heart-warming pictures of this or any other year."[73]

Another critic described it as a movie of "genuineness and sincerity,"[74] while the *New York Times* reviewer noted: "While this picture comes close at times to pathos, it is always skillfully rescued from the mawkish either by a line of humorous dialogue, of which scenarist Dalton Trumbo has contributed several effective examples, or by the adroit handling of these situations by [director] Roy Rowland."[75]

After he finished *Vines*, Trumbo did not return to his plan to focus on works other than screenplays. Instead, he accepted an offer from Columbia to adapt James Hilton's novel *And Now Goodbye*. This love story, written in 1931 and set entirely in the United Kingdom, was considerably broadened by Trumbo, who transported the lovers to Spain in the mid-1930s, where they became involved with the Republican side of the civil war there. At the end of the script, the male protagonist delivers a sermon that fully expresses Trumbo's hopes for the postwar period: "Teach us, Oh Lord, that the brotherhood of man . . . extends beyond nations, beyond creeds, beyond races. Teach us to share our goods with others, that they may be able to share theirs with us. Grant us the vision and the courage and the determination to live in peace with all nations and all peoples." And he warned against "the powers of darkness" that will try "to divide the unity which has been cemented by the blood of all the peoples of the earth."[76]

In April 1944, matching his residence to his salary, Trumbo purchased a house in Beverly Hills (620 North Beverly Drive) for $55,000. "It was," Christopher recalled, "a large, handsome place. It looked very much like Tara in *Gone with the Wind*, columns and all. At one point, we had a staff of three people keeping it in order. It had a tennis court, swimming pool, pool house, and eight or nine fruit trees." The house, like all the others in that section of Beverly Hills, had a racial segregation covenant attached to it, which Trumbo ignored.

A few months later, Trumbo again tried to develop a constructive plan for his writing. In a letter to Elsie, he acknowledged his bad spending habits:

> I am hopelessly extravagant. One may deplore this, as one would deplore a cancer, but like the cancer it is a fact and must be dealt with accordingly. I find that this extravagance has resulted in an increasing diversion of whatever talent I possess into the channel of original stories with which to bolster an already large but inadequate weekly income. Time which might

be spent on novels is thus wasted on originals for purely monetary considerations. This, we both agree, is bad.

The solution, then, would seem to be to increase the weekly
salary to such a point that increased revenue from the sale of
originals would be so small in view of taxes that it simply would
not be worthwhile. If this were true, then the time and energy
spent on originals once again would go into more serious writing. And this is exactly what I propose to do.

He intended to win a five-year contract with MGM that would pay him
$3,000 a week for fifty-two weeks a year, with no options and no mor-
als clause. He would have the right to suspend the contract at any time
to write a novel, a play, or short stories. If he used that time to write an
original screenplay, MGM would be entitled to only the courtesy of a first
look. "Thus my income will be such that the infernal temptation of originals will be removed, if for no other reason than that they will cease to
be profitable." In sum, he believed he could do "better work at a higher
salary and under less pressure at Metro than anywhere else," and the new
contract would allow him "to get back into more serious work."[77]

On August 21, 1944, Trumbo got what he wanted from MGM—a
contract increasing his salary to $3,000 per week and allowing him one
six-month leave of absence.[78] But as Oscar Wilde noted, the gods answer
only the prayers of those they wish to punish. Eight months after signing this contract, Trumbo told his mother that he was prepared to take
"drastic steps" to break it. He was growing "progressively sicker" of
his current assignment ("a consuming piece of idiocy for Clark Gable"),
of the studio, "and of the kind of life one lives when one has the constant feeling that each day one receives $500 and should, in all con-
science, show better results for it." He could no longer face the prospect
of "living out his life as a talented and highly paid hack-writer." So, he
claimed, he was prepared to leave the studio and Hollywood, sell the
Beverly Hills mansion, and write short stories, novels, and plays. "Ten
years at the bakery were enough. Ten years in Hollywood were enough.
The next ten years shall be devoted to serious writing—to my stab at
doing something worthwhile and enduring." And he planned to write
on the move: he and Cleo would live in Grand Junction for a year, New
York for a year, and England for a year.[79]

Fate, however, had other plans for Trumbo. War tasks and political
activity kept him tied to Hollywood, and he neither broke his contract
with MGM nor made much of a start on a novel or play.

7

Into the Communist Party

Joining the Communist Party had no more importance for him than joining the Catholic Church. It put him on the front line of the war against fascism. But, in his mind, he had not joined the worldwide Communist network, nor had he enlisted in all its battles nor had he become a propagandist for hire.

—Christopher Trumbo

Of course, Trumbo did not think of communism as a religion, but he was regularly derisive about the party's church-like aspects. Albert Maltz once heard Trumbo say, during an interview, that belonging to the Communist Party was like belonging to the PTA. An appalled Maltz exclaimed: "Well, that's bull shit! And he should have been ashamed of himself for saying a thing like that. Because if it was like being a member of the PTA, why was he a member?"[1]

Trumbo joined the Communist Party twice. He was a member from 1943 to 1948 and again for a few months in 1956. To anti-Communists of all eras, Trumbo's party membership is like the mark of Cain. To anti-Communists of his generation, Trumbo was a "Stalinist" who marched in lockstep with Soviet leaders, condoned some of the worst atrocities of the twentieth century, and refused to answer the reasonable questions of a legally constituted congressional committee. A later generation of anti-Communists is incensed that Trumbo, without apologizing for any of those "sins," became a hero to the New Left.

Thus, it is important to place Trumbo's party membership in its personal and historical context and emphasize that Trumbo, like most of his contemporaries in Hollywood who joined the party, was motivated by individual, albeit overlapping, ideals, hopes, and goals. Each responded differently to party doctrine and discipline. In other words, the Communist Party was not a gathering of preprogrammed robots.

132

One could be a member (just as one can be a member of the Catholic Church or the National Rifle Association) without believing all the dogma and every pronouncement of the organization.

Trumbo's decision to join the Communist Party was the direct outgrowth of his friendship with four other writers: Hugo Butler, Ring Lardner Jr., Ian Hunter, and Michael Wilson. In their letters to one another, they regularly used "Dear Lad" as a salutation and "Yours in Christ" as a valediction. Trumbo, Butler, Lardner, and Hunter became a tight-knit group sometime in 1938 (Wilson was not as close to the others as he was to Trumbo), and Trumbo was likely the linchpin. He probably met Butler at MGM in early 1938, and he probably met Lardner through Paul Jarrico or Alice Goldberg, both of whom were Communist Party members.[2] Trumbo and Jarrico worked at RKO at the same time, and Trumbo and Goldberg helped organized the Screen Readers Guild and might have dated for a short time. Lardner and Hunter (who later married Goldberg) were friends from their New York newspaper days.

Trumbo was the oldest of the core foursome by about a decade, and according to Nancy Schwartz, he served as both a mentor and a friend to the other three. Butler called Trumbo "The Knight" and referred to the younger men as his "squires."[3] As Trumbo later noted in a tongue-in-cheek letter to Lardner: "In 1942 or '43 . . . I was not only an older and therefore more experienced man than you; I was also a better drinker, drove a more powerful car, owned a bigger house and drew a larger salary."[4] But in terms of political engagement, Lardner claimed to have been the seigneur. He later wrote: "By introducing Ian to Alice [Goldberg], I not only helped him land a wife but laid the groundwork for his entry into the Communist Party, of which she was already a member. I played a more direct role in recruiting Trumbo and his friend Hugo Butler."[5]

"They had such fun together," Mitzi remembered. "They were all very funny, and they enjoyed each other's company. I don't think it was just about their common love for alcohol; there were bonds of brotherhood between them that lasted their whole lifetimes." When they were geographically separated, Trumbo exchanged long, humorous letters with Lardner and Butler.

Hugo Butler was born in Calgary, Alberta, in 1914. His father, Frank (1890–1967), deserted the family when Hugo was four years old, went to Hollywood, and became a very successful screenwriter. (He also helped found the Screen Playwrights, the sweetheart union that

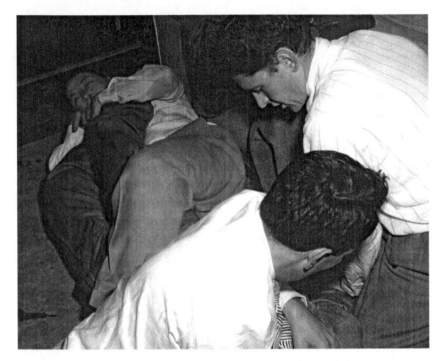

The Lads, 1945. Counterclockwise from bottom: Ring Lardner Jr., Hugo
Butler, Dalton Trumbo, and Ian Hunter (legs only). Photograph by Cleo
Trumbo.

nearly wrecked the Screen Writers Guild.) Hugo eventually followed
his father to Hollywood, and it seems likely that Frank helped him get
a screenwriting job at MGM. In 1937 Hugo received his first screen
credit, and he married Jean Rouverol. He was apolitical, but she was
a member of a Marxist study group. Under her tutelage, the couple
joined Popular Front groups and committees to improve conditions for
migrant workers. They were also, in Jean's words, "strong pacifists."
She did not say exactly when they joined the Communist Party, but
according to Jean, it was Hugo's decision, and they became very active
members. When the United States entered the war, Hugo went into the
army, and the party placed the Butlers "on leave." Shortly thereafter,
Jean gave birth to another child. When Hugo was discharged from the
army, he rejoined the party, but Jean did not.[6]

Their son, Michael, told me: "I thought my father was God. Everyone who knew him will tell you that he was charming and wise and
consistent and witty; he was also sensitive—uncannily attuned to the

distress of others. He was disciplined and ascetic but given to small indulgences (cigars, food, pre-Columbian art). This dialectic between the ascetic and the sensual was probably basic. He was capable of remarkable gentleness but also of sudden 'accesses' (as Joseph Conrad might have called them) of towering rage. This rage was over in a moment; almost never—in my experience—was his fury directed at another soul. He had extraordinary courage. His passions were sailing, jai-alai, and the bullfights (just as an observer in the latter two activities)."[7]

"Hugo was a big man," Nikola Trumbo recalled, "and he had black hair that he combed straight back on his head. None of them (except for my father) was small, but Hugo struck me as particularly large. My memories of Hugo are almost exclusively of scary stories (which he told us while my father was in prison). We kids—Trumbos and Butlers— would beg him for a story. When he would finally agree we would huddle together in the living room at the ranch, clinging to each other under blankets in makeshift forts of chairs while he terrified us with totally frightening stories. He was a gifted storyteller and I always believed that secretly he really enjoyed scaring the daylights out of us."

Ring Lardner Jr. was born in 1915. His father, Ring Lardner (1885–1933), was one of the best-known sports columnists and short story writers in the United States, renowned for his satirical humor. The younger Lardner attended Princeton, joined the Socialist Club, and dropped out of college in June 1934 to travel to Europe and the Soviet Union.[8] On that trip he met Budd Schulberg and Maurice Rapf, both scions of movie producers and both much further to the left than Lardner. When Lardner returned to the United States, he became a reporter for the *New York Daily Mirror*, where he met Ian Hunter. He moved to Hollywood in 1936 and was soon recruited by Schulberg to join the Communist Party. Lardner told me that he and the others kept quiet about their party membership, whereas Trumbo "broadcast his membership to every producer he worked for."[9]

Nikola Trumbo described Ring "as quiet and shy and tall and dark and handsome. He had a slight stutter and a hint of gravel in his voice. He was always interested in us kids, he seemed to me to be gentle and kind, and I always felt instantly comfortable with him." According to Lardner's daughter, Kate, he had stuttered as a child, and although he eventually overcame it, he remained a comparatively taciturn person.[10] He was probably the quietest of the quartet, but he was the wryest writer.

Lardner described Ian Hunter (born in 1915) as "a British sea captain's son who, after coming to this country with his family as a teenager, had proceeded directly from an American pre-school to a reporter's job [on the *Mirror*]." Hunter attended Princeton at the same time as Lardner, but he left after one year to return to the newspaper.[11] He followed Lardner to Hollywood, arriving in 1937. Soon thereafter he met and married Alice Goldberg. Joe Lardner, Ring's son, described Hunter as follows:

[He was an] affable, engaging man, friendly but in a discreet, cordial way, both a very good raconteur and an attentive listener. My impression was that he had the best heart of all of Dad's friends, but it was usually expressed through an entertaining observation or a kind of courteous, candid sociability, a youthful quality, which had a particularly charismatic effect on young adults. He was pleasingly handsome in appearance and manner, six feet when he stood up straight, which was not often, as he tended toward a relaxed, almost slouching posture, both standing and sitting. (His physical demeanor was expressive, like Trumbo's, but opposite in style: casual and companionable, whereas Dalton's was often hyper-expressive, taut and kinetic.) He had lived in the United States since he was a teenager, and his [British] accent was greatly moderated, mostly noticeable in his short a's and in certain expressions, like the term "lad," which, to my ear, seemed an easier, more natural form of address in his speech than it did in Trumbo's or Hugo's.[12]

Nikola Trumbo recalled that Hunter was "charming and fun and sophisticated. He had an unusual accent, decidedly cultured, and a honey-mellow voice that I loved to listen to. He had a shock of hair that fell over his forehead that made him decidedly handsome, and he paced a lot. I see him in my mind's eye chewing on a cigar and pacing, back and forth, back and forth, expounding." In Mitzi's memory, Ian was not handsome, but he was both charming and disarming. His manner, she said, "was more refined and subtle than Trumbo's, and he was enormously engaging." Kate Lardner was equally positive about Hunter, describing him as someone who "possessed a quiet charisma," was very easy to talk to, and "was sensuous and artistic."[13] Christopher considered Hunter one of those individuals who is naturally graceful and good at most things, especially athletics.

All the "lads" were very heavy drinkers. Their main form of relaxation, Lardner later wrote, "was to gather . . . in one of our Hollywood living rooms (usually Trumbo's, because he bought or rented huge houses), have a few drinks, eat a little something, and have a few more drinks. Some or all of our wives might also be on the scene, but as the liquid consumption added up, they tended to reassemble by themselves or go home one by one, leaving behind a group and mood that became increasingly more masculine." By all accounts, Ian's habit was the least controlled, sometimes reaching "the point of debilitation."[14] The others considered themselves "disciplined" about keeping their work and their drinking separate. "My father," Mitzi said, "never actually thought of himself as an alcoholic. He prided himself on not drinking during the day. But he knew he had a drinking problem, and Maud and Cleo were always trying to get him to change his ways." In a letter to Elsie McKeogh, posted during the autumn of 1942, Trumbo wrote:

> For the past two months I've scarcely had a drink. I didn't swear off—just lost my appetite for it. At first I was alarmed. Now I don't mind. It seems pleasant not to be fuzzy-headed most of the time. I do not think it is a permanent thing, for I have no intention of growing old and eccentric along such lines. . . . Cleo is the least bit worried, for I have become vain and proud in my abstinence, and refuse those before dinner highballs which are her particular delight. She suspects dyspepsia or another woman.[15]

Trumbo noted that Lardner had become "a dipso" long before the two of them had met.[16]

The last of the lads, Michael Wilson, was not an integral member of the original foursome, although he played tennis with Butler, Hunter, and Lardner and drank as heavily as they did; however, he was much less inclined to horseplay. He was, according to Herbert Biberman: "Quiet, intense, soft-spoken, precise, he was forever curling a lock of his prematurely iron-gray hair with his forefinger. When he was spoken to, his steel-blue eyes lifted, shot a hard glance at whoever addressed him, and then he replied tersely. When the intensity of look and speech subsided, a wry gaiety appeared."[17]

Wilson was born in Oklahoma in 1914 but was raised in San Francisco and Berkeley. He majored in philosophy at the University of Cal-

Trumbo and Michael Wilson (in France), 1960. Photograph by Cleo Trumbo.

ifornia, and while in graduate school there, he became the campus organizer for the Communist Party. He also decided to become a novelist, focusing on social and cultural subjects such as undocumented Mexican laborers. In 1939, however, his brother-in-law, Paul Jarrico, convinced Wilson to join him in Hollywood, not for the opportunity to write socially significant scripts but for the chance to earn enough money to support his novel writing. Wilson met Trumbo shortly after arriving, and the latter recalled: "We saw a lot of each other in those days, spending many evenings together planning ways of bringing down Warner Brothers by force and violence, injecting the noodles in MGM's chicken soup with a red dye, and writing subversive dialogue along the lines of 'share and share alike, that's democracy.'"[18] During the last two decades of Trumbo's life, he was probably closer to Wilson than to the others.

The lads frequently collaborated. Trumbo and Lardner cowrote one script, Hunter and Butler cowrote two, and Hunter and Lardner cowrote three movie scripts and later worked together on television scripts. Butler and Hunter fronted for Trumbo during the early years of the blacklist. Wilson and Trumbo worked together on several scripts while both were blacklisted and on one after the blacklist ended (see chapter 21).

During the early 1930s, the CPUSA would not have attracted Trumbo. Its leaders exhibited a schismatic, dogmatic, and violent bent. But Earl Browder, who became the party's general secretary in 1934, took it in a new direction after the Seventh Congress of the Third International (held in the summer of 1935). He moved the CPUSA decisively center-ward, toned down its rhetoric, tamed its tactics, announced that "Communism is the Americanism of the twentieth century," and offered de facto support for President Roosevelt. Via the newly created League of American Writers and League of American Artists, the party made a deliberate attempt to attract and cultivate intellectuals. This shift toward what is usually called the Popular Front made the party much more attractive. Its membership increased, as did the number of sympathizers and potential allies. Communists became major players in a new industrial labor federation, the Congress of Industrial Organizations. After 1935, hundreds of film industry employees joined the Hollywood branches of the party. Although Trumbo was not yet inclined to join, he worked alongside Communists in a small number of organizations, and many of his attitudes and beliefs clearly paralleled those of the Communist Party.

The date of Trumbo's joining is a matter of dispute. As noted in chapter 3, in August 1939, while under oath, Trumbo had told an examiner from the National Labor Relations Board that he was not a member of the Communist Party. Paul Jarrico claimed he recruited Trumbo sometime between September 1939 and June 1941.[19] Lardner's memoir corroborates those dates, but in an earlier interview he claimed that Trumbo and Butler had joined the party in 1943: "Either one of them would have been an unlikely member of the Party in the thirties. Trumbo, because he was pretty much of a Pacifist, and Butler because he . . . was interested in his work and his family and a lot of other things before he was interested in the Socialist movement."[20]

The FBI labeled Trumbo a "Communist fellow traveler" in October 1942, and six months later it referred to him as a known "associate of fellow travelers and Communist Party members."[21] However, the records of the Northwest (movie industry) Section of the Los Angeles County Communist Party, dated July 2, 1943, list Trumbo as a member of the Hollywood branch.[22] Trumbo himself, in an undated (circa 1957) draft of a letter, stated that he had joined the party in 1943.[23]

On several occasions, Christopher reiterated that date. (When Trumbo was interviewed by two FBI agents in January 1944 [see chapter 6], he denied being a member of the party, for obvious reasons. With tongue firmly in cheek, he also informed the agents that he had not even dared to join the League of American Writers, for fear that this "would have indicated a Communist sympathy.")[24]

Trumbo spoke publicly about his Communist Party membership for the first time in 1967. He told Helen Manfull, the editor of *Additional Dialogue*: "I joined the Communist Party in 1943 and left it in 1948 on the ground that I should in future be far too busy to attend its meetings, which were, in any event, dull beyond description and about as revolutionary in purpose as Wednesday evening testimonial services in the Christian Science Church."[25] Four years later, Trumbo repeated the 1943 date to an interviewer,[26] and in 1971 he gave the same date to biographer Bruce Cook.[27] But in his late 1971 interview with *Playboy*, Trumbo said he joined the party in the spring of 1944, just as it was being transformed into the Communist Political Association.[28]

Two years later, however, film historian Richard Corliss used the 1943 date to accuse Trumbo of lying about his membership. An incensed Trumbo reread the pertinent parts of *Additional Dialogue*, did some recalculating, and concluded that Corliss had been the victim of a printer's error and careless reading. In the hardcover edition of *Additional Dialogue*, Trumbo's draft of a letter to the FBI is dated "1942" in one place (22) and "ca. 1944" in another (26); the date of his party membership is given as 1943. Corliss, using the "ca. 1944" date, wrote that in "a respectful letter to some FBI agents," Trumbo had implicitly denied being a Communist, "which at that time he was."[29] Trumbo compiled a massive set of notes for his reply to Corliss, but he made only one comment about the date discrepancy, noting on a hand-written, undated piece of paper: "Joined in 1944 circa."[30] But for the paperback edition of *Additional Dialogue*, Trumbo not only corrected (wrongly, as we have seen) the date of his letter to the FBI (to ca. 1942) but also changed the date of his party membership to 1944.[31] Corliss then legitimately inquired: "Which of these assertions [1943 or 1944], if any, am I (or any fair-minded reader) to believe?"[32] (For more on Trumbo's exchange with Corliss, see chapter 26.)

A "fair-minded" (or generous) reader might believe that some thirty years after an undocumented fact, Trumbo simply forgot the exact date. Relying on a series of associations (the 1944 FBI letter and the 1944 party transformation), and perhaps blinded by his anger at Corliss's insinuations, Trumbo may have reconstructed an erroneous date. It is as if he said to himself: "I thought I joined in 1943, but now that I think about it. . . ." Nevertheless, the facts are that Trumbo joined the Communist Party in the spring or summer of 1943, and he wrote his letter to the FBI in January 1944.

When Cleo discussed Trumbo's party enrollment with Christopher, she did not provide a date. She only remembered that one spring (or early summer) night, Ted and Elsie Riner (Trumbo's uncle and aunt) were visiting at the ranch. "Trumbo came in full of energy and a little drunk. Not terribly drunk, but a little drunk. It's kind of like he blew in and announced that he had just joined the Communist Party and I was also a member, and then blew out again. And Ted just popped. He was so pissed. They were particularly mad because he said that I was now a member. 'He can't do that to you!' I thought little about it. I never became a part of the things he was doing. It was like I was a separate entity."[33] Christopher later wrote about this turnaround: "Cleo was angry about his decision to join, because they had agreed not to join, and then he had joined. She had no aversion to the party; many of her friends were members. But she was uninterested in communism or anything involving it."

Trumbo had not undergone a conversion experience. He had not been blinded by the celestial light of communism or Soviet Russia. He was, instead, "blinded by fascism" and motivated by loyalty to his friends.[34] According to Cleo, Dashiell Hammett convinced Trumbo it was time to join the party. The two had worked together organizing both the readers' and writers' guilds, and Trumbo had come to like, trust, and admire the older writer. It also seemed to him that, while he had been working alongside Butler, Hunter, Lardner, and Wilson as a nominal independent, he had been "traveling under false colors":

> I didn't want to have the advantage of those years of friendship and then to escape the penalties. That was part of my motive. If they hadn't been my friends, I wouldn't have joined. . . . To me it was not a matter of great consequence. It represented no significant change in my thought or my life. . . . I might as well have been a Communist ten years earlier. But I've never regretted it. As a matter of fact it's possible to say I would have regretted *not* having done it because . . . to me it was an essential part of being alive and part of the time at a very significant period in history.[35]

In addition, Cleo told Christopher, Trumbo was still trying to define himself politically. He wanted "to make a stand of some kind. To say I am opposed to what this country is doing and becoming."[36] Trumbo perceived that the United States was becoming politically reactionary. In particular, Republicans and southern Democrats in Congress and business organizations (such as the National Association of Manufacturers and the Chamber of Commerce) were loudly proclaiming their determination to reverse the gains made by organized labor during the 1930s.

Trumbo and his Communist friends wanted to create a better postwar world. Though Trumbo was not, in any sense of the term, a Marxist, he thought Marxian socialism was "a perfectly respectable philosophical system" and could serve as the basis for social change in the United States. He acknowledged that Marxism, like all philosophical systems, including Christianity, is "subject to distortion," and Soviet leaders had distorted it.[37] But he later said: "I felt that what the Soviet Union was doing had no relationship to me, and I had no responsibility for it. . . . I was never devoted to it." The only questions he consciously posed to himself about the CPUSA were: "What kind of people are in it, and what are they doing here and now?" He concluded that the party, like all groups, was made up of "a pretty courageous group of people, pocked and pitted with some frightful ideologues and generally nasty people," but the party members he knew were, by and large, "courageous, honest, intelligent people" who advocated socialism, racial justice, and the rights of labor and opposed anti-Semitism.[38] In sum, he was persuaded to join the party by the motivations and actions of the Communist Party members he knew, not by the worldwide goals of Soviet communism.

Trumbo was not, like Albert Maltz, a "good" party member. He refused to attend the weekly branch meetings that were held, he said, "with religious ferocity."[39] And he detested party oratory: "I disliked the solemn puritanical pedantry of Communist dogma as expounded in its press. I didn't swallow it. I tolerated it. I have a high regard for zeal; those who are zealous and zealots; and among zealots you will always find a certain percentage of morally arrogant—which is to say, disagreeable—people."[40] Cleo told Christopher that Trumbo attended only a few party meetings, and he was frequently drunk when he went—"at least I thought he was, since he drank every night."[41] She accompanied him only once, to a large, open meeting. But it was so boring, she said, that they quietly sneaked out a side door in the middle of it. When Cleo told that story to Christopher and Mitzi, she laughed out loud. Mitzi recalled that her father "hated meetings and the sorts of discussions that usually occur at them. They bored him. He liked to do his thinking on his own, by himself, at his typewriter. He didn't like to be harnessed or corrected or lectured. He did not like working in groups; he liked working for them, but not in collaboration with others."

Trumbo never expressed an ideological commitment to communism.[42] Though he could not be considered an apparatchik, he was a party loyalist in the sense that he did not criticize it publicly (although he regularly did so in private). That dichotomy puzzled Edward Dmytryk, a onetime party member and one of the Hollywood Ten who later became an informer. He could not understand "how such an inner-directed and unfanatical man [as Trumbo] could have maintained a loyalty to an organization as doctrinaire as the Communist Party." Dmytryk erroneously concluded that Trumbo must have been "blinded by a long-held dream and an ideal that never was."[43]

But Trumbo's loyalty was not to the Communist Party per se. More accurately, he was loyal to the belief that the party had a constitutional right to exist. He did not subscribe to the standard party doctrines of proletarian revolution and proletarian culture, nor to its veneration of Stalin. As Christopher sardonically noted:

> Trumbo never had a great identification with Mother Russia, and he always had differences with fellow leftists, because, one, he thought many of them were full of shit, [and two] he didn't like the kind of totalitarian ways in which they thought. He was always more of a theorist than anything else, open to argument and unbound by ideology. He paid no attention to party discipline. The idea of him taking direction from the party was laughable. He wasn't that kind of person. No matter what campaign or cause he was working for, he was not working for communism, but for that particular campaign or cause. He was not a propagandist for hire.

An anecdote told by Leonardo Bercovici reinforces Christopher's conclusion. Shortly after the war ended, Bercovici, who had been in the same branch of the party as Trumbo, delivered a strong speech about writers' unhealthy submission to the Los Angeles leadership group. According to Bercovici, "Dalton listened, and without telling anybody, sat down to write a thirty-page polemic about everything that I and others had said. He wanted it distributed to the various branches for discussion. But it fell into the hands of the Central Committee in Los Angeles. They decided that, while it was very interesting, the party was not 'sufficiently mature,' as they put it, to discuss it. The recommendation was that 'it be burned.' That's a quote."[44]

In June 1944, shortly after the Communist Political Association was created, Trumbo was assigned to the Beverly Hills Cultural Club and was then transferred to a "Special Group" comprising nine prominent movie industry Communists.[45] He and the other members of these groups devoted most of their political time to the campaign to reelect President Roosevelt, doing so via the National Citizens Political Action Committee, the Hollywood Democratic Committee, and Writers for Roosevelt, a group Trumbo had helped organize. Years later, Trumbo wrote: "For the truth of the matter is that whatever the policies of the national committee of the CP in New York, the main interest and activity of the great majority of Hollywood Communists lay in the practical politics of the Democratic party from the campaign of 1942 through the elections of 1946. From the time I joined the Party in 1943, I heard no talk about revolution, and very little talk about socialism; practically all I heard in the Party was the war effort and Democratic party politics."[46]

Actually, Trumbo's activities went beyond electoral politics. As part of his campaign to establish a peaceful postwar world, he addressed the anniversary dinner of American Youth for Democracy, participated in a symposium on "Culture and Democracy" sponsored by the Musicians Congress, and played a part in a dramatization of Wendell Willkie's book *One World*. He also continued to speak out in opposition to fascism both abroad and at home. He told a gathering of the Joint Anti-Fascist Refugee Committee that unless the Department of State "changed its pro-Fascist policy, the entire underground in Europe would be ruined."[47] He also chaired an event titled "The War Is Not over until Spain Is Free; Make Spain the Tomb of Fascism," sponsored by the American Committee for Spanish Freedom. In his effort to combat domestic fascism, Trumbo publicly attacked the Motion Picture Alliance for the Preservation of American Ideals (MPA).

The MPA had been formed in early 1944 by conservative writers Rupert Hughes, Fred Niblo Jr., and James K. McGuinness (who had been members of the Screen Playwrights) and by directors Sam Wood, King Vidor, and Clarence Brown, all of whom were fervent anti-Communists who were dedicated to eliminating "un-American" ideas and beliefs from Hollywood movies. The MPA's first public meeting received front-page treatment by the *Los Angeles Times*, and it was accompanied by a picture of Wood, Clark Gable, and Barbara Stanwyck.[48] One of the organization's most active members was Ginger Rogers's mother, Lela, who claimed the MPA had been formed "to educate Hollywood to the dangers of Communism which so many are too blind to see."[49] Several MPA members would be "friendly" witnesses at the October 1947 hearings of the House Committee on Un-American Activities, including Hughes, McGuinness, Niblo, Wood, Lela Rogers, Adolphe Menjou, Ayn Rand, Morrie Ryskind, Robert Taylor, and Walt Disney.

Communists were not alone in their hostility toward the MPA. On April 20, 1944, the Screen Writers Guild urged representatives of the film guilds and unions to meet to devise a strategy for "combating harmful and irresponsible" statements about the movie industry.[50] Trumbo worked closely with the four (non-Communist) members of the SWG who were organizing that meeting: Mary McCall Jr., Emmet Lavery, Howard Estabrook, and William Blowitz. In his lengthy analysis of their plan, Trumbo wrote that the aim "should be to smoke the Alliance into a public confession of their real motives, and of the essentially false statements behind which they mask these motives." The organizers should also present to the attendees "a definite constructive program, in sharp contrast to their [MPA's] destructive one," and emphasize MPA members' failure to name even one "subversive" movie. The latter, he wrote, was "a most vital point for us: because they dare not attack specific pictures without attacking specific production organizations, and the moment they do that, they're in the soup and have given us new allies. And if they fail to name pictures, as they previously have failed, they are naked." Trumbo also counseled the guild and union representatives not to allow themselves "to be jockeyed into a position" of defending the political affiliations of specific individuals. In sum, Trumbo wanted to ensure that the speakers focused on forming a broad-based, all-industry opposition to the MPA. They should not, he warned, allow themselves to get sidetracked into defending Hollywood against the MPA's red-baiting, nor should they attack the studios. They must recognize that the workers' postwar economic interests directly coincided with those of the producers and of the industry as a whole.[51]

When the representatives of thirty-eight industry organizations met on July 4 at the Hollywood-Roosevelt Hotel, Mary McCall Jr., following Trumbo's advice, told them that the purpose of the gathering was to make "concrete plans for the expression of industrial unity" in the face of a "dreary history of slander and abuse, which had begun in 1940 and was culminating in the bad press being generated by the MPA."[52] According to one reporter, "Speakers at the meeting denied that the industry was infested by communists and crackpots," and the participants voted to form a Council of Hollywood Guilds and Unions to defend the industry against charges such as those made by the MPA.[53]

In January 1945 Trumbo continued his efforts to promote Left-labor unity when he spoke at a banquet honoring union leader Sidney Hillman. Hillman was the founder of the National Citizens Political Action Committee (NCPAC), a liberal-labor Popular Front–type organization aimed at strengthening and extending New Deal reforms. Trumbo joined the NCPAC because he had "a deep personal desire" to affiliate himself "with the broadest possible group of Americans," one that "offered, not control *by*—but affiliation *with*—organized labor." It was one of the few organizations that provided "a mighty bulwark against intolerance and bigotry and the one-sided vilification which now passes—in some quarters—for a free press." He was confident that the existence of the NCPAC and organizations like it meant that "there can be no future Francos, no future Munichs, and consequently no future Pearl Harbors."[54]

But five months later, Trumbo's hope for a continuation of the war-time Popular Front was destroyed. In May the *Daily Worker* printed a translation of an article written by Jacques Duclos, a high official in the French Communist Party and a recognized annunciator of Moscow's dictates. In the article, Duclos criticized Browder for the direction the CPUSA had taken under his leadership, and he attacked the Communist Political Association as "a notorious revision of Marxism" that had "sowed dangerous opportunist illusions" among Communists.[55] The article provoked a heated debate among Hollywood Communists: some thought a more militant line was needed; others thought that such a change would be too sudden and too marked. The party's national leadership, however, fully embraced Duclos's critique and removed an unrepentant Browder from his leadership position. The CPUSA was reestablished in July with a new secretariat; seven months later, Browder was expelled from the party, and the new leadership engineered a sharp leftward swing in rhetoric and tactics. The heightened militancy drove a wedge between liberals and organized labor, on one side, and the party itself, on the other.

We have little evidence of what Trumbo thought about this significant shift in party politics. Since he rarely attended meetings of the

Communist Political Association, he may have viewed this change as irrelevant to his future activities. According to Jean Butler, Trumbo told her husband, Hugo: "It comes down to this—either Lenin was right and Browder was wrong, or Browder was right and Lenin was wrong. I prefer to believe that Lenin was right."[56] This statement, of course, does not make Trumbo a "Leninist"; he simply thought more highly of Lenin's thinking than of Browder's. Leonardo Bercovici commented on "the speed with which everybody [in the Beverly Hills branch] turned around after Browder was repudiated," but it is unclear whether this included Trumbo.[57]

Trumbo took little part in the party's transformational moves. He devoted his time to the reelection of the president, the organization of the United Nations, his visit to the Pacific theater of operations, and his role as editor of the Screen Writers Guild's new journal.

Trumbo "served" the US war effort between May and August 1945 in two different ways. His first service began in early May, when the US Army Air Force asked eight fiction writers to become war correspondents in the Pacific theater of operations. Those who organized the trip thought the experience would add authenticity to the writers' subsequent projects. It is unclear how and why these particular individuals were selected. The choice of Trumbo is bizarre if one considers his authorship of *Johnny Got His Gun* and his FBI file, but it is understandable if one considers his pro-war scripts. In any event, Trumbo was notified of his selection by Captain Robert Reeves, who must have gotten his address from Bertram Lippincott (the publisher of *Johnny Got His Gun*), who later wrote to Trumbo expressing an interest in any book Trumbo might write about the Pacific war.[58]

While he was filing his passport application and getting his inoculations for the Pacific trip, Trumbo received a summons for a different type of service. Robert Lynch, special assistant to Secretary of State Edward R. Stettinius Jr., asked Trumbo to come to San Francisco, where the United Nations Conference on International Organizations was meeting, and write a speech for a national radio address to be given by Stettinius.[59] According to gossip columnist Hedda Hopper, producer Walter Wanger persuaded Trumbo to go to San Francisco to write the speech, but Wanger did not tell Stettinius he had done so.[60]

When he arrived in San Francisco, Trumbo quickly learned that the major powers were beginning to divide on several key issues, while the smaller countries were becoming restive about their second-class status. Fearing that the conference was veering away from the agreements reached at Yalta, Stettinius hoped his speech would encourage the various delegations to act in a more unified manner.[61] In addition, the secretary had already yielded on two big issues—the status of regional agreements and the admission of the Argentine delegation—and he was determined to hold the line on three other contentious issues: admission of the delegation from Soviet-controlled Poland, the suspensory veto power awarded to the five permanent members of the Security Council (United States, USSR, United Kingdom, France, and China), and the trusteeship policy. Trumbo's assignment was to put a happy face on the two concessions Stettinius had already made, as well as on those he was not prepared to make.

Trumbo's experience in San Francisco was not a pleasant one. He spent the first night at the Mark Hopkins Hotel, where he met Thomas K. Finletter, a consultant to the delegation. He also reconnected with an old fraternity brother, Llewellyn Thompson, who was currently serving as an undersecretary of state. The next day Trumbo moved to the Fairmont Hotel, where the rest of the delegation was staying. "I was," he recalled, "given a room on the fourth or fifth floor between [John Foster] Dulles and [Harold] Stassen. It was a rather weird sensation to get off the elevator and look down the hall and see white-gaitered MPs standing guard in front of each room, and then, walking down the hall, to hear typewriters going behind each door." To his chagrin, he found two copies of the *Daily People's World* in his room, so he "went into the bathroom, . . . carefully tore both copies up and burned them and dropped them down the toilet."[62]

The following morning, Wednesday, Trumbo conferred with Finletter but spent the afternoon in bed, suffering from the side effects of his typhoid shot. Thursday he gathered as much information as he could, outlined it, and wrote the introduction to the speech, which he gave to Finletter on Friday. Though he received no response from either Finletter or Lynch, he continued to write and delivered the completed speech to Lynch three days later. By that time, Finletter had read the introduction, which he found "too defensive in its attitude." So Trumbo rewrote the entire speech and sent it to Finletter, along with a request for additional information. When Finletter failed to respond, Trumbo wrote to Lynch: "As you have perhaps surmised, I feel that I have been badly treated, and I am determined to bellyache about it. I did not solicit this work. I have gone to considerable trouble to undertake it." After listing the many speeches he had written for various political figures and causes, Trumbo stated:

In other words, I am not entirely an idiot in terms of understanding what the public wants to hear about men and issues,
and I am goddamned offended that a few Ivy Leaguers living
only temporarily at the Fairmont Hotel should have gone to
such extraordinary lengths to be rude to me. . . . Now that the
steam is off—steam which I assure you is personal and petty—I
should like to say only this: I believe this is the kind of address
which at this time would enormously enhance the stature of
any man who delivered it.

But if Lynch found fault with the finished speech, Trumbo vowed to
"take it south," where he was sure he could "find a good many officials
who will be eager to use it—minus, of course, its official implications—
for their own purposes."[63]

Lynch reassured Trumbo, and Finletter provided additional feed-
back, so Trumbo stayed four more days, rewriting constantly. He was
told to soften what he had written about the admission of the Argentine
delegation and the disagreement over the Polish government. He was
also instructed to use stronger language in the section on trusteeships
and to make the unequivocal statement that the United States would
continue to occupy "those strategic points in the Pacific which are necessary for the defense of the United States and for world security."[64]

When the speech was returned to him for a final polish, Trumbo
complained that there was "a good deal of awkward writing in the
draft."[65] "I have," he wrote, "gone over this thing four times, and I
have come to the conclusion that only rarely have I been witness to
such a vicious assault upon the lucidity of the English language." He
also offered a few unsolicited criticisms of its content. In his opinion,
the speech clearly implied that the United States and the United Kingdom were trying to control the conference, and it made the secretary
of state seem to be carping and whining that they were not achieving all their goals. Further, Trumbo complained about the deletion of
language emphasizing that Soviet foreign minister Vyacheslav Molotov
had "parted in friendship" with the United States and United Kingdom.
This omission left the impression that the problems of the conference
were the result of a breach among the three great powers, rather than
disagreements among all the participating countries. In sum, Trumbo
believed the revised speech implied that the United States was on the
verge of declaring war on the Soviet Union.[66]

The speech, as delivered by Stettinius, conveyed many ideas that were copacetic to Trumbo. The secretary stressed the need for all the countries of the world to promote peace, democracy, and economic and social development. He emphasized the importance of equal justice, individual rights, and freedom for all without respect to race, religion, or gender. He urged the leaders of the victorious countries to maintain their wartime collaboration, and he promised that the "the primary objective of United States foreign policy is to continue and strengthen in the period of peace that wartime solidarity which has made possible the defeat of Germany." But he qualified that statement in the next breath, saying: "We have the right to expect the same spirit and the same approach on the part of our great allies."[67]

On June 8 Lynch sent Trumbo a photograph of Stettinius inscribed: "To Dalton Trumbo, with best wishes." On an attached note, Trumbo later wrote: "For this man I did the United Nations Organization speech, living at the Fairmont Hotel in State Department rooms in May or June of 1945, at their request and my own expense. Several years later, [while I was testifying before the Committee on Un-American Activities], Edward R. Stettinius, Jr. [now Rector of the University of Virginia] issued a statement that he'd never had anything to do with me."[68]

On his return to Los Angeles, Trumbo put a positive spin on his experience in an editorial he wrote for *Screen Writer*, the newly created journal of the Screen Writers Guild. He congratulated the nations that had assembled in San Francisco for their efforts to forge an organizational structure to ensure "permanent peace which is the prime aspiration of mankind." He also urged filmmakers to do whatever they could—by writing better movies—to help the peoples of the world obtain "a full appreciation of the unity and cooperation" necessary to avoid future wars. Speaking for the editorial staff, Trumbo stated: "The motion picture is the most important of all international cultural mediums and . . . the screen writer is the primary creative force in the making of motion pictures."[69]

Privately, however, he expressed disappointment with what he had seen and heard in San Francisco. He told Elsie: "I saw the real seamy underside of life, things I'd read but never believed, feeling them to be the distortions of left-wing propaganda."[70] Trumbo did not go into detail, but he was probably referring to the nature of the realpolitik deals being made behind the scenes by the delegates. He had taken copious notes, and he intended to use them as the basis for a chapter in his war novel. He never wrote that novel, but his notes from the confer-

Trumbo and Earl Felton, ca. June 1945. Photograph by Cleo Trumbo.

ence express Trumbo's foreboding about the postwar world. "For all its worthy intentions, [the conference] was erecting the superstructure of peace"—the United Nations—on an undemocratic foundation. Contrary to what the US delegates were saying, the conference provided no "real representation to the populations of the world"; it excluded the soon-to-be-vanquished countries and colonial peoples and failed to give proportional representation to those nations that had contributed the most to victory. The conferees also turned a blind eye to the fact that only two great powers—the United States and the Soviet Union—were still standing, and they controlled or occupied many other countries. In sum, the conference "was rooted in unreality." In "its idealistic and equalitarian obsessions," it ignored the decisive factors—economic and military power—in international relations. Last, the organizers of the conference failed "to understand the direction of history" or how rapidly the forces of history were moving. As a result, what had been a "good" war, "a war of national defense . . . against unreason, bestiality, racism, crematoria," was being diverted to a bad end.[71]

Shortly after he returned to Los Angeles, Trumbo received his passport, and in June he and seven other writers began an eight-week,

22,000-mile journey that took them to Kwajalein, Guam, Tinian, Saipan, Iwo Jima, Manila, Tawi Tawi, Balikpapan, and Okinawa. In the letters he sent to Cleo,[72] Trumbo expressed his "awe" for the fighting men (June 6) and his horror at the war machine. He found "simply appalling the strength and organization and quantities of everything we have everywhere" (June 12) and "simply terrifying" the amount of construction and the concentration of power on the islands he visited (June 17). Some of his descriptions are vivid:

> Iwo [Jima] is the most appalling place on earth. . . . This little hell-hole is composed almost entirely of black volcanic dust and rocky bluffs. . . . 5,000 men died to take this place, and you wonder it wasn't 25,000 when you look at it. The rocky beaches are still littered with Jap ammunition, both live and expended, all kinds of abandoned equipment, and an occasional body rotting in the blistering sun. There are wrecked ships rusting in the harbor, and stacks of wrecked planes in the uplands. And remember, the island was secured March 17, and is considered pretty well cleaned up by now (June 20).

From the Philippines, Trumbo wrote to Cleo about the destruction in Manila:

> [It] is so terrifying and the disorganization [is] so complete. . . . [I]f you can imagine a city the approximate size of San Francisco in which every large building has been reduced by gunfire to rubble or gutted by flames; in which every residence has been shelled and burned; in which the people live 10 and 12 in a room; in which babies are bathed and families drink from the sewers; in which inflation and malnutrition have made the place a city of thieves—if you can imagine this and worse—with battles still going on within 23 miles of the city—with snipers still infiltrating into the city—with power still off—and a most difficult political situation numbing homesick G.I.s in the midst of what is professedly a near-independent nation—then you have a small idea of Manila. (June 22 or 23)

Aside from these letters, Trumbo took copious notes for his war novel, with special attention to the two air raids on which the correspondents flew. In the first raid, "The B-25 in which Captain Reeves was flying as aerial observer received a direct hit from 40 mm AA [antiaircraft] fire while attacking an enemy concentration. The plane exploded and fell into the sea with the loss of all aboard."[73] During the second raid, a bombing mission over the Japanese island of Kyushu, the "AA fire was radar-directed and heavy. We lost one B-25 and six Navy Corsairs who were flying escort."[74]

After returning from the second raid, the correspondents joined a fleet of some 300 vessels assembled for what would be the last amphibious assault of the war, on Dutch East Borneo. Trumbo described the landing to Cleo: "The first wave went in on schedule at 9:30 a.m. At 9:45 we [he, Ray Murphy, and Herbert Clyde Lewis] clambered into a Higgins landing craft, and waded ashore shortly thereafter. Smoke. Naval bombardment in the hills ahead of us. Ruined houses. Crazed and starved natives. Stripped coconut trees. Dazed, shell-shocked birds. Great oil fires. Almost intolerable heat. Heavy mortar fire from our own troops on all sides. Machines roaring through the surf onto the beach. Wounded being carried to first aid on stretchers" (July 1).

After they landed, the three correspondents decided to climb a hill to get a better view of the battle. The officer accompanying the writers declined to join them, "on the ground that it was a needless risk, justifiable for a correspondent but not for an escort." Perhaps fifteen minutes after arriving at the top, "a grim-looking Australian major charged up the other side of the hill at the head of an assault group, all bayonets heroically set. His pleasure in capturing the hill for king and country was somewhat diminished by the presence of three American correspondents already in firm possession." The next day, Trumbo and the other two correspondents joined another patrol, crossed the mountains, entered the port city of Balikpapan, and "penetrated halfway down its main waterfront street before cross-fire obliged us to return."[75]

Their "war" seemed to be over, and they departed on a small Catalina flying boat. However, somewhere off the Japanese-occupied Celebes islands, an alarm sounded in the cabin, signifying an imminent air attack:

> We in the cabin put on our helmets and lay down wherever we were. Our two gunners opened fire. The plane began to lose altitude rapidly, the only possible way for a slow-moving Catalina to escape a Zero being to get so close to the water that the Zero, in making its pass, will crack up. We who were in the cabin could do nothing; we could not see outside; we could not

Trumbo (back row, third from left) with his fellow war correspondents (Ray Murphy is at far right; Herbert Clyde Lewis is at bottom left), 1945. Courtesy of Trumbo family.

fight; we could not take shelter; we could not run; we could only lie quietly, realizing that our chances for life had all but run out, and wondering why we have ever permitted ourselves to be placed in such a position.

They soon realized there was no Zero. The nervous aircrew had only imagined it.[76]

Trumbo and Christopher, 1945. Photograph by Harry Baskerville.

One month after his return, Trumbo wrote a long article for the *Screen Writer* about his experiences in the Pacific, describing the servicemen and -women he had met and their feelings about the war and the coming peace. In one hospital he had visited on Guam, the patients had "heard, with a kind of contemptuous astonishment, that Negro and white blood is segregated in stateside Red Cross banks." In the war zone, they told him, "blood segregation would cost lives." Trumbo acknowledged that he had observed some examples of racial prejudice, but he tried to soften their import. Reporting on his time in Manila, Trumbo wrote: "G.I. Joe regards all Filipinos with a jaundiced eye. He is far from home and lonely, and he didn't ask to come here in the first place, and he is not inclined to search for reasons." As for the troops' thoughts about the larger political and social issues causing turbulence in the United States, Trumbo concluded that they had a more consuming interest: "They are working together at enterprises involving life and death. Perhaps this makes them less susceptible to subversive propaganda than we at home." Clearly, Trumbo was impressed by what he had witnessed—most of all, by "the men themselves."[77]

Shortly after his return to Los Angeles, the United States dropped two atomic bombs on two Japanese cities. Christopher recalled that his father initially approved of President Truman's decision, because it ended a horrible war. But after he had time to think about the negative consequences of one superpower having a monopoly on such a destructive weapon, Trumbo changed his mind, and he agreed to participate in a radio series sponsored by the Hollywood Writers' Mobilization to educate people about the atomic bomb and the need to create an international agency to deal with nuclear weapons. For the remainder of his life, Trumbo opposed the nuclear arms race and the testing of nuclear weapons.

The Hollywood to which Trumbo returned was not a peaceful place. There, a brutal jurisdictional strike pitted the Conference of Studio Unions (CSU) against the International Alliance of Theatrical Stage Employees (IATSE) and the studios. Because of his belief that the CSU was a democratic organization and the IATSE was a corrupt tyranny, he supported the CSU fully and publicly, even though the Communist Party was still enforcing its no-strikes-during-the-war pledge. On August 7 Trumbo delivered a forceful speech at a pro-CSU meeting at Hollywood Legion Stadium. And in October he and thirty-five other specially selected people stood outside the gates of Warner Bros. studios to witness the violence inflicted on CSU picketers by a squad of IATSE strikebreakers, supported by the Burbank police force. He and the other witnesses then signed a statement protesting the "outrageous violence perpetrated by hired thugs and police."[78]

As a result of his support of the CSU, Trumbo received a form letter from Roy Brewer, the international representative of the IATSE and a member of the Motion Picture Alliance, querying the recipient: "We now ask you whether or not you as an individual support the campaign of slander, vilification, lies and scurrility now being carried on against our officers and those loyal American workers who believe in and support the IATSE, and who, by doing so, have incurred the enmity and hatred of the entire Communist 'apparat.'" If, the letter implied, the recipient did not explicitly answer no, his or her future movies would be boycotted by IATSE projectionists.[79] The following day, Brewer publicly accused the Communists of launching a "gigantic conspiracy" in Hollywood.[80]

Unfazed by this threat, Trumbo spoke at a mass meeting sponsored by the Citizens Committee for the Motion Picture Strikers "to tell the truth about the strike, help end the reign of terror in Hollywood, and put the strikers back to work." Trumbo castigated the IATSE, which, he charged, was led by corrupt officers dominated by gangsters. To defeat the democratically run CSU, the IATSE had entered into an "unholy alliance" with the producers. The IATSE had created new locals to replace those of the striking CSU, and those newly chartered IATSE locals were being recognized by the studios. Trumbo called them "scab charters." The producers steadfastly refused to negotiate with the CSU locals; instead, they recognized the "unions which were set up for strike-breaking activities," discharged members of striking unions, and flouted a War Labor Board order for a cooling-off period. As a result of these tactics, the IATSE-producer alliance had converted a strike into a lockout. Trumbo urged "American labor" to pay careful attention to what was happening in Hollywood and to take heed of "the true nature of the dangers confronting it."[81]

At the end of 1945, Trumbo belatedly wrote to Elsie about his Pacific trip and reiterated his usual refrain about novel writing. The experience in San Francisco and the Pacific war zone had given him "a unique slant on war and peace," but before he could use that slant for a new novel, he had to "face the problem" he had been deferring for years: "The bakery [novel]. I have seven—wrong, six—novels on the bakery, all n.g. [no good]. . . . But the bakery must come first, then the stories of later on, the continuation of the bakery saga into other fields, efforts, communities until finally it becomes a part of history and of the world." He envisioned a series of novels, each based on a specific historical event: the Depression, President Roosevelt, the beginning of the war, the war at home, the United Nations conference, his Pacific trip, and, finally, "the conclusion of the mess."[82]

Meanwhile, Trumbo was "quarreling" with his bosses at MGM.

He had demanded a new contract without the standard morals clause. Fearing that a political investigation of the motion picture industry was on the horizon, he did not want the studio to be able to suspend him because of something he said during that investigation. Trumbo did not want to put his political activities at the mercy of his employer, which might become frightened and fire him because a particular speech or article caused the public to view him with contempt, ridicule, or scorn. When the studio denied his request, Trumbo refused all subsequent assignments. The studio suspended him for seven months, costing Trumbo more than $80,000 in compensation. But it was, he said, a sum "well lost," since the studio eventually gave in to his demand, and he signed a new contract that, he naïvely thought, guaranteed his "economic security in a rapidly darkening political situation."[83]

Between the signing of his new contract and his appearance before the Committee on Un-American Activities in October 1947, Trumbo was dissatisfied with the quality of the projects he was assigned. In fact, none of the scripts Trumbo worked on were made into movies. Ironically, the last screen credit Trumbo received before he was blacklisted was for a script he claimed he did not write—*Jealousy* (Republic, 1946). Trumbo later stated he had merely given the film's director, Gustav Machaty, an idea for a character. Machat was so grateful that he inserted an onscreen credit: "from an idea by Dalton Trumbo."[84] However, two years before the movie was made, an employee at Berg-Allenberg told Elsie that Trumbo had written the script for *Jealousy* "as a favor for someone," but he now thought it was "completely hopeless" and hoped it would not be made into a movie.[85]

8

Trumbo's Antifascist Persuasion

He was trying to get out of Hollywood. Cleo also wanted a different life. He has plans for a new novel. So, the plan is to move from Los Angeles and phase out a life centered around the movies.

—Christopher Trumbo

Between 1944 and 1946, Trumbo was more politically engaged than he had been at any time in the past. Fearing that his hoped-for democratic peace was being swamped by a wave of neofascist activity and deafened by a chorus of war talk, he spoke and wrote in a wide variety of forums. To make sense of Trumbo's political thinking and activity during those years, one must understand the role antifascism played in his thought process. To many leftists of the 1930s, antifascism offered the most appropriate means to preserve democracy and strengthen freedom via a series of progressive reforms. Though antifascism was a powerful motivating ideal in practice, it proved to be an unsteady ark, housing a wide and often conflicting passenger list of political ideologies, activities, and parties. This vessel was twice (in 1939 and 1946) run aground by its Communist passengers' unshakable loyalty and obedience to Soviet foreign policy. But—and this is crucial to understanding Trumbo's position—those Soviet foreign policy decisions did not, per se, undermine his belief in the value of antifascism.

This chapter attempts to explain the political ideas and values that motivated Trumbo from 1939 to 1947: his opposition to war in general (1939–1941), his support for US involvement in World War II (1941–1945), his postwar belief that fascism was on the rise in the United States, and his concern that the US government was trying to incite a third world war. Though my explanation is not intended as an apologia, it constitutes a conscious effort to challenge the many writers who have dismissed antifascism as an intelligible motive for political activity in the United States during those years, especially if it involved working in (or alongside) the Communist Party.[1]

Like many political observers during the 1930s, Trumbo feared both foreign and domestic fascism. Indeed, according to Tony Judt: "It seemed plausible in those years to fear that the final battle would be between communism and fascism, with democracy squeezed in the middle."[2] On the European front, the deeds of Benito Mussolini and Adolf Hitler were prominently featured in virtually every newspaper and magazine, as were the regular clashes between reactionary groups and the democratic governments of other European countries. On the home front, dozens of paramilitary, protofascist, and white supremacy groups formed, and several demagogic figures such as Huey Long and Father Charles Coughlin enjoyed a mass following.[3] The United States, United Kingdom, and France were standing by while Hitlerian Germany regularly violated the Treaty of Versailles and while Japan, Germany, and Italy pursued an expansionist foreign policy. Nor were the Western democratic governments doing much to quell the domestic fascist groups in their countries. Soviet leaders, in contrast, had taken several highly publicized steps to confront fascist aggression. The Seventh World Congress of the Third (or Communist) International (Comintern), which met during July and August 1935, called for the establishment of both a united proletarian front and a people's front to combat fascism. In response, the world's Communist parties created what was known as the Popular Front, and under its umbrella, a large variety of antifascist and pro-democracy groups formed, enrolling Communists, socialists, and liberals. In addition, the Soviet Union made two attempts to turn back the fascist tide in Europe. First, it tried, unsuccessfully, to build a peace front with the nonfascist European countries, and second, it was the only major power that offered aid to the Republican government of Spain, which was fighting for its very existence against a reactionary coalition of the army, the church, large landowners, and the Falangist (fascist) Party—a coalition openly aided by Germany and Italy.

To be sure, aligning oneself with the Soviet Union in the struggle against fascism required one to discount or ignore other perceptions, and this tunnel vision proved to be one of the main weaknesses of antifascism. At the height of the Popular Front, the Soviet government initiated a series of spectacular show trials involving many of the most famous leaders of the 1917 revolution, resulting in their condemnation as "enemies" of the Soviet state and their subsequent conviction and execution. At the same time, reports from Spain indicated that Soviet agents were murdering anarchists, socialists, and Trotskyists. Selective perception and rationalization reached a peak in late August 1939, when the world's Communists were told that the Soviet-German Non-aggression Treaty was the only means to avoid war and combat Western imperialism. It seemed to many antifascists that Soviet antifascism had taken a backseat to Soviet national interests, and Communists' efforts to deny this seemingly obvious fact and their attempts to justify the Soviet Union's sudden shifts from antifascism (1935–1939) to antiwar (1939–1941) and back to antifascism (1941–1945) raised some disturbing questions about their independent thinking and their reliability as political allies.

Trumbo, however, did not have to adjust his thinking about either fascism or the Soviet Union. He was not a member of the Communist Party, he had not joined any of the Popular Front antifascist groups, nor had he apologized for the Moscow trials or for Soviet activity in Spain. His political activity prior to 1939 consisted of union organizing and campaigning for progressive politicians. To be sure, he worked alongside Communists in pursuit of these activities, and after September 1939, his antiwar position and that of the CPUSA were identical. However, their reasons for being antiwar differed. The CPUSA was defending a Soviet foreign policy decision, whereas Trumbo, as he clearly stated in *The Remarkable Andrew*, did not believe the United States was making a genuine effort to defeat fascism. Only in December 1941, after the United States had been attacked and had formed an alliance with the Soviet Union to defeat the Axis powers, did Trumbo begin to support the war.

Trumbo's antifascism, his support for the war, and his notion of a democratic peace were tightly bound together. He opposed the postwar foreign policy of the United States because he thought the Truman administration, by failing to promote peace abroad and to protect freedom of speech and assembly at home, was acting in a warlike and fascistic manner. Looking back, one can say that Trumbo exaggerated the likelihood of both, but the depth of his concern was genuine. In the dedication to an unpublished short story written shortly after the war ended, he wrote: "For our children, Nikola and Christopher and Melissa / That their bright promises are not defiled / That they are permitted to live."[4]

The larger question is why postwar antifascists and war opponents chose to defend or ignore postwar Soviet activity, most of which was clearly not antifascist or antiwar. Why, for example, did they perceive the Soviet occupation or control of Poland, Estonia, Latvia, Lithuania, Romania, Hungary, Czechoslovakia, Bulgaria, and the eastern sector of Germany as the reasonable behavior of a state seeking to ensure its national security? Why did they fail to register the gross violations of civil liberties and human rights that were occurring in the Soviet Union and in the Soviet-dominated countries of eastern Europe? Two facts account for this blinkered perspective: higher expectations of the United States and its sphere of influence, and a lack of trust of the sources (mainly anti-Communists and the Truman administration) of the negative slant being given to the Soviets' true intent.

Trumbo viewed Soviet activity in central and eastern Europe in the most benevolent, one might even say purblind, manner possible. According to him, Soviet policy was no different from what the United States had done in Latin America and what the United States and the United Kingdom were presently doing—that is, continuing to support Western colonial empires and, in the countries they occupied, establishing or supporting regimes favorable to their interests. In one of his critiques of US foreign policy, he stated: "It is notable that the Russians, in Russian-occupied countries, have in no instance set up Soviet Socialist Republics." Rather, they had established governments that were more democratic than the one in Mississippi, and a larger percentage of the people in Soviet-occupied countries voted regularly than did those living in the Philippines. Furthermore, Trumbo noted, the Soviet Union did not represent a threat to the national security of the United States: there were no Russian troops in most of the places where US troops were stationed, no Russian fleets in the world's great waterways, no Russian air bases, "no Russian troops anywhere in the world engaged in putting down the movements of Colonial peoples toward freedom." And yet the US government, as well as "certain powerful segments of American life" and the media, had launched a campaign "of anti-Soviet fury," laced with bellicose rhetoric.[5] For that reason, Trumbo point-blank refused to criticize the Soviet Union. "If you wish to discover what is wrong with Soviet Russia," he said, "go to Adolf Hitler and *Mein Kampf*. Go to the hundreds of American journalists who make a very good living presenting such issues. . . . My neglect is corrected every morning and every evening by the editorial tirades and the angled news of the American free press."[6]

Fears of a pending third world war and the growth of fascism at home went hand in hand. Both were seen by Communists as the necessary products of the postwar national security policies and acts of the United States. When Communists in the United States spoke about postwar fascism, they regularly referred to acts by the government and by business corporations that, in their minds, mirrored those of Nazi Germany. They were convinced that passage of the Alien Registration Act (1940) was the keystone of a postwar policy intended to destroy the CPUSA; that resistance to strikes, the end of price controls, and the Taft-Hartley Act (1947) were all part of a coordinated campaign to break the power of labor unions and reduce the rights of workers; and that the investigations of the Committee on Un-American Activities was the opening wedge of a concerted effort to destroy all those groups that had campaigned against interwar fascism. In sum, after 1945, Communists used the term *fascism* to refer to a campaign backed by "finance capital" and aimed at strengthening the power of corporations and the government at the expense of workers and racial minorities.[7]

It should be emphasized that Trumbo's public warnings about a developing fascist conspiracy in the United States preceded those of the party by several months.[8] In a speech written in late 1945 or early 1946, Trumbo warned about a developing fascist conspiracy in the United States aimed against "the right of the writer, educator, scientist, to devote his work to democratic ends." This conspiracy functioned at several levels: at the national level, in the form of the Committee on Un-American Activities; at the state level, in the form of the California Joint Legislative Committee on Un-American Activities (aka the Tenney Committee); and at the municipal level, in the form of the relationship between Los Angeles city councilman Meade McClanahan and the America First Party of Gerald L. K. Smith. Trumbo vehemently denied that this "conspiracy" was a legitimate, if misguided, response to "Soviet aggression." It had an agenda of its own, he insisted, an agenda cloaked in the garb of anticommunism.[9] Reflecting on his postwar antifascism a decade later, he wrote: "I realize that fascism is an old-fashioned word today, but it wasn't in 1947, and since it always began first with the separation and then with the suppression of an unpopular minority, it seemed a lot wiser and easier to fight it in the opening stage than wait until it reached its second or third or final stage."[10] (Indeed, on November 2, 1947, writer Thomas Mann, a German émigré, said precisely that: "I am painfully familiar with certain political trends, spiritual intolerance, political inquisitions, and declining legal security, and all this in the name of an alleged 'state of emergency' . . . that is how it started in Germany. What followed was fascism and what followed fascism was war.")[11]

Nevertheless, their fight against "first-stage" fascism in the 1940s placed Trumbo and his friends in a predicament because it narrowed, in their minds, the possible outcomes to two: (1) fascistic, reactionary, or nondemocratic regimes, or (2) "people's democracies." Since they defined *fascism* as an opposition to civil liberties, the first outcome was unthinkable. However, they did not look closely enough at the second alternative. Rather, they viewed people's democracies through rose-colored glasses and excused them for doing what reactionary governments in the West were doing, such as curbing free speech and reducing the power of labor unions.

Trumbo's concerns about fascism in the postwar United States were reflected in some of the articles and editorials he wrote for *Screen Writer*, the new periodical of the Screen Writers Guild (SWG). Just before he went to San Francisco and the Pacific theater, he was selected as its editor, and he held that position for nineteen months. Other Communists held important positions: Gordon Kahn was the managing editor; Harold J. Salemson was the editorial secretary; and, for eleven of those months, the Editorial Committee included at least two other Communists. Did that make *Screen Writer* a "party-line" journal? If the percentage of articles written by Communists is the unit of measurement, the answer must be no. Only 19 of the 108 articles published during Trumbo's tenure were written by Communist Party members, and only two issues (July and October 1945) contained more than two articles by party members. Those who allege that *Screen Writer* was a party journal could point to the fact that the number of articles authored by Communists decreased markedly after Trumbo stepped down as editor. But that decrease coincided with the threat of an investigation of Hollywood by the Committee on Un-American Activities, leading a substantial number of guild members to want to lower the political profile of both the SWG and its journal.

Trumbo wrote editorials for most of the issues, but the majority of them addressed guild topics and had to be approved by the SWG Executive Board. There were a few controversies about rejected articles (see below), but Trumbo did not make those decisions unilaterally. He told the Executive Board that editorials "should be the direct expression of the Executive Board's wishes, and the Executive Board should be prepared to defend them as such. . . . [O]nly in this way can there

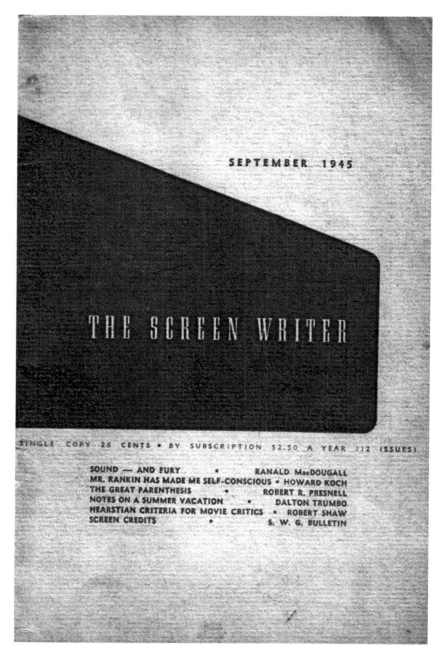

SEPTEMBER 1945

THE SCREEN WRITER

SINGLE COPY 25 CENTS • BY SUBSCRIPTION $2.50 A YEAR (12 ISSUES)

The Screen Writer, 1945.

be a continuity of official policy: only in this way can the monthly editorial perform what I consider to be its principal function—to prepare
the path for Guild progress."[12] The board concurred. In the June 1946
issue, Trumbo wrote: "Rejection or acceptance of an article is determined by a majority vote. All editorials are approved first by the Editorial Committee, and then by the Executive Board [of the Guild]."[13]

The next question is: was there a party line evident in the articles
written by Communists? To some degree, the answer is yes. For example, issues or personalities they disapproved of were regularly labeled
"fascist," and they tended to articulate the party's belief that the US
government was provoking a third world war. But in many cases, the
party line—that is, peaceful relations with the Soviet Union and opposition to militaristic talk and activity—was indistinguishable from the
positions espoused by liberals and non-Communist leftists.

In addition, many of Trumbo's editorials echoed industry-wide
attitudes. In the first issue, for example, Trumbo sharply attacked the
newly formed Motion Picture Alliance for the Preservation of American
Ideals (MPA). He noted that many MPA members were former members of the Screen Playwrights, which, during its campaign to destroy
the SWG, had acted as a mouthpiece for the studio heads. Now, however, these "assembled patriots" were venturing "to think boldly for
themselves," to proclaim, in the words of MPA president Sam Wood,
that Hollywood's war effort was the work of "Communists, crackpots
and radicals." Wood, a director, had denigrated screenwriters as "boil-
ermakers [and] apprentices," claiming that he dictated stories to them
and basically wrote their scripts for them. Trumbo recounted what took
place when the two had worked together on *Kitty Foyle*: "I was privileged to call at Mr. Wood's house and relate to him the contents of the
novel which he had not yet read. He agreed to direct it, and sailed the
next day for Honolulu, where he rested until the script was written.
Upon his return, he honored me with a half-day conference, after which
the cameras turned." Trumbo concluded with a two-fisted slam, sarcastically demeaning Wood's directorial skills and stating: "There seems to
be no way of confirming a report that he proposes to spend his twilight
years engraving the Lord's Prayer on the head of a Communist."[14]

Wood responded with a full-page advertisement in the *Hollywood
Reporter* titled "Portrait of a Patriot." It began with a completely capitalized statement—"COMRADE DALTON TRUMBO IS THE EDITOR OF THE
SCREEN WRITER"—and proceeded to comment that "Comrade Trumbo
is one screen writer who carries the deepest brand of the hammer and

sickle on BOTH HIS RUMP AND HIS TYPEWRITER." Wood then traced, in red-baiting language, Trumbo's adherence to the twists and turns of the Communist Party line after 1939. Wood ended his diatribe by labeling Trumbo's call for a second front in 1942 a blow for the Communist motherland and basically accused Trumbo of cowardice: "BUT COMRADE TRUMBO DIDN'T GET A GUN. NO SECOND FRONT BUSINESS FOR HIM. . . . BUT HE HAD TO DO SOMETHING WITH HIS TRIGGER FINGER. HE DID. HE PICKED UP A PEN WITH IT AND SIGNED A CONTRACT FOR $3,000 A WEEK." Herbert Clyde Lewis, a novelist and screenwriter who had accompanied Trumbo on the Pacific trip, wrote a tongue-in-cheek letter to the *Hollywood Reporter*, testifying, "There is no Hammer and Sickle branded on Mr. Trumbo's rump or typewriter."[15]

In the August issue of *Screen Writer*, Trumbo excoriated the vehement anti-Communist publisher of the *Hollywood Reporter*, W. R. Wilkerson, for enthusiastically welcoming Congressman John Rankin's (D-Miss.) call for an investigation of the motion picture industry by the Committee on Un-American Activities. Trumbo charged Wilkerson, one of the loudest anti-Communists in Hollywood, with "endorsing in advance an appraisal of Hollywood by one of the most dangerous fascist-minded men in America." Noting that Wilkerson's position coincided with that of the MPA, Trumbo accused them all of supporting "an 'investigation' which every decent and thinking American knows can only be anti-Hollywood, anti-Semitic and deliberately calculated to promote the fascist movement in this country."[16]

Another controversy sprang up following the publication, in the October issue of *Screen Writer*, of an article by Paul Trivers and an editorial by Trumbo, both of which criticized the radio program "Town Meeting of the Air." That program, sponsored by *Reader's Digest*, had featured a debate over the question: "Should Hollywood make pictures designed to influence public opinion?" Two members of the MPA had been chosen to argue the negative side, and the moderator had called on two other MPA members to ask questions from the audience. Trumbo wrote: "It is extremely interesting that the *Reader's Digest*, which published America's leading Fascist, the execrable Lawrence Dennis, should have sought out the MPA to express its point of view on contemporary films. For the *Digest*'s point of view is apparent from its long sequence of viciously reactionary articles. Similarly, the MPA's point of view becomes increasingly clear. Executive board members of the MPA have addressed meetings of organizations which have a proven record of isolationist, anti-labor and anti-Semitic activities." It is no wonder,

Trumbo concluded, that the MPA has received "enthusiastic support from the dark underworld of American reaction."[17]

One of the MPA members chosen to ask a question at the debate, Fred Niblo Jr., wrote a letter to *Screen Writer* denying Trivers's account of what had occurred and accusing Trumbo of conflating all anti-Communists and unfairly associating their reasonable anti-Marxist remarks with those of "embarrassing allies." Niblo categorically, and correctly, denied that an anti-Communist stance necessarily entailed an antilabor, anti-Semitic, anti-Negro, antidemocratic stance. He concluded by paraphrasing Sam Wood: "I believe that Mr. Trumbo and friends are talking through their hats—or through whatever part of their anatomy the hammer and sickle is branded upon."[18]

As a reflection of the widening ideological divide in the SWG, Ring Lardner Jr. (a Communist) came under attack for his negative article on the politics of director Cecil B. De Mille, who had created the Foundation for Political Freedom to oppose organized labor.[19] Trumbo wrote an editorial in defense of Lardner's article, noting that it was pertinent to guild members because "De Mille's political objectives would render American labor powerless to defend itself and such a threat directly concerns the Screen Writers Guild."[20] The gap widened further when Trumbo came to the defense of Alvah Bessie (also a party member). Bessie, who had fought on the side of the Spanish Loyalists, criticized *For Whom the Bell Tolls* (Paramount, 1943), a movie about the Spanish Civil War. In Bessie's estimation, the movie, directed by Sam Wood, was an excellent example "of a phenomena of silence, distortion, lying and betrayal" in the movie industry, which continues to produce films reflecting a dream world "that has no validity in terms of the lives most people live." Just as the makers of *For Whom the Bell Tolls* failed to honestly depict the real issues of the Spanish Civil War, postwar filmmakers refused to address important subjects such as the labor movement.[21] In effect, Bessie claimed that he and writers like him were blocked from expressing their ideas in current movies.

In a letter to *Screen Writer* titled "Who Censors What?" conservative screenwriter Richard Macaulay challenged Bessie's plaint that he was prevented from getting his ideas onscreen. Rather, Macaulay alleged, it was writers of Macaulay's persuasion who could not get their ideas in movies or in print. This was so, Macaulay charged, because "Mr. Bessie and his friends" will, "at the drop of an incautious or inaccurately reported quotation," launch "an organized, well-publicized stink." Macaulay cited as an example an article he had written about

American soldiers' negative attitudes toward Italians. It had been rejected by every magazine he sent it to because, in his words, the editors were "afraid of that segment of the 'Italian-American' population which, correctly enough, still placed the 'Italian' first in the hyphenation of their citizenship." In addition, they feared the wrath of Bessie and his friends, who also blocked all scripts about corrupt labor leaders; the uprising of the Polish Home Army, which had been crushed by the Germans while the Red Army watched; the villainy of Thomas Jefferson; or "Confessions of a Soviet Spy" (Macaulay was snidely referring to *Confessions of a Nazi Spy* [Warner Bros., 1939], which had been written by John Wexley, a Communist). Macaulay found it "amusing for Mr. Bessie to complain of something he can't write about, and here's why: There are so many things I wouldn't be able to write about because of Mr. Bessie."[22]

The Editorial Board of *Screen Writer* chose not to print Macaulay's letter, and Trumbo wrote a letter to Macaulay explaining why. The reason was not that Macaulay had attacked Bessie, he said. Rather, the editors had rejected it because of their belief that Macaulay had slandered 4 million Americans of Italian descent, attacked organized labor, taken the government to task on issues that had nothing to do with screenwriters, and made statements that could be construed as an attack on various religious faiths, especially the Roman Catholics. It seems clear that Trumbo misrepresented the truth. There is no question that Macaulay's controversially worded letter was rejected precisely because of his remarks about Bessie and his friends, and it was not surprising that Macaulay's politics played a large part in this so-called objective editorial decision. What was surprising, and inexplicable, was Trumbo's concluding remark: "It is difficult to support your belief in the 'inalienable right of man's mind to be exposed to any thought whatsoever, however intolerable that thought might be to anyone else.' Frequently such a right encroaches upon the right of others to their lives. It was this 'inalienable right' in Fascist countries which directly resulted in the slaughter of five million Jews."[23]

What provoked these words? The last sentence, with its strangely qualified description of free speech, is antithetical to Trumbo's most basic belief. I honestly do not believe that Trumbo was a hypocrite or that he was merely parroting a party directive. Perhaps it was a momentary lapse in judgment provoked by his anger at Macaulay's barely disguised red-baiting and blatantly false accusation. Like his 1944 letter to the FBI, the letter to Macaulay is anomalous. The two letters by themselves do not, by any objective measure, undermine Trumbo's stature as a defender of free speech.

Whatever caused Trumbo to respond to Macaulay as he did, he reverted to a more recognizable form a few months later when he answered a letter from SWG vice president Howard Estabrook to the Executive and Editorial Boards. Estabrook accused the editors of *Screen Writer* of making guild policy. In his reply, Trumbo argued that the *Screen Writer*'s columns should be open to the membership to discuss guild matters, even when such discussions are controversial. Trumbo posed a series of questions to Estabrook: "Just how far do you propose to stifle discussion of the Guild in the Guild's own paper? . . . Do you propose that the Executive Board govern by fiat, without the benefit of discussion within the membership, and then rigidly impose its fiat on the membership by propaganda articles carefully censored word by word to squeeze independent thought from them?" If the answer to the second question was yes, it would, Trumbo stated, introduce "perhaps a kind of Pecksniffian censorship" and restrict the members' freedom of expression. He vehemently denied that the editors followed a politically biased selection policy, but he acknowledged that "to some people, even to some Guild members, every action of the Guild to improve the conditions of writers has radical political implications."[24]

The following May the Executive Board, responding to growing criticism among centrist and rightist guild members that the magazine was becoming too controversial, restructured the Editorial Board. Three new members were appointed to the board: two were not associated with the Left at all, and one, Isobel Lennart, had left the Communist Party one year earlier. From that point forward, the only "subversive" article that appeared in *Screen Writer* was the transcript of a seminar on the Soviet film industry, featuring Russian writer Konstantin Simonov. That event had been sponsored by the Hollywood Writers' Mobilization and the Screen Writers Guild and chaired by Trumbo.[25]

Furthermore, all of Trumbo's subsequent editorials focused exclusively on SWG issues. Yet Hollywood had become so politically divided that one of those issues, a plan to establish an American Authors Authority (AAA), was labeled a "Communist plot" by opponents. The AAA was the brainchild of conservative writer James Cain, who modeled it on the music industry organizations ASCAP and BMI. It would have allowed screenwriters to own the rights to all their scripts and to receive royalties for every performance of movies made or remade from those scripts. Trumbo defended the AAA as "capitalism naked and simple"—but capitalism for writers, not for entrepreneurs. "If this be Communism," Trumbo sardonically remarked, "Guild members have a right to feel that Mr. Marx has been misquoted to them." He accused opponents of the AAA of distorting its origins and purpose in order to break the SWG, and he warned the members that they "must be prepared to fight hard and all the time, to sacrifice, to endure vilification and abuse."[26]

His words were prescient, because Hollywood anti-Communists launched a savage red-baiting campaign against the AAA, and Trumbo was one of their main targets. Gossip columnist Hedda Hopper, a charter member of the MPA, wrote in her usual wildly inaccurate manner: "The new writers' deal, seemingly thought up by James M. Cain, sounds as though it had been conceived on Joe Stalin's own desk. It's known as the Association of American Authors [sic] and would give one man the totalitarian power of controlling copyrights on all literary material. . . . Some of the names connected with this boldest of movements to throttle free speech in this country may surprise you but not us." Unsurprisingly, Trumbo's name was at the top of her list.[27]

Shortly thereafter, W. R. Wilkerson wrote three editorials in his *Hollywood Reporter*, red-baiting the SWG. His one-column editorials usually appeared on the left side of the first page, but these three took up two columns and were placed in the center. They were titled, respectively: "Red Beach Head!" "Hollywood's Red Commissars!" and "More Red Commissars!" In the first editorial, Wilkerson asserted that "90 percent of the Hollywood Communists look to the Screen Writers Guild as their most effective organ of propaganda." In the next two, he detailed the "Red" activities of past and present guild executives. In the third editorial, Wilkerson posed a series of questions to Trumbo: "Are you a Communist? Is your Party name (or alias) Hal Conger? Are you a member of Group 3, Branch A of the American Communist Party? Are you the holder of Communist Party Book No. 36802?" He then proceeded to list some of Trumbo's "Communistic" activities, including his novel *The Remarkable Andrew*; his membership in the American Peace Mobilization, the National Federation for Constitutional Liberties, and American Youth for Democracy; and his support for LaRue McCormick's campaign for the US Senate.[28]

Trumbo drafted a reply to Wilkerson's editorials, which presaged his response to the Committee on Un-American Activities, but he never sent it:

My last three films . . . have been highly recommended by your
journal. By soliciting and publishing advertisements calling
attention to their merits you have assisted in the dissemination of the ideas which they express. If these films contained
any elements of communist propaganda, I cannot believe that
you lack either the intelligence to detect them or the courage
to denounce them. Your failure to do so indicates that your
professed alarm about communist propaganda on the screen
is insincere and without basis in truth. Your real concern is
the growing strength of the Screen Writers Guild as it moves
toward its legitimate objectives, not one of which is political
nor ever has been. . . . We live in a country founded upon the
principle that a man's race, his religion and his politics are
his private concern, protected as such by law. Any answer to
your "questions," either positive or negative, would constitute
an admission on my part of your right to assume the function
of industry inquisitor. I deny that right, and have no intention
of collaborating with you to establish it. Your piece on me is,
in the main, a melange of inaccuracies, distortions and inven-
tions. Coming from one who has testified in open court that he
does not necessarily believe the editorials to which he affixes
his name, this should surprise no one.[29]

In October 1946, with an election for SWG officers pending, the
membership was openly divided. In past elections, individuals had nominated themselves for offices on a nonpartisan basis, but for the first
time in the SWG's history, an electoral slate was presented to the members, and its sponsors called a meeting to discuss why this slate had
been assembled. Hugo Butler presented a petition, signed by 200 members (liberals and Communists), objecting to this so-called balanced
slate because it deliberately excluded "certain candidates whose record
of service to the Guild would seem to entitle them to the most careful
consideration for Guild office." In particular, the slate "pointedly omits
every one of the nominees specifically mentioned by W. R. Wilkerson
and his *Hollywood Reporter*, with the single exception of Emmet Lavery," making it appear to be "a deliberate attempt to appease the Guild's
most notorious enemy." Everett Freeman defended the "balanced" slate,
saying that its supporters simply wanted to elect an Executive Board
that would be "more representative of the entire membership."[30] In the
ensuing election, Lavery was elected president, but several Communists

were also elected: Harold Buchman as treasurer and Lester Cole, Ring Lardner Jr., and Leo Townsend as board members. Shortly after the election, executive secretary William Pomerance (a Communist) was forced to resign.

It is likely that a highly publicized attack on free speech by party members affected non-Communists in the guild. In February 1946 the Communists in Hollywood were shaken by the party's response to an article that had appeared in *New Masses* (and was then serialized in *Daily People's World*).[31] Authored by Albert Maltz, the article criticized the Communist Party's dictate that art must be wielded as a weapon in the class struggle. But while Maltz was composing his article, which he saw as a contribution to the debate about the role of Communist writers, William Z. Foster (Browder's successor) was telling a meeting of the party's National Committee: "We must transform the Party into a Party of struggle. . . . [O]ne of the worst manifestations of Browder's revisionism was to kill the fighting spirit of our Party and to tend to turn it merely into a propaganda or agitational organization."[32] A few months later, Foster asserted that the party could be rebuilt only via "mass struggle."[33] As a result, according to Joseph R. Starobin, many party members became gripped with the "desire to reestablish that purity of commitment, that militancy, and that clarity which they believed had been eroded by their wartime errors and by the corruptions and enticements which the wartime policies had imposed."[34]

In the guise of this new purity, the Communist Party's cultural critics launched a series of ferocious written attacks on Maltz in the *Daily Worker* and *Daily People's World*, followed by an onslaught of vocal assaults at a series of meetings of Communist writers in New York and Hollywood.[35] Trumbo revealed to Jean Butler that he had been asked to write an article criticizing Maltz for *New Masses* but had refused to do so.[36] He also chose not to attend a meeting of Communist writers held at Abraham Polonsky's house to denounce Maltz. Leopold Atlas, who did attend, later told the Committee on Un-American Activities that the whole Maltz affair was "a nightmarish and shameful experience. . . . [T]he wolves were loose and you should have seen them. It was a spectacle for all time."[37]

Trumbo did, however, discuss his reaction to Maltz's article in "A Note to Myself at the Time," which he did not submit for publication. He was critical of Maltz's position, but, as it turned out, he misstated it. Maltz had addressed his remarks to writers of fiction, urging them to follow their artistic impulses rather than the current party line, but he did not advocate their withdrawal from political activity. In Trumbo's mind, however, Maltz had portrayed himself as an "'artist'—as a rare and complex creature whose problems are quite remote from those of ordinary people." Under the mistaken impression that Maltz was advocating art for the sake of art, Trumbo cited several foreign Communist writers as examples of those who had no difficulty using art as a weapon or mixing the artistic and the political. Trumbo then erected a straw man, which he proceeded to demolish. He had become impatient with

> the weeping and gnashing of teeth, the mourning and the lamentations, the frantic evasions and the eager search for a whipping boy—all of these have gone on overlong for my taste. If we [left-wing writers] have not lived up to our potentialities, well and good; let us try to do better in the future. But let us not insist that the measure of our own failure offers final proof that those who follow must also fail. Let us not make out of our own difficulties a cult for the future which must not even attempt to carry the ball we have fumbled.

Still misconstruing what Maltz had written, and probably voicing his own proclivities, Trumbo countered that writers should stay involved in political activity because "politics is life—politics is the real world, and the core of this real world is struggle." A writer who withdraws from that struggle withdraws from life and, in so doing, "draws more and more upon himself, rather than upon the day-to-day experience gained in political struggle. And inevitably—because of his enforced remoteness from life—he moves from the position that writers as persons must be excused from the struggle to the position that writers as writers must likewise be excused."

But Trumbo did concur with Maltz's main point: that a Communist writer must not "be compelled to write in a certain fashion, or to devote too much of his time to political work." Trumbo was certain that, to be effective, one must be "impelled toward his political life rather than compelled." That was why he had joined the party: to make himself more effective politically. Finally, Trumbo acknowledged that Maltz's article had done some good. Among other things, it highlighted the failure of left-wing writers to develop a new intellectual discipline; as a result, it demonstrated that some left-wing writers had begun to consider themselves "demobilized as citizen-participants" because they were "artists," leaving them unprepared "to cope with the most dangerous period in the history of America."[38]

It is not clear from these notes what Trumbo's intent was. He apparently wanted to articulate a middle position between "art as a Party weapon" and political art; at the same time, he wanted to locate his own personal position between the too-moderate Browder and the too-extreme Foster. But his argument lacked solid ground. He provided no procedural guidelines for a politicized writer (or for himself) in the increasingly frigid Cold War atmosphere.

Meanwhile, on March 26 *Daily People's World* and the Hollywood Forum announced that they would cosponsor a program titled "Art—Weapon of the People" on April 8, at the Embassy Auditorium in Los Angeles. Three days before the event, Maltz publicly repented,[39] and the April 8 program became a celebration of art as a weapon in the class struggle. Trumbo was one of the invited speakers, and he directed his remarks not to Maltz's words but to the screenwriter's role in the current political atmosphere. He told the 1,500 attendees that they must fight for freedom of the screen, but they must do so collectively, through their political and labor organizations. In essence, he was saying that a writer cannot be an effective political actor simply by writing as an individual. During the 1930s, for example, screen content had improved (and reactionary themes had declined) concurrently with "the great upsurge of the CIO and the general organizational advance of workers all over the country." In effect, whether he was conscious of it or not, Trumbo was defending Maltz's argument that the primary duty of the individual writer is, above all, to "defend his individual stories and their development."[40] At the end of April, Foster hailed the Maltz "debate" as a "healthy sign of the correction of our revisionism in the cultural field." Maltz's "right deviation," his assertion that art is free, had been "happily corrected by Maltz himself."[41] Maltz, of course, was far from happy with the outcome.

A few weeks later, Trumbo wrote a personal letter to Sam Sillen, editor of *Masses and Mainstream*. In it, he posed the same sort of question Maltz had asked in his recanted article: "How does he [the writer] use his art as a weapon in the destruction of fascism, of racial bigotry, of economic oppression, of the drive toward war?" It is both interesting and ironic to note that Trumbo also provided a Maltz-like answer: "First, of course, there comes the primary battle of the individual writer to defend his individual stories and their development into a finished screenplay. This is fundamental."[42]

Sillen must have recommended that Trumbo publish the letter, because in early May a rewritten version of it appeared in the *Daily Worker*. In what was perhaps the most Marxist-oriented of his writings, Trumbo reiterated some of the themes expressed in his private response to Maltz's article, but he retreated from some of the conclusions reached in his magazine articles from more than a decade ago. That is, he now defended the movie industry against charges it was corrupt and beyond redemption and argued that it was more important to analyze how it functioned rather than to denounce it:

> We have produced a few fine films in Hollywood, a great many which are vulgar and opportunistic, and a few which are down-right vicious. If you tell me that Hollywood—in contrast to the novel and the theatre—has produced nothing so provocative or so progressive as "Freedom Road" or "Deep Are the Roots," I will grant you the point. But I must also add that neither had Hollywood produced anything so untrue and reactionary as [Arthur Koestler's] "Yogi and the Commissar," [Jan Valtin's] "Out of the Night," [William Lindsay White's] "Report on the Russians," [Robert E. Sherwood's] "There Shall Be No Night," nor [John Dos Passos's] "Adventures of a Young Man." Nor does Hollywood's forthcoming schedule include such tempting items as James T. Farrell's "Bernard Clare," Victor Kravchenko's "I Chose Freedom," or the so-called biography of Stalin by Leon Trotsky.[43]

One cannot understand the film industry, Trumbo continued, unless one understands that it "represents monopoly capital in control of an art form. Five major producing companies control practically all the stage spaces in Hollywood." Because motion pictures are extremely expensive to make, and because producers want to make a profit on their huge investments, a film artist's freedom to express himself or herself is disproportional to the amount of capital investment required to produce that particular movie. Trumbo did not believe that the growing number of independent production units would "materially influence the social content of motion pictures"; in his estimation, they "mainly represent the drive of highly paid creative talent to participate in the profits of production; in other words, to become producers, capitalists, themselves." So, a "creative artist," whether employed by a major studio or by an independent production company, would remain, in effect, an industrial worker. Therefore, if such an artist wants to have an impact on film content, he or she must be organized. Better screen content will come only from "organized writers, striving individually and organizationally and politically in the closest possible relationship with the great masses of workers who represent the only direct, democratic, antifascist force in the world today."[44]

Alongside his work for the SWG, Trumbo, in his position as a member of the Executive Board of the Hollywood Independent Citizens Committee of the Arts, Sciences, and Professions (HICCASP), worked hard on behalf of progressive candidates and for a progressive agenda in the 1946 election. That year, the organization enrolled more than 1,300 members, collected $101,000, and spent $97,000.[45] In May one of the organizers of HICCASP, George Pepper, asked Trumbo to write two slightly different speeches for actress Olivia de Havilland, who was vice chairperson of the group. During the war, she had been a prominent supporter of the US-USSR alliance and a spokesperson for the Hollywood Democratic Committee. The first speech, which de Havilland was going to deliver at a dinner in Seattle, was specifically intended to urge people in the Northwest to rededicate themselves to "the principles of Franklin D. Roosevelt and Wendell L. Willkie." (Willkie, the Republican presidential nominee in 1940, was a powerful advocate of a decolonized, nonimperialist world.) The second speech, devised for a mass meeting, was supposed to encourage the audience to send a progressive message to Washington, DC. In the second speech, the focus was on the need to shore up the New Deal–World War II "domestic coalition of labor, liberals and progressive businessmen," which was being hammered at by "men of narrow interests and selfish aims" who favored "racial bigotry, union-busting and isolationism." These people, who represented "the darkest forces of reaction and confusion," refused to "extend democracy to our 13-million Negro citizens," were fomenting a war against the Soviet Union, and were voting for legislation to shackle American labor. That is, they were replicating the "same pattern of reaction which achieved its terrible finality in the Third Reich of Adolf Hitler." In conclusion, Trumbo wrote that democracy in this country could be preserved only by vigilantly protecting the rights of labor, establishing full democratic rights for the Negro people, and restoring the alliance among the three great powers that had, a few years earlier, "banded together for the destruction of fascism everywhere." Neither speech contained any mention of the Communist Party.[46]

However, after attending a June 2 HICCASP board meeting, de Havilland changed her mind about the organization. On that occasion, James Roosevelt stated that the organization must be "vigilant against being used by Communist sympathizers," for which he was sharply criticized by a few board members. After the meeting ended, ten of those sympathetic to Roosevelt's proposal, including de Havilland, met at her apartment, where Ronald Reagan proposed that they test the Executive Board's "redness" by introducing a resolution repudiating "Communism as desirable for the United States." De Havilland put forward this resolution at the next board meeting, held at Roosevelt's house in July. Trumbo was present, and he was one of the resolution's sharpest critics. When it was defeated, de Havilland and others resigned from HICCASP.[47]

De Havilland then contacted Trumbo about the speeches he had written for her. She informed him that she had decided "to frame the speeches in a different way," to allow herself to "speak as an individual" rather than as a member of HICCASP and to express her own point of view "regarding the problems of policy which face liberal organizations today." She had asked a screenwriter friend of hers to come to her "rescue" and compose a speech that would more accurately express her feelings about the political situation in the United States.[48] Her friend, Ernest Pascal, radically rewrote both speeches. In his revised versions, the sections on fascism were deleted and replaced by a strong condemnation of communism. Pascal also repudiated the idea of further alliances between liberals and Communists, implying that the latter were un-American. Communists, he wrote, "frequently join liberal organizations. That is their right. But it is also our right to see that they don't control us . . . or guide us . . . or represent us, for what we believe in is as thoroughly American as the farseeing programs of our pioneering forefathers."[49]

After seeing Pascal's changes, Trumbo wrote a strong letter of rebuke, saying: "You have devoted one-fifth of the speech to a denunciation of Communism, and have completely refrained from mentioning fascism. You have even deleted my own three unfriendly references to it. I think I understand your motives, Ernest, and to understand is, in some degree, to forgive. But don't you occasionally wonder, alone and late at night, who butchered the women of Europe and buried their living children and burned their men?"[50] To the HICCASP board, Trumbo wrote: "Since the last three meetings of the executive board and the council have been devoted to a discussion of the menace of Communism in America, I now feel that it is in order to propose that the next meeting of the board or council shall be devoted to a discussion of the menace of fascism in America."[51] This ideological schism widened rapidly; many other liberals left HICCASP, and two of the congressional candidates it supported began to move rightward.

Trumbo expressed his disgust with the new tenor of the campaigns being run by Will Rogers Jr. (for US Senate) and James Roosevelt (for US House of Representatives). They were, Trumbo wrote, behaving "with a resolute stupidity which offers few parallels in modern political history," and in a way that can only "delight" their opponents. There was, he continued, "a mindlessness about the[ir] campaign[s] which is almost terrifying." They were trying to woo the Right "by attacking the Left," and in the case of Rogers, he had utterly failed to distinguish himself from his opponent, William F. Knowland. Rogers's attempt to "out-conservative" Knowland would likely alienate "the great mass of liberally inclined voters," and it would distract him from the real issues, particularly the state and congressional un-American committees. Trumbo did not care if Rogers and Roosevelt defended the Communists, but he insisted that "they must attack the committees." Trumbo wanted Rogers to attack Knowland, place the blame for inflation squarely on him, advocate strong support for the Fair Employment Practice Committee, stop supporting Secretary of State James Byrnes's foreign policy, and cease red-baiting. (Trumbo also wanted Rogers to support Henry A. Wallace's message about détente with the Soviet Union, but he recognized that Rogers had moved too far right for that to happen.) Finally, Trumbo suggested that Rogers might take a "positive, progressive and decent" stand on the strike being planned by the Conference of Studio Unions by denouncing the producers as "monopolists" who had instigated the strike. If Rogers attacked their "unpatriotic undercutting of the American standard of living by transferring production to Europe to take advantage of lower labor costs there," he would, Trumbo believed, strike a blow against the producers' plan to "crush Hollywood labor by forcing it under the jurisdiction of the IA[TSE]" and to "ruin financially the independent producing organizations" that had sprung up in the last three years and represented an "enduring thorn" in the sides of the major studios.[52]

One other speech that Trumbo wrote for an actor at the request of HICCASP had two interesting elements, in terms of both the individual and the content of the speech. The actor, Edward G. Robinson, was a liberal who had been very active in the Hollywood Anti-Nazi

League, the Hollywood Democratic Committee, and the Committee to
Defend America by Aiding the Allies. During the war he gave a number of speeches, some in support of the Soviet Union and all of them
written by screenwriters he had employed or who had been assigned to
him for the occasion. At some point in 1946, Trumbo began to write
speeches for Robinson, one of which was for a pro-Israel rally at the
Hollywood Legion Stadium on September 18, 1946. On the copy of
the speech in Trumbo's papers, he wrote: "Eddie asked me to write
this speech for him—I did—he got an ovation and bowed to me from
the platform—then testified against me before the Committee on the
same day I entered jail!" (Actually, Robinson testified three times, and
only at the third hearing, by which time Trumbo was already in prison,
did he name Trumbo as a Communist.) The speech itself was brilliant.
Trumbo wrote it as if he were Jewish, but he used it to articulate all his
beliefs about racism, prejudice, tolerance, and liberation. In it, he called
Palestine "the testing ground of modern democratic faith," as well as
"the testing ground for a free America." That was so, Trumbo wrote,
because "the anti-Semite which curses Europe and strangles Palestine
will not be wholly destroyed until we here, in these free United States
of America, functioning under the protection of the Bill of Rights, in a
tradition of religious freedom and racial equality, destroy forever those
racial myths which flourish among *our* own people." The destruction
of any one form of prejudice "is quite impossible without the destruction of others which are related to it and, indeed, are a part of it." The
fight for a free Palestine would be futile—beyond that, hypocritical—
if its supporters failed to realize that it was only a portion of a larger
fight. Therefore, those who demanded freedom for Palestine "must also
demand the freedom of the Arab peoples from their feudal tyrants, the
freedom of Europe from the vestiges of fascist domination, the freedom of Indonesia and India and China from imperial overlords, the
freedom of American labor from any threat to its legitimate rights and
demands, the freedom of the Negro along with [the] Mexican, the Japanese, the Filipino, the Jew, the Protestant, the Catholic to live where he
wishes, to vote as he pleases, to educate his children and to safeguard
their future under a government which counts us all as equals before
the law." Trumbo concluded by stating that the prejudices against Jews,
Negroes, and workers "are closely related . . . part of the same pattern
of fascism which achieved its terrible perfection in the Third Reich of
Adolph Hitler," which we "must hate" and forever fight against. "Our
fight must be as broad as the earth. It must include all peoples of all

faiths and all races." A free Palestine must represent "both the symbol and the victory of a free world."[53] (Thirteen years later, in the concluding scene he wrote for *Exodus*, Trumbo reiterated some of those words. See chapter 19.)

The 1946 election was a disaster for the Left. The Republicans won control of both houses of Congress, and the new chairman of the House Un-American Activities Committee promised an investigation of Communist infiltration of the motion picture industry. After the election, Trumbo made plans to sell his house in Beverly Hills and move permanently to the ranch. He wanted to write his novel, and he hoped to loosen his ties to the Communist Party. He had begun "to receive ominous word from Washington about the intentions of HUAC from my friend, Ray Murphy, which indicated to me the possibility of some sort of future blacklist."[54]

The Trumbo family loved the Lazy-T. Christopher later said about it: "The ranch was a place of splendid isolation. Not until 1949 will another house be built in our part of the valley, and for the first time we can see a light in the night sky that is not our own. To the original structure my parents added another seven rooms, an electric generator, a third barn, a smoke house, two gasoline pumps and a vast butane tank—but no outside telephone line. The nearest telephone was twelve miles away."

Nikola remembered how carefree the days at the ranch were. She and Christopher especially looked forward to April Fool's Day and the tricks they would play on Trumbo. (They never played tricks on Cleo.) Nikola recalled one trick in particular: They dipped balls of cotton in melted chocolate and offered a tray of the "candies" to Trumbo. "'Would you like a piece of chocolate,' we offered, tendering our platter invitingly up at him. Trumbo smiled upon us benignly, perhaps a little too benignly, and then with exaggerated pleasure took a piece of candy and put it in his mouth. Then he reached for another, and another. And he swallowed them. We were astounded. Never had we imagined that he would actually eat the candy."

Christmases at the ranch were always something special. According to Nikola, "Trumbo loved that holiday and enjoyed making a great show of the season. He made it seem bigger than life." He made a production of everything: decorating the Christmas tree, concocting the eggnog, and roasting a pig or a goose. Trumbo spent hours in the kitchen preparing the eggnog. "He then poured it into a large silver punch bowl, which he took outside and nestled in a snow bank along with matching

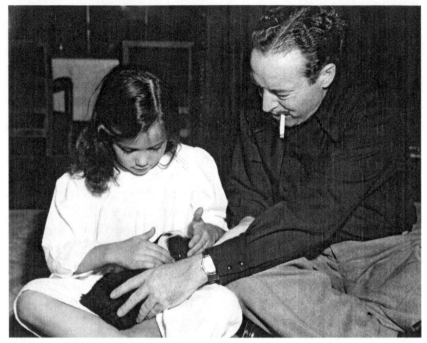

Trumbo and Nikola, 1945. Photograph by Harry Baskerville.

silver cups. When the eggnog was sufficiently chilled, Trumbo brought it in and grated nutmeg on it." One Christmas, Nikola recalled:

> Trumbo decided we would have suckling pig for dinner. He spent the entire day working on this meal, and the kitchen was filled with the smells of roasting meat. When it was finally done, it was delivered to the table by a proud Trumbo on a silver platter, ringed with pineapple and with an apple in its mouth. As it turned out, the hide was almost too tough to cut into and the meat not very good. Trumbo was applauded for the attempt and there was plenty of other food to complete the meal. Another Christmas, he decided we would eat goose. Again Trumbo served it with great show.

Michael Butler, who visited the ranch regularly as a young boy, remembered: "I felt as if one were entering a different world. I loved it, more than loved it. I craved the experience of being there." He and Christopher "built 'forts' high up in fir trees or concealed behind *bomas*

Christmas at the ranch, 1942. Courtesy of Trumbo family.

[enclosures] of mesquite and manzanita. One needed forts and look-outs in the wild; it gave one an edge against one's enemies: leopards, headhunters with blowguns and curare-tipped darts, the odd Hereford steer; imagined bad guys." Cleo, "the soul of aplomb," made sure that Michael and his two sisters (Susan and Mary) and her three children were kept busy. There were, Michael remembered, "a lot of quail and when Trumbo was absent Cleo would supervise our plinking at the quail from the flagstone patio. The rule was that if we hit one, we'd have to dress it, cook, and eat it. This deterred us from ever killing one. When Trumbo was at home—asleep, of course, during the day—we moved our shooting to an inside range in what had formerly been a chicken house." The same rule of silence applied when the children played canasta or Monopoly: "Trumbo was not to be awakened by our howls of victory or defeat."[55]

Because the ranch was a two-hour drive from Los Angeles, Trumbo's political activity lessened. In March 1947, at the Sixth Counter-Attack Forum sponsored by the Hollywood Writers' Mobilization, Trumbo spoke about the creative writer's responsibility regarding the treatment of minorities in films. In particular, he railed against the effect of racial untruths or caricatures on society. For example, the racial jokes in *Abie's Irish Rose* (United Artists, 1946) "are not funny anymore," he said. "There is too much blood on them." And "the promulgation of racial lies," such as those in *Duel in the Sun* (Selznick, 1946), is not "funny anymore" either. Those lies have "murdered too many people in the last ten years; and in our own South is still murdering too many." He chose, as his final example, the Disney-made film *Song of the South* (1946), which, he said, shows "Negroes in a false and libelous light." He did not accuse the filmmakers of racial prejudice, but he did charge them with ignorance—the form of ignorance that lends "validity to the Fascist myth of racial superiority." It is, he concluded, "our absolute obligation" to make certain that no films contain "even the hint of fascist ideology." (In a handwritten marginal note, Trumbo wrote: "We must still remain anti-Fascist.")[56]

Despite this lessening of Trumbo's political activity, FBI agents continued to pay close attention to him. The FBI director had ordered the special agent in charge of the Los Angeles office "to obtain admissible evidence tending to prove: 1. Subject's Party membership or affiliation; 2. Subject's knowledge of the Party's revolutionary aims and purposes." The agent's report, submitted in mid-September 1947, included several affiliations not previously listed and strongly indicated that the Bureau was looking for evidence to indict Trumbo under the Alien Registration Act.[57] Trumbo had also come to the attention of the California Senate Fact-Finding Committee on Un-American Activities. He was mentioned, as a supporter, sponsor, or member of Communist-front organizations, five times in the committee's 1947 report.[58]

To use a weather metaphor, the dark clouds of political suppression and censorship were rapidly scudding toward the isolated ranch and its inhabitants.

9

The 1947 Hearings of the Committee on Un-American Activities

We called it "the committee." We never capitalized it. We never called it HUAC or by any other initials. Other such committees, like the California one, we called by name—the Tenney Committee. "The committee" was reserved for the Feds.
                                                —Christopher Trumbo

One of the great mysteries that confronts anyone who studies the history of the early domestic cold war is how the small- and narrow-minded members of the House Committee on Un-American Activities (1947–1951) succeeded in imposing their rigid and humiliating version of Americanism (nationalism cum patriotism) on the political culture of the United States.[1] These men, not Senator Joseph McCarthy (R-Wis.), set the stage for official Cold War anticommunism. They did so by craftily melding together the power of a long-standing bogey (the Communist menace) and the virtually unchallengeable power of a congressional investigation (complete with subpoenas, the chairman's gavel, and contempt citations). An even greater mystery is why a larger group with arguably loftier intellects and ideals (federal judges) gave their imprimatur to these show trials. Without the contempt convictions, the committee might have been a nuisance but not a name-, status-, and job-destroying juggernaut.

On three previous occasions, 1938, 1940, and 1945, the chairman of the Special Committee on Un-American Activities had threatened to investigate Communists in Hollywood. Each time, nothing had transpired. But after the Republican sweep of the 1946 congressional elections, J. Parnell Thomas (R-N.J.), the new chairman of the now-permanent committee, launched an investigation into what he called

185

the "Moscow-directed fifth column" in the United States.[2] At the first hearing, held in March 1947, Eric Johnston, president of the producers' associations, told the committee that Communists had completely failed to capture the movie industry and their propaganda never reached the screen. Several committee members openly scoffed at Johnston's words,[3] and it was soon announced that a three-person subcommittee would be coming to Los Angeles. The subcommittee arrived on May 8 to investigate composer Hanns Eisler (whose brother, Gerhart, was reputed to be the leading Soviet agent in the United States) and, in Thomas's words, "to initiate an extensive and all-inclusive investigation of communistic activities and influences in the motion-picture industry."[4] The subcommittee held several closed-door hearings at the Biltmore Hotel, listening mainly to members of the Motion Picture Alliance, whom Thomas characterized as "friendly witnesses."[5]

The leftists mounted a counterattack in the form of a large rally sponsored by the Progressive Citizens of America. On May 19, at Gilmore Stadium, 28,000 people listened as Katharine Hepburn, "dressed in a sweeping scarlet gown" and speaking words probably written by Dalton Trumbo, accused Thomas of working closely with the Motion Picture Alliance for the Preservation of American Ideals to abridge the freedom of artists. Hepburn issued a dire warning: "The artist, since the beginning of time, has always expressed the aspirations and dreams of the people. Silence the artist and you have silenced the most articulate voice the people have." She was followed to the stage by Henry A. Wallace, who called the committee a "kangaroo court" before which people are "smeared without right of defense."[6]

The following month, the Hollywood Arts, Sciences, and Professions Council of the Progressive Citizens of America (formerly HICCASP) sponsored a five-day conference (July 9–13) on "Thought Control in the United States" at the Beverly Hills Hotel. Five of the nineteen future unfriendly witnesses participated, along with two of their attorneys, eleven future blacklistees, and three future informers.[7] (Trumbo was ill and did not attend.)

Trumbo was clearly beginning to feel the hot breath of the committee. The family was in the process of moving permanently from Beverly Hills to the ranch, and during the transition, Trumbo had rented a small house for them. According to Nikola: "The move was precipitated by warnings that the FBI was investigating us and my parents thought it prudent to move to less expensive quarters while they figured out what to do about a possible subpoena to testify before [the committee]."

While they were living in the rented house, Trumbo contracted diphtheria, and for the two-week duration of the quarantine, he mainly talked on the telephone, "ranting loudly" and "castigating the FBI for tapping his phone line."[8]

On September 17 Trumbo began his offensive against the committee. At a meeting sponsored by the Hollywood Arts, Sciences, and Professions Council, he warned that the Committee on Un-American Activities was perpetrating a "new intellectual terror" designed to instill fear and make people conform. The committee's investigation represented the "poisonous features of Fascism itself—the attack upon culture, the attack upon the worker, the sly and vicious anti-Semitism, the bitter hatred of the Negro—even beyond that, the hatred of people themselves and of all who speak for them."[9]

Four days later, the committee announced that it had issued forty-one subpoenas. The story in *Daily Variety* noted: "Some of the witnesses are friendly to the committee's purposes. Others are undoubtedly hostile."[10] There were nineteen men in the "hostile" or "unfriendly" group.[11] The manner of their selection was unclear then, and it remains so today.[12] Their ages varied; ten were unemployed at the time; three (Howard Koch, Lewis Milestone, and Irving Pichel) had never been Communists; two (Edward Dmytryk and Adrian Scott) claimed they had left the party years earlier; and one (Bertolt Brecht) was an alien. (Brecht had come to the United States in 1941 as a political refugee. He was a Communist and had worked closely with Hanns Eisler, but since he was desperate to return to Europe, he had to find a way to placate the committee and avoid a contempt citation. Also, he was in New York when he received his subpoena. Thus, he never met with the other unfriendly witnesses, but when he testified, two of the Nineteen's attorneys sat beside him at the witness table. Even though Brecht was not really part of the group, to avoid confusion, the unfriendly witnesses are always referred to as the Nineteen.)

Eric Johnston pledged the industry's full cooperation with the committee. If the industry did employ Communists or Communist sympathizers, he said, "We want to see them exposed."[13] One week later, Johnston sent a letter to Thomas, telling him that there were many other persons in Hollywood, aside from those subpoenaed, who possessed information about Communist infiltration of the industry, and he volunteered to supply their names.[14]

Trumbo was living at the ranch when the subpoenas were issued.

Christopher recounts the events of that fateful day when Trumbo's subpoena was delivered:

> The day our lives changed forever was predictably ordinary.
> The day was one of those hot, endless, late September days
> when the heaviness of the air and the deep stillness that settles
> in at 4 o'clock and seems to have no end makes you think time
> is standing still. Miles away the air shimmered where my sister
> and I [Niki was eight years old; Christopher had just turned
> seven] were staring, out where we knew the country road cut
> through the middle of the valley even though we couldn't see it,
> its worn gray surface lost in the sagebrush. In the afternoons,
> Niki and I would find the shade on the terrace, and stare out
> toward Mount Piños, across the steep wash [that] flash floods
> had carved out on the south side of the valley, and from there
> to its sagebrush-studded floor where the country road ran west
> from Frazier Park.
>
>   Niki pointed and I nodded, also seeing it. Miles away the
> flash of sunlight caught the chrome on a car, and then we made
> out the car itself as it crawled forward, disappeared in a dip cut
> across the valley hundreds of years ago by streambeds and flash
> floods, then reappeared, and, as the car inched along at an ago-
> nizing pace, we grew increasingly impatient. Days could pass
> without seeing a car, and we had no idea whether it was com-
> ing to us or if it would continue on, past the county line where
> the road was no longer paved and disappear into the mountains
> where it would eventually connect to Highway 33 in the high
> valley beyond.
>
>   At last we saw the car as it crept around the bend of Rat-
> tlesnake Hill and ran to pull on the heavy wooden gate that
> led the way into the ranch. Soon, a dusty prewar sedan came
> to a stop and a man in shirtsleeves [deputy US marshal David
> E. Hayden] climbed out from behind the wheel. "Hey kids,"
> he said, "your folks around?" We led him around to the door
> which opened into the kitchen, the one everybody used to go
> in and out of the house. Our father met us in the kitchen. "Mr.
> Trumbo?" the man asked. "That's right," our father said.
> "Mr. Dalton Trumbo?" He nodded and the man handed him
> an envelope. Trumbo opened it, removed the folded pink sub-
> poena inside. He nodded again as he read it and looked up.

"Would you like some water before you leave?" he asked the man. "That's kind of you—especially considering. It's a hot one out there." Trumbo filled a glass at the tap and handed it to him. It was water we pumped up from the creek, which wound down from the mountains behind the ranch.

Although Trumbo had told the children he wanted to avoid the subpoena as long as possible, he was not angry with them. Since then, Nikola has "wondered if he wasn't relieved to have the 'chase' finally ended and the next step of the drama engaged." The subpoena commanded Trumbo "to be and appear before the Un-American Activities Committee of the House of Representatives of the United States, of which J. Parnell Thomas of New Jersey is chairman, in their chamber in the city of Washington, on October 23, 1947, at the hour of 10:30 a.m., then and there to testify touching matters of inquiry committed to said Committee, and he is not to depart without leave of said Committee. Herein fail not, and make return of the summons."

Trumbo and Cleo were, Christopher recalled, completely frank with the children: "Our parents told Niki and me that our father was being investigated by a congressional committee. He said: 'It has subpoenaed me because of my political beliefs. We are Communists, and I have to go to Washington to answer questions about my communism.' 'What's that?' we asked. They answered: 'It's a system of government that provides to each person according to his need and that gives according to each person's ability. Capitalism, on the other hand, is based on making profits.' Our father said he might be going to jail. I had no idea what jail was."

Trumbo immediately notified MGM producer Sam Zimbalist, for whom he was writing "House on the River," about the subpoena. But Zimbalist and his superiors continued to treat Trumbo as if nothing had happened, and Trumbo continued to work on the script and attend script conferences at the studio. When he finished "House," he immediately began work on "Angel's Flight."[15] No unfriendly witness currently under contract was fired.

The reactions of the members of the Nineteen varied. Trumbo and Lardner met and began to devise a strategy to use against the committee. Dmytryk and Scott flew to San Francisco to retain Bartley Crum, a progressive Republican, as their attorney. The thirteen who were party members met and agreed to hire Ben Margolis and Charles Katz, who were Communists, as their attorneys. Margolis recommended that they add Robert Kenny (a progressive Democrat) to the legal team. As soon as Dmytryk and Scott returned to Los Angeles, eighteen of the unfriendly witnesses and their attorneys met at Lewis Milestone's house to discuss how they would deal with the committee.[16] Larry Parks told his wife, Betty Garrett: "It was strange that first meeting—19 [sic] men you'd never have been able to get together for a dinner party—I knew only two or three of them." They had "nothing in common but the conviction that this Committee was itself un-American and had to be fought."[17] According to Alvah Bessie, there was little initial agreement, even among the Communists, as to what their strategy should be. Lardner and Trumbo argued that the witnesses should, from the beginning, challenge the committee's right to ask any questions about their political beliefs or affiliations. This would accomplish two things: (1) They would not have to answer follow-up questions about other party members and thus would avoid becoming informers. (2) If they were cited and convicted for contempt of Congress, the guilty verdict might be overturned by an appellate court, thereby fatally weakening the committee's investigative power. Crum, Bessie, and Robert Rossen initially maintained that the witnesses should answer the questions truthfully. But when the other three attorneys told the Nineteen that they would be asked to name other Communists, they unanimously agreed to accept the Trumbo-Lardner approach—that is, to use the machinery of the courts to try to destroy the committee. There is no evidence to support Dmytryk's later claim that Moscow (via Margolis) instructed the party members what to do.[18] A few of them, notably Koch, expressed concern that a belligerent approach might get them fired, and Bessie recalled that two or three of the unfriendly witnesses signed, and deposited with their employers, statements swearing that they were not members of the Communist Party.[19] Margolis did not recall Trumbo or Lardner being too concerned about losing their jobs.[20]

Katz recommended that the witnesses use both the First and Fifth Amendments as the basis for their refusal to answer the committee's questions about their political and trade union affiliations. Though the wording of the Fifth Amendment—"no person . . . shall be compelled in any criminal case to be a witness against himself"—seemed to offer a shield against a contempt citation or a perjury charge, it was unanimously rejected. First, using it would not provide a platform on which to challenge the committee's right to ask such questions.[21] Second, the courts had not clearly defined how protective the Fifth Amendment would be in response to a question from a congressional committee. Finally, they believed that use of the Fifth Amendment suggested that membership in the Communist Party was criminal or incriminating, thus establishing what the committee was trying to prove. "So," Lardner recalled, "we decided to test the First Amendment and see if it meant what it said."[22] The lawyers were convinced that even if the witnesses were convicted of contempt of Congress, the Supreme Court would reverse the conviction. According to Katz, the lawyers believed the committee was being patently censorious and that the justices would rule its inquiry "an obvious instance of a prior government assault on freedom of the screen." They based that belief on two earlier cases (neither of which was fully on point, and one of which had been decided sixty-seven years earlier) and on their confidence that they could convince a slight majority of liberal-inclined justices of the validity of their First Amendment argument.[23]

In later years, two disgruntled members of the Nineteen and one of their lawyers claimed they had been muzzled by the so-called unanimity rule. According to Patricia Bosworth (Bartley Crum's daughter), Larry Parks had "earnestly requested" that all decisions made by the Nineteen be considered "unanimous," regardless of the size of the minority—meaning that the minority had to do whatever the majority advocated.[24] Dmytryk's 1978 memoir alleges that Parks had been asked to do this by "one of the Communist lawyers." Eighteen years later, Dmytryk wrote that Parks had been asked to do so by Dalton Trumbo.[25] Bosworth also puts the onus on Trumbo, based on what her father said: "The CP lawyers had secretly caucused about tactics and were getting their orders on how to proceed from Moscow, and . . . at the meeting at Lewis Milestone's house, Dalton Trumbo had spoken privately with Larry Parks (who worshiped him) and had persuaded the actor to make the request for group unity, and because Parks was so likable and unthreatening, the Nineteen went along with him." Only later did Crum "learn" that the "unanimity rule" was a Communist tactic to stifle dissent.[26] In his first memoir, Dmytryk also adopts the role of the innocent dupe, claiming, "Over the next few years, I learned that the unanimity rule was one of the major weapons in the Communist armory."[27] In his second memoir, Dmytryk blames his "naïveté" for his failure to realize that the two attorneys in charge—Margolis, whom he knew to be a "Red," and Katz, whom he suspected of being one—were being told what to do by "an unacknowledged source," namely, the Communist Party.[28] It is surprising that Dmytryk, who had been a party member, and Crum, who had been in many organizations with Communists, including the

National Lawyers Guild, could be so easily "duped" by a commonly used party tactic.

Bosworth also claims that Parks (again under party direction) instructed the Nineteen how to respond to the committee's questions. Instead of saying, "I refuse to answer, because the question violates my First Amendment rights," they should respond indirectly by criticizing what the committee was doing.[29] Lardner, however, maintained that it was Robert Kenny who persuaded them that the jurors in their contempt cases would be more sympathetic if the witnesses were perceived not as refusing to answer outright but as having been prevented from answering in their own way.[30]

Howard Koch also claimed he had been entrapped by the unanimity rule. In an affidavit he wrote in early 1958, while endeavoring to get off the blacklist, he stated, erroneously, that he had not met with the group until they arrived in Washington. (In fact, he had met with them at Milestone's house and appeared with them at a "Keep America Free" demonstration at the Shrine Auditorium on October 15.) Once in Washington, he stated, he had encountered a very strong "insistence" among the other men that he "act on their moral judgment" instead of his own. They had, he recalled, "decided on a group approach which was to be a refusal to answer the Committee's questions on the basis of the First Amendment. I never knew how this decision was arrived at, had no voice in making it, and, furthermore, disapproved of it." He proposed, instead, that each witness be allowed to declare and defend his own ideas. "This basic difference in our attitudes," Koch continued, "created a stalemate with most of the Nineteen against me. . . . Some of the more militant members of the group who later formed the nucleus of the Hollywood Ten brought considerable pressure on me to accept their policy, stating that my refusal to go along with the majority decision of the Nineteen would break the united front and play into the hands of the Committee."[31]

Crum, Bosworth, Dmytryk, and Koch all neglected one obvious point: eighteen strong-minded, very different men and four strong-minded lawyers were trying to confront a novel situation in a unified manner. As Trumbo later observed, all of them had unwillingly been thrust into political prominence at the dawn of a new, ultrareactionary era in US history. All were, in a sense, "virgins" confronted with "an unprecedented situation." They had anticipated a political battle, but they had not anticipated being tried, convicted, jailed, and blacklisted.[32] For sure, they "did not ask to play the parts assigned them by

Trumbo and Mitzi, October 4, 1947. Photograph by Cleo Trumbo.

the Committee, and, like any other group of even passably intelligent men, would have ducked the game altogether had the chance arisen. They were as confused as anybody else, and probably made more mistakes. They were, after all, down there on a ball field which is error's favorite breeding ground."[33]

In the course of my three-decade study of this subject, I have found no evidence that domestic or worldwide Communist organizations had any involvement with the Nineteen's defense. Indeed, every member of the Nineteen I spoke with expressly confirmed the lack of direct party support. Though it is likely that Lawson and Margolis discussed the matter with party officials, the agreed-upon strategy was very un-party-like, the unanimity rule notwithstanding.

On October 11 the committee sent telegrams to the Nineteen, advising them that their appearance date had been changed to October 27. Two days later, Trumbo sent a collect telegram to the committee, requesting expense money for the trip to Washington, "as specified by laws concerning such proceedings."[34] On October 15 seventeen of the unfriendly witnesses attended a fund-raising rally at the Shrine Auditorium, sponsored by the Progressive Citizens of America. Each of them was introduced, and several of them spoke, as did liberals Burgess Meredith, Marsha Hunt, Evelyn Keyes, and Norman Corwin. The attendees overwhelmingly approved a resolution asking the House of Representatives to abolish the committee.[35] The following day, the Nineteen took out a two-page ad in the trade papers, titled "An Open Letter to the Motion Picture Industry on the Issue of Freedom of the Screen from Political Intimidation and Censorship." They proclaimed: "The issue is not the historically phony one of the subversion of the screen by Communists—but whether the screen will remain free. . . . The goal is control of the industry through intimidation of the executive heads of the industry . . . and through further legislation. The goal is a lifeless and reactionary screen that will be artistically, culturally, and financially bankrupt."[36]

In mid-October the unfriendly witnesses took a train east, with stopovers in Chicago and New York. During the trip, the attorneys put them through mock interrogations. In Washington, they stayed at the Shoreham Hotel, where they gathered together in a large room to write the personal statements each man would make when he was called to the witness stand. "It must have looked pretty funny," Parks told his wife, "all of us crouched in corners, scribbling like mad."[37] According to Crum, Margolis regularly arranged meetings in the evenings, but Crum, Dmytryk, and Scott were not invited to all of them.[38] Dmytryk claimed that those witnesses who were still in the Communist Party held private meetings in Washington to decide "all procedural and positional matters."[39] Koch recalled the sinister atmosphere that enveloped them: "We were in our own capital, yet no foreign city could have been more alien and hostile. All our hotel rooms were bugged. When we . . . wanted to talk with each other or with our attorneys, we either had to keep twirling a metal key to jam the circuit or to go out of doors."[40]

The Nineteen's lawyers sent a telegram to committee chairman Thomas, demanding that he cancel the hearings because the investigation clearly violated the constitutional guarantee of free speech.[41] Thomas, of course, ignored them, and he refused to give them any information about the committee's procedure or the schedule of appearances. On October 19, the night before the hearings opened, the attorneys for the Nineteen were told by a studio attorney that the industry would resist ceding control of screen content and that no witness would "lose his job, forfeit his contract, or be blacklisted because of his position before the House Committee."[42] Thus, armed only with this promise, the First Amendment, and the questionable tactic of pretending to

Trumbo and Cleo watching the October 1947 hearings. Courtesy of
Associated Press and *San Francisco Chronicle*.

answer the committee's questions, the eighteen prepared to meet their
nemesis.

On the first day of the hearings, Thomas called to the stand the
three committee investigators, A. B. Leckie, H. A. Smith, and Louis
Russell; two studio heads, Louis B. Mayer and Jack Warner; and two
members of the Motion Picture Alliance, Sam Wood and Ayn Rand.
Wood used the occasion to exact a measure of revenge on Trumbo for
his critical remarks in *Screen Writer* two years earlier. When Wood was
asked, "Would you care to name any that you know yourself to be Communists?" he replied, "Well, I don't think there's any question about
Dalton Trumbo."[43] Wood was followed by Mayer, the head of MGM.
When asked if there were any Communists at MGM, he replied: "They
[the committee's investigators] have mentioned two or three writers to
me several times. There is no proof about it, except they mark them as
Communists, and when I look at the pictures they have written for us I
can't find once where they have written something like that."[44]

That night, Trumbo delivered a radio speech, sharply indicting the
committee. He accused the members of showing no interest in "truly
subversive conspirators" like the Ku Klux Klan, the Christian Front,

and the Silver Shirts or those who "deprive the American people of decent wages, fair prices, adequate housing, effective union organization, and a peaceful future." Instead of investigating those who undermined decent American traditions and the rights of the American people, this committee was investigating the individuals in Hollywood "who have been most actively concerned with the making of films which reflect decent American traditions and which, in many instances, defend the rights of American people." He accused the committee of being "in open *opposition* to labor," "a leading enemy of the Roosevelt tradition," and "clearly and consistently hostile to the Constitution of the United States." In sum, Trumbo declared, this committee had "degenerated into a conspiracy against the American people and their government." For their part, the Nineteen had "not come to Washington as the abject subjects of a police state. We come as citizens of a democratic republic. . . . We *will not submit* to intimidation. We *will not be* compliant to unconstitutional procedures. We will not surrender even the smallest portion of those immunities guaranteed us by the Bill of Rights. For if we should weakly surrender them today, you will be called upon tomorrow to perform a similar capitulation for yourselves and your children."[45]

The next day, October 21, writer John Charles Moffitt took the stand. Although he did not directly accuse Trumbo of being a Communist, Moffitt characterized him as one who fit the Communist "formula," which was based on what one had done between September 1939 and June 1941. According to Moffitt, after learning of the German-Soviet alliance, Trumbo had opposed war with Germany and then completely reversed his position when German armed forces invaded the Soviet Union. Moffitt also cited Trumbo's *Daily Worker* article of May 5, 1946, which Moffitt wholly misinterpreted. In Moffitt's construal, Trumbo "was pointing out and approving the fact that Communists had established an almost complete embargo in the world of thought, certainly in the world of fiction, against any criticism of communism in Communist Russia."[46]

Two days later, Richard Macaulay was called to the stand. When he was asked to identify those SWG members he thought were Communists, he too seized the opportunity to extract his pound of flesh, naming Trumbo and twenty-seven others. Macaulay also entered into the record his letter to the *Screen Writer* about Bessie's article, which had been rejected.[47] Another guild member, Fred Niblo Jr., called the *Screen Writer* "sort of a literary supplement to the *Daily Worker*" and offered his opinion that Trumbo was a Communist.[48] Lela Rogers made no mention of Trumbo during her short testimony on October 24.

Lardner later recalled that the Nineteen had been in the audience during the testimony of these "friendly" witnesses, and he described the atmosphere in the hearing room as "one-sided" and "frightening."[49] Two US senators, Glen Taylor (D-Idaho) and Claude Pepper (D-Fla.), characterized the hearings as fascistic, and Pepper advised the unfriendly witnesses "to stand up and say 'I am an American, and it's none of your business what I say, what I think or what I write.'"[50] In addition, unsigned editorials in the *New York Herald-Tribune* and the *New York Times* sharply criticized the committee's procedures, as did an ad sponsored by the Motion Picture Association of America.[51] (Congressman Richard Nixon, who had been an active and amiable questioner of several of the friendly witnesses, was not present after October 23. He flew back to California, probably to avoid having to meet with the delegation of the Committee of the First Amendment, due to arrive from Hollywood over the weekend.)

The first unfriendly witness, John Howard Lawson, was questioned on October 27. He was denied permission to read his prepared statement, and every time he tried to state his position, he was interrupted by Thomas's gavel. He grew increasingly angry and ended up in a shouting match with Thomas. Finally, Thomas terminated Lawson's testimony, cited him for contempt of Congress, and ordered him to step away from the stand. Thomas then called one of the committee's investigators to the stand, and he listed thirty-five of Lawson's "Communist" affiliations. Eric Johnston, who testified next, expressed alarm at the harm being done to the movie industry by the committee's investigation.

The following day, October 28, Trumbo was the lead-off witness. After watching the newsreel footage for the umpteenth time, Christopher described what he saw:

> The hearing room is crowded. He sits at a table flanked by his attorneys, Robert Kenny and Bartley Crum. There are two radio microphones in front of him. Photographers with speed-graphic cameras crowd forward. Flashbulbs pop. Radio commentators have their own section, with bulky vacuum-tube equipment in front of them. Across the table from him are two men, both stenographers; one will be taking down his testimony on a long stenographic pad, the other using a stenographic machine. To his right, as he looks past Crum, the committee staff is seated.

The committee members sit directly across from him, on a raised dais. This was Trumbo's destiny. Everything leads up to this. And in some ways, this hearing became the great clarifying issue of his life.

Trumbo sat down in the witness chair, wrote reporter Sidney Olson, "in a kind of nervous crouch."[52] In fact, he sat poised on the edge of the witness chair, looking like a well-trained gladiator, eager for the games to begin. The chairman drew first blood by denying Trumbo permission to read his statement because, Thomas told him, "it is not pertinent to the inquiry." When Trumbo observed that, at an earlier hearing, the chairman had considered an opening statement by white supremacist Gerald L. K. Smith "to be pertinent to its inquiries," Thomas angrily declared Trumbo's remark to be "out of order." Unfazed, Trumbo posed a reasonable question: "And where is mine different from that, sir? . . . I would like to know what it is in my statement that this committee fears to be read to the American people?" He got no answer.

In that unread statement, Trumbo accused the friendly witnesses of hearsay, slander, and perjury, and he reprimanded the committee members for allowing the friendly witnesses to enter into the record their "petty professional jealousies," "private feuds," and "intra-studio conflicts." He then proceeded to indict the committee's investigation of Hollywood. He accused the committee members of directly attacking the constitutional rights of property, management, and the free-enterprise system; the constitutional guarantee of "a free screen"; and "the right of the artist to express his ideas freely and honestly in his work." Trumbo then asserted that he and the other so-called unfriendly witnesses had discerned the committee's malign purposes and intended to challenge it, to remind the people of the United States that the "defense of constitutional rights is not simply a convenience to be invoked in time of need, but a clear and continuous obligation imposed equally upon all of us at all times. We are, as citizens, literally commanded by its implications to defend the Constitution against even the slightest encroachment upon the protective barrier it interposes between the private citizen on the one hand and the inquisitors of government on the other." Finally, Trumbo compared Washington in 1947 to Berlin in 1932, telling the committee that its hearings made the nation's capital like the German capital "on the eve of the Reichstag fire. For those who remember German history in the autumn of 1932 there is the smell of smoke in this very room."[53]

When Trumbo asked if he could introduce some evidence demonstrating that he had not spent his Hollywood years subverting the nation, he was again gaveled into silence. At that point, committee counsel Robert Stripling began the questioning process by asking Trumbo if he was a member of the Screen Writers Guild. Trumbo asked that he be allowed to introduce statements about his work made by General Hap Arnold and a municipal judge. The chairman's gavel continued to pound. Stripling then instructed Trumbo to answer the questions yes or no and advised him that he would not be allowed to make a speech in response to each question. Trumbo, in his best professorial tone, lectured Stripling about investigative committee protocol: "Your job is to ask questions and mine is to answer them. I shall answer 'Yes' or 'No,' if I please to answer. I shall answer in my own words. Very many questions can be answered 'Yes' or 'No' only by a moron or a slave." Trumbo again tried to introduce into the record statements "from responsible people as to the nature of my work," as well as twenty of his scripts, "so that it may be known what my work is, and what this committee may seek to prevent the American people from seeing in the future."

When Stripling repeated the question about his SWG membership, Trumbo again protested the chairman's refusal to allow him to read his statement or present his evidence. Then, turning to the committee counsel, he began his nonreply: "Mr. Stripling, the rights of American labor to inviolably secret membership lists have been won in this country by a great cost of blood and a great cost in terms of hunger. These rights have become an American tradition. Over the Voice of America we have broadcast to the entire world the freedom of our labor." Thomas queried, "Are you answering the question or are you making another speech?" Trumbo replied that he was "truly answering the question." Asked again about his guild membership, Trumbo answered: "You asked me a question which would permit you to haul every union member in the United States up here to identify himself as a union member, to subject him to future intimidation and coercion. This, I believe, is an unconstitutional question. . . . [It] is designed to a specific purpose. First, to identify me with the SWG; secondly, to seek to identify me with the Communist Party and thereby destroy that guild." When Thomas asked, "Are you refusing to answer the questions?" Trumbo replied that he was not. "Well," Thomas rejoined, "you are refusing to answer this question." Trumbo countered, "I am, indeed, not refusing to answer the question."

Thomas was prepared to excuse Trumbo from the stand, but Stripling insisted on posing the big question: "Are you now, or have you ever been, a member of the Communist Party?" Thomas concurred, and when Stripling posed that question, Trumbo crafted his reply in the form of a rhetorical question, asking Stripling if it was true that the committee had given the press an alleged Communist Party membership card with Trumbo's name on it. Thomas intervened, indignantly reminding Trumbo: "You are not asking the questions." Trumbo, in his sweetest voice, replied: "I was." Thomas attempted another reprimand, saying: "The chief investigator is asking the questions." When Stripling repeated the question, Trumbo replied: "I believe I have the right to be confronted with any evidence which supports this question. I should like to see what you have." Thomas told him: "Well, you will, pretty soon. The witness is excused. Impossible." As he was leaving the stand, Trumbo stated: "This is the beginning of an American concentration camp." Thomas retorted: "Typical Communist tactics. This is typical Communist tactics." After Trumbo left the stand, the chairman cited him for contempt of Congress. Stripling then read into the record the titles of the films Trumbo had written and thirty-nine items attesting to Trumbo's party "work."[54]

Dmytryk later claimed that "Trumbo's performance was the greatest disappointment of the week. . . . Dalton, normally an unflappable man, flapped like a flag in a gale that day. By the time he had finished, I knew we were dead."[55] Dmytryk seemed to be implying that Trumbo's usual cool demeanor had slipped, but it is clear from news footage of the testimony that Trumbo remained calm throughout the ordeal and calculatingly baited both Thomas and Stripling. Indeed, none of the major newspaper accounts of Trumbo's testimony echoed Dmytryk's assessment. Of all the unfriendly witnesses, Lawson's testimony received the most press coverage. The *New York Times*, for example, devoted only one sentence to Trumbo's testimony.[56] The *Los Angeles Examiner* devoted much more space to Bessie and Maltz, who also testified on October 28.[57] And the *Los Angeles Times* reporter neutrally remarked: "Trumbo set the pace with a demand for the right to 'introduce certain evidence bearing on this case' after defying the chairman to explain 'what in my statement is not pertinent.'" That reporter also noted Trumbo's comment about Gerald L. K. Smith.[58] However, an editorial in the *New York Herald-Tribune* made a point that many anti-Communists, liberal as well as conservative, later used against the unfriendly witnesses. By failing to reply to questions about their membership in the Communist Party, they ducked what had become

Trumbo leaving the witness stand, accusing the committee of creating "an American concentration camp," 1947. Bartley Crum is behind Trumbo; Robert Kenny is on the right. Courtesy of *Life* magazine.

a serious issue in the United States: the existence of a "political and pressure organization which conceals its membership," and the refusal of its members, when questioned, to admit or disavow membership.[59] Trumbo later told Christopher: "If the Committee had just allowed [the unfriendly witnesses] to talk, they would have run out of things to say and been forced to answer the questions."

After Trumbo left the stand, the hearings continued for two days, and nine more unfriendly witnesses testified. One of them, Edward Dmytryk, later claimed that he and Scott (with Crum's support) had once again proposed that they "tell the truth," but the other attorneys demurred.[60] The last unfriendly witness was Bertolt Brecht. Although he had urged the other unfriendly witnesses to tell the truth, Brecht did not do so himself. Most conspicuously, he expressly denied that he had ever been a Communist. In addition to being untrue, this answer made those who had refused to respond look very bad by comparison. Brecht later admitted that he had taken advantage of the situation: he had almost nothing to do with Hollywood, he was not involved in American politics, and the earlier witnesses had refused to answer the question directly.[61] Near the end of his life, Trumbo noted that a few of the Hollywood Ten had been somewhat miffed by Brecht's decision to answer the committee's questions, but most understood that if he had not done so, his status as an alien might have placed him in serious jeopardy. Speaking for himself, Trumbo had been "delighted" by Brecht's testimony, which "made total fools" of the committee members and staff.[62]

After Brecht's testimony on October 30, the hearings were adjourned. (Brecht flew to Europe on October 31.) Thomas stated: "I want to emphasize that the committee is not adjourning *sine die*, but will resume hearings as soon as possible." He noted that the committee had files on sixty-eight other prominent movie people who were party members or affiliated with party front groups, and he warned movie executives: "It is not necessary for the Chair to emphasize the harm which the motion-picture industry suffers from the presence within its ranks of known communists who do not have the best interests of the United States at heart. The industry should set about immediately to clear its own house and not wait for public opinion to force it to do so."[63]

Stripling later wrote that Larry Parks was scheduled to be the next witness, but he decided not to call Parks because "the entire hearing was taking on the overtones of a broken record. Further, I had every reason to believe that New York Communist circles were about to mass-picket the House Office Building and pack the caucus rooms."[64] But according to committee aide Louis Russell, the hearings had been discontinued for three other reasons: the committee was running low on funds; the "friendly" press had advised committee members that public interest was waning; and potential "friendly" witnesses among the Nineteen, such as Larry Parks and Waldo Salt, needed more time to prepare themselves.[65] Thomas told an FBI official that the hearings would not resume until a federal court had ruled on the contempt of Congress charges against the ten unfriendly witnesses.[66]

According to Parks, the Nineteen believed the hearings had ended because "reasoned opinion" against the committee had swelled. But, he added, the eight men who had not been called to testify "felt let down." They had been "prepared to face" the committee, and it would have been better for the ten if the other eight had also been cited for contempt.[67]

The Hollywood Ten have remained controversial, and they are regularly demonized by anti-Communists of all persuasions for the strategy they employed. First, they are criticized for failing to take a clear, forthright stand on the First Amendment. That is, they did not respond to the committee's questions about their political affiliations by forthrightly stating: "I refuse to answer your question because of my First Amendment right to private opinions."[68] This accusation is a fair one. They clearly harmed their case with the general public by evading the questions.

Others criticize the Ten's failure to stand, en masse, on the steps of the Capitol and announce to the press that they were members of the Communist Party. Had they done so, the argument goes, they would have undercut the committee (and Senator Joseph McCarthy), forestalled a blacklist, and weakened the domestic cold war. In his pamphlet *The Time of the Toad* (see chapter 11), Trumbo addressed this accusation: "For the witnesses to have revealed to the press that which they had withheld from the committee would have aided the committee in its objective [that is, the forcible disclosure of opinion] quite as effectively as direct revelation from the stand. The accused men made their stand before the committee to reestablish their right of privacy, not only in law but in fact." The Ten actually believed in that right, and a public statement about their political affiliations outside the hearing room would have rendered meaningless their assertion of that right on the witness stand. That right, Trumbo said, "must exist not only in law but in life itself; for it is only in the day-to-day actions of living men that laws achieve reality."[69] In other words, Trumbo believed that one cannot preserve the privacy of one's political beliefs and affiliations by publicly announcing them under pressure.[70]

This criticism also ignores two other facts. First, the Alien Registration Act made it a crime to belong to an organization advocating the overthrow of any government in the United States. The threat to those who openly acknowledged party membership became clear seven months later, when eleven leaders of the CPUSA were indicted and convicted under that act. (In subsequent years, dozens of secondary leaders were similarly indicted and convicted.) Thus, if the Ten had stood on the steps of the Capitol and announced that they were Communists, they likely would have been indicted, convicted, imprisoned, and blacklisted. In addition, after such an announcement, they likely would have been recalled to the witness stand by Thomas and asked the same question again. Then, they would have had to either refuse to answer on First Amendment grounds, which, as their attorneys had advised them, would have undermined their court cases, or take the

Fifth Amendment, which amounted, in their minds, to an admission of criminality.

A number of anti-Communists have argued that the Hollywood Ten, by concealing their political views, effectively opened themselves up to conspiracy charges and laid the groundwork for further congressional investigations of this sort. Indeed, they were responsible for McCarthyism. In notes he made for an interview, Trumbo made a distinction between concealment and self-protection: "The reason the Ten were called before the Committee," he wrote, "was that they had *not* concealed their views." Anyone who read the transcript of the hearings, he continued, would see that the committee did not ask any witness about his views, beliefs, or opinions. It was clear from the transcript that the committee "didn't want to hear our views, and every time we tried to state them on our own we were either gaveled down or thrown off the stand." The committee simply wanted the Ten to expose their political and trade union affiliations. The Ten, according to Trumbo, did not try to conceal their affiliations; they merely "refused to reveal them under compulsion."[71]

Several later commentators, especially those with a liberal bias, have accused the Ten of lacking "candor." In the afterword to his 1971 compendium of committee testimony, Eric Bentley wrote: "They lacked candor, and if that, humanly speaking, is quite a common lack, it is an impossible lack for real radicals."[72] In an early draft of his answer to this statement, Trumbo wrote: "When both of us have more time I'd also like to discuss with you the question of candor and what I conceive to be the difference between public assertion of political principles and public confession of organizational affiliation."[73] In the letter Trumbo actually sent to Bentley, he wrote: "I doubt that your remarks about radicals and candor (p. 945) in relation to the secrecy of political affiliation during hostile times can consistently be sustained by historical example." Trumbo cited the Sons of Liberty and Committees of Correspondence in the pre-Revolutionary North American colonies and concluded: "Candor may be the historical ideal for promulgation of doctrine, but it's not very practical for those who try—or think they're trying—to transform doctrine into reality."[74]

A few months earlier, Trumbo had also chastised film historian Richard Corliss for writing that Trumbo's refusal to admit he was a party member amounted to a lack of candor. In his letter to Corliss, Trumbo wrote: "Your use of the word 'admit' is pejorative: Did non-Communists who stood silent before the Committee (there were such) refuse to admit membership in an organization they had never joined? Obviously not: they *refused to answer* the Committee's questions about political affiliations. . . . To put the matter objectively rather than pejoratively, this was true of all witnesses who declined the Committee's gambit: they did not refuse to admit, they refused to answer."[75] In the notes he made for a subsequent letter to Corliss, Trumbo remarked: "Had I answered the first question 'are you now or have you ever been a member of the Communist Party?' affirmatively, the second question would have been 'who else were members?' and I should [have] been compelled to turn informer or go to jail." He did not consider his rejection of this path to be a heroic act on his part, since "it isn't heroic in any degree to refuse to become an informer: it is *natural*, it is normal, it is something we have learned from childhood."[76] In effect, Trumbo was restating his belief that he had both a natural and a constitutional right to say nothing at all.

Another group of liberals took the curious position that, by dint of being both highly paid screenwriters and Communists, the Ten rendered themselves morally unworthy of taking a principled stand. One of the first, and most condescending, accusations of this type was penned by Arthur Schlesinger Jr., who characterized Maltz, Bessie, Lawson, and Trumbo as "fellow-traveling ex-proletarian writers" who went "to Hollywood and became film hacks." In Schlesinger's imagination (he knew none of them personally), they had become burdened by "a pervading sense of guilt" and a feeling that they had sold themselves out. Therefore, beset with "qualms of conscience," they attempted "to buy indulgences by participating in the Communist movement." Then they refused to answer questions about that movement to a duly appointed committee of Congress.[77] Trumbo replied:

> I do not think it possible for a committee of the Congress to ask Mr. Schlesinger a question which would do violence to his conscience. He takes his stand squarely in the tradition of chronic confessors who have plagued the earth since the first establishment of orthodoxy. Wherever inquisitorial courts have been set up, Mr. Schlesinger and his breed have appeared in eager herds to proclaim: "I do not wish to imply approval of your questions, but I am not now nor have I even been a dissenter. I am not now nor have I ever been a Communist. I am not now nor have I ever been a trade unionist. I am not now nor have I ever been a Jew. Prosecute those who answer differently, O masters,

silence them, send them to jail, make soap of them if you wish. But not of me, for I have answered every question you chose to ask, fully, frankly, freely—and on my belly."[78]

Schlesinger responded that "it would be naïve, of course, to suppose that Mr. Trumbo thinks that Trotskyites and Klansmen should be accorded the same rights as Communists and fellow-travelers."[79] Trumbo countered: "I have always thought my stand on this issue [the constitutional rights of Trotskyists and Klan members] quite clear. I deny the right of Congress, or of any agent of government, or of any other group or persons to call American citizens to account for their political affiliations or sympathies. I affirm the basic constitutional principles that men may be questioned and prosecuted for their acts, never for their thoughts." Trumbo distinguished Trotskyist parties (political organizations that only printed pamphlets and newspapers) from the Ku Klux Klan, which he characterized as a criminal organization whose members murder, flog, and burn.[80] (Trumbo was consistent on this point. In 1961, when he was asked to comment on a draft of a pamphlet on the Nazi movement in the United States, he repeated what he had said to Schlesinger: "The moral and legal point of the First Amendment, as I see it, is that *no* kind of thought can be exposed, investigated, or punished; and that the same rule holds for association and public demonstrations arising out of such thought."[81])

Schlesinger never changed his position, and he and Trumbo continued to snipe at each other over the years.[82] Trumbo did, however, convince another well-known liberal, Murray Kempton, to alter his perception of the Hollywood Ten. In his 1955 book *Part of Our Time*, Kempton had denigrated the Ten:

Their story is a failure of promise; first, of the promise in themselves, and last, of the promise of the Hollywood which was so kind to them until they became an embarrassment and then turned them out. The promise at the beginnings of most of them appear now to have been tinsel, as Hollywood is tinsel. They were entombed, most of them, not for being true to themselves, but for sitting up too long with their own press clippings. . . . They were not very attractive witnesses; their habits were Hollywood's, and long training had reduced their prose to the muddier depths of a Nash-Kelvinator ad.[83]

But two years later, in response to a letter from Trumbo questioning the aptness of his remarks, Kempton expressed contrition: "I can only plead, pompous as it sounds, that I have come to believe that it is the greatest of crimes to write about a man whose face you have never seen, since writing is related to the subject more than the audience, and a man you have never seen is unlikely to recognize himself in what you say about him, and thus no engagement is possible. The book is full of that, and my only hope is that it taught me something."[84] Eleven years later, in his review of a book that was also critical of the Ten's position, Kempton criticized the author's use of irony. Kempton acknowledged that although irony had once been his preferred method of attack as well, he had come to realize that an ironic tone "is no longer adequate to our history. It can never be more than a refined expression of the very crude and philistine notion that the victim is usually guilty of something." As it happened, Kempton could not entirely disabuse himself of irony. He wrote, later in the review: "The rhetoric of the Hollywood Ten may have been inferior to their cause, as the rhetoric of victims quite often is. But it still ought to be said for them that, in their test, they did what they could with the remaining resources of language and dignity, and that they did better than we."[85]

Trumbo did not deny that the Ten's strategy was flawed. Years later he wrote: "There was something tragically wrong with the position of the Ten in those hearings, and I think it mainly stems from bad legal advice." He was correct that the Ten needed the stout legal shield of the Fifth Amendment, but he forgot that he and the other unfriendly witnesses had rejected its use, preferring instead "a club called the First Amendment."[86] If the Nineteen had relied on the First Amendment for their public campaign and reserved the Fifth Amendment as the main buttress of their legal argument, they would not have gone to prison, but they still would have been blacklisted. That outcome, Trumbo now believed, would have dealt the committee "a stunning setback, since it had sought to put men in jail and had failed, and the producers would have been handed a dirty legal problem: They would have been perceived as blacklisting men whom the Federal courts had exonerated. As a consequence, the producers might have been reluctant to extend the blacklist, in 1951, when the committee re-opened its investigation of 'Communist Infiltration of the Motion-Picture Industry,' and far fewer people might have suffered."[87]

All flawed decisions aside, Trumbo continued to believe that the Ten had accomplished something. They might not have halted the advance of postwar fascism in the United States, but at least they had not helped it: "We didn't do it any good. That's not much, but it's better than falling into a cataleptic fit every time the flag goes by." The Ten, by their refusal to answer, also upheld a very important principle about affiliations: if a government can force an individual to make public his or her affiliations, that ability can be used as a weapon "to destroy one's right not only to *express* belief but even to hold it. . . . Governments don't fear publicly expressed opinions half as much as they fear organization—i.e., affiliation—to make expressed opinions effective. That's why they're constantly after membership lists."[88] Finally, as Trumbo told the interviewer for the documentary film *Hollywood on Trial*, the Ten had purchased four years of continued employment for the other Communists and former Communists in Hollywood. Until the court decisions on the Ten's contempt charges were rendered, the committee could not go forward with its investigation of the motion picture industry, and the producers could not go forward with their blacklist. Trumbo did not mention that the Ten had also demonstrated, albeit unwillingly, the utility of invoking the Fifth Amendment. (Only a handful of subsequent friendly witnesses—notably, screenwriter Sidney Buchman and singer Pete Seeger—did not use the Fifth Amendment during their testimony. They were both cited for contempt, but those citations were overturned in court.)

Trumbo's final thoughts on the subject of the Ten's strategy were expressed in an angry exchange with Albert Maltz. Their dispute began in December 1972, when Maltz criticized Trumbo's acceptance speech for the Writers Guild Laurel Award for lifetime achievement (see chapter 22). In his reply to Maltz, Trumbo contended that the Ten had not behaved heroically, as Maltz had stated:

> [They did not] volunteer to perform heroic deeds, they were subpoenaed like all other witnesses and compelled against their wills to take the stand and testify. The best evidence that they appeared unwillingly is provided by their motions to quash the subpoenas that finally delivered them into the Committee's hands. A heroic position is clear, decisive, noble, bold, intrepid, etc. Once summoned, the Ten *could* have invoked the First Amendment at the outset, and refused to give the Committee anything but their names. Had they done so, their position would have been much clearer than it was and their punishment would have been no greater. Instead, for legal reasons and with

legal advice, they first invoked the Constitution, and thereafter pretended to answer questions which they were determined *not* to answer, and didn't.

So far, so good. But as he continued his remarks, Trumbo began to engage in some revisionist history, probably influenced by his changed perspective on informing. He insisted that the Ten had intended not to destroy the committee but to prevent the committee from destroying them. Rather than defending the sanctity of the First Amendment, they had used it both to avoid punishment for refusing to answer the committee's questions and to avoid becoming informers. He urged Maltz to recall that "our horror of becoming informers was so great that we would have refused even if there had been no First Amendment or, for that matter, no Constitution. Our primary aim was to avoid becoming informers. To defend and justify our refusals we used the Constitution as a shield. We needed that shield so we fought for it."[89]

Maltz justifiably avowed that the Nineteen's purpose had been, from the outset, to destroy the committee. They had invoked the First Amendment because their attorneys had advised them that no other amendment would lay the groundwork for the Supreme Court to declare the committee unconstitutional. Thus, their decision had nothing to do with becoming informers.[90]

Dissatisfied with Trumbo's letters on the subject, Maltz wrote to three of the attorneys—Margolis, Katz, and Kenny—asking for their recollection of the Nineteen's motives. Katz and Kenny concurred with Maltz's version, but Margolis declared that both Maltz and Trumbo were correct. According to Margolis, the Nineteen had used the First Amendment to advance their two principal objectives: (1) to protect the rights of the individuals involved, with respect to their jobs and possible criminal prosecution, and (2) to carry on the fight in a manner that would be most effective in politically defeating the committee and possibly destroying it. The policy of answering all questions, Margolis continued, "was rejected very quickly because it would require some persons to become informers or go to jail for refusing to name names. [In addition] this approach was not the one most likely to achieve the two principal objectives mentioned above because it was believed that broad support could not be gathered and maintained around this position."[91]

Shortly after this exchange, Trumbo privately acknowledged that the original nineteen unfriendly witnesses and their attorneys had agreed (more or less) on a common strategy and a set of tactics. However, in a series of undated, handwritten notes on the committee, Trumbo stated that the Ten had refused to answer questions about the Screen Writers Guild and the Communist Party "for various and sometimes different reasons (Albert Maltz to protect, preserve and defend the First Amendment; I primarily to protect, preserve and defend myself and others like me.)"[92]

As events would demonstrate, the legal system and public opinion became the final arbiters of the Nineteen's strategy, and the ten men who chose the pretend-to-answer tactic fared poorly with both.

10

Blacklisted, Indicted, Convicted

Hollywood is baffled by the question of what the Committee on Un-American Activities wants from it. People here are wondering, with some dismay and anxiety, what kind of strange, brooding alienism the Committee is trying to eliminate from their midst and, in fact, whether it was ever here. They are waiting hopefully for Chairman J. Parnell Thomas, Congress, or God, to tell them. They have been waiting in vain ever since last November.

—Lillian Ross

This is the Phony-War period of the blacklist. The battle lines have been drawn, but the situation is still quite fluid. Nobody really knows how the blacklist is going to work, or if it will work. It still applies only to ten men. . . . Other reds and radicals continue to work under contract.

—Christopher Trumbo

The Hollywood Ten constituted a group of relatively unknown men who had achieved notoriety in an unanticipated and unwanted manner. For three years, they shared an interest that was strong enough to overcome their differences, but each man dealt with the aftermath of the hearings in a distinctive manner. After his return to Hollywood, Trumbo had three goals: to carry on the fight against the committee, to continue his screenwriting career, and to pay bills totaling $27,000 for work on the ranch. Faced with foreclosure if the bills were not paid, Trumbo wrote a letter to Edward G. Robinson, his only acquaintance who was a millionaire, and asked for a loan of $10,000; he offered a first trust deed on the ranch as security. Robinson, according to Trumbo, "asked me to

211

come to his house, and I did. There he told me he couldn't lend $10,000, but would be glad to lend me five. I naturally agreed. Whereupon to my surprise he pressed into my hand *five one-thousand-dollar bills*. I then discussed with him the drawing up of a first trust deed against the ranch. *He refused to take one.* I next declared I would sign a promissory note. *He refused to take a note.*"[1]

Trumbo went back to work at MGM on November 6, 1947. He was told that his contract, which had been suspended during his three-week absence from the studio, had been extended for three weeks.[2] Trumbo participated in a series of conferences regarding the script he had written for "Angel's Flight" and the one he was writing for "House on the River." During one of those conferences, he and MGM vice president Eddie Mannix discussed the hearings and the conduct of the Ten, but Mannix gave no indication that Trumbo's tenure at the studio was in jeopardy.[3]

Before returning to the ranch, Trumbo spoke to a Mobilization for Democracy–sponsored "Stop the Witch Hunt" program at the Shrine Auditorium. Two days later, on November 11, Trumbo addressed an audience of 3,000 people at a PCA-sponsored meeting at Gilmore Stadium, telling them: "To accept the concepts of the Thomas committee is to yield to censorship, no matter how loudly it is protested that this is not being done." He declared that the Ten must be defended because they were doing more for a free screen than the producers, who were yielding to the wishes of the committee. The attendees were asked to sign petitions demanding that Congress dismiss the contempt citations and abolish the Committee on Un-American Activities.[4]

The next day Trumbo met with Howard Strickling, MGM's director of public relations, who later (under oath) recounted their conversation:

> I told him that as far as the world was concerned he was now believed to be a Communist; that the whole matter of his appearance before the Committee, in my opinion, had been handled very badly; and that he should have answered the Committee's questions. Trumbo said that his position had been misunderstood; that he was meeting with the other witnesses and was trying to get them to do something about the situation; that he had acted as a matter of principle, but that he was not a Communist. I replied, that if that was so, he should have testified that he was not, but that perhaps it was not too late yet; that he should come out with a public statement to that effect.

. . . Trumbo said he would not back down or give up his principles; that he didn't care if as a result he lost his job and had to
go back to doing what he had done before.[5]

Meanwhile, Trumbo and the six other screenwriters who had
refused to answer the committee's questions were learning that they
could not rely on the support of the Screen Writers Guild. At a guild
meeting on November 6, a report written by SWG president Emmet
Lavery was read to those in attendance. Lavery had testified at the
October hearings, and he had agreed to provide the committee with the
guild's membership list. In his report, Lavery accused the seven writers of trying "to make this a Guild matter, by giving non-responsive
answers to two questions of affiliation." Their refusal to answer questions about their guild membership was not, from Lavery's perspective,
intended to protect the SWG, and their doing so harmed the SWG by
linking it with their nonanswers about their membership in the Communist Party. Although he strongly urged the SWG not to support the
writers' legal cases, Lavery did recommend encouraging Congress to
reform the Committee on Un-American Activities and asking the producers' association to set up a public relations committee to defend the
industry from further attacks.[6] Lester Cole, Richard Collins, Gordon
Kahn, and Ring Lardner Jr. wrote a report challenging Lavery's version
of events: "In actual fact the Communist Party and the Screen Writers
Guild were tied together quite specifically, not by us, but by two other
unofficial Guild spokesmen, Fred Niblo, Jr. and Richard Macaulay." In
addition, they accused Lavery of testifying "more as a leader of a [guild]
faction" than as the group's president and admonished him for not protecting the guild's membership lists.[7]

Lavery had also been quietly assembling an "All-Guild Slate" for
the upcoming SWG election. Its candidates had pledged to unite the
guild, keep it out of politics, and obey the provision of the Taft-Hartley
Act that required union officials to sign affidavits attesting that they
were not members of the Communist Party. On November 19, this slate
won every executive position. The headline in the *Hollywood Reporter*
stated: "SWG Elects Anti-Red Officers."[8] At the same time, studio executives were putting terrific pressure on those Hollywood liberals who
had formed the Committee for the First Amendment, sponsored two
national radio broadcasts criticizing the House committee, and sent a
delegation to Washington to symbolize their opposition to the hearings.
According to director William Wyler, one of the main organizers of the

Delegation of the Committee for the First Amendment, leaving Los Angeles
to attend the 1947 hearings. Top left to bottom: Humphrey Bogart, Lauren
Bacall, Sterling Hayden, Paul Henried, and Shepperd Strudwick; top right to
bottom: June Havoc, Richard Conte, Danny Kaye, Evelyn Keyes, Jane Wyatt,
and Marsha Hunt. Courtesy of Judy Chaikin.

Committee for the First Amendment: "People got scared. The pressure
groups, the Motion Picture Alliance ([Roy] Brewer's group), scared the
hell out of everybody. All of our heads were going to be on a chopping
block."[9]

And then another blow came from an unexpected direction. On
November 26 Howard Koch publicly separated himself from the Nineteen. In a full-page ad that appeared in both *Daily Variety* and the
Hollywood Reporter, Koch stated: "I am not and have never been a
member of the Communist Party." In this "Letter to My Fellow Workers in the Motion Picture Industry," he praised the Ten for the position
they had taken in Washington, and he warned his "fellow workers" that
if they did not emulate the Ten and stand firm against the committee,
the result would be "a complete subjugation of the screen to the political
will of the Committee."[10]

As a result of these events, the Ten found themselves isolated in
Hollywood. The only organization fully behind them was the Freedom
from Fear Committee, sponsored by the Progressive Citizens of Amer-

ica. Located in a small house north of Hollywood Boulevard, it was run by Herbert Biberman and Pauline Lauber Finn. A volunteer staff raised funds, arranged national speaking tours, and organized a national "Stop Censorship" campaign.[11] This committee received no assistance from the CPUSA.

Some of the Ten, perhaps wistfully, expressed confidence that they would not be blacklisted. Biberman claimed that he had met with two MGM executives, Nicholas Schenck and J. Robert Rubin, and studio head Samuel Goldwyn, who assured him there would be no blacklist.[12] But Charles Katz had heard that Eric Johnston was prepared to support a blacklist and had convinced Spyros Skouras (Twentieth Century–Fox) and Schenck to go along.[13] The FBI had been told that people in the industry were "worried" and ready to fire any "Communists" exposed by the committee. Another FBI source claimed that Louis B. Mayer was concerned that box-office receipts were beginning to feel the pressure of public opinion, citing reports that several theater owners had refused to show Katharine Hepburn's *Song of Love*.[14]

Top movie executives met at the office of the Motion Picture Association of America in early November to discuss the public's belief that Johnston, Mayer, and Warner had, in their testimony, condoned communism and defended the presence of Communists in the industry. Convinced that Thomas was going to reopen the hearings, they decided they had to distance themselves from the unfriendly witnesses. Although the executives criticized the unfriendly witnesses for their "undignified" behavior, there was no talk of a blacklist.[15]

A few weeks later, a much larger group that included the heads of the studios and the production companies gathered at the Waldorf Astoria Hotel in New York City to discuss how to confront the bad publicity from the October hearings and the pending contempt citations in the House of Representatives. Eric Johnston told the gathering that, according to his sources, no further committee hearings were scheduled. Nevertheless, he advised the assembled executives that, for the good of "the public relations of the industry as a whole," the five unfriendly witnesses currently under contract must be fired. He also advised them not to hire anyone suspected of being a Communist. When asked who should make that determination, he answered, "each individual employer." He made it perfectly clear that the producers' association would not set up any "machinery" for that purpose. There was no recorded vote on the question of firing or refusing to hire the Ten. Rather, Johnston testified, the attendees reached agreement by "a kind of unanimous consent."[16]

On November 26 Johnston announced to the media: "We will forth-with discharge or suspend without compensation those in our employ [Trumbo, Cole, Scott, Dmytryk, and Lardner] and we will not re-employ any of the ten until such time as he is acquitted or has purged himself of contempt and declares under oath that he is not a Communist."[17] In a deposition later taken by Trumbo's attorneys, Johnston stated that he had acted in response to personal observation, press reports, and other comments that strongly indicated that the conduct and testimony of Trumbo and the other nine had "shocked and offended the community, brought himself and themselves into public scorn and contempt, sub-stantially lessened his and their value to their employers in the motion picture industry, and prejudiced the interests of his and their employ-ers and the motion picture industry generally." In addition, Johnston claimed he had seen evidence of a well-defined movement to boycott all the motion pictures connected with Trumbo and the other witnesses.[18]

As Johnston's words make clear, the blacklist was the brainchild of movie industry leaders. They created it, and they enforced it. In 1949 they established the Motion Picture Industry Council as their "holy synod," empowering its members to determine which suspected employ-ees could work in the industry. In essence, this council was granted the power to forgive an employee's political "sins" if that person submitted to the prescribed purification rituals and openly proclaimed his or her newfound faith. Under its mandate, clearance and absolution rapidly became a self-abasing process.

On the same day the Waldorf conference convened, J. Parnell Thomas asked the House of Representatives to certify his committee's contempt citations and send them to the US attorney for the District of Columbia so that the cited witnesses "may be proceeded against in the manner and form provided by law." He began with Albert Maltz. Three congressmen voiced their disapproval. Herman P. Eberharter (D-Pa.) argued against the resolution, stating that the committee had not dem-onstrated that any movie was Communist inspired or dictated; it had simply charged the witnesses with communism and then conducted a trial based on those unsubstantiated charges. George G. Sadowski (D-Mich.) denied the right of a congressional committee to ask a wit-ness about his political beliefs. And Chet Holifield (D-Calif.) accused the committee of invading "the field of thought, of opinion. Of politi-cal conviction." The House voted, 347–17, in favor of a contempt cita-tion for Maltz. Trumbo's citation was next. Five representatives spoke against it, but the House approved it 240–16. The next eight citations were approved by voice vote. Nothing was said about the ten men personally; the debate was strictly about procedure and substance.[19]

On December 2 MGM announced that Trumbo had been suspended. He received a telegram from his agent, Bert Allenberg, informing him that the studio had taken him off "Angel's Flight."[20] MGM also suspended Cole, RKO fired Dmytryk and Scott, and Twentieth Century–Fox fired Lardner. By this action, Trumbo later said, the producers had allied themselves with the committee as an enemy of the Ten, and the Ten had to fight both.[21]

That fight began on December 15 at a meeting of the Screen Writers Guild, where a committee sent by the producers' association tried to put the best light on the Waldorf statement. Dore Schary (a former screenwriter and head of production at RKO), Eddie Mannix (MGM), and Walter Wanger (an independent producer) were given the unenviable task of convincing the guilds that the industry leaders had acted to benefit the industry as a whole. Schary recalled telling the writers: "I was not there to either condone or condemn certain parts of [the Waldorf] statement in relationship to individual companies firing or not hiring communists. I think I mentioned that I, myself personally, was opposed to this part of the statement, that what I was there to discuss with them was their cooperation in the formation of a public relations organization that would, in some way, help create a different impact in the future for Hollywood in connection with attacks that might be leveled on it."[22]

Paul Jarrico and some other writers who were present said that Schary told them, in effect: "This is not a blacklist. The five men were not dismissed because they were believed to be Communists, but because it was believed that they have impaired their usefulness to the industry by their actions."[23] An FBI informant quoted a furious Trumbo's remarks: "These three men [Schary, Mannix, and Wanger] have come here to force their weasel-minded policies down the throat of this Guild. I want to denounce them for what they are—liars, hypocrites and thieves. . . . Now they come here and ask you, my fellow Guild members, to turn your back on me when I am fighting for a principle that concerns every man in this room. . . . [A]re we going to be swayed by this lying hypocrisy?"[24] Alvah Bessie referred to it as "Trumbo's fighting, delightfully obscene extemporaneous speech."[25]

After Schary and his cohorts left the meeting room, the writers voted to combat any type of industry blacklist and to have the SWG appear as an amicus curiae in any breach-of-contract suit filed by the three fired writers (Trumbo, Cole, and Lardner). They also voted to

table a policy statement condemning the unfriendly witnesses.[26] A few
months later, the SWG Executive Board voted to seek injunctive relief
from the producers' conspiracy to create a blacklist. But the board's
resolution clearly stated that this suit was "not in any way connected
with the defense of the writers held in contempt nor with their individual suits."[27]

A key element of the Ten's strategy was to argue their position in a
book, which Trumbo had agreed to write. In November 1947 Adrian
Scott wrote to his friend Bennett Cerf, the president of Random House,
asking for his comments on an enclosed outline of a book about the
hearings. "I hope," Scott wrote, "the book can be finished within a
three-week period. We are asking Dalton Trumbo to do a benzedrine
job—which is the way he works anyway—and I do think he is the best
fitted for it." Trumbo intended to write the book as a "first-person-
singular account" of the hearings. It would also ask and answer several questions: What is the road from here? Why did the Nineteen take
the position they did? What will they do now? And how can they keep
America a free country? According to Scott, Bartley Crum would be
listed as the author.[28] Cerf replied at length, saying he would not publish such a book unless Crum, or whoever wrote the book under Crum's
name, was willing to state "with absolute clarity" the political affiliations of the unfriendly witnesses, as Howard Koch had recently done.
Cerf, and others to whom he has spoken, believed that the unfriendly
witnesses had failed "to state their position clearly" and seemed to be
hiding behind their constitutional rights. No book of this sort would be
taken seriously, Cerf continued, "unless Mr. Crum's side states its own
position in the most unequivocal terms." Then he posed some questions
of his own that the book's author must answer: "Are they Communists
or are they not? . . . Also, if they are Communists, *why* do they persist
in this philosophy in light of their own careers? Just what do Hollywood Communists believe anyhow? Do they owe their first allegiance
to America or to Soviet Russia? Are they planning only a change in
this government by legal voting procedure or do they advocate force?"[29]
Unfortunately, Scott's response is not among his papers, but it is clear
that the Ten rejected Cerf's suggestions. Cerf was not surprised at their
response, and he acknowledged "all the pitfalls" the Ten might encounter if they followed his outline.[30]

At this point, for reasons that are unclear, Trumbo dropped out
of the project, and Gordon Kahn was chosen to write the Nineteen's
version of the October hearings. When the manuscript was completed,

Scott sent it to Cerf, soliciting his comments. Apparently, Cerf had met with some members of the Nineteen just prior to receiving the manuscript, and it is clear from his response that his position had hardened against them. The manuscript, he wrote, is "completely one-sided, and, in fact, suspiciously close to the 'party line' in spots. . . . Its obvious partiality destroys its appeal to the general public, who, for the most part, will, I feel, agree with critics of the right who will undoubtedly dismiss the book as 'blatant Red propaganda.'"[31]

Cerf's letters to Scott represent strong evidence that the Ten had failed to convince the vast majority of observers that members of a congressional committee had neither the right nor the responsibility to ask the questions they did, much less that doing so was a harbinger of fascism. As the months passed and the Ten did not moderate their positions, despite the increasingly frigid domestic cold war, Cerf became more and more hostile toward them, and his fondness for Scott ebbed noticeably.

Although there had been previous blacklists in Hollywood, and Trumbo himself had been blacklisted for a few months during the 1930s, this one was clearly different. Most notably, it was the first publicly announced refusal to hire. Thus, no one was sure how it would function or whether it would extend beyond the Ten. In the interim, the blacklisted men inhabited an economic twilight zone, and the other Hollywood Communists could only wait and wonder. According to Christopher:

> The blacklist changed all Trumbo's plans. After thirteen years, he had finally reached the point where he was going to concentrate, where he knew what he was going to try to do. His future course was now out of his control. As far as the rest of us were concerned, nothing really changed for us. If we had lived in Los Angeles, things might have been different, but we lived in a very small mountain community. People knew us, and they either liked us or didn't. We were not subject to a lot of outside pressure; we were not subject to daily newspapers, people coming to our house and throwing things at our windows. We were, in a sense, buffered.

Nikola and Christopher were further protected by the principal at the four-room El Tejon School in Lebec. Nikola recalled that the principal was aware of their identity and took steps to ensure that they were

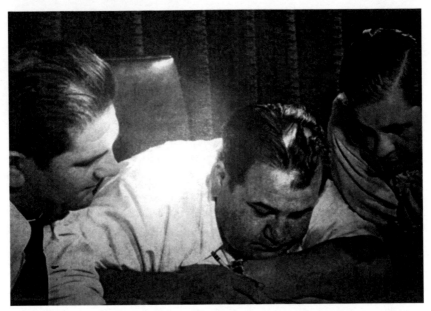

The King brothers—Morry, Frank, and Hymie—ca. 1948. Courtesy of *Life* magazine.

not bullied or made to feel different. In 1949 or 1950 school authorities gave Nikola a Good Citizenship Award, sponsored by the American Legion. Given that the legion was one of the most zealous proponents of Americanism—and thus supported investigating, exposing, blacklisting, and deporting "Communists"—Trumbo considered the award "an amusing irony."

By December, Trumbo began to feel the economic constraints of the contempt citation and the blacklist. His application for a passport was denied, and his agents had started to ignore him. As a consequence, when Frank King asked Trumbo to work for King Brothers Productions, albeit at a sharply reduced salary, Trumbo leaped at the opportunity. This deal initiated what came to be called the black market. Its buyers came mainly from the hundred or so independent production companies, none of which had signed the Waldorf statement. (For more on the King brothers, see chapters 13 and 14.)

Trumbo knew he would not receive screen credit for the script he had agreed to write for the King brothers, and he decided he should come up with another name to write under. In a letter to Elsie McKeogh, he said that when he traveled east for his trial he wanted to discuss pseudonyms with her, remarking, "I don't know how such things are done, but I suspect that will be necessary."[32] At the same time, he hired Martin Gang, who had crafted his contract with MGM, to challenge his suspension. Gang informed Loew's Incorporated, MGM's parent company, that there was no provision in Trumbo's contract allowing the company to suspend him or to withhold the money owed him (Trumbo was owed $14,000 for the screenplay of "Angel's Flight").[33]

Trumbo had convinced himself that he could earn an adequate living without regular script assignments. When William Pomerance, former executive secretary of the SWG, invited him to join a company of left-wingers to make movies, Trumbo replied: "Count me out, old boy, I never did like that racket and although I'm not especially fond of the *way* I got out of it, still and all I'm glad I *am* out. I may steal a little now and again on a piece of shit, but I'll never work for them [studios] again. Life's too short and movies are too long."[34]

To commence his new, independent life, Trumbo decided to write a play, which he titled "The Aching Rivers." The title came from Walt Whitman's poem "From Pent-up Aching Rivers," the first lines of which were undoubtedly the key ones for Trumbo: "From pent-up aching rivers, / From that of myself without which I were nothing, / From what I am determin'd to make illustrious, even if I stand sole / among men." (He did not seem to find the next line—"From my own voice resonant, singing the phallus"—significant.)[35] As Trumbo conceived it, the play would have a "social point" and carry "a certain import" in line with his convictions," but it would not contain exhortations or social declamations, and it would not make any obvious political statements. He told Elsie: "Whatever meaning the audience carries home I hope shall come from their interpretation of events which occurred on the stage, rather than from any blue-print formula predigested for them by the author."[36]

Trumbo also decided, for a variety of reasons, to leave the Communist Party, but he wanted to do so quietly and informally. He had always found the party's ideology and oratory boring, and he hated going to party meetings. By late 1947, he had become impatient with the party itself. It was, he later told an interviewer, "being wiped out as an effective medium of action." In addition, "there were discouraging events within the Party—the transition from Browder to William Z. Foster— disgraceful, vitriolic debates, where people who had stood shoulder to shoulder through years of hardship and hard work suddenly rending each other to pieces, and this was pretty sad to see." However, he did not hate the party or what it stood for, nor did he consider himself an enemy of the party The time factor was probably the most significant reason for his leaving: he was now living permanently at the ranch, an eighty-five-mile drive to Los Angeles, and most of his time and energy were concentrated on earning a living and fighting his contempt citation. Thus, he chose not to make a public announcement; he did not want to look like an opportunist—that is, someone who had joined the party in good faith but then denounced it in a spectacular way to clear himself.[37] He told Bruce Cook: "I just drifted away. I changed no beliefs. I just quit going to meetings and never went back—with no more feeling of separation than I had before I started with the Communist Party."[38]

At some point after the October 1947 hearings, Trumbo wrote a poem titled "Confessional." It is about a writer who has resigned from the party, "Not in a public way, you understand, / Not in a way to harm a soul who stays. / But quietly." The writer had worked with the party "in many ways," fighting where it fought "with perfect faith." And yet, when the writer came under fire for those activities, he did not receive the party's support; instead, he was sneered at:

> As if a clear-won reputation gone,
> All blackened and degraded by the smear—As if this were a simple
>   battle-loss
> To be shrugged off, accepted and forgot
> With no repudiation of the cause
> Which brought it all about.

And yet, the confessor declares: "Never, I swear to you, shall I oppose / The ends we both desire."[39]

Trumbo also had to reconceive his relationship with the SWG. It had began to dun him for his dues, and in his typically tart manner, Trumbo wrote to Harry Tugend, the guild treasurer: "I thought it [your last letter demanding payment] rather loud and more than ordinarily witless, but to deny you those qualities would be to silence you altogether; and that, for constitutional reasons alone, I should not like to see happen. I can't clearly make out whether your main quarrel is with me or the Mother Tongue, you have damaged us both almost beyond repair."[40] But, being a loyal guild member, Trumbo made an arrangement to pay a yearly sum, based on an estimation of his gross earnings. When the blacklist ended, he promised to provide an accurate accounting. This agreement was based on a mutual recognition that he could not, as a blacklisted writer working on the black market, reveal his pseudonyms or the producers he was writing for.[41]

In February 1948 Trumbo asked to dissolve his contract with Berg-Allenberg. He started work on an original screenplay and began to revise a script titled "Gun Crazy" for King Brothers. He did not, however, intend to "put out feelers" for more black-market work. As he told Sam Zimbalist: "Just as I do not wish to hock the ranch, neither do I wish to fall into the trap of getting money by anonymous work in which there is no merit, no satisfaction and no real gain. I have my eyes on other goals." The main goal was to write a Broadway play, and the prospect of doing so invigorated him. He told Zimbalist:

> One of the nicest things that has happened is the discovery that I have a reputation outside of Hollywood. Although I am as full of vanity and arrogance as the next one, still I had never realized it. I have been approached by two top New York producers. . . . They appear to have no fear about my name driving customers away, or how it may affect movie sales. . . . You better than most—and certainly better than the gentlemen who have sought my services—know how little I understand about the theatre; you know the six plays I have seen in my life. However I set to work in the long night hours trying to learn. Instead of going to Norman Krasna, Garson Kanin and F. Hugh Herbert [all screenwriters], I began an intensive reading of Ibsen, Shaw, Chekhov and the Irish playwrights. . . . I cannot tell you how much pleasure it gives me to be writing on something which is mine, something over which I possess complete control, and something which is new to me and fraught with danger and speculation. I am transported back to the time when I was trying to write novels—the same nervous interest, continuing and mounting from day to day; the same wonderment as to whether it is good or whether it stinks; the same trepidation of the thought of failure and the same dreaming of success. My mind is actually working—I am on my own—hammering at the doors of an entirely new way of writing. And I must say—whether I win, lose or draw—I have the feeling of living and of pitting myself against the best that others are able to do. I had forgotten how it felt, and it feels good.[42]

But before Trumbo could finalize the play deal or sell his original screenplay, he had to find a way around his suspension from MGM. Since he had not been fired, his contract remained in force, and it allowed him

to write original material only during a leave of absence. But according to Gang, if Trumbo asked for a leave of absence, it would compromise his civil case against the studio. Trumbo told Charles Katz, who
was overseeing the sale of the original screenplay: "I want this to be the
darkest kind of secret between us, not only so that Metro won't discover
this violation of their contract, but also to protect the guy under whose
name it is being sent out, since the faintest rumor might harm his career
in the sense that whatever good work he has done in the past or might
[do] in the future could, by such rumor, be attributed to me, hence spoil-
ing his own reputation."[43] In August his lawyers finally worked out an
agreement with MGM, allowing Trumbo to sign, without prejudicing
his civil suit against the studio, a contract with Lee Sabinson to produce
a play titled *The Biggest Thief in Town*.[44]

Although Trumbo reported total earnings of $34,258.50, from sales
and royalties, on his 1948 income tax return, he was unable to meet
his expenses.[45] To support his family, Trumbo asked to borrow money
from his friends ($3,000 from Katharine Hepburn, $3,000 from Lewis
Milestone, $1,000 from John Garfield, $2,000 from Charles Katz, and
$2,000 from Yip Harburg) and took on more black-market work.[46] He
now had to juggle both his time and his projects. He told his business
manager that although he had earned $1,000 for Project A, Project B had
earned him nothing because "the promoter had no money to pay for it,
and will not pay. It has nothing to do with the quality of the work, which
is first-rate. It is simply that a shoestring operator has run out of cash,
has defaulted on a verbal contract, and, for a number of reasons, I have
no legal recourse against him. I must take the loss in silence." Trumbo
had to stop working on Project C when the producers of his play flew in
from New York for conferences, and by the time the meetings were over,
"there was not enough time to bring Project C to the point where it would
offer me any significant financial relief. . . . Therefore I reversed my field
completely, temporarily dropped Project C, and addressed myself to a
new long shot." That gamble, on Project D, succeeded, netting Trumbo
$20,000 when he sold it to a major studio.[47] During the first quarter
of 1949, however, he earned no money, and his debts were in excess of
$12,000. In June he anticipated "four more weeks of panic living,"[48] but,
to his surprise, he ended up earning nearly $50,000 that year.[49]

On December 5 Trumbo and the other nine witnesses who had been
cited for contempt of Congress were indicted by a federal grand jury on
two counts. Trumbo's indictment read:

> Dalton Trumbo, having been summoned as a witness by the
> authority of the House of Representatives of the United States
> to give testimony upon a matter under inquiry before the Com-
> mittee on Un-American activities of the said House of Rep-
> resentatives, and having appeared before the said Committee
> at its session within the District of Columbia on October 28,
> 1947, refused to answer a question put to him by the Com-
> mittee, namely, whether or not he was a member of the Screen
> Writers Guild, which question was a question pertinent to the
> question under inquiry. . . . [And] refused to answer a question
> put to him by the Committee, namely, whether or not he was or
> had ever been a member of the Communist Party, which ques-
> tion was a question pertinent to the question under inquiry.[50]

The ten indicted men had to travel to Washington for their arraign-
ment. Lawson and Trumbo, the first two witnesses who had been cited
for contempt, were also the first two arraigned, on January 9, 1948.
Both men pleaded not guilty. On January 30 Robert W. Kenny filed a
motion to dismiss the indictments against all of the Ten, citing the committee's wholesale violation of the defendants' First Amendment rights.
The motion was denied, and the trial was set for April.

In the intervening months, Trumbo made speeches about the case
in Boston and at Yale University. He and Scott were also scheduled to
address an audience at the University of New Hampshire, but the trust-
ees banned them from speaking anywhere on campus. Dartmouth College opened its doors to them the next day.[51]

The Ten's cause was dealt a stunning blow on March 18, when
they learned that the US Circuit Court of Appeals (for the District of
Columbia) had upheld the contempt of Congress convictions of members of the executive board of the Joint Anti-Fascist Refugee Committee. They had refused to provide the Committee on Un-American
Activities with records of the organization's contributors and aid recipients. In the court's majority opinion, Associate Justice E. Barrett Pret-
tyman, bowing before the powerful winds of the domestic cold war,
wrote: "We are considering a specific question only, which is whether
this Congressional Committee may inquire whether an individual is or
is not a believer in Communism or a member of the Communist Party."
He answered in the affirmative, stating that Congress has the power
to inquire "into threats to the existing form of government by extra-
constitutional processes of change." Since the Communist ideology is

"antithetical to the principles which underlie" the forms of government in the United States, Congress also has the power "to identify individuals who believe in Communism and those who belong to the party." Further, Congress does not have to wait until the danger posed by the Communist Party becomes a clear and present one. Congressional investigating committees have the authority to decide how pressing the current danger is and how intensive their inquiry should be.[52] Associate Justice Henry White Edgerton dissented, arguing that this particular congressional investigation abridged freedom of speech and inflicted punishment without a trial. The US Supreme Court denied certiorari. In effect, the majority opinion destroyed the basic pillar of the Ten's legal edifice. It established that the First Amendment did not protect witnesses from being compelled to disclose their political beliefs to a committee of Congress.

In the court of public opinion, the Ten's position was substantially weakened by the deepening of the Cold War, a spate of scary newspaper headlines, and a surge in anti-Communist sentiment. In March 1948, for example, the Communists staged a coup in Czechoslovakia, overthrowing an elected government. A headline in the *Los Angeles Times* read: "[Secretary of State George C.] Marshall Declares World Situation 'Very Serious'—Czech 'Reign of Terror' Denounced; Great Alarm Raised in U.S. Cited."[53]

Lawson was tried first. Although he was found guilty of contempt on April 20, the lawyers used the same legal strategy in Trumbo's case. But Philip Dunne, who had agreed to appear as a character witness for Trumbo, warned the lawyers that one of their key exhibits, the tape of Trumbo's committee testimony, would not have the intended effect. The lawyers expected the tape to prove that Trumbo had done his best to answer the questions posed to him. But after listening to the tape, Dunne told Robert Kenny: "To play the tape for the jury would be disastrous. What came through was a loud and obstreperous witness obviously evading the questions posed to him by a kindly and fatherly Congressman Thomas. There was nothing kindly and fatherly about Chairman Thomas, but that was how he managed to sound on that particular tape."[54]

Trumbo's trial commenced on April 29. In his opening statement, William Hitz, the assistant US attorney assigned to prosecute the case, stated: "The charge here is the intentional refusal to answer a question that was a proper question for the committee to ask of a particular witness." He then listed the elements that constituted the prosecution's case: Did the defendant appear as a witness? Was the defendant asked whether he was a member of the Screen Writers Guild and the Communist Party? Did the defendant give responsive answers to those questions?[55] The prosecution called only one witness, committee member John McDowell (R-Pa.).

The defense called several witnesses: Dunne; Louis B. Mayer; Herbert Blankenhorn, a labor economist; Gerard M. Cahill, an employee of the Motion Picture Association of America; and Richard Griffith, executive director of the National Board of Review of Motion Pictures. Judge David Andrew Pine, however, sustained every objection made by the prosecution challenging the materiality of the defense attorneys' questioning of these witnesses, ruling that "it is no concern of the jury whether this man is a Communist or not a Communist; whether he is a good screen writer or not a good screen writer; whether the House Committee on Un-American Activities has conducted its hearing according to their concept of fairness or otherwise."[56]

At the end of its case, the defense submitted seventy-eight prayers related to the jury instructions. Judge Pine treated them with scorn, questioned whether they had been submitted in "good faith," and reprimanded the defense attorneys. The purpose of such prayers, he said, "is to enlighten and illuminate, not to confuse and becloud. Aside from your constitutional questions, the issues before the jury and the principles of law which this jury will have to have given them are extremely few and simple. I shall look over them during the night, but if I feel tomorrow as I feel now, I shall deny them all and instruct the jury in my own way."[57] On May 5 Pine rejected all seventy-eight prayers and issued his own instructions to the jury:

> You are not called upon to decide whether the defendant is or is not a member of the Communist Party; nor whether or not his work as a writer is good or bad; nor whether he is or is not a member of the Screen Writers Guild; nor whether or not there has been any infiltration of communism in the motion picture industry; nor whether the Committee on Un-American Activities conducted its hearing in a fair or unfair manner; nor whether or not certain members of this committee, or its chief investigator sought to blacklist or cause the discharge of this defendant by his employers. . . . The truth or falsity of [the statements the defendant made to the committee] is not before you.[58]

Judge Pine instructed the jury that it could consider only the following "essential elements": that defendant had been summoned to appear by a legally constituted subcommittee of Congress, that he did appear, that "a legally constituted sub-committee" was sitting during the defendant's appearance, that the defendant was asked whether he was a member of the Screen Writers Guild and the Communist Party, and that the defendant refused to answer those questions. Pine then defined what he meant by an "answer." It was, he said, "a responsive reply; it does not mean any kind of reply that a person desires to give. So a witness may refuse to answer by making an unresponsive reply or statement when he does so not accidentally but intentionally, knowingly, with full understanding of the question and after being given a reasonable opportunity to answer responsively. His motives, as distinguished from his intent, in making the statements may not be considered."[59] Charles Katz objected to that definition, saying: "We think properly a witness can be guilty of contempt only when he actually refuses to answer, and that refusal means more than the mere giving of a non-responsive reply." The objection was denied.[60]

The jury arrived at a guilty verdict that same day. Katz remembered that when he and Trumbo left the courtroom, they spied three black women jurors standing on the steps of the building. When Katz and Trumbo approached them, they ran. It was, Katz remarked, a kind of visual testimonial that, in the minds of some jurors, he and Trumbo "were the devils."[61] Many years later, in the documentary film *Hollywood on Trial* (Cinema Associates, 1976), Trumbo stated: "As far as I was concerned, it was a completely just verdict. I had contempt for that Congress and have had contempt for several since. And on the basis of guilt or innocence, I could never really complain very much. That this was a crime or misdemeanor was the complaint, my complaint." When the interviewer asked whether he would have acted differently had he known the outcome, Trumbo replied: "I don't know. I don't believe anyone knows. It's hard enough for me to predict what I am going to do in an ordinary event, in the ordinary course of circumstances. I hope I wouldn't have, and I think probably I would not have. But I really can say no more than probably, because you don't know. I had three children, I had a nice wife, why should I go to jail?"

Trumbo's attorneys filed a motion for a new trial that listed seven classes of errors, including the sustained objections to the defense attorneys' questions and the judge's charge to the jury. On May 21 Judge Pine denied that motion and then pronounced sentence on Trumbo:

"imprisonment for a period of Twelve (12) months in a Common Jail" and a fine of $1,000. In his statement to the court, Trumbo said: "I have searched my conscience deeply—and I have discovered there no word or act of thought which departs in any degree from those obligations which citizenship imposes equally upon us all."[62] The attorneys immediately filed a notice of appeal, and to avoid the expense of eight more trials, the remaining eight defendants stipulated their guilt. One judge sentenced six of them to one-year prison terms; a different judge sentenced Biberman and Dmytryk to six months.

As a result of these verdicts, ten professional men ranging in age from thirty-two (Lardner) to fifty-seven (Ornitz) were going to prison because they had refused to answer two questions. These questions, they believed, had been political, not legislative, in intent, and neither of them had any bearing on the national security of the United States. None of the men had engaged in any conspiracy or criminal activity; they had not impeded, in any way, Congress's authority to legislate.

Trumbo wrote to Cleo: "It is a curious thing, this business I have been through. As you get into it, you begin to disassociate yourself from it. You are there, in that chair, before that tribunal, only in body. The rest of you has become remote. You watch the stately, formal little dance of legality as if it were someone else involved. You become so scornful of it you can no longer take it seriously. So all that is left is a detached interest, polite and very cool."[63] And he told the *Daily Worker*: "You can't hope for a fair trial before a jury, the majority of which are government employees. They're subject to the loyalty test and are operating under the possibility that they themselves may be persecuted." Two consequences of his trial and conviction bothered him deeply. First, he felt that the media had lowered an ominous curtain of silence on the trials. Second, he predicted a reappearance in Hollywood movies of the "more vicious and calculated" stereotypes, such as "the comic Jew, the Uncle Tom Negro and the ignorant worker," which the Ten had largely removed from motion pictures.[64] (Actually, new stereotypes would appear: the murderous female, the gold-digging female, and the psychopathic soldier.)

Trumbo did, however, wax optimistic during his interview with a reporter from *PM*. He claimed to be "happier since this thing happened than I have been in the last 10 years. I am one of the few people in the U.S.A. for whom there is no wavering in the future," one of the few who knew how to defend "such a basic principle as civil liberties." He had no regrets, he continued: He would not, even if he could, go

Christopher, Cleo, Mitzi, Trumbo, and Nikola, 1948. Courtesy of Trumbo family.

back and change one word or one line from the time the hearings were announced to the time he was convicted. And if his pending prison sentence was not overturned by either the appellate court or the Supreme Court, he would still be at peace because, under the current political circumstances, "there's no other place [than prison] right now for a man in my situation. . . . But peace doesn't mean acquiescence. When this thing is over, whether we win or lose, these guys will know they've been in a fight. You've got to keep slugging. Once you stop slugging, you're a cooked goose." He predicted, with some degree of accuracy, that if the Ten's appeals failed and they went to prison, the Committee on Un-American Activities and federal prosecutors would have free rein against others like the Ten. The result would be a fascist country, and he accused the committee of being "the advance agency of American fascism." Every future witness called before that committee, he said, would be forced to decide whether to "cooperate with the objectives of fascism." Finally, Trumbo said that he stood forthrightly beside the twelve leaders of the Communist Party who had recently been threatened with indictment under the Alien Registration Act.[65]

Shortly after he returned to Los Angeles, Trumbo spoke at a rally for Henry A. Wallace, the presidential candidate of the Independent Progressive Party. Wallace was a staunch advocate of détente with the Soviet Union, and for several months he had been speaking out against the Truman administration's foreign and domestic Cold War policies. One of his campaign's pamphlets was titled *Stop the Drive to War.*[66] Although only a few Hollywood Communists had worked openly to organize this third party, many had contributed money. Two of the Hollywood Ten, Herbert Biberman and Albert Maltz, connected their campaign to stay out of prison with Wallace's presidential campaign, deeming it "part of the larger engagement in which the entire American people are involved."[67]

Two months later, Trumbo spoke at another Wallace gathering. He also wrote a letter to C. B. (Beanie) Baldwin, Wallace's campaign manager, stating that he hoped to travel east in September and remain there until the election: "I shall be happy and honored to write for, speak for, fight for or pick up the floor for Mr. Wallace."[68] Financial and other concerns kept him from making that trip, but he stated in October: "I am for Wallace because it is not possible for me or my family or any other decent person to live under the gathering cloud of fascism which presently envelops America." This "gathering cloud" included the generals and bankers who had usurped the powers of a democratic government; the Thomas Committee, which had flaunted the Constitution; those who murdered Negroes, reviled Jews, and broke workers' strikes; and Congress, which failed to provide veterans with homes but granted tax relief to the wealthy. Unless Wallace were elected, Trumbo was certain that "millions of young Americans" would soon be fighting and dying in support of "the United States' alliances with the world's dictators."[69] In the election, Wallace received 2.4 percent of the popular vote, and Truman won by a narrow margin.

Many years later, Trumbo admitted that the seeming success of the Wallace rallies had been deceptive. He wrote to Maltz: "When the shooting match was over the Progressive party didn't even represent a healthy political splinter." The people who had crowded Gilmore Stadium "represented only themselves."[70]

11

The Time of the Toad

His pamphlet *The Time of the Toad* demonstrated the depth to which the United States had, in his estimation, fallen, as a nation of laws, and his belief that those who resisted the committee and the blacklist and those who condemned both were the ones trying to save the country from its current fit of insanity.

—Christopher Trumbo

Shortly after his trial, Trumbo turned down, perhaps "rashly," he wrote to Charles Katz, "another black market venture." He explained, "I see no profit in putting in time and whatever talent I have on such projects, when I feel that my big gamble and my main chance lie in the play, which simply must be finished by the end of June."[1] The play, titled *The Emerald Staircase*, was based on Trumbo's experience as a cub reporter for the *Daily Sentinel* covering the mortuary beat. Corruption loomed large, and he used the practices of the undertaking industry to dramatize "the absurdity of the idea of commercial ethics." Undertakers were particularly ripe for dramatization because, in his words:

They have selected an enormously profitable business, not because they love it, not because they have a priestly feel for it, but because it is a damned good way to get rich. . . . The last struggle of society to extract money from the individual therefore occurs over the dead body. Vast establishments are incorporated for this single purpose, and millions of dollars are spent to attract customers. The go-getter gets lots of bodies and gets rich; the drudge gets few and stays poor. And the clearest way, it seemed to me, to show all of this was to take an impoverished undertaker and let him try to operate—as logically he

233

must—under the same set of ethics that govern, say, the real estate salesman, the stockbroker or the wildcat oil driller. Then the thing can be seen most clearly. And also the piety which conceals the commercial aims of the undertaker only a little better than it conceals the aim of the banker (whose advertising also reeks with piety), appears in the case of the undertaker to be more shocking and therefore funnier.[2]

The play contained only one direct comment on Trumbo's recent experience with the Committee on Un-American Activities, and it reflected his thinking about informing. One of the characters, pondering how to avoid a criminal indictment, says: "If it wasn't me, it had to be Joe. You can't clear yourself just by saying I didn't do it. Nobody'll believe you. You've got to tell on the guy that *did* do it."[3]

When Trumbo read the completed script to the Lardners, the Hunters, and Hy and Rheata Kraft, they collectively agreed that the first half was superb, and the second half was terrible. Trumbo acknowledged that he "had made the unforgivable error" of shifting the focus from one set of characters to another, resulting in "a disastrous dichotomy of feeling, and a complete letdown of interest." What had started out as "essentially a humane comedy" had morphed into an angry and heavy-handed drama. Convinced that the play's structure was "well-conceived and dramatically sound," he began a revision designed to return "the last half of the play to the people to whom it belongs."[4] This proved to be more difficult than expected. He told Lee Sabinson in late August: "Whether or not this damned thing can be salvaged I do not know. Perhaps I should start another at once; or again, perhaps I am not a playwright. You would be doing me a favor if you relieved my mind on these matters."[5] Trumbo persevered and finished the revised version in November; however, he had not resolved the comedy-drama dilemma, and the comic parts were not, at least by modern standards, consistently witty or amusing.

Just before he traveled to New York City on January 22, 1949, to watch the rehearsals, the Ten's defense committee asked him to make some speeches about the case. He agreed but added: "I am determined that nothing should interfere with the play, or with my work on it. Not that the play is such great shakes, but rather that it is important that it be successful if it has the seed of success in it. My authority for this is the decision taken by the Ten a year ago, in which it was declared that the greatest service any one could, during the blacklist, do the Ten would be for one of them to produce a hit novel or a hit play."[6] (Christopher estimated that his father delivered more than fifty speeches between the hearings and his imprisonment.)

The Emerald Staircase opened in New Haven, Connecticut, on February 23, 1949. It achieved moderate success there and in Philadelphia but received poor reviews in Boston. The critic for the *Boston Globe* characterized it as "a jumble of farce, melodrama, sentiment, sob story, social preachment and corn on the cob. Some of it is very funny, some of it is dull. There are flashes of brilliant writing."[7] After watching the previews, Trumbo concluded that he had failed to correct the play's original flaw: it was still an awkward combination of "a serious piece and a comedy." He therefore decided to cut the serious portion before the play opened in New York.[8] The night before the play—now renamed *The Biggest Thief in Town*—opened there, he told the *New York Times*: "The play started out as a drama of frustration. Then the audience and other factors changed it into what it is today. We hope it's a comedy. . . . It concerns a modest, decent, honest man badly in need of money for his daughter's education. And for this most moral of reasons, he commits an immoral act."[9]

After its March 30 opening in New York City, Brooks Atkinson, the *New York Times* drama critic, wrote: "To enjoy 'The Biggest Thief in Town' . . . you have to do Dalton Trumbo one favor. You have to agree that an undertaker's parlor is a comic place and that body-snatching is hilarious." Atkinson did not include himself among that group; nor did he admire Trumbo's construction skills, describing him as "an industrious joke-smith who knows how to pound a comedy together" but had to use "scotch tape" to keep it from falling apart.[10] Howard Barnes said the play lacked "sustained merriment."[11] Wolcott Gibbs wrote: "Mr. Trumbo, whatever his gifts as a political thinker may be, is a fairly primitive humorist, and his treatment of the subject strikes one as dull and objectionable to a really spectacular degree."[12] Other reviews were equally unflattering, except for the one in the *Daily Worker*, which called it an "amusing play" that had fallen victim to the "critics' bias against progressives and attacks on the powers that be."[13] The play closed after only thirteen performances in New York City, and Trumbo deemed it a "historical flop."[14]

Even before the play flopped, Trumbo was, as he informed two correspondents in July, "broke as a bankrupt's bastard." Of necessity, he had to return to the black market. He wrote to agent Bob Coryell: "Do any of your clients have a quick polish job or a sick script they'd like to have a coat of rouge put on? I'm their boy. I'd hate to take a project from scratch for the kind of money they're paying but I presume I'd even do that if I had to."[15] To George Willner, another agent and friend from the party, Trumbo took a more direct approach: "I shall be on the hunt for a little black market money. . . . The deal would be darker than dark—nothing in writing, no correspondence, toilet-meetings, etc. . . . Destroy this letter, too. Too goddam many things are getting subpoenaed these days. And mention it, when you solicit, as darkly and round-aboutly as possible—even in your own cozy little agency."[16] But despite his best efforts, someone told the FBI in 1950 that Trumbo was writing on the black market, although the informant was unable to name the scripts he had written.[17]

In early September Trumbo wrote to Elsie McKeogh that he had "put out my feelers on the black market which exists here rather sparsely, on fast, emergency jobs." In addition, he had begun work on an original screenplay—"Remember, O Remember," under the pseudonym Emmett Doyle—which he hoped might be salable to some magazine. He lamented: "My fingers are scummed with black market work. . . . My God, how bad a writer can become after ten years in the movies! It will take some time and hard work and an evener temper than I presently possess before I complete the job of intellectual re-tooling."[18] When Elsie responded that, to avoid deceiving her friends in the publishing world, she would have to reveal Trumbo's authorship, Trumbo decided he would submit his pseudonymous magazine stories either directly or through Willner.

By early autumn, Trumbo had completed the revision of the "Gun Crazy" script for Frank King. The script was based on a 1940 *Saturday Evening Post* story by MacKinlay Kantor that related the crime spree of a Bonnie-and-Clyde–type duo. Kantor had been hired by the Kings to adapt his story, and by the end of May 1947, he had written a first draft and revised it twice. According to notes in his papers, Kantor owned 25 percent of the film, but he had grown increasingly angry with the Kings, who constantly outvoted him on script decisions, and eventually sold his share of the project to them.[19]

Trumbo, who had agreed to forgo screen credit for his work, needed a front, so he asked Willner to sound out another of his clients, Millard Kaufman. Trumbo was not personally acquainted with Kaufman, but he probably knew about the pamphlet Kaufman had written for the United Auto Workers and the story he had written for the short-subject film *Expanding World Relationships*.[20] The Kings sent Kantor copies of the rewrites with Kaufman's name on them. In June 1948, when Kantor read the final version, he exploded in anger and proceeded to berate the brothers for employing "an apparent half-wit named Millard Kaufman to ruin my script. Mr. Kaufman was given to such original little turns as having the gunman kill time in his room by tossing a coin into the air. . . . Frankly, the only decent thing that survived in this picture were the scenes that Mr. Kaufman never got his fumbling fingers upon. Even though I was disassociated from production on this picture, it was a terrible pain to find myself sharing a screen credit with a writer of this caliber."[21] Kantor's assessment was unfairly harsh. Although the dialogue may have been stilted, Trumbo skillfully described the vagaries of sexual attraction and the relationship between sexual desire and violence, and his depiction of the pursuit and killing of the couple was chilling.

Trumbo was satisfied with the results. He wrote to Willner: "Those fellows [the King brothers] are hooked, I think. They have a good script, and they appear to respect me. The final draft [of "Gun Crazy"] goes to them in the same mail that this letter goes to you. Which brings up the matter of credit. They are willing for Kaufman to have credit, and I think he should take it. It will be no great shakes, but it will be a good production of its kind, and might lead to better things." He also enclosed a copy of his novella "Remember, O Remember," written by "Emmett Doyle," for which he wanted $6,000. Trumbo told Willner that Emmett Doyle was a nom de plume of "Beth Fincher," who "writes either under it or her own name." He added that "Beth Fincher" (aka Trumbo) wanted Willner to be her agent and to negotiate her next deal with the King brothers.[22] Trumbo told Sabinson that he had been offered a few other projects and had "a number of other ideas I have cuddled through the years, and I shall do nothing but sit up here in my mile high beauty and isolation and hammer them out."[23]

The film was originally released in October 1949 under the title *Deadly Is the Female*, with Kaufman and Kantor sharing the writing credit. The reviewer for *Daily Variety* wrote that the movie "starts slowly but eventually gets around to generating plenty of excitement."[24] That reviewer and the one for *Motion Picture Daily*, however, thought the characters and their motives remained superficial.[25] The *Hollywood Reporter*'s reviewer called the film "a dramatic and compelling adaptation" and described the story as "tightly-knit . . . fast, actionful, frequently thrilling, and always suspenseful." He congratulated the King brothers for "their most effective production since stepping into the Hollywood field a short decade ago as newcomers in Poverty Row."[26]

The movie became a cult film during the 1970s and is frequently cited as the precursor of Warren Beatty's *Bonnie and Clyde* (Warner Bros., 1967). However, most later commentators credit the director, Joseph Lewis, as the film's "creator."[27]

Even before *Deadly Is the Female* reached the screen, Trumbo realized he had become a hot commodity on the widening black market for scripts. He told his aunt and uncle: "I have signed for three pictures. . . . It appears that through one of the jobs, I shall be able to get as much work as I wish, with a percentage of the picture as a future backlog. It simply requires that I work three times as fast for about one-fifth my former price. But this is okay, since I don't need so much to live on as formerly, and work doesn't hurt me."[28] Willner, Gang, and Katz were finding assignments for him, and Trumbo was also writing original scripts and circulating them under the names of various fronts.[29]

When Trumbo learned that "Remember, O Remember" had been turned down by *American Magazine*, he told Elsie he was not surprised; it "is no good. . . . I would not publish it under my own name even if I were to be decorated rather than jailed by the Thomas Committee." He resolved to study the magazine market more carefully and do a better job in the future.[30] He then gave Willner the okay to peddle "Remember" to the studios and to be the "sole judge, sole distributor, sole tactician" of whatever Trumbo sent him. All Trumbo wanted in return was "sums, however small or large, derived from your chicanery, minus commission."[31] Kaufman agreed to act as Trumbo's front for "Remember,"[32] and Willner was able to sell it to Joe Cohn, a producer at MGM, for $35,000. Trumbo bragged to Elsie about the sale: "It's a very handsome relief. . . . I also feel smug about being able to command such a price under the name of a new writer. They're going to have to figure out new ways of blacklisting before they starve me out entirely."[33] "Remember" was not made into a movie. Indeed, Trumbo wrote on the script's title page: "It was impossible for anyone to make a film of it—and still is—because the story is preposterous. But people who are stupid enough to blacklist are also stupid enough to buy ridiculous stories. I wrote it to their taste out of revenge, and they bought it."[34]

In April 1949 Trumbo, in a much less smug mood, wrote to Willner: "I am laboring, with God knows how many groans, over the shittiest original that ever came along. . . . It is terribly difficult to write this crap without any enthusiasm at all, but only under the compulsion of the most deadly kind of necessity." He mentioned several other possible projects, but none of them excited him.[35] Two months later, Willner brought Trumbo a script titled "The Prowler" that producer Sam Spiegel wanted rewritten. It was similar in theme to *Double Indemnity* (Paramount, 1944), except that the male character was the initiator and manipulator of the scheme.[36] Spiegel promised to pay him $7,500— one-third up front and two-thirds within ninety days of delivery of the final draft. Hugo Butler, who was moving from one hotel room to another in an attempt to duck the subpoena he expected, agreed to put his name on the script. Although Butler made some changes, his wife, Jean, later called the script "much more Trumbo" than Butler.[37] It was an excellent script—dark, tense, and full of suspense—an expressionist depiction of the effect of displacement, unsettlement, and the decline of traditional values in postwar Southern California. Both "The Prowler" and "Gun Crazy," Christopher noted, captured a society in transition, the diminution of the American dream, and the suspicion and distrust that resulted. They reflected Trumbo's vision of "the cunning of the irrational individual, obsession (with guns, sexuality, and ambition), and the nature of evil and amorality."

The *Weekly Variety* reviewer called *The Prowler* "a bawdy, daring story" and lauded Joseph Losey's direction as "intelligent and sensitive to the story's broad theme."[38] Philip K. Scheuer called it "an eye popper . . . an extraordinarily persuasive job of movie making, in writing, direction and performance."[39] Trumbo, however, was disappointed with the final product. He saw the movie shortly after his release from prison and told Charles Katz, "I don't think 'The Prowler' will pay off, simply on my judgment that it is such a bad picture."[40]

The Prowler job also entangled Trumbo in a dispute with Spiegel (and, later, Losey).[41] Spiegel was notorious for not paying his employees, and Trumbo and Willner had failed to discuss payment terms for the second draft. Trumbo wrote to Willner: "I crawled on my belly to Sam for $500, and when I left Wednesday, he told me he had arranged with [Martin] Garbus for it to be given to me as a loan (not an advance on [the] second draft). It was to be sent in cash the following day, $100 to my mother in law, $100 to my mother and $300 mailed to me at the ranch. However it didn't arrive. . . . I simply must have money from these people immediately, or I am going to have to blow the deal," even though "it's a small stinking deal."[42] As it happened, Spiegel reneged on the final $2,500 he owed Trumbo. After years of fruitless efforts to collect, Trumbo took legal action, but he had to keep his name out of it. He assigned the claim to another person, who carried it through the courts and won a judgment. (Losey also had to sue Spiegel to get what was owed him.)

Before he learned about Spiegel's improbity, Trumbo agreed to adapt Frank Harris's *My Reminiscences as a Cowboy* for him. He was supposed to be paid $5,000 up front and $5,000 on delivery. Once again, Hugo Butler agreed to be the front. But Spiegel paid Butler only $4,000, and while Trumbo was in prison, Katz wrote to Cleo and Butler: "That bastard Spiegel finally, and after the most awful kind of procedure on my part, sent a check for $500. . . . He promises to make another payment on Wednesday, taking care of the balance, but I do not believe the son-of-a-bitch."[43]

Weary of these constant problems with small, independent producers, Trumbo made a resolution in August 1949 that he would find difficult to keep: "to have no more of these little deals, of which there is always a plethora, since they are no real solution to my truly heroic needs. I therefore intend, during the next three months, to gamble recklessly on original screenplays."[44] He did so partly because of his personal financial situation and partly because of the Ten's need for money to pay their legal fees. In line with this determination, he wrote an original script titled "Roman Holiday," for which he wanted $40,000. He told Willner: "I am now a fiendish machine, starting on another [original script], and if God is good and time lasts for me, I shall have three in your hands before I leave [for prison]."[45] He explained to Biberman the reasons for, and the physical costs of, writing one original work after another:

> I have the immediate problem of figuring out [how to earn] enough cash to provide for a wife and three children for nine months, plus the total support of two elderly women [his mother and mother-in-law] living in separate Hollywood apartments. The only way I have figured out how to solve this purely practical and, to me at least, absolutely urgent problem, is to spend 13 to 14 hours each night at my typewriter, and to continue this routine without break until the day I have to leave. In order to maintain it, I take drugs to put me to sleep without loss of time, and other drugs to awaken me promptly.[46]

One of these originals was a comedy about the girl who invented the Toni permanent wave (fronted by Butler), and another was a drama about a man executed for a crime he did not commit (fronted by Guy Endore). The latter sold for $40,000 but was never made into a film. In addition, Trumbo outlined the plot for a stage play that was a political parallel to *The Prowler*. It illustrated how a petit bourgeois type of individual, unable to move up in social class, comes to fear communism and "unconsciously to lean toward Fascism."[47]

While he was writing and revising *The Biggest Thief* and writing scripts for the black market, Trumbo was also working on his brilliant political pamphlet *The Time of the Toad*, which was published shortly after the circuit court denied Lawson and Trumbo's appeal and affirmed the committee's power to inquire into the political affiliations of witnesses.[48] The pamphlet was, Trumbo told his mother, aimed "mainly at intellectuals, the universities, the churches, the professions"—the people and institutions Trumbo considered most vulnerable to future committee investigations and, hence, those most likely to support the Ten.[49] He could have subtitled it "The Duty of a Loyal Citizen in a True Democracy Is to Work for the Destruction of the Committee on Un-American Activities." Since Trumbo was writing it on behalf of the Ten, it was agreed that Herbert Biberman and Ring Lardner Jr. would edit the pamphlet. Although they both approved of what Trumbo had written, Biberman wanted Trumbo to revise his statement that the Hollywood Ten's case was the first of its type. He reminded Trumbo of the similar cases involving the Joint Anti-Fascist Refugee Committee and Communist Party leaders and pointedly told him: "[the] weakness of pamphlet is that by posing ours as only important one—they resent it and we lose support—and it is *not true!*"[50]

Trumbo opened the pamphlet with a definition of what he called "toad-time." That designation was based on Émile Zola's article "Le Crapaud" (The Toad), in which he advised a young writer to swallow a live toad every day. Only by doing so, Zola sarcastically wrote, could the writer strengthen his stomach sufficiently to digest all the abusive remarks his work would receive in the press. Trumbo defined "toad-time" as "an epoch long or short as the temper of the people may permit, fatal or merely debilitating as the vitality of the people may determine, in which the nation turns upon itself in a kind of compulsive madness to deny all in its traditions that is clean, to exalt all that is vile, and to destroy any heretical minority which asserts toad-meat not to be the delicacy which governmental edicts declare it. Triple heralds of the Time of the Toad are the loyalty oath, the compulsory revelation of faith, and the secret police."[51]

As two examples of toad-time, Trumbo cited Nazi Germany and the United States from 1938 to the present (the era of the Committee on

Un-American Activities). Since 1938, that committee "has flouted every
principle of Constitutional immunity, denied due process and right of
cross-examination, imposed illegal sanctions, accepted hearsay and
perjury as evidence, served as a rostrum for American fascism, impeded
the war effort, acted as agent for employer groups against labor, set
itself up as a censor over science, education, and the cinema and as arbiter over political thought, and instituted a reign of terror over all who
rely in any degree upon public favor for the full employment of their talents" (6). It has, Trumbo continued, "arrogated to itself at the expense
of the Constitution" the right "to inquire into the realm of political
thought, affiliation and association." Its power lies specifically in its
asserted right to ask a single question: "'Are you now or have you ever
been a member of the Communist Party?'—a question to which thirty
years of propaganda has lent a connotation so terrible that even the asking of it, regardless of the answer, can imperil a man's career and seriously qualify his future existence as a citizen free from violence under
the law" (7).

The people of the United States could weaken or destroy the committee's immense power, according to Trumbo, but only if they directly
confront it—"only if the dread question is faced and the servile answer
refused; only if the courts, by reason of the individual's refusal to surrender to the committee, are obliged once and for all to rule on the
validity of the Bill of Rights as opposed to that of any inquisitorial body
however constituted" (7). The issue is a simple one, Trumbo insisted:
Either the committee or the individual witness will be destroyed. An
individual who is called before this committee "must either collaborate
with its members in their destruction of civil rights, or by his refusal
attempt to destroy the committee's fraudulent power and mark out its
limitations" (7). And the times are such that it falls to every committee
witness who is concerned about the dissemination of ideas and unre-
stricted inquiry "to provoke the legal conflict which alone can restore
the rule of law. . . . [H]e stands in solitude between the Constitution and
those who would destroy it. He can surrender or fight. He can assert his
rights, or answer the question" (17).

Trumbo acknowledged that every witness, regardless of his or her
affiliation, faced difficult dilemmas. It should be recalled that he was not,
in this pamphlet, addressing the issue of the "stool pigeon"—a former
Communist who named his or her former comrades. Rather, Trumbo
was mainly concerned with the two types of witnesses—"friendly" and
"unfriendly"—he had seen at the 1947 hearings. The latter individual—

a Communist (meaning someone who is still a party member or has quietly resigned) who is asked the question, "Are you now or have you ever been . . . ?"—has no safe harbor. If he or she denies party membership, the penalty is perjury; if he or she refuses to answer, the penalty is contempt of Congress; if he or she answers the question, the next question is inevitably, "Who else is in the party?" This involves the witness in such a nauseating "quagmire of betrayal that no man however sympathetic to his predicament can view him without loathing" (17). (As it turned out, some "betraying" witnesses became well-paid agents of the Department of Justice, while others were heralded as real patriots.)

The situation of the "friendly" (non-Communist) witness was no better: "He must determine for himself whether, by casting aside the immunity with which he is clothed, he wishes to assist the committee in its pursuit of an illegal end. He must consider the precedent which his act establishes. He must decide whether he wishes absolution and approbation at such hands. He must consider the frightened men of Germany. . . . He must consider the texture of the toad, and its desirability for his children. Then he must say no to the question, or he must not answer at all" (18).

The second major target of Trumbo's animus, after the committee, was the liberal "intellectual" of the Schlesinger stripe—those who constituted what Trumbo called the "new Liberalism" or the "non-Communist Left." These types of people, he wrote, have "no stomach for liberalism itself, save on a high and almost theological plane. When the battle is actually joined on a specific issue involving the lives and rights of existing men . . . they are not to be found in the lists. They abandon such earthy matters to organizations designated 'subversive' by the attorney-general." As a result of their cowardice, these "new liberals" have become the "non-anti-fascist-left," subscribing to a dogma that is "nine parts anti-Communist to one part anti-Toryism, or anti-reaction, or comically enough—anti-anything-but-fascism. For fascism is the dirty word of the sect: it must not be used because it has been willed out of existence" (23–24).

If these liberals truly wanted to defend the Constitution, Trumbo argued, they would have to defend Communists. But they must do so

> not with the high-piping invective of a Schlesinger, not while calling him a scoundrel worthy of hell's own damnation, for if you defend him in this manner your case is fatally weakened.
> . . . The legal principles which protect one against the force of

the state protect all. If a Communist comes first under attack
and is overwhelmed, the breach opened by his fall becomes
an avenue for the advance of the enemy with all his increased
prestige upon you. You need not agree with the Communist
while you engage in his and your common defense. You may,
indeed, oppose him with every honorable weapon in your arsenal, dissociate yourself from his theories and repudiate his final
objectives. But defend him you must, for his defeat in the Constitutional battle involves the overturn of principles which thus
far have stood as our principal barrier, short of bloodshed,
against fascism. (37)

Trumbo then shifted to the fate of the Hollywood Ten and the
consequences of their defeat in the courts. As a result of the guilty
verdicts pronounced by his and Lawson's juries and the circuit court's
upholding of those verdicts, the US government had been handed
the power to regulate political speech. Frightened by how this power
might be used against them, cultural, artistic, and professional institutions had begun censoring and purging their members. Although the
Ten's case was not the ultimate battle, it represented "a direct challenge to the censorial power of government over the human mind . . .
the immediate outpost in a long line of battle." If people fortify that
outpost, it might continue to stand, and if it does, "all will hold, and
even advance a little. If it falls, all will share in the defeat and in the
hard years of struggle to make up for it" (38). These words proved to
be an accurate prediction of the atmosphere in the United States for
the next seven years.

The Time of the Toad was very well received by the Left. It was
reprinted twice and sold 50,000 copies. Biberman, in his typically over-
optimistic manner, announced that it was "going to pay off in every
conceivable way," by which he meant it would keep the Ten out of jail,
allow them to win their breach-of-contract suits, and improve "the total
political climate in the country."[52] Albert Maltz thought it was "juicy,
sassy, and wonderful. A quite extraordinary achievement" that would
help the Ten very much.[53] Future informers Pauline and Leo Townsend
concurred, pronouncing it "the best damned piece of political journal-
ism since Tom Paine."[54] Marsha Hunt, a member of the Committee for
the First Amendment who was blacklisted when she refused to apologize for her opposition to the committee, later said she found it "brilliant, gutsy, irreverent, cynical, furious, absolutely outraged."[55] Joseph

THE TIME OF THE TOAD
A Study of Inquisition in America
by Dalton Trumbo

The Time of the Toad, 1992 British edition.

Morton reviewed it favorably in *Daily People's World* but criticized Trumbo for failing to document all the government's prosecutions and failing to emphasize that the trial of the Communist Party leaders was the "keystone" of the present fascist drive. Although Trumbo acknowledged that Morton was correct in these criticisms, he challenged Morton's claim that "toad-times" were solely the work of a ruling minority. While they are never initiated by the majority of the people or the workers, toad-times are often accepted by them.[56]

While he was writing this pamphlet, Trumbo agreed to be a cosponsor of the Cultural and Scientific Conference for World Peace, which met in March 1949 in New York City. The conference, sponsored by the National Council of the Arts, Sciences, and Professions, was intended to "smash the artificial iron curtain erected by the cold warriors" and to summon people of whatever nationality "to resume the free interchange of ideas, of art and of science." It was, in effect, a call to end the Cold War.[57] Years later, in response to a letter from Cedric Belfrage inquiring whether Trumbo still felt proud of being a cosponsor, Trumbo replied:

> The word "proud" has always troubled me. People are "proud" to be Americans, "proud" to be Russians, "proud" to be Republicans or Democrats or Communists, "proud" to be black, white, brown, or yellow. Why such things make them proud I have no idea, and because I do not understand the word as they use it I try to avoid it altogether in describing my own feelings. I am glad that I sponsored it, I have never regretted my sponsorship of it, and doubt that I ever shall. I am quite content that in the midst of those first wild salvos of the Cold War, I chose to stand for peace. I still do.[58]

In May he told an emergency meeting organized by the California Legislative Conference and the National Lawyers Guild: "We have come to this meeting for the purpose of protecting ourselves against the merchants of fascism in the United States. We are no longer fighting fascism, we are now facing open tyranny, the same as once existed in Germany. . . . No degree of caution will satisfy these new agents of totalitarianism."[59] In November he spoke about the Ten's case in St. Louis, Minneapolis, Madison, Duluth, Milwaukee, and Chicago.

During this time, Paul Jarrico, head of the Film Division of the

Free the Hollywood Ten rally, 1949. Left to right: Lester Cole, unidentified woman, Dalton Trumbo, Alvah Bessie, Nikola Trumbo, Albert Maltz, Christopher Trumbo, Cleo Trumbo, Frances Lardner, Ring Lardner Jr., Ben Margolis, unidentified woman and man, Herbert Biberman, unidentified woman and man. Courtesy of Trumbo family.

Hollywood Arts, Sciences, and Professions, produced a film about the Ten to raise money for their legal fees and to warn the people of the United States about the threat to their civil liberties. The Ten cowrote the script, and John Berry directed it. The first half of the film focuses on the Ten's private lives and their professional achievements; during the second half, each man delivers a speech of warning. Trumbo asks rhetorically: "Why didn't we avoid all this? Why didn't we answer the questions, 'yes' or 'no,' as the Committee demanded? Because we wanted to challenge the right of the Committee to ask such questions." A few minutes later he warns: "When we were asked, 'are you now, or have you ever been, a member of the Communist Party?' the Committee was really preparing to ask you, 'are you now, or have you ever been, in favor of peace?'"[60] Some of the wives were asked to speak at showings of this film, and Cleo agreed to be one of them. She told the audience: "I am not accustomed to speaking in public. However, neither am I accustomed to having my husband in prison, and I must take whatever course will hasten his release. We've all got to find new ways to free the Ten."[61]

On October 19, a few months before going to prison, Trumbo spent two hours in a municipal jail on a charge of public drunkenness. In Trumbo's version of events, he had been searching for a drink for most of the day, without success. That evening, he met Ian and Alice Hunter for dinner, after which the three of them repaired to the Hunters' home, where Trumbo consumed two highballs. At 1:30 a.m. he decided it was too late to return to the ranch, so he prepared to spend the night there. Before going to bed, however, he needed to urinate. That, Trumbo told his uncle, is when things took an interesting turn:

> I don't want to urinate in the only toilet, because the thing goes dribble-dabble for hours afterward unless one jiggles handle violently. Violent jiggling invariably awakes baby in next room. I go outside to curb. Very remote little residential section, a G.I. community. No moon. No streetlights. No lights in any house except ours. No traffic. No people. Haul out and urinate as my father taught me to. Car turns corner, catches me like moth in powerful light. Try quickly to insert penis back in pants. Car stops. Am trapped while still buttoning.
>   Police want identification. I give. Want to know what I am doing. I say urinating in gutter, pardon the expression. They say why. I say toilet jammed, dribble-dabble, jiggle, child, disturbance, innate courtesy, here I am. They say drinking? I say yes. They say when last. I say two minutes ago. They say drunk! I say no. Then I say, with anger, the way they talk would think I'd been drinking since six-thirty in the morning. (This choice quote comes out in one paper as saying boasted of capacity, said had been drinking since six-thirty a.m.) They say climb in car. I do. Hunter comes flapping out in bathrobe crying outrage, snatch, violation of rights. I tell him not to worry, I'll take sobriety test, be back in twenty minutes.[62]

The police refused to give Trumbo a sobriety test and locked him in a cell. Hunter arrived and called an attorney, who advised Trumbo to just pay the $20 fine. Trumbo did so, but as soon as he was released, he drove immediately to the home of a doctor, who gave him a sobriety test and took a blood sample.

The *Los Angeles Times* headlined its four-paragraph story about the incident: "Contempt Case Screen Writer Held as Drunk." It ran a photograph of Trumbo but did not quote anyone involved.[63] The newspaper stories depicted Trumbo as being "in [a] fighting mood." He told his uncle: "With lawyers I make plans for trial and acquittal, which is a cinch. Prosecution lets it be known if I testify in court I was urinating in gutter in defense of drunk charge, they will then file charges of indecent exposure. This is a nasty charge, generally associated with waving genitals at young children. Can't stand trial on that too. Publicity not good."[64] Finally, the two sides reached a compromise: the police would not prosecute, and Trumbo would not plead guilty to drunkenness. On the day of the trial, neither side appeared, and the case was dismissed.[65] Trumbo told his uncle: "Bail was forfeited. I am not guilty of any misdemeanor. On the records I am guilty neither of being drunk nor of urinating in gutter. Seemed best solution to get thing out of headlines, keep my aging puss out of pictorial section."[66]

Years later, at Trumbo's memorial, Hunter told a slightly different version of the story. When he arrived at the police station to provide bail, Hunter discovered:

> Bail was not the problem. Trumbo had enough cash for that on him. The problem was that Dalton had made various stands on principle, the final one being that Trumbo would not allow himself to be let out unless his cell mate of the previous evening, with whom he had established instant rapport, was let out with him. I think the cops kind of wanted to get Trumbo the hell out of there by this time, and they let me talk to him through the bars of the cell. He accepted my proposal that we use my cash for his bail, so that he, when he regained his wallet, could use his cash for the cell mate's bail. That was done and the incident ended.[67]

On April 10, 1950, the Supreme Court refused to grant certiorari to the Lawson and Trumbo appeals. A petition to reconsider was also rejected. Two days after this decision was announced, all the members of the Hollywood Ten and the eleven defendants in the *Barsky* (Joint Anti-Fascist Refugee Committee) case, whose appeal had also been rejected, appeared at three "Deadline for Freedom Rallies" in New York City. They told their audiences: "Until the Un-American Activities Committee is declared unconstitutional no individual can be safe from smears

and threats, the blacklists and even prison terms for which this Congressional body is responsible." They urged all citizens to sign petitions
to the Supreme Court, demanding that it rule on the constitutionality
of the committee.[68]

Just before Trumbo left the ranch to travel east for his incarceration,
he was approached by Bob Roberts, the nominal head of Roberts Pictures (actually owned by actor John Garfield), to adapt a novel by Sam
Ross. Trumbo was to receive $5,000, deferred until January 1951, and
5 percent of the producer's profits.[69] According to Christopher: "Guy
Endore fronted at first and did some work on it. The director, John
Berry, made many changes. Then, Hugo Butler came on board, restored
much of Trumbo's work, and made his own contributions." Trumbo
later wrote to Roberts: "At your solicitation and upon your promise to
make immediately a picture called 'He Ran All the Way' at a *price not
to exceed $400,000* and possibly to run as little as $300,000, I agreed
to spend my last two weeks out of jail doing the script. . . . However you
exceeded the maximum budget we had agreed on by almost a quarter
of a million—and that came right out of my pocket. I ended up with
$5,000 for a backbreaking job. Everybody else on the picture got more.
. . . I have only that worthless 5%."[70] However, according to one of
Garfield's biographers, Roberts made every effort to hold expenses to a
minimum, and the picture was completed in six weeks.[71]

The movie's profit potential was actually torpedoed shortly after
shooting ended, when Garfield was subpoenaed by the Committee on
Un-American Activities. He testified on April 23, 1951, avowed that he
hated communism, denied being a party member, and claimed he did
not know whether anyone he was asked about, including Hugo Butler,
was a Communist.[72] Sharply criticized by many of his former friends, an
obviously exasperated Garfield replied: "Why can't you people understand? . . . I have this picture scheduled for release and my own money
riding on it. If I queer myself with this committee, we're wiped out. . . . I
have to do it this way, and besides, I'm *clean*."[73] He was not asked about
Trumbo because the committee was unaware Trumbo had written the
script for *He Ran All the Way*.

After Garfield left the witness stand, a committee spokesperson
announced that a transcript of Garfield's testimony would be sent to
the Department of Justice so the FBI could compare it with the Bureau's
files on him (to establish the basis for a possible perjury indictment).[74]
As a result of the subpoena and Garfield's committee statement, theaters refused to book *He Ran All the Way*. Criticized by both the Right

and the Left and seemingly blacklisted, the now-desperate Garfield met with Arnold Forster of the Anti-Defamation League in the hope of finding a way to clear himself. Forster recommended that he write a tell-all confession and arrange to have it published in a major magazine. Garfield completed his confession on May 18, but he died of a heart attack three days later. He was thirty-nine years old.[75]

Many years later, Cleo told the members of a committee of the Writers Guild of America, West, assigned to restore the credits of blacklisted writers: "[*He Ran All the Way*] was a screenplay Dalton was proud of and asked Hugo to see that no one tampered with it while he was in jail. I don't think Hugo did rewrites, but if he did they would have been minor."[76] Berry later stated that he and Jack Moss had tried to "fix up" Trumbo's script, but no one liked the result, so they hired Butler to restore what Trumbo had written. Berry then shot it, using an effective combination of neorealist and noir techniques. He later said it was "a helluva movie" and the best one he had worked on up to that time.[77] *He Ran All the Way* was one of Trumbo's darkest scripts, centered on an insecure sociopath who takes a family hostage. It captures well the paranoia of the early 1950s. Trumbo tipped his pen to his past by making the female lead a bakery worker. He also included a conversation between Garfield and the father of the hostage family (Wallace Ford), regarding resistance to a stronger force. Garfield buys dinner, but the family refuses to eat it. When Garfield insists, Ford says: "There's some things you can't make people do, Nick. Everybody gets to the point where they draw a line, and when that line is drawn, you can't force them any farther, even with a gun. Even if you beat them to death. People are like that." Garfield replies: "You read that in a book somewhere. You're dead wrong." When Garfield threatens to kill one of the family members, Ford relents. Clearly, Trumbo recognized that sometimes principles do bend to a force majeure, and different people have different bending points.

In June 1951, just before the movie opened, the Committee on Un-American Activities issued subpoenas for John Berry and Hugo Butler. Roberts immediately removed their names from all official advertising.[78] (Six of the people who worked on this movie ended up on the blacklist: Trumbo, Roberts, Endore, Butler, Berry, and associate producer Paul Trivers. Three actors were "graylisted": Garfield, Selena Royle, and Norman Lloyd.) Berry went to France to avoid his subpoena. In September, Roberts was named by Martin Berkeley, and he moved to England soon after.

The reviews for *He Ran All the Way* were generally positive. Most critics thought it was a suspenseful and exciting movie. Edwin Schallert called it "one of the deadliest and most relentless crime melodramas every fashioned,"[79] and Bosley Crowther congratulated Endore and Butler for having "penned a shock-crammed script."[80] Robert Hatch described the plot as "an ingenious idea" and the script as "well-written," but he faulted the ending: "a whole hierarchy of moral problems which the plot so neatly contrives is neatly evaded."[81] Though it did not fare well at the box office, *He Ran All the Way*, like *Gun Crazy* and *The Prowler*, is now considered a classic noir film. When it was shown at the San Francisco Film Festival in 1998, the brochure called it "one of the most ideologically charged films ever to come out of Hollywood."[82]

Thus, in a two-year period fraught with blacklisting, a contempt trial, financial ruin, and a looming prison sentence, Trumbo crafted four remarkable film scripts (three noir classics and *Roman Holiday*), a Broadway play, and a brilliant indictment of the domestic cold war. It is a feat that has rarely been matched in the annals of his profession.

No sooner had he completed *He Ran All the Way* than Frank King asked Trumbo to write a screenplay about a carnival, based on a story by Marcel Klauber and C. B. Williams titled "Backfire." Trumbo said no, but when King drove to the ranch and offered to pay Trumbo $8,000 for the script, he changed his mind.[83] Trumbo read dozens of books on circuses and carnivals, but he went to prison before he could begin writing.

Meanwhile, Trumbo was taking steps to ensure that his family had enough food to last them through his year of incarceration. Nikola recalled:

> We had a back porch, a kind of larder, which housed a large freezer and many shelves stocked with canned goods. To provide meat for the family he bought an incubator and 100 fertilized eggs and put the entire operation in the hands of Jim Martin, the ranch caretaker. When the eggs hatched and matured he split their number between our household and the Martins' in return for their labor when it came time to butcher the chickens. When that day came a kind of assembly line was set up with huge buckets of boiling water, a plucking area, and a gutting area, and of course a killing area. I remember it as a bloody and busy day. I was on the assembly line with the job

of cleaning gizzards. In the end we had 50 chickens which we froze and ate over the year he was gone. This was done with typical Trumbo flamboyance (don't order 50 chickens—instead hatch them and grow them) but also was born out of an emulation of his grandparents and an earlier time which I think he in some way was re-creating at the ranch.

Trumbo also left behind several guns. He had given Nikola and Chris .22-caliber rifles, along with "a rigorous gun safety course," according to Nikola. "We learned how to fire them, how to clean them, how to carry them, and how to store them. As a result we were incredibly careful with guns." On one occasion, while Trumbo was in prison, Cleo and the children thought they might have reason to use those guns. Nikola and Chris were on their way home from school when they heard that several convicts had escaped from jail, somewhere near Bakersfield, and were still on the loose. Nikola remembered:

When we got home we gathered together the weapons we had in preparation for a night's vigil, and we all climbed in Cleo and Trumbo's bed, which was always a treat. Chris and I each had two .22-caliber rifles, plus we had Trumbo's arsenal. But I think it was only our rifles that we had with us at the ready that night. I remember it as a great adventure. I don't think we believed that anything bad would happen to us. The event was more like the *Inner Sanctum* radio episodes we were so fond of listening to on Sunday afternoons, in which we outwitted the bad guys.

In early May 1950 Bob Roberts and his wife invited the Trumbos, Lardners, Richard Collins, and Carey McWilliams, among others, to their house. According to Collins, Trumbo looked "much older," but he joked a great deal. Trumbo said about Robert Kenny: "He didn't even have a conviction before [our trial]. I don't know why he had to break that cherry [with us]." Collins also noted that Trumbo was "anxious to get to jail and get it over with."[84]

12

Incarceration and Drift

> Each man owes his country
> At least a little time in jail,
> So it cannot be a matter of surprise
> That I have arrived at last before these gates
> Which have closed so many times on better men,
> And daily close upon my brothers.
>
> —Dalton Trumbo

On June 7, 1950, Trumbo and Lawson flew to New York City. They attended several farewell parties and a rally at Madison Square Garden sponsored by the New York Civil Rights Congress. More than a thousand people came to Penn Station to watch them board a night train to Washington, DC. There, Trumbo wrote, "Jack and I had the rather grotesque experience of being carried aloft through the crowd like a pair of startled, sacrificial bullocks on the way to the altar." (Ten days later, seven other members of the Ten spoke in New York City at a meeting sponsored by the National Council of the Arts, Sciences, and Professions.) When Lawson and Trumbo arrived in Washington, they held a press conference, went to the court building, and from there were taken to the district jail. Trumbo described himself as being "clean, well-fed, and getting lots of sleep."[1]

Despite their request that they be sent to federal facilities in the West, so they could be near their families, the Ten were all incarcerated in eastern prisons. Lawson and Trumbo were held for eleven days in Washington's District Jail. From there, Trumbo wrote to Cleo that he had only two regrets: contributing to Harry S. Truman's vice presidential campaign in 1944, and his "financial carelessness—the thousands of dollars I gave away, or contributed, or lent; with them, we would be much more comfortable economically."[2]

Trumbo (left) and John Howard Lawson at Penn Station, 1950, on their way to Washington, DC, and imprisonment. Courtesy of Trumbo family.

On the evening of June 20, he wrote: "We were dressed out in our own clothes, handcuffed to each other, and conducted by four gun-toting marshals to the Washington Station, where all six of us boarded a Baltimore and Ohio Pullman bound . . . for the Federal Correctional Institution in Ashland, Kentucky. Once aboard we were conducted to a compartment in which he [Lawson] and I spent the night leg shackled together in a single upper berth. Two marshals slept in the compartment's lower berths. One marshal slept in a compartment to our right, another in a separate compartment on our left."[3] They arrived at Ashland on June 21.

Trumbo was assigned prisoner number 7551. FBI director J. Edgar Hoover wrote to the special agent in charge of the Los Angeles office: "In view of the short period of incarceration of the 'Hollywood 10' it is believed advisable to retain their Security Index Cards," and he instructed the agent to change Trumbo's Security Index Card to read: "Residence address: Federal Correctional Institute, Ashland, Kentucky."[4] Trumbo would be eligible for parole in October; if he were denied parole, he would be eligible for release on April 9, 1951 (taking into account time served in the DC jail and time off for good behavior in both institutions).

Trumbo, in the poem cited in the epigraph, wrote that he came to

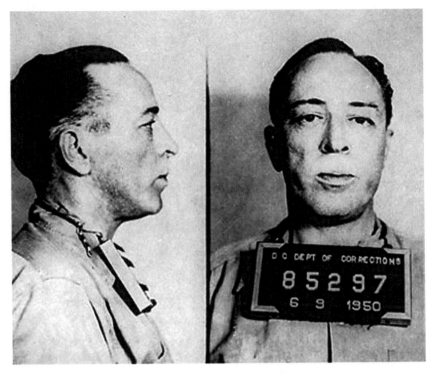

Trumbo mug shot, 1950. Courtesy of Trumbo family.

jail "not willingly, / And lay / Most easily upon my conscience." Rather than "crawl on his knees / In freedom to a bowl of buttered slops / Set out for him by some contemptuous clown, / He walked to jail on his feet." The conditions were not displeasing to him: "From what I have seen of the institution and its personnel, one could not wish for a pleasanter place, granted that one must be imprisoned in the first instance."[5]

Shortly after Trumbo arrived at Ashland, he was visited by Cleo, Christopher, and Mitzi (Nikola was at summer camp). "My ideas about jails," Christopher said, "came straight from the movies—Jimmy Cagney, the Big House." He expected to see fifty-foot stone walls, a guard tower looming over the road, and a mounted machine gun pointing down at them as they approached the entrance. Instead, the prison was surrounded by a tall wire fence with barbed wire on top; the layout resembled an army base, with a series of barracks. Christopher recalled, "We met him in a large room, one family among several who were visiting that day. I was secretly relieved that he was not wearing a uniform with gray and white stripes. He was dressed in khakis similar to those he had worn when he returned from the South Pacific. Despite my pleading, the guards would not let me go with my father into the barracks dormitory where he lived."

Most of the citizens of Ashland did not realize they had subversives in their midst. According to Allison Anders, "the prison had always been very low key about itself." When she asked her mother, Rachel Young, whether she knew about the men's presence, her mother replied: "No idea, and I'm glad we didn't know, because we would have been scared to death—you have no idea what it was like during that time and how scared we all were of Communists. We were so stupid."[6]

But one citizen, Bill Smith, was very much aware of them. Smith was a railway clerk, a lay pastor at Pollard Baptist Church, and a huge movie fan. Several days a week he ministered to the inmates, and during his first visit after the arrival of Trumbo and Lawson, he asked a trustee to identify Trumbo. Smith walked over to him and said, "Mr. Trumbo, I'm Bill Smith from Pollard Baptist Church. Is there anything I can do for you?" Trumbo responded, "Well, Bill Smith from Pollard Baptist Church, you could tell me what you are doing walking around with Montgomery Clift's head perched on your shoulders." (Smith told his son that, sans glasses and mustache, Trumbo resembled Humphrey Bogart.) Smith asked Trumbo about the movies he had written, and on one occasion he asked if Trumbo would like to see a cowboy movie being shown by a local man who owned a 16mm projector and a stack of old movies. "See it? I probably wrote it," Trumbo replied. Smith recalled Trumbo's "personal flair." Sometimes he looked almost regal, reading or writing in bed propped up with a pillow behind him, rolled-up blankets under each arm, and a sheet across his lap. Other times he buttoned the top button of his shirt and tied a bandana around his neck, like a short necktie. Smith was allowed to bring some of the inmates to his church and then home to dinner. When it was Trumbo, Lawson, and Scott's turn, they skipped the service and walked around town. Smith's mother remembered that Trumbo wore a yellow dandelion in the frayed hole of his prison work shirt.[7]

Trumbo was allowed to subscribe to as many newspapers and magazines as he could afford, and he could read whatever books he desired. Removed from "twenty-five years of the most intensive work, the sudden shucking off of all responsibility," he felt "a sense of almost exhilarating relief" at being in prison.[8] However, he hated the censorship of his letters, and he later observed: "Like all censorship, this knowledge of constant snoopery produces self-censorship, inhibits spontaneity, limits the areas in which truth can be spoken, and tempts the inmate to manufacture small, cheerful lies about prison life to please the warden. You're really not writing to your wife, you're writing to *him*."[9]

Trumbo said he felt safe in prison—"never safer"—but it is not clear what he felt safe from, and he could not stop himself from counting time:

> First, like a fool, by days—until I was approached by another con who said to me, "Look, bud, count by weeks, then by months; you'll never build up time by days." After a while you just don't think about it when you're in there. After all, you know how long you're in for and you know when you're going to get out, so there's really nothing to think about. You don't get depressed; you don't get morose: you just do your job. And I liked my job. I had a typewriter to use and I could sit down all day.[10]

He seemed to be popular with the other inmates. Many were illiterate, and Trumbo wrote letters for them. He later wryly commented: "Our conversations never seemed to dwell on our personal problems. The men were always able to sum up the world situation in a few choice words. They would talk about the friggin' President, the friggin' Russians and the friggin' A Bomb—and hope that if the friggin' bomb were to drop on this friggin' country, it would fall right in the middle of this friggin' prison."[11] Neither in his letters from prison nor later did Trumbo talk about his relations with Lawson and Scott, the other members of the Ten who were incarcerated at Ashland.

Though he was assigned a clerical job and given regular access to a typewriter, Trumbo did not find it easy to develop a steady work rhythm. In mid-August he wrote to Cleo:

> At last I have got down to work. As you probably gathered, it has been quite a problem. After my first impressions of conditions here, I concluded that the want of privacy would prevent serious work, and that I must therefore do strictly movie stuff and trivialities. However, I tried the trivialities, and not only were they extremely difficult to do, but, upon reading them, I found they were also extremely bad. Followed a period of inactivity and brooding. Then I concluded that precisely because of the conditions and interruptions, a serious work was the

only project that could possibly engross my attention so completely that I wouldn't notice the conditions or the interruptions. Accordingly, I started the war novel. . . . Miracle upon
miracle! It absorbs me completely, and neither wind nor rain
nor the hounds of hades can distract me from it. . . . [I]t is the
best prose I have ever written. . . . [A]nd if I am denied parole, I
shall have a finished novel to hand you when you pick this poor
depraved convict up on the front steps.[12]

A few days later he wrote: "Time absolutely rushes by. Every spare
moment is spent on the novel."[13]

In early October, as his parole review date approached, Cleo contacted more than a dozen people and asked them to write letters of
support to the parole board; only a few of them, including Bertram
Lippincott (Trumbo's former publisher) and Bert Allenberg (his former
agent), refused.[14] When Trumbo learned that all their applications for
parole had been denied, he was, according to Martin Popper, "as angry
as a fighting cock."[15] He was particularly angry with the eastern attorneys, whose approach to the parole board "had been formal, legalistic,
and perhaps a little timid." Deciding to take a more active role in the
parole proceedings, Trumbo proposed that the Ten's defense committee organize a "group of very distinguished citizens," represented by a
high-profile attorney, to petition the parole board to reconsider its decision. This petition should state that the board's rejection of the applications for parole had "set up the principle of No Parole for Political
Prisoners, which is a perversion of the very principle of parole."[16] Ben
Margolis suggested that the attorneys file a plea for executive clemency,
but Trumbo rejected that idea because, he said, it was a continuation
of "past errors, and diminishes our hope for release." In other words,
Trumbo did not want to ask for forgiveness; he wanted the authorities
to act responsibly. For this reason, he told Margolis that "all possible
emphasis" must be placed on an application for reconsideration of the
parole decision.[17]

In the months that followed, Trumbo was overtaken by a feeling
of melancholy. His novel writing bogged down because, as he wrote
to Cleo in early December: "It is very difficult, in terms of my work,
to develop ideas because I have no one to throw them to and help me
clarify them. At that point I am victim of the occupational disease of
all writers—the fear that I am drained of all ideas."[18] He tried to write
an original screenplay but found he could not do even that. "I think

the reason is that basically I hate them [screenplays], and in order to do them at all [I] must plunge in, hypnotize myself completely, concentrate exclusively on the story, and emerge five or six days later with the thing completed. Here I cannot do that, and the result is that working an hour or two a night, my dislike of the story gets the better of me and I am simply too nauseated to finish it."[19]

Money worries also weighed heavily. He told Cleo:

> More and more I realize that when I emerge from this place I must at last make the choice of whether I want to live at the rate of $35,000 a year as we always have, or whether I want truly to become a writer. I think it would be better for all of us if the latter course were taken, although it would entail certain sacrifices, including (unless we won a whopping law suit) the ranch. It seems very clear that with the kids growing into high school age as they are, we can't live at the ranch more than a year longer anyhow. Selling it, we could live practically anywhere in the world we wished for a year or two or three, during which I could accomplish the rather difficult but pleasurable task of shifting literary gears. But, with everything so unpredictable these days, exactly the opposite might work out. I am getting quite resigned here to surrendering myself amiably to events.[20]

Nor were his spirits lifted by a telegram he received at the end of December, signed by twenty Soviet writers congratulating him on his struggle for peace. "I thought," he later said, "Jesus, why me? The FBI has got it (it came by cable), and the guard was smiling like a child as he handed it to me, saying 'Happy new year from your friends.'"[21]

In mid-February Trumbo regrouped. He decided to stop working on the novel and start working on "one good original" movie script and two stories for what he called "the slick magazines." For the latter, he planned to create a "new person" (pen name); then, after his release, he would go to New York and find an agent willing to handle him and his pseudonym. As for the original script, he would submit it to a producer as soon as he arrived back in Los Angeles. Those tasks accomplished, he would complete the carnival script for the King brothers.[22] Two weeks later, he asked Cleo to get in touch with Hugo Butler and have him tell the Kings, "I'm their boy immediately upon my return to the old hunting grounds."[23] During his last two months at Ashland, a revitalized Trumbo wrote two stories and two scripts. Neither of the stories was published, but he later sold one of the scripts, titled "West from London."[24]

On March 21, three weeks before Trumbo's release date, Larry Parks (one of the Nineteen) was chosen to be the lead-off witness for a new investigation by the Committee on Un-American Activities into what it called the "Communist infiltration of [the] Hollywood motion-picture industry." The committee selected Parks because he would generate the biggest headlines. Two of his recent movies had been huge hits: *The Jolson Story* (Columbia, 1946) and *Jolson Sings Again* (Columbia, 1949). In a session that was both long and agonizing, Parks pleaded, without success, to be allowed to talk about himself and no one else. Each time he was asked whether a specific actor or actress was a Communist, he demurred, although he did provide the name of the person who had recruited him into the party. Finally, in an executive session, Parks caved in to the committee's demands and named twelve actors and actresses who had been in the same party branch with him.[25]

Christopher retained a fondness for Parks, whom he described as "handsome, younger than my father. He once came to the ranch on a motorcycle. The next time it was in a Piper Cub. Nobody had ever landed a plane up there. Niki and I ran out, ahead of our parents. I remember him helping me get up into the cockpit, which was even better than getting up on the Caterpillar tractor. I was intrigued by the dials, the levers, the steering mechanism. My father liked Larry Parks, and he felt sad and awful when he heard about Parks's testimony. He felt terribly sorry for him and thought of him as an involuntary informer." (Twenty years later, Trumbo bumped into Parks, greeted him, and shook his hand. He could not, Trumbo said, turn his back on Parks.)[26] By the time Trumbo walked out of Ashland in April, three other witnesses had also informed, including Richard Collins, another of the Nineteen. (None of them named Trumbo, but ten of the witnesses who testified over the next several months did so, putting him in ninth place on that particular hit parade.)

One can only guess what Trumbo was feeling or thinking when he walked out of Ashland a free man again. A few days before his release, in his "final notes," he wrote that the main character of his novel would discuss all the contradictions of the history of the United States, but not in a hateful manner. The novel, he noted, "should literally be saturated" with her love of this country.[27] He was not bitter. He did not hate the United States. He knew its government frequently made mistakes. He was, however, determined to wage war against this particular deviation. On their way home, he and Lawson stopped in New York, where they participated in a meeting sponsored by the New York Arts, Sciences, and Professions Committee. Trumbo pledged to continue the fight and told the audience: "The end of our careers, hell! This is the beginning of our careers. We're going to write the goddamnedest books and plays this country has ever seen. We're going to have a real people's culture at last."[28]

But when he returned to the ranch, he discovered that the world had become much more hostile, even though the family seemed to be in relatively good spirits. Cleo had worked hard to maintain the children's normal routines, and she constantly assured them that their father would be home soon. Two lengthy stays by the Butlers alleviated the intense strain she was feeling. The effect on the children, who ranged in age from six to twelve, is more difficult to ascertain. Certainly, their memories of that time are not dire. Nikola did not recall missing her father very much, and Christopher said life on the ranch went on pretty much as before; Mitzi's memories were hazy, but she remembered playing with the Butler children and how much she loved Hugo's "terrifying" ghost stories.

During his incarceration, there had arrived at the ranch "week after week . . . from all over the country threats and obscenities, of which anti-Semitism was the common denominator. Many of them were on penny postcards (which were naturally read by the personnel of the village post office) and almost all of them were anonymous." He learned that some of his neighbors had formed an organization "for the announced purpose of clearing the community of subversives when 'the time' arrived." In addition, Cleo had employed a retired policeman to accompany the children to school and elsewhere and to generally watch over them. FBI agents constantly came to the area asking questions; the American Legion sent emissaries to photograph the ranch, which were then printed in its magazine; and "a succession of men appeared at the ranch house door on vague missions which were never made quite clear."[29]

One of the more disturbing pieces of news Cleo shared with Trumbo concerned Edward G. Robinson. He had been listed in *Red Channels*, a smear publication, and in a frantic effort to clear himself, he had spoken to the FBI and appeared twice before the Committee on Un-American Activities. He must have told either the FBI or the committee that he had loaned money to Trumbo, because Robinson sent two of his attorneys to the ranch to ask Cleo for a copy of the letter Trumbo had written asking for $10,000. When she said she had no such letter, the attorneys asked her to sign certain documents. She refused. Then they asked her to speak with Robinson on the telephone, but she hung up when she realized he was recording the conversation.[30]

On June 8 Trumbo drove to Los Angeles to deliver a speech at the Embassy Auditorium. He reminded the audience what he and the Ten had said about how their blacklisting and imprisonment would affect the movies: "The American screen has become not only the home of force and violence, it has become the principal teacher and the most powerful advocate of force and violence. It has become the conscious spokesman for the cult of blood, brutality, perversion and war." (He was referring to the raft of war movies being produced by the studios, many of them about the Korean War.) He also warned his listeners that the Supreme Court's decision in *Dennis v. United States* (June 4, 1951)—to uphold the conviction of eleven leaders of the Communist Party—would further blight the freedom of communication in the United States, which now stands "on the threshold of Fascism."[31]

In September 1951 the FBI changed Trumbo's Security Index Card to read "unemployed."[32] In fact, he was employed, but on the black market. In January 1951 he received no income, but Hugo Butler owed him $2,300, and his checking account had a balance of $800.85. The next month he received another $1,800 from the Butlers, and his account balance was $695.68. In March he received $1,000 from Jean Butler, but his account now had a negative balance of $269.47.[33] He earned $4,410 between January 1 and June 3, 1952. He also received $75,000 from Loew's, in return for his agreement not to sue the studio for suspending him. After he had paid his attorneys and allocated small sums to the members of the Ten who had not been under contract in 1947, Trumbo netted $28,000. At his direction, his attorneys had crafted the settlement so that the money was paid neither as income nor as a settlement of the contract; rather, it was "recompense" for the damages inflicted on him by Loew's.[34]

Trumbo also settled, in a much less satisfactory manner, his increasingly troubled relationship with the Screen Writers Guild, which seemed unable to appreciate the nature of the motion picture blacklist. Guild staff repeatedly haggled with Trumbo over dues, pseudonyms, and credits. Finally, in mid-1952, Trumbo allowed his membership to lapse. The guild had agreed to grant studios the power to refuse screen credit to any writer publicly identified as a Communist by a friendly witness or

anyone who had appeared before a congressional investigating committee and invoked the Fifth Amendment. Trumbo later said: "I preferred
being a non-member to a dishonest one; I frankly did not wish to pay
money to an organization which spent a fairish amount of its income
enforcing rules that had the effect, though perhaps not the design, of
pauperizing me."[35] But more was at stake than credit. The guild's position on dues had placed Trumbo in a difficult situation: if he were honest about who had hired him to write black-market scripts, he would
have to dishonor the secrecy required by those who had hired him. If
the names of those hiring writers on the black market became known,
they might be blacklisted themselves, resulting in the end of the black
market.

In fact, the necessity for secrecy had increased markedly as a result
of the 1951 hearings. Since then, fewer producers were willing to buy
black-market scripts, and on April 13 George Willner was named by a
friendly witness. He appeared before the committee eleven days later,
invoked the Fifth Amendment, and was immediately blacklisted; the
studios refused to deal with him. Trumbo described the new situation
in a letter to novelist Nelson Algren, whom he had met during a speaking tour in 1949. Algren's best seller, *The Man with the Golden Arm*,
had just been published, and he was the head of the Chicago defense
committee for the Ten. The purpose of Trumbo's letter was to inquire
whether Algren—"on the off-chance" he might be interested "in an
occasional piece of dirty money"—would agree to front for Trumbo:

> Since I have been released from jail I find that most of the
> friends who accommodated me have either left town or are
> themselves blacklisted or are under some kind of cloud—the
> variety of clouds in Hollywood is enormous. Likewise my agent
> [George Willner] has been forced out. I hasten to add that none
> of the misfortunes befalling these people had anything to do
> with their black market connections with me, for the whole
> thing was quite secret. In considering how to resume opera-
> tions again, it has occurred to me that you might find such an
> arrangement acceptable. The procedure would be very simple.
> I would write a story which I considered saleable and mail it to
> you. You would send it to your agent in Hollywood as yours. If
> it sold, you would transfer to me my end of the cash made out
> in my wife's maiden name. You would report the whole sum
> as received in terms of your income tax, and deduct therefrom

the sum remitted to my wife, either as payment for her literary services, or as your outright purchase from her of a literary property. My wife, in our own income tax, would report
the money as received from you, and all the legalities would
be satisfied. . . . I am obliged to warn you in advance that an
original story, designed for sale on the local market, involves a
combination of prose and construction and sentimentality and
vulgarity that appalls even me, who am used to it, and would
appall you even more. The only thing which makes it possible
for a self-respecting writer to engage in such an enterprise is
that the story is never published, and is read only by Hollywood. A good rule, which I have always observed in the sale
of such material, is never to permit oneself to be inveigled into
taking a job to develop the material for the screen, because such
stories are not really designed to *make* motion pictures; they
are only designed to *sell* to them. . . . I need not add that secrecy
is the first element of your success in such a scheme. If I sent you
a story, you could be assured that no one would have read it.
. . . If you have any moral compunctions about such a procedure in relation to motion pictures, please forget them. Hollywood is a vast whorehouse, and any scheme by which tolerably
honest men can abstract money from it for their own purposes
is more than praiseworthy. If, however, you have compunctions
in terms of your own personal convictions about such matters,
then of course I shall forget about the matter entirely and with
complete understanding.[36]

Algren agreed, telling Trumbo that "anyone who'd reject such an offer
requires immediate medical attention." He assured Trumbo that he
knew all about the required secrecy, having earlier worked with Edward
Dmytryk on a King Brothers film that Willner had arranged.[37] Although
Trumbo wrote two other letters to Algren, promising to send him a
script each time, they never collaborated on any project. Two months
later, Trumbo wrote to Ray Murphy, his friend from the Pacific trip,
and offered him a similar arrangement: "I have a story idea I think I'll
do. It won't be any good, but it might sell. If you are still interested in a
bit of gentlemanly theft, I'll holler when it's done."[38]

Mainly, though, Trumbo was working for King Brothers, reading
scripts and writing the carnival story. He was, however, "badly broke,"
and he asked the brothers for an advance of $500, telling them: "I am

aware that you have already paid a generous advance, and are under no obligation at all to pay any attention to the problem." But if they were amenable to his request, it would save him from "the humiliation" of trying to borrow that amount.[39] Three days later they sent a check in that amount to "Beth Fincher." They also asked Trumbo for his advice, free of charge, on a script Michael Wilson had written for them.

Trumbo completed the first draft of the carnival story on July 11, for which he should have been paid $2,500. When he asked Frank King when he would receive the money, King asked him how much he actually needed. Assuming that the brothers were temporarily short of funds, he asked for only the $1,000 in back taxes he needed to pay the IRS to avoid its placing a lien on the ranch, which would prevent Trumbo from using the ranch as security for a loan. King promised to mail Trumbo a check for $1,000, but instead he sent only $500. Trumbo was forced to telephone the brothers, explaining that he would be forced to put the ranch on the market for a quick sale or lose everything.[40] The brothers immediately sent Trumbo a check for the balance. It should be noted that the King brothers were not, like Sam Spiegel, chronic defaulters. They were, however, tight-fisted and often insensitive to the financial plights of the blacklisted writers who worked for them.

The ongoing financial pressure led Trumbo to consider selling the ranch and moving out of the Los Angeles area. But where would they go? Mexico was a possibility. One of the Nineteen, Gordon Kahn, had already moved to Mexico City; another, Albert Maltz, had gone directly from prison to Cuernavaca; and the Butlers were enjoying a temporary stay in Ensenada. In June, Maltz wrote to Trumbo about the cost of living and the quality of schools in Mexico,[41] and Trumbo told Butler he was strongly tempted to move there, "but not to your fishy little community [in Ensenada]. To Mexico City." For some reason, he had convinced himself that he "could spend the next five or ten years in Mexico City or its environs and earn say forty or fifty thousand a year, which isn't at all improbable, and pay Mexican incomes taxes, and stash enormous sums of cash away."[42] Butler responded that he too was seriously contemplating a permanent move to Mexico, where he could live cheaply and avoid jail; however, he did not like the idea of living so far away from his close friends.[43] He later sent Trumbo a detailed letter in which he answered a series of questions about Mexico.

In July Trumbo told Biberman that he was leaning toward a move to Cuernavaca. He noted that although he was finding enough work in Hollywood, he did not enjoy any of it, and he found himself stalling a great deal of the time. "I am impatient for something to happen to us, good, bad or indifferent. I want to move somewhere."[44]

Trumbo also considered going to Europe, where a number of other blacklisted people had already moved. But he ran into an insurmountable obstacle: he could not get a passport. He applied for one in September 1951 so he could go to London to consult on his play *The Biggest Thief in Town*, which had opened in a small theater and then moved to a larger one in the West End. He also wanted to meet with the foreign publishers of his novels. He wrote to Ruth Shipley, chief of the Passport Department:

> The present political climate in this country has made it impossible for me to earn a living at my profession. This climate, however, does not prevail in England nor in those countries on the continent through which I plan to travel (Denmark, France, Switzerland, Italy). For example, my play "The Biggest Thief in Town" was excoriated by every New York newspaper and forced to close after a 1949 Broadway run of thirteen days. The same play, without a word changed, opened at the Duchess Theatre in the West End of London on August 14, 1951. It was enthusiastically received, not only by all of the London newspapers, but by all of the cultural reviews which thus far have dealt with it. It is now an established success . . . accumulating author's royalties which it is impossible for me to earn in the United States. . . . In a word, my passport applications are made for business reasons essential to my continued existence as a writer. I am not undertaking a speaking tour. I have not been invited, nor is it my purpose to attend, any congress, conference or assembly of any kind.[45]

Willis H. Young, acting chief of the Passport Department, rejected the application because, he told Trumbo, "the Department is of the opinion that your proposed travel abroad would be contrary to the interests of the United States."[46]

Trumbo also made some inquiries about moving to the East Coast, but, he told Butler, "There is practically nowhere in the U.S. where we can live much more cheaply than at present, unless we are willing to take a five room bungalow and live in dishwater clear up to the nose line. This being impractical, as well as self-defeating, since I cannot write and decently share household work at the same time, plus see my kids, I should be as bad off as at present, only on a more miserable scale." He had therefore decided that Mexico was the answer, but he noted it would be a more desirable option if the Butlers moved to the same city, "within a reasonable distance of each other." Trumbo was convinced that each of them could earn "an absolute minimum of 15Gs apiece each year directly out of Hollywood—with plenty of time left over for serious work." For Trumbo, the latter concern was paramount: "I want, and must have before I die, the opportunity to learn whether or not I can become a successful writer in my own terms. That is primary with me."[47] Shortly after writing that letter, Trumbo put the ranch up for sale, and the family began packing for the move to Mexico.

While he was still deciding about the move, Trumbo was approached by Herbert Biberman, who, along with Adrian Scott and Paul Jarrico, had established the Independent Productions Corporation (IPC). They wanted to make films from a leftist perspective, and they were particularly interested in films about racial minorities and racial issues. Biberman had become interested in the story of Jean Field, a divorced mother of two children who had moved to Santa Monica from Oklahoma and married a black man. In the summer of 1950 (just as the Korean War started) her two children returned to Oklahoma to visit their father and their paternal grandparents, who were appalled that Field had been encouraging her children to be friends with black children. During their stay the children received two letters from their mother that further aggravated the grandparents. In the first, Field expressed her support for the People's Democratic Republic of Korea and criticized those who directed the policies of the United States, which supported fascism the world over, killed all progressive legislation, and muzzled free speech and a free press. In the second letter she stated: "We are all so proud of the people's army in Korea." Her ex-husband, goaded by his parents, alleged that Field was teaching the children "Communist ideology" and sued for custody. Before the case came to trial, Field traveled to Oklahoma and took the children back to California with her. When an Oklahoma court awarded custody to the father, Field filed a custody case in California and asked the court for an injunction to prevent the children from being taken to Oklahoma. A defense committee was formed to help her.[48]

Biberman wrote to Trumbo, telling him that Field's story would be the company's first project. He also asked Trumbo to write the script: "Within a month I will come to you with a check and offer you the story. I feel strongly that this is a story for you—that you should do the first story—and Simon [Lazarus, IPC's president] feels strongly if we can strike out strongly—make a film that sings with truth and unobfuscated emotion—even in these times—we will make a lot of money . . . which also means more films."[49] Initially, Trumbo agreed, and on July 19 Biberman sent him the transcripts from the Field trials but added, "the real material will come from the talks with Jean herself."[50] Shortly thereafter Trumbo changed his mind, telling Biberman:

> I should, in the first place, never have taken this assignment, for the simple reason that I knew it would consume a minimum of two months of intensive work and probably longer. I now, somewhat belatedly realize that I can't afford to do it. I sired these kids of mine, and I've got to support them, and even the noblest intention to write a screenplay with social content cannot excuse me for not having at present the money to buy their needed clothes for the new school term. That is a primary obligation, and, in accepting the assignment for reasons which were perfectly decent, made it secondary. That was wrong. Since the problem is exclusively mine, I am the only one I know of who can solve it, and the first step to solution is clear. I am, from today on and for some time in the future, not interested in pamphlets, speeches or progressive motion pictures. I have got to earn money—a considerable sum of it—very quickly. I cannot and will not hypothecate two or three months, or even a month, for any project that doesn't contain the possibility of an immediate and substantial sum. . . . Hence, dear fellow, I pass the torch back.[51]

At some point before leaving for Mexico, however, Trumbo reconsidered and decided to write the Field script after all. So he had two writing commitments to take with him: the Field story for IPC, and the carnival story for King Brothers.

13

Oh, Oh, Mexico

I dreamed of living in luxurious exile in Mexico City. Well it was luxurious for the first year but absolutely hellish during the second year. . . . I was heroically broke.

—Dalton Trumbo

It turned out that we did not fit into the larger community. There wasn't a flow of black market work then, and he could not make the force of his personality felt at a distance. We came back with a lot less than we went with.

—Christopher Trumbo

According to Jean Butler, the decision to leave the United States emanated from fear: Hugo feared he was about to be subpoenaed by the Committee on Un-American Activities, and Trumbo feared he might be subpoenaed again, asked the same questions, and indicted on a brand-new charge of contempt.[1] Trumbo had received letters from Gordon Kahn and Albert Maltz, both of whom were currently living in Mexico, telling him how secure they felt there. "In short," Christopher recalled, "Mexico offered a modicum of safety from government interference with our lives." In addition, they did not need passports to enter Mexico, the film industry there was growing, and Hugo had recently finished an adaptation of Daniel Defoe's novel *Robinson Crusoe*, which George Pepper (who was already self-exiled in Mexico) promised to produce.[2]

Escrow closed on the ranch in October; the King brothers loaned Trumbo $3,000, even though he had not completed the screenplay for the carnival story; and Trumbo and the Butlers agreed to meet on November 1 in San Diego.[3] Jean Butler described their exodus:

Four adults, seven children, a dog, and a cat set out in a caravan: [the Butlers in their] tall, ancient Cadillac; Cleo and her three children in their relatively new Packard; and Trumbo—with the sheepdog, which unhappily proved prey to car sickness—in a Jeep pulling a teardrop trailer filled with his books. . . . By virtue of age, experience, and general panache, Trumbo had assumed the position of tribal leader, and Hugo, who within his own family structure was absolute monarch, fell comfortably into place as his second in command. He and Trumbo made all substantive decisions, which Cleo and I never questioned: they were the cartographers, planning the stops and the side trips and seeing to the general care and upkeep of the cars. Cleo, who over the last few years had become a skilled photographer, took pictures at each stop.[4]

The children were plagued by illness on every leg of the journey: Nikola contracted strep throat in San Diego, Mitzi came down with it in Gila Bend, and all the other children suffered from it in Mexico.

They entered Mexico around mid-November. From Guadalajara,

En route to Mexico, 1950. Left to right: Michael Butler, Hugo Butler (face hidden), Christopher Trumbo, Nikola Trumbo, Mitzi Trumbo, Mary Butler, Emily Butler (head turned), Jean Butler, and Susie Butler. Photograph by Cleo Trumbo.

Trumbo and Hugo flew to Mexico City, where they found two houses not too distant from each other. At the end of December the Hunters and Lardners arrived (but they stayed only six months). It was a happy reunion of what Jean Butler called "a close quadrumvirate." The male foursome worked together, played together, drank together, and spent "their evenings philosophizing, arm wrestling, and trying to top each other's jokes. . . . It was a friendship so close, so satisfying, that it almost superseded the four marriages." The four couples regularly dined together in Mexico City, and after dinner "the men, fueled by liquor that was gratifyingly cheap in Mexico, got into another of their heated, witty, outrageous discussions. I lingered on the outskirts of the talk with the uneasy conviction (which I never told anyone, not even Hugo), that we wives were not quite members of the club."[5]

Jeannette Bello, then married to George Pepper, recalled the close relationship among the Trumbos, Butlers, Lardners, and Hunters:

> [They] were very close friends, had to be invited to dinner all together. That made life a bit difficult for George and me, who had a very small apartment in those first years. But parties with them all were marvelous. The four men were marvelously funny and very, very smart. . . . They were all great raconteurs. Hugo would take an amusing topic, recount it, and then revise it steadily until it was hilarious. Just as he might a script. Whereas, Ring, who spoke rather slowly, from the remains of a stammer, might not utter a word all evening. But one night, he suddenly said something and everyone shut up at the extraordinary event. They said the most appalling things to each other. Trumbo described this practice as "character strengthening," to which end he contributed his best efforts.[6]

The Mexican interlude lasted twenty-six months. Financially and socially, it proved to be a big mistake; nor did it completely shelter them from the storm of political reaction in the United States. Trumbo had taken $28,000 to Mexico, and he earned about $15,000 while he was there. But he was spending $21,000 a year in back taxes, medical and educational expenses, support of his mother and mother-in-law, and a variety of loans to friends in need.[7] In addition, the sale of the ranch had fallen through, and Trumbo found himself saddled with the property taxes on it. Indeed, the lack of money trumped all other concerns. He later said: "There were times of infuriation when I was broke. There

George and Jeanette Pepper, visiting the Trumbos in Mexico City, 1952.
Photograph by Cleo Trumbo.

was a time in Mexico when I was so broke it seemed there was no hope,
no possible hope, but there seemed something funny about it. I've never
been in worse shape than I was in Mexico, and even flat tires attack you
at times like that, and it is *funny*."[8] He borrowed money from several
friends, and he tried and failed to borrow from several other blacklisted
people, using the trust deed on the ranch as collateral. On several occasions, only a desperate plea or a last-minute cash infusion from a script
saved him from complete ruin.

The children felt they had no links to anything or anybody in

Mexico. "We were," Christopher remembered, "separate from the actual country, not part of the culture, and thrown back upon whatever resources we had brought with us. We were foreigners, just kind of floating there. We had no connection to the society in general, and Trumbo felt no sense of community with the other exiles." Nikola had few friends at the American School, and "because of my father's political affiliations [I] was blackballed from a club I hoped to join."[9] Mitzi, who was very young, enjoyed her stay. She learned Spanish quickly, and because her father had no interest in learning the language, she often interpreted for him. "This pleased and annoyed him. He was pleased that he could show off my language skills, but not so pleased to have to lean over and listen to my translations, and wait for me to translate back. It was a thrill having this power over my father, the man with all the words."

In addition, the exiles realized all too quickly that they had not escaped the domestic cold war. Their community was rife with rumors about informers and surveillance, and a high level of fear reigned. They were not, as it turned out, paranoid, because the US legal attaché in Mexico City had been instructed by FBI headquarters "to ascertain [Trumbo's] residence and activities in Mexico City, as well as determining the probable extent of his residence there."[10] Then, several months after their arrival, anti-Communist screenwriter Richard English reported in the *Saturday Evening Post* that the Mexican FBI maintained a file on every US Communist living in Mexico and that it had arrested and repatriated CPUSA leader Gus Hall and suspected spy Morton Sobell. "In Cuernavaca," English wrote, "there is a loud cell of American Reds," largely made up of expatriate Hollywood writers and directors. He claimed, inaccurately, that Gordon Kahn and Albert Maltz, abetted by Trumbo, Lardner, and Butler, had shattered the tranquility of Cuernavaca by their antics.[11]

Trumbo and Butler were not harried by the Mexican police or the FBI, and they were free to pursue their writing careers and their newfound obsession for collecting pre-Columbian artifacts. Shortly after the Trumbos and Butlers arrived in Mexico City, the families made an excursion to Teotihuacán to see the pyramids there. Trumbo and Butler were, according to Jean Butler, "approached furtively by a local townsman who offered to sell them '*cabecitas*,' tiny, ancient stone heads unearthed by the hundreds from the soil thereabouts and peddled illegally to tourists." Thereafter, the two men made regular trips to brick pits, and "after some homework on the subject, it was only a few steps to the clandestine acquisition from dealers of more impressive and expensive trophies."[12] They each amassed impressive collections and, in the process, drove up the prices other collectors had to pay.

Life was not completely grim there. Christopher recalled that the families played a weekly softball game: "There was a large vacant lot near the Butlers' home, and Ian decided that it should be a softball field, even though there was a pepper tree in center field and an eight-foot drop in left field. All the adults and children would go there on Saturday afternoons to play. My father went once, as an indication of his interest in athletics." Cleo and Ian were the best players.

For Trumbo, the Mexico interlude was most notable for an unproduced script (the Jean Field story), the opening of a movie for which he had written the script (*Roman Holiday*), and the idea for a script that would give him the opportunity to undermine the blacklist (*The Brave One*).

As soon as they were settled, Trumbo resumed work on the Jean Field script. He sent some pages to Biberman, who expressed his enthusiasm and said IPC wanted a final draft by March 4.[13] Trumbo, disconcerted by the short time frame, replied that the partners had placed on him "not only the normal burden of a man who has an obligation, but also a moral and political burden. . . . [Y]ou want a good script and good scripts are *not* written in two months. . . . And I, like a damned fool, am trying to do it. And we are presently operating on precisely the same speed-crisis which accounts for all the bad motion pictures ever made— we, who as [independent] artists, are to make the best!"[14] Nevertheless, Trumbo managed to complete the script in March and wrote to Biberman: "I have never had so difficult a job nor, now that it is finished, so pleasant a one. It's greatest difficulty, which I want you all to understand, lay in this: that it is not and cannot be a work of the imagination. It is a work of fact." He had, he noted, read four volumes of trial records, and he had decided to frame the story around Field's friendship with a black woman she meets during the trial (a character invented by Trumbo). Together, counting the various drafts, Trumbo estimated that he had written 600-plus pages.[15]

I have not found a completed script for the Jean Field story, which is puzzling, given that both Trumbo and Biberman were savers. I did find forty-three random pages of what seems to be a first draft.[16] They indicate that Trumbo had not solved the story's problems. He created the fictional Helen to be a friend and political adviser to Catherine (Jean Field), but the two women do not converse with each other; they

declaim. When Helen talks about racism, she does so in a stilted, dogmatic, political manner. And Catherine's conversations with her children and the defense committee take the form of long speeches. The
trial sequence, which is the heart of the script, is pure politics. The lawyer for Catherine's ex-husband introduces a letter signed by fifty-four
black soldiers claiming that the US Army practiced racial discrimination against them during their service in Korea, and he asks Catherine
if this is the sort of message she sends to her son. Catherine replies in
the affirmative.

> Attorney: You know, of course, that is what Communists teach?
> Catherine: I hope they do.
> Attorney: You would like Communists to teach that?
> Catherine: I would like everyone to teach that.

When she is asked about her political affiliations, she channels Trumbo's feelings about such questions: "I have to trample over someone,
don't I? If not my children, if not Negroes, if not Koreans, then someone else—I must deliver some group up as a victim to you or I can't be a
real American! I must offer up some scapegoat, mustn't I? That's the last
thing you'll take from me, isn't it? If I wish to escape, I've got to give you
someone else to terrorize—someone for Operation Killer!"

Biberman did not like the script. In a six-page analysis, he identified the main problem: Trumbo had relied too much on the actual
court record and, as a result, had surrendered control of the story. "Not
only is flexibility absent, and real realistic invention, but every human
being in the story is formalized into a witness. All integration between
people is gone. Every individual is limited to answering questions. . . .
[I]nformation does not come crisply and in active, sequential fashion."
Catherine's interrogation is "ponderous and interminable," the script
lacks drama and clarity, and the main characters are "not complex
enough."[17] But Biberman suffered an unfortunate failure of nerve, and
he did not send this analysis to Trumbo. Instead, he waffled, telling
Trumbo on April 1 that the partners had not yet read and discussed the
script. Trumbo, who was very adept at reading between the lines, wrote
to Biberman: "Now that the script has been delivered, the tone and
unwonted brevity of your response indicate that the season of phony
enthusiasm has passed, and the time for calm disillusionment is at hand.
In this you follow the classical pattern of any studio in dealing with its
enemy, the writer."[18]

Even worse, from Trumbo's point of view, Biberman had given the script to Jean Field to read and then passed along her very negative comments to Trumbo. Field said she "found in this script RANK CHAUVINISM," and she accused Trumbo of "selling a Tenney brand of Americanism." In his accompanying letter, Biberman tried to soften Field's remarks by telling Trumbo that although the IPC partners agreed, in substance, with her basic criticisms, they did so "with the understanding" that her remarks were directed against IPC as a group, not against any individual. Furthermore, the partners did not accept, "in any large part," Field's proposed solutions.[19]

Trumbo was furious. He wrote to Biberman: "I am so *very* glad I received a copy of Jean's Report before I came North. Now I am prepared for the worst." He enclosed a thirty-page rejoinder in which he rebutted, point by point, each of her criticisms. From the quotations Trumbo cited, it is difficult to understand why the partners took Field's comments seriously; they were remarkably trivial. But, as Trumbo pointed out, the main problem was not his so-called "errors of CHAUVINISM" but the manner in which those errors were presented to him. His detailed response illustrates Trumbo's thoughts on how leftist intellectuals should discuss ideas:

> There is a fine tradition in the left wing that whenever a book or play or film is produced which is harmful to the best interests of the working class, that work and its author should and must be attacked in the sharpest possible terms. There is another fine tradition that when divergent views break out in the left-wing press, one view has to be wrong and one has to be right, and that the search for the right one must be resolved through the widest and sharpest criticism. This latter is called "self-criticism," and is often sharp and sometimes hurtful, as it must be if it is to be effective. I presume that in agreeing in substance with this report, you thought you were standing firmly in this tradition. You were not. You were not even within gun-shot of it. This script was submitted to you before production for the express purpose of *preventing* it from being made in a form which would be harmful to the working class. This [is something Friedrich] Engels calls "mutual criticism." It is searching and friendly and kind. It recognizes the necessity upon and the responsibility of all concerned to *prevent* the work from *needing* to be attacked in sharp and often unnecessarily

unkind terms. That is its purpose. Your report violates this. It is unfriendly, angry, vindictive, envenomed, careless, inaccurate and often inventive. It bears no relation to decent left wing "mutual criticism." . . .

You were not kind enough to suggest that I might have been *unaware* of my RANK CHAUVINISM. You were not kind enough even to put it in normal type: you capitalized it. You made it deliberately the worst possible charge of chauvinism that can be made against a man: a charge that could not be made more extreme if it had been applied to Congressman Rankin or Governor [Herman] Talmadge of Georgia. You accused the script of CHAUVINISM IN THE HIGHEST DEGREE. EXTREME CHAUVINISM. GROSS CHAUVINISM. UTTER CHAUVINISM. And all of you agreed with it in substance. You say: "In accepting her basic criticism. . . . " Nonsense! If you had taken it as directed against yourselves, and if you are decent men, you would have spent sleepless nights, as I have, and have searched your consciences with agony. But you haven't. You did not take this horrible charge as really directed against yourselves. Nor could it have been. You had not even seen the script until it was finished. You had no control over the words. I wrote the script, and I wrote the words that are RANK CHAUVINISM, and a writer's words are a reflection of his life. When I gave you this script, I trusted you with my reputation—not as a writer, for that isn't of very much consequence; but with my reputation as a decent man—and you have fulfilled the trust by throwing a bucket of filth over me. To me this is one of the most shameful and serious moments of my life. . . . The script I agreed to write had to do *with peace, with war, and with the rights of accused Communists which encompass the rights of all minorities.* Oddly enough, these matters aren't dealt with in your report. Is anybody thinking about them?[20]

I have not found an account of what transpired between the partners and Trumbo when the latter flew to Los Angeles to discuss the script. In any event, the IPC partners decided to drop the Field project and focus on *Salt of the Earth*, and they sent Michael Wilson's script to Trumbo for his comments.[21] The partners paid Trumbo a kill fee of $2,000, but his anger lingered. In the margin of his copy of a letter he sent to Biberman later that year, Trumbo wrote that he never would have accepted the Field project from a Hollywood producer, and the

IPC partners' reasons for not producing it "were probably as irrelevant as any a Hollywood producer could have thought up."[22]

This experience further divorced Trumbo from his Communist Party past, as did his reading of John Howard Lawson's newly published book *Film in the Battle of Ideas*. Trumbo had been asked to review it for *Masses & Mainstream*, but he declined, saying he could not do it "justice." In fact, he declined because he did not want to publicly criticize Lawson, who had, in Trumbo's mind, conformed his arguments to agree with the current party line of sectarian class struggle and was uncritically parroting V. J. Jerome, the party's so-called cultural commissar. In doing so, Lawson had thrown a pessimistic shadow over left-wing screenwriters' accomplishments during the Popular Front and thereby cast a pall over the future. According to Trumbo, Lawson's implication that they had accomplished "practically nothing" lent "credence to the theory that no accomplishment is possible." Furthermore, Lawson had failed to emphasize the successes of the Hollywood Left: their guild organizing, their mobilization of industry-wide antifascist political action, and their modifications in the content of film itself. Progress was made, and "if all this is ignored, if it is actually derogated—then regardless of the theoretical soundness of an injunction to fight for content and employment—regardless of statements that it can and ought to be done—still there will be immobilization and inactivity, because there is no evidence that it ever was done, or that it is actually possible." It was important to remember, Trumbo concluded, that "the Committee attacked Hollywood for a *reason*."[23] In a letter he wrote directly to Lawson, Trumbo noted that the Hollywood Ten must not "reject the past because of our mistakes; it was a part of our growth; it was honorable; it had results; and it [this past] cannot be rejected, eliminated or passed over for any reason. It is perhaps less than good, but it is better than bad. It *was*. And what it was constituted such a danger to fascists that they had to stir the earth for five years to destroy it—and they haven't destroyed it yet."[24]

As Trumbo desperately struggled to stay afloat financially, Paramount Pictures, a coauthor of the Waldorf blacklisting agreement, released a movie written by him. *Roman Holiday* opened in September 1953 and was a huge box-office and critical success, but given the constraints of the black market and his distance from Hollywood, Trumbo could not take advantage of it. Trumbo had written the script in the autumn of 1949, but of course, his name was not on it. It was based on an idea given to him by Ian Hunter, who had read newspaper accounts of a trip Princess Margaret (Queen Elizabeth II's sister) had taken to Rome.[25] "We were broke," Cleo later said, "so Dalton did what he knew how to do so well; he went to his typewriter. The result was *Roman Holiday*."[26]

After Hunter agreed to be his front, Trumbo gave the script to George Willner and instructed him to sell it to a major studio. In October 1949 Willner entered into an agreement with Liberty Films, an independent production company owned by Frank Capra, William Wyler, Samuel Briskin, and George Stevens that had become a wholly owned subsidiary of Paramount Pictures. Liberty agreed to purchase the script for $35,000 and hired Hunter to do eight weeks of additional work on it, for which he would be paid $5,000.[27] When that contract expired, Paramount signed Hunter to a separate contract for $750 a week.[28] For a variety of reasons, Capra's interest in the script lessened. In March 1951 he settled his contract with Paramount and bowed out as director, and William Wyler inherited the project.[29]

The first official record of a script with the title "Roman Holiday" bears Ian McLellan Hunter's name; it is dated March 1, 1950, is 174 pages long, and is labeled "revised."[30] One copy of it is enclosed in a cover with the name of the Goldstone-Willner Agency on it. (There is also an undated, nine-page treatment by Hunter in the collection.) There is no way of knowing to what extent Hunter revised Trumbo's script. Many years later, when a committee of the Writers Guild of America, West (WGAw), had been established to determine who wrote what during the blacklist, Ring Lardner Jr. told Cleo that Hunter "did considerable work rewriting the screenplay with Frank Capra," but he had "no specific knowledge of how much Dalton's screenplay was changed by Ian."[31]

In any event, Wyler never seemed satisfied with the Trumbo-Hunter script. He first asked Ben Hecht to rewrite it, and Hecht wrote two drafts (dated July 7 and November 5, 1951). Hecht's scripts had the same structure and main characters as the Trumbo-Hunter script, but he rewrote much of the dialogue and changed the names of some of the characters. Then, in April 1952, Preston Sturges did a rewrite. While traveling by ship to Italy, Wyler asked Robert Wyler (his brother) and Lester Koenig to rewrite one of the previous versions. Once they arrived, two Italians, Enzo Flaiano and Suso Cecci D'Amico, also did some rewriting. Their revised script, dated May 1952, was partly in English and partly in Italian. Wyler then brought in an English writer, John Dighton. The "final" script, dated June 4, 1952, bears the names of Dighton, Flaiano, and D'Amico. When it came time to assign the screen credit, a studio employee compared the various scripts and decided to credit Hunter for the original story (which had never existed) and Hunter and Dighton for the screenplay.[32]

As it happened, Ian Hunter received an Academy Award for best motion picture story, and he and Dighton were corecipients of the SWG's award for best written comedy. Lardner told Trumbo that Hunter was not pleased: "His greatest cross is the revival of publicity about the authorship of that royalist thing [*Roman Holiday*]. Someone twitted him about an item in Hy Gardner's column in a public restaurant and he [Hunter] reacted with an instant nosebleed. Never has a man been so appalled by the success of work credited to him."[33] In fact, Hunter kept the Oscar statuette in the bottom drawer of his filing cabinet. (Trumbo's name was added to the WGAw award in 1993, and the Academy awarded Trumbo an Oscar for best story that same year. In 2011 the WGAw added Trumbo's name to the screenplay credit. See chapter 27.)

Trumbo could not, however, exploit these awards. *Roman Holiday*, Christopher told me, "came too early in the game to do him any good. There was no thriving black market; there was no backdrop of screenplays with rumors attached. He knew that there had to be accompanying circumstances, and that they had to lead somewhere."

All the necessary "accompanying circumstances" merged around Trumbo's script for the movie released as *The Brave One*. The idea had come to Trumbo after he and Cleo, at the invitation of the Butlers, attended a bullfight. According to Jean Butler, "One of the kills had been clumsy. . . . The Trumbos, who had kept a cow and several horses on their ranch that they'd been quite fond of, were pro-bull from the outset and came away from the plaza white-faced and outraged." Trumbo and Hugo argued regularly about the difference between sending a bull to the slaughterhouse and giving it the opportunity to win in the ring and be retired to a ranch.[34] Trumbo decided to write a story about a bull that had received an *indulto*, a pardon or grant of clemency that spectators awarded to a bull that had fought particularly well. Shortly after he conceived the story, Trumbo had to fly to Los Angeles; the sale of the ranch had fallen through, and he had to make a deal with the IRS for the payment of back taxes. While he was there, Trumbo outlined his bull story for the King brothers, who were immediately interested. But first they wanted him to finish the script for the carnival story.

Carnival Story was released in April 1954, with principal writing credit going to Marcel Klauber. It was one of the least humane of Trumbo's scripts. The characters use one another without scruple, and virtually no one acts morally. Christopher commented that his father had become fascinated with "the strange kind of misfit lives these people led." The movie received positive reviews in the trades and in local newspapers, and it proved to be one of King Brothers' most profitable films. Trumbo, however, had to beg for the $2,000 he was owed for writing the script.[35]

By this point, Trumbo had lost patience with Mexico. In early April 1953 he wrote to Hy Kraft: "I was a fool for coming down here. The line of supply to my living source is so tenuous that when I do work the people who owe me for it mistake my absence for my death, and simply do not pay without the strongest kind of pressure being exerted. I went flat about June. Then I wrote an original screenplay [the bull and boy story] and sold it for $10,000. But the bastards didn't pay. I had to make two trips to enforce collection, and still have not got it all. Then Cleo got sick. She went from bad to worse, into a complete malnutritional breakdown."[36]

In late autumn Trumbo decided the family should return to Los Angeles. He realized that, for the foreseeable future, the only way he could earn a living was as a screenwriter, and he told his family: "If you want to suck, you better get close to the tit."[37] He wrote to Michael Wilson:

> As for our condition, we are living out an old truism: "The first time you see Mexico City you are struck by the horrible poverty; within a year you discover it's infectious." I am as broke as a bankrupt's bastard. I am now an old customer of the Monte de Piedad (Mount of Pity), so called because it is the government pawnshop and charges only 36% interest per year. We have at the moment reposing in the vaults of this benign institution a diamond ring, two gold cigarette lighters, a gold cigarette case, my watch, a Leica camera, as well as certain objects of the Butlers' I hocked for them in a moment of need. . . . Precisely how we are going to get back I don't know, but we keep up our brave intentions to try. Indeed we have no other course, for I cannot make it here. . . . My general plans are this: return in January, rent some large, gloomy, drafty, run-down old house, get my furniture out of storage, and try to devote half my time

to earning a living and the other half to serious work. I am not too sure of pictures any more, and therefore am trying, through a front, to open up the magazine market.[38]

Wilson replied that the market for movie scripts in Hollywood "is shrinking on all fronts, and particularly in the thieves' [black] market. However, there remain certain thieves whose need occasionally overrides hysteria, and whose respect for your probity could bring them around to venturing a dollar. I'm not kidding. There is not a market here for most folks. I believe there is for you. It's even possible I could lead you to the proper booth in the bazaar."[39]

Another reason behind Trumbo's decision to return to the United States was his determination to break the blacklist. In Christopher's words:

He couldn't see things going on this way, being always in a defensive position, kind of like a beggar or the village outsider. He set breaking through the blacklist as a goal. He did not yet envision how it would occur. One thing was certain, however: He would not sign a letter of contrition or explanation. He told us: "I'm not going to tell the producers a damn thing that I wouldn't tell the committee. That's it. Those freedoms that I alleged in all the legal briefs I filed, I still believe those things. They were just." He thought he could win his way back into the industry in another way. . . .

Though the move to Mexico had been permeated by a spirit of spontaneity, even lighthearted adventure, the return was more subdued. We felt the same sense of relief that any exhausted vacationing family does at finally going home. Cleo, still rocky after a rough surgery, left first, taking Mitzi with her and flying to Los Angeles shortly after Christmas in 1953. Not long afterward, on a crisp January morning, Trumbo, Niki, and I—along with the dog and the cat—took off from Mexico City in a hired car with a driver, headed for Texas. In an effort to escape the fees, regulations, and red tape that trailed after American cars in Mexico, our Jeep and the trailer had already been driven north where they awaited our arrival. The Jeep was housed in Brownsville, immune from Mexican harassment, while the trailer languished across the border in Matamoros waiting for us to claim it and shepherd it through Customs. The task proved more complicated than anticipated.

Trumbo at the brick pits, looking for figurines. Photograph by Cleo Trumbo.

The main complication was Trumbo's plan to get his collection of pre-Columbian sculptures out of Mexico, despite the ban on removing "archaeological treasures." According to Jean Butler, Trumbo packed his teardrop trailer by hand and with great care, "putting his beloved antique *figuras*, well wrapped, at the bottom, then above them a layer of *falsos* (imitations, sold to tourists by the thousands) as decoys, and above these, a gallimaufry of household items, clothing, and suchlike. This he had shipped in its entirety to a warehouse in Matamoros, the Mexican border point facing Brownsville, Texas, to await his arrival."[40]

Trumbo picked up the story of what happened after he arrived in Matamoras in a long, tongue-in-cheek letter he wrote to the Peppers and Butlers. (The Butlers stayed in Mexico until 1960.) He found that the trailer had fallen off the truck, and the transporters had repacked it with "all light and crushable items being expertly stowed away at the bottom; all heavy ones on top of them." Trumbo hastily reorganized the contents of the trailer, "at [the] cost of God knows what labor and profanity." But in his haste to get moving, Trumbo had made a mistake. He had planned to attach the trailer to the Jeep, which was waiting across the border in Brownsville. But when the Jeep was delivered to Matamoros, Mexican custom officials demanded to see a current license for the Jeep, and Trumbo could not produce one. They accused him of illegally using the Jeep in Mexico during his entire stay. Then, according to

Trumbo, "there ensued a long argument, during which I engaged some six or eight different persons in my fluent conversational Spanish. They demanded papers; I countered with a storage receipt. They threatened jail and nationalization of the car; I countered with yelps for the American counsel. Finally I got hold of a man who understood decent Spanish, and this part of the situation was cleared up." (According to Mitzi, her father knew very little Spanish. He had spent his entire life learning English, he told her, and he was not about to waste his time learning another language.)

The border guards then inspected the trailer. "Every blessed thing was unloaded and carefully pawed through . . . , and my whole boodle was kept, and I was given a receipt for it, together with an appointment for Monday with the Aduana [customs official]. Then, amidst savage shrieks, they threw everything [except the valuable figurines] together again and heaped it into the trailer in such a fashion that the doors wouldn't close. I tied them together, and crept across the border at about midnight." On the US side, he had to unload the trailer for inspection by customs officials and then reload it, and he had to explain why he did not have current California license plates for the Jeep. When that issue was resolved, Trumbo continued: "I stepped on the starter. Nothing happened. The battery was out. It was three o'clock in the morning, and I just collapsed over the steering wheel and began to sob. The children consoled me." The Jeep had to be towed—all over Brownsville, it seemed—since the first four motels they tried did not have enough rooms for Trumbo, the children, and the pets. On Monday, Trumbo returned to Matamoros, where he was "now widely known and making fresh enemies by the hour." He finally agreed to send the art objects back to Mexico City (although they eventually found their way back to him in Los Angeles). On Tuesday morning, with "the children munching hamburgers and Hershey bars as they have been steadily doing ever since striking the auld sod," they headed west to Los Angeles. They covered the 1,500 miles in three days, and on his arrival, Trumbo "threw himself into the blessed arms" of Cleo, who was "snuffling from a cold."[41]

The family holed up in another motel room until Trumbo found what he called "an old Spanish fort" to rent. It was located in La Cañada, an upscale Republican community close to Pasadena. But as Christopher remembered, it was "more a run-down house than a fort, drafty and not terribly comfortable." (The house, located at 2001 Los Amigos Street, in what is now La Cañada–Flintridge, has since been

torn down.) Trumbo borrowed $1,200 to get their furniture out of stor-
age and to pay for moving expenses. Although Cleo and the children
were relieved to be back in Southern California, none of them, according to Christopher, came to think of La Cañada as "home":

> Perhaps because of its dilapidated state and the reluctance of
> the landlord to improve existing problems, to say nothing of
> the new ones which mysteriously appeared at an accelerating
> rate the longer we stayed, it wasn't long before the urge to move
> took hold. The problem, however, was not only where, but
> how. Finding the right place for the right rent was a daunting
> problem, and the idea of buying a house lay in the realm of fan-
> tasy, if not delusion. Deeply in debt, blacklisted, with no source
> of steady income, certainly without cash for a down payment,
> Trumbo was a ludicrous candidate for a bank loan.
>
> The solution to this predicament came through the unlikely
> figure of Frank King. As it happened, a friend of Frank's, Lio-
> nel Sternberger, had a house he needed to get rid of in Highland
> Park, a neighborhood just north of downtown Los Angeles.
> Lionel, credited by many as the inventor of the cheeseburger,
> had lived in that house with his mother, until she died. Not
> long after her death, at about the same time we returned from
> Mexico, Lionel had become romantically involved with a
> woman who, sensing that the house held too many memories of
> [Lionel's] mother, wisely refused to live there. Frank arranged
> for Lionel and Trumbo to get together, and a deal was made.
> The King brothers vouched for Trumbo, but the clincher may
> have been his stand against the committee. Sternberger was an
> unabashed health advocate, possessed of unconventional ideas
> about nutrition and food supplements and drugs which he was
> eager to share with all who might be interested. This enthusi-
> asm had brought him to the attention of the authorities, who,
> suspecting he might be guilty of giving medical advice with-
> out a license, had tapped his phone. His outrage at the govern-
> ment's meddling intrusion produced an instant sympathy with
> Trumbo's plight, which expressed itself in an extraordinarily
> generous fashion: He required no down payment on the house,
> carried the note personally, and lent Trumbo another $2,400
> to get the rest of our belongings out of storage where they were
> being held captive as surety against default.

Trumbo paid Sternberger $200 a month, plus a balloon payment of $3,000 every September 1, for seven years. Mitzi and I recently visited the house, at 6231 Annan Trail, Highland Park. It is still owned by the family the Trumbos sold it to. Perched high on a hill, it has a great view of the city. Trumbo's office was located in a converted shed that had been cut into the hill. It is now, sadly, a ramshackle storage room.

When Nikola and Christopher were young, they called their father "Daddy." When Christopher was in high school, he decided they were too old to use that term, so all three children started calling him "Pop." But in our conversations, Christopher usually referred to his father as "Trumbo."

Trumbo spent most of his children's growing-up years in that converted shed, writing his way off the blacklist. During that time, he became a distant and sometimes stormy presence. Christopher described him as "a larger-than-life figure who was somewhat remote. I would not describe him as 'a loving individual.' Though he felt responsible for us, we were not the center of his life. He had his own space in the house, and we left him alone; we did not go rushing to him with our problems. Cleo was the go-to parent. We had to be careful when informing Trumbo about our crises and issues because of his propensity to use an elephant gun to swat a fly." Mitzi concurred: "Pop did not take an active part in our childhood, and he treated me with distracted affection. He worked all the time, fighting his battles or writing his scripts. It seemed to us he was always in his office. He even went there after dinner. He'd find out what the three of us were doing by asking Cleo. Unless there was some sort of crisis, he stayed in his world and didn't interfere in mine." One night, however, when Mitzi was in tenth grade, Trumbo accompanied her to a father-daughter banquet at her high school. She was very nervous about how he would behave with the other fathers. Trumbo, however, thought he had behaved very well, asking her during the drive home, "Aren't you proud of me? I didn't once say 'fuck.'"

When Trumbo was present, Mitzi continued, "he was captivating to be around, even, to a large degree, to us. We admired and wanted to please him; a compliment from him, for anything, but especially for something smart or insightful that we said, was always highly prized and hard-won. Sometimes, in conversation, he would set an unseen trap with honey then pounce on the victim. We kids learned to sidestep those traps pretty well, but others weren't as experienced as we were." He did not, Christopher said, "understand children and was not very interested in them. He treated children as though they were small adults. My sisters and I always had adult conversations with him, and he believed we could handle whatever came along."

Those "adult conversations" did not include Trumbo teaching his children about Marx, Lenin, and Stalin or romanticizing the Soviet Union when he talked about it.[42] He subscribed to the *Daily Worker* and *Daily People's World*, which the children were free to read if they wished. In the spring of 1956, when those newspapers extensively covered the speech by Soviet party leader Nikita Khrushchev, delineating some of the crimes of the Stalin era, Trumbo thought Christopher might be upset and tried to reassure his son. But, Christopher recalled, "I was not upset at all. I had never identified with the Soviet Union in any way. Nor had my parents identified with it in any way that influenced me." Mitzi remembered that there was "a lot of political talk in our family, mostly about what was going on in the world. There was lots of talk about the blacklist, but there was never any more talk about Russia or communism than there was about any other news of the day." Nikola was aware, from an early age, of the evils of racism: "I knew my father was a Communist, and he thought racial discrimination was wrong." But, she emphasized, "we were not instructed in any of this. If I asked, Trumbo would explain, and his explanation was what he understood the situation to be. By that I mean that he never couched his words, but always made clear what he believed in or thought was right."

Being a Trumbo was not always easy, as evidenced by Christopher's "furnace story":

Wherever we moved, recognition of my father's name followed. The question was never if, but only how quickly, it would surface. But I was completely unprepared for what occurred one morning, shortly after our return from Mexico, during the home-room period at Luther Burbank Junior High School. My home room was metal shop. Mr. Unger, the home-room teacher, had left the room. Without warning, I was grabbed and wrestled from my seat by several boys, dragged across the floor toward the shop furnace where metal was heated, and thrown in. The door was slammed shut. Flames shot up from the gas jets around me. A wall of hot air hit my face. I knew, since it was the start of the day, the furnace had yet to warm up. I also knew it was hot and getting hotter, and that I was in a lot of trouble. Then the door opened, and Mr. Unger reached in and hauled me out. My hair, eyebrows, and eyelashes were singed. My clothes were torn. Mr. Unger took me to the office of the boys' vice principal, where I telephoned my mother, asking her to meet me a few blocks from the school with a change of clothes.

I walked up Figueroa Avenue getting angrier with every step. Never had I felt so powerless or so frustrated, but I knew I had to go back.

My mother spotted me on the sidewalk and pulled the car onto a side street. I climbed into the back seat. She turned in the driver's seat, watching me as I changed clothes.

"What happened?" she asked.

"Nothing."

"Come home with me. We'll talk about it."

"I'm all right."

I slipped my belt through the loops of the pants she had brought. I knew that if I went home I might never go back. She was silent, watching me, trying to read my mind.

"Come home."

I was buttoning my fresh shirt. "I'm late for first period already." I met her eyes. "I'll be all right."

She looked at me for a long moment, then reached out and put the palm of her hand to my cheek. "Call me if anything happens. I'll be there right away."

I got out of the car and started back to Luther Burbank. As I walked down Figueroa, I began to sort out my feelings and figure out what kind of choices I had, if any. I was absolutely certain that if I told my parents what had happened they would leap immediately into action. I had no doubts. I knew I could count on them. But also, if I told them, I was aware that everything that had happened and its consequences would pass beyond my control. What father wouldn't react with fury after learning that his son had been thrown into a furnace? I envisioned angry confrontations, lawsuits, criminal proceedings. I imagined myself stuck with the title of Furnace Boy for the rest of my time in school, and since I was only in the ninth grade, as far as I was concerned, that might as well be the rest of my life. I saw my face plastered in the newspapers with some lurid caption beneath it. On the Left I would become the poster boy for anticommunism run amok. None of these things appealed to me.

For my own part, what I wanted was to be left alone. No more harassment. I didn't care about revenge, or justice, or some kind of apology. The kids in my home room hardly knew me well enough to dislike me, much less hate me. McCarthyism was a plague on the land—I knew it even if they didn't—and I happened to have the wrong last name. I just wanted the whole incident forgotten and a future where I didn't have to look over my shoulder every ten seconds. For me, that would be a win.

The next day in home room it was as if nothing had happened. Mr. Unger never spoke about what had happened to me; neither did the vice principal. Nobody else did either. It was as if nothing had ever happened, and that suited me fine.

One year later, when I went to Franklin High School, I tended not to make friends with those for whom my father's identity might be a problem. I don't remember being ostracized by anyone there. I was a member of the band and orchestra; I played B football; I was the president of the honor society; I was an Ephebian [an honor society whose members are selected on the basis of good character, citizenship, and scholastic achievement].

Being Trumbos also created problems for Cleo and Mitzi. When Mitzi was in fifth grade, her parents' political views were discovered by the neighborhood parents. Thereafter, secret PTA meetings were held, with the intent of barring Cleo from that organization. At one parents' meeting, Cleo had the unforgettable experience of "sitting down and finding everyone getting up and moving away from me so that I was alone." She was also told she could no longer be the coleader of Mitzi's Camp Fire Girls troop.

Mitzi remembered: "My life at school was changing; at first I was ignored by individual friends, but eventually in the classroom, and especially the playground, I was taunted and ostracized. I didn't tell my parents for months, believing that whatever was happening was because of my own failings. Soon, I was getting sick every morning and begging not to go to school. I finally had to tell my mother what was happening." Cleo told Trumbo, who immediately wrote a letter to Mrs. Eleanor Barr Wheeler, the principal of the elementary school. In that letter he sharply criticized Wheeler and the Annandale PTA for holding secret meetings to discuss his and Cleo's "characters" and for not warning them "of the shocking torment which a coterie of grown persons was preparing to inflict upon . . . Mitzi." Although he and Cleo had become accustomed to such treatment and understood the mindlessness behind it, they now realized "that the taint was hereditary," and it had been passed down to their daughter. As a result, Trumbo continued, Annandale "has become to her a misery and a wound." Trumbo, at his most eloquent and coldly furious, described what Mitzi had suffered:

> At the beginning of the 1955–56 school term we entrusted to your care a happy, healthy, comparatively well-adjusted and demonstrably intelligent child who loved school, adored her teachers and enjoyed the friendship of her small circle of contemporaries. Eight months later you have returned to us a spiritually devastated human being who begs us not to send her to school. . . .
>
> Small childish conspiracies are directed against her—patterned in secret after the conspiracies of the parents—and she is quietly and incessantly persecuted and boycotted and shunned as long as the school day lasts. . . .
>
> This slow murder of the mind and heart and spirit of a young child is the proud outcome of those patriotic meetings among a few parents in Annandale School under the sponsorship of the PTA and the Bluebirds [junior Camp Fire Girls]. It is a living test of the high principles of both organizations—principles noble in word, ignoble and savage in application. The principles are what they say: Mitzi is what they do. . . .
>
> I should like you to see the lines of nervous exhaustion on our daughter's face when she returns home from school each day; I should like you to watch how decently and bravely she tries to suppress her bewilderment at her first encounter with barbarism parading as American virtue. Barbarism which began at your school among adult persons.[43]

Trumbo threatened to send letters to the superintendent of schools, members of the school board, the entire PTA, the Camp Fire Girls, the American Civil Liberties Union, and the Ministerial Association of Los Angeles. But first he gave a copy of this letter to Robert Kenny, who passed it on to a school board member.

After a school nurse visited the Trumbo home, Mitzi was allowed to withdraw from Annandale Elementary School, with the assurance that she would be promoted to the sixth grade in her new school. When she enrolled at Rockdale Elementary School in the fall, there were no further incidents. "At my new school," she recalled, "the atmosphere was peaceful, and the following six years in junior and senior high school in Eagle Rock were relatively happy ones. But school friendships seemed fragile, since there was so much I couldn't reveal. I was guarded about my personal history, my political beliefs and background. I just wanted to get by. So I flew under the radar of the blacklist as best I could."

Nikola, the oldest, also had some unpleasant experiences, but they seemed less traumatic than those suffered by her younger siblings. She did, however, have the most contentious relationship with Trumbo. In 2005 she wrote: "Over the years I struggled to understand my father's inconsistencies—a political hero to me and to many others, but at home just a father whose action was based not on his beliefs but on his most deeply held prejudices. . . . He and I clashed frequently; he was determined to control me and I refused to be controlled."[44] When she told her parents she intended to work for the Sobell defense committee (see chapter 15), Trumbo cautioned her that she would "be marked for life, not as her father's daughter, but on her own as an adult." That was what she wanted. Trumbo wrote to Hugo Butler, expressing his pride in Nikola and saying that he and Cleo would allow her to "develop as she wishes."[45] For her part, Nikola remained very proud of Trumbo: "Despite his inconsistencies, my father's ethical orientation, his sense of morality, and his determination to stand with what he believed was right provided a role model I studied and followed in my own [life]."[46] Mitzi, too, deeply admired her father's strong moral sense: "It was as if he were driven by some powerful inner force, clear and strong and bright. He had strong convictions and the courage to stick to them no matter what was thrown at him. He certainly instilled in me the desire to do what he had done, to fight the good fight in my life."

In the autumn of 1956 Trumbo's protective instincts toward his children were expressed in a different way. He began to amuse himself by composing a series of letters in which he offered advice to offspring leaving home. In so doing, he followed a long, hallowed tradition that can be traced back to Marcus Tullius Cicero (106–43 BCE). Trumbo's first two letters of advice were *études* (warm-ups), and to me, they seem somewhat crude expressions of a form of male humor that is no longer in fashion. On the occasion of Christopher and Mitzi's visit to the Butlers in Mexico City, Trumbo wrote a letter to Christopher in which he imparted "certain basic truths" to "guide his actions, solve his difficulties, enrich his mind and increase the scope of his activities" with women.[47] Having warmed to the task and the intricacies of the double standard, Trumbo wrote to Nikola, who was in Europe, and warned her about "men of all colors and dimensions and temperature, men as various as the sands of the sea are many, yet each one of them as like unto the other as new-coined dimes in that most urgent aspect of their lives which, if they have any brains . . . deals, my dear, with you." Trumbo discussed the sexual proclivities of twelve foreign nationalities, described the predatory instincts of American men abroad, and advised Nikola to purchase a good stiletto. He then instructed her how to use it.[48]

His most notorious advice letter was written two years later, when Christopher was a sophomore at Columbia University. It was subsequently immortalized in Christopher's play and in the film based on it. It is a lengthy disquisition on masturbation, and it is embellished with so many infrequently used words that Christopher had to use his dictionary to make sense of it. After he had read and translated what came to be known as "The Letter," and after his laughter had subsided to an occasional chuckle, he immediately shared it with everyone he knew. Forty-five years later, Kate Lardner can still remember the day he brought it to the Lardners' apartment on West End Avenue. It is, from beginning to end, an example of Trumbo's wit and playfulness with the English language.

The first (and smaller) piece of advice Trumbo offered his son was to read Henry O. Yardley's *Education of a Poker Player*. He told Christopher: "Read it in secret, hide it whenever you leave quarters, and you'll be rewarded with many unfair but legal advantages over friend and enemy alike, not to mention that occasional acquaintance who has everything including money." His second (more extensive) piece of advice was to read Albert Ellis's *Sex without Guilt*, which he had "mailed in plain wrapper under separate cover." Trumbo urged Christopher to share it with all his friends. Trumbo extolled Ellis as an author, stating:

> [He] will take his place in history as the greatest humanitarian since Mahatma Gandhi. . . . This good man has written what might be called a manual for masturbators. That is to say, in one slim volume he has clarified the basic theory of the thing, and then, in simple layman's language, got right down to rules and techniques. This in itself is a grand accomplishment; but what most compels my admiration is the zest, the sheer enthusiasm which Dr. Ellis has brought to this subject.

It is Dr. Ellis' idea to spring masturbation from the bed-
room's crepuscular gloom, where for endless generations it has
lain a saprogenic curse of millions of little lechers, and turn
it loose in the parlor where it rightfully belongs. This chap
doesn't find anything wrong with it at all: indoors or out, he
ranks it right up there with ping-pong, gin rummy and "Maverick" [the television western] as a time-honored, red-blooded
patriotic pastime.

Several wildly baroque pages follow, in which Trumbo describes his
own adolescent tangle with the enterprise, including this wonderful
passage:

I (sneaky, timorous, incontinent little beast with my Paphian
obsessions) was never wholesomely at home with my penile
problem, nor ever found real happiness in working it out—all
because of that maggoty, mountainous pustule of needless guilt
that throbbed like an abscess in my young boy's heart.

On warm summer night's while exuberant girl-hunting contemporaries scampered in and out of the brush beneath high
western stars, I, dedicated fool, lay swooning in my bed with no
companion save the lewd and smirking demons of my bottom-
less guilt. Cowering there in seminal darkness, liquescent with
self-loathing, attentive only to the stealthy rise and Krafty-Ebb-
ing of my dark scrotumnal blood, fearful as a lech yet firmer
of purpose than any rutting buffalo, I celebrated the rites of
Shuah's son with sullen resignation. Poor little chap on a summer's night, morosely masturbating . . . !

Claiming (tongue fully in cheek) how painful it had been for him to
relive, for Christopher's instruction, the calamitous tale of his youth, he
asked, rhetorically: "What is pain compared to the immeasurable satisfaction of being a proper dad to you?"

Trumbo acknowledged that he had written this letter while "still
too deeply under the literary and erotic spell of *Lolita*," which he had
read "four straight times in four straight days." Trumbo compared
Lolita's author, Vladimir Nabokov, with Ellis: He is "a way-shower,
one of those spirits who understands that everything under the sun
has its time and place and joy in an ordered world." Trumbo then seg-
ued into a brilliant parody of Humbert Humbert's descriptions of the

nymphets encountered in *Lolita*, which Christopher did not include in his play:

> Now that *Lolita* has brought nymphetophilia into the world of fashion and made it, thank God, as respectable as ornithology, I'm willing to place it on record that my own sexual taste in young girls runs strongly to larvines, beside whom your average nymphet seems gross and dissolute. A larvine begins to glow at five-and-a-half and generally is quite hagged out before her eighth birthday. Perhaps it's the very brevity of her flower that so attracts me. The man fortunate enough to catch one of these delightful creatures at the very peak of larvineal bloom—provided, of course, no one catches *him*—will be rewarded indescribably.
>
> A pair of them approach even as I pen these words. They live two houses down. I spy on them night and day with a 40-power Stankmeyer-Zeitz. They're on the point of passing my study door en route to Sunday School. One of them's already in third grade. Soon they'll be too old. Closer and closer they come. My excitement mounts like the fires of Krakatoa.
>
> Now (squish-squish-squish) they draw even with the door. Glowing grandeur of tiny milk-fleshed thigh. Liquescent breath of gay vulvaginous pearl. (Psst! Speak to the nice old man. Come into my parlor. Ice cream? Morphine? Exciting photographs?) They continue down the drive. Patter of footsteps fainting with my heart. Nubescent rumplets winkling wild their nappled wonder. Scent of loinwine sighing, crying, dying on soft amber-tawny singing little legs. Oh my God—.[49]

When I asked Mitzi if she had received a "special advice letter," she told me: "I did not, and I bitched about it. So Pop wrote me a short (two-page, I think) letter about the perils of working for the New Christy Minstrels, which was my summer job. But it was done under pressure and he just wasn't really inspired." After reflecting on his letters to and about her and her siblings, Mitzi said: "We all knew that he truly loved us, but we also knew how single-minded he could be. Sometimes he became so wrapped up in what he was doing that he may have had no room for thinking about how to direct us. He did not know how to sit down and *talk* to us. He could be roused to battle on our behalf—that's what he did best! And he loved writing those letters of advice.

They were intended to amuse Niki and Chris; they were not meant to be 'personal.'"

I once asked Christopher if it was difficult for him to be the only son of such an incandescent, larger-than-life father. He said, "No, I always had a firm sense of who I am." In one of his audio notes to himself, he said: "My father is different from other people. Many of them looked up to him and sought his company, which was reasonable, because, after all, I looked up to him. I sought his company." One of Christopher's favorite stories, which he told repeatedly, was about the first time he realized that his father was not an ordinary man. When Christopher was nine or ten, Trumbo took him and a young friend to the Santa Monica Pier. The two boys went on the various rides at the amusement park there, while Trumbo had a few drinks at a bar. On the way home, Trumbo drove the wrong way down a one-way street and was stopped by a motorcycle policeman. The officer approached the car and asked for Trumbo's driver's license. The officer looked at it, looked at Trumbo, and walked back to his motorcycle. He returned with a copy of *Johnny Got His Gun* and, instead of giving Trumbo a traffic citation, asked him to autograph the book. A few years after that event, Trumbo began to pay more attention to Christopher, and they would sometimes travel together. In particular, Christopher remembered their trips to the Frontón Palacio in Tijuana to watch jai alai games. And when Christopher was playing football for his high school's B team, Trumbo secretly attended the home games, but he never talked to his son about his athletic efforts.

Those who knew Christopher well are unanimous in saying that he loved and respected his father and appreciated the quality of his writing, his political work, and his battle against the blacklist. Michael Butler remembered that when he and Christopher were working together during the early 1970s, "Chris would now and then refer to Trumbo as 'The Master.' Chris would suggest that if he and I encountered a story problem we couldn't lick, he'd take it to 'The Master.'"[50] Christopher, however, was not blindly appreciative. When asked to appraise his father's writing, he replied: "On the whole, what I liked most about his work is the intelligence and the humor. What I find most distressing is when he becomes overly sentimental."

For most of his life, Christopher was reluctant to talk about his relationship with his father, but near the end, he tried to articulate how he felt:

[Trumbo] felt he had placed a special burden on his children because of his stand before the committee. That colored his relationship with us. I don't know if Niki or Mitzi would agree, or how it worked itself out with them, but with me he was less willing or unwilling to jump into my affairs or direct me than he might have otherwise. Also, I think he was too aware of his own faults to try and impose his values or ideas upon me. There was also his separation from children that he was aware of. Even though he liked us, loved us, he was awkward at expressing those emotions. He often said about himself, or others said it about him, that he went to extremes, and he wanted to guard against this in one way or another. Not that he always succeeded, of course. But I think it was a cautionary idea in the back of his mind. I also think that, in one way or another, the guilt he felt about his life in general made him reluctant to set himself up as an arbiter of my own attempts to handle the world. Sometimes, looking back, I wish that at some point he had actually told me what he expected of me or what he wished for me. But that was not an easy thing to breach. Perhaps I should have done it, but I didn't know what I wanted from him. That what I had was plenty, and was enough.

Perhaps Trumbo's greatest gift to Christopher was a deep respect for thinking and speaking precisely, for striving to find the apt words or phrases, then composing them into model paragraphs. "Trumbo was," Nikola remembered, "very careful in his use of language, and we three kids were expected to speak well and we were chastised for using slang." Mitzi recalled that he "presided over the family dinner table with flair and theater, but he could be merciless when he felt that we were not thinking and arguing clearly." Christopher, like his father, was a master of the subtle—and sometimes not so subtle—riposte. He was not as flashy, but he could be just as effective. Mitzi considered her brother "the most thoughtful, the most careful, and the most serious of us."

Christopher, like several other screenwriter progenies, dreamed of becoming a novelist, and Trumbo encouraged that effort and offered to support him. Instead, Christopher became a writer for the screen (*Brannigan*, *The Don Is Dead*) and television (*Naked City: A Killer Christmas*, *Amy Prentiss*, and *Ishi, the Last of His Tribe*). He wrote episodes for a variety of television drama series, including *Ironside* and *Quincy M.E.*, and served as executive story consultant for three television programs: *Dark Justice, Mrs. Columbo,* and *Quincy M.E.* He and his father worked together effectively and happily while making the film version of *Johnny Got His Gun,* and Christopher completed two of his father's scripts (*Papillon* and *Ishi, the Last of His Tribe*). Trumbo also gave one of his movie scripts ("Mr. Adam") and one of his play scripts ("A Married Man," aka "Morgana") to Christopher to rewrite and market. But it seemed to me that Christopher derived little satisfaction from those undertakings. Perhaps his disappointment with his writing career was one of the reasons why, in his early thirties, he succumbed to the disease of alcoholism.

When Nancy Escher met him in 1979, Christopher was almost forty and had been in and out of Alcoholics Anonymous for ten years. She joined Alanon, and together they struggled to find recovery. They slowly rebuilt their lives, moved to Ojai, and traveled. Christopher began to work again, this time mining the subject he knew best: his family's life on the blacklist. He remained sober and productive for the rest of his life. The success of his play *Trumbo: Red, White and Blacklisted* and the loss of a kidney to cancer gave him a new purpose and direction. He worked closely with Peter Askin on later versions of the play and on the documentary film *Trumbo,*[51] and he started the biography-memoir-history of his father. While he was working on that project, Nancy recalled, Christopher regularly "found himself caught in a twilight zone between memory and history." During one of those moments he wrote: "It is as if the ghost of Trumbo had appeared to me and said, as did the ghost of Hamlet's father to Hamlet: 'Adieu, adieu, remember me.' In a way all sons have the same duty, but Trumbo's ghost wants more than to be remembered, it wants its mortal life to be justified, through the eyes and memories of its son. The son's eyes that have seen him and known him, those are the eyes the ghost chooses."

But the cancer returned. As Mitzi noted sadly, both her father and her brother "died before completing what they wanted to do most—Pop, to write *Night of the Aurochs* [see chapter 26]; Chris, to write his and our father's story."

14

Negotiating the Black Market, Working with the King Brothers

I have sampled the waters here briefly, and have reason to believe I shall be able to earn a living. . . . I am going to work like hell for two or three months to get back on my economic feet, and after that try your trick of apportioning a certain time to Christ [novels] and a certain to Caesar [scripts].

—Dalton Trumbo

Trumbo returned from Mexico an angry man, his anger stoked by the effect the blacklist was having on him and his friends. For the most part, he effectively and productively channeled that anger: he wrote pamphlets and articles and delivered speeches criticizing the domestic cold war, he wrote dozens of scripts for the black market, and he devised and implemented a grand strategy for breaking through the blacklist. From time to time, however, his anger erupted, and he lashed out at blacklistees and attorneys whose actions he deemed inimical to his strategy to fully exploit the black market in scripts (an approach, it should be noted, that only writers could take advantage of and profit from, since unlike actors and directors, writers did not have to appear at the studios to do their jobs; they could use pseudonyms or employ fronts).

Since writing was the only weapon he and the other blacklisted writers possessed, he decided they should try to defeat the blacklist by outwriting the white market. If enough people on the blacklist wrote enough black-market scripts that were filmed, they could undermine the system because their underground market would devalue the aboveground market. A second tactic was the employment of rumor and ridicule. Toward the end of 1956, when it became clear that Michael Wilson's script for *Friendly Persuasion* (for which he did not receive screen credit) would be nominated for an Academy Award (see chapter 17), Trumbo devised a way to use that event to illuminate the black market. If Wilson were nominated, the industry would experience not the glowing publicity that usually surrounded its award ceremonies but, instead, a series of disquieting rumors. When reporters asked Trumbo, Wilson, and Albert Maltz (the most likely suspects) if they had written the script in question, each refused to either confirm or deny that rumor. That way, they could get their names associated with the good pictures and not with the bad ones.

Trumbo's strategy required an expanding black market, but when he arrived in Los Angeles, he found that the black market had shrunk in size, forcing dozens of screenwriters to seek better opportunities in Mexico, Europe, San Francisco, and New York City. Many of those who remained in Hollywood had taken other types of jobs. Robert Lees, cowriter of many of the Abbott and Costello films, had opened a dress shop with his wife; Fred Rinaldo, Lees's writing partner, sold stationery; Adrian Scott, who had produced *Cornered* and *Crossfire*, worked for a toy manufacturer. They did not live in the same neighborhoods, did not enjoy the same lifestyle, and did not socialize extensively with one another. Some had been close friends and remained so (Ring Lardner Jr. and Ian Hunter, Paul Jarrico and Wilson, Lester Cole and John Howard Lawson). Some friendships foundered (Trumbo and Hugo Butler, Jarrico and Scott). But they constituted a community of sorts. With very few exceptions, they readily responded to appeals for loans from other blacklistees, even if they had to borrow from someone else, and they rarely demanded repayment. In addition, they helped one another get jobs, and in a few cases, they even stepped in to finish scripts that, for one reason or another, a friend could not. The litigious few sometimes met to plan strategy and talk about their current court case. By the time Trumbo returned from Mexico, Communist Party membership in Hollywood had probably declined to a few dozen. Two years later, in 1956, following Khrushchev's speech about the crimes of Stalin and the Soviet invasion of Hungary, the Hollywood branch ceased to exist.

While Trumbo was in Mexico, the blacklisted, without any assistance from the Communist Party, had devolved several strategies to fight the blacklist and the domestic cold war. They organized a picket of the September 1951 hearing of the Committee on Un-American Activities held in Los Angeles. They instituted nearly a dozen individual and collective legal actions against the producers. Philip Stevenson cofounded *California Quarterly*, a left-wing cultural journal, and Sylvia Jarrico and Helen Levitt created *Hollywood Review*, which printed critical analyses of films and the film industry by some of the blacklistees (Wilson, Scott, and Lawson, among others). And, as noted earlier, Biberman, Scott, and Jarrico founded an independent film company.[1]

Though Trumbo would have preferred to write novels and plays, Christopher said:

> He returned from Mexico determined to write screenplays. One reason was earning a living. The second was his determination to break the blacklist. But he did not, at first, know how. He did not think that the legal path would work, and after his breach-of-contract suit was settled, he bowed out of further litigation. After all, it's very difficult when you're trying to get your job back, to sue the people who are going to [re]employ you. He did not oppose the litigants, but he refused to be associated with them.
>
> Trumbo knew he had to concentrate on means not ends, focus his gaze, and not allow himself to be sidetracked. He and the other writers had to learn to be satisfied with small achievements. He developed a series of tactics by which blacklisted writers might improve their condition, pushing each forward at different times, and remaining flexible enough to respond to the constantly shifting conditions in the black market. He was not interested particularly in who broke through the blacklist or how, but only that it be ended.

As it happened, the blacklist was not broken, but it was progressively weakened by a series of events, many of them cleverly utilized by Trumbo. These began with Wilson's screen credit for *Friendly Persuasion* and extended to Otto Preminger's public announcement that he intended to give Trumbo screen credit for *Exodus* (see chapter 19).

Trumbo's strategy was based on the belief that the producers were using the blacklist to economically intimidate those who were likely to be subpoenaed by the Committee on Un-American Activities. Witnesses facing the loss of earning power, a drastic reduction in living standards, and economic insecurity were more likely to cooperate. And the more witnesses who cooperated, the more it appeared that the industry was cleansing itself of Communists. The blacklistees would become, in effect, nonpeople. Therefore, raising the salaries and the standards of living (and hence the stature and presence) of those writing for the black market became Trumbo's immediate goal. It could be labeled the "we are still here, you bastards" plan. To accomplish that goal, he and the other blacklisted writers had to write a lot of scripts very quickly; accept, at least initially, a much lower rate of pay than they were used to; and be extremely stealthy. Trumbo, for example, never cashed a check in his own name because he suspected that government agents were watching his bank accounts. And he had learned from his experiences with Sam Spiegel and the King brothers that some producers, whether because of a lack of money, bankruptcy, miserliness, or greed, would renege on their promises to pay. When that happened, the writer's only recourse was to plead. For example, Benedict Bogeaus, an independent producer, signed a contract with "Sam Jackson" (one of Trumbo's pseudonyms) to write a script: $5,000 to be paid up front, and another $5,000 if Bogeaus liked the script. Bogeaus did like the script, but he remitted only $3,000 to Trumbo. In desperation, Trumbo wrote:

> I need this money, Ben. I don't have the chance that you have to make big money. I gamble my time, and in that sense, a small portion of my life, on very little money. Less money than any other writer within a mile of me would charge. I count on the money. I have to budget the money out. And I do very much need that two thousand. Please, please treat me in this matter as you would the least shit-heel actor. Please pay me. . . . If you don't, I won't do anything about it anyway. Because I can't. So all I can say, having waited, having been honest and prompt, having done the best I could according to my agreement—all I can say is *please*.[2]

(See below for the one occasion Trumbo allowed himself to vent his anger directly to a producer.)

To be successful, the strategy of writing one's way off the blacklist required a new way of doing business and of writing and revising scripts. First, one had to develop a dependable circle of producers. Then one needed to find people to act as fronts. Prior to going to prison, Trumbo's friends had served as his fronts, but when they too (Butler and Hunter) were blacklisted, Trumbo began to use Cleo as his front. When he returned to Los Angeles, he continued to use Cleo, made arrangements with some nonblacklisted people, and invented a long list of pseudonyms. Trumbo had so many pseudonyms (thirteen in all) that Mitzi told her then-boyfriend, comedian Steve Martin, "There were no wrong numbers in their household because any unknown name the caller asked for was assumed to be one of Trumbo's aliases."[3]

Once producers and fronts were secured, Trumbo had to find a way to protect them from exposure. To break up the money trail, Trumbo opened several bank accounts under different names. "As soon as I was able to drive a car legally," Christopher recalled, "I was drafted into black-market service, delivering messages Trumbo didn't want compromised by a paper trail, picking up cash and checks, then depositing my various collections into various bank accounts opened under the names of the pseudonyms Trumbo was using. After a decent interlude, I would transfer the money from those accounts to my parents' bank. Occasionally, I'd have to concoct an explanation to satisfy a bank manager who was wondering what someone my age was doing with all that money, but the scheme usually ran smoothly." Trumbo recalled one cash run in particular: "Chris used to go over to Ben's [Bogeaus] house to collect the money, which was always paid in cash so there would be no record of any transaction with me. . . . Ben handed him an envelope with $10,000 in cash in it and told him to count the money. Chris almost collapsed. He was then in high school. He counted the money with trembling fingers and drove home at the rate of about five miles an hour to make certain he delivered it safely."[4]

Black-market screenwriting also required Trumbo to promise to do as many revisions as the producer demanded, free of charge. Though he might, on occasion, defend a scene or a story line he believed in, he always let the producer have the last word. "He knew that was what he had do to," Mitzi recalled, but it "didn't stop him from storming around after a conference in his office, ranting about the absurd alterations he was obliged to make."

During the period from 1954 to 1960, Trumbo wrote (or consulted on) more than sixty stories, treatments, and scripts. (For a list of Trumbo's black-market work, see the appendix.) In addition, he worked on a variety of novels and wrote several plays, four well-researched political pamphlets, hundreds of detailed letters, and many pages of political reflections. These Herculean (and low-paid) labors made it necessary for Trumbo to juggle projects, take time from Peter to assuage Paul, and lie to both.

He was in his office at the Highland Park house by six o'clock every morning. He drove Mitzi to school at eight o'clock on weekdays, but otherwise he spent the entire day writing and reading. (He was a terrible driver, and Mitzi was relieved when she turned sixteen and got her

The Trumbo home in Highland Park. Photograph by Larry Ceplair.

driver's license.) At six in the evening he returned to the house for what Cleo called "drinking time." After dinner he returned to his office and worked late into the night. "He was never without a cigarette," Nikola told me, and after 6:00 p.m., "he was never without a glass of scotch."

Trumbo rarely collaborated because of the complications it involved, but shortly after his return from Mexico, as a means of reimmersing himself in the black market, he cowrote a few scripts with Michael Wilson. They found it impossible to work together in the same room, so they developed what they called the "pony express" method to meet their tight deadlines. Zelma Wilson, Michael's wife, called it "a kind of shuttle operation. Mike developed the script's structure" or outline, and Trumbo wrote the dialogue; then "Mike would do more outlines." They mailed material back and forth every day. Using that process, they completed three westerns in a one-month stretch, receiving about $3,000 a script.[5]

Trumbo was then hired by Frank Seltzer, co-owner of Seltzer Films, a small independent production company. The contract was signed by Cleo, using her maiden name: Fincher. For a payment of $1,000, "she" agreed to revise a screenplay based on the life of the late Tom Pendergast, former political boss of Kansas City, Missouri. "She" agreed to make any changes Seltzer desired, "without limitation of any kind," until Seltzer declared himself satisfied. If a B (low-budget) film was made from the script, Seltzer agreed to pay an additional $9,000 on the day principal photography began; if an A film was made, he would pay an additional $19,000. In either case, Fincher was guaranteed 2.5 percent of the producers' share of the profits.[6] Nothing was said about screen credit, but Ben Perry later agreed to put his name on the script. Trumbo discarded the original screenplay and, using the research Seltzer had given him, wrote an original titled "The Boss," which he completed in March 1956.

That script was one of his better black-market efforts, perhaps because it was based on characters familiar to him from his earlier magazine articles and screenplays: corrupt city officials, venal businessmen, gangsters. When *The Boss* opened in theaters in October, it was well reviewed. Ruth Waterbury wrote: "It is powerful and outstandingly honest in its character portrayals. Its people are not rubber stamps, but forcefully original human beings. Their speech is never trite, and neither are their reactions. The credit for this, obviously, belongs to Ben L. Perry."[7] It was also lauded by the reviewers for *Daily Variety* and *Hollywood Reporter.*[8] Following its recent DVD release, Paul Mavis wrote that it was "lean and crude and tough."[9]

Unbeknownst to Trumbo, one of the producers with whom he was working was an FBI informant. George Templeton, who had purchased the "West from London" script Trumbo had written while in prison, contacted Trumbo in late 1955 and asked him to rewrite a television script titled "Citizen Soldier." Templeton then told an FBI agent he had hired Trumbo. Templeton also told the agent that "Trumbo has considered going to the FBI in order to discuss his full history but there appears to be one friendship connection that Trumbo is waiting to have cleared up before doing so."[10] The latter comment was typical of the nonsense that fills much of the FBI files on the motion picture industry.

Trumbo's most dependable employers on the black market were the King brothers: Maury, Frank, and Herman (Hymie). They were born in New York City to immigrant parents named Kuzinsky in 1911, 1914, and 1916, respectively. The family later moved to Chicago and then to the Boyle Heights section of Los Angeles. When their father died, Maury became a boxer to support the family and allow his brothers to finish high school. After they graduated, the three brothers became newspaper vendors, and a few years later they borrowed $250 and went into the candy, tobacco, and arcade game business. Within ten years, they were known as the pinball kings of Los Angeles. Unhappy with the supply of movies available for their penny arcade machines, they began to make their own. They rented an office and learned the movie business. "They were all over the lot," an early associate recalled, "asking questions from cameramen, grips, directors, laborers—helping hoist something while asking why it was being hoisted." Another acquaintance said the brothers would "ask everybody everything. . . . Then they['d] hash it over with their mother and decide."[11]

Their first movie, *Paper Bullets*, was made in 1940 at a cost of $20,000. It grossed $400,000. With those profits in hand, they left the pinball business, changed their name to King, and signed a distribution deal with Monogram Pictures Corporation. Over the next five years they made nine pictures; all were shot within two weeks, and only one cost more than $250,000. They all earned a profit. Their biggest success, *Dillinger*, returned $2.5 million. After that, the brothers and their mother moved to Beverly Hills.

Philip Yordan, who wrote *Dillinger*, later said he loved working for the King brothers. When asked if Frank had any "story sense," Yordan replied: "Frank, story sense? He would say, 'I like it' or 'I don't like it.' . . . But he very seldom commented [beyond that]. . . . Frank was intelligent. . . . [H]e could read, he could understand." Yordan added that Frank, who resembled "a 300-pound Chinaman," always had "a big cigar in his mouth and his drawer full of Hershey bars, and he always wondered why he was so fat, because, he would say, 'I don't eat.'"[12]

Robert Lewin, a reporter for *Life* magazine, described the brothers in a less picturesque manner: "Maury is generally conceded to be the spark plug of the trio, the idea man with good story and publicity sense. Frank is quieter, holds down Maury's wilder flights [and] handles their business deals shrewdly. Herman is the quietest of the three, spends much of his time on the road finding out what the exhibitors want, making friends where they'll do the Kings the most good." Maury, the "sparkplug," told the *Life* reporter: "We ain't going to stop until we get an Oscar." Yordan told Lewin: "They worship a guy with a name, no matter if he's a success or a has-been."[13]

Because of their frugality and because of their desire to work with famous writers and directors, even if they were well past their prime, the King brothers assiduously mined the black market. Indeed, for many years they *were* the black market. At various times they employed Edward Dmytryk, Michael Wilson, John Howard Lawson, Lester Cole,

Robert Richards, Guy Endore, John Berry, Ian Hunter, Al Levitt, and Ring Lardner Jr. According to Lardner, the King brothers were "not at all unpleasant to work with," although they were not particularly sympathetic to the plight of the blacklistees.[14] Dmytryk recalled: "Between them, Frank and Maury had all the attributes of a top producer, except one—they refused to risk much money on any film, no matter what its potential."[15] Levitt thought the brothers were "ridiculous" but "extraordinary"; he found them "very vulgar in every way and unprincipled."[16]

The Kings were certainly a fount of assignments for Trumbo. In April 1954 they agreed to pay Cleo Fincher $3,000 for a rewrite of a script titled "The Indian Fighter."[17] In July the brothers paid Trumbo $4,000 for an original story,[18] and they agreed to pay him $5,000 to write an original screenplay under the title "The Syndicate."[19] In August 1955 the Kings hired Trumbo to write "Heaven with a Gun," which was fronted by Robert Presnell Jr.; Trumbo received $10,000 for that assignment—half up front.[20] One year later, Trumbo contracted to adapt Pat Frank's comic novel *Mr. Adam* for the brothers; he got $5,000 up front, plus a percentage of the net profits, if any, and a percentage of the net profits if the script were sold to another film company.[21] Whenever Trumbo completed a script for the King brothers, they required him to sign a letter waiving his rights to a screen credit.

Trumbo generally used the name "Doc Abbott" (the protagonist of his novel *Eclipse* and his screenplay for *A Man to Remember*) in his correspondence with the Kings, but the checks they issued for his work were usually made payable to Beth or Cleo Fincher. The relationship between Trumbo and the brothers was not, however, always a harmonious one, particularly with regard to the movie released as *The Brave One* (aka "The Bull and the Boy" or "The Boy and the Bull"). As noted previously, Trumbo flew from Mexico to Los Angeles to pitch the story to the Kings, who agreed to buy it for $10,000: $3,500 up front, another $1,500 when they received the script, and an additional $5,000 if they decided to make the movie. When Trumbo sent them the script, they promised to remit the $1,500, and they also sent him a contract calling for the deferment of the other $5,000, "to induce the Chemical Bank and Trust Company to advance monies for the production and completion" of the film. Trumbo was not happy with that arrangement, and he wrote to the brothers to explain why:

> In our first verbal agreement about my writing original screenplays and giving you exclusive option on them without charge,

the price was to be $10,000, and no mention of deferment was made, nor, on my part, intended. In our telephone conversation setting up the present deal on "The Bull and the Boy," no mention was made of deferment. On the contrary, it was agreed that if you decided to make the picture, you would pay me the remaining $5,000. I had no idea you would send papers giving me a deferred payment if, when and how such monies should later become available. However, as you see, I have signed the papers because, to put it very simply, my wife is going to the hospital as soon as the $1,500 arrives, and I have no alternative.[22]

The Trumbos received a check for $1,500 on September 22.

In January 1953, when the Kings could not come up with the deferred money, Trumbo had to borrow $3,000 against the deferment, at 6 percent interest. The loan was cosigned by Seniel Ostrow, a wealthy mattress manufacturer who helped out many of the blacklistees.[23] When Trumbo sent the final draft of the bull story to the Kings a few months later, he once again had to plead for the money they owed him:

This letter is not a reproach, because I know that you are decent men and I value our relationship. It is not written in anger, for anger will do no good. It is actually written to beg you—to supplicate you to pay me the $1,800 if you possibly can, and before the fifteenth, so I can save my trust deed. And to please write me, telling me what the situation is, and what future there is, if any, for me with your organization. If you really want me— that's the point; and perhaps you don't, in which event kindness would dictate that I be told so. Because this worry, this loss, this dread of tomorrow, this slow stripping away of everything one has simply because one cannot get the money already due—is too much for a human being to bear. Please—in God's name, write me quickly and tell me.[24]

Trumbo received $300 on April 24, $1,410 on April 28, and $3,090 on August 10.

The Brave One is a variant of a traditional genre: young person saves adored pet from death. Trumbo told the story in a naturalistic manner, sharply reducing the bathos normally associated with this genre. The movie is not profound, Trumbo later wrote, "and not in any way innovative." It is, rather, "a very simple and simply made family film."[25] The King brothers employed two writers to revise Trumbo's script—Harry Franklin and Merrill White—and assigned them screen credit. The original story was credited to Robert Rich. Maury King later said: "I needed a name for the script, so I picked my nephew's. He knew as much about writing as I know about fixing cars, since he was working as an assistant bookkeeper someplace."[26] The movie opened on October 26, 1956, at the Four Star Theater in Los Angeles. Edwin Schallert called it a "gem-like picture,"[27] and it performed well at the box office. To everyone's surprise, the movie received three Academy Award nominations: best achievement in sound recording, best achievement in film editing, and best motion picture story.

Shortly after the film was released, Trumbo's patience with the Kings came to an abrupt end. In late December 1956 he wrote them an angry eleven-page letter in which he gave full rein to his flair for the melodramatic. "This is," he began, "a painful letter to write, but it has to be written. The sleigh ride is over. The horse you refuse to feed can no longer haul your wagon. . . . I can no longer afford the crushing burden of supporting the King Brothers out of the product of my mind and the contents of my bank account." Although they had paid him $9,750 for *Carnival Story*, he had rewritten it four times, and it had earned a large profit for the company. *The Brave One*, however, was a different matter: it would earn even more than *Carnival Story*, and it would establish the Kings as prestige producers. And yet, Trumbo fairly shouted, *"at no point in the whole period while that script was being got out of me and produced was I treated fairly or decently. . . . You violated every single clause of* [our original] *agreement."*

Trumbo then outlined his grievances. The Kings had agreed that if they did not like the script, they would return it immediately, without showing it to anyone outside the family. Instead, they had copied it, labeled it "property of King Brothers Productions," and spread it around Hollywood and Spain. Then, Maury had sneaked down to Mexico City and tried to make a deal behind Trumbo's back, thereby ruining any chance Trumbo had to get a fair price in the open Hollywood market. All told, as a consequence of this betrayal, Trumbo had no money to feed himself and his family, he had to liquidate assets at well below their market value, and he had to wait nine months to receive full payment for the script. The Kings got what they wanted "by almost destroying" the Trumbo family. He asked, dramatically: "How was your family eating during those days, Frank? . . . How were your assets during those days while you operated with my property, Frank?—were they doing fine?"

But that was not the end of the Kings' fiscal shenanigans. Trumbo had asked Frank King to reimburse him $1,420—the amount he had spent trying to collect the money the Kings owed him for *The Brave One*. Frank had agreed to pay him $1,000 but then never sent it. Again, Trumbo waxed dramatic: "What are you doing with my $1,000, Frank? Are you making a little money with it? I hope so. I hope you make a lot with it. I have a little daughter who is eleven years old. She's going to need a college education. That's her money you have, Frank. You took it from her. Keep it, and may God rest your soul."

As the grand finale to this letter, Trumbo recounted the series of events that had provoked him to write it: "It was the present Maury gave me the day before Christmas in the form of a telephone call urging me and my wife-secretary to work days and nights [on 'Mr. Adam'] straight through the holiday season in order that you . . . could make another million or two out of our blood." That admonition from Maury had come directly after Trumbo's doctor had warned him that his "mental fatigue" was "very marked" and that he was expending far too much "nervous energy." That nervous energy, Trumbo claimed, "had gone out of my life to enrich the King Brothers. I realized that after giving them (for a disgraceful sum) $8,000,000 to $10,000,000 of grosses, they still weren't satisfied. Speed it up, Doc; work nights, Doc; get your wife on that typewriter, Doc; forget Christmas, Doc; forget your family, Doc; forget your health—*we're in a hurry to get more money out of you*."[28]

This letter did not destroy Trumbo's relationship with the King brothers. Both parties had come to know, appreciate, and tolerate the other's idiosyncrasies, and both realized the value of their connection. A series of discussions followed the Kings' receipt of the letter, and four months later, Trumbo wrote a conciliatory letter to the family, apologizing for his one-sided letter:

> I remembered everything I felt you had done *to* me, and I forgot everything you felt you had done *for* me. This is a common failing of angry men, and I displayed in my letter a full share of it. I forgot that just before I went to jail you gave me an advance on a script [*Carnival Story*]; and that immediately thereafter the court decision went against me; and that I went to jail without writing the script I had agreed to write; and that you did not

ask for your money back for non-performance as you had every right to do; and that when I got out of jail the commitment still stood with you, so I stepped out of jail into a job.

"You are," he concluded, "honorable men of great integrity."[29]

As a result of this and the myriad other frustrations associated with working on the black market, Trumbo was constantly searching for a way to increase his independence. He thought he had found such a way when, in mid-1955, he crossed paths with Eugene Frenke, an independent producer. Frenke had been born in Moscow in 1907, fled to Germany in 1920, and became a movie producer. He married Russian-born actress Anna Sten, and when Samuel Goldwyn signed her to a contract in 1932, Frenke and Sten moved to Hollywood. Frenke had coproduced or produced five movies between 1943 and 1954, but by the time he met Trumbo, he was a packager of film deals: he would find a story, hire a writer to develop it, sign stars to play the roles, and then sell the package to a studio. He had just sold the *Heaven Knows Mr. Allison* project to Twentieth Century–Fox, for which he had sought Trumbo's advice on the script. Satisfied with Trumbo's response—a seven-page analysis and suggestions for some minor revisions—Frenke asked if he would be interested in writing a movie about Franklin D. Roosevelt that would be produced by a company he and Trumbo would own. Trumbo was enthusiastic about both the story and the company. He wrote to Frenke: "I've been going over my pre-blacklist record to discover for myself whether that record justifies on my part a gamble that my films in the future will make money. For in forming a company, we are essentially gambling on our ability to choose subjects and deliver scripts that will *earn* money. We cannot afford a single flop." To persuade Frenke of his profit-making potential, Trumbo reviewed his own record as a screenwriter. Trumbo calculated that during his entire career, he had written scripts for twenty-five films: "1 lost money, 2 broke even, 22 made money." In addition, between 1947 and 1950, he had sold $200,000 worth of stories. Having demonstrated that he could generate money-making ideas, Trumbo proposed that he and Frenke make two movies a year. Trumbo would tailor each script so that it could be filmed economically, in black and white, to fit a conventional-sized screen.[30]

When Frank Seltzer learned about the deal, he warned Trumbo against any type of connection with Frenke: "He is not rated top-drawer ethically or socially and I beseech you to check and recheck any negotiations in which you may become involved with him. . . . I happen to know certain things about him that puts him beyond the pale of the kind of people that I would care to do business with."[31] Many other people warned Trumbo about Frenke, but he disregarded all the negative comments. A few years later, he even made Frenke his business manager. Although Frenke was tremendously loyal to Trumbo and to Trumbo's interests, Frenke's methods frequently caused problems, and several of the financial transactions he recommended cost Trumbo a great deal of money.

Trumbo was not alone in his efforts to break through the blacklist. His cause was helped by Elizabeth Poe Kerby's groundbreaking article for *Frontier* magazine titled "The Hollywood Story," which appeared in May 1954. She was the first journalist to interview blacklisted people, and she exposed the mechanisms of the blacklist in Hollywood. Two years later, the Fund for the Republic published John Cogley's two-volume work on blacklisting, for which Kerby was one of the main researchers and writers.[32]

Also in 1956, the suspicious circumstances surrounding black-listed writer Carl Foreman's reappearance before the Committee on Un-American Activities provoked Cogley and Paul Jacobs to write articles intimating that at least one movie studio might be arranging clearances with the committee. Foreman had appeared on September 24, 1951, invoked the Fifth Amendment, been blacklisted, and moved to the United Kingdom.[33] In early 1956, according to Jacobs, Columbia Pictures decided it wanted to change its production and distribution operation in the United Kingdom, and it wanted to hire Foreman to produce films there. Columbia negotiated a contract with him, conditional on Foreman's voluntary reappearance before the committee and his not invoking the Fifth Amendment. Then, Foreman's lawyer, the studio's lawyer, or both met with committee chairman Francis E. Walter (D-Pa.), who agreed to allow Foreman to reappear and admit his former party membership without having to name anyone else. However, committee director Richard Arens claimed that he was unaware of this "arrangement," and when Foreman met with Walter and Arens, Arens, following standard committee procedure, asked Foreman about other party members. Walter immediately intervened and told Foreman he was not required to answer Arens's question. Although the committee did not publicly announce that Foreman had been cleared, Columbia signed him to a four-picture deal. The *Hollywood Reporter*, Veterans of Foreign Wars, American Legion, and Aware attacked Columbia, but studio executives did not retreat. Walter, to save face, said: "I wasn't interested in getting names from Foreman of people who had already been identified as Communists. I wanted someone who could get up and tell what a sucker he'd been [to join the Communist Party]. I thought Foreman was the kind of important man we needed for this, and I think he did a service to the country in his testimony."[34]

When news of this event reached Hollywood, a number of blacklisted people were suspicious, especially since, just a few months earlier, the Department of State had inexplicably ceased its opposition to Foreman's passport application.[35] Foreman agreed to meet with about two dozen blacklisted writers at Michael Wilson's house, and Trumbo asked Christopher to drive him to the gathering. It was, Christopher recalled, "an all-night meeting. Foreman said that it was his unique value to Columbia that allowed him to do what he did. He had made no deal with the committee; his lawyer had made a deal with the studio. And he had not publicly abased himself. Trumbo believed Foreman, because not believing him led nowhere and believing him revealed a chink in the blacklist. He also saw that Foreman's situation was unique and represented only one individual's end run around the blacklist." Trumbo later said: "Obviously there was corruption somewhere, but so long as a man didn't inform, if he had been fucked by a corrupt system and could take advantage of that corruption without harming anyone else, possibly without harming himself (except to the degree he did something that he preferred not to do), I see no harm in it. It seems a mild sin, a venial one. And with a few exceptions forgiveness can be granted. I don't admire it, but then I'm not called upon to admire it."[36]

15

From the Communist Party
to the New Left

> I do not . . . mean that Communist writers should have pro-
> claimed their affiliation aggressively . . . : only that they should
> not have concealed it.
>
> —Dalton Trumbo

While he was hard at work on the black market, Trumbo had little time to participate in political activities. He later said he had a "fear of activism" because every time he spoke, the sponsoring organization was attacked by anti-Communists.[1] Nevertheless, he made a few speeches, kept himself fully informed about events, wrote letters to periodicals (especially in opposition to the testing of nuclear devices), and, on several occasions, agreed to write pamphlets defending people who were being persecuted by state or federal government agencies. As a result of the confluence of his research and writing, the conversations he had about informing, and Khrushchev's 1956 speech, Trumbo also devoted a significant amount of time to rethinking his attitude toward the Communist Party.

In the summer of 1954 Lou Goldblatt, vice president of the International Longshoremen's and Warehousemen's Union (ILWU), asked Trumbo to write a chapter for his organization's forthcoming pamphlet challenging the government's perjury case against union president Harry Bridges. In 1949 Bridges had been convicted of criminal perjury for stating, in his naturalization papers, that he was not a member of the Communist Party; four years later, the US Supreme Court overturned that decision.[2] One year after this reversal, the Department of Justice brought a civil perjury charge against Bridges. Goldblatt gave Trumbo a mass of research material and outlined the arguments the ILWU attorneys intended to make, and Trumbo agreed to contribute to the pamphlet. Ironically, when *The ILWU Story* was published six months later, none of the authors received credit for his or her work.

In the portion of the pamphlet authored by Trumbo, he characterized the government's campaign against Bridges as "twenty-one years of the most shameful and unprecedented persecutions in the history of the United States." After reviewing the history of the indictments, Trumbo concluded that the campaign had been nothing less than an effort to weaken a successful, democratic, racially tolerant labor union. But, he emphasized, in each of the cases brought against Bridges, officials in the Justice Department had been aiming at a larger target: "They have aimed to stifle the independent voice of the union and to shackle the rank and file nature of its operation. To silence, restrict and confine this union because of what it is and what it stands for, and to change it into a compliant and conforming body."[3]

Trumbo also became peripherally involved in perhaps the most notorious trial of the Cold War—that of the so-called atomic spies. The US government had arrested Julius and Ethel Rosenberg and charged them with espionage. Morton Sobell, a friend of Julius's, had been named a coconspirator by a government witness. Then, depending on whose story one believes, Sobell either took a long-planned vacation to Mexico or fled there to avoid his imminent arrest. Two months later, he was picked up by the Mexican police, turned over to the FBI, and brought back to the United States to stand trial. In early 1951 Sobell was tried alongside the Rosenbergs. He invoked the Fifth Amendment but was convicted of conspiracy to commit wartime espionage and sentenced to thirty years in prison. The Rosenbergs were sentenced to death.

Trumbo was approached by Widge Newman, a member of the Los Angeles Committee to Secure Justice for Morton Sobell, to write a pamphlet challenging the government's case. Trumbo read the transcript of Sobell's trial and decided not only to write a political pamphlet but also to make a "definitive" statement about spying. In it, he intended to present two theses: (1) espionage is as old as world history and is practiced by every country in the world; and (2) Sobell and the Rosenbergs cannot be guilty because "it is inherently improbable that the Soviet Union would employ a Communist as an espionage agent, or the American Communist Party as a vehicle of espionage." Trumbo was convinced that the more evidence he could find that linked Sobell and the Rosenbergs "to the general left and the Communist Party," the stronger the

proof of their "probable innocence."[4] Although Trumbo received a large
amount of material from Newman and made several pages of notes on
the subject of espionage, he never wrote the pamphlet. The reasons are
unclear, but if he had done so, the final product would have undermined
his reputation as an astute political analyst. Material unearthed over
the last two decades from the Soviet archives clearly demonstrates that
there was a very close tie between the CPUSA and Soviet spying in the
United States. Moreover, Sobell later admitted he had passed military
secrets to the Soviet Union.[5]

The third pamphlet assignment Trumbo accepted during this period
resulted in one of his best political efforts. In the summer of 1951 the
Department of Justice arrested fifteen leaders of the California Communist Party and indicted them for violating the Alien Registration Law.
(One defendant was eventually dropped, owing to poor health.) The
California Emergency Defense Committee to support the "California
Fourteen" was formed. It published pamphlets; circulated petitions;
sent speakers to address unions, churches, and community organizations; and organized groups to observe the trial.[6] In August 1952 the
jury found all the defendants guilty, a decision that was upheld three
years later by the Circuit Court of Appeals. However, in October 1955
the US Supreme Court issued a writ of certiorari.

Trumbo had been following the case closely, and he regarded the
entire trial process as a travesty of justice. In addition, he was well
acquainted with Dorothy Healey, one of the defendants. (The two of
them had formed a mutual admiration society.) So, when the defense
committee asked Trumbo to write a pamphlet to rally support for the
California Fourteen's case, he readily agreed. As an additional act
of solidarity with the defendants, he rejoined the Communist Party,
which he considered a political statement rather than a quixotic gesture. Unlike the liberals in 1947, Trumbo refused to dissociate the people under attack from the principle being defended. As he said a few
years later: "They were leaders of a party I had belonged to, and they
had been sentenced to savage prison terms in a phony trial because of
that leadership, and I felt a personal obligation to support them in every
possible way. I felt the Communist Party was finished and that all that
remained to do was clean up the wreckage, try to save those victims still
buried in its rubble, and close shop. I do not regret that decision. I identified myself thereafter in every possible public way with the fourteen
convicted persons."[7]

Trumbo's pamphlet, *The Devil in the Book*, was a sharp critique

Dorothy Healey, one of the fourteen California Communist Party leaders arrested and charged with violating the subversive activities section of the Alien Registration Act, ca. 1951. Courtesy of Richard Healey.

of the Smith portion of the Alien Registration Act and the indictment and trial of the California Communists. For the epigraph, he used the same quotation from von Jhering he had used in *The Time of the Toad*. And he repeated the theme of that pamphlet, except that he substituted "the Smith Act" for "the Committee on Un-American Activities" and "Communists" for "the Hollywood Ten," stating: "The Smith Act has become the hallmark of a decade of repression and restriction not only of Communism but of the entire national community. The means by which Communists are imprisoned therefore becomes the concern of the whole people since it is their liberty which is diminished by each conviction under the act."[8]

The gravamen of Trumbo's argument was that the California Fourteen had not been charged with perpetrating any act of violence, committing any crime, or doing or saying anything in secret. Therefore, to get a conviction, the government had to convert its case into a dubious conspiracy: The appellants were not, at the time of their arrest, charged with teaching and advocating some doctrine; they were instead charged with conspiring to teach that doctrine at some unstated time in the future. In other words, they "were to be punished not for what they did but for what they might do" (11). Their common belief in Marxism constituted the foundation of the "evidence" introduced in support of this "conspiracy." It followed, according to the syllogistic logic of the government's case, that since all Marxists advocate conspiratorial revolutions, and since the appellants were Marxists, they must be advocates of conspiratorial revolutions. Thus, the only evidence needed to convict them was a lengthy compilation of quotations gathered from a large stack of Marxist books and pamphlets. As a consequence of this syllogistic argument, Trumbo stated, each appellant became responsible not only for the words and deeds of every other appellant "but also for Marxist thoughts committed to paper twenty or fifty or a hundred years ago by men long dead in historical circumstances which have ceased to exist" (11–12). Their trial became, therefore, a trial both "of individuals and of philosophic principles. And because of this it inevitably degenerated into what [John] Milton [in *Areopagitica*] held to be the ugliest and most hateful of criminal prosecutions—a trial of books," one in which "the dead became more real than the living, the past more vivid than the present. The government had found devils leaping from these Marxist books, and it sought to exorcize them by punishing living people" (12, 15).

Trumbo concluded *The Devil in the Book* on a much more confident note than he had *The Time of the Toad*. He wrote that he perceived the dawn of a "heartening new atmosphere," and he encouraged his readers to exploit this new atmosphere, "take new stands," "give expression to long-held faith," and "enter the struggle to overthrow" these convictions. It was past time for the citizens of the United States to become fully aware that "the old and not very valorous strategy of tossing Communists to the wolves in despairing hope that the civil rights of all others will then be spared has not worked" and to acknowledge that the "appetite of the Department of Justice and the FBI has proved insatiable." The Smith Act had become "the keystone of the whole structure of suppression," and "its collapse will undermine all other parts of the hateful edifice" (40–41).

Shortly after Trumbo completed his pamphlet, US Attorney General Herbert Brownell Jr. asked the Subversive Activities Control Board to require the California Emergency Defense Committee to register as a Communist front organization, thereby forcing it to reveal its members and donors.[9] In June 1957, however, the Supreme Court overturned the convictions of five of the appellants and remanded the cases of the other nine for new trials.[10] The Department of Justice immediately filed charges against those nine, but it later dropped them. The defense committee dissolved without ever registering with the Subversive Activities Control Board.

After the charges were dropped, Trumbo resigned from the party. He later wrote about the pamphlet: "Now that five of the fourteen have been set free by the Supreme Court, now that all charges have been dropped against the others, now that the judge of that phony trial has been reversed sixteen times [mainly on bail decisions] by higher courts, I look on my pamphlet with a certain pride. Changing times, generally so fatal to political polemics, have not touched it. Not one word needs changing."[11]

Trumbo's political magnum opus, a detailed discussion of his views on the Communist Party, the Soviet Union, secrecy, and socialism, was not published or publicly read aloud. It consisted of a series of drafts he wrote in 1957 for an article he naïvely hoped would be printed in the Communist journal *Mainstream & Masses*. In this manuscript, Trumbo attempted to do what few former Communists had accomplished: he tried to think his way out of the belief system he had followed for more than a decade rather than simply walk away from it, trash it, or transmogrify himself into an anti-Communist. He also wanted to draw lessons for the future of the Left in the United States.

The Devil in the Book, 1956.

In the first part, "My Own View of the CP," Trumbo revealed the main reason he was no longer a party member: he had lost patience with the constant errors and miscalculations of party leaders and their insistence that those errors were "dialectically necessary" in the short run but would be proved correct, in the long run, by "the verdict of history." He concluded that the party had become an organization clinging to life by means of an annual recitation of "last year's errors." (In a draft of a letter to John Howard Lawson, written at about the same time but never sent, Trumbo criticized Lawson for continually asserting "that nothing is more dangerous and more softening to the morale of engaged persons than a victory." So, Trumbo replied sarcastically, are we to derive from that statement the lesson that nothing uplifts and strengthens party members like defeat and, "as Stalin so disastrously put it in tragic action, that each victory increases the peril of the victor"? No, Trumbo answered, "the reverse is true. Each victory adds strength; each defeat detracts from strength.")[12]

Trumbo next addressed the question of how a disillusioned Communist should properly leave the party. This portion of the draft was intended as a direct attack on those Communists (particularly the higher-ups) who had recently resigned from the party in a noisy fashion. In particular, Trumbo cited a mimeographed circular he had just received, signed by nineteen prominent California Communists (including some he had defended in *The Devil in the Book*). The circular announced the signatories' resignation from the party and their reasons for doing so. But by resigning in such a public way, they undermined the decisions of many Hollywood blacklistees who had secretly resigned from the party. Had those individuals publicized their resignations, they might have "hastened the day of their open return to professional careers." Now, to their chagrin, the circular demonstrated that they had maintained a fruitless secrecy "on behalf and at the behest of at least nineteen theoreticians who had no respect for it at all." For his part, Trumbo chose to leave the party quietly, without picking a quarrel with anyone and without making an announcement. He had done so for two reasons: (1) to adhere to the blacklistees' "long-standing" vow of silence about their political affiliations; and (2) to avoid adding to the tribulations or violating the secrecy of those who had chosen to remain in the party.[13]

Thus, Trumbo wrote, because of the party's almost complete disregard for the Hollywood blacklistees, he did not "feel any loyalty or obligation to the Communist Party." He did not feel tied to it in any

way. He had given the party as much as it had given him, "and possibly
a little more. The score is even." He did, however, continue to "feel loyalty to the principle that any political party has the right to unharassed
existence and activity. So long as there remain two persons in the United
States who wish to call themselves a Communist Party, so long must I
defend their right to do so" (23).

That said, he did not feel obligated to continue to defend the Communist Party's "most glaring stupidity, which was its thralldom to
the Soviet Union, and the mystique that arose therefrom." Trumbo
acknowledged that he had defended the Soviet Union, particularly its
foreign policy, between 1939 and 1949, but he had never considered
himself to be in bondage to that country. He next made the excellent
point that, in its own way, the Department of State had been just as
enthralled and mystified by the Soviet Union as CPUSA leaders had
been. Both the State Department and party leaders had suspended
"rational thought" and "abdicated all power of independent judgment.
Having fallen together into the delusion that every act must be predi-
cated on a prior Russian act, both were rendered incapable of perceiving
their own best interests, much less of formulating policies to advance
them. . . . When Russia moved, the State Department and the American
CP turned lively as crickets. When silence enveloped the Kremlin, they
were paralyzed. They had surrendered their intellects in a fit of voluntary self-immolation so insanely wonderful that only metaphysicians
dare dwell on it." As a result of their respective tunnel visions, the State
Department beheld the Soviet Union as the implacable enemy of world
peace, while the Communist Party perceived the United States as the
fomenter of war. "And each saw *only* these things, and *nothing* of what
the other saw—and neither saw the truth" (23–24).

In Trumbo's opinion, although greater odium attended the mystified vision of the Communist Party, that vision had caused much less
harm to the country than did the State Department's mystified vision.
After all, the Communist Party had only "deluded tens of thousands,
[whereas] the State Department triumphantly infected scores of millions. If those who embraced the Communist mystique could tear themselves from the mourning wall for a glance at the visible world, they
would find solace in the fact that though they were not more innocent
of evil than their opponents, their efforts at least produced immeasur-
ably less of it" (24).

Trumbo titled the second part of his long draft "Secrecy and the
Communist Party." There are two versions of it, as well as some unpagi-

nated leaves. The first version (which I call "Secrecy 1") is more focused on Hollywood; the second version ("Secrecy 2") is more universal in scope. Both open with the same sentence: "The question of a secret Communist Party lies at the very heart of the Hollywood blacklist." In "Secrecy 2" Trumbo goes on to state: "There was a secret party and people did belong to it. The question of whether or not the party should have been secret is not as academic as it may seem, since secrecy is a principal issue between it and the American public it sought to reach." In the past, he continued, many organizations had "wisely" used secrecy, but they had done so only when popular or official opposition became "fierce enough to interfere with, or threaten to interfere with, their legal but popular activities." The CPUSA, in contrast, was the only organization that, to his knowledge, had maintained for more than three decades "the secrecy of its general membership regardless of external political circumstances and apparently on a permanent basis."[14]

The kind of secrecy practiced by the CPUSA gave it the appearance of being "a conspiracy to overthrow despotism" (which did not exist in the United States), "while its activities gave it the *function* of a political party in a free country" (which did exist). The party's "refusal" to recognize the impact its conspiracy was having on its prospects and to alter it "finally rendered it incapable of fulfilling its political function." Had Lenin lived to see what the CPUSA was doing, Trumbo mused, he "would have hooted" at its rule of secrecy, and he would have told party leaders that the open politics practiced by the European parties offered much greater opportunities to advance the party's program. Instead, the party's secrecy mandate ended up driving the "secret" Communists in the labor movement from their union positions, from their jobs, and ultimately from the party. "Could greater disaster," Trumbo asked, "have attended an open course?" (1:2–3).

Looking back, Trumbo concluded that the Hollywood Communists "should have been open Communists, or they should not have been members at all." Had they been forced to face the prospect of open membership when they were contemplating enrolling in the party, the Hollywood party would have been much smaller, because a significant number of potential recruits would have weighed their careers in the balance and "prudently . . . refused to join" (1:3):

> The promise of secrecy, however, eliminated the necessity of such a choice. They joined feeling their careers were protected. Their moment of choice was delayed until the illusion of secrecy

collapsed—and by then the quality of choice was radically changed for the worse. Instead of voluntary choice between party and career, they now faced compulsory choice between informing and the blacklist. The number of those who chose the blacklist is impressive evidence of the honor and integrity which they brought with them into the Communist Party.

That they were never given an opportunity to face the first and the real choice is a tragedy. Whichever decision they at that time might have made, they would have emerged from the past decade with more dignity—as men and women, as political persons, as writers, as members of the community—than by submitting to a process which has separated them into informers on the one hand, and professional and social exiles on the other. In a certain sense even the informers can be counted among the victims of a policy which gave them no realistic moment of choice. (1:4)

Fifteen years later, Trumbo used this insight—that both the blacklistees and the informers were victims—as the centerpiece of a speech that provoked sharp criticism from other blacklistees (see chapter 22).

Secrecy also disserved the Nineteen as they were planning their strategy in 1947. The staff of the Committee on Un-American Activities knew from their investigations that the "secret" members of the Hollywood party had focused most of their time and energy on openly supporting progressive Democratic candidates for political office. That is, they had not acted any differently from any other "ardent Democrat." But when they were subpoenaed by the committee, they were faced with a dilemma: should they talk about all their affiliations or remain silent about them? Secrecy, in other words, made their testimony "as perplexing to the public as it was painful to them" (1:2).

Furthermore, because of secrecy, Communist screenwriters who had written political articles or speeches about political issues were faced with an ethical problem. Speaking as partisans of a political party, while claiming secrecy for the party membership that had generated that partisanship, had tainted their written political work. According to Trumbo, "the associations and beliefs" that animated a writer's work needed to be acknowledged "if his ideas and art are to be fairly conveyed and evaluated" (1:6).

The last deleterious effect of secrecy on the Hollywood Communists was that they got no credit for writing some of the decade's (1935–

1945) finest films and for altering film content for the better. Without party-imposed secrecy, the Hollywood community, the nation, and the world would have known "that many of the films it applauded most came from a small political minority whose views they questioned." Trumbo was not saying that Communist writers should have aggressively proclaimed their party membership, "only that they should not have concealed it" (1:6).

While Trumbo was contemplating the effects of secrecy on the organized Left, the domestic cold war had begun to thaw. In 1954, even though the Committee on Un-American Activities and the FBI were still in hot pursuit of "Communists," two of the most notorious red hunters were silenced: Senator Pat McCarran (D-Nev.), chair of the Senate Internal Security Subcommittee and sponsor of the most significant anti-Communist laws, died; and Senator Joseph McCarthy was condemned by the Senate. The following year, President Eisenhower and Soviet premier Nikolai Bulganin met in Geneva to discuss how to lessen global tensions.

Parallel to these developments, radical pacifist A. J. Muste began to prepare the ground for a new, nontotalitarian Left in the United States. He organized a series of meetings on the subject and, with the assistance of other radical pacifists, founded the publication *Liberation* in early 1956. The editors lamented "the decline of independent radicalism" in the United States and "the failure of a new radicalism to emerge." Seven months later, the editors called for a new political organization or alignment, one that was "essentially revolutionary in its program" and based on "fresh thinking in a non-sectarian and non-dogmatic spirit."[15] That last phrase was quoted in an article titled "The New Left: What Should it Look Like?" published in the October 29, 1956, edition of the *National Guardian*, a newspaper that Trumbo regularly read.[16] The author of the article did not answer that question, but one month later, in a speech to a *Guardian* anniversary meeting, Trumbo did. The main task, as he saw it, was to save socialism from its association with the Soviet experience. Socialism, he said, "offers the most humane and intelligent solution to the problems that presently affect the world," and he expressed his "belief that the American people will eventually establish socialism in these United States of America." He was "maddened that the first socialist nation in history permitted its government—temporarily [he hoped]—to degenerate into a dictatorship." Then, in a direct challenge to anti-Communist orthodoxy, he stated: "I know of nothing I could have done to prevent what has happened there; nor do I know of anything I can presently do to hasten the Soviet government's return to those standards which I, and perhaps you, have set up for it."

He did, however, offer a means for the Left in the United States to free itself from the "intellectual orbit of the Soviet Union" and to make the case that just because the type of socialism practiced in the Soviet Union had led to dictatorship did not mean that socialism everywhere would inevitably produce the same result. But to accomplish these tasks, the Left would have to discuss "the real needs of the American people" and learn from them "how they wish to go about the job of improving affairs." In addition, this "new left" must abandon the "swamp lands of emotion, invective and empty rhetoric" and climb to "a higher ground more hospitable to the practice of logic and the restraint of the reasoning intellect." During this climb, no existing leftist organization must be allowed to "assume a position of leadership," and some current leaders would have to become followers. Finally, "for moral reasons and for its own survival," the first order of business for this "new left" must be the winning of civil rights for black people. "There can be no genuine American Left until there is a free Negro community in the United States." Here again, Trumbo issued a warning about avoiding past practices: the "new left" must not expect the Negro people to merge with it. He closed with the adamant assertion that the "fight for Negro freedom is the great historical task of our time."[17]

In sum, by looking backward and forward, Trumbo endeavored to produce a critique that might serve as a bridge connecting the Old Left and the New Left. As it happened, the Old Left proved unwilling to cast a critical eye on its own past, and Trumbo became increasingly critical of its failure to learn from past defeats. Meanwhile, the New Left was still in embryonic form. But, just as Trumbo had predicted, the developing movement for black civil rights would enlist many young white people, some of whom would form the nucleus of a New Left.

16

Blacklist and Black-Market Politics

> My obligation to myself is to write a script with which the producer states his satisfaction; my duty to others is to see that I'm not lured into any conflict which will close some future door on me or someone like me.
>
> —Dalton Trumbo

Trumbo's reflections on communism coincided with his efforts to closely supervise the blacklist and the black market. As a result, his thoughts evolved about the nature of informants and the role of informing in the maintenance of the blacklist. He went to great lengths to instruct other blacklistees how to work on the black market as well as how to resume work on the white market. In terms of the latter, he explicitly rejected making a deal with the Committee on Un-American Activities and pursuing legal action. However, not all members of the blacklisted community accepted Trumbo's self-appointed position as the maker and interpreter of the rules of engagement or his views on informing and informants.

The occasion for Trumbo's first major pronouncement on informing occurred a few days before Christmas 1956, when several blacklistees met at the home of Ben Maddow to listen to Guy Endore's plea that they develop an honorable plan to get what he called "minor people" off the blacklist (though he failed to mention that he considered himself one of those "minor people"). Endore proposed that these people be encouraged to appear before the committee, admit to party membership, and, when asked about other party members, offer the names of previously identified Communists. But, he continued, that approach would not work unless a prominent blacklistee (i.e., Trumbo) interceded with the editors of *Daily People's World* and with the blacklisted community as a whole and convinced them not to publicly criticize those appearances. Endore later wrote: "I said to Dalton: 'At least let's not have those shameful columns they have in the *People's World*,'" and "Dalton felt that I was justified in this request and that there were people, economic borderline cases, you know, who should be allowed to earn a living. . . . So, he said he thought that he could appeal to the editors of the paper and so on. . . . Well, he agreed to it and the following day, I got a special delivery letter. It was a long letter, full of self-bravado, saying he wasn't going to [do it]."[1] In fact, Endore received the letter not the following day but one week later.

Trumbo had not intended his reply to Endore to be widely circulated as an open letter to the blacklisted community. He had decided to write the letter only after hearing that Maddow and Endore had attached Trumbo's name to ideas he could not "possibly approve." He therefore "felt obliged to correct their misapprehension at some length" and to clarify his statement, made at the meeting, that although he favored people seeking clearances, he did not condone "informing" as a means of doing so. He mimeographed the letter because he intended to send it to the fifteen people who had attended the meeting.[2]

Trumbo began the letter by describing the various factors that might have contributed to the "misunderstanding": he had come to the meeting prepared for a discussion of a very different topic; he was suffering from a viral infection; and he had spoken, as was his wont, intemperately. He then summarized events at the meeting as he recalled them:

> I stated at the outset that I had no interest in taking action of any kind to reinstate myself. I also stated my anger at the lost careers and the unused talents of this community, as well as my grief that certain persons have been hastened to their graves by what has happened.
>
> I stated I felt ways must be found as quickly as possible to get people back to their jobs; that I felt the problem should be widely and openly discussed; that all possible areas should be investigated; that all kinds of thinking should be devoted to it. I stated I thought such a search for ways was necessary, not only because it was desirable, but also because I had the feeling that in certain areas of blacklisted people [i.e., among certain elements of the blacklisted community] there was a trend toward getting back at any cost, and that people affected by such feelings should very quickly be presented with the possibility of honorable alternatives.

Trumbo noted that although he had agreed with others at the meeting that informing had been "an act of capitulation" in the early 1950s, he now regretted giving the impression that he was receptive to the notion that "informing now had only ritualistic significance" and that "the damage inflicted by informers today is far less than it was several years ago." He was particularly chagrined by what he had done next: "entirely on my own, I went much further: 'thinking out loud,' as I believe I explained it, I summarized arguments *for* informing." To correct any perception that he advocated any type of informing as a means of getting off the blacklist, Trumbo embarked on a long disquisition on the topic. He condemned it in very general terms as an act that undermines "the very heart of the social compact" and labeled it a "crime . . . worse than murder or rape." Murderers and rapists harm only specific victims, "while the informer poisons and destroys the spiritual life of whole peoples." He condemned in particular "the man who informs on friends who have harmed no one, and who thereafter earns money he could not have earned before." That man, he wrote, is "not a decent citizen, not a patriot, but a miserable scoundrel who will, if new pressures arise and the price is right, betray not just his friends but his country itself." Trumbo also wanted to reverse any impression that he agreed with "the thesis that informing no longer harms those who have often been informed upon." Since he was still a prominent candidate for being named a Communist, he wanted to make it clear that "he who informs on me, privately or publicly, adds to the cumulative burden I already carry, and postpones or possibly destroys my chance to break through." Yes, he wanted as many blacklisted people as possible to return to work as quickly as possible, but if they did so by informing, they would destroy the possibility of open and honest discussion among blacklistees, because everyone would suspect everyone else of being a potential informer.[3]

Endore expressed his gratitude for Trumbo's clarification, writing to him:

> I am really honored to be the recipient of so beautiful a letter. . . . It is more than beautiful, it is impressive and persuasive. . . . I cannot deny to myself what I know to be true: that I called you up, that I got you exercised, that I invited you to a meeting, that I have been the gadfly in all this flurry. . . . I thought that my plan for ending the blacklist was not too bad. And I felt your offer to take away some of the onus from informing was good.

. . . I would not have said so much to you if you hadn't castigated yourself so severely for your really generous impulse the
other day, when you said you would not hold it against people
if they should inform. The correct thinkers will hold it against
you. But I am not one of them. I respect you for it.[4]

But seven years later, Endore reversed himself. In an oral history interview, he claimed that Trumbo's letter "didn't sit well with" him because
it raised "a kind of flag of Trumbo's devotion to the cause of humanity," and it made Endore feel as if he had "proposed something very un-
human." Then, shifting to a pejorative mode, Endore called Trumbo a
two-faced party hack who expressed one set of ideas in private conversations and a different set "in the Party and as a Party representative."[5]
Then, probably without realizing he was doing so, Endore revealed one
of the reasons he had changed his mind about Trumbo and the letter.
Endore was envious:

Since that time [December 1956], of course, Dalton has become
one of those particular cases of a blacklisted person who is in
tremendous demand, and he makes an enormous amount of
money. He is very generous with his money, but he makes an
enormous amount of it. . . . So, I think that when I spoke about
Trumbo and said that he must have a certain *arrière pensée*
[hidden agenda] about the Communist Party, I don't know
if that is so or not, but I think it must be so. If it wasn't, he
wouldn't have spoken to me one day one way and then written
me a letter with a completely different import the next.[6]

Trumbo's disquisition on informing was circulated more widely
than he had intended. Herbert Biberman showed it to several blacklistees who had not been at the December meeting. One of them, John
Bright, responded with an "open letter" to the blacklisted community.
Although Bright was no longer in the Communist Party, he used the
reprimanding language of a party ideologue. "In terms of gravity,"
Bright wrote, "I maintain that Dalton's most unfortunate error lies in
a somewhat static interpretation of history." This "static and cloudy
view of history can lead, through vulgarity, to . . . dangerous obscuran-
tism [of the] bourgeois-romantic nonsense given off by the Communist
Party rationalizers during the reign of [Earl] Browder"—an obscuran-
tism that had debased "the basic character of the Leninist dialectic."

And yet, Bright continued, despite the fact that Browderism has "long since been exposed and routed by the thoughtful minds of the Left everywhere[,] all sorts of hangovers from this intoxication have persisted, and I find evidences of them in Dalton's argument." By implication, Bright was characterizing Trumbo as a "bourgeois intellectual" who felt compelled to fortify the betrayal of his own class with lofty praise for democratic values. In an addendum, Bright, now sounding like Arthur Schlesinger Jr., asserted that Trumbo's thinking had been contaminated by the "moral corruption that is the quintessence of life in the motion picture industry on the higher echelons."[7]

Trumbo sent two replies to Bright. The first was, by Trumbo's standards, very short: "You should take pride and much comfort in the knowledge that you alone remained incorruptible and correct through all those years that found your companions so dismally sunk in error. It's a cozy feeling and rather unique these days."[8] Two months later, Trumbo wrote a longer letter to Bright. In one of the drafts of that letter, Trumbo accurately stated that he had made no "reference to any kind of revolutionary thinking or activity in the United States," nor had he categorized as fundamental and consistent "the democratic tradition in American life." Indeed, Trumbo wrote, Bright had "imagined all of these things. . . . To plainly say [as I did] that people don't like informers and have never liked them is not, as you imagine, to assert 'a consistent U.S. morality'; for informing is much less a question of morality than you think, and much more a question of self-preservation. That is why mistrust of the informer is implicit in all cultures and amongst all peoples."[9]

In the letter he actually sent, Trumbo listed six reasons why he had not responded specifically to Bright's letter: (1) "It refutes in great detail a point I never made or hinted at." (2) It was ad hominem, a logical fallacy that cannot be refuted. (3) "It misquotes me." (4) "Your main argument is based upon that pompously invincible ignorance of the history and conditions of Americans which for three decades has so unhappily distinguished the American left. Nothing I might write could undeceive you." (5) "You've made an obvious attack on my honor. If I truly have honor, your words cannot destroy it and mine certainly can't save it." (6) "Your letter stinks of Calvinism—dull, savage, repressive, joyless Calvinism."[10]

The letters he wrote to Endore and Bright motivated Trumbo to think more deeply about how to fight the blacklist. At some point in early 1958, he composed a long exegesis in the form of a letter titled

"Present State of the Blacklist," analyzing the conditions of the black market and the blacklistees' situation. In his opinion, they had arrived at a fork in the road: one sign pointed to continuation of the black market, and the other to breaking through the blacklist. Conditions, Trumbo argued, were favorable for both. But if the blacklistees continued on the black-market road, they might arrive at two potentially undesirable destinations: (1) if the black market became almost a legitimate institution in Hollywood, it could become a permanent feature of the movie industry; (2) having spread to England, France, and Italy, it also threatened to establish a worldwide black market. In contrast, the road to breaking the blacklist was not nearly as difficult to traverse as it had once been. Trumbo pointed to several promising developments that worked in the blacklistees' favor: (1) the motion picture industry was no longer a monolithic business that was tightly controlled by six big corporations, and it could no longer effectively enforce the Waldorf statement; (2) the anti-Communist movement had weakened; (3) public opinion had turned against the blacklist; and (4) the Communist Party no longer existed in Hollywood.[11]

What was needed, he continued, was "a strategic plan" that would permit every blacklisted person to return to work. Trumbo's plan explicitly excluded apologizing or informing. No blacklistee should make a public statement concerning his or her party membership, nor should any of them ask to reappear before the Committee on Un-American Activities. If they did the latter, even if they carefully qualified what they said, they ran the risk of revitalizing a weakened institution. The committee, Trumbo maintained, could no longer blacklist because the public hysteria against communism had greatly diminished and the committee had run out of new Hollywood victims to subpoena. But a parade of witnesses seeking clearance from the committee might grant it power over the process of rehabilitation and, perhaps, allow it as much "control over the decline of the blacklist as it held over its rise." In other words, any strategy for breaking through the blacklist had to bypass the committee and the Motion Picture Producers Association of America.[12]

Trumbo believed he had devised such a plan. It stemmed from his new relationship with Eddie Lewis, a freelance producer, and Kirk Douglas's Bryna Productions. One of Lewis's poker-playing friends had told him about Trumbo's work ethic and rate of production. Lewis arranged a meeting with Trumbo and gave him several books to consider for adaptation, and Trumbo signed several contracts with Lewis.

He also learned that both Lewis and Douglas opposed the blacklist, and Trumbo's inventive mind and fertile imagination devised a plan: "Jones" (aka Douglas), the hypothetical owner of a hypothetical production company (aka Bryna), loathes the blacklist and decides it would add to his luster and reputation to be known as the producer who broke the blacklist. So "Jones" offers Trumbo a contract containing an option as to whether Trumbo's name will appear onscreen; the contract does not require Trumbo to write an exculpatory letter. Meanwhile, production company executives make "special surveys and analyses of possible public reaction"; they have "private discussions with certain persons of great influence in the motion picture industry." But "Jones," who is also an actor, is justly afraid that "a strong, adverse public reaction" will damage both him and his company. It is likely, therefore, that at the time of the film's release, "Jones" will decide against giving Trumbo screen credit. If that happens, Trumbo will try to convince "Jones" to release the film with Trumbo's name on it. If the response of the industry and the public is hostile:

> Jones, approached by the press, would say: "I hired the man as a writer, not a politician. Hence I asked about his record as a writer rather than as a politician. I know nothing about his politics, and have asked him nothing about them." The press would come to me [Trumbo], and I would confirm what Jones previously has said. Then, depending on the pressures being exerted on Jones, I would say: "However, if it's going to hurt the picture, or if a man like Jones, who isn't remotely interested in my politics, is going to suffer because of these speculations, then I don't at all mind telling you that I am not a Communist, and haven't been for a very considerable length of time."

Should the Committee on Un-American Activities decide to exploit the occasion and subpoena Trumbo, he would again decline to answer its questions, this time invoking both the First and Fifth Amendments. He would then hold a press conference and frankly discuss his political affiliations. As a result, Trumbo fancifully projected, "the Jones organization, in return for my having protected their film, would announce my employment for a second [one]."[13] (For more on Trumbo's dealings with Bryna and Douglas, see chapters 17 and 18.)

It is unlikely that Trumbo's plan would have worked for any other blacklisted writer, since none of them enjoyed the kind of personal relationship Trumbo had with Lewis and Douglas. Also, Trumbo might not have received screen credit for the movies he wrote for Bryna (*Spartacus, Lonely Are the Brave,* and *The Last Sunset*) if Otto Preminger had not unexpectedly announced that he was giving Trumbo screen credit for writing the script for *Exodus*. Finally, Trumbo's breakthrough proved only wide enough for him (at least initially). These contingencies were apparent to some of the blacklistees and their lawyers, who continued to believe that legal action was the only effective tool. As noted earlier, Trumbo had explicitly rejected the filing of suits against the major studios, and he was especially up in arms against *Wilson v. Loew's,* which had been filed in July 1953 in Los Angeles Superior Court by twenty-three blacklisted film industry employees. They alleged that the studios had conspired to blacklist them, and they were asking for $51 million in damages. The superior court judge dismissed the complaint, the California District Court of Appeals sustained that decision, and the California Supreme Court refused to hear the case. In February 1957 the US Supreme Court issued a writ of certiorari, but one year later the justices dismissed that writ "as improvidently granted because the judgment [of the California Supreme Court] rests on an adequate state ground."[14] For Trumbo, the *Wilson* case was simply the latest example of "a staggering sequence of [legal] defeats" resulting from bad legal advice. Even if, he asserted, the plaintiffs had won a monetary award, none of them would have been rehired. He urged members of the blacklisted community to be realistic about their situation and to "abandon all hope of future legal relief."[15]

For the present, then, until his "Jones" plan reached fruition, Trumbo insisted that exploiting and manipulating the black market remained the most viable path for screenwriters, and he was quick to admonish those writers who unwittingly did anything to undermine it. In this matter, he was particularly tough on John Wexley. According to Trumbo, Wexley had signed a contract with director David Miller (who would later direct *Lonely Are the Brave*) and attorney Sam Norton (Bryna's lawyer). Miller and Norton hated Wexley's script, and they asked Albert Maltz to do a rewrite. Wexley, in turn, hated Maltz's revisions, and a now-desperate Miller and Norton asked Trumbo to do another rewrite. Trumbo, who found himself caught in "a four-cornered spat" among Norton, Wexley, Miller, and Maltz, agreed to do the job "to help my friends and vindicate the black market." He made it clear, however, that he would accept no money for his work.[16]

Wexley was not appeased by this solution, and he asked Trumbo to back out of the project, hoping to force Miller and Norton to return to his own script. Trumbo responded with a long, admonitory letter. For starters, Trumbo took Wexley to task for griping about his remuneration of $6,000 up front and $10,000 deferred. It was "an excellent deal, and you will find few experienced black market writers whose hearts will be moved because the sum you are receiving is less than that which you formerly received. It took years of weary hacking and price-raising on their parts to make your present deal even possible." Next, Trumbo chastised Wexley for refusing to complete the job, arguing with the director, angrily terminating the deal, and seeming to threaten blackmail by asking his attorney to write a letter to the producer's attorney. Worst of all, from Trumbo's perspective, by asking Maltz and Trumbo to refuse to work on the script, Wexley had foolishly tried to use "the weak and scattered forces of the black market . . . to impose upon producers a working rule which the Screen Writers Guild at the apex of its power would never have dared impose." Wexley's notion that he could boycott "a producer into working always with the same writer on a given project" was not only unfair to the producer but also "unfair to the writers, unfair to the ultimate product." Furthermore, such an act could drive that producer from the black market. Trumbo concluded with a slap at Wexley's lament that his "pride" had been damaged, delivering a small lecture on the subject:

> My experience with "pride" is this: people who can afford it have it; people who can't don't. I can't afford the "pride" that led you into this situation, hence I don't have it. Once I am through with a script, and the producer has stated (truly or falsely) his satisfaction with the job, my feelings come to an end. I shall never receive credit for it, hence I don't give a damn whose name appears on it. Neither do I give a damn who rewrites it or why or for how much more or less than I received. I don't give a damn whether the script is improved or ruined or tossed into the nearest furnace.[17]

In sum, Trumbo was proposing a monolithic strategy for overturning the blacklist, and he was setting very high standards for work on the black market. Only a few blacklisted writers—those who were most in demand on the black market (Maltz, Wilson, Nedrick Young)—fully

agreed with his approach, and on occasion, Trumbo had difficulty living up to his own standards (recall his frequent quarrels with the King
brothers). But his insistence on protecting the producers who employed
him (notably, Kirk Douglas) from public exposure would pay off handsomely over the next two years.

17

Using and Revealing Robert Rich

> By the late 1950s Trumbo became convinced that it was only
> a matter of time before the blacklist fell, and that it would be
> one of four writers (himself, Albert Maltz, Michael Wilson, or
> Nedrick Young) who would provide the extra push to topple it.
> He didn't care which one it would be.
>
> —Christopher Trumbo

The burden of his black-market work and his feeling of frustration that
the blacklist showed no signs of ending led Trumbo to, in his words,
"totally revolt against the sense of martyrdom that lay so heavily over
all of us. Nobody likes a martyr. They're a living reproach to have
around the house. And we were falling into that. There's nothing so
destructive to a person." He realized that if he did not "get out of that
trough of martyrdom" immediately, he never would.[1] With that thought
in mind, Trumbo began a new anti-blacklist campaign at the end of January 1957. He sent letters to a number of well-known novelists whose
books had been adapted for movies—William Faulkner, A. B. Guthrie,
Ernest Hemingway, William Saroyan, John Steinbeck, and Thornton
Wilder—asking each to send him a statement condemning the Hollywood blacklist, which he would then forward to the press as he saw fit.
None of those writers replied. He also sent a letter to President Dwight
D. Eisenhower, urging him to publicly condemn the blacklist. Eisenhower's special counsel, Gerald D. Morgan, replied that the president
"could not comment on the employment practices of any industry,
unless such practices constituted a violation of federal law."[2]

Shortly thereafter, the Board of Governors of the Academy of
Motion Picture Arts and Sciences unexpectedly provided Trumbo
with a new means of mocking the blacklist to great effect. He later
commented that there was always someone in the industry "opening

his foolish mouth who you could just ridicule and have fun with."[3] In this case, the governors were determined to prevent blacklisted writer Michael Wilson from winning an Academy Award for writing the script for *Friendly Persuasion*.[4] In 1947 Wilson had adapted Jessamyn West's novel *The Friendly Persuasion* for Liberty Pictures, and although several other writers had subsequently worked on it, including West, a Writers Guild arbitration committee had given Wilson sole credit. But executives at Allied Artists, the production company, took advantage of a clause in the collective bargaining agreement between the Motion Picture Association of America and the Writers Guild, which allowed studios to withhold screen credit from Communists and Fifth Amendment witnesses. When the film was released in late November, it credited only one writer: Jessamyn West (the credit read, "from the book by Jessamyn West"). Two months later, the Academy's Board of Governors, fearing that Wilson might still be nominated for an Oscar, approved a motion by B. B. Kahane, the newly elected vice president of the Association of Motion Picture Producers, "that a By-Law be written so that no Communist or Communist sympathizer can win an Academy Award." The board voted to add a new clause to article VIII, section 1, of its bylaws: "Any person who, before any duly constituted Federal legislative committee or body, shall have admitted that he is a member of the Communist Party (and has not since publicly renounced the party) or who shall have refused to answer whether or not he is, or was a member of the Communist Party, or who shall refuse to respond to a subpoena to appear before such a committee or body, shall be ineligible for any Academy Award so long as he persists in such refusal."[5] When the Academy Award nominations were announced on February 18, Wilson's name was not among them. But in a completely unanticipated development, "Robert Rich" was nominated for best motion picture story for *The Brave One*. One month later, the members of the WGAw voted to give Wilson the organization's award for best written drama. At the WGAw awards banquet, Groucho Marx joked that the producers of *The Ten Commandments* "were forced to keep Moses' name off the writing credits because they found out he had once crossed the Red Sea."[6]

But the real shocker came at the Twenty-Ninth Academy Awards presentations, when Robert Rich was announced as the winner of the Oscar for best motion picture story. As soon as the presenter, Deborah Kerr, announced Rich's name, Jessie Lasky Jr. leaped from his aisle seat and strode to the stage. When he reached the podium, Ms. Kerr read

"Robert Rich," aka Dalton Trumbo, 1957. Photograph by Cleo Trumbo.

from a card in the results envelope and said, "Mr. Jessie Lasky Jr., vice president of the Screen Writers branch of the Writers Guild, will accept the award for Mr. Rich." Lasky accepted the Oscar and said: "On behalf of Robert Rich and his beautiful story, thank you very much." Trumbo sardonically commented years later: "That it [*The Brave One*] should have been voted the best original story that year is a comment on the Academy's idea of originality."[7] Among the writers who lost to "Robert Rich" were future Nobel Prize winner Jean-Paul Sartre (*The Proud and*

the Beautiful) and the highly regarded Italian neorealist Cesare Zavat-
tini (*Umberto D*). (The Board of Governors eliminated the award for
best motion picture story shortly thereafter.) Mitzi remembers jumping
up and down and saying, "Daddy, let's go pick it up tomorrow." He gently explained to her why they could not and why she could not share her
joy with anyone outside the immediate family.

Even before the award was announced, rumors had begun to spread
about the "real" Robert Rich, and Trumbo used those rumors to great
advantage. They started when Rich, under pressure from his girlfriend
and without telling his uncles (the Kings), went to the Academy offices
and asked for tickets to the awards ceremony. But prior to the event he
telephoned the Academy to say that his wife was sick and he would be
unable to attend. The Academy's secretary, Margaret Herrick, became
suspicious, and she related the story to a few people. Thus, questions
about the "real Robert Rich" began to circulate.[8] Trumbo later said the
Academy Award and those rumors gave him "the key" to unlock the
blacklist:

> You see, all the press came to me, and I dealt with them in such
> a way that they knew bloody well that I had written it. But I
> would suggest that maybe it was Mike Wilson, and they would
> call Mike and ask him, and he would say no, it wasn't him. And
> they would come back to me, and I'd suggest they try somebody
> else—another blacklisted writer like myself who was working
> on the black market. And I had a whole list of them because we
> kept in close touch. It went on and on and on. I just wanted the
> press to understand what an extensive thing this movie black
> market was. And in the midst of this, I suddenly realized that
> all the journalists—or most of them—were sympathetic to me,
> and how eager they were to have the blacklist exploded. There
> had been a certain change in atmosphere, and then it became
> possible.[9]

Within a month of the awards show, rumors about Robert Rich
were buzzing around Hollywood. A reporter from *Daily Variety* asked
Trumbo if he was Robert Rich. "'Hell, no,' he retorted cheerfully, 'I'm
Dalton Trumbo.'" Frank King "hotly denied" that Rich was actually
one of the Hollywood Ten. King acknowledged having a nephew named
Robert Rich, but he claimed that was merely a coincidence. The actual
author of the story, King revealed to a reporter, was "a boy he bought

the script from in 1951 in Germany. He's a photographer and writer, and is goateed. We are trying to locate him and bring him here. I've sent out five cables looking for him, and expect him in town the latter part of the month." Harry Franklin claimed he had simply been given a script with Rich's name on it. In another *Daily Variety* story, Trumbo announced that Robert Rich was the pseudonym of Michael Wilson, who was so incensed by the Academy's new bylaw that he had written *The Brave One* "to have something to show for his year's work."[10] A few days later, the *Daily Variety* reporter asked Trumbo again if he was Robert Rich, and Trumbo refused to either confirm or deny the rumor. The same question was posed to Paul Jarrico, who also refused to confirm or deny it. Albert Maltz denied it outright.[11] An unnamed Academy source declared, "On advice of counsel we are going to keep out of this situation"; one week later the Board of Governors met and officially decided to do nothing.[12]

Though the Oscar for *The Brave One* gave Trumbo leverage and the opportunity to use his charm and charisma on reporters, he could not, he told Christopher, come right out and say he had written the story. That would have dishonored his agreement with the King brothers, and it would have put them in a very difficult position. In addition, a premature admission of that sort might have had serious political repercussions. Such an announcement would have been a "romantic gesture" in what was still a "dangerous and ugly time" in the United States. After all, as Trumbo later noted, the Motion Picture Alliance for the Preservation of American Ideals "still stood bull-watch over the town. The Americanization Commission of the American Legion were on call for picket lines in every town and city in the country," and the Committee on Un-American Activities "had maintained a standing threat to return for new hearings . . . at the first sign of a weakening blacklist." If the committee chairman carried out his threat, Trumbo feared he would subpoena the producers and "totally destroy the subterranean market for blacklisted work it had taken almost a decade to develop."[13]

So Trumbo contented himself with brilliantly manipulating the media. He found a very capable ally in Bill Stout, one of the best television reporters in the Los Angeles area. "My father," Mitzi told me, "carefully developed a close relationship with Stout. He enjoyed working out strategies with Bill; it was like a chess game for them. They even orchestrated a ridiculous blind date for me with Bill's son, when we were both thirteen years old." (It was not successful.) On April 9 and 10, 1957, Trumbo appeared on Stout's *Assignment America* and

revealed that he had been working on the black market for years and
that at least one of his scripts had been nominated for an Academy
Award. When Stout asked Trumbo, "Did you write *The Brave One?*"
Trumbo answered: "Well, you see, I've been accused of writing many
pictures in the last ten years, during the period of the blacklist. So I've
had to make a policy about such questions. My policy is that I, modestly, refuse to either confirm or deny. In this way, I receive just a little
bit of credit for every good picture that is made, and for some reason I
never get blamed for the scamps [flops]."[14]

When a reporter from *Life* asked Trumbo the "Robert Rich" question, Trumbo responded with a short poem he had written for the
occasion:

> Come back, Robert Rich, wherever you are,
> Return so the ghost can be shriven.
> Do you live on the moon, do you live on a star?
> Is that where your legends are scriven?[15]

For his part, Frank King told several conflicting stories about the
script's provenance: he bought the script from a bearded Spaniard; he
bought a six-page outline from a man named "Robert Rich" he had
met wandering around Europe; he bought the script from an ex-GI in
Europe. When asked by a *Life* reporter about his nephew's contribution to the script, King spluttered that the names were "a pure coincidence. So what if it's the same name? How many Frank Kings are there?
It's crazy, that's all. It's nuts, that's all." When asked why Robert Rich
had not appeared to accept his Oscar, King replied that he was still in
Europe. The reporter pointed out that King had earlier placed the man
in Australia.[16]

An unexpected dividend from all this publicity arrived in the form
of a letter from Ilse Lahn, who worked at the Paul Kohner Agency. She
sent Trumbo a story about Tahiti that had appeared in *Esquire*. It had
been given to her by producers Martin Melcher and Michael Meshekoff, who, she told Trumbo, "want Bob Rich to read it in hopes that he
may want to undertake the writing of a screenplay based upon it for
them." Lahn had told the producers that Rich was traveling abroad, but
he might take the assignment if he could write the script wherever he
was currently staying. In addition, she said, in light of Rich's Academy
Award, "he may want some real money for the job or at least a decent
amount in cash and profit participation in the picture." Melcher and

Meshekoff told Lahn that if Rich's salary demands were too high, they might decide to use another fellow named Flexman, who was currently writing a script for them ("The Green-Eyed Blonde"). The delicious irony is that "Flexman" was one of Trumbo's many pseudonyms.[17]

As part of his stepped-up campaign of ridicule, Trumbo wrote an article on the blacklist and the black market for the *Nation*. It was the third of his four great anti–Cold War political writings. His extensive research included interviews with William Wheeler, the West Coast investigator for the Committee on Un-American Activities, and Dorothy Furman of Harshe-Rolman Inc., the Academy's public relations firm. (Trumbo's telephone calls to the public relations department of the Motion Picture Association of America were not returned.) Furman told Trumbo she could not give him the details of the board's deliberations on nominations and awards. In a note to himself, Trumbo wrote: "I pointed out to Miss Furman this ruling was an act of high patriotism and that it seemed odd that the assembled patriots were so loathe to tell how many of them were there, and what the vote was. It seemed to me a refusal to stand up and be counted which was precisely what they are penalizing [Michael] Wilson for."[18]

The editor's introduction to the article (which may have been written by Trumbo) stated: "Mr. Trumbo has become a prolific and anonymous contributor to Hollywood's black market in scripts, and for all anyone knows (other than Mr. Trumbo and his producers, who aren't saying) he may have won more Oscars in the last ten years than Walt Disney." Trumbo began this article by starkly noting that Hollywood "finds itself celebrating, willingly or unwillingly, the tenth anniversary of a blacklist." The movie blacklist, he continued, was part of an immense official blacklist mechanism that he characterized as "an illegal instrument of terror which can exist only by sufferance of and connivance with the federal government." But a crack had recently appeared in the Hollywood blacklist: scripts written for the black market were starting to get nominated for industry awards—notably, Michael Wilson's for *Friendly Persuasion*. The Academy, in an attempt to avoid the embarrassment of a blacklisted writer being nominated for or winning an Oscar, had instituted a new prohibitive bylaw. But when nonblacklisted writer "Robert Rich" won an award that year and could not be identified, the Academy was flummoxed:

> The Academy, giddy by now with patriotism, flushed with its
> victory over Wilson, anxious to proclaim itself Cerberus of

the blacklist, and sensing that a second barbarian might have breached the defenses and profaned the sanctuary, rushed into print with the most disastrous publicity release of its twenty-nine-year history.

"Robert Rich," it announced pompously, "credited by the studio which produced *The Brave One* with authorship of the motion-picture story and winner of the Academy Award in this category, stated today he was not the author of the story." There followed a series of dire warning from Mr. [George] Seaton [president of the Academy] and his underlings. The original story, it was hinted, wasn't original at all, or if so it was very likely a plagiarism, and the Academy would probably withhold the Award, punish the King Brothers by giving it to the owners of another story who were suing the Kings, or even declare Robert Rich, like Wilson, a non-person, and turn the Oscar over to the next highest man in the vote, or maybe shoot craps for its custody.

But when it became known that "there are literally hundreds of valid, free-born, no-[takers-of-the-Fifth-]Amendment Robert Richs scattered throughout practically every country in the Western world," the Academy decided to say nothing more, and silence descended on Hollywood. Trumbo and William Stout, "a brilliant young news commentator," decided that this stillness "call[ed] for a little noise." They decided to make their feelings known to the world via a filmed interview about the blacklist and the black market. At almost any other time in the past, Trumbo's televised interview with Stout would have raised a loud fuss from the industry, but, Trumbo wrote: "I heard not one yelp of anger nor a single denial. All over town publicity departments worked furiously and overtime at the job of saying nothing." Nevertheless, the "black market flourishes and the producers know it and dare not deny it and pray each night for a court decision, please God just one decision, that will give them an excuse to . . . regain control of the organizations they head."[19]

John Bright, still on the prowl against Trumbo and his increasing prominence, again misinterpreted Trumbo's intent. In a letter to the editor of the *Nation*, Bright wrote: "In his otherwise effective and impish piece on the blacklist and black market, Dalton Trumbo allows his sense of personal gloating to run away with the reality." By doing so, Bright claimed, Trumbo "blithely exempts writers from the pervasive suffering" of the blacklist and implies not only that the black market is "flourishing like a green bay tree but [also] that its fruits are a basketful of Oscars." Trumbo and a few others might be doing well, Bright acknowledged, but most blacklisted writers were experiencing great hardship, and despite the existence of the "'cunning' and 'secret'" black-market channels Trumbo was heralding, the majority of blacklisted writers, if they were fortunate, experienced only "haphazard success" and suffered "savage cuts in the value of their wares."[20]

The article, Trumbo explained to Bright, "was a public relations job applying to *all* blacklisted persons. When you are operating toward public relations, you *never* present yourself as a martyr. The public hates martyrs. To have appeared as one would have defeated the whole purpose of the piece." Besides, he added, "we are *not* martyrs, and any effort to present ourselves as such is simply disgusting." Trumbo was not, he emphasized, gloating about the Robert Rich affair, and even if he had been, his gloating had "proved beneficial to many people":

> I can introduce you to a dozen who are working today, who were not working before the Rich pop-off, and who attribute a considerable portion of the change in the community attitude toward the blacklist to all the "gloating" that went on. The black market, treated as it was during the Rich thing, became almost an open market . . . ; and producers, who formerly had been afraid to enter it, suddenly awakened to the realization that they were fools if they longer desisted from what they now felt every other producer was sampling. The result: a *great* gain in employment.[21]

When Alvah Bessie complained that Trumbo had not been hard enough on the producers, Trumbo replied: "I didn't jump the producers because I've never thought they were really the heavies, and in that, of course, I may be wrong. Also, I think one can in some circumstances make a better case with ridicule than with indignation."[22] Maltz thought the article was "splendid."[23]

The next month, *Frontier* magazine printed a condensed version of the speech Trumbo delivered to the Citizens Committee to Preserve American Freedoms. The author identification (again, probably written by Trumbo) stated: "Rumor has it that Oscars decorating the mantelpieces of several homes in Hollywood belong to Mr. Trumbo." Trumbo opened his speech with comments on how silly the black-market situation had become and went on to express his hope that ridicule might be a way to kill the blacklist. But then his tone shifted, becoming impassioned, angry, and, above all, gloriously eloquent as he incisively exposed the cancerous heart of the blacklist experience:

> I, for one, am afraid that ridicule alone is not enough. For although the case of Robert Rich lends itself magnificently to jokes, and may even be the invention of a jokester, it nonetheless contains, as every really good joke must, an essential element of tragedy, or horror, or of disgrace or doom. I choose to think of Robert Rich as a symbol of disgrace; as the personification of a nation-wide blacklist. . . . Robert Rich, therefore, is the generic name of all persons who must somehow escape their individual identities if they are to continue working at their professions. As such, he has as many faces as the blacklist itself. . . . I have seen the blacklist that produced Robert Rich. I know its pain and its frustration and its horror and its shattering cruelties. . . . I have long served in this lonely, marching army of the anonymous. . . . I can make no more jokes about Robert Rich. They turn sour on my tongue. I can invent no more witticisms about the Oscar he does not claim, because—that small, worthless, golden statuette is covered with the blood of my friends. I cannot laugh about it any longer because my belly is filled with the poison of this blacklist, and my heart is filled with its grief, and my ears roar with rage at its injustices, and my heart, for the first time is filled with something very close to hate. Ten years of this accursed thing is enough. . . . Let us not yield to them [the Committee on Un-American Activities, the movie industry, the FBI, the attorney general] one more inch. Let us not give them one more life.[24]

In September 1957 Trumbo traveled to New York, where he spoke at Carnegie Hall. At this event, sponsored by the Emergency Civil Liberties Committee to Abolish Congressional Inquisitions, Trumbo again expressed his anger, telling the audience, "Robert Rich is the Unknown Artist—the man who has been suppressed so mercilessly by his own government that he has forsaken not only his own name but all honors which may accrue to his work. He is the Quiet American of our time, and it is my purpose and determination that his name shall be remembered as a symbol of this national sickness long after the Committee itself has been abolished and the blacklist destroyed."[25]

While in New York, Trumbo was invited to appear on a radio show called *Night Beat*, hosted by John Wingate. Trumbo investigated Wingate, learned that he was a "hard-ball" interrogator, and carefully prepared for the show. According to a review of the program, Wingate "failed to make the elusive gentleman [Trumbo] come clean and emerge from his smooth line of patter about the rights of the individual." By the end of the broadcast, it was clear that Wingate "had met his intellectual match in Trumbo, who at times succeeded in making him [Wingate] sound foolish." During the program, Trumbo refused to confirm or deny that he was Robert Rich, continued to defend an individual's right to privacy about his or her political beliefs, and stressed the misery caused by the blacklist. He ridiculed Wingate's accusation that Communists had invaded the entertainment business, emphasizing instead the malign effects of the anti-Communist hysteria gripping the country. At the end of the program, Wingate asked Trumbo why he had agreed to do the show if he did not intend to answer Wingate's questions. "I came because I was asked," Trumbo replied.[26]

Although everyone else continued to guess at the identity of Robert Rich, an FBI informant told the special agent in charge of the Los Angeles office "that Dalton Trumbo . . . was the true author of 'The Brave One.'"[27]

Following his return to Los Angeles, Trumbo initiated another phase in his anti-blacklist campaign. He instructed his attorney, Aubrey Finn, to contact the producers with whom Trumbo had verbal agreements and request that they put those agreements in writing. George Bilson acceded to Trumbo's request, and for the first time since his last deal with MGM, Trumbo signed his own name on a contract. He was to be paid $3,000 on delivery of the script, plus an additional $3,000 on the first day of production.[28] The movie, about the plight of illegitimate children, was never made.

But Trumbo was no longer acting alone. The blacklist was coming under attack from several directions. One of the major offensives was led by Ingo Preminger, the younger brother of Otto. Ingo had come to the United States from Austria in 1938 and arrived in Hollywood in 1947. He worked one year with the Goldstone agency before setting up his own shop. According to his son, Jim, blacklistees were an important part of Ingo's business, and he loved spending time with them. Even though Ingo was not a political person, he believed he should help them;

his home became a refuge for many blacklistees, and he liked looking after them.[29] Ingo's first, and arguably his most important, victory
was his sale to Stanley Kramer of a script written by Nathan E. Douglas (pseudonym of blacklisted writer Nedrick E. Young) and Harold B.
Smith titled "The Long Road." Preminger had informed Kramer that
Young was on the blacklist, but Kramer did not give a damn. According to Josh Smith, Harold's son, "Kramer did not insist on any credit
fictions, fronts, or coffee shop exchange of rewrites." Instead, he moved
the two writers into the studio adjoining his offices and paid them the
going aboveground rate.[30] One year later, on April 30, 1958, Kramer
announced that he had hired Douglas and Smith to adapt the play
Inherit the Wind. And in August Kramer appeared on NBC's *Youth
Wants to Know* and publicly admitted that he employed many people
who had been subpoenaed by the Committee on Un-American Activities.[31] Earlier that year, Michael Wilson's agent had written to him that
Otto Preminger was "very eager to get you to write a screenplay for
him," and "he'd even give you screen credit, because, as he puts it: 'he
doesn't give a dam what anybody says.'"[32]

In New York City, radio commentator John Henry Faulk filed a
suit against Aware Inc., alleging that the company had caused him
to be fired from his radio job and was actively preventing him from
obtaining another job in that field. (The suit dragged on for five years,
and although Faulk won a judgment, Aware had no money to pay it.)[33]
Edge of the City, directed by blacklistee Martin Ritt, was distributed
by MGM in January 1957; *Time without Pity*, directed and written by
blacklistees Joseph Losey and Ben Barzman, respectively, was released
by Astor Pictures in November. Another small tear in the fabric of the
blacklist appeared in 1958 when Alfred Hitchcock hired graylisted
actor Norman Lloyd to be the associate producer of his television show.

Meanwhile, Trumbo was trying, without success, to convince the
King brothers to make a public announcement revealing the identity
of "Robert Rich." Initially, he hoped the numerous plagiarism suits
brought against *The Brave One* might force their hand. It seemed that
every writer in Hollywood had a boy-and-bull story in his or her filing cabinet. In the first suit, filed in February 1957, the plaintiffs asked
for $750,000 in damages. The Kings settled out of court for $25,000
because, as Maury King later said, "If it had gotten out that Trumbo
was the writer, RKO would have stopped distribution. You know how
Howard Hughes was."[34] Trumbo also had reason to fear a deposition,
which would force him to reveal his other black-market employers and

fronts. Plagiarism suits of this type were, according to Trumbo, "the constant ghost: that haunted the house of black-market work."[35]

Trumbo also tried to leverage "Robert Rich" in other ways. For instance, he tried to persuade the Kings to put the name "Robert Rich" on the "Mr. Adam" script he had written for them. When that ploy failed, he tried to take advantage of the "Robert Rich" pseudonym by having his attorney draw up articles of incorporation for Robert Rich Productions.[36] His grand stroke in this phase of the campaign was a confidential letter he sent to Academy president George Seaton. It was enclosed in a sealed envelope with a cover letter in which Trumbo wrote, "Forgive this touch of melodrama." The sealed letter opened with this remark: "Forgive the ambiguity of this letter." Without mentioning names, Trumbo encouraged Seaton to persuade the Board of Governors to cooperate in resolving the "Robert Rich" problem. Trumbo believed it would be in the best interest of the blacklistees if the board acknowledged that Trumbo was "Robert Rich" without seeming to cave in to obvious outside pressure. But, Trumbo told Seaton, if the board did not act, the real author of *The Brave One* script would make the announcement "in the most public way possible," and the King brothers would confirm it. In effect, Trumbo told Seaton, Robert Rich's identity was going to be revealed one way or another, and he hoped they could manage the revelation so that it occurred "at the most propitious moment for all concerned, and in a fashion which reflects no discredit on any person or organization."[37] Although Seaton did not respond to Trumbo's invitation to meet and discuss the situation, Trumbo's letter got Seaton thinking about how to resolve this problem and prevent any future embarrassment.

In March 1958 the blacklistees received another major boost when the Academy Award for best adapted screenplay, for *The Bridge on the River Kwai*, was given to the author of the novel, Pierre Boulle. Many people in Hollywood knew that Boulle did not speak or write English very well, and virtually everyone in the blacklisted community knew that the script had actually been written by Carl Foreman and Michael Wilson. The day after the presentation, *Los Angeles Times* columnist Philip K. Scheuer quoted director David Lean as saying that both Foreman and another American writer (whom he declined to name) had contributed to the script. In the same edition of the *Times*, Foreman stated that he had written the screenplay.[38] Bill Stout spoke about the blacklist in his television commentary, and CBS's *Studio One* did a story on "Robert Rich." Trumbo seemed to have mixed feelings about the award and the stories that followed it. On the one hand, he described Scheuer's article as being "really a major statement coming at exactly the right moment from probably the most powerful right-wing newspaper in the country." In addition, he was pleased that "the writing Awards were gloriously screwed for a second time running, and . . . I've been quietly active in stimulating the whole thing. All in all, the results have been excellent." But, he continued:

> In all other directions, I am extremely po'd. After eleven years of investigation, blacklist, jail, pamphleteering, platform rhetoric, TV debates and interviews, I lift my shaggy old head above the horizon and I behold—nothing. Only a bunch of blacklisted artists doing work they shouldn't do because they're prevented or forbidden from doing work they should. Everybody else seems to be fat and happy. . . . The only persons to whom no real change has occurred in this time of adventurous change are the intellectuals, and specifically the writers and artists of Hollywood. . . . [W]e have established no rights at all. Worse than that, we have no support: neither local nor national, neither in the courts nor in the press, nor among those very groups and persons whose fights we have supported and paid for with our careers.[39]

Trumbo was also unhappy with his work pace and remuneration. He decided in early 1956 to do something drastic "to get off the dreary necessity of working for mere wages," of always coming in on the tail end of a series of poorly written drafts, many by famous writers. He decided to concentrate on original screenplays. On the one hand, this would give him more control over content and asking price; on the other hand, the market for original scripts written on speculation was unpredictable. In addition, with an increasing number of producers "having the courage to look in on the black market," sales were taking much longer than usual. As a result, the sale of his first original screenplay had taken five weeks, and he had been forced to take whatever job came along that promised immediate cash. Three such jobs came his way, but they barely covered his operating expenses through the summer. Plus, he had to hire a secretary, "simply because this sudden rush" no longer permitted him "the luxury of typing" the screenplays himself.[40]

The "sudden rush" also forced Trumbo to farm out two assignments. (He rarely said no to an offer; he always tried to find another blacklisted writer to do it.) The first was a western, "Terror in a Texas Town," that he had received from Frank Seltzer. Trumbo gave it to Mitchell Linde-mann and John Howard Lawson, but when their work proved unacceptable to the Seltzers, Trumbo stepped back in and rewrote it in a mere four days. The cast and crew of this film included an interesting combination of characters: it was directed by Joseph H. Lewis, who had directed *Gun Crazy*; it starred Sterling Hayden, an informer; and it featured Ned Young, a blacklisted writer, as the killer (Young had also appeared in *Gun Crazy*). It was a B version of *High Noon* and a variation of another B movie, *Johnny Guitar* (which also starred Hayden). In all these films, one brave individual is forced to face the evildoers alone, because the townspeople are too afraid to do anything. Thus, they all could be read as commentaries on the domestic cold war.[41] In terms of quality, *Terror* was a distant third.

Trumbo also ran into difficulty with the second farmed project, "The Girl with the Green Eyes," a story about a girls' reform school. When Adrian Scott and Sally Stubblefield brought Trumbo the script assignment, he asked Paul and Sylvia Jarrico to prepare the step outline. Dissatisfied with their work, Trumbo wrote a new outline as well as the script. When *The Green-Eyed Blonde* was released in December 1957, the screenplay was credited to Stubblefield. On the cover of his copy of the script, Trumbo wrote: "This I wrote on the black market for Sally Stubblefield. It was [co-]produced at Warners by Marty Melcher and utterly ruined by the director [Bernard Girard]. Because Mr. Melcher published music he wrote a horrible song for the film called 'The Girl with the Green Eyes.'" Since Trumbo claimed he "never saw the picture," someone must have told him how bad it was.[42]

The pace and extent of his black-market work were eroding Trumbo's health, and he tried, without success, to lessen the strain. In response to an inquiry by Arthur Landau about a possible writing assignment, Trumbo wrote: "For the first time in my life I am going to have to back out completely from an assignment. . . . On the 5th of July I suffered a mild heart attack which knocked me down for a few days. . . . A check-up revealed high blood pressure, and I have, as of yesterday, been ordered to take a complete rest for a minimum period of three months." The checkup also revealed that Trumbo had hemorrhoids.[43]

But Trumbo ignored the doctor's warning and did not slow down. Months later, he wrote to Hugo Butler:

> In order to keep this madhouse going, I awaken each morning between 3 and 5 a.m., although rarely as late as five. I work

steadily until about one. Then I take a half-hour nap. Work
steadily until 7 or 7:30 p.m. After that I take three stiff belts of
whiskey to uncoil on, eat dinner, and go to bed. This schedule
is absolutely unfailing, Saturdays and Sundays included. I was
never a social person, but I am much less so now than formerly.
I dread going out because it means drinking and lowered vitality for tomorrow.[44]

He confessed to Bob Roberts: "I myself made the mistake of grabbing
too many things, and am, at the moment, utterly swamped beneath the
burden of six simultaneous assignments. Thus my skills, both as writer
and liar, are taxed to the breaking point."[45] But sheer necessity kept him
from slowing down: he was supporting two children in college, sub-
sidizing four other college students, supporting his mother, repaying
debts, paying taxes, and so forth. He was fifty-two years old, the blacklist had not yet ended, and he feared his savings would be insufficient to
carry him through the inevitable fallow periods to come.

The incessant work was paying off, however. During those years,
Trumbo's black-market income steadily rose. In 1956 he received $7,000
from the King brothers, $15,200 from Sally Stubblefield (for *Green-
Eyed Blonde*), $6,850 from Frank Seltzer (for *Terror in a Texas Town*),
$3,750 from George Templeton, and $10,000 from Ben Bogeaus.[46]

During the summer of the following year, another Alice-in-Won-
derland event occurred. Alec March hired Trumbo to rewrite the script
for *The Philadelphian*, a novel by Richard Powell. Like *Kitty Foyle*, the
story was set in Philadelphia, but in this case, the man came from the
working class and the woman from the upper class. Since the producing studio, Warner Bros., required its writers to work in an office on the
lot, Trumbo and March hired Ben Perry to sit in the writers' wing at
the studio and attend conferences while Trumbo wrote at home. It was
not a happy arrangement. Sometime in the late summer Trumbo sent
some pages to March, accompanied by an angry remark about Warner
executives: "Fuck those bastards."[47] Trumbo completed his treatment
in September and the script in November, but the studio executives did
not like it, and they fired March and Perry (and, of course, Trumbo).
Shortly thereafter the new director, Vincent Sherman, and the movie's
lead actor, Paul Newman, called on Trumbo. They cursed the script
Perry had written and pleaded with Trumbo to rewrite it. One wonders
what went through Trumbo's mind when he declined their offer, claiming he had too many other contracts to fulfill.[48]

Trumbo, Aubrey Finn, and Cleo, 1957. Photograph by Mitzi Trumbo.

Following this experience, Trumbo again resolved to work only on originals. Using the name "James Bonham," Trumbo signed a service agreement with Eugene Frenke Productions to write five scripts. Frenke would pay "Bonham" $2,000 per month plus 50 percent of the net profits of each movie made. The following year, in October, Trumbo and Frenke created Springfield Productions Inc., which, in addition to making "loan-out" deals for Trumbo's services (under the name "Theodore Flexman"), invested Trumbo's money in real estate and stocks. Trumbo guaranteed his exclusive services to Springfield. The contract contained no options, no cancellation clause, and no morals clause; it gave Trumbo the absolute right to choose or refuse all assignments. He was to be paid $80,000 per year ($50,000 in cash and $30,000 deferred), and Cleo was to be paid $100 per week.[49] (Trumbo's ongoing relationship with Frenke puzzled many of his friends, including his attorney, Aubrey Finn. Trumbo told Finn that he thought he could earn more money from the studios, via Frenke, than he could on his own, even using a dozen agents. In addition, Trumbo liked Frenke and trusted him, although he harbored doubts about Frenke's "stability."[50])

And yet it was not a Springfield production of an original script that cracked the carapace of Trumbo's blacklistee status. The gamebreaker arrived unexpectedly in January 1958, when Eddie Lewis offered Trumbo a contract to adapt Edward Abbey's novel *The Brave Cowboy* for Bryna Productions. According to the contract, Lewis and "Sam Jackson" were to collaborate on the first draft and all necessary revisions. Trumbo was to be paid $2,500 up front, $1,250 on completion of the first draft, and $1,250 on completion of all revisions. He would also be paid $10,000 at the start of production, plus 5 percent of the producer's share of the net profits.[51] Lewis subsequently contracted with Trumbo to write "Spartacus," "Showdown at Gun Hill" (aka *Last Train from Gun Hill*), and "Sundown at Crazy Horse" (aka *The Last Sunset*). In 1958 Trumbo received almost $53,000 from Bryna: $35,979 for "Spartacus," $6,500 for "The Brave Cowboy," and $10,000 for "Showdown at Gun Hill."[52] Trumbo also tried to sell two scripts he had written for the King brothers to Bryna, as the basis for coproductions. Trumbo later said: "During most of the year 1958, my principal work was the writing of *Spartacus* for Bryna [see chapter 18]. Due to the peculiar circumstances surrounding my name, I worked under the pseudonym of Sam Jackson, for Mr. Edward Lewis, who was producer of the film. Both Bryna and Mr. Lewis were aware of my identity. I received payment in the following fashion: Mr. Lewis would secure money from Bryna, and convey it to me, sometimes in the form of a check on his personal bank account, sometimes in cash. I would give him a receipt for each sum paid."[53]

During that year, Mitzi recalled:

My father was deeply preoccupied with all issues relating to the blacklist. He seldom came up to the house from his office before 10 p.m. Niki and Chris had both left home for college, so it was just the three of us. My father was on edge and easily angered, and he would pick fights with my mother. He was drinking too much, smoking too much, taking Dexedrine to stay awake and Seconal to sleep, and there was no time for anything but writing. He worked day and night and weekends, seemingly indefatigable, but it took a toll on family life, his health, and his marriage.

Cleo's health also declined under the strain of keeping secrets, maintaining the household, and protecting her children. In October Trumbo took her to the Mayo Clinic. When they returned, Trumbo informed their doctor, Murray Abowitz, that Cleo had been diagnosed with exhaustion and needed several months of absolute rest. Trumbo himself had been told he was diabetic.[54] He vowed to make long-overdue changes in his routine: "The fact is that my fantastic work schedule of the past eighteen months, involving almost monastic isolation from sun-up to nine at night, has thrown upon her shoulders too many tasks, burdens and decisions that I should have shared with her. Now she must rest, and I must cut down on work and resume my rightful portion of family cares and pleasures."[55] That resolve was short-lived.

While Trumbo was at the Mayo Clinic, a golden opportunity to reengage with the Academy appeared: *The Defiant Ones* (produced and directed by Stanley Kramer, distributed by United Artists) opened in September 1958 to much critical acclaim. It became the favorite for a number of year-end awards and Oscars. As soon as he was back in Los Angeles, Trumbo met with the two screenwriters, Harold B. Smith and Nathan E. Douglas (Nedrick Young), and they began planning a campaign to use the expected awards as a lever against the Academy. In a letter to Maltz and Wilson, Trumbo wrote:

> About 2 weeks before Xmas Hal and Ned were approached at a luncheon by George Seaton and Valentine Davies, representing the Academy. They recognized the possibility of *Defiant* being nominated for the Academy [Award], wished to avoid a third scandal in as many years, said they were going to try to get the Academy rule rescinded, and asked Hal and Ned to help them by giving a friendly interview (non-political) to Tom Pryor of the *NY Times*, which would reveal Ned's true identity, and permit them to go to work within the Academy to get the rule abolished.
>
> Ned, Hal and I held a conference. I contended that, this being the season for honors and silver plate, Hal and Ned should wait until they had picked up a number of other awards before considering breaking anything. I felt it was the Academy's problem, not theirs; and that they should save all their fire for a fight if one developed, rather than wasting a single inch of newspaper space when they did not need it. They agreed. They gave no interview.[56]

On December 31, however, their plan went awry when it was announced that Douglas and Smith had received the New York Film Critics Award, and Pryor threatened to break the story, with or without them. The principals decided it would be better to cooperate, so they met with Pryor later that day in Ingo Preminger's office, where Young revealed that he was Nathan E. Douglas.[57] Trumbo immediately called Bill Stout, who invited Young and Smith to be on his television program that evening. During that broadcast, the two screenwriters broke "the news locally in a most dignified and advantageous way." According to Trumbo, "for 45 minutes after the show [Stout's] board was clogged with calls—all for, only one (Dick Macauley) against! For 3 days the industry greeted this with a silence which convinces me (and still does) that we have the best chance of our lives." Trumbo then met with Lew Irwin, a radio news announcer for KPOL and a TV news commentator for KABC.[58] On January 8–10 Irwin devoted "City Final," his KABC-TV commentary segment, to a report on the blacklist. In the first part, Irwin focused on Ned Young's possible nomination for an Academy Award and the Academy's possible response. Irwin, perhaps at Trumbo's suggestion, compared the blacklist to the Soviet government's treatment of Boris Pasternak, and he quoted Frank King. Probably at Trumbo's request, Irwin did not mention the Robert Rich affair, but he did allude to Trumbo, noting that a local television station had aired *Kitty Foyle* one week earlier and received no complaints. Irwin declared that the blacklist was "dead," and he quoted Ward Bond (one of its most dedicated supporters): "They're all working now, all these Fifth-Amendment Communists. We've just lost the fight. It's as simple as that."[59]

Bond would have been even more distraught had he known that George Seaton had launched a campaign to convince the Academy's Board of Governors to rescind the bylaw preventing blacklisted people from receiving Academy Awards, and Stout and Trumbo were planning to have the real "Robert Rich" appear on one of Stout's upcoming shows. But when Trumbo learned of Seaton's intentions, he decided to delay his Robert Rich revelation until after the next Board of Governors' meeting. If the board rescinded the rule, Trumbo wrote:

> The story will be told without rancor, without attacks on anyone, with good humor, *and with no digs at the Academy or its leaders*. (This I think is the tone for everyone who has anything to say from the blacklistees' side—restraint, cooperation with pleasant professional relations, etc., etc. Nobody's a martyr, nobody's mad, history hurt everybody, all made mistakes, and

la-de-da-da-do.) The reason I make a point of this is that there can never be an *official* end to the blacklist—this is as close as we shall presently come. Therefore, we must pretend that is the end (which it damned near is), and pose not as angry martyrs, as the persecuted, but as good *winners*. In this guise we assume our victory at last, and carry no grudges into the future.[60]

But if the board failed to revoke or substantially revise the rule, Trumbo intended to use the Rich announcement and *The Defiant Ones* "to blast hell out of them."[61]

The Board of Governors met on January 12, 1959, to consider a request from the Academy Writers Branch to drop article VIII, section 1(f), because "it is impractical to administer and enforce." Seaton advised the board members that they were facing a very difficult situation this year. Unlike in 1957, when Michael Wilson had been the sole person involved, nominations were anticipated for two writers (Harold B. Smith, cowriter of *The Defiant Ones*, and Edmund North, cowriter of *Cowboy*); although neither of them had been accused of Communist affiliations, they had collaborated on scripts written by Communists. Seaton also pointed out another potential source of trouble: what if a foreign-language film were nominated and it was later learned that its producer, director, or writer was a Communist? Following a lengthy discussion, Seaton's motion to repeal the bylaw carried by a vote of eighteen to one. The article announcing the decision was titled: "Ban Lifted on Red Candidates for Oscars," and it included a quotation from the board's official announcement: "The board of governors decided that experience has proved the bylaw to be unworkable and impractical to administer and enforce in view of the fact that control over the engaging of talent for films does not rest with the Academy. . . . [T]he proper function of the Academy is only to honor achievements as presented."[62]

The stage was now set for Trumbo's announcement that he was "Robert Rich." To prepare the Kings for the upcoming press conferences, Trumbo provided them with a list of possible questions and some suggested (sarcastic) responses:

Q. Have you done any other films with blacklisted people?
A. I'll answer that question when the rest of the town comes clean. Get all the producers in Hollywood together, and we'll have a truth session.

Q. Are you going to hire Trumbo in the future?

A. If I ever hire him again, I promise you it'll be in the open.
   Everybody in town is up to his armpits in the black market.
   We just happen to be the only ones who are willing to come
   out and admit it. I don't understand what all the noise is about.
   There are more ghosts in Hollywood right now than there are
   in Forest Lawn. Nobody in Hollywood wanted the blacklist in
   the first place. There isn't a producer in town who wouldn't be
   secretly glad to get rid of it. We've got more [Boris] Pasternaks
   running around in Hollywood than any other town in the
   world outside Moscow.[63]

Trumbo then arranged for Frank King to meet with *Time* reporter Robert Jennings, and he again supplied King with a few pointed answers about the blacklist.[64]

Stout and Trumbo then proceeded to film their carefully orchestrated show on which Trumbo would reveal the identity of "Robert Rich." The night before, Trumbo asked Stout to allow him to tell Irwin about the pending broadcast and arrange for Irwin to interview Frank King. Trumbo wanted to do this because so few reporters had "been willing to go out on limbs on this issue that I shrink from the idea of letting any of them down." Stout concurred. Trumbo then suggested several questions Stout might ask him, including about the Academy, to end Trumbo's part of the show. He also apologized to Stout:

> [I'm sorry to be] such an old maid about the thing; but at this
> point the blacklisters need as much help as the blacklisted in
> finishing the dirty business off. Seaton and his friends, who rep-
> resent probably the largest and most influential group within
> the industry, are now apparently determined to wash the thing
> up and end it—not only in the Academy, but in the Guilds, and
> finally, among the producers themselves. Therefore, in pretend-
> ing to be the victor in a ten year fight, I must be more cunning
> than Satan, more generous than Jesus. I'm not well fitted for the
> role, so I fret about it.[65]

Bill Stout devoted two segments (January 16 and 17) of his "Special Assignment" to the Robert Rich case, interviewing Trumbo at length on both broadcasts. The interview took place at Trumbo's house, and Nikola recalled it was "a big deal" for the family. When Stout asked

Trumbo if he was the author of *The Brave One*, Trumbo showed one version of the script and said he had four or five others plus the contracts to prove it. "There is no problem in proving authorship, the problem in Hollywood is to admit authorship." Stout asked if Trumbo intended to disclose any other films he had written under the name Robert Rich or some other pseudonym. "Well, no," Trumbo replied. "You see, these pictures were protected by anonymity, by agreement with the producers who needed that protection, and I, of course, would never violate that agreement. I couldn't do it. But there were many, comedies, melodramas, westerns, all kinds." As for the future, Trumbo said: "I have contracts covering work for approximately the next year, and, of course, these contracts call for pseudonyms and I will naturally honor those contracts. But once I have [finished them], I will never again write anything for anybody without using my own name," or, he added, the name "Robert Rich." When Stout asked, "Why Robert Rich?" Trumbo replied: "Through a grotesque chance, Robert Rich is probably the best-known screenwriter in the history of motion pictures. I should like to be associated with him, because I should like to be as well known myself."

Next, Stout asked if Trumbo intended to ask for the Academy Award Rich had won. To this query, the diplomatic Trumbo responded: "You don't ask the Academy for awards. The Academy is a private institution that confers awards. I must say that the whole uproar over Robert Rich, two years ago, was not the Academy's fault. They voted the award; they had it on hand physically; they tried to present it; they tried to find someone to give it to; and I didn't arrive. I assume they still have it. I imagine if they consider me qualified, they, in their time and in their way, will make arrangements to confer it." Pushing the line of questioning a bit further, Stout asked Trumbo what he would do if the Academy presented him with the award for *The Brave One*. To this question, Trumbo gave a very emotional answer:

> I have a daughter [Melissa], thirteen years old. I've been black-listed since she was three. She has known the title of every motion picture I've written in this study, and she has kept those titles secret. She's been a soldier. When her friends say to her, as children do, my father does so and so, what does your father do? this confronted her with a very real problem. It confronted her with the problem, and has since she was three, of who her father really is. What her father really does. I think I will give this Oscar, if I get it, to that girl. I think I will tell her, "Well,

here is one secret you no longer need to be burdened with." I'll tell her, we have our names back.

It was only when Stout posed the inevitable question concerning Trumbo's politics that he allowed an angry tone to enter his voice. His politics were his own business, he said:

But the point is I have never made a point of political secrecy. I have always been interested in politics, have had many political discussions with many people. And I have always voluntarily told many people what my affiliations are. But, of course, I will not do it for money, and I will not do it to get a job, and I will not do it for any little group of vigilantes, and I certainly will not do it under legal threat by a committee of congressional snoops, who have been condemned in terms of their questions and their methods by the Supreme Court itself. I just won't do it. There are chances, of course, in any man's life, when he may change from time to time his political affiliations. Many men do. But that again would be my own personal concern, to be revealed when I wish to, on a personal basis. I will not make public confessions of error, and I will not make recantations of error. It's not American; it has no relation to this country; and I will just have no part of it, no part at all.

At the end of the interview, Trumbo compared, in emphatic terms, his situation to that of the out-of-favor Soviet writer Boris Pasternak, who had won the 1958 Nobel Prize for literature:

The parallel is the power of the government, any government, to assert this control of the mind of a man, his writings, his thoughts, his beliefs, his affiliations. It's the same thing. It's the power in a different degree, but it is power, and that's the evil. Pasternak didn't go to jail, but on the other hand I wasn't thrown out of the Screen Writers Guild as he was thrown out of his union. But the real problem all over the world, here, there, and everywhere, is this assertion of power over the most private thoughts of men and the assertion by government that it has the power to compel men to tell, to recant, to disgrace themselves, to swear they were idiots, to revoke their past, and to spit on their work. This is what government wants in greater or less degree all over the world, and this is what nobody, nobody, can do.[66]

That same evening, as previously arranged by Trumbo, Lew Irwin interviewed Frank King, who confirmed that Trumbo was Robert Rich. The Kings had hired Trumbo, King told Irwin, because their company was a public corporation and they had "an absolute obligation" to their stockholders to buy the best scripts they could find. They would continue to buy the best material available to them, regardless of the politics of the writer, he stated. Besides, King added, "I'm not hiring their [the blacklistees'] politics, I'm hiring their writing talent. I'm no policeman." When Irwin asked if King was aware that Trumbo had refused to answer the committee's questions, King replied: "Certainly I knew that. I also know he was convicted for contempt of Congress and served a year in jail. As far as I'm concerned, that closed the books. If a man was wrong and paid for his crime—contempt is only a misdemeanor—then I say everything is square. You're not going to punish him for the rest of his life, are you?" Irwin then queried, had King ever asked Trumbo if he was a Communist? King replied: "Of course not. I'm not interested in his politics or his religion or his color. I was interested in his work. It was good work. It [*The Brave One*] was the story of a little Catholic boy and his pet. Is there anything Communistic in that?"[67]

There remained one more fire to extinguish—the one lit by current Academy president George Stevens in the January 16, late-night edition of the *Los Angeles Times*. A story about Stout's pending broadcast carried a quotation from the director, attacking Trumbo's "deception" about the identity of Robert Rich. Trumbo prepared a scathing response that he intended to use on Stout's program that evening. He showed it to Seaton, who advised Trumbo to let him handle the problem. Seaton then persuaded Stevens to withdraw the quotation from later editions of the paper. Trumbo wrote to Seaton, saluting his "astonishing talent for mediation" and proposing another way that Seaton could pour oil on the troubled Academy waters:

> I wonder if it wouldn't be helpful if you explained to Stevens that my breaking of the story had nothing whatever to do with the Academy? To that end you have permission to show him all or any part of my recent correspondence, including the present letter, if you think it wise. As for the award, that should be no

issue between us. It would be absurd for me to "claim" it, and
I will not do so. I have documents establishing authorship and
Stevens or any representative of the Academy may request and
examine them.

It seems to me it will be rather difficult for the Academy to
withhold the award and still maintain its dignity. If, however,
they do decide to withhold it, I shall cooperate with them so
that the least harm possible be done to everyone concerned. I
cannot, of course, hold silent for any attack upon my personal
or professional integrity. My objective, as you know, is much
more important than the physical possession of any award
which can never be dissociated from my person anyhow.[68]

An unmollified Stevens announced a few days later, on behalf of the
Academy, that if the authorship of *The Brave One* could be verified, he
saw no reason for the Academy to withhold the award.[69] But then he
told a *Los Angeles Times* reporter that the Oscar for *The Brave One*
was not one the Academy would be happy to give.[70]

The "Robert Rich" announcement was big news nationally. *Time*
and *Newsweek* both ran stories about it.[71] Coincidentally or not, shortly
after the interviews aired and the stories were printed, someone broke
into Trumbo's study and stole some of his private papers. He was also
physically attacked in front of his house by two boys and a girl, sustain-
ing two black eyes.[72]

In February 1959 Trumbo surveyed the situation in Hollywood. He
concluded that both the industry and the political forces in Hollywood
had fragmented. There is, he wrote to Michael Wilson, "no longer a
left, and there is no longer a right, and there is no longer a centralized
control of the industry tight enough to enforce the blacklist." Yet he
remained convinced that a collective breakthrough of the blacklistees
was not possible; he did not believe that the current studio bosses, many
of whom had signed the Waldorf statement, were disposed to offer a
general amnesty. Such an announcement on their part would imply that
a blacklist had existed. Therefore, in Trumbo's opinion, the best tactic
of the blacklistees was "straight guerrilla warfare." The "guerrillas" he
had in mind were himself, Wilson, and Maltz. They possessed, through
the "sheer excellence" of their work—their talent, competence, ability, craftsmanship, "or what you will"—the only "practical weapon" in
the armory of the blacklisted screenwriters. Trumbo believed the three
of them, acting individually and in a coordinated manner, could com-

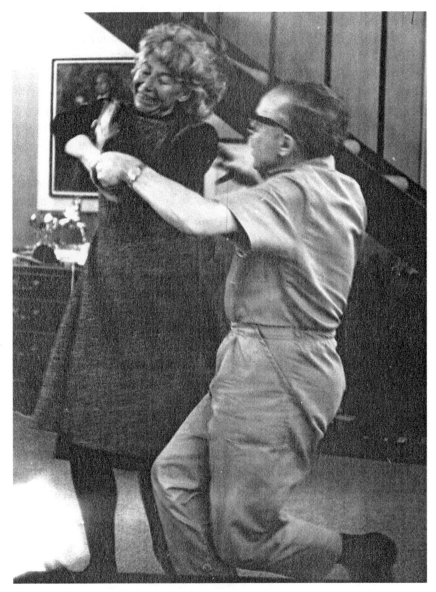

Trumbo doing his knee dance with Pauline Finn, 1957. Photograph by Cleo Trumbo.

pel the producers of their scripts to use either their real names or their established pseudonyms.

Trumbo was certain that an aboveground, frontal assault on the studios, similar to that promoted by the "die-hard elements of the left," would surely fail and would "frighten off the center forces which are actually doing the job [of ending the blacklist] without anybody's assistance." He feared that the slightest appearance of any organized or organizational effort by the Left would give "the old right an opportunity to reactivate itself and bring to the forefront issues and arguments" from twelve years earlier that had no relation to the current situation and would only muddy it. "No greater service to the idiot right could be rendered," Trumbo declared, "than to give them the opportunity to revive the argument as it was."[73]

Ned Young and Hal Smith fully agreed with Trumbo, and when they won their Academy Awards and the WGAw award for *The Defiant Ones* in March 1959, they made no public statements about the blacklist. None were needed. One by one, just as Trumbo had predicted, the industry's blacklist mechanisms were ceasing to function. An industry spokesperson announced that its blacklist oversight group, the Motion Picture Industry Council, would suspend operations in July,[74] and the WGAw announced that it was renewing its fight against the clause in the Minimum Basic Agreement that allowed producers to deny screen credit to unfriendly witnesses.[75]

Still hoping to arrange some sort of compromise that would settle all the issues that had emerged since 1947, Trumbo accepted an invitation to meet with Mendel Silberberg, known as the "rabbi" of the movie industry, in July 1959. (Silberberg was the attorney for the producers' association, had helped craft the Waldorf statement, and was Louis B. Mayer's personal attorney. In addition, his firm Mitchell, Silberberg & Knupp represented Columbia and RKO.) At that meeting, Trumbo told Silberberg: "The crumbling blacklist, which no one wants, *can* be eliminated altogether" if management "quietly and with dignity asserts its rights and responsibility and duty to employ personnel on the basis of skill alone." Silberberg did not disagree, but he told Trumbo that he would have to take the first step in this "compromise" and write a letter revealing his membership in the Communist Party. Trumbo refused. He explained why to his attorney: "(1) to deliver now a statement one has for twelve years refused on principle to write savors more of surrender (as when virginity is compromised) than of true compromise; and (2) compromise involves reciprocity which I find altogether missing from the current discussions, in that Mr. Silberberg would get specifically what he wants for the defense of his producer-clients, while he offers nothing tangible in return for my spiritual clients—the blacklisted personnel of Hollywood." From Trumbo's perspective, Silberberg failed to understand that now, as in 1947, the producers' interests (in strengthening the movie industry) coincided with the interests of those they had blacklisted. Trumbo authorized his attorney to arrange another meeting with Silberberg that would, Trumbo hoped, "put a civilized end to a situation which presently is far more embarrassing (as distinguished from painful) to producers than to blacklistees."[76] Silberberg failed to reply.

A few months later, Trumbo used revelations of cheating on several television quiz shows to once again expose the hypocrisy of blacklisting. In it, he was at his sarcastic best:

> In only one aspect of the scandal can we take real satisfaction: all who participated in the fraud were certified, loyal Americans. The elaborate system of blacklisting, by which the networks deny use of publicly-owned channels to those with whom they disagree, makes certain of that. Everybody connected with the shows had been cleared by the House Committee on Un-American Activities, the Senate Internal Security Committee, Aware, Alert, *Red Channels*, sponsors' check-ups, the agencies' private eyes, the networks' corps of dedicated snoops. And Heaven knows how many nuts, crooks and crackpots. . . .
>
> To the last child they were authenticated patriots, well-oathed and clean as the whistle that finally blew them up. . . . [T]he Republic could take comfort that it hadn't been gulled by a gang of subversives.[77]

As for his "guerrilla war" against the studios, the efforts of his small "gang of subversives" were on track: Wilson had just started work on *Lawrence of Arabia*, Maltz was adapting *Exodus* for Otto Preminger, and Trumbo was finishing his work on *Spartacus* for Kirk Douglas. In February 1959 he had told Wilson: "I think it is not at all unlikely that the credit for this picture will fall to me or my pseudonym like a ripe fig. I doubt that by the time credits are to be determined there will be found one person in Hollywood who will be willing to let his name go on the film. Hence I stand a chance of inheritance by default."[78]

The blacklist was clearly weakening, and Trumbo was being offered contracts with production companies that could pay higher rates for better-quality projects than the Kings could give him. But Trumbo knew enough about the contingencies of the script market to maintain good relations with the Kings. He thought carefully about how to address his strengthened bargaining position, and in a letter he drafted but did not send, he deftly sketched the symbiosis of the black-market relationship:

> You said that after the blacklist was over, and I was in a position to claim for my work its fair market price, I should remember that it was you who became the first to buy my services and work and make advances during the days of the blacklist. This is true. I do remember it, and always will. But . . . there is another aspect of it [the past] that you yourself must remember. I sold my work to you at very low prices, and from it you produced two films which, as you have told me, not only saved your company from closing its doors, but also returned such large profits that it has, in effect, become self-supporting and self-financing from its own earned capital. So each of us has something to remember and be grateful to the other for.

As a result, in any future contracts, the Kings must offer him "the very highest price a prosperous corporation can afford."[79]

As it happened, Trumbo did not write another script for the King brothers, but he did a variety of small jobs for them and continued to negotiate with them on other projects. In gratitude for the profits Trumbo's scripts had earned them, in March 1968 the brothers offered Trumbo the opportunity to buy 5,000 shares of King Brothers International, their new production company, at one-third its par value. They also gave Christopher several jobs. Christopher told Nancy Escher that when he went to their office for his first interview, Mama King was present, and Frank told her they were considering hiring Christopher as a reader. "Yeah," Mama King asked, "but is he as smart as his fadda?" "Of course he is," Frank replied, "it is in the genies [sic]."

18

Spartacus

Both *Spartacus* and *Exodus* deserve extended treatment, not only for the timing and the place they occupy in the defeat of the blacklist, but because of the scope and thrust of each picture and the particular problems they posed for Trumbo. He wrote both of them in less than nine months [eight on the first draft of *Spartacus*; one on *Exodus*]. It is also worth noting that he has sole credit on both films, a rarity for writers rewriting other scripts; they opened within five months of each other; and both were huge box-office successes. They gave him momentum.

—Christopher Trumbo

The "Spartacus" project was Trumbo's finest hour as a screenwriter and as an agent of historical change. But, Christopher said, "it was an awful push and pull, a tremendous struggle, and it was not just because of the personal antagonisms. It was simply a whole bunch of things getting shoved into place. It is amazing that a picture came out the other end." "My father was," Mitzi recalled, "completely obsessed" with it in 1959—driven to write a great script, procure screen credit for it, and thereby deliver a fatal blow to the blacklist. For reasons discussed later, the quality of his script was compromised by others; still, Trumbo's screen credit further weakened the blacklist, though it did not break it. In addition, he wrote hundreds of pages of brilliant (frequently witty and acerbic) letters, memos, analyses, and arguments that, collectively, provide a fascinating look at this writer's passion for his work, his understanding of his craft, and his tactical genius.

It is important to remember that when Trumbo began to work on "Spartacus," the blacklist was still firmly in place, and blacklisted writers were having an enormously difficult time obtaining film assignments, and they continued to be paid well below market rates for the work they did get. Even those producers who regularly hired blacklisted writers feared the relationship might become known. But one production company seemed to be a little less fearful than the others.

In 1955 actor Kirk Douglas created Bryna Productions. One of its first movies, *The Indian Fighter* (1955), was based on a script by Ben Kadish (fronting for the blacklisted Robert L. Richards). There is no indication that Douglas was aware of the true author of the script or that he took much interest in the blacklist or the black market. Two years later, however, independent producer Eddie Lewis began to bring projects to Bryna that he assigned to blacklisted writers. His initial connection with the blacklist came through blacklisted writer Frank Tarloff, with whom Lewis played poker. Tarloff and Paul Jarrico had written a script that Lewis tried, unsuccessfully, to sell to Bryna. However, Douglas did accept Lewis's next project, *The Careless Years*, written by two blacklisted writers, John Howard Lawson and Mitch Lindemann, and fronted by Lewis. Lewis never became an employee of Bryna. He was, in effect, an independent contractor who brought projects to the company. In late 1957 he brought two novels to Douglas's attention: *The Brave Cowboy; An Old Tale in a New Time* by Edward Abbey, and *Spartacus* by Howard Fast.

Lewis cannot remember how he and Trumbo first met, but they could have connected in a number of ways: writers on the black market openly exchanged information about prospective employers, a few agents were directing black-market scripts to independent producers, and independent producers knew which writers were blacklisted. In any case, on January 14, 1958, Trumbo, using the pseudonym "Sam Jackson," signed a letter of agreement with Eddie Lewis to adapt Abbey's novel. The first sentence reads as follows: "This will confirm our understanding regarding your collaborating with me in the writing of the screenplay based upon the novel by Edward Abbey entitled BRAVE COWBOY." The agreement called for Trumbo to write a first and a revised draft in four months and to receive in payment $5,000. The agreement then stated:

> You understand that the producer of the photoplay based upon the said literary material will not be required to give you screen or advertising credit. However in the event that the producer does not give you such credits and providing a photoplay is produced based substantially upon your screenplay, then you will be entitled to receive the following:

(a) Ten Thousand ($10,000) Dollars, payable upon com-
mencement of principal photography of said photoplay.

(b) Five percent (5%) of the producer's share of the net profits derived from said photoplay.

In the event the producer desires to give you screen and
advertising credit, you may designate any name you wish to
receive such credit.[1]

This may have been the first domestic black-market deal to introduce
the possibility of a screen credit for a blacklisted writer.

The other novel Lewis brought to Bryna was the story of Spartacus,
the leader of a slave rebellion against the Roman Republic in 71 BCE.
Its author, Howard Fast, had been a member of the Communist Party
and had worked for several Popular Front organizations, including the
Joint Anti-Fascist Refugee Committee. In March 1946 he and that committee's other board members were served subpoenas by the Committee
on Un-American Activities. Citing the First Amendment, they refused
to answer the committee's questions or provide it with the requested
documents. They were charged with contempt of Congress, indicted,
and found guilty. Fast was sentenced to three months in prison. Following three years of unsuccessful appeals, Fast commenced serving his
sentence in June 1950, alongside Edward Dmytryk and Albert Maltz at
Mill Point, West Virginia. While there, he developed the idea for a novel
about the great Roman slave revolt, which he intended as an allegory
for the terror that gripped the United States from 1945 to 1952.[2] After
seven publishers rejected it, Fast published the book himself. Despite
very few reviews, it sold exceptionally well: 45,000 copies in the first
three months.[3] But, for obvious reasons, no movie producer showed any
interest until Lewis convinced Douglas to do so at the end of 1957.

Douglas, however, had difficulty obtaining a production agreement, mainly because his regular distribution company, United Artists,
was already committed to another Spartacus project based on Arthur
Koestler's novel *The Gladiators*. It was being developed by Yul Brynner,
who would play Spartacus; Martin Ritt would direct, and Abraham
Polonsky was going to write the script. (Koestler was an ex-Communist,
Ritt had just gotten off the blacklist, and Polonsky was still on it.) Polonsky's diary entries indicate his lack of enthusiasm for the project and his
difficulty in finding a dialogue style that pleased him. By the end of the
year, he pronounced himself "bored with it."[4]

When Trumbo learned that Bryna was negotiating with Fast for the movie rights to his novel, he suggested that Lewis assign the adaptation to either him or Albert Maltz. Trumbo then wrote to Maltz about the assignment. "I think," Trumbo wrote, "it would make a hell of a film: it would also have a vast budget, big stars, and a piece would make some dough. As I say, I've got my claws in it, but I may be obliged to disgorge it, and they'd be just as happy, or happier for all I know, to have you."[5] Maltz replied that he was occupied with other projects and expressed doubt that a good film could be made from the material. As it turned out, Fast preferred to do the adaptation himself and made it a condition of the sale of the rights to the novel.

A few months later, Douglas approached Universal-International with the "Spartacus" project, but Ed Muhl, the executive vice president in charge of production, expressed reservations about making a movie from a book (and a script) written by a notorious ex-Communist. Muhl said he would put out the word that the studio was interested in making the movie, and if there were no big negative reaction, he might agree to use Fast's script.[6] Apparently, Muhl heard no discouraging words about Fast, who turned in a 102-page step outline on May 27. It was written as three acts, and the third act was 57 pages long. Like his novel, it contained very little about Spartacus, and Fast told the entire story of the uprising from the Romans' point of view; he placed most of the emphasis not on the defeat of Spartacus's uprising but on the personal defeat suffered by the Roman leader Crassus. Fast modestly acknowledged that he had incorporated large sections of his book into the outline because the novel "was written so concisely and tightly" and was difficult to improve upon.[7] No one who read Fast's outline liked it. Mel Tucker, a Universal executive, said later that Fast's first draft "was not very good"; it was too wordy and "very poorly balanced in form."[8] Douglas called it "a disaster, unusable."[9]

Fearing that they were losing ground in the competition to hire the same trio of British stars (Laurence Olivier, Charles Laughton, and Peter Ustinov) that Brynner wanted to play the Roman parts, Lewis and Douglas had to come up with a script that would appeal to those actors, and to do so, they needed "the quickest and most skillful writer in the business."[10] So Lewis took Fast's novel and outline to Trumbo, who speed-read both while Lewis waited. Trumbo immediately identified the major problem: there was no central Spartacus character, the story was told from the Romans' point of view, and Spartacus existed only in their memories.[11] After Lewis reported back to him, Douglas had Lewis ask Trumbo to prepare a new step outline that they could give to Fast under

Lewis's name. Douglas also compiled a list of writers he might hire to replace Fast (Paul Osborn, Arthur Laurents, Dudley Nichols, Irwin Shaw, Lillian Hellman, or Maxwell Anderson).[12]

Lewis and Douglas agreed that Fast should not be privy to their deal with Trumbo. Douglas would soon need to renew his option with Fast, and he did not want to alienate the writer. Furthermore, at their first meeting years earlier, Trumbo had publicly humiliated Fast. At a welcome-home-from-prison party hosted by attorney Martin Popper, Fast had loudly bemoaned the hardship of his three-month prison sentence. According to Katherine Popper, Trumbo verbally sliced Fast "to ribbons."[13] Ben Margolis recalled that "Dalton took over, and for about two hours engaged comically with Fast," during which time "he absolutely destroyed him."[14] Trumbo, for his part, did not care whose work he was rewriting. When Douglas (or Lewis) asked Trumbo how he felt about working on this project, Trumbo replied, "You cannot fight a blacklist for as many years as I have and retain any desire to install a new one."[15]

On June 13 Trumbo gave Lewis a new step outline and, on his own initiative, a detailed set of suggestions that included a "Chronology of Servile War" (nine pages), "Notes for U-I Research" (three pages), "General Notes (for the consideration of Mr. Fast)" (three pages), "Suggested Step Outline" (fifty-two pages), and "Afterthoughts" (three pages).[16] Having done much more than had been asked of him, Trumbo wanted to ensure that the quality of his work was not undervalued either creatively or monetarily. He wrote to Lewis:

> You have countered [Fast's work] with [my] detailed, step-by-step treatment, indicating every movement and scene, even sketching in the dialogue possibilities. This "step outline," as we modestly call it, is actually a complete map for a movie, and runs longer than any script—approximately 30,000 words, which is the length of a *Saturday Evening Post* serial, or even some novels. It is, in my opinion, worth money. [Universal-International] mustn't think it's simply Eddie's notes thrown into the pot as a part of his executive supervision of the job. They should understand it as that which fundamentally creates a motion picture for them.[17]

Trumbo framed the "General Notes" section very carefully, using, as he put it, "chaste and placatory words" and making it seem as if the notes had been the work of a committee: "We have all gone over the outline, and pooled our various opinions and suggestions." The first sentence read: "These notes are based on the excellent outline you [Fast] have given us, in which the complex structure of the novel has been transformed so well into the sequential narrative form which most often suits the needs of a motion picture." The "Suggested Step Outline," however, clearly changed the focus and direction of the project. Again, choosing his words carefully, Trumbo wrote: "The form and concept of the novel, while it dealt with Spartacus as the perpetrator of overwhelming events, concerned itself mainly with the reaction of the characters to what an off-scene Spartacus was doing and had done to the Roman world. The motion picture must, of course, reverse the emphasis"— that is, it must show Spartacus acting and the Romans reacting. "To this end it is felt we shall have to open up and develop the campaigns of Spartacus, to show the immensity of the forces that were called into action, and to show Spartacus directing them in a way we have not yet achieved." In addition, Trumbo wrote, we must "extend the struggle in time, lest it seem like merely a heroic skirmish extending over a few months. We must show, or account for, or give the impression of, four years of devastating war in which hundreds of thousands of men were slain on both sides—four years of terror for Rome herself, a terror that can only be measured by the frightfulness of the final punishment she exacted for it."[18] Trumbo then detailed the stages of development of Spartacus's character. (It should be noted that the lack of material about the historical Spartacus had defied the best efforts of both Koestler and Fast. Trumbo's attempt to invent a satisfactory "character" for him was a problem that concerned, and seemingly bedeviled, everyone else involved in the production.)

In one of his "notes between scenes," Trumbo pointed out that Fast's outline focused solely on the collision between two worlds (the Romans and the slaves), it lacked direct conflict between the main characters in those two worlds, and it failed to emphasize the historical importance of all the conflicts. "The gladiators' revolt," he stated, "must mark, in the personal story of Spartacus, his rise from animal to leader; in the overall story, the slave world's challenge to the Roman world." That climax will make no sense, he continued, unless the movie provides much greater detail of the lives of the escaped gladiators and slaves during their four-year rebellion.[19] In the "Afterthoughts," Trumbo stated his main thesis: "In a certain way, one might say that Spartacus actually won the war. Or, to put it differently, at least his enemy, the Republic, did not long survive."[20] Indeed, after the last battle, in which the Romans beat Spartacus's army, Trumbo wanted the Roman general Crassus to say: "The slave world has fatally wounded the Republic."[21]

Though not all of Trumbo's ideas and suggestions were used, his step outline became the matrix of the finished film. However, when Douglas gave "Lewis's" step outline to Fast, the writer exploded in anger and threatened to cancel the contract. After talking with his agent and learning the penalties involved if he quit, Fast returned to work and reluctantly followed "Lewis's" outline. But when Fast's second draft also failed to satisfy Douglas and Lewis, they decided to hire an established screenwriter to write a draft based on Trumbo's outline and then give that draft to Trumbo for a final polish.[22] Lewis provided Trumbo with the list of writers Douglas had compiled in March and asked for Trumbo's advice on which writer to select. Trumbo replied: "Most of the names on your list are extremely expensive writers, and will run up fatly on the budget. Some of them are superb at dialogue, some at construction, and some are all-round professionals. It is just possible that the one you choose will give you a fine and a finished script you'll not wish to change in any way. However, the complexities of the historical film and the fallibility of human nature inclines me to think that in any event, the script would terminate with a minimum of two writers attached to it." To avoid that problem, Trumbo recommended that Bryna hire "someone not quite so flossy on the first draft" and then give that draft to Trumbo to revise and polish.[23]

Douglas, however, did not have the luxury of making that choice. He did not yet have a production deal with a studio, his option on the novel was about to expire, and Fast was threatening not to renew the option unless he were allowed to write the screenplay. So Douglas decided to employ a device used in the old studio system: he would assign the same project to two different writers, unbeknownst to them. On May 28 Bryna signed an agreement with Fast to write a treatment and a draft screenplay for the sum of $75,100. Three days later, Lewis signed an agreement with "Sam Jackson" to write a screenplay for *Spartacus*. For the next six weeks, Fast and Trumbo were writing separate scripts.[24] Mel Tucker later said about Jackson's real identity: "All I remember is that it was well into the shooting of the picture that we were informed of it, and I think it was when Eddie Lewis told Ed Muhl, for reasons of protecting Universal at that time, I guess, as it was becoming more and more rumored and I think that they owed it to us to make us privy to the information. But it was well into the shooting of the picture."[25] But according to Douglas, he told his agent, Lew Wasserman (MCA), about Trumbo just before Bryna and Universal signed their *Spartacus* contract, and Wasserman had allegedly replied, "I know."[26] However, Ronnie Lubin (another MCA agent) told Wasserman's biographer that Wasserman learned of Trumbo's authorship only when Muhl called him, just as the film was about to wrap, with the news that an anti-Communist organization was threatening to publicize Trumbo's involvement unless Universal fired him. Wasserman doubted the anti-Communist group would do anything, but he left the decision about Trumbo to Muhl.[27] Whichever account is correct, both indicate that Douglas, who was facing a host of other problems, was not eager to publicize Trumbo's participation in the film.

In early July, Fast and Trumbo turned in their respective drafts.[28] Bryna executives thought Trumbo's draft was "far superior in concept, narrative line, dialogue, etc. to anything in the Fast version."[29] Douglas then exercised his option to terminate Fast, and Lewis flew to London with Trumbo's draft in hand. There, he met with Olivier, Laughton, and Ustinov and, on the basis of Trumbo's script, convinced them to sign with Bryna. With those actors under contract, Universal-International agreed to produce the movie. Bryna then contracted with Trumbo to write a second draft.

According to Douglas, Trumbo was writing at "breakneck speed," making revisions without complaint. The two met regularly and secretly at their respective houses and exchanged a host of memos. Douglas described Trumbo as "wonderful to work with, [he] never had any hesitancy about rewriting a scene."[30] At some point in 1959, Mitzi recalled:

> Kirk Douglas gave my father an African gray parrot, which lived in his office, usually perched on his shoulder while he typed or lay on the sofa reading. Its wings had been clipped, but it could travel fast by foot, and it reputedly could bite through a person's finger. Whenever I entered the office, usually barefoot, the parrot would race towards my feet, head down, terrifying me as I scrambled onto a chair. It learned to mimic my father's voice, and its rendition of my father's cough was uncanny. My father enjoyed teaching the bird tricks and occasionally, since it couldn't fly, the bird was brought up to the house to show him off. The parrot's most famous deed was interrupting Laurence Olivier by saying, in my father's voice, "Oh, shut up, shut up!"

Trumbo with the African gray parrot given to him by Kirk Douglas, 1959. Photograph by Cleo Trumbo.

At the end of July, Trumbo was clearly feeling the strain of this process, and he was concerned about the murky arrangements regarding the manner and schedule of his compensation. He wrote to Lewis, asking specifically about his fee: "During a telephone conversation, after I had finished my treatment and while Fast was working on [a] first draft of his screenplay, you mentioned a payment of $75,000—was that for both of us or for me alone? When we spoke yesterday, you mentioned that I was to receive $25,000 for first; $25,000 for second, and that you would try to get me another $25,000."[31] Trumbo also requested a change in the nature of their arrangement, to relieve "both of us of the painful embarrassment of working with each other in an artistic relationship while at the same time being compelled to deal with each other as businessmen."[32] Later that same day, Trumbo wrote a second letter to Lewis, apologizing for the earlier one: "I am so very heartily sorry for the mental state into which I let myself drop, and this morning's letter which resulted."[33]

Trumbo's mental state would have been considerably more agitated

had he known that Douglas was regularly consulting Fast about the
script's progress. It is not clear why Douglas did so, given his thoughts
about Fast's outline and draft and his belief that Fast "was an incredible
egomaniac, the only person who was always right."[34] His dependence
on Fast probably reflects Douglas's insecurity and his lack of control
over the direction his multibillion-dollar project was taking. Whatever
the reason, Douglas does not mention any of his conversations with
Fast in either of his autobiographies. The first discussion occurred on
November 3, 1958, after Fast had read Trumbo's second draft and complained that the writer had thrown away his book, keeping only the
names of the characters. "Is it too bad?" Douglas asked. Fast replied:
"I'm going to give you the straight truth—not try to be diplomatic.
Worst script I've ever read. . . . So bad it's insulting and tragic. . . . A film
based on this script will be disastrous. . . . I don't want my name on it,
in any case. . . . Not one line in the script is mine." When Douglas asked
Fast to write a detailed, candid letter, Fast replied:

> What's the use of my writing to you? Eddie Lewis is the world's
> worst writer—no talent, no imagination, ignorant. He has a
> compulsion to prove he can write. . . . This terrible piece of work
> must not be represented as my work. . . . This terrible script—
> with its silly adolescent notion of what dialogue should be. . . .
> The only barrier to getting a good script is Eddie Lewis—he is a
> literary and dramatic half-wit. Bring in another writer, another
> editor—if you can do that, I'll break my neck to do all I can.[35]

In a follow-up letter to Fast, Douglas remarked: "If time and situation
permitted, I would love to have you out here."[36]

Fast, who concluded (wrongly) that "Lewis" had turned Spartacus
into "a petulant savage," intended to remake Spartacus into "a person of force and dignity." Many years later, Fast reiterated his strong
objections to Spartacus being depicted as a brute rather than as "a man
of compassion and understanding."[37] In effect, Fast wanted Spartacus's
humanity to be evident from the beginning of the movie, rather than
having it evolve during the movie (as it did in Trumbo's script).

Trumbo completed his "final" draft of "Spartacus" on December
9, 1958, and a revised "final" draft on January 16. According to Trumbo's note on the cover, the January draft was the one used by director Anthony Mann when principal photography began.[38] Mann knew
that "Sam Jackson" was Trumbo's pseudonym, and he considered the

whole masquerade "too ludicrous for words." So, when Ustinov asked Mann if he could talk to "Jackson" about his part, Mann intentionally blew the carefully contrived cover. He telephoned Trumbo and asked if he and Ustinov could come over and talk about the script.[39] Trumbo agreed, thinking they must have received permission to do so. But when Trumbo told Douglas and Lewis about the visit, they responded, "That's it. We're in trouble."[40] Ustinov then told Olivier, who also wanted to talk to Trumbo about his part. Douglas and Lewis approved that meeting.[41]

A few weeks later, Mann either left the production or was fired, depending on whose version one believes.[42] Mann's departure proved to be a double-edged sword for Trumbo. On the one hand, after he left the movie, Mann told everyone that Trumbo was writing the script, and soon the gossip columnists were writing about it.[43] On the other hand, Douglas replaced Mann with Stanley Kubrick, who had directed Douglas in *Paths of Glory* (1957). Prior to *Paths of Glory*, Kubrick had directed three short subjects and three features, the latter produced by companies he co-owned. He had then been hired by Marlon Brando to direct a much more expensive feature, *One-Eyed Jacks*. After six months of work on that project, Kubrick resigned, citing artistic differences. Kubrick and his producing partner, James B. Harris, were involved in an adaptation of Vladimir Nabokov's novel *Lolita* when Douglas called. Kubrick and Harris decided to put *Lolita* on hold and accept Douglas's offer. But to seal the deal, Douglas had to agree to release Kubrick and Harris from their four-picture deal with Bryna. Harris called that deal "a life sentence," especially since they believed *Lolita* would be a big hit. In addition, Kubrick's salary for *Spartacus* would give his company a much-needed injection of cash (he was paid $5,000 a week and received $155,000 in total).[44] Kubrick also liked the idea of directing the three British actors, and he was eager to direct a big picture.[45] *Spartacus* would be the biggest, longest, and most expensive movie he had directed to date.

Douglas regarded Kubrick as a brilliant director, but he also knew from previous experience that Kubrick had a "tremendous ego" and an obsession with rewriting other people's scripts, even though he was not, in Douglas's opinion, a good writer.[46] When Trumbo learned about the change in directors, he wrote to Douglas: "If Kubrick can give it visualization, and I think he is a budding Eisenstein, you will have a great film."[47] Kubrick read the script over a weekend and began shooting on February 16, but he and Trumbo did not meet until three weeks later. After that meeting, Trumbo changed his mind about Kubrick. He

was not, Trumbo later said, "quite the right man" to direct this movie.
"His career was at stake," he jumped into the assignment without having read the script, and "he was a little mystified the first three or four
days."[48] Christopher later said: "Kubrick's hiring changed everything.
All of the problems *Spartacus* encountered began with Kubrick. They
are of his manufacture. He was hired to do a job and then subverted
what he was supposed to do."

Christopher could have cited Douglas for subversion as well. Shortly
after hiring Kubrick, Douglas sent a revised copy of Trumbo's script to
Fast (without telling Trumbo) and asked for "constructive" suggestions.
Fast replied that although the first sixty-five pages were vastly improved,
the whole story bogged down after that, mainly because it departed
radically from his book.[49] Douglas also sent the revised script to novelist
Romain Gary, who pointed out a basic weakness: the "lack of characterization of Spartacus himself."[50] Trumbo knew about the "character"
problem, and he had already offered Douglas "many suggestions" for
strengthening the role of Spartacus. First, he noted, Spartacus must discover his purpose, to be "a leader who must exercise inner discipline,"
to do what "leaders from Moses to Lenin have had to do." Second, at
the end, he must "realize that he will be defeated but that the fight is an
inexorable and necessary part of his fate."[51]

Three weeks after Trumbo's first meeting with Kubrick, Lewis
showed him the "final" shooting script, which differed significantly from
the one Trumbo had completed in January. Worried about what these
changes portended, Trumbo wrote to Douglas: "I've read your final
script and find myself with the occupational hazard of the onlooker—I
want to get into the act! So please understand my more minute suggestions about Spartacus." Trumbo reiterated some comments from his
February note: "The Spartacus character flags badly in the middle of
the script. The slaves revolt but their lack of purpose and building up
of the Gracchus (Laughton) and Crassus (Olivier) characters leaves the
hero merely a muscle man who has been tamed by love."[52] In another
set of notes, Trumbo focused on the film's final scenes, particularly the
confrontation between Crassus and Spartacus.[53] Trumbo wanted the
audience to leave the theater with the belief that "Spartacus is not a
tragic figure, because he wins."[54] He wanted Spartacus to be killed in
the final battle and then placed on the cross, but Trumbo did not want
Spartacus to be crucified.

A few weeks later, Trumbo added a scene designed to strengthen
his victory-in-defeat concept of the slaves' revolt. In that new scene,

Crassus comes to the battlefield to view the captives. He approaches Spartacus and Antoninus (his former slave) and asks their names:

> Spartacus: You asked my name. I give it to you. Spartacus.
> Crassus: And you, Antoninus—are you Spartacus, too?
> Antoninus: One name's as good as another. We're all Spartacus.

On May 7 Douglas sent a memo to Lewis, Kubrick, Stan Margulies, and Jackson (Trumbo) with an idea for a variation on this scene: "Suddenly, Antoninus, with a twinkle in his eye, jumps up with his arms waving; 'I am Spartacus.' David the Jew follows suit. In short order, the hundreds and hundreds of slaves are all jumping up, yelling in a happy vein, 'I am Spartacus.'"[55]

As the weeks passed, Trumbo felt increasingly cut out of the script revision process. He expressed the pain and isolation he felt in a long letter to Lewis: "I don't know what we've shot, what we're going to shoot; speeches are cut rather than being re-written for cuts; effects are being lost; I write five versions for five different people, and don't know which has been found acceptable, which has been changed, or in what way." He had never been invited to visit the set; he had not been shown one foot of film, and now he was finding it *"absolutely impossible to get script changes as they come through."* He assured Lewis that he was not being a prima donna; he was willing to cut and rewrite. His only concern was that too many good parts of the original script were being cut. He was, he said, "heartsick" about losing them, and he feared the loss of others in the future. Then, in an unusual show of emotion, Trumbo told Lewis: "I have sweated. I have given up family life, social life, everything, in my absorption. And when ten hours of my life is casually snipped out of existence—I begin to think it isn't worth it." He continued, "I'm not referring to fairness, or any of that crap; nor to the writer's sanctity, nor any of that shit; I merely mean that I am obsessed with this film; that I am giving it far more time and devotion and thought than any other film I've ever written; and that a thing like this cuts so deep into me psychologically I shall have to break the obsession if I am to avoid the shock of preparing the best that I have—for somebody's wastebasket." Furthermore, no one working on the movie seemed to understand the structural elements of scriptwriting. His original lines had been, "by and large, constructed like a crossword puzzle. Each line is there by intent (in most instances), and when it's cut, something is lost. Some cement that makes one follow another is gone." As a result, Trumbo concluded: "I don't know anything. I have lost all thread of the film. . . . I *love* this picture . . . and I don't think anyone else does."[56]

On April 27 Trumbo sent a two-page memo to Douglas, commenting on the most recently revised script pages. A few weeks later, fearing he was not being heard, Trumbo sent out a seven-page memorandum titled "General Broadcast: Copy to All Concerned," referring to the final confrontation between Crassus and Spartacus. In it, he wrote: "I am absolutely convinced that our scene, in any of its present forms, is dead wrong. Worse than wrong, I think it degrades our theme, it degrades the picture, it degrades the actors. I think it is fraudulent, unbelievable, and vulgarly melodramatic. It degrades the character of Spartacus, it destroys the character of Crassus, it completely evades the valid emotional and intellectual problems of the film." Trumbo specifically criticized Kubrick, who, at the moment of Spartacus's "supreme moral, spiritual and physical agony," had him mock his conqueror, boasting and spitting. The scene is "false and melodramatic and in abominable taste." To this memo, Trumbo attached a new scene depicting "a calm, intelligent, inquiring Crassus . . . , pitted against a physically exhausted, spiritually drained Spartacus in his final moment of absolute defeat."[57]

Douglas was not satisfied with the way the movie was developing either, so he sent the latest version of the script to Fast, marking the scenes that had already been shot. Douglas told Fast: "I have been hoping to work out some way to get you out here to do more work on the script, in an official capacity. For a multitude of reasons, I have not been able to present this type of proposal to you." But, Douglas assured him, "we have gone back to many of your scenes in construction. . . . [W]e intend to make many more changes, based on your version." Douglas asked Fast for some suggestions, particularly in the farewell love scene between Varinia and Spartacus, where Spartacus's dialogue "doesn't have the simplicity that you usually write for the character."[58] Two weeks later, Douglas brought Fast to Los Angeles and paid him $4,000 for one week's work.[59] One month later, Fast did more rewriting at his home in New Jersey.[60] Fast later claimed that Trumbo's script "had no real continuity and no climax," requiring Fast to write twenty new episodes to sew the movie together.[61] Trumbo was not told any of this.

Nor was Trumbo aware of the extent of Ustinov's revisions. In his memoir, Ustinov wrote: "I rewrote all the scenes I had with Laughton, and we rehearsed at his home or mine. . . . Kubrick accepted what I had done more or less without modification." Douglas and Lewis also knew this was happening.[62] Trumbo, thinking that Ustinov was rewriting only a few lines, expressed no qualms about it to Kubrick: "The material written by that scoundrel Batiatus [Ustinov] is so stunning one is tempted to use it all, and dislike losing any of it. . . . I think the scoundrel Batiatus does us a very large favor, adding wit to our script and pleasure to our lives: I feel like a vandal when I touch any line of his. Why, then, do I do it? Only the dear Gods know."[63] Finally, at the end of May, Trumbo learned that Ustinov had rewritten all his dialogue with Laughton. An enraged Trumbo sent two telegrams to Lewis. In the first, he canceled a scheduled meeting and accused Lewis and Douglas of allowing two actors, "neither of whom is a writer, to meet and decide about how a writer should write. . . . I have rewritten as much as I intend to. Let the real creative people take over and improve my feeble efforts. And let them also take a credit for which it has been mutually assumed shall be assigned to no one." In the second telegram, sent twenty minutes later, Trumbo wrote: "I quit the picture absolutely. Inadvertent or unintended insults do not disturb me. Calculated ones, in which what I have always felt to be an honorable profession, are too degrading for me to endure."[64]

In *I Am Spartacus!* Douglas claims that as soon as he heard about the telegrams to Lewis, he drove to Trumbo's home. (Douglas does not mention this significant event in *The Ragman's Son*.) The gist of this alleged conversation concerned Douglas's sudden realization that, to convince Trumbo to return to work, he would have to rehire him as "Dalton Trumbo." When Trumbo asked Douglas point-blank whether he would tell Universal that Trumbo was the writer on *Spartacus*, Douglas replied no. But once the film was finished, he offered to give Trumbo credit as sole screenwriter, and he swore Trumbo to secrecy about that promise.[65] It is more likely that the exact opposite occurred: Trumbo refused to go back to work unless Douglas promised to give him screen credit. After all Trumbo, had been maneuvering for credit since the beginning of the assignment. As Lewis recalled, "Trumbo was determined to leverage this opportunity. He constantly gave me cues about how to handle Douglas. 'Don't tell him it's a moral issue. Tell him it's the smart move; it will help him not hurt him.'"[66]

The principal photography on *Spartacus* was completed on August 1, and a cutter's continuity (rough cut) was prepared on September 14. That cut pleased only Kubrick. Everyone else was unhappy. Douglas and Lewis arranged for Trumbo to come to the Universal lot to view the rough cut, and Trumbo was, in Mitzi's phrase, "livid." He asked

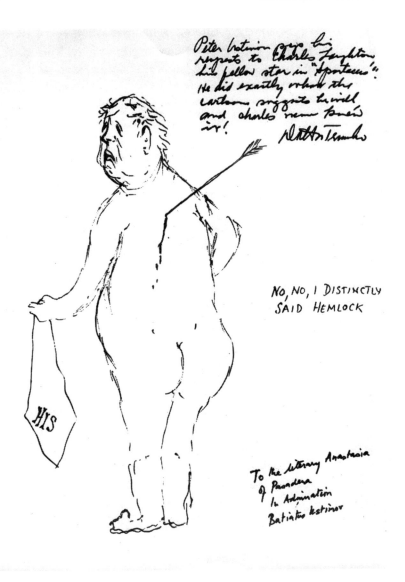

Drawing by Peter Ustinov of Charles Laughton, 1960. Courtesy of Trumbo family.

to return the next day to watch it a second time, after which Trumbo wrote a note to Douglas (which he did not send): "Now you've had your fun. Whether it is you alone, or Stanley gently and convincingly encouraging you, or Stanley alone, you have had already $3-million worth of fun. One or both of you must stop this horseplay, and take serious thought to your careers."[67]

Please return

Peter came to my house during the early shooting of Spartacus (1959) and told me through this cartoon what he was going to do to Charles Laughton. He, like others, knew my house was in Highland Park rather than adjacent and more prosperous Pasadena but they always preferred the latter.

Inscription by Trumbo on the back of the drawing: "Peter came to my house during the early shooting of *Spartacus* (1959) and told me through this cartoon what he was going to do to Charles Laughton. He, like others, *knew* my house was in Highland Park rather than adjacent [to the] . . . more prosperous Pasadena, but they always preferred the latter."

Trumbo spent the next few days feverishly writing a long treatise on the failures of the film. He rarely stopped, even for meals. In both his memoirs, Douglas raved about Trumbo's report, calling it "the most brilliant analysis of movie-making that I have ever read." He claimed, "I had never read anything like it. As I turned each page, mesmerized, I thought, *They could teach this. It should be required reading for every would-be screenwriter, actor, or director.*"[68] When Kubrick asked if Trumbo had liked the rough cut, Douglas replied: "He *didn't* like it, and he's right."[69]

Trumbo was the only one to see that the combination of Douglas's vacillations over the script and Kubrick's directorial vision had resulted in a compromised picture. In this respect, Trumbo's report was, in Christopher's words, "a counterrevolutionary document." It was also a clear indication that Trumbo had decided not to quietly fold his tent and retreat into the hinterlands. As an epigraph to his report on *Spartacus*, Trumbo repeated Winston Churchill's exhortation: "Never give in! Never give in! Never, never, never—in anything great or small, large or petty—never give in except to convictions of honor and good sense."[70] He then opened his report with the statement: "I have never before in my life had such an almost physical reaction to a rough-cut film."

Trumbo's "Report on *Spartacus*" comprised two sections. The first, titled "The Two Conflicting Points of View," ran eleven pages.[71] From the beginning, Trumbo wrote, there had been "two perfectly honest points of view on the nature of the Spartacus story" (1-a). A five-page, side-by-side comparison of the two views followed. The "large" view, which was Trumbo's, posited the slave revolt as a major rebellion that shook the Roman Republic, lasted one year, involved a series of brilliant military maneuvers by the slaves, and required the entire Roman army to defeat it. The "small" view (Kubrick's) saw the revolt as a quick jailbreak and a dash for the sea, requiring only one Roman detachment to quell it. In the "large" view, Spartacus fought for the freedom of every person in his army and never doubted the rightness of his cause. In the "small" view, he fought only for the freedom of himself and Varinia. The "large" view depicted the slave revolt as affecting the entire social structure of Rome, whereas the "small" view gave it no such dimension.

Turning next to the character of Spartacus, Trumbo acknowledged that it was the major unresolved weakness in his script. Douglas and Lewis had asked Trumbo to focus on the Roman scenes to entice the British actors to sign on. They all thought they would have sufficient time before the beginning of principal photography to attend to the Spartacus scenes. But for some reason, the character of Spartacus was never filled out. And once Kubrick was hired, "the small view took over." Thereafter, there were "what amounted to three complete plot re-writes of the Spartacus scenes." Trumbo admitted his complicity: "For such elements of the Spartacus small view, as I have permitted myself, under pressure of time or persons or arguments, to write into the script, I bitterly blame myself. I should have found some better way to make my point of view clear." And yet, "no matter how I sought in the writing to preserve the large view, every scene in which it appeared would be re-written by others, hastily and on the set. . . . And I have no reason to believe that any Spartacus scene I write in the future will be shot as written" (7). Trumbo blamed Kubrick for the despair he was feeling. Kubrick had not followed the script as Trumbo had written it. He had displayed no appreciation for "the dangers of haphazard set re-writing," and he had allowed Ustinov "to dabble mercilessly" with his and Laughton's parts, to both their detriments (8). Trumbo concluded the first document with this statement: "I have every confidence that if my work is left alone, I can write a Spartacus that will be the equal of any other part in the film. The question is—do *you* have that confidence?" (9).

In the second document, titled "Scene-by-Scene Run-through" (sixty-eight pages), Trumbo was not wholly negative.[72] He thoroughly approved of ten scenes; in those he criticized, he did not aim his guns solely at Kubrick. About the "First Varinia-Spartacus Scene in Cell," Trumbo wrote: "I bow to the director for a brilliant concept" (2). And for the "Cutting of After-the-Battle Sequence," Trumbo congratulated Kubrick for "the awesome mood of death" he had "so magnificently evoked" (47–48). In an addendum that Trumbo titled "P.S. to Stanley K. Junior Kubrick," he wrote:

> You talked to me the other day about the character of Sparta-cus? What was it really? I thought about it until I saw the film for the second time. I suggest you get over to the projection room and look at the first hour all by yourself. *That's* what Spartacus's character is! You conceived it, you created it, you directed it, and you shot it—it's all yours, and it's all there, and it's wonderful. Spartacus is *gentle*. For having character-ized him thus, we are all in your debt. We must not depart from that basic characteristic of our hero: *Spartacus is gentle!* (68)

Indeed, in this portion of the report, Trumbo was far more sharply critical of Ustinov's writing and Tony Curtis's acting than of Kubrick's directing. He referred to Ustinov as *Père* Ustinov, and in his comments on the "First Gracchus-Batiatus Scene," Trumbo wrote: "Charles [Laughton] put himself in Peter's hands for certain re-writes in this scene. He could not have been unluckier in his choice, since Peter was determined to give Charles a screwing, and did so" (14–15). Later, in his comments on the "Second Batiatus-Gracchus Scene," Trumbo wrote: "Père Ustinov, in fact, maimed two birds with one stone in this instance" (52). As for Curtis, Trumbo described him as "one of the least talented, most deplorable actors" he had ever seen (57).

The main motifs in the second part of Trumbo's report were his insistence on returning to the "large" Spartacus theme and his criticism of Kubrick's distrust of dialogue to explain the characters' motivations. In Trumbo's comments on the scene "The Matched Pairs [of the Gladiators]," he noted: "This is the first scene in which we have the blessed chance to replace the Small concept of Spartacus with the Large one. We must not fluff it. . . . [W]e must in this scene establish a logical plan for the slave army, and that plan *must* include the question of the army's ultimate objective, its destination." The slave plot, he continued, has "always been fundamental" to the concept of the slave story. But Kubrick had continually thrown this plot out, thereby crippling the story or making it nonsensical. He did so because the slave plot, to be fully understood, had to be spelled out—"it involved the use of *spoken words*—and spoken words are, *ipso facto* [in Kubrick's mind], dull and to be avoided." Trumbo then asked to be given the green light to rewrite those scenes using words, because without those words, the movie would fail. The movie, in its current cut, juxtaposed "a now-plotless slave story (against a strongly plotted Roman story)" (9–10). What was needed, Trumbo said, was a scene in which Spartacus spoke to his followers in a quietly persuasive, confident, tolerant, and understanding manner. "He should speak affirmatively, morally, intelligently—and even brilliantly," but he must not speak (as he did in the current cut) as though he were the graduate of a Roman school of rhetoric. "Here we have the great moral speech of Spartacus in this scene—and it begins with six rhetorical questions! What is this Spartacus," Trumbo asked rhetorically, "a debater on points?" Because Kubrick had allowed this rhetorical method to be used throughout, "over every objection" Trumbo had made, "the point of view of the Small Spartacus permeates this film." If the filmmakers "want the Large Spartacus," they must allow Trumbo to write him. "He must speak as a man with a brain and a heart rather than the boy upon the burning deck" (11–12). Trumbo reiterated his "large" thesis in his comments on "Encampment at Vesuvius," where his effort to depict the slave army as a community had been altered, making it instead a slave army with camp followers. "The nobility of the slaves, the dignity of their enormous efforts, and the tragedy of their final defeat is thereby fatally diminished. When you diminish the cause, you diminish the stature of the leader. You produce the Small Spartacus" (21). The "small" view also emerged in the meager screen time allotted to the slave community. Deprived of a detailed look at the slave community, the audience, Trumbo predicted, will not "give a damn about what happens to such a dull *crowd* . . . of people" (18).

Kubrick continued his diminution of Spartacus's achievements in the scene titled "Caesar Discusses Metapontum in the Baths," where he failed to show the Romans' reaction to the slaves' victory at Metapontum. By doing so, Kubrick refused to acknowledge that Metapontum had been a great victory for Spartacus's army; it had "stunned Roman society, and opened the first visible fissures in the stability of the Republic as a form of government." Trumbo was "driven wild at the thought of losing" the scene he had originally written, because of what it did for the character of Spartacus and for the movie as a whole (42).

Detailed analyses of other scenes followed, but Trumbo reserved his strongest words for his bête noire: the Crassus-Spartacus confrontation at the cross. In one note, he had mildly written: "There is absolutely no reason after the Olivier-Douglas scene to hold on Douglas getting strung up on that silly cross."[73] In another note, he gave full rein to his anger:

> I can't allow it [this scene] to pass without telling you once more—indeed it is my *duty* to tell you—that this speech is a gut-turner, a festering, vomitous heap of garbage, an obscene catastrophe. It would have been a catastrophe for the Small view of Spartacus. It is even a greater catastrophe for the Large view. I will keep saying this until I drop in my tracks—not out of vanity, not out of stubbornness, but because I have too much respect for Kirk Douglas as [a] man and an actor than to permit his public degradation without protest.[74]

In the report, however, Trumbo concluded, "There is nothing Spartacus can say at this point in his life that is half so eloquent as his *complete silence*."[75]

In "A Last General Note on *Spartacus*," Trumbo emitted a final cri de coeur:

> For the past three months the script has been written by a com-
> mittee rather than by a writer. Everything has been thrown at
> me: hostile Koestlerian ideas derived from quite another book;
> rhetorical speeches and character gems from the newly discov-
> ered [*sic*] Fast script which should have been read months ago;
> psychiatric observations which I have found of immense value;
> the rival opinions of actors; the director's opinion (possibly cor-
> rect) that the words don't matter anyhow so long as they're
> simple, and that any attempt with speech to provoke thought or
> illuminate intellectual, political, or moral concepts simply con-
> fuses the audience; a wide-spread conviction that complexity
> has no place on the screen, and that simplicity is best brought
> out by action alone; every possible attempt at swift and easy
> solutions to the problem of a script which is essentially com-
> plex, and therefore is bound to have a certain complexity of
> motives (as you have discovered in ten versions of the climax).

The time had come, Trumbo asserted, for some person to step forward, call a halt to the never-ending process of speculating about how many ways a particular scene might be written, and decide, once and for all, "on the way it *will* be written." He nominated himself for that job: "I therefore move that I be advanced from the status of stenographer to writer." And, in his closing plea, he implored his readers, "Let us go back to the old-fashioned idea that by and large the best man to invent a story and write a script is a writer."[76]

Douglas and Lewis accepted Trumbo's conclusions, consulted with him, and authorized him to write as many additional scenes as nec-essary to improve the movie. Universal approved another half a mil-lion dollars to allow Kubrick to go to Spain and shoot more big battle scenes, and additional filming commenced on November 2, 1959.[77]

As for the more intimate battle between Trumbo and Kubrick, the director had three distinct advantages: he was on the set, directing, every day; he was overseeing the editing; and he could talk publicly and freely about the picture. Trumbo, confined to his office, could only fume and write angry memos and notes. At some point during the shoot, Trumbo typed an "After-Note: Spartacus-Crassus Confrontation Scene," which was a parody of Kubrick's insistence on "visual" scenes:

Spartacus (sneeringly): Did'st thou, great Crassus, truly think
To look upon the face of mighty Spartacus
And laugh at his discomfiture—and spit?
But soft, great lord; thy star has gone a -wry,
For my expectoration's in *your* eye,
And were I acrobatic, 'twould be shit.
(He spits a burpet of spattle.)

Trumbo made another not-so-veiled comment about Kubrick in a note he titled "Directors and Their Delusions":

Practically all of these cunning scamps truly believe that worm-eaten old chestnut which extols the effectiveness of one picture over ten-thousand words. They're fanatically convinced that their silly camera angles are more interesting to the audience than the actor's spoken dialogue. They hate dialogue because it presents ideas (which directors abominate), causes a thought reaction, and diverts attention from the visual contemplation of the scene (which, to a director, is the only valid reason for making the film in the first place). The result: letting a director scissor a decent script is like turning a starved weasel loose in a hen house. Phrases and feathers all over the place, and very little life remaining.[78]

In one of his undated notes on "The Mass-Marriage" scene, Trumbo gave full rein to his antagonistic feelings, referring to the director as "Stanislav Kubrick," "Stanwick Kubrick," "Dr. Kupper," and "Kupprock."[79] In another undated set of notes, Trumbo became personal and rather mean:

Stanley Kubrick is a guy who is a Jew, and he's a man who hates Jews. He has said to me that the Jews are responsible for their own persecutions because they have separated themselves from the rest of humanity. He has said this to me in relation to the slaves and Spartacus. Yet on the other hand, Stanley, who is thirty years old, has married a German. The question in my mind is this: Did he marry her because he loved her or did he marry her because he wanted to marry a German girl in order to punish the Germans (through her) for what they had done to the Jews? Therefore we have the problem about Stanley which

is terribly important in relation to this picture. What is he trying to prove? It may be that he is a more devoted Jew than any
other. It may be that he is the essential renegade. . . . In the
meanwhile the essence of the picture that I see [him making] is
cruelty. Tony Mann was fired because of bad taste in relation to
cruelty. Stanley is trying to do it in good taste.[80]

But it was only after viewing the rough cut that Trumbo perceived a
second front in Kubrick's campaign to diminish the character of Spartacus. Trumbo wrote about it in the six-page prelude to his "Report,"
which was a distillation of the thirty pages of notes he took while viewing the rough cut. In that prelude, Trumbo accused Kubrick of reading
Koestler's novel and adopting Koestler's thesis about the nature of those
who are caught up in revolutions. In *The Gladiators*, Koestler made
the people appear "stupid, corrupt, and altogether responsible for their
own miseries," whereas the leaders "are the elite of mankind, tragically
frustrated, tragically pulled down and destroyed by the decadence and
vulgarity of the very rabble they sought to lead to freedom." Trumbo
acknowledged that Koestler had "a perfect right" to express that theory
about revolutions:

> And Stanley has every right to agree with it. The point at issue
> is not whether the Koestler theory is philosophically and his-
> torically right or wrong; it is rather that all theories are debat-
> able, and that the Koestler theory is directly antipathetic to the
> theory of the script on Spartacus. . . . I think it is dead wrong
> to transmit any part of Koestler into Spartacus. Nonetheless,
> the Koestler theory still pops up, not as a "conspiracy" but as
> a conviction on Stanley's part, and I think we must recognize
> it, and decide to accept it or reject it, since it is impossible to
> compromise with it.

But if the Koestler-Kubrick thesis were accepted, it would invalidate the
story Trumbo was trying to tell. In Trumbo's story, a united army of
slaves had stood up to the might of Rome. They had been "defeated by
Rome, not by their own weaknesses."[81] In other words, the slave army
depicted by Trumbo was not a demoralized rabble led by corrupt leaders.
     Whereas circumstances confined Trumbo's criticisms of and angry
outbursts toward Kubrick to his personal notes, letters, and reports,
Kubrick, in his denigration of Trumbo, had full access to an uncritical

media. In one instance, Kubrick told Dick Williams, a reporter for the *Los Angeles Mirror*, that various members of the production crew had "improvised a lot on the set." He was, of course, referring to the script revisions made during the shoot. As an example, Kubrick cited Tony Curtis's part, which had "started out with a brief scene or two and a few lines of dialogue" but just kept building.[82] (In fact, an extensive part for Antoninus, Curtis's character, had been in Trumbo's first draft.)

After reading this newspaper story, Trumbo wrote to Lewis:

> I don't mind Stanley publicizing himself. It is his duty to do so. Neither do I mind his cautious avoiding of my name in relation to those minor portions of the script that possibly may not have been improvised . . . on the set. . . . However, I will not allow him to take credit for the screenplay. . . . Neither will I permit him to disparage my work and my profession for the aggrandizement of his own, nor to make false statements concerning the development of the film and its characters, nor to throw doubt of any kind on my professional qualifications. There is quite as much room in his own field as Stanley can occupy, and hence no need to move cheaply and feloniously into mine.

Trumbo demanded that Douglas and Bryna correct this "injury" at once and take steps to prevent a recurrence. If Kubrick continued to make such public statements, Trumbo threatened to publish the notes he had accumulated "detailing the entire film-making process, along with a factual commentary, in book form."[83]

Kubrick, however, proved irrepressible. One week later he repeated his new mantra to a reporter for the *Los Angeles Times*, claiming: "We did a lot of improvising on the set." He then added: "I spent eight months in the cutting room. I always cut my own pictures."[84] That last boast was challenged by the business representative of Motion Picture Film Editors Local 776, who stated that the members of his union had done all the editorial work on *Spartacus* and had been duly credited for it.[85] (However, Irving Lerner, an uncredited editor, and Douglas both stated that Kubrick had worked with the editors.)[86]

In early October Kubrick told a *New York Times* reporter: "I think the film will be a contender for awards. . . . It's just as good as 'Paths of Glory,' and certainly there's as much of myself in it. I don't mean to minimize the contributions of the others involved, but the director is [the] only one who can authentically impose his personality into a picture, and the result is his responsibility—partly because he's the only one who's always there." Not satisfied with glorifying himself, Kubrick took the opportunity to denigrate Trumbo. He claimed that when he accepted the assignment to direct *Spartacus*, he immediately saw that Trumbo's screenplay was "in need of repairs." So, Kubrick told the interviewer, he "took control with icy aplomb." He alleged that he had worked "with Mr. Trumbo on the script, changing it, as he put it, 'to a more visual conception.'" He then falsely claimed that he had deleted, against the protests of everyone else involved, all but two lines of Kirk Douglas's dialogue during the film's first half hour.[87] (In fact, in Fast's novel, Fast's script, and Trumbo's first draft, Spartacus had very few lines.)

The *Daily Variety* film reviewer accepted Kubrick's version of events. While acknowledging that Kubrick "had a remarkably good screenplay with which to work," the reviewer noted, probably after talking to Kubrick, that the script "was not at first entirely to his [Kubrick's] satisfaction and he worked it over several times during filming with the writer." But the reviewer did emphasize the most significant fact: Dalton Trumbo had written *Spartacus*, and Dalton Trumbo's name had appeared on a film "for [the] first time in about a decade since he served a prison sentence for contempt of Congress because he refused to declare whether he was or was not a member of the Communist Party." And, the reviewer declared, "there is no ignoring that the man is a helluva craftsman."[88] (For the details of Trumbo's screen credit, see chapter 19.)

The reviewer for *Time* observed that the movie's quality owed more to its script than its direction, and he lauded Trumbo for writing "with humor, eloquence, sophistication and a corrosive irony."[89] Philip K. Scheuer thought that although Kubrick's direction was "pictorially strong and interesting," it hardly compared with William Wyler's work on *Ben Hur* (MGM, 1959). Scheuer noted that Trumbo's screenplay progressively departed from Fast's novel, "though not necessarily with any loss to the film as a concept."[90] Bosley Crowther, however, flung brickbats at all concerned, calling it "a spotty, uneven drama" and "a romantic mish-mash" that bristled "with patriotic fervor" and "heroic humbug." He characterized Trumbo as an "aggressive" writer who had written a "freedom-shouting script."[91] A conservative ideologue, reviewing the movie for an academic journal, ignored Kubrick altogether and castigated Fast and Trumbo's politics: "The political bias underlying left-wing author Howard Fast's *Spartacus*—a shallow, rather silly and thoroughly uninformed piece of parlor pink propaganda—has been faithfully reproduced in left-winger Dalton Trumbo's screenplay."[92]

A few years later, Trumbo told a French interviewer that his relationship with Kubrick had "been quite cold." He noted their disagreement about Spartacus's character, "especially in the last scene of the film"—the crucifixion scene. According to Trumbo, having Spartacus die on the cross created "a certain ambiguity," reminding viewers of "a similar (though inappropriate) antecedent"—the crucifixion of Jesus Christ, which had "nothing to do with the uprising" of the slaves against Rome.[93] Several years later, Trumbo told a different interviewer that Kubrick was "a very talented guy, but talent isn't everything."[94]

Neither Trumbo nor Kubrick was pleased with the finished film. Trumbo's comments were much more muted, however. He told Michael Wilson that the movie "was a disappointment," mainly because of Kubrick's treatment of the character of Spartacus and the acting of Tony Curtis.[95] For his part, Kubrick regularly voiced his displeasure. He told one interviewer: "It was the only one of my films over which I did not have complete control; although I was the director, mine was only one of many voices to which Kirk listened. I am disappointed in the film. It had everything but a good story."[96] And he told another interviewer: "In *Spartacus*, I tried very hard with only limited success to make the film as real as possible but I was up against a pretty dumb script which was rarely faithful to what is known about Spartacus."[97] And yet James B. Harris recalled that, during the filming, Kubrick had voiced only one complaint about the script—it lacked a big battle scene.[98]

Given Kubrick's manifest intent to disown this movie, it is astonishing that historians (both classical and film) almost unanimously refer to it as "Stanley Kubrick's *Spartacus*."[99] What was a Douglas-Trumbo-Kubrick film would have been much better if Douglas had known what he wanted and if he had trusted Trumbo to give it to him. Douglas should have been the one to resolve the Trumbo-Kubrick conflict, but he was wearing too many hats, listening to too many voices, and blind to what was happening on the set after he hired Kubrick. Further, by surreptitiously seeking Fast's input and allowing Kubrick and Ustinov to make changes in the script, he allowed too many cooks to season the brew without having a master recipe in mind.

Many of the film's commentators believe that Trumbo had a political agenda in his "master recipe." He, however, maintained that he never intended to write a political script. When an interviewer complimented him on the boldness of the *Spartacus* script, Trumbo demurred, claiming that he had deliberately been "very restrained" because he was keenly aware that every sentence would be carefully scrutinized. Knowing that he was likely to be accused of trying to sneak in propaganda, he wrote what he considered "a very mild script."[100]

It is clear from Trumbo's first draft that, for him, the story of Spartacus was a tale about freedom, not revolution. From the outset, the theme of freedom clearly dominates Spartacus's outlook. For example, in one of the early scenes at the gladiator school, Draba defeats Spartacus but refuses to follow their owner's order to kill him. When Draba attacks the Romans instead and is killed by them, Spartacus asks Varinia: "Why did he do it? Why did he throw his life away?" She replies: "For a moment of freedom." "No!" Spartacus rejoins: "A moment's not enough. He had no chance of freedom. It was foolish. Until there's a chance for freedom, a man must keep living." If five or even ten gladiators had tried to do what Draba did, "That would be worth dying for!" (This scene did not make it into the finished film.) Later, after the gladiator-slave army defeats a Roman army, Spartacus tells them that they must march to the Alps. Once they are out of Italy, he says, "Every man and woman and every child can go in peace to the land where he was born. . . . To breathe once more the air that filled our lungs at birth. . . . [T]o be remembered by our children as those who gave them freedom. . . . Is there more? Does anyone ask for more? To the Alps and Freedom!" Later, when Spartacus realizes that his followers cannot escape Italy and must face the Roman host, he tells them: "Rome will not allow us to escape from Italy. We have no choice but to march against Rome herself and end this war the only way it could have ended, by freeing every slave in Italy. I'd rather be here, a free man among brothers."[101] Trumbo's focus on freedom is obscured only in the scenes he did not write, including the dialogue between Antoninus and Spartacus as they await their fate, the duel between Spartacus and Antoninus, and the spitting scene.

In a letter to Pablo Picasso, written after the movie was finished, Trumbo expressly reiterated his freedom concept: "The theme of the film, for which I take full responsibility, is simple and, I feel, curiously appropriate to our times: in waging a life-and-death struggle to keep Spartacus and his followers enslaved, the senate and people of Republican Rome inevitably produced the conditions for their own enslavement under a dictatorship of the right."[102] In other words, Trumbo's message to Picasso was simple: Those who try to suppress freedom create slavery. And even if the present battle for freedom is lost, it will have positive consequences in the future.

19

Exodus and the Credit Announcements

> I am not an authority on the Hollywood blacklist. But assuming that such a thing exists, I will not participate in it. In my opinion, it is illegal and immoral.
>
> —Otto Preminger

Trumbo met producer-director Otto Preminger in November 1958, and they agreed that Trumbo would adapt two novels for the screen: Pierre Boulle's *The Other Side of the Coin* and Ugo Pierro's *The Camp Followers*. A contract for the first project was signed on May 1, 1959, between "Peter Flint," as author, and Carlyle-Alpina, S.A., as purchaser. (The contract stated that the producer would not be required to divulge the writer's name on the screenplay or in any advertising or publicity.)[1] Before Trumbo signed the contract, he informed Preminger that his first obligation was to the *Spartacus* script. But, Trumbo being Trumbo, he found time in between the *Spartacus* drafts to compose and deliver "Coin" drafts to Otto's brother Ingo. Trumbo assured Otto that he would do as many rewrites as necessary and that he did not expect to be paid unless and until Otto was satisfied with the final draft. There came a point, however, when Lewis and Douglas were steadily pressing Trumbo for revisions on *Spartacus*, and he had to stop working on the "Coin" script. Otto, who was facing script problems and a fast-approaching deadline for the start of principal photography on his next project, *Exodus*, did not raise any objections.

Around the same time Otto signed the "Coin" contract with Trumbo, he also signed a contract with Albert Maltz to adapt Leon Uris's novel *Exodus*. Otto stipulated that he needed a completed script by December, and he promised to give Maltz screen credit.[2] And yet, within one or two months of signing the contract with Maltz, Otto signed a contract with Trumbo to adapt *Exodus*. (There is another version of this story, recounted later.) In December 1961 Trumbo told Burt Prelutsky that, during the summer of 1959, Otto had offered to pay him $50,000 and to give him screen credit for writing the *Exodus* screenplay.[3] This statement was documented by Trumbo in his letter applying for reinstatement in the WGAw. In that letter, he wrote that he had signed a new contract with Springfield Productions on July 1, 1959, and three weeks later, Springfield had loaned him to Otto's company to write *Exodus*.[4] Sometime later that year, Otto told an interviewer that he had contacted Trumbo in July 1959 and "discussed with him the various problems in translating the story of *Exodus* into a film." After a week of conferences, a writing contract was signed.[5] (Christopher told me that Trumbo started working on the script in November.)

Ten years later, however, another story surfaced. In that version, Trumbo told an interviewer that he received a telegram from Preminger on December 12, 1959, stating: "Buy Exodus. Read it at once. You must help me. I will arrive on Dec 16." Otto subsequently came to Trumbo's house carrying a 400-page script written by Maltz.[6] Otto did not want to shoot that script, but he had to begin filming in four months. Trumbo told him: "Otto, I cannot write a script in so short a time. I would need at least one month to outline it. You should try to cut what you already have." Otto agreed, saying: "Tell me simply the scenes I ought to use, and in which direction I ought to go." And that is how they proceeded.[7] Trumbo gave the same date to Ingo and explained that he had leaped into the breach not because he was generous but because he owed Otto "a script ['Coin'] anyhow, and was late on it."[8]

At that point, Otto telephoned Maltz to tell him that he was being terminated and Trumbo was being hired to write another script for *Exodus*.[9] Then, on January 4, 1960, Trumbo also notified Maltz that he had been hired to write a script for *Exodus*. He wrote: "I've read the material carefully, and accepted the job for the following main reasons: (1) I think your script is what happens to all [of] us now and again—a miss; (2) I don't like any assignment to slip out of the black market, as this will unless I take it; (3) I think I can do a better job on it than others he would go to; and (4) . . . it is a subject that moves me and seems urgently important." Maltz made no objection.[10]

It is unclear why Trumbo and Otto changed their stories. If they had wanted to spare Maltz's feelings or assuage his anger, they would not have told the earlier interviewers about Trumbo's summer starting date. Whatever their thinking, this episode does not cast a flattering light on either Trumbo or Otto. Both kept Maltz in the dark about Trumbo's parallel writing of the script.

In any event, using the book and Maltz's script, Trumbo wrote every night for a month, stealing time from his other writing assignments and forcing him to "lie and deceive those people" he owed work to, "all the while, illegitimately and unethically and quite dishonestly, I was devoting my time and energies to *Exodus*. I behaved dishonestly from what I considered to be necessity. I heartily wish I had not had to do so, but I did."[11]

According to Trumbo, Preminger knew exactly what he wanted, and Trumbo "followed him like a dog through the construction." If a scene Otto wanted to include was not working, Trumbo would jump ahead to later scenes.[12] One such scene came at the end of the movie. Uris's novel ended rather abruptly, and it was decided that the movie needed a dramatic peroration. Perhaps drawing on his memory of the speech he had written for Edward G. Robinson twelve years earlier (see chapter 8), Trumbo wrote a two-minute eulogy delivered by Ari over the common grave of Karen (a sabra) and Taha (a Palestinian), both killed by fedayeen. Ari, surrounded by a few dozen armed Israelis, does not deliver a pacifistic speech. He ardently desires peace and bemoans "the world's insanity," "our [Jewish] slaughtered millions," and "senseless killing." He looks forward to a time when Arabs and Jews "will share a peaceful life in this land they have always shared in death," but he (and the audience) knows the war will continue.

Otto arrived at Trumbo's house each morning to read aloud what Trumbo had written the previous night. On Christmas morning he tapped his foot impatiently while gifts were distributed and unwrapped. Trumbo later recalled, tongue in cheek, a typical conversation:

> Otto: No, not quite right here. It does not have your usual flair. It
> does not have your genius. It somehow lacks the genius that the
> other scenes have, and we must have that genius.
> Trumbo: Otto, for God's sake, if we have every scene equally
> excellent do you realize how monotonous this picture is going
> to be? It will be impossible to sit through. There must be
> variety, and that's the reason I made the scene this way.
> Otto: I'll tell you what, you make all the scenes excellent and I will
> direct unevenly.[13]

Trumbo said about his collaboration with Otto, "We are very sweet and very gentle together (although we can be violent elsewhere)."[14] A few years later, he told another interviewer: "I'm verbose and sentimental. He has a sharpshooter's eye for verbosity and he knows how to assassinate sentimentality. He's also most helpful in construction. I had more pleasure working with Otto than with anyone in my life."[15]

Otto Preminger and Trumbo on Cyprus, 1960. Courtesy of Trumbo family.

Trumbo and Christopher on Cyprus, 1960. Courtesy of Trumbo family.

Despite their mutual respect, Trumbo was unable to convince Otto to drop some portions of the novel, especially the scenes involving Kitty (played by Eva Marie Saint). According to Christopher, even after one month of cutting, the script was still too long. Therefore, during their last night together, the two men had to make some radical cuts and ended up with a 246-page script. (While on location, Otto and another writer revised 72 pages but made no significant cuts.)[16]

When the film was released, reviewers praised Trumbo's script. The reviewer for the *Hollywood Reporter* wrote: "Trumbo's screenplay is superior to the book as a dramatic structure, and if the film fails, it is not the fault of the writing."[17] In *Film Daily* the reviewer congratulated Trumbo for weaving the novel's many stories "skillfully into a unified and imposing pictorial document."[18] But the *Daily Variety* reviewer thought the movie needed "more dramatic incisiveness."[19] And although Stanley Kauffmann praised the first part of the film, he criticized the second part for its "self-conscious momentousness and its contrivances."[20]

Trumbo thought the final version was "far too long" and that "the love story fails altogether."[21] He later said: "We just cut, cut, cut, cut. . . . We should have cut more." He also thought *Exodus* suffered from the same structural problem as *Spartacus*: the climax (the announcement of partition in the former, the battle scene in the latter) occurred long before the film ended. The result was that each film had to proceed from its natural climax to what Trumbo considered a false ending.[22]

The *Exodus* assignment gave Trumbo an expedited, direct path to a screen credit. Preminger had full authority over credit assignments, and he was seemingly unconcerned about the repercussions of crediting a blacklisted writer. Whether Preminger or Douglas can claim priority in the matter of screen credit for blacklistees depends on the respective weight one assigns to Douglas's earlier decision and Preminger's subsequent action. What is clear is that neither of them "broke the blacklist." Christopher, in what was intended to be his introduction to this topic, wrote: "Kirk Douglas, on many occasions, has laid claim to breaking the blacklist, and whether that distinction belongs to him is worth exploring, for he is not the only claimant. After all, Frank King said in 1959 that he broke the blacklist; and Milton Friedman has put forth the curious idea that the free market broke the blacklist." Writer-director Jules Dassin also staked a claim because his name was on *Rififi* when it was shown in June 1956 at the Plaza Theater in New York.[23] And Harry Cohn could also demand a seat at the head of this particular table. (To the best of my knowledge, Preminger did not nominate himself as a contender.) And yet, as Christopher correctly asked: "Beyond those claims, what does breaking the blacklist actually mean? What does it entail?"

To put Christopher's questions differently: How can a collusive, unwritten but institutionalized agreement not to hire a particular group of people be "broken"? The obvious answer is for the legal system to declare the blacklist an illegal conspiracy. But all attempts to convince a series of judges to do so had failed. Alternatively, breakage could have been achieved if the producers had announced: "The blacklist has been rescinded; all is forgiven; come back to the studios and sign new contracts." They did not do so, for two reasons: (1) such an announcement would have exposed them to hundreds of civil and criminal damages suits; and (2) the producers had, under the cover of the blacklist, established a new way of doing business and a tighter means of controlling their workers and screen content.[24] Thus, by 1960, industry executives had a vested interest in this new corporate model.

The producers' determination to maintain the blacklist was made evident in August 1959, when the producers' association sent vice president B. B. Kahane (who was also vice president and head of the clearance department of Columbia Pictures and president of the Academy) to Minneapolis to mollify attendees at the national convention of the American Legion. In particular, Kahane was supposed to defuse a pending resolution from the California chapter condemning the industry for hiring "subversives." When Kahane arrived at the convention, he told the group's Americanism Committee: "We're just as anxious to keep Commies out of Hollywood as you are." He also said that of the 224 persons on the American Legion's 1955 blacklist, only 4 (Charles Chaplin, Jules Dassin, Dalton Trumbo, and Nedrick Young) were still working in the industry. According to Ed Magnuson, a reporter for the *Minneapolis Tribune*, Kahane described Trumbo as a "hard-core Communist" who had used an assumed name to obtain employment with Bryna. Kahane also said that Kirk Douglas and Universal Pictures had been unaware "that Trumbo was doing 'undercover work' for Communism" and had no "knowledge as to his true identity."[25]

Furious with Kahane's statements, Trumbo drafted a letter that accused him of lying.

> You and I both know that in your eagerness to win the Legion's approval of Columbia you lied to the Americanism Commission. . . . Columbia has not only released the work of blacklisted persons, it has *knowingly* produced such work. . . . I will not permit you to make of me a public scapegoat for the shameful and probably illegal conduct of your principals. For too many years the social climate of American has been poisoned, and

the moral atmosphere corrupted, by just such remarks as you so freely made before the Legion.

I am compelled to ask what sort of American are you, whose patriotism must be rekindled every year or two by the threat of an outside organization? What sort of character is this, who appears before the Legion to defend the efficiency of his patriotic blacklist, and, there, in that most holy of patriotic holies, speaks not the truth, but a series of cunning evasions, malicious half-truths, and forthright lies? What sort of man is he who passes from perjurious premises to forthright bargaining for his corporation's right to patriotic accolade?[26]

Probably following Cleo's advice, Trumbo did not send the letter.

Instead, he wrote to Aubrey Finn and explained that, "in this most delicate phase" of his career, he could not permit statements that he was a "hard-core" Communist doing "'undercover work' for Communism" to be made about him. But at the same time, Trumbo insisted, he did not want to publicize this issue; nor did he have any wish to damage Kahane or to sue him. Trumbo instructed Finn to contact Kahane and request that he write a letter retracting or denying the offensive quotations attributed to him. Copies of Kahane's letter should then be sent to Bryna Productions, the Academy of Motion Picture Arts and Sciences, and the presidents and executive producers of every studio that was a member of the Association of Motion Picture Producers. For his part, Trumbo would promise to show his copy of Kahane's letter only to those producers who refused to hire as a result of Kahane's allegations or to the press, in the event that any officer or member of the Association of Motion Picture Producers or the American Legion subsequently red-baited him or *Spartacus*.[27]

Kahane consulted with Mendel Silberberg, and they composed a letter in which Kahane denied making any of the statements regarding Trumbo or his connection (if any) to the Communist Party attributed to him by the *Minneapolis Tribune* and *Weekly Variety*. In the letter, Kahane admitted that although he "did state that Mr. Trumbo was considered a Communist," he had "no personal knowledge" regarding Trumbo's connection to the party. Kahane also denied that he had told anyone that Trumbo had done or was doing undercover work. Trumbo wanted three paragraphs and several sentences deleted from the proposed letter, because he thought they undercut the substance of Kahane's denials.[28] (No signed copy of any such letter from Kahane is in the Trumbo Papers. He died in September 1960.)

Even if the blacklist could not be "broken," it could be weakened and breached. And despite the studio owners' efforts to maintain it, the blacklist began to develop cracks owing to a combination of events and circumstances and Dalton Trumbo's leveraging of those events and circumstances.[29] The first sign of its weakening was the growing number of producers who were willing to hire blacklisted people. The blacklisted did not return en masse, however; they came back in a slow single file, by way of a series of individual deals. As Christopher once noted, "The blacklist ended again and again and again as one by one those on the list returned to work. Not all of them did."

As for Kirk Douglas's repeated claims that he "broke" the blacklist, the evidence is incontrovertible that, at some point in 1959, Douglas decided that he would try to give Trumbo screen credit for the *Spartacus* script. However, Douglas did not have the final say in the matter. Universal's head of production, Ed Muhl, did. In his second memoir, *I Am Spartacus!* Douglas reveals that in early December 1959 he met with Lewis and Kubrick to talk about the writer's credit (even though he had already decided to give it to Trumbo). When Douglas asked them who should be given that credit, Lewis refused to take it, but Kubrick offered to do so. Kubrick's opportunistic grab at the credit was the catalyst for Douglas's next decisive move.[30] (In his first memoir, *The Ragman's Son*, Douglas places this meeting in August, and he claims he was so incensed by Kubrick's offer that he decided to give Trumbo screen credit then and there. Douglas reportedly called the front gate at Universal Pictures the following morning to leave a pass for Trumbo.)[31] After the meeting, Douglas telephoned Trumbo and invited him to come to lunch at the studio commissary, under his own name. It was that invitation, Douglas maintains, that "broke" the blacklist.[32] According to Lewis, however, no such meeting took place. He never heard Kubrick say that he would take the writer's credit, and he never heard Douglas ask for anybody's opinion on the subject.[33]

Lewis did meet with Muhl on three occasions to discuss the issue of a writer's credit. At the first meeting, Muhl asked Lewis whether Trumbo would agree to meet with attorney Martin Gang, who was orchestrating the unfriendly witnesses' return to work. All Trumbo had to do was answer, in writing, a few questions concerning his party membership, and Muhl would declare Trumbo "cleared" for employment by Universal. Trumbo told Lewis he would do so, but only if Gang charged Trumbo a fee; in other words, Trumbo would answer such questions only if attorney-client privilege prevented Gang from revealing Trumbo's responses. At the second meeting, Muhl advised Lewis that the studio simply wanted a statement from Trumbo that he "was no longer what he once was." Trumbo agreed to meet with Muhl to discuss writing such a statement, but only if Muhl agreed to first read Trumbo's 1949 pamphlet *The Time of the Toad*. Trumbo gave Lewis a copy to pass on to Muhl, but when Lewis put it on his desk, Muhl refused to touch it. At the third meeting, Muhl asked Lewis to assure Trumbo that no blacklist existed and that a written statement from Trumbo would simply be a formality. Trumbo agreed to sign any letter Muhl prepared, but only if Muhl took out a full-page ad in the trade journals announcing that no blacklist existed in the industry and that he intended to cast Gale Sondergaard, a blacklisted actress (and wife of Herbert Biberman), in an upcoming movie.[34] Muhl did not accept any of Trumbo's counteroffers.

While those conversations were occurring, Bryna executives and Eugene Frenke negotiated a loan-out agreement for Trumbo's further services on the *Spartacus* script on November 2, 1959. It included a paragraph stating: "Springfield specifically agrees that [Bryna] shall have no obligation to accord employee any screen and/or advertising credits in connection with the photoplay."[35] One month later, Sidney Skolsky's gossip column stated that Trumbo had written the screenplay for *Spartacus*.[36]

But all these maneuvers became pointless when, on January 19, 1960, Otto Preminger told a reporter from the *New York Times* that Trumbo was writing the screenplay for *Exodus* and that he "naturally will get the credit on the screen that he amply deserves." When asked why he had chosen to reveal this news, Otto replied, "Simply because your newspaper asked me." The story also included the information that Trumbo had worked on the script for *Roman Holiday* and was working on the script for *Spartacus*.[37]

Preminger was interviewed on February 1 by Tom Duggan on his KCOP-TV show. The director said he had hired Trumbo because he was "the right man for the job"; Trumbo had paid for whatever he did, "and he had a right to come out clean and free like you or anyone else." When Duggan asked if Preminger knew whether Trumbo had been or was still a Communist, Preminger replied: "It is absolutely un-American . . . to ask people what political beliefs they have." Preminger added that in giving Trumbo screen credit, he was acting much more honestly than other producers who had employed blacklisted writers and did not give them credit.[38]

In his autobiography, Preminger notes that prior to his announcement he had lunch with the heads of United Artists, Arthur Krim and Robert Benjamin. At that meeting, Preminger told them: "Trumbo has done a first-rate job on this script. You people are always saying that the blacklist is fiction, so I will give him the credit he deserves. I shall use his real name as the sole author of the script." Krim replied: "You have the right to do this. We can't support you, but we are not going to stop you."[39] In a press statement issued the day after Preminger's announcement was reported, Krim said: "Mr. Preminger has complete autonomy in the selection of writers. United Artists has no right of consultation or approval. We respect these contractual obligations."[40] (Because United Artists was not a production company, its executives had not signed the Waldorf statement.)

There are no memos in the Bryna files specifically referring to Preminger's announcement. Lewis recalled that no one paid much attention to it.[41] And the evidence indicates that the announcement changed no one's mind. A Universal interoffice memo dated January 25 stated that the screenplay credits for *Spartacus* had been assigned to Lewis and Fast. "There are," the memo writer continued, "four or five other writers, some of whom will probably be given screen credit. This is a matter which must be adjudicated by the Screen Writers Guild [*sic*]. . . . It will be three or four months before final credits are determined."[42] According to Trumbo, at some point in late 1959 or early 1960, Universal executives asked the polling firm of Sindlinger and Company to ascertain Trumbo's name recognition and notoriety with the moviegoing public. Only 12.5 percent said they would not pay to see a movie written by Trumbo.[43]

Douglas, who disliked Preminger intensely, has consistently downplayed the significance of Preminger's public announcement. In *The Ragman's Son*, Douglas characterizes Preminger's press conference as a "clever" ploy to overshadow Douglas's earlier "fait accompli"—his decision to give Trumbo credit for *Spartacus*.[44] And in *I Am Spartacus!* Douglas writes that a furious Preminger called him within hours of his "now-widely-talked-about lunch with Trumbo in the Universal commissary" and exclaimed: "Vat are you doing?! You *know* who my writer is? It's Maltz! If you put Trumbo's name on *Spartacus*, this will kill both pictures. You cannot do this thing!" When the news of Preminger's announcement reached Douglas, he reportedly said to his wife: "You've got to hand it to Otto. He saw that the train had already left the station with *Spartacus* breaking the blacklist. Not only did he run to catch up with it, he jumped into the front car and claimed to be the engineer."[45]

Hollywood's response to Preminger's announcement was muted. An unnamed spokesman for the Motion Picture Association of America denied that a blacklist existed and that his association told studios who they could hire. He acknowledged, however, that the major film companies had, purely on an individual basis, instituted a policy of not hiring "known Communists" or any other persons who had "identified themselves in such a way that they are not employable."[46] The *Hollywood Reporter*'s anti-Communist publisher W. R. Wilkerson congratulated Preminger for having "the guts to publicly, openly acknowledge the Trumbo assignment," but he condemned Preminger's failure to take seriously "his responsibility to the motion picture industry or the American people he seeks to entertain."[47] A writer for *Weekly Variety* reported that a number of industry insiders were "suspicious" of Preminger's motives, and many regarded his announcement as "an opportunistic publicity gimmick." The reporter also noted that a number of Jewish people had expressed their "disappointment" that Preminger had chosen to use *Exodus* "to upset the blacklist." These critics feared that *Exodus* would have enough problems among anti-Semites and did not need any "unnecessary" issues.[48]

The only Hollywood executive to speak publicly about Preminger's announcement was Harry Brandt, president of the Independent Theatre Owners Association. Brandt forthrightly called for "an end to the era of the blacklist," which he called "a shameful chapter in the industry's history." Alluding to the American Legion, Brandt stated that if the motion picture industry "is ever going to throw off the shackles of the private pressure groups which have taken onto themselves a special guardianship of the screen, the Kramer-Preminger position is entitled to support from other motion picture producers, distributors and exhibitors. . . . Kramer and Preminger have shown the way to write an end to a shameful chapter in the industry's history."[49] (And yet Stanley Kramer, who had knowingly hired blacklisted writers, chose not to comment on Preminger's announcement.)[50] At least one other person in Hollywood was elated by what Preminger had done—blacklisted producer Adrian Scott, who told Preminger: "How is gratitude expressed to one who has provided the conditions that mean life again can be resumed in terms of his own choosing? For this is the essence of what you have done, for me as well as for others."[51]

Rumors surfaced that Francis E. Walter, chairman of the Committee on Un-American Activities, had threatened to schedule a hearing on the hiring of Trumbo. Muhl asked Trumbo what he would do if the committee subpoenaed him, and Trumbo responded: "I would take a full-page ad in the *New York Times*, announcing that I would not answer any of its questions about my politics and urge them to save their money."[52] Trumbo proceeded to prepare a press statement to issue in the event he received a subpoena. In it, he repeated many of the same ideas that had motivated him thirteen years earlier, including his First and Fifth Amendment rights not to answer questions related to his writing, employment, political thoughts, or affiliations. "So long as the Constitution stands," he wrote, "I shall never reveal to Congress information which the Constitution permits me to withhold; and never will—as I never have—make a political declaration to any employer as a condition for practicing my profession." However, for the first time he would "volunteer information" he had never desired to keep secret but had determined never to "reveal under threat" of punishment: "For seven of my 54 years I was a member of the Communist Party. I made no secret of that membership. . . . I would have made no secret of it these past 13 years of the Hollywood blacklist, had not this committee, by its authoritarian passion for turning free men into informers, compelled witnesses to the very secrecy it hypocritically deplores."[53]

Walter did not follow through on his threat, but the American Legion redoubled its efforts to intimidate any would-be employers of blacklisted screen employees. According to Murray Schumach, the Legion was "relentless in its determination to impose its will upon the industry."[54] Several spokespeople for the California Legion publicly denounced Preminger,[55] and Tom Holt, chairman of the Counter Subversive Committee of the American Legion, accused Preminger of "helping to support the [Communist] Party." And then, without realizing that he was helping Trumbo get another credit, Holt stated that Trumbo had written the screenplay for *Spartacus*.[56]

When Walter Winchell also reported that Trumbo had written *Spartacus*, Trumbo advised Lewis to immediately acknowledge that fact and get Winchell "into your corner." If Lewis denied it, Trumbo warned, Winchell "will hit you every day because he must." In other words, Bryna and Universal executives had a simple choice: announce that Winchell was correct, or allow the story to drag on for weeks.[57] Lewis was unable to convince the decision makers at Bryna or Universal to follow Trumbo's advice, and Trumbo probably decided to push the envelope by leaking information about the credit situation to a friendly newspaper reporter. A few weeks later a *New York Times* story was headlined: "U-I Is Pondering Credit to Trumbo." Its writer, Murray Schumach, stated that executives at Universal knew Trumbo had been hired to write the script for *Spartacus*, but "officially, Universal, Bryna Productions, Mr. Douglas and Mr. Trumbo have nothing to say on the subject."[58]

At the end of May, Schumach reported that Trumbo had written "The Hot Eyes of Heaven" (released as *The Last Sunset*) for Bryna and Universal and that he was currently in Mexico revising it. Nevertheless, Schumach reported, there "was no indication that Universal intends to give screen credit for this movie to Trumbo, nor for *Spartacus*, even though there is no doubt that Trumbo wrote that script." Schumach also reported that three of the other major studios had already made deals involving blacklisted writers and directors.[59] One of them, Twentieth Century–Fox, announced that blacklisted writer-producer Sidney Buchman would be making pictures for it in Europe as an independent producer. Another, MGM, had acquired the distribution rights to Jules Dassin's *The Law*; it was also reported that Dassin was negotiating a contract with United Artists.[60] In June, Stanley Kramer's *Inherit the Wind*, written by Nathan E. Douglas and Harold B. Smith, opened without incident, and Sam Spiegel announced that he had agreed to give Michael Wilson "partial credit" for writing the screenplay for *Lawrence of Arabia*. This meant that Wilson would receive "full credit" on all prints shown in the Eastern Hemisphere but no credit on those shown in the Western Hemisphere.[61] The most significant news item that month was the report that, after a six-month strike, the WGAw had negotiated a contract with the producers' association that eliminated article 6 (allowing producers to refuse to give credit to Communists or Fifth Amendment witnesses).[62]

Even in the face of all these cracks in the blacklist, Universal and Bryna executives maintained their silence on the *Spartacus* credit,[63] but they kept fully informed about public reactions to the subject. On June 20 a Universal interoffice memo called attention to an item in Sidney Skolsky's *Hollywood Citizen-News* gossip column. Skolsky had written: "Any time you see the name, Sam Jackson, on the screen you'll know that Dalton Trumbo wrote the screenplay."[64] Also in the Bryna files are four letters condemning Douglas for hiring Trumbo, along with a copy of an American Legion press release criticizing Preminger, Douglas, and Kramer.[65] On June 23 Universal-Bryna submitted its "Analysis of Film Credit" form for *Spartacus* to the Production Code Administration, with a question mark on the line designating the screenwriter.[66]

Trumbo and Cleo, meanwhile, took a much-needed vacation to Europe. Securing a passport had been a difficult process. Their first application in 1951 had been rejected. When they applied again in August 1956, the Passport Office sent them two non-Communist affidavits, which, of course, they refused to fill out. Trumbo explained to the director of the Passport Office the constitutional basis of their refusal: "The affidavit solicited from us relates to our past or present political affiliations or sympathies. Not wishing to lend ourselves to a violation of the First Amendment to the Constitution, or of the many State and Federal statutes which derive from Constitutional affirmations of freedom of association, action and thought, or of that proud tradition of resistance to bureaucratic encroachment upon the realm of conscience which has for almost two centuries characterized the government and people of the United States, we have refrained from executing the affidavits you request." He also pointed out the limitations of the affidavit: it made "no inquiry as to whether we are now, or have been in the past, or when we ceased to be, engaged in the commission of murder, rape, mayhem, assault, robbery, theft, embezzlement, perjury, usury or dozens of other pernicious enterprises which, if undertaken by us in foreign countries, might be 'extremely prejudicial to the interests of the United States.'" Additionally, he called attention to the striking similarity between the sections of the Code of Federal Regulations requiring non-Communist affidavits and "practices existing now or in the past under dictatorial governments—practices which have been denounced with great vigor by Secretary [of State John Foster] Dulles as an offense against the conscience of mankind calculated to reduce the world and all its peoples to a state of blind and monolithic orthodoxy." In effect, he concluded, the Passport Office's affidavit was nothing more than a "test oath for passports."[67]

The department head, Frances G. Knight, replied that the Trumbos' failure to file completed affidavits terminated their application process. When they reapplied in June 1958 and were once again told they must sign the affidavit, Trumbo referred Knight to a recent Supreme Court decision establishing that the US government could not arbitrarily deny passports to applicants. On July 2 Trumbo was informed that such an affidavit was no longer required.[68] But the Passport Office notified the FBI about this and every other trip Trumbo took abroad.

During this trip, Trumbo and Cleo traveled to Cyprus and Israel to watch Preminger shoot *Exodus* and to visit Christopher, who was working on the production. From there, they met Mitzi in Italy and Nikola and Christopher in Paris. They stayed at the best hotels, and Trumbo was spending money lavishly—much more than he could afford—and was having some difficulty with the exchange rates. In Paris, John Berry visited the Trumbos in their hotel room. (Mitzi recalled Berry as "a big bear of a man, and a really funny guy. He gave great bear hugs to everyone. We all liked him very much.") Berry offered to go out and buy a bottle of scotch to drink in the room, rather than paying the exorbitant rates for drinks at the George V. Trumbo gave him a fistful of francs, and five minutes later Berry burst through the door, shouting, "Jesus, Trumbo, you gave me $800!" (The franc had been revalued in January 1960, and 1 new franc equaled 100 old ones.)

While Trumbo was in Europe, Muhl decided to give sole credit to "Sam Jackson." When Fast learned of that decision, he asked the WGAw to appoint an arbitration committee, contending that he had written at least 50 percent of the script. Following standard procedure, Lewis submitted the names of all the writers who had contributed to the final script, including Peter Ustinov's. Trumbo wrote to Aubrey Finn that although he understood why Fast would seek an arbitration, he was concerned that Ustinov's name was on the list of writers. Trumbo was not actually worried that Ustinov, who had written no more than five pages, might get a credit; rather, he feared that an anti-Communist writer might be appointed to the arbitration committee and leak Ustinov's name to the press. That, Trumbo told Finn, "will make copy, and his contribution to the script will be vastly exaggerated. Given this publicity, Ustinov, regardless of arbitration in my favor, would automatically receive credit for every witty line in the script. This would be a little hurtful to me, and of course it's never good for a picture, in terms of critics and reviews, to have it known or rumored that the script was a multiple-writer proposition."[69]

After reading Fast's novel and all the scripts, the WGAw arbitration committee decided that the credit should read as follows: "Written by Dalton Trumbo, based on the novel by Howard Fast."[70] A few years later, Trumbo wryly commented that he had won the arbitration because "people hated Howard Fast more than they hated me—people in the Guild, I mean."[71] (Trumbo clearly exaggerated his unpopularity, because in early 1961 the WGAw membership nominated Trumbo's screenplay for *Spartacus* in the category of best drama.)

As soon as Universal received word of the arbitration committee's decision, an interoffice memo was prepared, blandly stating: "Dalton Trumbo has been awarded sole screenplay credit on *Spartacus*. . . . The matter of answering queries to Trumbo receiving screenplay credit was discussed." It was decided to answer all inquiries as follows: "Mr. Trumbo is a gifted writer. He worked under careful supervision. The picture will speak for itself."[72] Five days later, a studio press release announced that Trumbo's name would appear on the screen. Fast expressed his hope that this would "help to break the disgraceful black-list that is so degrading to everyone."[73] Trumbo did not think it was proper to comment, although he later said that Universal executives finally decided to put his name on *Spartacus* because of the "impetus Otto gave."[74] In an effort to put the best spin on the subject, Stan Margulies (a Bryna executive) told Douglas that Universal-International was "the first major movie studio to give screen credit to a blacklisted writer." According to Margulies, because United Artists (the distributor of *Exodus*) was not a signatory of the Waldorf statement, Preminger's announcement did not, technically, "break the blacklist."[75]

Trumbo was always grateful for Douglas's decision, and he understood the need to move cautiously. One year after the Universal announcement, Trumbo told Ring Lardner Jr., who was writing a story about the blacklist for the *Saturday Evening Post*:

> It has always been Eddie Lewis's policy, and mine, and Universal-International's, to keep Kirk out of the picture as the man who made the decision. There is sound reason for this, I think, since an actor is far more vulnerable than a man like Otto. The facts are that Universal-International made the announcement, and that as a matter of personal public relations policy, Kirk did not. The whole point was to divert the responsibility of choice from the shoulders of a vulnerable man to those of a group of corporate executives. I think the policy was sound, and I would much prefer that Kirk's name not even be mentioned. There is no reason to increase the flow of Birch Society mail to his house when no significant purpose is achieved thereby.[76]

Trumbo did not, however, ever believe or state that Douglas had "broken" the blacklist.

Spartacus and *Exodus* opened in August and December, respectively, and attracted huge audiences, despite the presence of American Legion pickets at both. (When I saw *Exodus* at a benefit screening in Hollywood that December, the audience burst into applause when "Written by Dalton Trumbo" appeared onscreen.) In late January, Attorney General Robert F. Kennedy viewed *Spartacus* and recommended it to his brother. One week later, President John F. Kennedy and Secretary of the Navy Paul Fay made an unannounced visit to a neighborhood theater to watch it. They too enjoyed it.[77]

Those successes did not noticeably weaken the determination of most studio bosses to continue the blacklist, and the "Communist letter" became their fallback position. The *New York Times* reported in September that producers were asking writers who were under consideration for assignments to write letters simply stating that they were no longer members of the Communist Party.[78] Two months later, Eric Johnston assembled the members of the Motion Picture Association of America in Washington to decide what to do about the blacklist and the American Legion. This time around, the participants chose not to reaffirm the Waldorf statement of November 1947; however, they resolved that none of the members would "knowingly hire a Communist," and it was the responsibility of each company "to determine for itself whether any person it employs is a Communist."[79] In other words, they decided to maintain a diminished form of the blacklist.

As a result, Trumbo's breakthrough remained, for the moment, a solitary one. In early 1961 Adrian Scott told Paul Jarrico: "Many thought that after Trumbo's breakthrough there would be many more. Not so. . . . Trumbo is secure now, mining a narrow vein but of pure gold."[80] During the following years, a trickle of blacklisted people signed contracts with major Hollywood studios: writers Marguerite Roberts and Waldo Salt and director Jules Dassin in 1962; writers Ben Barzman and Sidney Buchman and actor Jeff Corey in 1963; writers Ring Lardner Jr. and Michael Wilson, director Joseph Losey, and actor Lionel Stander in 1965. Others never did, including Alvah Bessie, John Bright, Hugo Butler, Lester Cole, Guy Endore, Ian Hunter, Paul Jarrico, John Howard Lawson, and John Wexley.

20

Back on the Screen

The economic argument for the institution of the blacklist was exposed as a chimera, the empty threat of empty men. Dalton Trumbo, a man who had not retreated one inch from the stand he had taken thirteen years before, had his name on the screen once more, and the American public did not recoil in horror. Though he was, in effect, "unblacklisted," it would take several more years before he was able to make an over-the-table deal with an American producer. Thus, there was no victory—perhaps there was vindication, but no more. He had regained something, but other things cannot be regained.

—Christopher Trumbo

Trumbo did not feel triumphant, and he had no time for bitter reflections. He remained starkly realistic about what lay ahead, and he continued to tread very carefully through the minefield of the blacklist and the black market. After all, *Spartacus* and *Exodus* (and the actions of Douglas and Preminger) might have resulted from a unique alignment of the fates, or he might have been an exception. Three problems in particular concerned him: (1) the box-office success of *Spartacus* and *Exodus*, (2) the possibility that frustrated blacklistees might write recantation letters for the studios, and (3) new legal actions by blacklistees. Shortly after *Exodus* opened, Trumbo sent a telegram to Michael Wilson, telling him: "If these films are economically damaged by my name the ban against everyone will be absolute."[1] But one month later, after seeing that the American Legion's boycott had failed to dent the receipts of either *Spartacus* or *Exodus*, Trumbo observed that this would prove "to the banks, the distributors, the studios, and the organizations and press of the right that, ordinarily, good films cannot be financially damaged by political attack, threatened boycott, and actual picketing. Not in today's climate, at least. This *has* to be, in one degree or another, a victory for every blacklisted person, since it knocks the props out from under the principal economic reason for blacklisting him."[2]

Second, Trumbo was concerned that some blacklistees—perhaps growing impatient with the strategy he had laid out—would try to regain regular employment in the studios by stating in writing that they were not members of the Communist Party. He was especially concerned that Wilson might have done so. According to Trumbo, Sam Spiegel (producer of *The Bridge on the River Kwai* and *Lawrence of Arabia*) had urged Kirk Douglas to get Trumbo to sign a non-Communist letter and claimed that Wilson had signed such a letter before beginning work on *Lawrence of Arabia*. In a telegram, Trumbo asked Wilson whether Spiegel's comment was true.[3] Wilson immediately wired back that it was not. In a follow-up letter, Wilson explained that Spiegel had asked him to write such a letter, and Wilson speculated that Spiegel might have told the executives at Columbia that he actually had one in his possession. Wilson, in turn, expressed his concern that Trumbo might be tempted to write such a letter, and he urged Trumbo not to do so: "I fear that any such statement would annul the tremendous victory you have achieved in your fight for credit. When Dalton Trumbo signs a letter it isn't the same as Ian [Hunter] signing a letter. I apply a different and harsher set of standards to Trumbo. You've been the pathfinder in this long trek; you scratched and clawed your way through the jungle, emerging at your destination still dragging your canoe behind you— and to me at least it would be a pity if now you felt impelled to kick a hole in the canoe."[4]

Trumbo's last major concern focused on a new damage suit against the studios, filed in late 1961 by a group of blacklistees. He feared it would have the effect of closing the door to reemployment that he had pried open. This lawsuit had been proposed by David Shapiro, a New York antitrust lawyer, and had been approved by three of the Hollywood Ten's attorneys: Ben Margolis, Martin Popper, and Robert Kenny. Blacklistees Ned Young, Herbert Biberman, John Howard Lawson, and Lester Cole were among the plaintiffs.[5] In *Young et al. v. Loew's et al.*, the plaintiffs alleged that the production companies, distribution companies, and producers' association had unlawfully conspired to restrain interstate trade by circulating a blacklist and refusing to hire people on that list or to distribute their films. The plaintiffs were asking for an immediate injunction and $7.5 million in damages.

At the suit's inception, Trumbo told Wilson that Shapiro and Biberman had come to him to explain their reasoning and to get his "bless-ing." Trumbo refused to participate in such a suit and claimed he would not have done so even prior to Preminger's announcement about the *Exodus* credit. He simply did not believe that, in the current Cold War climate, any federal judge would look favorably on employment claims by "Communists."[6] After this visit, Trumbo wrote to Margolis: "I do not favor this suit although I recognize as completely justified any effort by any blacklisted person to bring an end to the injustice of it, and seek recompense for the personal and economic damage it has brought upon him." Trumbo also noted that it would be unethical of him to sup-port a suit that included Universal-International among the defendants, because the company had treated him honorably, and he advised Mar-golis to exclude United Artists and Universal-International as defen-dants, since both companies were now openly employing blacklisted people.[7]

Margolis agreed with him about United Artists but not about Uni-versal. After all, Margolis noted, the so-called highly commendable behavior of Universal-International "thus far has been limited to Dal-ton Trumbo," and that could bestow "neither absolution for its black-listing of others nor a license to continue such blacklisting." Margolis then questioned Trumbo's strategy: "I am sure that you hoped that your own successful campaign to break through the blacklist would end it for everyone. It didn't work out that way. It is not even clear that on an industry basis you have ended it for yourself." What was now required, Margolis concluded, was a legal action to widen the breach made by Ned Young and Trumbo and to take "a step forward benefitting all blacklistees" by wiping out the blacklist completely.[8]

A few months later, Trumbo vented his wrath about the *Young* suit and its lawyers in a letter to Wilson:

> The trouble with these goddamned left-wing lawyers is that they try to figure the odds instead of the law, and they're the worst handicappers on earth. The case of So-and-So, equated with a recent political amnesty in Outer Mongolia, modified by the death of [Patrice] Lumumba, illuminated by the Con-gress of Vienna, viewed from the perspective of *The Eighteenth Brumaire of Louis Bonaparte*, indicates a qualitative change, a new period, and great days comin'. So they gather up eight or a dozen suckers and gallop off to court with a whole batch of new magic. Then—boom!—three decisions in a row and the odds

shift. The vision of plaintiffs-as-victor becomes plaintiff-as-martyr, and noble ends are served even though the complainants all end up as dead ducks.

[This case has] tightened the blacklist. And I think it has pretty well killed the plaintiffs. I think especially of Ned Young, who entered it for God knows what motives, and who, had he continued with patience and hard work as he was doing, could have won through on his own. For those who wanted to end the blacklist in a coldly practical way and were prepared to work their asses off to do it, I think, in all modesty, mine was far the better system, and it was beginning to pay off not only to me but to others. But to some people the blacklist is a comfort and a cover and an excuse to such an extent that they have acquired a vested moral and spiritual interest in it. Frankly, I loathe them, and they most heartily reciprocate.[9]

As we will see, this letter marked the first of several critical comments Trumbo would make against the Left. His antipathy stemmed from his belief that several members of that amorphous group were murmuring that Trumbo's method of weakening the blacklist was not sufficiently inclusive or confrontational. He had also become convinced that the Left regularly sacrificed individuals (in this case, the Hollywood blacklistees) for loftier—"dialectically necessary"—ends. In addition, Trumbo had concluded that this group of leftists was unfairly blaming the informers for the endurance of the blacklist. This last divergence would culminate in Trumbo's controversial Laurel Award speech (see chapter 22).

The *Young* suit was announced at a Carnegie Hall meeting in September 1961 and was filed at the end of December.[10] It is clear that Murray Schumach spoke to Trumbo before he wrote his article commenting on the case. In an oblique reference to Trumbo's position, Schumach wrote: "Many in Hollywood think the plaintiffs are mistaken in taking their case to court at this time. They argue that the blacklist was doomed because of ethical and economic reasons." Those same people cited the American Legion's failure to keep moviegoers from *Exodus* as evidence of the weakening of the blacklist. Schumach concluded, clearly paraphrasing Trumbo: "Those producers and directors who consider a blacklist unethical—and there are many in Hollywood—can now point out to studio executives that it is no longer dangerous, economically, to employ writers opposed by such groups as the American Legion."[11]

Further evidence of Trumbo's belief that he still had to tread lightly came in the form of a letter he wrote to *Time* reporter Robert Jennings. Jennings had just interviewed Trumbo, who was having second thoughts about some of the information he had revealed. In the letter, Trumbo urged Jennings to consider as privileged anything Trumbo had said about the writing and filming of *Spartacus* and *Exodus*, as well as anything that might reflect negatively on the integrity and intelligence of the executives of Bryna, United Artists, and Universal-International. He cited two reasons for asking Jennings to exercise restraint: because those companies had behaved extraordinarily well toward him, and because "the whole blacklist situation at this moment is in such a delicate state of balance, and the careers of so many people depend on tipping the balance against blacklisting, that I could never forgive myself if an act or work or interview of mine should backfire to the disadvantage of all." He was not, Trumbo assured Jennings, asking to be "whitewashed (who's got that much whitewash anyhow?), and I know that a certain amount of defiance on my part is inherent in the story. I only hope the defiance will seem amusing rather than grim, not altogether extraordinary, but actually a defiance that comes quite naturally to a normal, healthy American male of my advanced years."[12]

Jennings respected Trumbo's wishes, and his published piece described Trumbo as "one of the hottest potatoes every baked in Hollywood." Trumbo was, Jennings wrote, "hated by many" and "adulated by some as a political martyr. At 55, the once-flaming Trumbo appears quiet, gentle and humorous. But . . . he rarely answers except with a speech, and anything will set him off." Jennings did, however, include one defiant statement that Trumbo clearly meant to be humorous—a quotation about lying framed like his advice letters to his children: "Let the lie be delivered face to face, eye to eye, and without scratching the scalp, but let it, for all its simplicity, contain one fantastical element of creative ingenuity."[13] This remark would come back to haunt Trumbo.

As noted earlier, Trumbo had also asked Lardner to tread carefully around the subject of *Spartacus* in his *Saturday Evening Post* article. When the *Post* sent a photographer to California to take a picture of Trumbo for the article, Trumbo wrote to the editors: "I presume that there will be some brief identification beneath the photo your representative has just taken. I hope it will not be pejorative in nature, since my position, in the sense of public relations, is quite delicate." Besides, he continued: "I date all my troubles from the day" in 1936, "when the *Post* published my first short story. So the whole damned mess is your

Trumbo with some of his favorite pre-Columbian sculptures, 1961. Courtesy of *Saturday Evening Post*.

fault. Since I'm thus established as your baby, if you can't be proud, at least be merciful."[14] (The magazine printed two photographs of Trumbo, accompanied by bland captions.)[15]

Lardner, per Trumbo's request, did not mention Kirk Douglas's name. He did, however, laud Trumbo in his uniquely wry manner:

> A breach in the iron screen [of the blacklist] has been effected almost singlehandedly by the fertile talent, capacity for hard work, imaginative flair for publicity and unswerving devotion to a high living standard, of a writer named Dalton Trumbo. Like the rest of us, he is still officially anathema to the major studios that joined together to launch and maintain the blacklist, yet in a three-month period last year more thousands of feet of film were released under his openly acknowledged authorship than any screen writer has ever inflicted on the American public in a similar space of time in the history of the business.[16]

Trumbo applauded Lardner's openness in writing an article about his membership in the Communist Party and his life on the blacklist: "It is a real coup, and its impact on the present situation can be almost shattering. I really don't think it is possible to overestimate the good it will accomplish, and your approach to the material is, as always, exactly right."[17]

When an official of the American Legion offered to debate Trumbo publicly, he declined because, as he told Maltz: "To debate with the Legion now, or at any time, would, in my opinion, revert the dialogue to the level of 1947, which would be a great step backward. To defend myself against an attack which had no power and no effective distribution would have been, in this instance, to publicize for the Legion what they, without my assistance, could not have publicized." As far as his own situation, Trumbo's main fear was receiving another subpoena from the committee.[18]

Trumbo was also careful to avoid putting nonblacklisted people on the spot when he happened to bump into them in public. He referred to this predilection in a letter he wrote to actor Peter Lawford, whom he had met on the set of *Exodus*. After returning to Hollywood, the two men had encountered each other, and Lawford had greeted him cordially. Trumbo explained:

> Events have persuaded me that I am not a well-loved figure in our community. That's why, with the exception of someone like Otto (who asked for it and got it), when dining out I never recognize or greet acquaintances who are in the public eye. I feel somehow that they have enough trouble on their own, without some half-drunk ex-con bellowing hellos at them, slapping their backs, and hovering over the table in lingering appeal for introductions all the way around. Your courtesy the other evening—perhaps gallantry is the better word—suggests cautious revision of my rule, to wit: If in the future our eyes chance to meet in some public place, let us nod our greetings and be done with it. Exception: If either of us is dining with Hedda Hopper [the anti-Communist gossip columnist for the *Los Angeles Times*], the glassy eye of non-recognition prevails.[19]

Movie offers were pouring in, and because Trumbo was getting more work than he could accept, he recommended other blacklistees for the jobs he had to decline. He was also sending scripts and treatments written by blacklistees to producers he knew, and he was lending money to those who needed it. He remained convinced that only a few individuals—Wilson, Lardner, Jarrico, Maltz, and Hunter—had the capacity to do what he did: namely, to write one's way off the blacklist. And he believed that their success would open the door for others. But his old friend Hugo Butler, who was currently living and working in Italy, reacted pessimistically to Trumbo's plan. In an angry, bitter, occasionally witty letter to Lardner, Butler forecast no end to his blacklisting "short of the grave," and he recommended that Trumbo "get himself some other hobby because between that thermo-fax machine, his scripts, the grey parrot and our blacklist, he is plain wearing himself out—and for me the blacklist is serious and not a hobby at all." Perhaps, Butler suggested facetiously, if Trumbo persisted in writing every black-market script in Hollywood "just to break the blacklist for the rest of us," the other blacklisted writers should send a petition reminding him that he was no longer blacklisted and suggesting "that he is ruining his health and doing the less highly priced and low down honest members of the blacklist out of a decent, if scratchy living." The petition "should try and prove, to Dalton's satisfaction, that he is *not* blacklisted, and that trying to muscle in on the glory of the situation just won't go with the rest of us anymore."[20]

Trumbo was not fully unblacklisted until September 1961, when Walter Mirisch and Frank Ross simultaneously asked United Artists, the distributor for both producers, to allow them to employ Trumbo to rewrite their respective scripts: "Hawaii" and "Mr. Moses." United Artists executives agreed to accept Trumbo's employment on either project, leaving the decision to him. Trumbo chose to adapt James Michener's novel *Hawaii*, for which he was to be paid $175,000. But, fearing that the news of this contract might not be well received in the blacklisted community, he once again outlined his strategy in a letter to Wilson (with copies sent to Jarrico, Maltz, and Hunter):

> When the news of the really extraordinary demand for my services creeps out, as it is bound to although I myself shan't publicize it, I'm sure there will be mutterings on the left. "It just isn't possible for him to get away with all that without having compromised honor (sic!) in some direction." Well, for the information of you [Mike] and Paul whose opinion of me I cherish, it is possible. There is no letter of any kind anywhere, neither in the past nor the present, nor will there be (since there's no need for one in the future). The subject doesn't ever come up any more. Perhaps they think it is in bad taste. I say this once again

because I insist that my strategy for breaking the blacklist was and is absolutely correct, and that the left's strategy is, as usual, absolutely wrong. That is if breaking the blacklist is actually a real objective of the left, which sometimes I doubt.

Although the personal profits of my situation presently accrue only to me, I think in the long run they accrue to you and Paul and everyone else who doesn't give up. The thing is to work the trick of that first credit as cunningly as Satan himself would do it—and then the same miracle of acceptance will occur. There appears to be something so final about a fait accompli that the boys [the producers] seem to throw down their barriers with actual relief. They accept the status quo as if it had never been anything different.

So I choose to believe, in spite of such exalted spirits as Mitch Lindemann and Lester Cole [two of the most vocal "left-wingers"], that my personal good fortune can and will rub off on others in the same situation from which I emerged only a year ago. On the other hand, I think you know my view about decent letters of clarification: i.e., that I take no position of reproach or of moral superiority over those who feel that such letters are necessary to employment. It's a matter which is absolutely up to the individual, and uniquely his to decide. I, for one, have had a bellyful of gratifying this damned Fascist minority with the sight of decent artists unemployed and unrecognized. . . . I feel Ring's forthright statement of the truth and its meaning [in the *Saturday Evening Post* article] creates an area of presumptive innocence (as to present politics) for everyone else. And realistically, the presumption of innocence is an excellent weapon in the struggle of the blacklisted for open credit.[21]

Maltz expressed surprise at Trumbo's statement about the Left. During his visits to Hollywood, Maltz had never "heard anyone suggest" that Trumbo's strategy of writing scripts as a means of getting himself off the blacklist was incorrect. So, Maltz concluded, Trumbo must be referring to the criticisms directed at him by some of the *Young* plaintiffs. Maltz then posed the following questions to Trumbo: "Aren't you forgetting that blacklisted actors and directors cannot break through the blacklist by writing scripts as you have? Their only hope lies in a judicial decision that would end the blacklist for everyone. What hope does your strategy offer *them*? And, as a matter of fact, isn't it clear that your strategy will work only for the most talented amongst the blacklisted writers?" It seemed to Maltz that Trumbo might be "beating a non-existent dead horse," and he surmised that Trumbo was doing so because he anticipated "mutterings on the left" in response to the "Hawaii" assignment. Maltz reiterated that in all his conversations with Hollywood leftists, he had "never heard from anyone the slightest suggestion" that Trumbo had achieved his present position by signing a non-Communist letter. Nor had Maltz ever "heard anything but admiration for what Trumbo had achieved." Everyone was aware that Trumbo's achievements "were helping everyone." Perhaps, Maltz concluded, Trumbo's distasteful experiences with John Howard Lawson and Mitchell Lindemann on *Terror in a Texas Town* had caused him to feel embattled and unfairly criticized.[22]

Be that as it may, Trumbo was the only blacklisted writer who had his choice of quality assignments. Before he could start work on *Hawaii*, he had to finish three projects, all involving Kirk Douglas: one of these he considered a disaster, another proved to be painful, and the third turned out to be what he and others considered one of his best scripts. The "disaster" was *The Last Sunset*, a western costarring Douglas and Rock Hudson. Trumbo adapted the script from Vechel Howard's novel *Sundown at Crazy Horse*.[23] After reading the novel, Trumbo decided to make what he called a "plot variation": instead of following the novel's romantic triangle of two women and one man, Trumbo decided to explore the love of an older man for a younger woman who happened to be his daughter. In other words, he wanted to work a variation on the Oedipus theme. But because of the demands of *Spartacus* and *Exodus*, he was unable to write the first draft of the script properly, from beginning to end. Instead, the script "was done in bits and pieces, amidst constant interruptions for services needed by other scripts." He completed a first draft in October 1959, but he knew it did not work; in an effort to improve it, he asked for input from Kirk Douglas, director Robert Aldrich, and coproducers Gene Frenke and Eddie Lewis. He said to them: "Since none of us concerned with making this a good movie is an idiot, I shall not strive to out-argue or over-rule opinions or decisions. I shall accept the majority decision when it is mutually made."[24] Aldrich, who had done a few screenplays, made many comments, which he expressed in two long memos.[25]

Despite this collaboration, the shoot did not go smoothly. Douglas did not want to work with Hudson but was forced to do so by Universal executives, who also demanded that Douglas "beef up Rock's part" and "put in scenes that really didn't suit the story."[26] Aldrich's ideas were not working, so Trumbo was summoned to Mexico, where he tried to weave homespun into silk. After seeing a rough cut of the film, Trumbo told Lewis that he wanted to relinquish the writing credit because keeping it would cost him "a great deal in terms of critical esteem and public approval." It was only his "sense of fairness and honor" toward Douglas that stopped him: "Having been associated with him in a success, I could not and would not withdraw from him in disaster."[27] In a letter to Wilson, Trumbo described the finished movie:

> [It is] as frightful a piece of shit as one can imagine. I chant several excuses to myself each night before toppling off to sleep: I agreed to do it three years ago without the slightest idea my name would ever be on it; the script was shamelessly juggled during the course of shooting, whole portions of essential scenes were not shot at all, with resulting incomprehensibility; it was distorted by entry into the cast of Rock Hudson; etc., etc. Even so it wasn't a very good script to begin with, and the critics have dealt me some pretty harsh and wholly justified slaps.[28]

In a 1964 interview Trumbo candidly admitted: "I am principally responsible for it. It is my very worst film . . . ; the screenplay was bad."[29] One year later he told another interviewer: "It was a lousy script for one thing and there was nothing I could do with it. That's the one I went down [to Mexico] and mothered. But it was hopeless, utterly hopeless."[30] His script was, he lamented, "too sentimental," and he had treated the incest idea too feebly.[31]

When *The Last Sunset* was released in June 1961, Philip K. Scheuer was one of very few reviewers who liked it. In his eyes, it was "as slickly contrived a western as Hollywood (via Mexico) ever turned out." And he even had kind words for Trumbo's script, remarking that it contained "unexpected flashes of poetic prose with just-what-you'd-expect-'em-to say."[32] The reviewer for *Daily Variety* wrote: "It is apparent that Trumbo has made an earnest effort at three-dimensional characterization, at least insofar as the central character (Douglas) is concerned. However, the tricky story he is attempting to bring to dramatic life is burdened by serious unlikelihoods, and the artificial strain is compounded by the fact that a number of key scenes have a distractingly postured appearance and deliberate pace."[33] The reviewer for the *Hollywood Reporter* stated that the script "has some characteristic Trumbo touches. . . . But the careful construction and solid character this screen-writer usually achieves do not come across."[34] The reviewer for *Lime-light*, however, called it "one of the worst Westerns ever made" and expressed disbelief that Trumbo could have been "responsible for the borrowed plot devices."[35]

The Last Sunset is not a terrible movie, but the story is weak and Aldrich's direction is mediocre. The pace of events is very slow, and there is virtually no chemistry among the four main actors (Douglas, Hudson, Dorothy Malone, and Carole Lynley). Only Douglas delivered a believable performance.

The second project, *Town without Pity*, was unpleasant from beginning to end. It was supposed to be based on Manfred Gregor's novel *Das Urteil* (The Verdict), the story of the trial of four US soldiers charged with the gang-rape of a sixteen-year-old German girl. German director Gottfried Reinhardt brought the project to Douglas, and in 1960 Bryna, Mirisch Brothers Productions, and two German produc-tion companies (Gloria-Film GmbH and Osweg) agreed to coproduce the film. The first draft of the screenplay was written by the director's wife. Neither Douglas nor Harold Mirisch liked it, and they demanded radical revisions. Douglas insisted that Trumbo be hired to make the necessary revisions, but the Mirisches were "at best neutral about his being hired, and perhaps, negative on the ground that this would increase the cost of the picture and possibly delay its shooting date." As for Reinhardt, he "was opposed for a number of reasons," including the fact that his wife had written the script; in addition, he feared Trumbo's involvement might complicate and delay the production schedule.[36] For his part, Trumbo described himself as being "wryly amused that I, who had been considered to be anti-American, was assigned to correct" a script bristling with anti-American overtones.[37]

Trumbo was given three weeks to complete his work, at a salary of $10,000 per week. When he and Cleo arrived in Munich in early November, he quickly ascertained that the Germans were "indiffer-ent and uninterested in his role."[38] Indeed, Reinhardt immediately informed Trumbo that the Germans were operating on a very tight bud-get and that every script change must fit their plan of production and their shooting schedule.[39] After one week's work, Trumbo sent a revised draft to Reinhardt, who acknowledged the "sheer quantity" of Trum-bo's work, which was much greater than expected, and then criticized several aspects of it.[40] Apparently, Reinhardt and other members of the crew showered Trumbo with suggestions, because a few days later,

Trumbo wrote an angry note to himself at 4:00 a.m., revealing that he had spent "22 straight hours of work" assembling a final script from all the correction and amendments, "without once leaving this fucking hotel. Without once discarding the bathrobe in which I began the day." At that point, he told himself, he no longer cared what happened with the final version: "Let Gloria [one of the German production companies] revert to its original script, and *shoot* the son-of-a-bitch. Let them do it! And let me sleep." He had, he concluded, "highly misjudged" his own capacity, and he was exhausted.[41] Looking back on the experience, Trumbo wrote: "Gottfried hated me, the entire German crew wanted to get me out of town, and the Mirisches wired almost daily asking why the hell I didn't finish."[42]

Trumbo completed his revisions on November 15, and when he arrived home he told Frenke: "This trip was all work and no pleasure—seven days a week without respite, and I hope I draw no more such assignments."[43] But his agony was not over: he was not invited to the preview, and he soon learned that screenplay credit had been given to Silvia Reinhardt and Georg Hurdalek. On May 4 he sent a telegram to Mirisch Brothers Productions, complaining about the preview and threatening to ask the Writers Guild to arbitrate the writing credits.[44] Harold Mirisch claimed that the failure to invite Trumbo to the preview was "purely an oversight," and after looking into the credit assignment, Mirisch discovered that the decision to keep Trumbo's name off *Town without Pity* was Douglas's.[45] Douglas had apparently concluded that Trumbo's name was on too many films in which Douglas appeared, so he chose to remove it from *Town without Pity*. "I have," Trumbo told Lewis, "yielded to Kirk's wishes in this matter," even though the loss of this credit, combined with the poor reviews and box-office receipts for *The Last Sunset*, had harmed him professionally. In Trumbo's mind, Douglas's decision represented a new type of "blacklist," precisely "when others seek my services with credit regardless of the blacklist."[46]

Trumbo agreed to relinquish his claim to credit, on one condition: he wanted a letter from Reinhardt acknowledging the quantity and quality of Trumbo's work on the script. Such a letter was necessary, Trumbo told Lewis, to enable him "to emerge from this sleazy affair with any self-respect at all."[47] Reinhardt complied, but not in a manner that appeased Trumbo. In his telegram, the German director said: "If material of yours was not used this was not due to lack of its quality. That which was used certainly contributed to picture's quality." That phrasing, Trumbo wrote to Harold Mirisch, "in addition to being incomprehensible, . . . is pure Reinhardt, so fragrant of his character that the stench has been electronically transmitted with the words. It is, of course, quite unsatisfactory from my point of view, and I could make things rather nasty for him if I wished." Nevertheless, he preferred to "consider the matter closed, and the credits, as they presently (and fraudulently) appear on the screen, to be final."[48]

The movie received mixed reviews but was not successful at the box office. Since no one knew about Trumbo's contribution, Reinhardt received most of the criticism. John L. Scott, for example, wrote: "It is difficult to determine just what producer-director Gottfried Reinhardt is trying to do."[49] The reviewer for *Newsweek* said (paraphrasing the title song by Gene Pitney), "It isn't very pretty, and it isn't even very real."[50] But Brendan Gill and Bosley Crowther both admired its honesty.[51]

Douglas's curious behavior toward Trumbo took on another dimension when the actor was interviewed by Murray Schumach for a *New York Times* article titled: "Trumbo Backed by Kirk Douglas: Writer's Use on Series of Movies Is Defended." In the article, Schumach essentially celebrated Douglas's use of Trumbo, while Douglas celebrated his own courage in doing so. Douglas said his associates had warned him that it would be unwise to hire Trumbo, but he had ignored their advice because he wanted the best possible talent and Trumbo was, in his estimation, an extremely gifted screenwriter. Besides, Douglas remarked in a self-congratulatory manner, "People who hire other people under pseudonyms have no guts." And then, in a rather perplexing and remarkably tone-deaf fashion, Douglas offered his thoughts on the hiring of Communists: "If a guy is a Communist—and I don't think Trumbo is a Communist—he is no less a Communist than if he uses another name." In any case, Douglas was certain that neither Trumbo nor any other Communist writer could slip Communist propaganda past him and into a script for Bryna.[52]

Even though Trumbo was sure that Douglas's remarks had been made innocently, Trumbo was equally certain that the article would have a harmful effect on him. He explained why to Lewis:

> 1. It called embarrassing attention to my "talent" at a time when reviewers everywhere were validly pointing to "Sunset" as valid evidence I had very little, if any. 2. It revealed publicly for the first time that Kirk "has been warned by associates that it is unwise to have scripts written by Mr. Trumbo." Who

could have given Murray Schumach that confidential information except Kirk himself? Kirk reveals, as background material, hitherto unpublished attacks upon me, and then proceeds
publicly to defend me from something that could not have been
known but for his defense. 3. It thus allowed another rehash of
the events of 1947 and the committee, which it has always been
my public relations policy to ignore and hence de-emphasize. 4.
It implies that I am still very dangerous, in that it takes great
courage to use my work, whereas the truth is that other stars
and several studio heads seem to think it is no risk at all. 5. It
publicly defends me and calls attention to me at a time when
the attacks against me have failed—which is to say, when the
last thing I need or want is a public defense. 6. It quotes Kirk as
saying, "I could not have stood the hypocrisy of not using his
name" (on "Spartacus") at the very time when he is insisting
that my name not be used on "Town without Pity."[53]

Trumbo's one purely happy experience with Douglas was the work
he did adapting Edward Abbey's novel *The Brave Cowboy*. According to Trumbo, Douglas and Lewis had offered to let him direct the
movie (released under the bizarre title *Lonely Are the Brave*) as well, but
Trumbo could not do so because he had a prior commitment to write
another script for Otto Preminger (*Bunny Lake Is Missing*).[54] Trumbo,
ended up juggling the *Bunny* and *Cowboy* assignments and, in the
process, irritating both Preminger and Douglas. At one point Douglas said to Trumbo, "I hear you are also working on a script for Preminger." Trumbo replied: "Well, Kirk, when I was working on *Spartacus*,
I screwed him, now it's your turn."[55] (Preminger's reaction is described
later.)
       One of the reasons the assignment was copacetic for Trumbo was
the story's minor character Paul Bondi, a friend of Jack Burns, "the
brave cowboy." Bondi was very Trumbo-like in his attitude toward the
justice system. Indeed, in a letter to director David Miller, Abbey characterized Bondi's main trouble as being "his passion for justice." Like
Burns, Bondi "loves liberty, but even more intensely he demands justice,
whereas Burns, while sympathetic to this peculiar passion, is a little too
embittered by personal experience to seriously expect justice."[56] In the
novel, Bondi is indicted for refusing to register for the military draft,
and even though he believes the draft requirement is not a reasonable
or legitimate act of government, he accepts the guilty verdict. Accord-

ing to Christopher, Trumbo was told to change Bondi's crime, probably because the studio executives did not consider it good politics to glorify draft resistance. In the first draft of his screenplay, Trumbo slyly changed Bondi's crime to refusing to testify to a grand jury about a conspiracy to smuggle parrots across the Mexican border. Apparently not tickled by Trumbo's humor, a studio executive demanded that the crime be changed to harboring illegal immigrants from Mexico.[57]

Trumbo's screenplay followed the book closely and captured Abbey's vision: "I simply took a cowboy and his horse—the romantic symbols of American freedom—and set them down in the midst of the modern world. They didn't make out well at all. Just as all the old concepts of freedom (mostly horseshit anyway) won't make out in the midst of the different freedoms in the last half of the twentieth century."[58] Trumbo told an interviewer that *Lonely Are the Brave* is "the film with which I am most pleased. . . . [I]t is an appeal to freedom, to respect of the individual, a defense of friendship and love. . . . Jack Burns, the cowboy played by Kirk Douglas, is a free man. The mountains, his horse, represent freedom, better than the highway, the sanitation truck: the modern world, society. At the end, when his horse dies, he must also die."[59]

Trumbo completed a first draft at the end of August 1960 and a final draft the following June. Douglas raved about it, saying: "Of the seventy-five movies I've acted in, and all the others I've produced, and all the movies I've heard of, it's the only time that I know of a writer producing a perfect screenplay: one draft, no revisions. Like a hole-in-one."[60] Lewis agreed. Abbey also liked it, and they shot it as written. Trumbo later said that he, Lewis, and Miller had made a pact: "no changes, no changes, no changes." During filming, however, Douglas regularly called Trumbo to tell him about some "cute" (amusing) bits of dialogue he had conceived and wanted to add to the script. Trumbo, who did not think Douglas had a gift for "cute," always replied: "Kirk, when you get up in the morning, take two Seconals, and go out on the set, and it will be just fine."[61]

No one, however, liked the title. Trumbo queried: "What does lonely are the brave mean? I don't know who was brave. Nobody was brave, really."[62] Abbey had pleaded to Miller: "Please don't change the title. Please. *The Brave Cowboy* is just right, has just the proper ingenuous and myth-evoking quality, and furthermore, in the setting of the story, adds the note of irony that every good book—and movie—should have."[63] Douglas also objected to the title change and wrote, "To this day, I'm not quite sure what it means."[64] The film title was chosen by someone at Universal, from a list of fifteen possibilities.

Lonely Are the Brave is one of those rare films in which everyone concerned is covered with glory. It is a gem, imparting two universal themes—courage and freedom—to a seemingly small incident: a cowboy goes to jail for an act of civil disobedience. As Trumbo saw it, each character is seeking a particular type of freedom, and when their paths cross, no one's ideal can be completely realized. Trumbo did not embellish the story; the script was devoid of sentimentality. Trumbo presciently told Michael Wilson that he had high hopes for the movie but feared he had priced himself out of the market for writing any other "'distinguished,' or 'interesting,' or 'unusual'" films of this type.[65]

As it happened, *Lonely Are the Brave* (which was released in June 1962) was a critical success and a box-office failure. Douglas complained that Universal had shown little interest in the film from the outset and had simply dumped it in theaters.[66] The critic for the *Saturday Review* called Trumbo's screenplay "the finest Western script since 'High Noon' and 'The Gunfighter.'"[67] One of the few negative reviewers of the film, Brendan Gill, took a polemical swipe at Trumbo, stating that the "screenplay, by Dalton Trumbo, struck me as a shoddy and remarkably simple-minded song of hatred for twentieth-century American society." Gill had obviously not read Abbey's novel, because he accused Trumbo of fabricating the "vulgarity" of the scene in which the cowboy is run down by a truck carrying portable toilets. (In fact, that collision is a central structural element of the novel.) Gill concluded: "There may be a lot wrong with this country, but Mr. Trumbo is plainly not the man to point it out."[68] Trumbo, infuriated by Gill's remarks, warned him: "If you'll call me a Communist in *The New Yorker* instead of implying it, I guarantee a trail of Gill-feathers all the way from 25 West 43rd Street [the magazine's address] to Bronxville, New York. You can lead off, crying—as apparently you're apt to—'Nonsense! Plenty of fun to be had along the way!' and I'll be right behind you having it."[69]

Several months later, Trumbo sent a telegram to Douglas: "Once in a while when God smiles and the table is tilted just slightly in our favor something happens. It comes from inside and reveals what we really are. I think it happened with you and Cowboy. I think they [the viewers] are going to leave the theatre saying 'That is what I really am. Or at least it is what I want to be in my finest hour.' You did it. You showed the heart of a man. Do you dig me amigo? Old Sam is grateful and sends you love."[70] Douglas replied: "Your wire was warmer than the Italian air and came at a time when I needed it most. Thank you, friend, but what have you written for me lately?"[71] Douglas later cited *Lonely Are the Brave* as his "favorite movie."[72]

Trumbo's working relationship with Douglas ended with *Lonely Are the Brave*, but he continued to write scripts for Preminger. At some point in 1961, Ingo Preminger sent a copy of Harold Robbins's novel *The Carpetbaggers* to Trumbo, asking if he would like to adapt it. In a draft of his response, Trumbo thoroughly skewered the novel, rejected the assignment, and sarcastically remarked: "I'll return it [the book] as soon as the kids finish it. They're chanting passages in unison upstairs right now, hoping to memorize the poetry before they surrender it."[73] Ingo then sent him another book, *Bunny Lake Is Missing* (by Merriam Modell, who had written it under the pseudonym Evelyn Piper), along with Ira Levin's adaptation of it. Otto hoped Trumbo would agree to rewrite Levin's script, but it proved to be a very unhappy experience for all concerned.

First of all, Trumbo encountered great difficulty with the adaptation. It turned out that Otto had a higher opinion of Levin's script than Trumbo did. Trumbo thought he should write a completely new script, but, as he soon learned, Otto was not sure what he wanted. Second, Otto decided that Trumbo was taking too long to complete the script. Based on the *Exodus* experience, Otto was convinced that because Trumbo regularly stole time from one assignment to work on another, he could revise a script in one month.[74] Trumbo completed the first draft of the "Bunny" screenplay in May, but he was not happy with it. He wrote to Otto:

> I came home, bearing my two copies of Bunny; I put them on my desk and left them there for four or five days. Friday I opened the top copy and read it carefully from beginning to end. I took a nap. I awakened and read it again. My first feelings were confirmed. This script is no good. We have wasted our time. The script is not *about* anything. . . . I think you should postpone this film for a least a year—or conceivably drop it altogether. . . . It is bad enough that you and I, working very hard and for a protracted time, should have come up with a bad script; but to go ahead and compound the error by deliberately making a bad picture would be unforgivable. If you are sure—*if you are absolutely certain*—that you can make a successful film based on all or part of this script, then I will stick with you to the bitter end;

I will write and re-write till the day you begin to shoot, and even after; I will do everything in my power to improve chances which I now think so slim. I will even demand a full card on the screen, with my name in enormous letters, and credit in all advertising, if for no other reason than to inform the world that I am as willing to share a disaster with you as I was to share a success. Call the scripts in and burn them, cancel or post-pone the picture, fire my son, post a notice in the press that I have perpetrated an obscenity, circularize the Screen Producers Guild with warnings against me—but do not make this film![75]

Michael Wilson, to whom Trumbo had sent a copy, agreed with Trumbo's assessment of the script: "The problem is deep-rooted and pervades the entire screenplay . . . [it] has no theme. . . . [I]t is not *about* anything. . . . [T]he sorry truth is that my judgment of the screenplay, while not as harsh as your own, is pretty negative and sweeping. I no longer believe that it can be easily fixed. . . . [A] fairly drastic re-write is involved."[76]

Trumbo told Ingo: "If Otto's going to make it, I'm going to be with him until he throws me off. . . . I will not abandon this script until it is

Christopher, Nikola, Trumbo, and Mitzi at Nikola's graduation, University of Colorado, 1962. Photograph by Cleo Trumbo.

the best that can be done."[77] But Otto decided that Trumbo's script was "very theatrical and wrong,"[78] so he hired John and Penelope Mortimer to do a complete rewrite. The movie was released in October 1965, to mixed reviews. (Nor could Trumbo and Otto solve the problems that had plagued them on *The Other Side of the Coin* since 1959. Otto finally decided to abandon it in 1963, and the two did not work together again, although they remained friends.)

The FBI continued to compile reports on Trumbo and maintained his name in its Security Index, purportedly because "of his active and substantial participation in . . . Communist Party front organizations."[79] The Bureau knew that Trumbo had left the party years earlier, but it took seriously the inaccurate statement of an informant that Trumbo "remains sensitive to what the Communist Party thinks," and he "still wants to stay on the right side of the Party in case the Party might be useful to him. [H]e does not want to be labeled a 'renegade' by the Party." The special agent in charge of the Los Angeles office suggested it might be worthwhile to interview Trumbo, but it is not clear why, since he went on to note: "while there is some indication that Trumbo would not refuse to be interviewed by Bureau representatives, there is no reason to believe he has any potential as an informant and because of his apparent flair for publicity and self-aggrandizement, it is entirely possible he might publicize any interview by Bureau Agents."[80]

FBI director J. Edgar Hoover was seriously worried that blacklisted writers, directors, and actors were returning to work in the motion picture industry and being reinstated in their respective guilds. He ordered the Los Angeles office to submit a written report every sixty days "concerning this most important field."[81] Then, in an astonishingly ill-informed and bizarrely worded memo to one of his aides, Hoover unfolded yet another in his long line of anti-Communist tactics. Hoover had received information that Communist Party leaders were worried that Trumbo "may make a number of antic statements as part of a promotional scheme for the picture he is working on." Hoover was convinced that none of these "antic statements" would represent a real change in Trumbo's "thinking," given that "he still embraces the communist philosophy." Based on that premise, Hoover concluded that Trumbo would "simply be attempting to erase his heretofore disreputable position in the Hollywood community." To forestall this tactic, Hoover ordered his agents not to send Trumbo's "antic statements" to the Bureau's stable of pet journalists; instead, they should utilize them in its Counterintelligence Program (COINTELPRO), which was designed to cause disruption in the Communist Party. "If Trumbo is sincere" in his fidelity to the Communist Party, Hoover chortled, "it represents a major break in the hard-core Communist Party in Hollywood and exploitations of this break could influence other Communist Party members and sympathizers to leave the Party." (At this point, it should be noted, there was no Communist Party in Hollywood, and virtually all its "hard-core" members and sympathizers were in their sixties.) However, if Trumbo was insincere, the Bureau could use its "friendly press contacts to expose Trumbo as the opportunist he is and this in turn could act as a deterrent to other Communists who may be considering making weak antic statements in an obvious self-serving manner."[82] Twelve days later, Hoover ordered the Los Angeles office to "alert confidential agents and sources" to keep the Bureau cognizant "of any antic statements by this individual."[83] The following year, Hoover suggested that Trumbo's name be placed on the Bureau's mailing list of people designated to receive anonymous mail describing incidents of anti-Semitism in the Soviet Union. "Such mailings might have a further disillusioning effect on Trumbo which might prepare him for possible interview at sometime in the future."[84] As it turned out, Trumbo was not interviewed by the FBI, and the Bureau did not use any of his "antic" statements. (My guess is that Hoover's agents did not know what an "antic" statement was.)

Trumbo, of course, knew nothing about Hoover's rants, and they had no effect on him. He did, however, feel the hot breath of another government agency: the Internal Revenue Service. Its agents gave Trumbo his most anxious post-blacklist moments when they opened an investigation of his tax returns in 1960. The large number of bank accounts he had been using to hide the money trail during the days of the black market had caught the attention of an IRS examiner, and he turned Trumbo's amended 1958 federal tax return over to the agency's Intelligence Division. The investigating agent, who was satisfied that nothing was amiss, submitted his completed report, and it was duly approved by the Los Angeles office. However, another examiner in the San Francisco regional office, who had read Trumbo's 1961 *Time* interview with Jennings, attached that interview to Trumbo's tax return, with his remarks about the art of lying marked in red pencil.[85] Another, more extensive investigation was subsequently opened.

Years later, Trumbo told an interviewer: "I believe the blackest despair I ever felt was the day that a special intelligence agent for the

IRS subpoenaed every record I had. . . . The despair came from what I felt would be the squalor of the crime—for *money*, income tax evasion. I felt that really my life would not be worth living, if this thing [a trial] occurred." Trumbo feared that his political record and his previous federal conviction might lead a jury to pronounce him guilty. It was, he recalled, a miserable experience: "I had to examine every paper in my life, reconstruct every financial transaction of a decade. I worked for months like a maniac. This time there would be no riding off to jail on people's shoulders as a political martyr. You are just a chickenshit chiseler."[86] After examining Trumbo's records, the regional office determined that there had been no criminal intent to evade taxes.

21

Hawaii and *The Sandpiper*

> After all those years of fighting, I think he was exhausted. He wasn't able to return to the mind-set of his younger self, when his ambition was clear and unencumbered and the future seemed limitless. He had started late; he was making up for lost time; and then came the blacklist. He was angry. He knew he could not get back those lost years.
>
> —Mitzi Trumbo

After getting out from under *Bunny Lake*, Trumbo looked to the future with some optimism. He wrote to Michael Wilson that, at age fifty-five, he was probably in the midst of his "last big whirl" as a screenwriter, and he intended to reap as much money as he could from it. His contract with Frenke would terminate in early 1964, and he expected to receive substantial deferred salary payments for five years thereafter. He and Frenke were making what Trumbo thought were good investments, and for the first time in his life, Trumbo was convinced he had a "good set-up"; if all went according to plan, he would not have to write a single movie between 1964 and 1969. But he was afraid he might have become ensnared in two of the traps of Hollywood screenwriting: (1) he had "dulled the edge of whatever talent" he possessed by too "much hard work, for too much money"; and (2) he was too easily lured by an enormous salary into doing the type of film that, given its cost and size, was unlikely to be a "fine" one. In sum, he wondered whether it was possible to "make money from one medium come hell or high water, to purchase the freedom of expressing oneself in another media more receptive to original thought." If he were trapped, he concluded, "So be it."[1]

But his thirteen-year war against the blacklist had taken a greater toll than Trumbo realized. Even though a truce had been declared in his own case, he was frustrated that others were not so favored; his health was not good, and he was drinking heavily. The workload of the black-market years had eroded both his patience and his tolerance. His state of mind was also affected by the dramatic change that had occurred in Hollywood moviemaking. Most films were now made by independent producers in the form of package deals, and the delays and frustrations were magnified. In particular, many projects had several directors and writers, resulting in a dramatic increase in the number of WGAw credit arbitrations. Trumbo found himself enmeshed in two such credit disputes, one of which involved his close friend Michael Wilson. He also had a falling out with Hugo Butler.

Hawaii, the massive novel (in both size and sales) by James Michener, was published in the autumn of 1959. It is a six-part history of the islands from their geological beginnings to the present. Even though its size and structure presented a major problem for any writer attempting to adapt it to the screen, the Mirisch Company purchased the movie rights for $600,000, and it contracted with Fred Zinnemann to direct the film and Daniel Taradash to write it (the two had worked together very successfully on *From Here to Eternity* [Columbia, 1953]). After reading the novel, Taradash realized that dramatizing it would be "a very massive job," but he thought he had found a theme—"all men are brothers"—that might serve as a unifying device for the movie. But, he told Zinnemann (and the Mirisches), that theme would work only if they made two movies.[2] They concurred.

Taradash labored for two years and finally completed a 237-page treatment in June 1961, at which point he informed Zinnemann and the Mirisches that three three-hour films would be required to tell the full story. Taradash did not have the stamina to write the second and third scripts, and he recommended Dalton Trumbo for the job.[3] When Walter Mirisch told Taradash that his company was going to make one long film and that he wanted a 300-page shooting script for it, Taradash was unwilling to start over. Instead, he proposed cutting his current 250-page script to 150 pages and writing "a rapid, master-scene, 'dummy-dialogue' screenplay of the rest of the treatment." But shortly thereafter Taradash decided to drop out of the project altoghether.[4]

The Mirisches offered the job to Trumbo, who quickly accepted. It was a prestige assignment, it paid well, and it had a guaranteed screen credit. In addition, Trumbo was attracted to what he perceived to be the theme of Michener's book: "I considered its story of racism and the evils that spring from it the most important theme of our century.

I felt that I knew how it should be dealt with and I was determined to do everything in my power to bring my ideas to bear upon it."[5] When the news of Trumbo's hiring became public, a headline in *Daily Variety* asserted that the American Legion "Threatens 'Battle' if Trumbo 'Allowed to Screenplay.'" Thomas Hoag, chairman of the California Legion's Counter-Subversive Committee, promised that his organization and the American public would wage "the most serious kind of battle" against the movie if Trumbo wrote the screenplay.[6] By this time, however, proclamations of this kind were being met with yawns in the movie industry.

The Mirisches had returned to the idea of making two movies, so Trumbo wrote a script for each. He also provided a shorter version of each script, just in case the producers decided to make only one movie. When he delivered the four scripts on March 1, 1963, he and the Mirisches agreed that Trumbo would not have to start on the final drafts until the fall. In May, however, Mirisch informed Trumbo that United Artists would agree to finance only one film, and he asked Trumbo to immediately revise the script for the first picture, comprising the Bora Bora, missionary, and Chinese sections of the novel. But Trumbo, relying on his March agreement with the Mirisches and believing he had five or six free months, had accepted two other assignments, neither of which had "stop clauses" in their contracts that would have allowed him to return to work on "Hawaii." He informed Walter Mirisch that he would be unable to resume work until January 1964 but promised to have a completed script by June 1 of that year. He did not, he told Mirisch, "want any other writer touching what by now I feel is so intimately mine."[7]

Mirisch agreed, but when Zinnemann withdrew from the project in February 1964, his replacement, George Roy Hill, decided to write a completely new script. Trumbo, meanwhile, was working on "The Sandpiper" script. Apparently, Hill's script satisfied neither himself nor the Mirisches, because when Trumbo wrote to Walter Mirisch in August, seeking reinstatement as the screenwriter, Hill readily concurred.[8] Trumbo wrote steadily from September 1964 to May 1965, but he was concerned about the credit. Trumbo wrote in a note to Taradash that some of the script had been written "by you, some by George Roy Hill, and some by me. In what proportion only God, time, and the Continental Congress can tell."[9]

The film began shooting in February 1965, but weather problems and Hill's slow and erratic pace caused the film to go way over budget.

Desperate to get costs under control, the Mirisches replaced Hill with Arthur Hiller, but when all the Hawaiian actors and extras and the entire casting crew walked off the location in protest, the Mirisches were forced to rehire Hill. They then dispatched Trumbo to Hawaii to reduce what remained of the unshot script. According to a story in the *Los Angeles Times*, Trumbo had "to unwrite his script by hindsight. With the film being shot in continuity, he started at the last page and worked backwards eliminating characters which had not yet been established and telescoping events that had not yet taken place." By the time he had finished, the story had been trimmed by twenty years, and the entire Chinese section had been eliminated.[10] Hill was very grateful and thanked Trumbo profusely "for so goddam much on this film—not the least of which is the gorgeous job of writing on the last part under tremendous pressure."[11] Walter Mirisch was even more grateful, noting the "mammoth amount of work" Trumbo had done on the script and his support "in helping me manage the situation."[12]

The finished movie essentially tells only one of Michener's stories: that of the missionaries who came to the islands from New England to save the Hawaiians for Jesus but ended up nearly annihilating them in His name. Since the missionary section of the novel lacked an "ending" (i.e., a satisfactory dramatic conclusion), Trumbo had to invent one. He decided to soften the Reverend Abner Hale's "radical racism" through a theological disputation.[13] At the end of the movie, after a measles epidemic has been contained, Abner blames himself because, during one of his religious rants, he called the wrath of God down upon the sinful Hawaiians. Jerusha, Abner's wife, reminds him of God's role in human events and calmly tells him it is just a disease; the words of the Bible should not be taken literally. If Abner is correct in his belief that the Bible is the inerrant word of God and that a Christian must follow it, Jerusha says she will no longer call herself a Christian. She does not believe in a wrathful God; nor does she believe that the unbaptized Hawaiian people actually reside in Hell. They are too full of the Christian spirit, loving, and generous. When Abner replies that their fate is "God's will, not mine" and asks, "What else but God's wrath has the power to annihilate them?" Jerusha has a ready answer: "Disease, despair, our lack of love, an inability to find them beautiful, our contempt for their ways, our lust for their land, our greed, our arrogance. That is what killed them and that is what you must save them from." She advises Abner to shelter and protect them and "win them to a merciful God, with bonds of charity so strong that they will be bound to Him forever." Abner must, she pleads, give them what he has denied both them and her for all these years—his love. After Jerusha dies, Abner does what she asked of him.

Michener later wrote to Trumbo: "When I read the adaptation of *Hawaii*, I thought that you had captured most of what I wanted to say in the portions you were using and that you heightened the dramatic impact of those portions. In particular, I thought that the ending of the screen play, which was an addition to my novel, was better than I could have devised."[14]

One reviewer, Vincent Canby, wrote: "Not since Rev. Mr. Davidson went after Sadie Thompson [in *Rain*] has Protestant Christian proselytism come off so poorly on screen. There's nothing wrong about that. It's just a surprise that when the film finally lumbers to its close to find Mr. Von Sydow [Abner] . . . still a figure of unexplored pathos."[15] Taradash said the casting of Max Von Sydow as Abner ruined the movie for him.[16] The members of the Hawaiian Mission Children's Society (all descendants of the first missionaries) absolutely hated the film. They prepared an eight-page pamphlet in which they accused the filmmakers of misleading the film's audience and provoking "malicious" and "uninformed" opinions about the missionaries and the islanders.[17] Trumbo thought it was "a rather courageous film by Hollywood standards" because it painted an honest portrait of a crusading missionary and did not idealize his religion; rather, it clearly condemned "the super-aggressive religionists."[18] Given the many vacillations of the filmmakers, it is remarkable that *Hawaii* turned out as well as it did. Contrary to the opinions of Canby and Taradash, the Abner Hale character, as written by Trumbo, rivets one's attention, probably because Hale exemplifies the bigotry, rigidity, and dogmatism Trumbo detested. Trumbo not only graphically depicted the contradictions inherent in the missionary impulse but also offered an alternative, benevolent image of God.

On December 8, 1965, the Mirisch Company awarded Trumbo sole screenwriting credit. Taradash, however, thought he deserved cocredit and asked the WGAw to appoint an arbitration committee to hear his claim. Mirisch executives and Hill strongly supported sole credit for Trumbo,[19] and he became convinced that Mary Dorfman, the guild's arbitration secretary, had changed, bypassed, or abrogated altogether the arbitration procedure to favor Taradash. According to Trumbo's view of events: "Mr. Taradash stands before the Credit Arbitration Secretary as an honorable man; I stand as a parvenu whose work, like his check, must be certified by his betters (before anyone will accept it)."[20]

In their respective briefs to the arbitration committee, Trumbo claimed he had written an original script based on Michener's story and characters, whereas Taradash staked his claim for credit on the similarities in continuity, construction, selection of material, and characterizations in the two scripts submitted to the committee.[21] In mid-January the arbitration committee arrived at a unanimous decision: Taradash and Trumbo would share the credit.[22] When Hill heard about the decision, he wrote to Trumbo: "You must absolutely fight it. . . . [T]he decision is terribly, terribly unjust. . . . There is something *wrong*, Dalton. I don't pretend to know yet what it is . . . but goddam it, *something is wrong somewhere*, and it must *not* stand unchallenged.[23] The difficulty was that the WGAw's bylaws allowed a review of the arbitrators' decision only on the grounds of bias, fraud, and so forth, but since the guild would not reveal the arbitrators' names, evidence was difficult to amass. Undaunted, Trumbo filed an appeal, basing it on two grounds: (1) he was still engaged in rewriting and thus his script was incomplete, and (2) bias on the part of the arbitrators. Trumbo's determination to pursue an appeal must have worried the guild. According to Aubrey Finn, who was representing Trumbo, Mary Dorfman "seems most anxious to satisfy you, or to avoid controversy."[24] The guild's executive secretary, Mike Franklin, did not think Dorfman had acted arbitrarily, or even if she had, he did not believe it had impacted the committee's decision. Nevertheless, he feared the bad publicity if Trumbo went public with his claim. Taradash was requested to submit to a second arbitration with a different panel of writers.[25]

For the second arbitration, Taradash's statement and list of scene comparisons totaled 39 pages, whereas Trumbo's statement consisted of 104 pages plus a 109-page appendix. Taradash reiterated what he had written in his first statement: "The *continuity* and *dialogue* are so identical as to make the use of that word proper here. The *selection of material* and its use is the same. The *characterizations* are no different. The *story line* is exactly as it was."[26] Trumbo, in effect, said "so what?" Because both writers were adapting the same novel, it should come as no surprise that both writers "directly and legitimately appropriated scenes, incidents, characters and dialogue which were written and conceived by Michener." Trumbo pointed out that the central question was reducible to "which writer is to receive credit for Michener's work?" The problem, Trumbo legitimately stated, was the guild's tradition that the first writer was given credit for any material from the source that was also used by the second writer. Trumbo conceded the similarity among major scenes and characters in all three scripts (his, Taradash's, and Hill's): "The selections of all three were predictable because they were necessary, and necessary because they were inescapable: without them Michener's story could not be told." Trumbo argued further that 35 percent of the material in his final draft was not replicated in Taradash's, and the stories "are told from such different points of view and

Trumbo and Mitzi, Reed College, 1964. Photograph by Cleo Trumbo.

arrive at such different conclusions that I cannot imagine the author of either one of them desiring or deserving credit for the other."[27]

The second arbitration committee met in September and awarded cocredit to Trumbo and Taradash. A few years later, Walter Mirisch hired James R. Webb to revise Trumbo's second script, which was based on the Chinese section of Michener's book. After reading Webb's script, "The Hawaiians," Trumbo told Mirisch to give Webb solo credit.[28]

As previously noted, Trumbo had begun work on "The Sandpiper" in between stints on *Hawaii*. This project did not bring out the best in Trumbo. He was, especially during the postproduction process, contradictory, cantankerous, and ungenerous. The most curious aspect of his behavior was that he did not think he had written a particularly good script. His captiousness was probably fueled by the problems encountered during the long stint on *Hawaii*, his poor health, his heavy drinking, and difficulties he and Hugo Butler had with a script they had agreed to write for Dino De Laurentiis.

In October 1962, with the *Hawaii* project still uncertain, Ingo Preminger notified Trumbo that De Laurentiis wanted to hire him to write a treatment and a screenplay, adapting Mika Waltari's historical novel *The Dark Angel*.[29] De Laurentiis offered Trumbo $150,000. Trumbo declined, explaining that his other assignments would not allow him the time necessary to travel to Rome and adapt a long novel. Trumbo proposed that the assignment be given to Butler. Ingo passed along the suggestion, but De Laurentiis wanted Trumbo and offered him $175,000. Trumbo still declined. Ingo informed De Laurentiis that both Trumbo and Michael Wilson agreed that Butler was the best writer for this job, but De Laurentiis persisted, this time offering Trumbo $200,000, travel expenses, a villa, and groceries for his family. Trumbo again declined. Finally, De Laurentiis agreed to accept Butler as the screenwriter, but only if Trumbo worked with him. Trumbo had trepidations about such a collaboration, but he knew how much this job meant to Butler, so he accepted the proposition. The contract called for the exclusive services of Butler as screenwriter and the "nonexclusive services" of Dalton Trumbo as "story consultant." Trumbo agreed to work on the treatment with Butler and director Richard Fleischer for a fee of $20,000 and on the first draft for an additional payment of $10,000.[30] Unbeknownst to Trumbo and Ingo, however, Hugo had begun to fall apart. In his wife's words, "He began losing his temper in odd ways, and when we got to Italy [in late 1960], he really became a different guy."[31] He had begun to decline physically and mentally, but it was not until years later that he was diagnosed with arteriosclerotic brain disease.[32]

When Butler, Trumbo, and Fleischer met in Los Angeles to begin work, something untoward occurred between Trumbo and Butler, and the arrangement fell apart. As a result, Trumbo was forced to go to Rome and write both the treatment and the screenplay. He was drinking more heavily than usual, which produced tension between him and Cleo and between him and Christopher. A few months before going to Rome, Christopher had told his father that he wanted to get married, and Trumbo had tried to dissuade him. In a postscript to a letter on that subject, Trumbo wrote: "And so, old boy, you can possibly understand this note, begun in sobriety at 5 p.m., has terminated at 10:05 p.m. in the area of intoxication. For which, I no longer ask forgiveness (which you have always extended to me, and which I hungrily accept), but understanding. Permit me to offer understanding back to you if you ever want it."[33]

Trumbo arrived in Rome in a very discouraged state, and the time he spent there only worsened his frame of mind. As usual, his financial circumstances played a large role in his despondency. He realized he had lost all control over his personal finances, and his liabilities far exceeded his assets. In March 1963 he instructed Frenke to cancel the lease he had negotiated for a house in Beverly Hills, where Trumbo and Cleo were planning to live when he returned from Rome:

> The truth is that I cannot afford to live in Beverly Hills, or in another of the better residential districts in that general area. Indeed, I can scarcely afford to live in the heavily mortgaged house I have just barely been able to maintain in Highland Park. . . . The truth is that I have become discouraged with a life of exactingly strenuous work each year of which pushes me farther into debt. I am discouraged to think that at the age of 58 all I have in this world is a small equity in a heavily mortgaged house, a small equity in a business building, a few shares of stock . . . , and mountainous debts. . . . I have very little chance of ending my career with a dime for myself, and will be lucky even to pay off what I owe. This being the case I will forget all these dreams about millions for "just one good script." Instead, I will live as modestly as I can . . . [and] arrange some kind of regular income.[34]

Trumbo finished the treatment for "The Dark Angel" in May. Seeing that he had a few idle weeks in front of him while De Laurentiis read it, Trumbo asked Ingo to arrange for "an easy polishing job, one or two weeks, to be paid for by a Rolls Royce." It just so happened that Ingo knew of such a project involving director William Wyler and producer Martin Ransohoff (who had produced three movies and the hugely popular television series *The Beverly Hillbillies*). Trumbo's interest was piqued, and he flew to London to meet with Wyler and Ransohoff and, to his surprise, Elizabeth Taylor and Richard Burton. They showed Trumbo the story and script for a movie titled "The Flight of the Sandpiper."[35] Ransohoff had written the original story, and a husband-and-wife team (Louis and Irene Kamp) had developed it into a script. Everyone at the meeting agreed that a completely new script was needed, but Trumbo was contractually committed to "The Dark Angel" project, and Burton was about to begin working on *The Night of the Iguana*. So Trumbo dismissed the idea and returned to Rome, where he spent another eight months on "The Dark Angel."[36] He completed a second draft in February 1963, and De Laurentiis announced that he was satisfied with the results. The movie was never made.

Trumbo's physical health continued to deteriorate, as did his morale. He complained to Frenke that he seemed to be continually ill or injured. He had broken his hand, contracted the flu, suffered from a "low backache" and "a hideously painful sciatic nerve," and sensed "a gradual seepage of energy and ultimately even of interest." In December he caught a cold that would not go away; he ran a low-grade fever and developed scabs on his scalp, canker sores in his mouth, and a swollen tongue. When he finally saw a doctor, he learned that he was suffering from chronic arthritis, bronchitis, and emphysema, but not, as he had been told in 1958, diabetes. According to this doctor's diagnosis, Trumbo's current poor health was partially caused by the diabetic diet he had been following for five years. He was suffering from a lack of sugar and a deficiency of minerals and vitamins. Trumbo resolved to give up cigarettes and return to a normal diet.[37]

While Trumbo was finishing his work on "The Dark Angel," Ransohoff met with Michael Wilson, who had just completed a long screenplay for him, and offered him "The Sandpiper" assignment. Wilson declined, claiming he did not want to write another long screenplay. However, Wilson made a counterproposal: he would write a new treatment, and Trumbo would write the script. Ransohoff and Wilson telephoned Trumbo, who accepted the arrangement. They agreed that

Trumbo and Wilson would share screen credit. Ingo set Trumbo's price at $125,000.[38] During the course of writing the treatment, Wilson and Trumbo conferred regularly by telephone. Wilson then took his completed seventy-three-page treatment to Rome, where he and Trumbo discussed it. (They ate at the same restaurant every night. If Trumbo arrived first, he would arrange for the musicians to play the theme from *Lawrence of Arabia*; if Wilson arrived first, he had them play the theme from *Exodus*.) Trumbo approved Wilson's work and began to write the screenplay.

Meanwhile, Wyler had dropped out of the project and had been replaced by Vincente Minnelli; in addition, Ransohoff had moved his production company from Columbia to MGM. Trumbo finished his first draft in May 1964, just as Minnelli and Ransohoff convinced Burton and Taylor to star in the movie. Elated by that news, Trumbo sent an effusive telegram to Burton: "The parts were written for the two of you and I had become so involved I simply could not imagine the possibility of any other man or woman intervening."[39] According to a variety of sources, Taylor liked the script, but Burton thought it was a potboiler and remarked that "the words were torture. The dialogue was so awful that you'd die a little each day from sheer embarrassment. We only got into the picture because Elizabeth wanted to work with William Wyler and we didn't read the script first."[40] (Burton omitted from his ex post facto tale of woe that he was looking for a part he could mail in, and both stars were handsomely compensated—$1 million for Taylor and $500,000 for Burton.)

When the shooting was completed in August, Trumbo became involved in an unseemly conflict with Wilson over screen credit. It began when Ransohoff reminded Trumbo that Wilson wanted cocredit for the screenplay. (Wilson had not received a screen credit since *Five Fingers* in 1951.) Trumbo initially agreed. But the next day he experienced "strong second thoughts," prompting him to ask Ransohoff to postpone the credit assignment until the movie was ready to be released. Trumbo, however, did not send Wilson a copy of this letter to Ransohoff. Three months later, Trumbo admitted he should have sent Wilson a copy, but, he explained lamely: "You had approached Marty [Ransohoff] rather than me, which indicated perhaps you wanted him as a go-between." Reflecting on the history of their involvement in the project, Trumbo acknowledged that he had suggested a cocredit for Wilson. "I did so," he explained, "out of gratitude for your excellent treatment. I did not, however, believe that any normal arbitration would have awarded you co-credit. I felt, in short, that the screenplay credit was mine to give, and that a certain amount of generosity went into the giving of it." Since their meeting in Rome, however, Trumbo had changed his mind. One reason was that, "as a matter of professional policy," he had not willingly shared a screenplay credit with anyone since 1940. And second, he had done an incredible amount of solo work on the script. Besides, Trumbo rambled on, Wilson's intent from the beginning had been to earn some fast money and a fast screen credit. He had therefore chosen to write a treatment because he knew it required substantially less time and work than a screenplay. Conveniently forgetting how much time and work he put into his own treatments, Trumbo emphasized his own burden: writing the screenplay, revising it, discussing it with Ransohoff and Minnelli, and viewing the rushes. Having weighed all those factors, Trumbo concluded: "I would be unfair to myself if I did not say that I now feel more strongly that under Guild rules I alone have written the screenplay and deserve sole credit for it." That said, Trumbo had no objection to Wilson receiving an "adaptation by" credit.[41]

Wilson denied approaching Ransohoff about the matter, and he characterized Trumbo's decision not to send him a copy of the letter to Ransohoff as "a pity . . . and significant." Wilson then addressed Trumbo's arguments. From the start of the project, Wilson had been certain they were engaged in a collaborative enterprise because Trumbo had told Ransohoff that a cocredit was "the primary condition" for his taking the job. "You were determined," Wilson continued, "you said to both of us, to get my name up there on the screen alongside your own." Wilson then demolished Trumbo's burden-of-labor argument, noting that the "structure, plot and continuity of the screenplay derive entirely from the treatment. Furthermore, roughly forty percent of the dialogue in your first draft was taken *intact* from the treatment." Nor was Wilson impressed with Trumbo's reasons for changing his mind. "Why," he asked, "do you stoop to petty argument in presenting your case? Why does the fact that you spent a few alcoholic conversations with the Burtons in a hotel suite entitle you to knighthood? Why does the fact that you've had to put up with a Minnelli or a Ransohoff erase what I put on paper?" To be sure, Trumbo had contributed ideas to the treatment, but Wilson had done likewise for the screenplay. Wilson acknowledged that Trumbo alone had viewed and commented on the rushes, but that was only because Wilson had not been invited to do so and Trumbo had not insisted on his being there. (The Wilsons had returned to Southern California that summer.) Thus, for Trumbo to imply that Wilson had withdrawn "from this project a long time ago, and left you [Trumbo] to be the sole watch-dog over the screenplay, is a piss-poor argument for solo credit." Wilson had no argument with Trumbo's statement that the usual guild arbitration panel would probably deny him cocredit for the screenplay, but "such speculation . . . is idle," he added, "for it has never crossed my mind to put this matter to arbitration, and I shall never do so. . . . I accept your proposal. The solo credit for the screenplay is yours. The reason for my wordy preface is that I'm trying to clear the air. I feel that you've handled the situation without grace or candor."[42]

Wilson then wrote to Ransohoff: "I move that Dalton have solo credit on the screenplay. Let it be seconded and so ordered." But, Wilson added, he deserved some type of screen credit because he had done more than simply adapt Ransohoff's story. He had taken Ransohoff's original idea and developed it into a "full-blown film story." Wilson proposed that he and Ransohoff share the story credit.[43] Wilson sent a copy of this letter to Trumbo, who began to feel deep remorse about the situation. Telling himself that Wilson had acted out of haste "and perhaps to his own disadvantage" in renouncing the cowriter credit, Trumbo wrote to Ransohoff and again asked him to postpone sending the notice of tentative credits to the Academy.[44]

Trumbo had not changed his mind; he merely wanted more time to convince Wilson of the validity of his position. So Trumbo wrote another letter to Wilson in which he defended most of his previous arguments, splitting hairs in every sentence. But he did end the letter with an apology of sorts, telling Wilson: "I am not proud of the silence which accompanied my second change of mind during the period of the American rewrites. . . . It was affection for you that made me hesitate to speak up. I didn't want to dispute with you, or incur your anger, or hurt you. So I delayed the unpleasant moment in an idiotic hope it would either go away or solve itself by ESP." But on one point Trumbo remained adamant: "We were *not* collaborators."[45]

Wilson terminated this epistolary duel with a killing shot. While seeming to accept Trumbo's main argument about the nature of collaboration, Wilson subtly eviscerated it:

> I was badly mistaken from the start. You state emphatically that we were not *collaborators*. You say that your objective in this project has *never* been to share a screenplay credit with me. You declare that my work was completed when I finished

the treatment, and that you would have vigorously rejected any offer of help on the screenplay.

Your declarations become true the moment you assert them. No collaboration is possible unless both parties are consciously aware of it, and one of us was not. . . .

I did not accuse you of lying or credit stealing. The charge I made was serious enough without resorting to slander. . . . I accused you of lack of candor as a collaborator, and it is now apparent that this collaboration existed only in my imagination. A retraction is called for, and I make it; an apology, too, and I offer it sincerely.

Wilson then explained that his expectation of a cocredit did not arise from any promise made by Trumbo:

[It] arose from the mistaken notion that we were *collaborators*; I therefore tried to write the treatment as if it were a capsule screenplay in narrative form. . . . I can see now that I had insufficient grounds for assuming that we had undertaken a collaboration. I borrowed on affection to construct an imaginary professional rapport that was never spelled out. For me to take for granted that we were *collaborators*, and not to discuss this matter with you long ago, smacks of opportunism or insensitivity or vanity, and I may be guilty of all three. You make the same point in your last letter, when you say that from the earliest beginnings of *Sandpiper* I expected more of you than a thoughtful friend should have wanted to receive.

Wilson concluded: "I don't want the credit anymore. (I once wanted it badly, and I don't like myself for wanting it so much.) Since we were not *collaborators*, I don't deserve it, and I would never feel right about accepting it."[46]

At some point during this exchange, one of them suggested that they submit the question, informally, to a mutually agreeable third party. When Wilson nominated Christopher for the task, Trumbo had a change of heart, writing to Ransohoff: "I have concluded that Mike Wilson should receive co-screenplay credit on *The Sandpiper*. I therefore waive all rights, whether real or asserted, to a sole credit."[47] When Wilson learned what Trumbo had done, he wrote to Ransohoff: "I still feel . . . that Dalton should have sole credit on the screenplay. If none of the other writers protest the tentative credit, there will be no arbitration. In that event, Dalton and I can reach an agreement by ourselves."[48] Wilson sent a copy of this letter to Trumbo, who wrote at the bottom of it: "This sorry business ended with a justly shared credit. Our friendship was perhaps reinvigorated by the knowledge we had both been wrong in certain areas (I probably more greatly wrong)."[49] The Kamps, however, demanded an arbitration. In January 1965 a WGAw arbitration committee awarded Trumbo and Wilson cocredit for the screenplay, Ransohoff story credit, and Irene and Louis Kamp adaptation credit.[50]

But Trumbo had one more battle to fight on this project—with Martin Ransohoff. The producer did not invite Trumbo to watch any of the rough cuts, and when he invited Trumbo to a sneak preview, Trumbo refused to go. This was the first time in more than eight years, Trumbo informed Ransohoff, that he had been invited to a sneak preview of a film he had written without first seeing and discussing the rough cuts. In a sarcastic tone, Trumbo wrote: "Although I salute the exuberance of a talent that of itself can do anything and everything without assist, I have no intention of exposing myself to those ugly little surprises with which your art may inadvertently have booby-trapped my craftsmanship."[51] Ransohoff quickly arranged for Trumbo to view the current rough cut, after which Trumbo sent Ransohoff thirty-eight pages of "notes." In the cover letter, Trumbo wrote:

> Not once in a practice of my craft that extends over three decades have I consciously sought to achieve money or success by catering to the sex fantasies of that essentially onanistic segment of the movie audience that pays to see them. . . . Now I find my name about to appear on a film in which every creative effort—the actors', the director's, the costume designer's, the editor's—appears directed toward the single purpose of transforming a pleasant and rather moving love story into a monotonously repetitive sequence of copulative technicolored postcards. It's as if the makers of the picture had simultaneously, and for the first time in their lives, discovered how to fuck, and simply couldn't wait to notify the outer world that pleasures hitherto unheard of in the relationship between man and woman have at long last been made possible.

Trumbo complained about Minnelli's direction, Elizabeth Taylor's acting, and her wardrobe. He also accused Ransohoff of cutting Richard

Burton's part to the bone and thereby misusing the movie's greatest
asset, whom Trumbo described as "one of the best actors in film, and
probably the greatest romantic star in the eyes of women." Trumbo
readily acknowledged that his "script was never good enough to offer
hope for a great film," but in his opinion, Taylor's performance made
even a first-rate film impossible. However, the "fair film" he had seen in
the projection room could be refashioned into a good film if Ransohoff
followed Trumbo's suggestions.[52]

Ransohoff replied in a Trumbo-like manner: "I have read your glowing epistle and as always, find you erudite, brilliant, flowery, impetuous,
hostile and quite amusing. However, I must also state quite emphati-
cally that you are *full of shit*." Ransohoff suggested that Trumbo search
his office for the script he referred to in his letter, because, Ransohoff
stated: "It appears that we shot the wrong screenplay. *The hip, daring, exciting (even actually prurient) story* that you allude to must still
be sitting on your desk, because I have never received a copy of such a
screenplay." Ransohoff avowed, untruthfully, that Minnelli "did not in
any way tamper with your script—not hardly at all—not even like an
inch." The movie's problems, Ransohoff contended, should be blamed
on him and Trumbo. They had failed to find an effective way to dramatize the story and justify the behavior of Burton's character in human
and understandable terms.[53] It should be noted that Ransohoff took
Trumbo's comments seriously and made several changes in the movie.
After viewing the new cut, Trumbo declared that the main defects had
been cured, but he submitted six more pages of small changes that,
he assured Ransohoff, would "add a certain polish, a certain elegance
which is never harmful to a film."[54]

Nothing could have improved the quality of this movie; its weaknesses were inherent in the original, trite story of temptation, sin, regret,
and repentance. None of those who contributed to the dialogue had the
faintest idea how a post-Beat, pre-hippie woman and a horny Episcopa-
lian minister-headmaster thought or spoke. The latter's motivation to
commit adultery is not probed. But the biggest problem was the casting of Taylor and Burton. In the original story, the female protagonist
was described as a woman of scant means of support, with "uncoiffed
hair" and a "ruddy" complexion; she lived in a cabin in Big Sur that
"appeared to be the work of patient, impoverished and determined
amateurs." The male protagonist was "vigorous, muscular, crew-cut."[55]

The critics were justifiably harsh. Philip K. Scheuer wrote that
the work of Trumbo, Wilson, and Minnelli was "old timey," and the

script had some good and some clichéd dialogue.[56] Eleanor Perry wrote: "Any publisher could comb through their script and come up with a best-selling dictionary of clichés."[57] Hollis Alpert termed the script a "mass of windy platitudes and stale stereotypes."[58] On the plus side, the movie fared well at the box office, and composers Johnny Mandel and Paul Francis Webster earned Academy Awards and Grammies for best original song ("The Shadow of Your Smile") and best original score, respectively.

Robert Jennings, who had moved from *Time* to *Esquire*, informed Trumbo that the movie "made Elizabeth . . . 'ill' and Richard claims not to have seen it at all." Trumbo replied: "The pleasantest news in your letter is that seeing *Sandpiper* made Elizabeth ill; the wildest falsehood Richard's claim he didn't see the film (he sat through the whole thing in Paris)."[59] (And Taylor, after seeing *The Sandpiper* in London, noted, "It is not quite as bad as I thought."[60]) When Jennings asked Trumbo if he would allow the magazine to publish his notes about *The Sandpiper*, Trumbo declined. Although Trumbo blamed Ransohoff for his "gutlessness as a producer which resulted in that vomitous mess," he would not undercut him in public: "I ate his bread, and must, in all decency, wait till the feast is over and the film's first-run terminated, before regurgitating it so publicly." Trumbo did not want to give the impression that he was trying to escape the onus of bad reviews; nor did he wish to "align" himself "with that squalid company of self-serving scroungers who have not hesitated to balloon a chance acquaintanceship with the Burtons into a publicity bonanza for themselves."[61]

Once the movie's first run ended, Trumbo freely condemned it. In an undated note, probably from sometime in late 1965, he wrote: "I find the film triumphantly vulgar, incorrigibly dishonest, and faintly loathsome."[62] In another note he described Burton's performance as "the triumph of integrity over intelligence" and Taylor's as falling "midway between Goldilocks and Madame La Farge."[63] Several years later he referred to the movie as "one of the most frightful cinematic abortions of recent history," and he placed most of the blame on Minnelli for caving in to the demands of Taylor and Burton.[64] He did not absolve himself of all blame. At one point he said to an interviewer: "Christ! Do I hate that movie. Let's just start by saying the script *was* lousy, though I'm not sure it was *that* bad."[65] The experience also made him leery of love stories. Thus, when Paul Gregory of Paramount sent him a script about a romance and asked him to revise it, Trumbo declined: "The truth is, as the reviews on *Sandpiper* may convince you, that I have had a bellyful of adulterous love stories, and the mere thought of doing another sends waves of nausea through this aging frame. I just couldn't face up to it, and I'm probably off the genre for the rest of my life."[66]

Trumbo's unseemly tussle with Wilson over *The Sandpiper* writing credit must be put into context. First of all, he hated shared screenplay credits. Second, as a result of his previous battle with the guild over the *Hawaii* credit, he became temporarily blinded by the percentage formulas used by the guild's arbitration committees and focused only on the words in the script he had written, failing to consider Wilson's treatment and their extended discussions. Trumbo was not, as a rule, credit-hungry. He readily relinquished claims to material that had been thoroughly rewritten by others, and he did not seek credit for all his work, especially the hurriedly produced scripts written during his early years on the blacklist. For example, at the end of 1963 Trumbo read an article in *Weekly Variety* reporting that he was going to receive cocredit for a movie titled *The Cavern*, and he wrote to Ingo Preminger to explain why he did not want it: "Several years ago, in the depths of the Black List, a man named Petchnikoff (I think) [Michael Meshekoff], who had been associated with Jack Webb's original television series [*Dragnet*], together with a man named Edgar Ulmer, signed me to do a script on a subject which was called 'The Cavern.'" For $5,000, and using a pseudonym he no longer remembered, Trumbo had dashed off a script that was probably not very good; the contract had obliged the producers to use a pseudonym for the writer, and they had not asked permission to use his name. Trumbo wanted the filmmakers, Edgar Ulmer and Franco Reggiani, to remove his name from the credits, all advertising, and all publicity.[67] Preminger wrote the appropriate letters, and the filmmakers acceded to his request.[68]

A few years later, Trumbo learned that the rights of another of his black-market scripts, "Something for Nothing," had been sold by Samuel Bischoff to Allied Artists. Trumbo had signed a release of his rights (for a $1 payment) and had added a paragraph of his own composition stating that his name could not be used on the released film. Trumbo subsequently read in the trade newspapers that Bischoff's production company was going to make the movie from Dalton Trumbo's script.[69] Trumbo instructed Finn to write to Bischoff, "suggesting . . . that he shouldn't do it." Finn went a little further, telling Bischoff that the use of Trumbo's name would constitute a moral breach of confidence as well as a breach of contract. Bischoff replied: "We have every intention, if and when we produce this picture, to use the name of Dalton Trumbo as the author of the screen play. If you will please note the copy of the assignment, you will note that Dalton Trumbo personally stapled on a condition which he initiated. But, this condition was never discussed by Dalton Trumbo with me, nor did I ever initial it." Bischoff proceeded to make a convincing moral case for his right to use Trumbo's name:

> 1. At that particular time, Mr. Trumbo was considered and publicized throughout America as a communist. 2. He was one of the so-called "unholy ten" and was indicted as such by the Federal Government. 3. He was black-listed in the motion picture industry along with the other nine members of that group. Mr. Trumbo could not get a job and when I hired him to write a screenplay, I was breaching that so-called black-list. I took a great gamble when I hired Mr. Trumbo through his agent, the late Arthur Landau. Nothing was discussed at our first meeting about a pseudonym. We naturally could not put Mr. Trumbo's name on the screen for the obvious above-mentioned reasons. The pseudonym was not an established thing with Mr. Trumbo prior to his indictment as a communist. We merely used it as a cover-up so that he could write the script to get money to feed himself and his family, which he needed badly at that time . . . otherwise he would not have done the script for that kind of money. The morals in this situation seems [*sic*] to me to be on the other foot. The fact that we gave him the opportunity to earn this money should have made him grateful to us for the rest of his life. The chance that I took for him was tremendous, as I could have been black-listed as well as he, by doing just what I did.[70]

But this movie, like so many other projects hatched on the black market, was never made.

22

The Fixer and the Laurel Award

I look back on three decades through which good friends stood together, moved forward a little, dreamed that the world could be better and tried to make it so, tasted the joy of small victories, wounded each other, made mistakes, suffered much injury and stood silent in the chamber of liars.

—Dalton Trumbo

When Trumbo returned from Rome, he and Cleo moved to a house on St. Ives Drive, a very narrow street off Sunset Plaza, in West Hollywood. The exterior of the house, as seen from the street, looked plain. "It is hard to get a grip on it from the outside," Mitzi said, "but it went down three stories, and my father took the lowest floor for his office—a big room, a bathroom, a sauna (never used) and a room for a secretary and his enormous copy machine." Nikola recalled that Trumbo "never went to the stationery store, the hardware store, etc. He almost never drove. Cleo or I ran his errands, and, if he had to go out, Cleo did the driving."

Trumbo was starting to feel his age. He told Robert Jennings: "For myself, I have been noticing lately that I sneak small naps in the afternoon. It's just a little more difficult to summon the energy to write now than it was five years ago. Wine goes to my head more quickly than it used to. I walk forward instead of running, and although there is much life in me, much has also gone."[1]

Comedian Steve Martin has provided us with a whimsical view of the sixty-one-year-old Trumbo. Martin and Mitzi began dating in the spring of 1967, and he was a regular visitor to the Trumbo house. In his memoir, Martin notes: "My first glimpse of Dalton Trumbo revealed an engrossed intellect—not finessing his latest screenplay but sorting the seeds and stems from a brick of pot. 'Pop smokes marijuana,' Mitzi explained, 'with the wishful hope of cutting down on his drinking. . . . Pop doesn't know how to smoke pot. He thinks you smoke it like a cigar, and he never gets high.'" Martin remembered looking down from a balcony in the house and seeing Trumbo "walking laps around the perimeter of the pool. He held a small counter in one hand and clicked it every time he passed the diving board. These health walks were compromised by the cigarette he constantly held in one hand."[2]

Trumbo talked about pot smoking in his unpublished *Playboy* interview:

> I love to drink, and I found that my two double scotches can quickly double to four, and it's too much for me at my age, so I thought I'd try grass. So, I bought a kilo and began to smoke at six instead of drinking. I didn't get a helluva lot out of it, so I would smoke more and more, six, eight, ten joints. . . . [T]hen I would lace it with hash because I didn't have to smoke so much, but there's something about the effect of it I don't like, because unlike drinking after dinner, even people who are drinking can keep to the subject, even if they're sharp and argumentative about it, but everything recedes, and even under pot, I wanted to stay on the subject and no one else would.[3]

One other interesting aspect of Trumbo's life in these years was his fondness for and patience with wounded birds. When the family had lived in Highland Park, the cats would often bring home wounded birds, which Trumbo always tried to save. Before leaving for Rome, he had given away his African gray parrot, but at the St. Ives house he began to care for the wounded birds Mitzi occasionally found in the yard. She would put them in a shoebox and bring them to his office. He would grumble that there was nothing to be done, but then he would always try to do something. "He made nests of torn newspaper and fed them his own concoction of egg yolk, bread crumbs, and water, inserting the food in their tiny beaks with an eyedropper. Most died of shock but occasionally one survived and was released. It seemed that there was always a wild bird flying around in his office, landing on his shoulder, and pecking at his ear." (And, of course, there were bird droppings everywhere.) When he was ready to release a mockingbird that was a particular favorite of his, he was concerned that an owl might grab it. "So," Mitzi recalled, "he erected several large spotlights outside to

Trumbo with mockingbird, 1965. Photograph by Cleo Trumbo.

shine into the trees all night, and the bird cage was put outside with the door open. It took a couple of weeks for the bird to leave the cage and fly away."

Though Trumbo worked on many projects during the late 1960s, he had only one major screen credit. According to Mitzi:

> My father had become a notorious procrastinator when it came to writing. He was always thinking about the project at hand, but would spend weeks and often months without writing a single word. He would find distractions. One summer he spray-painted forty wooden file boxes all different colors to organize them, leaving spray marks all around the pool and diving board in the backyard. Mostly he would read. He ordered books by phone from a local bookstore, and bundles of hardcover books would arrive at the house—research for projects, contemporary political commentary, books that he had read about in the *New York Review of Books*.
>
> He was always under the pressure of deadlines, and he regularly missed them. Often he didn't start writing an assignment until the weekend before it was due, and he would then have

his secretary, or me, or my sister, typing in shifts until it was done. He had an IBM dictabelt machine, and we would listen and type up his newest scenes as he would hand us each a plastic dictabelt. He would then lay the typed scenes end to end on the carpet in his office, often stretching across the entire floor, then cut them into pieces with scissors. When a scene was organized, he would scotch tape the parts together. Then he would rearrange the scenes and cut them into the appropriate format and send them to be mimeographed.

His method of writing had changed. He now used a storyboard to keep track of the continuity of the script, repositioning or replacing scenes as the script progressed. It was about ten feet long and mounted on a wall behind his desk. Nikola did a lot of the transcribing and retyping for her father: "He always typed a first draft, and then he made corrections with a pen or pencil and sent the corrected pages to me to retype. Since I worked in another room, he would call me (either by intercom or buzzer) when he had more pages for me." Mitzi remembered that "he often talked to himself," claiming that "was the only way to be sure of getting an intelligent answer."

Three major projects collapsed during those years. Two of them, "Montezuma" and "Will Adams," had been in the works since the late 1950s, and both were supposed to be directed by John Huston. Eddie Lewis and Kirk Douglas could not get a studio to finance the "Montezuma" project, and Huston did not like Trumbo's final draft of the "Will Adams" script.[4] The third project was slated to be the first of three scripts for MGM—Kathleen Winsor's *Wanderers Eastward, Wanderers West*, an epic novel about the discovery of gold, silver, and copper in the West and the exploitation by Wall Street speculators. It was a project that appealed to Trumbo, a self-identified westerner who had written many articles criticizing eastern encroachment on western culture. He and Winsor met shortly after she sold the rights to MGM. As Trumbo was writing the script, he kept Winsor apprised of what he was doing, and their correspondence clearly reveals Trumbo's process of adaptation. It was necessary, he explained to Winsor, "to wield my knife on the corpus of your novel if I am to fulfill my obligation to Metro, the novel, and, ultimately, to you." He told her he was encountering the same ratio of novel length to movie time as he had with the *Hawaii* project:

Trumbo sketched by John Huston, 1965. Courtesy of Trumbo family.

I shall be obliged to: 1. Cut 93% of your novel's total wordage, and tell the story with the remaining 7%. 2. Cut approximately 88% of the novel's direct-quote dialogue, . . . 88% of your dialogue by volume, and condense, condense, condense the background, characters, events, and scenes. The novel's dialogue is not rewritten because it is bad (it may very often be better), but because it cannot be cut or condensed to the necessary length and still make sense. Hence the screenwriter must compensate for the cut and condensation by capturing the essence of the dialogue in six or seven rewritten speeches. It's the only way. If I preserve its *essence* I have preserved its truth, and in doing so shall have been more faithful to the novel and to you than had I sought, scene by scene, to preserve its physical reality.

Anyhow, whether you hate or merely despise the way I am manhandling your child, please understand that I do it gently and with the kindest intention. . . . Yet the instant I write these words I realize what a poor guarantee they are. How many times have I written something I thought good and found it aroused almost universal detestation? More times than I like to remember. How many times have I written something I thought was bad and found it hailed as excellent? Never.[5]

Winsor replied that Trumbo's letter "leaves me wondering, even more than before, why anyone would try to make a motion picture of so long and intricately knotted a book, when it would be so much easier just to write one off the cuff." She admitted that she had wanted to write the script herself, but the producer had convinced her to leave it to the experts. She then listed those parts of the book she hoped Trumbo would retain.[6]

Trumbo agreed with some of her suggestions and disagreed with others. He concluded by saying:

You seem to be asking me "just for once not to make a trashy film of your novel. . . . " I realize—or at least I hope—that you did not mean precisely this, but it is incontestably what you say. Since neither Christopher Morley [*Kitty Foyle*], Leon Uris [*Exodus*] nor Jim Michener [*Hawaii*] made such a suggestion when I adapted the biggest sellers they ever wrote, I am somewhat startled that you should. Not that you haven't the right to, only that I doubt you have the reason. . . . I suspect the problem might be that you regret having disposed of the film rights to *Wanderers* as you did.

Given her feelings, he suggested that Winsor might want to return the money the studio had paid her and regain the rights to her book. If she chose to do that, he, in turn, would either refund what MGM had already paid him for the adaptation or ask the studio to apply it as a credit against some other script.[7]

Winsor assured Trumbo that she had not meant to appear tactless, and nothing she said about movies or Hollywood applied to him. After making a few more suggestions, she announced her intention to leave him free to adapt her novel as he saw fit. "I wrote a novel. You will write a screen-play."[8] Trumbo, in turn, assured her that she had not been tactless; "it was simply a frank expression of your thoughts, hopes and fears about a project you have every right to comment on. The job goes slowly, because these big, many-charactered novels are absolute brutes to organize." He enclosed a copy of a letter from James Michener, congratulating Trumbo on his adaptation of *Hawaii*.[9] As it turned out, Trumbo did not complete the *Wanderers* adaptation, and he had to refund some of the money MGM had paid him.

That same year, Frenke sent him Terry Southern's novel and screenplay for *Candy*. Trumbo strongly disliked both, and he expressed his antipathy to Frenke:

> If ever I need money so urgently that I'm tempted to put a thing like *Candy* on the screen, I hope Almighty God will give me the strength to open an honest whorehouse instead, and staff it with my wife and daughters. . . . I have wasted three hours of my life reading [the novel and screenplay]. . . . That I myself am not a pornographer, as I tried to explain to you when I twice rejected *The Carpetbaggers*, does not mean that I hate pornography, for often I rather enjoy it. But it must be good pornography, which is to say it must contain some element of art. Without art, without wit, without a point, pornography becomes what the screenplay of *Candy* actually is—a dull, clottish attempt at cock-teasing.[10]

Trumbo spent most of 1967 adapting Bernard Malamud's prize-winning novel *The Fixer* for Eddie Lewis and John Frankenheimer. The two men had formed their own production company and had been working on an adaptation of Malamud's earlier novel, *The Assistant*, but they altered their plans when Malamud sent them the proofs of *The Fixer*—a tale of injustice that they found more appealing. Malamud's story was based on the 1911 case of Mendel Beilis, a Russian Jew charged with committing blood libel (killing a gentile boy and using his blood for a religious ritual). Malamud's protagonist, Yakov Bok, is depicted as "a man (not necessarily a moral man) who is arrested for a crime he didn't commit and spends years in prison." The "idea of freedom" grows in the mind of this man, who is "subjected to a gross injustice."[11] Lewis and Frankenheimer contracted with Trumbo to adapt the novel, who read it as "the story of an uncommitted man who learns that life itself is a commitment; that it is better to risk disgrace or even death than to involve oneself and others in the terrible consequences of a state-demanded lie. I can think of no more important theme for a world in which governments and ideologies, without exception, glorify the expedient lie as passionately as they fear the inconvenient truth."[12]

It was perhaps the most difficult adaptation Trumbo had undertaken. Length was not the problem: *The Fixer* was about one-third the size of *Hawaii* and *Wanderers*. Rather, the bulk of Malamud's novel takes place inside the mind of Yakov Bok, and Malamud's language was not easily translatable into film dialogue. (In addition, as Malamud's daughter later wrote: "It is a hard book to read, demanding an almost masochistic attention from the reader."[13]) Trumbo decided the screenplay needed to "open" the novel and provide a more historically detailed account of what was happening outside Bok's prison cell (and his mind). He also decided to treat Bok's numerous fantasies, dreams, flashbacks, and hallucinations as realistically as the rest of the story, and he urged Lewis and Frankenheimer to avoid using any camera tricks in the movie. Last, Trumbo reworked the ending to give more emphatic meaning to Bok's suffering.[14]

As he was nearing completion of the first draft, Trumbo asked Malamud to read it. "I want very much," Trumbo said, "for the film which evolves from it to be worthy of the novel."[15] Malamud agreed, and Trumbo sent him the script in mid-March, noting: "It's always a delicate business for one man to adapt another's work to a different medium, and much blood has been spilled because of it. I risk spilling a little more because I am certain that the script and film will be improved by your comments."[16]

Malamud assured Trumbo that no blood would be spilled, as he understood "the enormous difficulty" of Trumbo's task. Malamud thought the first part of the script was "good enough," but the second part, especially the ending, disappointed him. Trumbo had, in Malamud's opinion, failed "to deal adequately with the spiritual quality of the book . . . Yakov's anguish, growth, change," and he recommended that Trumbo "steep" himself in the book, "mine the truth of it," and use more of the book's dialogue.[17] Trumbo replied at length, devoting four pages to Malamud's letter and eight pages to his comments on the script. In terms of Malamud's advice about mining, Trumbo wrote: "I assure you that by the time I've finished with this job, I'll have mined all the truth of it that's filmable." As for using Malamud's dialogue, Trumbo explained the difficulty of doing so: "Sometimes it is not dramatic. . . . Sometimes a beautifully dramatic speech occurs in a context from which it cannot be abstracted without using too much of what precedes and follows it."[18]

Malamud, in his reply, pleaded with Trumbo not to add scenes showing what was happening outside the prison. To do so, Malamud insisted, "will destroy the truth of Yakov's [solitary] experience," because he "didn't know what was going on on the outside." Malamud also expressed his concern that Trumbo had injected too much of what he had learned about the real Mendel Beilis. This "documentary realism," Malamud complained, was destroying the integrity of Bok's novelistic experience. "Please," he implored, "translate my *fiction* to the screen. . . . Please simplify, avoid the temptation to be grandiose."[19]

When Trumbo offered to send him a revised draft in May, Malamud declined. But one year later, after the shoot was completed, Trumbo again reached out to Malamud. Perhaps fearing that Malamud did not understand the difference between a novel and a screenplay based on that novel, Trumbo tried to explain the process of adaptation:

I'm sorry you weren't able to read the second and third drafts, which generally reveal the process of changing a novel into a film much more clearly than the first. The problem is illustrated by your request that I "translate" your fiction to the screen. Unhappily that cannot be done. The art of fiction is narrative; the art of film is dramatic. It follows that my task was not to transcribe your fiction to the screen, but to transform it into something altogether different—into a drama, into a motion picture.

The difference is even better illustrated in the last paragraph of your first letter: "you ought to steep yourself in the book so that you can mine the truth of it." The only metal I know of that can be mined by the process of steeping is sulphur; the gold which I was determined to mine from the ore in your book requires smashing, sluicing, refining, and God knows what else. I would have been untrue to the book had I not fulfilled that requirement. . . .

I'm afraid this business of making the film "worthy of the novel" has been somewhat overdone by us and perhaps misunderstood by you. [That phrase] was a conventional literary courtesy rather than a vocational vow. The truth is, that my object from the outset was to make the film better than the novel rather than merely worthy of it. . . . The point is that a serious man—and I *am* serious—undertakes such a task . . . to improve on his source material rather than to equal it. Otherwise, why bother? . . .

Cleo, Trumbo, and Eddie Lewis, Budapest, 1967. Courtesy of Trumbo family.

Trumbo walking his poodle, Budapest, 1967. Photograph by Cleo Trumbo.

Despite what I have been compelled to do to your lovely book, I have tried to the very best of my admittedly small ability to preserve its essence, its spirit, its purpose.[20]

Trumbo ended up writing five drafts. MGM executives decided that his third draft (154 pages) was too long and would be too costly to film, so they demanded that he eliminate and shorten several scenes.[21] The fourth draft, completed in August 1967, was 120 pages long. Lewis and Frankenheimer, fearing that the radical cuts had created continuity problems that would not be evident until principal photography began, asked Trumbo to come to Hungary to be available for more rewriting. Trumbo, Cleo, Mitzi, and their miniature poodle arrived in Budapest in October and stayed four months. Mitzi remembered how amusing it was to watch Trumbo "walking the poodle through the snowy streets of Budapest. Somehow, he never looked right with a little poodle on a leash." Trumbo and Frankenheimer met almost every day, and Trumbo rewrote every night. By December, the script had grown to 173 pages.

Trumbo left Hungary before shooting was completed. When he was shown a rough cut of the film in March, he expressed his disappointment with certain elements in a long, detailed letter to Frankenheimer. According to the director's reading of the letter, Trumbo turned on him and wrote "one of the most scathing letters I [have ever] received, telling me all the things that were wrong with the movie that were obvious."[22] In fact, Trumbo wrote a three-page cover letter and a thirty-page inventory of changes he hoped would be made. The letter and the inventory were far from "scathing." Unlike the *Sandpiper* letter, it contained no polemical statements or personal attacks. Almost all the changes Trumbo listed were qualified by "I think" or "I suggest." When he did use "strong" language, he did so because: "I love THE FIXER as deeply as you do and wish as passionately as you for it to represent the best that is in all of us." Trumbo's main complaint was Frankenheimer's "dénouement," which departed from both the novel and the script and was, in Trumbo's opinion, "a shocking disappointment and betrayal of the entire film." In sum, Frankenheimer had eliminated Trumbo's ending that appeared in every draft of the screenplay—the huge procession of Russian soldiers and officials accompanying Yakov from the jail to the courthouse. Indeed, Trumbo had devoted seven detailed pages to that ending, for the purpose of contrasting "the confrontation of one lone, tormented, stubborn, honest man with all the panoply and power and majesty of the Russian Empire—a confrontation which, in the novel as in the script, is *immensely* visual." Without that immensely visual scene, there was no "dénouement," by which Trumbo meant the movie lacked "that essential moment of unknotting, of disclosure, of discovery—that urgent and imperative moment in which good and evil, man and fate, stand fully revealed in their eternal opposition—that ultimate moment of recognition in which the protagonist at last perceives the truth of his own condition and the audience, through him, perceives the truth of the drama." Trumbo strongly urged Frankenheimer to reshoot the ending.[23]

Lewis and Frankenheimer agreed with many of Trumbo's suggestions. Trumbo and Frankenheimer spent the spring and summer working on a new ending, and Frankenheimer returned to Hungary for one week to shoot it. Trumbo wrote to Lewis: "Did the hours I spent and the 51 pages I have contributed to *The Fixer* since my return from Budapest bring results that pleased you? . . . If not . . . I feel that I must return the money you paid for the work [$25,000]."[24] A few days later Trumbo wrote to Lewis again, complaining about the ads in the trade papers: they announced the Frankenheimer-Lewis production of Bernard Malamud's *The Fixer* but omitted the name of the screenwriter.[25]

After the retakes were shot and the move was reedited, MGM executives decided it was too long. In response, Frankenheimer and Lewis removed most of the early flashback scenes depicting Bok in happier circumstances. After seeing the new cut, Trumbo wrote to Frankenheimer, "You and Eddie have completely solved the problem of length. We can now look at the film free from that pre-occupation with length which thus far has overshadowed all other considerations."[26] But a few months later Trumbo expressed second thoughts, telling an interviewer that the final cut had unbalanced the movie. Those scenes of Yakov in happier circumstances, Trumbo said, might have provided some relief for the audience. Instead, the movie became "two hours of unremitting cruelty."[27] He told another interviewer that the movie had been edited "for straight torment."[28]

Frankenheimer told an interviewer in 1995 that *The Fixer* is "a severely compromised picture." He and Trumbo had "made a movie that was much too long, and we had to cut the whole first part of the movie. . . . We had beautiful scenes that all went in the cutting." Frankenheimer blamed the cuts on Lewis and regretted that he had not resisted making them. Echoing Trumbo, he said *The Fixer* was "so unrelenting" that he had no desire to see it again.[29] But three years later, Frankenheimer told another interviewer: "I feel better about *The Fixer* than anything I've ever done in my life. . . . I think Dalton Trumbo's screenplay is a masterpiece. If I'd messed up that masterpiece, I should have been shot, it is such a beautiful work. . . . [T]here is hardly a single scene that does not please me. . . . *The Fixer* is one of the few films which I have never compromised on."[30]

The film did not do well at the box office, and reviews were mixed. Charles Champlin called Trumbo's script "passionate and often eloquent,"[31] but Renata Adler heaped scorn on it. She called the script trivial and said that Trumbo had regressed to using "the old sentimental Hollywood formula." She failed to identify which formula she meant; nor did she explain how Trumbo had demeaned and vulgarized the "oppression, suffering, and inexplicably secular courage" shown by

Yakov Bok. Continuing her polemical assault, Adler complained that Trumbo's use of "hack-plot fiction approximations of eloquence" proved that Malamud was "an infinitely better writer than Dalton Trumbo." Then, committing a momentous non sequitur and misstatement of fact, Adler declared that "Trumbo's experience of McCarthyite persecution has not made him equal to a subject as grand as this." By referring to Bok as an innocent man "who seems to have drawn his courage mostly from the injustice done to him," she implied that Trumbo was neither innocent nor courageous.[32]

Justifiably angered by Adler's remarks, Trumbo wrote directly to her: "The statement [about Bok's innocence] contains one quite unnecessary error of fact. Yakov was, indeed, an innocent man. I am a guilty one who never proclaimed his innocence, called his experience 'persecution' or asserted that his misadventures made him equal to a subject as grand as 'The Fixer' or any other." With regard to her statement that Bernard Malamud "is an infinitely better writer than Dalton Trumbo," Trumbo tut-tutted her: "Oh come now, Miss Adler, we're different things. I'm an infinitely better screenwriter than Malamud, and he is an infinitely better novelist than I." Then he offered her some free advice about her writing style: "watch the cloudy sentences, use a few more periods, and stick to the facts."[33]

A contemporary reading of the script reveals it to be a very good adaptation of *The Fixer*. Perhaps Trumbo stuck too closely to Malamud's narrative, but he succeeded in his overall goal—to replicate onscreen the novelist's meta-statement about the nature of injustice and the meaning of freedom. The studio executives, by demanding major cuts in the film, were responsible for its problems.

A few months before *The Fixer* came out, Lewis and Frankenheimer asked Trumbo to adapt Joseph Kessel's *The Horsemen*, a novel set in Afghanistan. They agreed to pay him $125,000 for the completed script and another $125,000 in ten equal installments.[34] Kessel wrote to Lewis: "I am delighted to learn that Dalton Trumbo is going to make the adaptation of my novel. I consider him to be in the first rank of screenwriters."[35] It is clear from a set of conference notes that the novel's protagonist (Uraz) appealed to Trumbo because he was a person who challenged the code of behavior by which he had been raised.[36] But for reasons that are not clear, Trumbo either misinterpreted or misread the book's dénouement. In Kessler's novel, Uraz, like Mark Twain's Huck Finn, goes through a learning experience and realizes at the end that the social and cultural values of his society are inhuman. Uraz, like Huck, decides to head for the frontier, where he can live according to his own values. Trumbo, however, characterized Uraz as a self-destructive person who learns nothing from his mishaps. Once Trumbo completed the first draft, Lewis questioned his depiction of Uraz's motivations and suggested a better way to dramatize them.[37] After reading the script, Christopher also commented to his father that it failed to show Uraz's motivations.[38] Frankenheimer, in contrast, called Trumbo's script "perceptive" and "damned good." However, *The Horseman* suffered the same fate as *The Fixer*. Studio executives demanded that the rough cut be reduced from slightly over three hours to two hours, and according to Frankenheimer, they had to "totally restructure it."[39]

When the film was released in June 1973, it was not well received by the critics, and Trumbo's script was singled out as the culprit. The *Daily Variety* reviewer called it a "cliché script" filled with "mock-poetic dialog."[40] Kevin Thomas congratulated Frankenheimer for absolving the movie from "some of the more purple passages" of the script.[41] And the review in the *Hollywood Reporter* stated that the script "vacillates between flat banalities and inflated, flowery passages of 'deep' dialogue that could bring a blush to the face of even the hairiest camel."[42]

During these years, Trumbo paid fitful attention to the publication of a collection of his letters. He had mixed feelings about exposing the wide variety of moods the letters expressed. The anthology was the brainchild of Helen Manfull, an archivist at the Wisconsin Center for Film and Theater Research who was assigned to process the Trumbo papers. She began reading them, took some home at night, and became convinced that they told a wonderful story—"the story of what a blacklist can do to a man's career." She wrote to Trumbo and asked for permission to edit the letters. He immediately agreed.[43] In his preface to the published collection, Trumbo wrote:

> It didn't take much blocking or tackling to bring me around. I was, after all, a writer, or at least I call myself one, and while writers dearly love to work, they stand with parsons and painters and philosophers in loving just as dearly to be paid for it. What were all those letters entombed in Madison, Wisconsin, but the accumulated residue of past work thrown into the pot for nothing and by now almost forgotten? The idea of being paid for them so many years later in real money . . . was too

staggering for a mere journeyman-outsider to resist. Instant autobiography, so to speak. And on the cheap.[44]

In that nondigital age, Manfull spent hundreds of hours at the typewriter, copying the letters she had selected. When she completed the task in 1966, Trumbo sent her a glowing response; then two years passed without a word from him. She finally wrote him a reproving letter in April 1968. In his response, Trumbo confessed that after reading the manuscript, comprising "eleven pounds of ancient, annotated correspondence," he had second thoughts about publishing it:

Guided by greed, I had actually wanted to view this austere, wart-hummocked landscape in the exact center of which, I'd been told, at precisely five o'clock in the afternoon, every pilgrim confronts at last his moment of truth. Surely these pages, obsessed with money, filled with endlessly reiterated objects, lost clauses, metaphors not merely mixed but macerated, trivial grievances, contradictions, false prophesies, unkept resolutions, high purposes brought low and low ones here and there brought high—surely these letters weren't the me I know so well and remembered so differently. For two years I pretended I hadn't yet found time to read them through to the end.[45]

It took another two years for Trumbo to send the final edits and annotations to her.[46]

When the collection, now titled *Additional Dialogue*, appeared in print in 1970, it was reviewed widely and well. Eric F. Goldman wrote: "Trumbo is a man of a dozen sides, principled and petty, funny and oracular, cantankerous, charming, wily, self-righteous and mocking of himself and everything around him."[47] Philip French thought the Trumbo that emerged from the letters was "a generous, honest, amusing man, a firm friend, a trustworthy employee, an admirable husband, a lovably understanding father, as modest in times of good fortune as he is cheerful and resilient in adversity."[48] Richard Schickel, who was not a fan of the Hollywood Ten, wrote that Trumbo "is surely one of the most engaging characters ever nurtured by the industry. . . . Trumbo is a tremendously shrewd, though entirely casual, sociologist, and his style—rich and funny—is an accurate measure of the man."[49] And Emile Capouya penned an appreciation of Trumbo's unique brand of radicalism, praising him as a person who gives "vigorous expression to

what one would have thought was the common American ethic, a sort
of cranky and pugnacious independent, at its worst naively provincial,
at its best—as before Congressional committees—manly in its refusal
to blubber before our elected bullies." He characterized Trumbo's type
of radicalism as one that displayed "a certain charity and mannerliness,
and a decent formality all the more striking in a choleric personality."[50]

The harshest criticism came from his former fellow indictee Lester
Cole, who was angered by the selection of letters printed in *Esquire*. In
reference to Trumbo's description of his arrest for public urination (see
chapter 11), Cole wrote: "Whatever the merits of your defense of the
time you wet the curb outside of Hunter's house, your letter leaves little
doubt about your compulsion toward indecent exposure. To piss in public on the legs of old friends and comrades certainly suggests the need
for some manner of restraint." Trumbo replied: "As for all that piss you
seem to have discovered on your legs, I'm afraid you're so far out of
local range that it simply can't be mine. The problem (a messy but not
uncommon one in men of our years) is best solved, I'm told, by having
oneself measured for a catheter."[51] Lardner, however, thought the letters
showed Trumbo's many sides: "wise, funny, greedy, generous, vain, biting, solicitous, sentimental, devious, petty, altruistic, superbly rational,
prophetic, shortsighted and indefatigable"[52]

Trumbo continued his close observation of political events and movements. He spent most of 1965 writing a long article for the centennial
edition of the *Nation*. It was, in effect, the last in his series of political
pamphlets criticizing the domestic cold war. He researched it extensively and rewrote it multiple times. He began with a summary of the
Hollywood Ten's battle against the Committee on Un-American Activities, followed by a discussion of those who had deserted them in that
struggle. As the Ten had predicted, their political isolation and imprisonment had given the committee's hunt for "Communists" in the United
States free rein, allowing it to rage "at blood heat, roving wherever its
members wished, summoning whomever it pleased, demanding answers
to questions never before heard in chambers that displayed the American flag . . . in every area of American life that dealt with ideas and
their dissemination." This hunt had transformed the Cold War United
States into a closed society and altered its political dynamic. Anti-
Communists had created and then exploited a hysteria about the
"threat" of communism, thereby making this country's politics "ritualistic, tribal, propitiatory and sometimes magical; they had created a

new language of incantation," and their magic word—*Communist*—polluted "the fount of honor" at its source. That incantatory word, which packed "the killing power of a bullet," had transformed the once "simple act of staying out of trouble" into a complex exercise requiring "more guile than most men have on call." This "whole degrading process of politics-as-magic and incantation-as-intellect," Trumbo predicted, "will continue until that terrible word is wrested from sorcerers and robbed of its necromaneous power to drive men mad."

Trumbo correctly noted that the whole anti-Communist crusade had been and remained a fraud: "The American Communist Party . . . posed about as grave a threat of revolution as the Ancient and Honorable Order of Nobles of the Mystic Shrine, which out-manned it ten to one and had a lot more fun." And the organized Right knew that; their real goal had not been the eradication of communism but the destruction of the radical Left and the vigorous coalition of leftists that had elected reform-minded candidates to office during the New Deal and World War II. But the Right could not have succeeded if not for the apathy of US citizens, who, faced with the Right's assault on their rights, had remained "silent, contented, alienated, frightened, and acquiescent." Trumbo had watched, with a sense of foreboding, the people of the United States "slipping into a stupor, no longer caring about being free."[53]

Peter Bart, who interviewed Trumbo in December 1966, referred to him as a "benign radical," whatever that meant.[54] To be sure, Trumbo was not marching or writing pamphlets, but he was supporting a number of radical causes. Apparently, none of those activities worried the FBI, which removed Trumbo's name from its Security Index in October 1968. The last report in Trumbo's FBI file is dated October 15, 1968, but Mitzi remembers that the following year, Danny Arnold (a television producer who lived next door) told Trumbo that two FBI agents had come to his house and requested that he take down the license plate numbers of all cars that carried visitors to the Trumbo house. Arnold refused to do so, but he wanted Trumbo to know about the FBI's request.

Trumbo was an early, constant, and vigorous opponent of the war in Vietnam. In an undated note to Senator Wayne Morse (D-Ore.), the most outspoken and consistent congressional critic of the war, Trumbo declared "that no national, international, or moral law justifies our presence in Vietnam, nor our military defense of a sequence of squalid dictatorships which command neither the support nor the respect of their own people."[55] On Christmas Day 1966, as part of a protest against the war, Trumbo spoke at a meeting at the First Unitarian Church; on Veterans' Day 1968 he read a portion of *Johnny Got His Gun* on the Los Angeles radio station KPFK; and he contributed money to the Student Mobilization Committee to end the War in Vietnam. In 1970, in a letter to the *New York Times*, Trumbo wrote: "I agree with today's protesting students. . . . I'm against burning down libraries, but we burn down more than that in Vietnam. After all, who is it that is using violence?"[56] The following year he chaired a rally organized by the Entertainment Industry for Peace and Justice to End United States Involvement in Southeast Asia. It took place at the Beverly Hilton Hotel and featured Jane Fonda and Noam Chomsky. Trumbo told the gathering: "We hope in a general way to cooperate with other peace organizations around the country."[57]

But Trumbo's most important contribution to the antiwar movement was via *Johnny Got His Gun*. Sometime during 1967 Trumbo allowed a section of *Johnny* to be used in the antiwar film *A Conscientious Objection*. And in his addendum to the 1970 reprint of *Johnny*, Trumbo graphically expressed his deep anger about the death and wounding of US personnel in Southeast Asia and US citizens' seeming indifference to it:

> Numbers have dehumanized us. Over breakfast we read of 40,000 American dead in Vietnam. Instead of vomiting, we reach for the toast. . . . Do we scream in the night when it touches our dreams? No. We don't dream about it because we don't think about it; we don't think about it because we don't care about it. We are much more interested in law and order, so that American streets may be made safe while we transform those of Vietnam into flowing sewers of blood which we replenish every year by forcing our sons to choose between a prison cell here or a coffin there.[58]

The following year he granted permission to actor and antiwar activist Donald Sutherland to recite the last four pages of the novel in performances of the antiwar troupe created by Sutherland and Jane Fonda. Dr. Howard Levy, a former army captain who had been court-martialed and sentenced for refusing to teach medical techniques to Green Berets, had urged the two actors to present an alternative to Bob Hope's traditional shows for the troops. He suggested they call themselves FTA (Fuck the Army). Fonda and Sutherland put together a troupe of very talented singers and comedians, and they gave their first performance in March 1971. All told, the show was performed twenty-one times on the East Coast and in Okinawa, Japan, and the Philippines, before more than 64,000 military personnel.[59]

At the end of each performance, Sutherland held up a well-worn copy of the paperback edition of Trumbo's book and said: "I want to read from a book. The book is called *Johnny Got His Gun*." After providing a short synopsis of the story, Sutherland recited from memory the words of the last four pages. "His reading of the last passage of 'Johnny Got His Gun' brought GI's to their feet in a standing ovation wherever the 'F.T.A.' played."[60] Sutherland recalled: "I loved those pages of Dalton's. I still say them. They're poetry. They sing like those high-tension wires he writes of. Ron Kovic [author of *Born on the Fourth of July*] told me that hearing my reading of those words at an anti-war rally had helped catalyze his political convictions, but they were not used in the film Tom Cruise made of Kovic's life."[61]

Trumbo continued to support the black civil rights movement, but he also wrote favorably about and contributed to advocates of Black Power. He did so because he had come to believe that nonviolent resistance had its limitations. When David L. Wolper contacted Trumbo about adapting William Styron's novel *The Confessions of Nat Turner* (about the leader of a bloody slave revolt in Virginia in 1831), Trumbo expressed interest and described Turner as "a far more contemporary figure than Martin Luther King. . . . In his resort to violence Nat Turner is truly a man of the Twentieth Century, which Martin Luther King, unhappily, is not." Turner's violence, according to Trumbo was "completely modern in everything but its origins." Trumbo characterized Turner "as a prophet, strong in faith, fierce in action, and mercilessly obedient to the wrathful commands of an outraged and insulted God." Turner, "in carrying through his rebellion, did nothing more than accept a principle of white Christian violence which had enslaved all of Africa, and used it for the first time in American history as a weapon against white Christians."[62]

Trumbo contributed $35 a month to the Student Nonviolent Coordinating Committee, and he also contributed money to the Black Panther Party's free breakfast and free clinic programs. In February 1970 he sent a letter to the *Los Angeles Times* calling attention to the juxtaposition of two stories: one describing the prison sentence imposed on defense counsel William H. Kunstler for contempt of court (he had represented Black Panther leader Bobby Seale during the conspiracy trial of the Chicago Eight), and the other describing an anti-integration rally in Macon, Georgia, at which Governor Lester Maddox had urged the state's citizens to disobey the latest integration order of the US Supreme Court. "Two questions immediately arise," Trumbo wrote: "(1) who conspires to violate the public law and who does not? (2) who is truly contemptuous of the federal court system (hence of 'law and order'), and who is not? I suggest that until we find honest answers to these questions, we stand on extremely treacherous ground in hectoring youthful dissenters for lack of faith in political judicial processes which have harried thousands of their contemporaries into jail or exile."[63] The following month Trumbo, along with Jane Fonda, Donald Sutherland, Dennis Hopper, Sydney Pollack, Michelle Phillips, and Angela Y. Davis, signed a "Protest of the Political Persecution of Black Panthers."[64] According to one of Fonda's biographers, her meeting with members of the Black Panther Party at a fund-raiser at the Trumbo house helped jolt her "out of her [political] indecision."[65]

One year later, in a note to an interviewer from *Playboy* magazine, Trumbo angrily pronounced the culture of the United States to be "fundamentally" racist, and he called racism "the keystone of national policy, both domestic and foreign—so profoundly a part of our national psyche that we accept it as the natural order of the universe rather than a violation of the natural order." This racism was not confined to black people; in fact, it was especially noticeable in this country's treatment of Asians. During World War II, for example, the US government had put Japanese but not Germans in concentration camps; it did not "drop atomic bombs on the populations of Munich and Dusseldorf." Trumbo asked, "How many gooks have we killed in Korea? How many slopes in Vietnam, Laos and Cambodia? Millions, and we're still killing more of them. Our thirst for the blood of dark-skinned sub-humans is insatiable."[66]

Trumbo also kept his eye on international affairs, and in private, he occasionally criticized some aspects of Soviet behavior; however, he wrote no anti-Soviet articles. In response to a postcard asking him whether he would ever "permit himself" to adapt a book about the crimes of the Stalin regime, Trumbo replied: "It is entirely conceivable that I would . . . do so," adding that he had protested the imprisonment of writers opposed to the Soviet invasion of Hungary (1956), the resumption of nuclear testing (1961), and the prosecution and sentencing of dissident Soviet writers Yuli Daniel and Andrei Sinyavsky (1966).

He told this correspondent that he had also written letters protesting the suppressive acts of non-Communist states such as Turkey, Spain, Greece, and South Africa.[67]

Later that year, after the Warsaw bloc countries invaded Czechoslovakia, Trumbo sent a telegram to the Writers Union and Association of Film Makers in the Soviet Union condemning that act.[68] In a telegram to the Czech Writers Union, Trumbo said: "As one of many American writers who have protested the invasion of Vietnam by the USA, I extend my heartfelt sympathy to the writers and people of occupied Czechoslovakia. Your struggle for intellectual integrity has won the open or secret admiration of writers all over the world. I salute you through the darkness which has descended upon all of us . . . and look forward to a new day which cannot be long deferred."[69]

Early in 1969 the Trumbos were again victimized by Cold War anticommunism, this time by a liberal. It was, in many ways, a very peculiar episode. Tom Bradley, a black city councilman, was running for mayor of Los Angeles against the ultraconservative incumbent Sam Yorty. A representative of a committee working on Bradley's campaign asked the Trumbos to host a fund-raising party. At least four of the twenty-four members of that committee (Steve Allen, Burt Lancaster, Budd Schulberg, and Bill Stout) knew about Trumbo's political past, but either they were not consulted or they saw no reason to object. Invitations were duly sent, cordially inviting the recipients to "an intimate cocktail party in honor of Tom Bradley . . . at the home of Mr. and Mrs. Dalton Trumbo" on Friday, March 14. The minimum donation required to attend the event was $20 per person, which included supper and cocktails. Football player O. J. Simpson was to be a special guest; Mahalia Jackson, Jack Lemmon, and Buddy Collette were listed as entertainers. For more information, invitees were requested to call Beata Inaya.

At that point, Steve Allen, who had never met Trumbo, decided that a serious mistake was about to be made. He wrote a letter to Inaya, positing that if Dalton Trumbo had been a Communist, and "*if* (a) Mr. Trumbo is today of the Communist persuasion (something he has every legal right to be), and *if* (b) this fact is publicized by Mr. Bradley's rightist political opposition, then (c) the March 14th affair will almost certainly be used in such a way as to cost Mr. Bradley a perhaps significant number of votes." A Bradley campaign official abruptly canceled the party. Trumbo placed all the blame on Allen, but he should have directed some of his anger toward Inaya, who had clearly sent Allen's letter to someone higher up the chain of command.

Trumbo remained uncharacteristically silent about this incident for two months, at which point he received an invitation from the Arts Division of the American Civil Liberties Union (ACLU), asking him to sponsor a playwriting contest. Seeing an opportunity to have some fun with Allen, Trumbo made a direct reference to the cancellation of the Bradley cocktail party in his reply, stating: "Although no one had mentioned the matter [of the cancellation] to Mrs. Trumbo or me, and the invitations were already at the printers, the party was canceled forthwith, and we, quite after the fact, were notified of our undesirability." Because of this, Trumbo said, he dare not commit himself to sponsoring this contest until the ACLU had secured the written consent of Steve Allen. He added: "I know this seems odd, but it is the only way I can think of to avoid another spasm of nastiness, and, perhaps, disavowal." Trumbo sent a copy of the letter to Allen.

Allen then wrote to the Arts Division, admitting that his letter to Inaya "did indeed recommend against the holding of the fund-raising party" at the Trumbos' home, but, he emphasized, "the party was not canceled on my instructions, though primary blame for the cancellation rests on my shoulders. If he [Trumbo] were a Communist, I would not wish to be politically allied with him. I concede my strong anti-Communist bias." A true liberal, Allen averred, must be anti-Communist. (Meanwhile, Bradley had lost the election, partly because of Yorty's blatant appeals to the racial prejudices of white Angelenos, and partly because of Yorty's emphasis on law and order. However, Bradley defeated Yorty in the 1973 election and was reelected four more times.)

Trumbo responded with five sarcastic, funny letters that were clearly intended to ridicule Allen. In one, Trumbo asked Allen's advice about accepting an invitation to speak at a dinner honoring civil rights activist Julian Bond. On June 13 Allen finally responded to Trumbo's spate of letters, exhibiting his own brand of humor. He spoke about a nightmare he was having that Trumbo's correspondence went on "ad infinitum, ad nauseam, Ad Wolgast [a world-champion boxer]." There the matter might have rested. Trumbo had had his fun, and he was busy trying to secure financing for a movie version of *Johnny Got His Gun* (see the next chapter). But unbeknownst to Trumbo, Allen had sent copies of their letters to Trumbo's old sparring mate Arthur Schlesinger Jr.

On August 4 Schlesinger wrote to Allen, stating that he "would be in strong agreement" with Allen's action and reasoning. "I have never,"

Steve Allen and Dalton Trumbo, ca. 1969. Courtesy of *Esquire* magazine.

Schlesinger continued, "understood how people who uphold Communism can without incongruity associate with an organization dedicated
to civil liberties." That is, both men—both of them liberals—without
any evidence in support of their position, assumed that Trumbo had

been and might still be a member of the Communist Party; that even if he were no longer a member of the party, he was still a "Communist"; and that there was only one type of Communist—one who uncategorically supported a Stalinist tyranny and lied about his or her belief in civil liberties. Allen's secretary sent Trumbo a copy of Schlesinger's letter, and Trumbo's nine-page response was equal parts funny and angry. Trumbo began by parsing Schlesinger's language usage. In his opening sentence ("I would be in strong agreement"), Schlesinger had paired "a volitional auxiliary with a volitional verb" when he should have used "an auxiliary of simple futurity such as *should*." Trumbo then noted several other grammatical errors and rewrote Schlesinger's letter correctly.

But the heart of Trumbo's letter focused on liberal stereotyping, and it was a deadly serious political statement, a kind of coda to his Cold War pamphlets. In response to Schlesinger's stated inability to understand how people who defended communism "could" (Trumbo noted that "can" would be more appropriate in this context) consistently associate with an organization dedicated to civil liberties, Trumbo asked: "Why doesn't he [Schlesinger, understand]? Why can't they [Communists, associate]? What holds them [Communists] back?" In effect, Trumbo asked, how can anyone's belief in communism, which is defined by most dictionaries as a philosophy or a system, "possibly be considered inimical to the defense of civil liberties?" It can be so considered, he answered implicitly, only if the askers of that question are dogmatic liberals whose thinking processes are obscured by unexamined cant. Furthermore, Trumbo queried, what qualified those two liberals to write about Trumbo's "present political convictions"? After all, Allen had confessed at the outset that he knew nothing about them, and Schlesinger simply followed along. Thus, "everything in their thesis which flows from this anarchic demolition of valid inference and reasoned thought is, by definition, fallacious, illogical, irrational and, for men of such enormous integrity, morally degrading and intellectually disgraceful." As a consequence, they have written "sheer mindless gabble; garbage, as some call it; dreck, pure merde." What is it, Trumbo then asked, "that impels a ranking intellectual like Mr. Allen and a Schweitzerian humanitarian like Mr. Schlesinger to write all this gabble and dreck or whatever one calls it?" Again, he answered his own question: "the vincible companion of sloth called ignorance; that infallible solace of closed minds which has sometime been called the voluntary misfortune." And the "pity of it is that their ignorance could have been so easily dispelled":

Had Mr. Allen approached me for enlightenment . . . , I should cheerfully have told him all my secrets and blessed his warm, inquiring heart. Had he confided to me his misgivings about the effect on the Bradley campaign of a party at my house, I should have consented at once to its transfer from my address to his. Not because I share his fears or admire him over-much for harboring them, but because as a rational man I should have been compelled to recognize the objective fact of their existence and to deal with them on that basis.

Trumbo would have been "happy to accommodate" Allen and Schlesinger if they had come calling with a request to exchange ideas on any subject of mutual interest. And he would be happy to do so in the future:

[But] I don't think either of those aging and obsessed evangels will come tapping at my door, because knowledge is the killer of faith, and they are of the faithful. They have hallucinated God as the greatest anti-Communist of them all and been completely unhinged by the sight of His glory. It is no longer important to them that they know what they're talking about. It is important only that they talk, since in their ideology the act of speech proves the truth of what has been spoken. Trapped thus between nightmares of qualified good and unqualified evil, they have become what they hate.

Allen's reply confirmed Trumbo's point about blinkered thinking on the subject: "I am obviously more-or-less cemented into my view that Communists—*acting as such* cannot be trusted." In addition, he repeated the tired anti-Communist syllogism: "liberals must oppose communism; I am a liberal; therefore, if Trumbo is a Communist, I must oppose and hamper all his political endeavors."[70]

In September 1969 Trumbo negotiated with *Esquire* to print the exchange with Allen. The magazine agreed to pay Trumbo $500 and Allen $100. Allen requested that his payment be sent to the ACLU. Trumbo said he was willing to split the $600 fee with Allen, but he intended to keep his half, having just spent $200 for a family table at an ACLU event honoring Tommy Smothers. Trumbo then waggishly asked the *Esquire* editor: "Have you considered the idea of printing Mr. Allen's letters in black ink and mine in red, so that the reader, if he wishes, can skip great chunks of his last letter and rush forward to the goodies in mine? Or does red trouble the eye?"[71]

Trumbo had one last significant statement to make about the effects of the Cold War. The occasion was the bestowal of the WGAw's Laurel Award, honoring Trumbo's lifetime achievement as a screenwriter. Trumbo's acceptance speech eloquently and poignantly encapsulated many of the ideas he had been meditating on since the mid-1950s (see chapters 15 and 16). But what he had to say about the blacklist era and informers was not kindly received by some of his former comrades.

He was notified in February 1970 that he had been chosen to receive the award, and the headline in *Daily Variety* read: "Trumbo Wins Laurel Award: 3rd Once Blacklisted Writer to Be Given It."[72] (The other two were Sidney Buchman and Carl Foreman.) In early March, Allen Rivkin, the guild's publicity director, asked Trumbo for a copy of his acceptance speech, which was to be printed in the guild's *Newsletter*. Trumbo sent him a copy, noting: "The small changes (attached) which I beg you to make in this accursed speech reflect but the last of a life-long series of lethal and generally losing struggles with the English tongue. I sternly remind you that it is also your obligation as my editor to correct misspellings, keep a sharp eye on the who-whoms, and unfuck the punctuation." Rivkin replied: "Your acceptance remarks are deeply moving—and I'm glad you're saying them."[73] In his notes for a letter he did not send, Trumbo wrote:

> This speech is an example of why I always seem to get in trouble. Its true intention is to bury all hatchets in contemplation of a time which I fear may be one of troubles for all. I confess to you that I face the evening with a certain amount of trepidation, because when I see on the late late show some of the films I've written, I am filled with revulsion. Nothing I've ever written has been as good as I hoped it would be or as it should have been. My sense of failure—of true failure—gives poor promise that Laurel will become me.[74]

Just before the ceremony, Trumbo showed the speech to Cleo. According to Mitzi, "She did not like parts of it, because she thought his intent would be misunderstood by their friends. She tried to get him to change some of the wording, but he was extremely stubborn, and he was mad at her for not embracing it as it was written."

On March 13, when Trumbo took the stage to accept the award, he received a standing ovation. His speech, the reporter for *Daily Variety* wrote, was delivered "more with sadness than bitterness."[75] In this brilliant distillation of his years of experience in Hollywood, Trumbo spoke movingly about the courage of the men and women who had founded the Screen Writers Guild and of those guild members who had fought in World War II. And yet, within six years of the war's end, a significant number of those veterans of the fight for unionism and against fascism had been "denounced as un-American, stripped of their names and passports, and blacklisted." The most controversial element of this speech, his comments about the blacklist, came next. He addressed those remarks to members of the guild who had no memory of the blacklist:

> To them I would say only this: that the blacklist was a time of evil, and that no one on either side who survived it came through untouched by evil. Caught in a situation that had passed beyond the control of mere individuals, each person reacted as his nature, his needs, his convictions, and his particular circumstances compelled him to. There was bad faith and good, honesty and dishonesty, courage and cowardice, selflessness and opportunism, wisdom and stupidity, good and bad on both sides; and almost every individual involved, no matter where he stood, combined some or all of these antithetical qualities in his own person, in his own acts.
>
> When you who are in your forties or younger look back with curiosity on that dark time [the blacklist], as I think occasionally you should, it will do no good to search for villains or heroes or saints or devils because there were none; there were only victims. Some suffered less than others, some grew and some diminished, but in the final tally we were *all* victims because almost without exception each of us felt compelled to say things we did not want to say, to do things we did not want to do, to deliver and receive wounds we truly did not want to exchange. That is why none of us— right, left, or center—emerged from that long nightmare without sin.

Lost in the controversy over Trumbo's "only victims" remark was the following key part of his speech:

I said "almost without exception" because those who were
killed in World War II escaped the blacklist altogether, and
therefore lay beyond its reach. In July of 1947 the Guild published the names of its five war dead and established, in memory of them all, an annual honor which is called the Robert
Meltzer Award. Lieut. Robert Meltzer . . . served with a specially trained, specially equipped volunteer attack group called
the Rangers. He survived the Normandy landings only to be
killed while leading a later assault on the fortress of Brest. . . .
During the 1951–52 hearings of the House Committee on Un-
American Activities, reference was made to the existence of a
Meltzer club or branch or cell of the Communist Party in Hollywood. The last Meltzer Award was presented in 1952; the
first Laurel Award was announced and given in 1953. As its
22nd recipient I ask you permission to accept it in the names [of
the five men killed in the war].

Also lost was his concluding paragraph: "I assure you—I assure you
most sincerely—that what I have said here is not intended to be hurtful
to anyone: It is intended rather to repair a hurt, to heal a wound which
years ago we inflicted on each other, and on ourselves most of all."[76]
The speech received, according to the account in *Daily Variety*, "hefty
applause."[77]

Christopher thought long and hard about how he would describe
this speech. In his last formulation, he wrote:

What Trumbo said was unexpected and misunderstood. He
was neither forgiving nor condemning the informers, nor was
he inviting them to lunch. He simply wanted people to become
more accepting, to think before calling someone a "stool
pigeon." The informers were not agents of some kind sent in
to gather information; they were already in the game. The
blame for the blacklist should be put on the committee, not
the informers, because it had put them in a place where they
had to answer a question they should never have been asked.
He believed that to focus on the informers was a sideshow; the
committee was the main event. In that sense, the speech both
worked and didn't work. It did not please those who had been
blacklisted, but it did force some of them to think about what
the blacklist was all about.

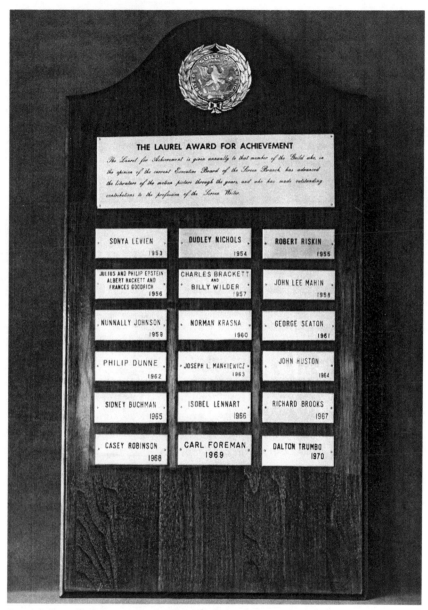

Laurel Award plaque, 1970. Photograph by Mitzi Trumbo; courtesy of WGAw.

Christopher concluded that his father's meaning would have been clearer and his speech less controversial if he had said "we were all casualties of the Cold War." (I prefer Primo Levi's phrase "guiltless victims.")[78] Trumbo's point was that neither those who resisted the committee nor those who cooperated with it had done anything that merited being brought before an unholy tribunal and forced to make an infernal choice. He was trying, once again, to draw a sharp line between persecutors and victims. The informers were not perpetrators: they did not send the subpoenas, ask the questions, or create and administer the blacklist. All that can be said about the informers is that, when confronted with the choice of collaborating or not with the persecutors, they opted for the former—not because they believed in the anti-Communist crusade but because they did not wish to suffer materially from the blacklist.

When Eddie Huebsch, a blacklisted writer, sent Trumbo a copy of a letter he had written to the guild, complaining that the Meltzer Award had been replaced by the "craven Laurel Award," Trumbo responded:

> I spoke of the Meltzer Award as I did because to exorcize an evil one must first identify it, and I felt that no harm could come from recalling the cruelties and idiocies of which all of us are capable. . . .
>
> As for the rest of my speech that night, I meant every word of it:—that none of us has lived a life so blameless, so virtuous as to permit him, twenty years after the fact, to hurl maledictions at his enemies in the presence of a Guild now largely composed of persons who had nothing to do with the events at issue. I made the point because I am convinced that American liberties presently stand in greater jeopardy than ever before in our history. . . . I am convinced that only by an alliance between today's left and center can the growing assault from the right be turned back.
>
> To forget old grievances and forgive old enemies is not too high a price to pay for that alliance.
>
> I do not delude myself that the future of the country will pivot on the unity or disunity of a comparatively small and powerless Writers Guild of America. However, it is an organization of some importance, and was, on that night, the only organization that was willing to listen to what I had to say. It would, I presume, have been easy to spit in their faces . . . , but it would also have been irresponsible, unjust, and divisive—in short, a scandal.[79]

The public response from other former comrades was vituperative. Lester Cole called the speech an "outrageously lofty, ecclesiastical

benediction" from "on high."[80] Albert Maltz thought it was "an absolutely dreadful perversion of history."[81] And Arthur Laurents stated: "I
thought Dalton Trumbo was disgraceful when he said . . . that it didn't
make any difference who were the victims. . . . That's absolutely balls.
. . . I thought that was a disgusting thing to say."[82] Privately, many
of Trumbo's friends were dismayed. Michael Wilson, for example,
"vehemently disagreed" with him.[83] Yet Leo Townsend, who had once
fronted for Trumbo and then became an informer, called to praise him.
This astounded Trumbo, who couldn't believe he had said anything
that would please Townsend.[84] Trumbo would have been even more
astounded, and deeply chagrined, if he had lived to hear Schlesinger's
praise.[85]

But Trumbo was speaking only for himself; he was not granting
absolution to anyone. He used the Laurel speech to encourage the old
members of the Hollywood Popular Front groups to stop clinging to
past grievances and to move forward on the serious social and political
issues facing the country. He was trying to promote a reunited Left. It
may have been a naïve effort, but it was a laudable one.

23

Johnny Got His Gun—The Movie
Preproduction

I feel that the great war picture has not yet been filmed. And I feel that it will not be filmed until some director with stark genius transplants pure insanity on the screen. I do not know how he will do it, or when. But it will be done eventually, and when the task is accomplished motion picture art will have something which will rank favorably with the best that the other arts have produced.

—Dalton Trumbo

Making a movie about *Johnny Got His Gun* was the best response Trumbo could make to the carnage of the war in Vietnam. He felt he had to do something; he had to find a way to add his voice to the voices of others who opposed the war. He put aside everything else and put all his time and energy to getting it made. He decided to take personal control of the project, because he feared losing control of the material and this occasion to express his thoughts about war.

—Christopher Trumbo

Trumbo had never lost interest in *Johnny*. It was his master work, and he delighted in the reprints and the recurring interest shown by new generations of young people. His efforts to make a movie based on the book and his ideas about both the book and the film provide glimpses into Trumbo's thoughts on several subjects, among them philosophy, aesthetics, finances, and the art of moviemaking. It is also another demonstration of his determination to succeed and his work ethic.

Trumbo waited fourteen years before trying to get *Johnny* republished. In March 1954 he wrote to Cameron and Kahn, one of the few firms willing to publish books by left-wingers, informing the editors that he had in his possession the printing plates for the novel and asking: "Do you think this might be of any help in bringing out a cheap edition?"[1] There is no copy of the editors' response in the Trumbo Papers, but it must have been no. Three years later Trumbo received a letter from Bob Roberts, who had produced *He Ran All the Way*. Roberts wrote: "I have been reading *Johnny* again and feel strongly that this might make a fine movie and that now may be the time to have it done." He asked whether Trumbo would be interested in doing a screenplay if Roberts were able to set up a production in England (where he was living at the time). Trumbo replied: "As to making a movie of it—I've thought about it for years, and simply don't know how it could be done. Once in a while I have a wild idea, but close analysis generally convinces me that it was only wild and no idea at all."[2]

A few days after this exchange, Paul Krassner, editor of the *Realist*, sent Trumbo a letter raving about the novel and calling it "the best book I've ever read." Krassner also wondered whether Trumbo wanted to have it republished. "There is," Krassner wrote, "a whole new generation—a whole new audience—for 'Johnny Got His Gun.' It is more than an anti-war document; it is a treatise for the times if only in terms of putting basic values into perspective in an era when traditional beliefs are becoming more and more unacceptable."[3] Trumbo agreed, and in 1959 *Johnny* was published by Lyle Stuart, with a new preface by Trumbo. He wrote:

> Reading it once more after so many years, I've had to resist a nervous itch to touch it up here, to change it there, to clarify, correct, elaborate, cut. After all, the book is twenty years younger than I, and I have changed so much and it hasn't. Or has it?
>
> Is it possible for anything to resist change, even a mere commodity that can be bought, buried, banned, damned, praised, or ignored for all the wrong reasons? Probably not. *Johnny* held a different meaning for three different wars. Its present meaning is what each reader conceives it to be, and each reader is gloriously different from every other reader, and each also is changing.
>
> I've let it remain as it was to see what it is.[4]

When a theatrical agent in London inquired about the rights to *Johnny*, Trumbo wrote: "I have no present intention of disposing of any of the rights connected with it. It could be that an especially attractive offer, including a substantial control of the material by me, might interest me—although it's doubtful."[5] Other requests for the film rights were met with the comment: "I can't see how to make it into a film, and I'm a fair pro at turning books into movies. So if I can't, I don't see how you can." But he changed his mind in late 1963 when a Mexican producer named Gustavo Alatriste approached Trumbo with the news that Spanish film director Luis Buñuel wanted to make a movie based on the novel. Trumbo, who had met Buñuel during his Mexican sojourn and appreciated his work, was "delighted." He considered Buñuel the only director he could "implicitly trust" with his novel. Trumbo told Alatriste: "I'd do a screenplay, and be his secretary, and carry his briefcase and do his laundry," and he immediately authorized Ingo Preminger to negotiate Buñuel's purchase of the film rights to *Johnny*. Trumbo then traveled to Mexico City, where he and Buñuel enjoyed, in Trumbo's words, "two marvelous weeks together."[6] Buñuel's son, Jean-Luis, recalled that his father and Trumbo spent a few months together, with Buñuel doing most of the talking while Trumbo took notes. They also drank copiously. At one point, Trumbo admired a parrot belonging to Señora Buñuel. She warned him that it was a vicious bird, but he assured her that he loved birds and they liked him. As he put out his hand for the parrot to perch on, it bit Trumbo's hand to the bone. Undaunted, Trumbo tried to kiss the bird, which proceeded to bite him twice on the lips. Jean-Luis described what happened next: "There was blood everywhere, but Dalton didn't care. . . . The last thing I remember seeing is Dalton waving from the back of a taxi, drunk, with blood down his chin and all over his shirt."[7]

After his return to Los Angeles, Trumbo worked on the script for another sixteen months, completing it in September 1965.[8] In it he solved one of the problems he and Buñuel had discussed—namely, finding a cinematic way to break the monotony of a long shot of a covered figure lying in a dark room and, at the same time, offer some respite from the relentless misery of his fate. They had decided on the inclusion of what they called "Joe's Image." When Joe awakens for the first time and asks, "Where am I?" the script describes a camera shot: "medium shot toward a darkened corner of the room." Then, the script says: "The light is somewhat better here than in the area surrounding the bed. Something sits on the floor. As we INTERCUT back and forth between this corner area and the bed area we realize that JOE'S IMAGE (i.e., Joe as he was before his accident) has been lying unconscious in the corner on the floor, waiting for the WOUNDED JOE on the bed to regain consciousness, thus permitting Joe's Image also to awaken." Joe's Image is awake only when Joe is. According to a note in the script, "Joe actually has four identities in the film. They are: (1) Wounded Joe on the bed in the hospital; (2) Joe's Image, unwounded but trapped in the hospital with the Wounded Joe; (3) Flashback Joe . . . as he was in those incidents from his past which he thinks about and which we dramatize on the screen; (4) Fantasy Joe, or the Joe of his dreams, of fantasies, nightmares and hallucinations. All but Wounded Joe are physically identical, although it may be found desirable to costume them differently."[9]

Trumbo also decided not to include the last four pages of the novel, where Joe speaks about himself as a new kind of Christ, a man of the future, a man of peace who represents the will of people and who, in the next war, will turn the guns against the war makers. Instead, he ended the film as the drug that will permanently silence Joe takes effect. The direction for the last camera shot states: "Sadly, Joe's image crawls to its usual place on the floor against the wall, and reluctantly surrenders to slumber."[10] But in a revised version dated May 24, 1965, Trumbo has Joe moaning and tapping in Morse code: "SOS. Don't give me dope. Help me—don't knock me out! SOS. SOS. . . ."[11] By the time Trumbo had finished the script, Buñuel was working on another movie, and Alatriste reported that he was unable to secure financing.[12]

In January 1968 Trumbo decided to make a concerted effort to get a movie made from his script. He sent a copy to Maltz, asking for his comments.[13] Thereafter, word began to circulate that Trumbo had a script ready to be filmed. John Bright, who was working as the story editor for a television production company run by Bruce Campbell, Roy Silver, and Bill Cosby (CSC),[14] heard about it. Knowing that Campbell and Silver were looking for another movie project, Bright asked Trumbo for a copy of the "Johnny" script. Trumbo sent him a copy, noting that it was "based on a series of discussions which I had with Buñuel in Mexico several years ago." Trumbo explicitly told Bright that he wanted complete control over script revisions, casting, directing, and the final cut. He also specified that the film must be shot in black and white, using completely unknown actors.[15] Bright brought the book and the script to Campbell's attention. Campbell pronounced himself "very taken with" the novel, and when he read the script, he was convinced that CSC should produce it.[16]

Bruce Campbell is one of the most fascinating characters in this saga. His original enthusiasm for the script would transform into an obsession with the movie. Mitzi, who was married to him for three years, described him as follows:

> He was wiry and energetic, extremely upbeat, always moving, hands waving as he talked and paced. His enthusiasm was contagious. He had many friends, and people he met believed in him, at least until things began to fall apart, which they always did. He was manic-depressive, and he would alternate between the two states—a few weeks being wildly and feverishly enthusiastic, planning more and more extravagant projects, followed by weeks in bed, barely speaking or moving. He had a good psychiatrist and medications that worked, when he took them, but he only took the prescribed lithium for a short time, because he missed the excitement of his highs.

On April 20 Trumbo signed a letter of agreement with CSC to make *Johnny* into a movie.[17] At that point, Trumbo articulated his three primary goals for the movie. First, the film, like the novel, was to be a sort of paean to his childhood. For that reason, the film had to include the scene in which Joe loses his father's dearest possession, his fishing rod; in Trumbo's mind, that scene evoked the strong bond between father and son. He acknowledged the "sentimentality" of the scene but denied that it was "mawkish sentimentality."[18] Second, the movie must convey Trumbo's strong antiwar message. When asked if that theme was still relevant, Trumbo angrily responded to one interviewer: "Darn right! . . . The problem is universal. Whether in Greece, Africa, or just about anywhere, some poor sonofabitch is holding out, saying, 'I won't do it.' He can't do otherwise. It isn't that he doesn't want to; it is simply that he *can't* give in. It's relevant to the Vietnam War, to the people who say, 'I can't do it. I can't go fight.' And it's relevant to the Negro. For 300 years it has been relevant and now they are saying, 'We can't do it.'"[19] He insisted, however, that the antiwar message must be delivered without using "battlefield gore." Trumbo considered graphic depictions of violence to be "aesthetically unsatisfying." "Real drama," he said, "lies in that which has been violated rather than in the act of violence itself."[20] Third, he wanted Marcel Marceau to play "Joe's Image," but after meeting with Trumbo, Marceau declined the offer (and Trumbo later dropped the idea of using an image).[21]

During the summer of 1968, Campbell made contact with Robert Haggiag, a Libyan-born producer who owned a movie studio in Rome.

Haggiag wrote to Campbell: "If you would find it of interest to produce the picture at my studios in Rome, I would be very happy to consider it, as well as a co-production in Italy."[22] Meanwhile, Trumbo had revised his script and sent copies to fourteen people, asking for their comments. Albert Maltz responded negatively to the idea of making *Johnny* into a film because "it transgresses a fundamental aesthetic law: that people can read and endure and be moved by materials in a novel that become unbearably painful for them in film and theatre form. So it is my feeling . . . that you will not find audiences for this film." He forwarded no suggestions for changes because, based on Trumbo's remarks, he assumed Trumbo wanted "to shoot the whole wad without compromise." Maltz also wondered whether Trumbo could write the same sort of pacifist statement today.[23] In a lengthy reply, Trumbo affirmed his nonviolent mind-set:

> I'm afraid that I've come to the conclusion in my twilight years that murder is absolutely bad, and that mass murder by warring groups of human beings is a culturally acquired and culturally inherited phenomenon rather than a "national" one. I feel that violence—i.e., mass murder—is not and never has been a solution to any of the problems to which it has been applied; that probably, on the contrary, it has exacerbated, embittered and deepened the problems which existed before violence was resorted to. I think this incessant resort to violence has made the world steadily worse [rather] than steadily better. The pacifism which I admire and perhaps to which I subscribe, is not a passive ideal; it does not simply refuse to participate in war, it actively opposes war. Any kind of war. Had there been sufficient pacifism of this sort—a true pacifism—there would have been no World War II. . . .
>
> I've come to believe that all wars are irrational to the point of insanity . . . and must be actively opposed by men who believe them to be so. *Johnny* as a film—if it is even made—thus becomes my own personal act of opposition. That, of course, is why (in terms of content) I feel that I must carry it through to the bitter end.[24]

Trumbo repeated that credo in a CSC prospectus titled "An Immodest Argument in Behalf of 'Johnny Got His Gun.'" The subject matter, he wrote, is "Peace." It is "neither pro nor anti any country; it is solely anti-

war [and] entirely pro-American . . . [It] is a love song to America and
to the lives and hearts of all of its people."[25]

In late October 1968 Trumbo and Campbell met with Haggiag.
They agreed that Haggiag would form an Italian company (collectively
owned by Haggiag, Trumbo, and CSC) to make the film. Shooting was
projected to begin in April 1969. According to Sherry Sonnett (who
was married to Christopher at the time), the family began taking Italian classes.[26] Campbell and Trumbo began to think about casting the
parts, and at some point in December or January they contacted Kenneth Hyman at Warner Bros./Seven Arts to discuss a distribution deal.[27]

Walter Matthau was Trumbo's first choice to play Joe's father.[28]
Trumbo later said about him: "Ever since he played the sheriff in *Lonely
Are the Brave* I have considered him the finest actor on the American
scene. . . . He is the keystone, the anchor, the rock on which my present thinking about this film relies."[29] But when Matthau declined (for
unspecified reasons), Trumbo suffered his first serious crisis of confidence. He wrote to Haggiag in a "melancholy vein," confiding that he
was "a bit thrown by the Matthau rejection." He needed to clarify his
thoughts by putting them down on paper:

> I am terribly disappointed and, beyond that, deeply troubled. I
> am disappointed because there is simply no other actor on earth
> who can play the role as well as Matthau. . . . I simply cannot
> think coherently about casting the part without him.
>
> When I say that I am also troubled, I refer to something even
> more serious. I know nothing about Mr. Matthau as a private
> person, nor do I need to: I only know that as a public person, he
> is an artist of impeccable sensitivity. And, apparently, *because*
> of this sensitivity to the script, he has felt obliged to reject it.
>
> This, I fear, speaks ill of the script itself. By this I mean that
> although I *want* actors of great sensitivity, I begin to feel that
> the very quality of sensitivity I'm after will cause other artists
> of integrity and worth to react as negatively as Mr. Matthau
> has done, and for the same reason.
>
> This, of course, raises the final and most depressing ques-
> tion. If the impact of the script is so strong as to repel first-rate
> artists, isn't it possible that the public also will be repelled by
> the finished product?
>
> To put it frankly: *is the impact of the script so strong that it
> should be abandoned altogether as a film?*

To answer that question, Trumbo had read and reread the script and could find no repellent qualities in it. The "Johnny" script is not, he insisted, "a tale of horror, it is a story of love. It is not a death-song, it is a hymn to life. I swear that when we are finished with it, it will—and *must*—overflow with gentleness, with aspiration, with sexual and parental love, and, to the very highest degree, with love of life and respect for every living thing." In his postscript, Trumbo asked:

> Do you suppose there could be something in my political past, something relating to the various battles I have felt myself obliged to engage in, which may have offended Mr. Matthau or, perhaps, wounded someone he esteems? There are, as you know, wounds all over this town—all over this country in truth—which sometimes flare up with all the old pain ten years after the fact, or fifteen, or, as it has been in my case, twenty-one. I don't know. I'm simply speculating. I speculate because I want so very much to believe that the rejection was not caused by the quality of the script itself.[30]

Shortly after Trumbo wrote this soul-searching letter to Haggiag, Matthau changed his mind and agreed to take the part (again, for reasons unknown).

At this point, a much bigger question than the casting of Joe's father arose: should Trumbo direct the movie? He was ambivalent at first, telling John Bright: "This is my one chance to do something with the one purely creative product of my life, and I must strive for the best in everything that touches the film."[31] But shortly thereafter, Trumbo told an interviewer: "Twenty years ago I had the vague idea I might like to direct. And perhaps it has hovered on the fringes of my mind ever since." But after watching John Frankenheimer direct *The Fixer*, he realized he would be old and feeble before he could learn everything Frankenheimer already knew about directing. Thus, after returning from Budapest, he had abandoned the notion of directing.[32]

A few months later, he changed his mind again, motivated by all the articles he had read about the director's primary role in filmmaking (the auteur theory). He expressed his frustration with that idea in a letter to Allen Rivkin:

> We have encountered, in our declining years, the rise of the director to a position from which I think it will be impossible

to topple him. His ascendancy has been accompanied by the
simultaneous arrival of a new school of young critics who have
no idea of how movies are made and rely almost exclusively
upon the French [auteur] school to tell them. The prospect is so
depressing that I, who have never leched to direct, am going to
take over *Johnny Got His Gun*, not merely to assure that my
contribution as its writer must then be recognized, but to make
certain that if it is fucked up by muddle-headed direction, I, for
a change, shall be in charge of the fucking.[33]

"He was," Christopher said, "well aware that he had never directed a
film. But he knew how to write a script, and he was confident that if he
followed his script, it should work. He told himself: 'If I can film the
script I wrote, the footage will be easy to edit.'"

Trumbo
with his first
grandchild,
Dominic
Taylor
(Nikola's
son), 1966.
Photograph
by Cleo
Trumbo.

In early February 1969 Haggiag backed away from the project. He wanted to make the film at his studio in Rome, but Hyman wanted to make it in Burbank. Trumbo did not seem to be upset by Haggiag's withdrawal. He was much more perturbed by the telephone calls he had received from two Warner executives. In the first, Hyman told Trumbo that Warner Bros. had decided to cut Campbell's proposed budget from $1.55 million to $1.2 million. In the second, the head of the story department, William Fadiman, informed Trumbo that he would have to make twenty-two specific cuts in the script. In Trumbo's mind, these cuts portended "a mass assault upon the screenplay as it presently stands." If, he noted, "we keep only the 'necessary' scenes we shall end up with a film of about forty-seven minutes running time. The story, or plot, is, after all, extremely simple. The truth is that I consider every scene we have a necessary one because each scene is part of a general mosaic without which this will not be a complete film or even a successful one." Trumbo informed Campbell that he would not make a deal with Warner Bros. until Hyman and Fadiman "accept the script *'scene for scene'* as we have presented it to them, with the specific understanding that every scene in the script will be shot as it is written."[34]

A much more damaging setback occurred three months later when Trumbo learned from a front-page story in *Daily Variety* that Bill Cosby had moved out of the CSC offices, saying, "I no longer have anything to do with them. That's it, simply."[35] Mitzi recalled that Cosby "had become unhappy with the company: it had too many irons in the fire and was spending too much money too fast. He wanted to go back to the earlier arrangement, with Roy Silver as his manager. Roy said no, Cosby pulled out his money, and CSC fell apart very quickly." As a consequence of this rupture, all sources of financing vanished, and Trumbo could not find a studio or a distributor willing to take a chance on an antiwar film with a first-time, sixty-three-year-old director. (At this point, no major studio had produced a film about the Vietnam War. Four independent production companies had done so, but only two films, *The Quiet American* and *The Green Berets* [John Wayne's panegyric epic], had been distributed by a major studio.)

Trumbo later said: "I don't think there was anything particularly discriminatory against me, or against a picture by me; it was simply the fact that they didn't think the character of Joe Bonham could provide a film that would return their money. And if that were not sufficient hazard, attached to it was an albatross, named me, who had not directed a picture before."[36] And when a new source of funding, Allied Art-

Trumbo writing in his bathtub, 1969. Photograph by Mitzi Trumbo.

ists, appeared on the scene, Trumbo was bluntly honest about his failed efforts to secure financing. He drafted a letter to one of its executives, telling him that the project had been rejected by every major American producing company for the unstated reason that it would not turn a profit. "With this history," Trumbo ruefully stated, "it must be apparent to you as to me that when I undertake on my own to arrange for a production, I shall be negotiating from weakness rather than strength. My only strength lies in my ownership of the novel and script, and my determination that if it can't be made honestly and well I shall not permit it to be made at all." He then stated his firm conviction that he was the only person who could make an honest movie from the book: "All of the book (aside from the war experiences) is autobiographical, and . . . for this reason alone I know more about the film and its characters— how they should look, feel, think, behave—than any other man, director or not, can possibly know. Joe's small town was mine, his childhood memories are mine."[37]

None of what Trumbo said in his letter dissuaded William Dodd (the president of Allied Artists), who in January 1970 made a serious offer to finance and distribute the film. Dodd told Trumbo that *Johnny* was "the most important project that I have come across since I have been in charge of production for Allied Artists," and he assured Trumbo that there would be no changes in the basic budget or the script, and the studio would not impinge on Trumbo's artistic freedom. But Dodd did stipulate two conditions: (1) Trumbo must agree to shoot the picture in Europe, because it would be less expensive to do so; and (2) he wanted Campbell to work "under the supervision of a production expert." Although Dodd had been favorably impressed with Campbell, he was concerned that Campbell "may not have the necessary experience at this time to effectively produce."[38] On January 30 the Allied Artists board approved an $800,000 budget for *Johnny*, with Trumbo as the director and Campbell as a coproducer. They were to receive 35 percent of the gross profits and were to be paid salaries and living expenses during the European shoot.

But then a silver-tongued devil appeared in the person of Simon Lazarus. Lazarus was an old friend. He had once owned four movie theaters and now owned a shopping center and a substantial amount of land in the San Fernando Valley. He had backed *Salt of the Earth* (made by blacklistees Paul Jarrico, Herbert Biberman, and Michael Wilson) and *Slaves* (directed by Biberman), neither of which had made a profit. On February 5 Trumbo and Cleo had dinner with Lazarus and his wife, and Trumbo described what happened: "I mention our A.A. [Allied Artists] deal. Simon jumps on the thing like a crocodile. A.A. is no good. Independent financing, which he can arrange simply by picking up the telephone, is the only way to go. He must see the script at once. I tell him no. . . . He remains at fever pitch throughout the evening." After several more entreaties, Trumbo made the mistake of agreeing to send Lazarus the script.[39]

On February 13 Lazarus came to Trumbo with a counteroffer, saying he could raise $600,000 from an investment group headed by Harry Margolis (a lawyer and the brother of Trumbo's friend Ben Margolis). Trumbo later wrote:

> I warned the investors' representatives that seven out of eight motion pictures lose money. I also projected at that time a preview schedule, a series of European showings, and the possibility of trying for the Cannes festival—a schedule which clearly ran into May of 1971. I also pointed out that *Johnny* was a delicate and difficult project; that it was at all times subject to political attack; that it had been rejected by some seventeen top-ranking studio executives; that the only offer we had received for its production came from Europe; and that its subject matter was such that it would always require special treatment.

Trumbo was assured that the investors "understood the gamble they were taking, that they were prepared to lose their last invested dollar if affairs turned out badly, and that the production money would be available for a year."[40] Believing that he and the Lazarus-Margolis group (hereafter referred to as the Investors) fully understood each other, Trumbo rejected the Allied Artists contract. Several factors motivated his decision: (1) he knew Lazarus and Ben Margolis better than he knew the Allied Artists people, and he trusted them; (2) he preferred to shoot the film in the United States, to "give the picture a more American look"; and (3) he thought that he and Campbell would have greater control over the making of the movie.[41] Thus, on March 3 Trumbo and Campbell signed a production agreement with the Investors. It was written by Ben Margolis and stated:

1. . . . A budget has been prepared indicating that a motion picture to be directed by Trumbo can be produced from said script for a total cost of approximately $600,000 in cash plus $325,000 in deferred payments.
2. The investors will make available to Trumbo the sum of $600,000, which sum it is expected will be borrowed from a bank and guaranteed by the Investors. . . .
3. Trumbo will undertake to complete the motion picture including all aspects of the production thereof. Thereafter Trumbo will undertake to arrange for distribution of the

picture. . . . The Investors will be consulted with respect to distribution and financial problems relating [to] the production of the motion picture but the final decision shall be with Trumbo.

4. The Investors will be repaid the sum of $610,000 plus interest on such moneys as will have been borrowed from a bank, the repayment to take priority over all other payments to be made from Trumbo's share of the receipts from the motion picture.

5. Trumbo will organize a corporation in the United States to which the script and all rights with respect to the motion picture to be produced shall be transferred. . . . The agreement referred to herein will then be entered by the said corporation and by a foreign corporation to be designated by the representatives of the Investors.

6. In the event the cash cost of producing the motion picture exceeds $600,000, Trumbo shall be solely responsible for raising the amount in excess . . . [but the Investors would be given first opportunity to match any funds promised].[42]

Several years later, Trumbo told Ben Margolis this was "the worst decision I ever made and probably the worst one you ever made."[43] The problems inherent in this agreement should have been obvious: the movie was badly underfunded, and fully one-third of the final cost had to be deferred; the Investors had first crack at the gross profits; Trumbo had no control over the foreign corporation; and Trumbo was responsible for all cost overruns (in the end, he had to use his house as collateral for a completion bond). The agreement also lacked a clear and detailed distribution clause. Why Campbell and Trumbo did not seek Aubrey Finn's expertise or the advice of an experienced entertainment attorney is one of the many unanswered questions that plague the history of *Johnny* the movie. Equally puzzling is why Trumbo failed to take into account the numerous conflicts of interest involved. Several years later, when asked in whose interest he had acted during the *Johnny* project, Ben Margolis replied: "Well, that is a little hard to say. . . . At that point I was sort of middle man between Trumbo . . . and my brother." He acknowledged, however, that he also represented some of the investors and was an investor himself.[44]

As per the agreement, Finn filed articles of incorporation for a new embodiment of Robert Rich Productions Inc. on March 4.[45] At the first board of directors meeting, Finn was named president; Campbell and

Trumbo and Bruce Campbell, 1970. Photograph by Mitzi Trumbo.

Frenke, vice presidents; Cleo, secretary; and Lazarus, treasurer.[46] The company's office was located in a house on Harper Street, in West Hollywood. On the house's exterior, only a paper sign indicated that it was the site of Robert Rich Productions. All the casting and secretarial work was done there. The cutting and projection rooms were situated in the basement of a building located directly across the alley.

Then, on the advice of several attorneys, Trumbo made another ruinous decision: he put all his financial affairs into the hands of Harry Margolis and Sol Scope (Ben Margolis's partner). Harry Margolis, an expert in creating overseas tax-shelter trusts, began to set up a series of Caribbean-based trusts for Robert Rich Productions and for Trumbo, including a lifetime employment contract between World Entertainers Limited, a Bahamian corporation, and Trumbo.[47] At one point, while he was attempting to explain the financing structure to Campbell and Trumbo, Harry Margolis finally gave up and admitted that it was "horrendously complicated." Even Finn did not "thoroughly understand it." To Campbell, it was just a bunch of names, and he could never remember "which company owned what."[48] Thoroughly confused about the financial plan, Trumbo wrote to the attorneys and posed twenty-nine questions. The third question asked: "If I go into the plan, is there any conceivable chance that because of it I shall in future risk the possibility of criminal prosecution?"[49] He did not receive an answer.

It soon dawned on Trumbo that he had undertaken a potentially disastrous financial endeavor. The prospect of failure began to weigh heavily on him. In a note addressed to "my dear colleagues," he stated: "I am making a far greater sacrifice of property, invested-time and lost income (past and future) than anyone else connected with the film. I am taking less cash out of it than others, and absolutely no deferments. I have put myself down for so little because this film *must* be made cheaply. I intend to fight for every penny, every quarter, every dollar that is spent."[50] Two days later, Finn told Trumbo that he was "personally responsible for every penny spent," that he had guaranteed to deliver a completed film, and that everything he owned had been "placed on the line as a completion bond."[51]

Meanwhile, money from the Investors began to flow in, and a production staff was assembled. (Trumbo had instructed Campbell that at least 10 percent of the production staff had to be black or Chicano.[52]) Shooting was scheduled to begin on May 4 and end on July 10. (Trumbo and Campbell anticipated they would need fifty camera days.) The total projected cost, including salary deferments, came to $1,087,340.[53]

Trumbo spent a great deal of his preproduction time assembling the cast. As already noted, Walter Matthau had accepted the part of Joe's father. For the role of Christ, Trumbo wanted Donald Sutherland, whose latest movie, *M*A*S*H*, had just opened. Trumbo approached Sutherland as "a bare-assed beggar" and asked him to play the part. "I am willing," Trumbo wrote to the actor, "to rework the scenes to your taste and feel, to bend or break it altogether for your convenience, to provide you with champagne baths, nubile dancing girls, little boys, pot, hash, horse or dirty pictures: in short, I am prepared to endow you with anything and everything but money."[54] Sutherland, who greatly admired the book and its author, accepted the part gratis, even though he was considered one of the hottest actors in Hollywood.

The most significant casting decision concerned the young actor who would play Joe. Trumbo later told a radio interviewer: "Joe's whole task is to rediscover the exterior world. He had to be real, not a professional actor. I tested about 100 people."[55] Trumbo even considered casting Steve Martin, because he liked Martin's face and open manner. (Martin and Mitzi were no longer dating, and Martin was struggling to succeed as a stand-up comic.) The last person tested was eighteen-year-old Timothy Bottoms, a recent high school graduate who had only

begun to act in his senior year. An agent who had seen him play the
male lead in *Romeo and Juliet* had told Bottoms: "I can get you a job in
the movies." The agent arranged an audition for a television program,
and Bottoms was offered the role, but he turned it down, explaining
that he wanted to begin his career in a movie. Although the agent was
understandably unhappy about losing the commission, he mentioned to
Bottoms that there was a role for someone his age in an independent,
very low budget, highly controversial movie production—*Johnny Got
His Gun*. Bottoms had not read the novel, nor did he know who Dalton Trumbo was. Bottoms's mother, however, had read the book, and
she considered Joe a hero. She strongly urged her son to audition for the
part.

Bottoms's agent gave him the address of Robert Rich Productions,
where he was interviewed by Tony Monaco, the casting director. During their conversation, a door opened and a man wearing a white jump-
suit, sporting a white mustache with nicotine stains under each nostril,
suddenly stuck his head out, looked around, and then closed the door.
When Bottoms returned the next day to audition for the part, the mus-
tachioed man greeted him and gave him some lines to read. When Bottoms had finished, Trumbo told him, "You have the part," but he added
that, during the shooting of the film, "you must turn into a man, lose
the softness of a boy."[56]

Jules Brenner, the director of photography, was a late hire, but
he turned out to be one of the most important members of the crew.
Brenner had worked as a camera operator on several documentary and
feature films, and he had been the director of photography on a low-
budget feature film. He loved the novel: "It's a book that leaves indelible images and impressions. I thought it was more intense and satirical
than I would have expected from a screenwriter. I appreciated the style
and historical context of the book—that it was an important anti-war
commentary with sly humor and not a little irony." When Brenner happened to see a reference to the proposed film in *Daily Variety*, he telephoned Campbell and asked for a job. According to Brenner, Campbell
"saw me as a new, young director of photography, who was passionate about this project (and who could be taken advantage of, I think)
and recommended me to Trumbo." Trumbo, however, was planning on
using a variety of film stocks and had decided that he needed a veteran
director of photography, so he hired Stanley Cortez. Cortez was one
year older than Trumbo and had accumulated more than seventy credits, including *The Magnificent Ambersons* (RKO, 1942), *The Night of*

the Hunter (United Artists, 1955), and *The Three Faces of Eve* (Twentieth Century–Fox, 1957), as well as two Academy Award nominations. But during the screen tests, Trumbo saw that Cortez was attempting to assert control and decided that he might be better served by a young, eager, unknown director of photography—someone who would not tell him what to do but could help him translate his inventive ideas into cinematic reality. Campbell reminded Trumbo about Brenner, who was then working as a second-unit cameraman on a Paul Newman movie (*Sometimes a Great Notion*) that was just beginning to shoot in Oregon. When Campbell called him, Brenner faced a dilemma. He later recalled: "From a career standpoint, there was only one thing I could do, in spite of the fact that I had to burn a few bridges to do it." Brenner gave his notice, jumped into his car, and drove back to Los Angeles, where he met Trumbo for the first time:

> I was captivated! In his script he had set up three different visual concepts and so indicated them for each sequence: "the color of memory"; "the color of fantasy"; and "present-day reality." This got my creative juices to a boiling point, given my desire to explore film and lighting possibilities to underlie the mood and subject matter of a film. But, subtly, mind you. Never to draw attention to itself. I think Trumbo picked up on the fact that I understood and loved the concept and was an eager collaborator in his intentions. His only warning to me was that we would not be shooting through things, like trees and other foreground objects. He had an aversion to that technique, which he might have associated with the "new breed" of cameramen. I committed to him that I would not originate such a shot unless he demanded or strongly recommended it.[57]

The same day he hired Brenner, Trumbo received a telephone call from someone who identified himself as "cop-out Matthau." The actor, who had a serious cardiac problem, had been strongly advised by his doctor to bow out of *Johnny*. A disappointed but grateful Trumbo subsequently wrote to Matthau: "But for you *Johnny* simply could not and would not have been made. For two discouraging years . . . you alone have kept this project alive. The fact that you were going to play in it, the use of your name, the altogether extraordinary generosity of your offer to hang on when the budget sank to scale—it was this and only this which kept our sputtering little flame alive and enabled us to pull

it off."[58] Trumbo then turned to Jason Robards, who agreed to play
the part of Joe's father. Most of the actors worked on a minimum scale
as "day players," earning $120 a day. Timothy Bottoms (Joe) received
$420 per week; Kathy Fields (Kareen), $600. Some of the actors—Jason
Robards, Diane Varsi, and Marsha Hunt—were guaranteed (in addition
to their day rate) deferred payments. A schedule of deferments was completed in July, indicating that a total sum of $199,605 had been deferred
(this included $40,000 for Robards, $15,000 for Frenke, $10,000 for
Brenner, and $80,500 for the companies supplying the equipment and
crews.)[59]

The day before shooting began, Trumbo sent Brenner a set of
"Camera Notes," telling him that "aside from an occasional and unique
instance of absolute physical necessity, I wish the camera to be the abject
servant of the actors. It follows that the actors must be positioned and
moved about for *dramatic* effect rather than for *camera* effect." Whenever possible, Trumbo wanted Brenner to hold the camera stationary
and to avoid any unusual or odd lighting effects, visual distortions,
over-the-shoulder shots, and too frequent use of full-face close-ups.[60]

Thinking that the worst was behind him, Trumbo anticipated a
very successful shoot.

24

Johnny Got His Gun—The Movie
Principal Photography and Editing

> He asked me to work on it, because he knew nothing about
> making a movie, and he knew that I did. He had never directed,
> did not know the mechanics of working on a set, and he was
> not accustomed to telling people what they should be doing.
> —Christopher Trumbo

Shooting began on July 2, 1970, a few days sooner than anyone wanted, because Donald Sutherland had only two days off between two other films (*Alex in Wonderland* had just wrapped, and he was leaving for New York to shoot *Klute*). "We shot for a week," Campbell remembered, "filming all of his [Sutherland's] scenes and some others that didn't involve him. Then we shut down for a week, with everyone on salary, in order to complete our preparation. That seemed like an unfortunate waste of the time, but it worked out so well for us that we intend to do it again. That week gave us a chance to breathe and to study the film we had shot."[1]

A few days later, Trumbo received a telegram from Luis Buñuel: "I know you are shooting now Johnny the most moving book ever been written. I violently wish the film can be as good as the subject deserves."[2] Trumbo replied: "I will never be able to do Johnny as well as you would have made it, but your good wishes will help me more than you'll ever know."[3]

Trumbo arose very early each morning and typically worked twelve-hour days. While on the set, he spent many hours revising the script. Each night he would write copious "production notes" about the day's shoot. In addition, as detailed in the next chapter, he composed many long letters to the Investors. Mitzi, who was photographing the production, recalled:

My father lived and breathed that film. It completely absorbed him, and it was all new to him—hiring the crew, casting, production details, rewriting every day and during every break on the set. His total attention was fixed on filming, rewriting, micromanaging the set, and working with the actors. He smoked constantly. Chris was at his side the entire time, translating Trumbo's plans into action as well as keeping his eyes and ears open to spot problems. Chris picked him up every morning and brought him home every night. The two of them stayed up late, drinking and talking, preparing for the next day, worrying over the schedule and all the details that had to be managed and altered continuously.

Christopher quickly realized that his plan to stay in the background and clean up any messes was not going to work:

The official first assistant director did not understand what my father wanted, nor could he translate my father's words for the crew. At lunchtime, I said to him [the assistant], "I think I should be doing what you're doing." He agreed. So, from that point on, I picked Trumbo up every morning and told him what we were going to do that day. I was his untitled troubleshooter. I made things go faster and more efficiently, and I translated between him and the crew. I knew the crew's language, and I was also the only one who knew his language. He was the decision maker, and I was the transmitter of his directions. We worked together well. We had always gotten along, but this was a new—professional—experience.

Christopher received an associate producer credit, and Mitzi (under her married name, Melissa Campbell) received a still photography credit. Cleo should have been credited for still photography processing, since each night she developed the rolls of film Mitzi had shot.

According to Timothy Bottoms, Trumbo was not a "Prussian-like" director. Jules Brenner and Tony Monaco set up the scenes, and then Trumbo talked to the actors about what he wanted from them; he was very specific, but he was also open to their suggestions. He spent a great deal of time with Bottoms, who felt like Trumbo's grandson by the end of filming. Trumbo wanted Bottoms to be "real, to put himself into Joe's mind, to identify as fully as possible with the horror and desperation of

Trumbo and Christopher on the set of *Johnny Got His Gun*, 1971.
Photograph by Mitzi Trumbo.

Joe's situation." Bottoms spent much of the shoot in bed with a bandage over his face, his arms and legs poking through holes made in the mattress. Oxygen had to be piped into the "mask" so he could breathe.[4]

Jerry Fielding, the film's music composer, recalled that those working on the movie were very loyal to the project and to Trumbo. He told his wife, Camille, that he never saw Trumbo take out his irritation or frustration with the Investors on the cast or crew.[5] According to Campbell: "All of the people working on the picture held a very reverent attitude toward the subject matter and were very dedicated."[6] Brenner said, "We all had a feeling that we were engaged in something of special significance and shared a total commitment to his satisfaction with our work on behalf of realizing his vision."[7] Pepe Serna, an actor whose scenes were edited out entirely, described the atmosphere on the set as "great." He characterized Trumbo as a congenial, easy-going director who behaved like a *currandero* (the spirit of a shaman) or *abuelo* (grandfather). At one point, Serna was having his makeup applied when the lighting cues for his scene were being marked, so Trumbo, cigarette holder firmly in place, laid down on the set to aid the lighting technicians.[8]

Jules Brenner and Trumbo on the set of *Johnny Got His Gun*, 1971.
Photograph by Mitzi Trumbo.

Brenner approached the film "with something bordering on reverence—to the work itself, that is, and to its creator. . . . Above all, I tried
to define what he had been seeing in his mind's eye for the 32 years
of the book's existence."[9] As for his opinion of Trumbo as a director,
Brenner said: "He was the writer of the literary classic on which the
movie was based, so that put him in a very special category. It was probably the reverence I felt for him, his history and accomplishments that
made him, to me, a once-in-a-lifetime director. I felt and still feel that
becoming the person to translate his images to the screen was a rare
privilege and the highlight of my career."[10]

The shoot took forty-two days, and the company used twenty-three
locations. When it became obvious in August that the film was going
over budget, Trumbo met with Ben and Harry Margolis, Simon Lazarus, and Sol Scope. They agreed to provide an additional $40,000, with-
out penalty.[11] At about the same time, Trumbo sent a note to Aubrey
Finn, stating: "I have taken time out for a cool-headed inventory of
myself, my life, and my financial health. The latter, I'm sure you'll be
surprised to discover, is too ludicrously catastrophic for normal men to
contemplate. Contemplate it, nevertheless, I have."[12]

On August 23 Trumbo wrote in his diary: "Saw last week's rushes.

. . . They are good. I begin to think we have a *good* film."[13] Principal photography was completed three days later, at which point Campbell informed the Margolis brothers that an additional $110,000 was needed to pay for the rights to the negative and the music. If those payments were not made, Campbell told them, they could not obtain a print to show to potential distributors. Campbell also informed them that he had agreed to very expensive penalty payments if the deferred fees of the film's suppliers were not paid on time. If he had not done so, Campbell explained, the production could not have been finished on time; he also assured them that the distribution advance would cover the deferments before the penalty payments became due. Harry Margolis went into a rage, accusing Campbell of mismanagement and incompetence, while Ben Margolis criticized Campbell for making deals that were "unfair to the production."[14]

When Trumbo learned what had transpired, he lashed out at the Investors, accusing them of failing to pay, "promptly and graciously," the debts of the production company. He also resented their attack on Campbell. As Trumbo reminded the Investors:

> [Campbell] has been my friend and trusted business associate for almost three years. He has been my son-in-law for less than a year. . . . I want it thoroughly understood that I know Bruce to be a decent, honest, truth-telling man with no more defects of character than you or you or you and I. I want it understood that neither of us could have made *Johnny* without the other; that having made it together, we shall stand together in resisting attack upon it or upon either of us, no matter where or by whom the attack is launched; and that from this point forward each of us will regard a slur upon the character of one of us as a slur upon the character of the other.[15]

Bottoms recalled that Campbell was the "guns behind the whole thing,"[16] and Brenner said that Trumbo was very dependent on Campbell.[17]

Harry Margolis promised Trumbo that the Investors would provide the funds required to complete the movie, but he also informed Trumbo that his "financial affairs are in sad disarray for a variety of reasons." In addition, Margolis made it clear to Trumbo that he could not seek any remunerative employment that interfered with his "valuable contributions to the sale and promotion" of *Johnny*.[18] Taken aback by Margolis's insensitivity to what Trumbo had accom-

plished on a shoestring budget, Trumbo reminded him and the other
Investors:

> For over two months I have got out of bed no later than 5:30
> a.m., prepared my day's shooting, left the house before 7 and
> returned to it and my neglected bed far more often after mid-
> night than before it. This is also true of Saturdays and Sun-
> days. . . . I make no complaint. Any *professional* director in the
> world would have added three weeks to the shooting schedule
> for the excellent reason that he quite simply would have refused
> to work such inhuman hours. These hours, however, are what
> must be spent if one is to bring in a film of this caliber for under
> a million dollars. I spent them cheerfully because that was what
> I was hired out to do, and because every moment of the work
> was, to me, sheer joy.
>
> My pay for the novel, the script, the music and the direc-
> tion—$10,002—has not been exorbitant, and I have not laid
> off one cent of my personal expenses against the picture. . . .
> This is the way *Johnny* has been produced all along the line—
> by human sweat and free of cut-price labor. It was brought in
> at whatever price it presently costs (or will) only because of
> (1) Bruce's enormous talent for securing concessions and nego-
> tiating advantageous deals, and (2) the willingness of every
> actor and every member of the crew—to cut their normal sala-
> ries and accept deferments for overtime because they liked the
> script and wanted to be associated with the production.[19]

In Trumbo's estimation, the crew's work had paid off. Otto Preminger had seen some of the rushes and was amazed that, on a budget of
less than $1 million, they had managed to achieve the production values
of a major film. For that reason, Trumbo did not understand why several of the Investors—Ben Margolis in particular—continued to complain about Campbell's "unreliability" as a budgeter. What they did
not realize, Trumbo asserted, is that "there is not and never has been
a scientific or absolutely accurate way in which to budget a picture."
Trumbo then listed seven unpredictable mishaps that had occurred during the shoot, none of which could have been anticipated. Turning to
the Investors' charge that he and the project "face a grave and urgent
financial crisis," Trumbo offered to sell his share of the movie to obtain
the necessary funds.[20]

The Investors did not respond to this offer, which may have been a bluff on Trumbo's part. But less than a month later, on October 2, 1970, perhaps to forestall a unilateral move by Trumbo, the Investors transferred the 100 outstanding shares of Robert Rich Productions to another offshore trust, the Aruba Bonaire Curacao Trust Company, which thereby became the sole shareholder in the company. The Investors had effectively stripped Trumbo of his ownership rights in the film. He was now a mere trustee.

A few weeks after the end of the shoot, the crew and the Investors were shown a rough cut of the film. Brenner was dissatisfied with the way the film had been edited, and he expressed his disappointment to Trumbo:

> My overall impression was that much was sacrificed in the name of brevity. The attempt to keep the pace up produced losses greater than the gain. . . . What I am principally concerned with is the intent. Does the cut I saw indicate an intent on the cutter's part that might be in contradistinction to that of the two people who shot the film? . . . I, in fact, sensed some discomforting things, such as a possible lack of respect for the basic material, for the strength of the script, for the importance of values the film itself indicates. . . . Everyone so far has respected *your* script, *your* vision, *your* creativity.[21]

Ring Lardner Jr., who also saw the rough cut and had read the final script, urged Trumbo to rethink the ending.[22]

Trumbo did not like the rough cut either. In early November he wrote to the three editors (Bill Dornisch, Millie Moore, and Elizabeth Buxton). He pronounced himself satisfied with the editing of the individual scenes but dissatisfied with the "choppy" editing of the continuity. He blamed himself for allowing the editors to alter the basic structure of the script, and he stated that the movie had to be recut in accordance with the original structure.[23] Dornisch, feeling that he had been relegated to the sidelines, left the project. He wrote to Trumbo: "I've never been so depressed by what is being done to the most important film I've ever seen."[24]

Trumbo told the Investors that a print would be ready to show to potential distributors in early December. Campbell and Lazarus suggested that the asking price be set at $1.5 million in advance and another $1 million to pay for prints and advertising. The Investors then stipulated "that the present financial needs of Dalton and Bruce have to be considered in setting forth a minimum cash position." At that point, matters took a turn that would negatively affect the sale of the movie. Trumbo and Campbell suggested that Don Kopaloff of Donburry Management Ltd. be hired to conduct the negotiations. Ben Margolis, however, objected on the grounds that the Investors could do a better job than a professional agent.[25] A few weeks later, one of the Investors, Elaine B. Fischel, told Trumbo and Campbell that Popularch Productions, one of Harry Margolis's investment consortiums, had "acquired" the distribution rights and had retained Ben Margolis to act as its representative.[26]

When it turned out that a postproduction print would not be ready until January 7, the producers and Investors decided to schedule a private showing on that night and sneak previews on January 8–10. The print that was previewed in early January consisted of seven reels and had a running time of 129 minutes.[27] The viewers thought the movie was too long and contained too many scenes depicting Joe's fantasies. After reading the preview cards, Trumbo decided to recut the movie, reorganize the scenes, and rewrite some of Bottoms's voice-over narrations.[28] Trumbo then told Campbell and the two editors who were still working on *Johnny*:

> It is sad to the point of heartbreak that our investors' necessity for immediate negotiations has compelled us to speed up our final cut and dubbing at the precise point when most film makers are permitted the luxury of a slow-down for critical contemplation. Working six twelve-hour days a week under the almost intolerable pressure of deadlines, we have been compelled to make final decisions in action and on the spot—decisions which should have been arrived at deliberately after a decent pause for critical screenings, experimentation, and reconsideration.
>
> The only resistance on the part of distributors which I foresee—and I think it is a *real* one—is their feeling (whether right or wrong) that *Johnny* is too powerful, too relentless, too painful an emotional experience for a general audience: in short that its appeal will be restricted to a special—and therefore limited—audience. I *know* this will be one of their considerations because it is also one of mine. We must therefore do everything possible with the film—and do it *now*—to diminish anything which will serve to fortify such a feeling.[29]

Determined to make a "quality" cut, Trumbo sequestered himself with a Moviola for twelve consecutive days, watching the film "frame by frame and action by action."[30] The new cut required Bottoms, who was in Texas shooting *The Last Picture Show*, to fly to Los Angeles on several Sundays so that his new lines could be taped. (He did not, however, have to don the mask and bandages.) Trumbo deleted two extended scenes involving the bakery workers, two scenes with Marsha Hunt (Joe's mother), all the scenes involving an elderly black woman wandering through the railroad station (intoning over and over, "Where's my boy?" and then prostrating herself on his gravestone), a scene in which the black woman's son and Donald Sutherland appear together, and the scene of Joe's father's funeral. Trumbo also shortened the Greco-Roman garden fantasy and rearranged some of the other scenes. He did not enjoy the process; he especially hated having to telephone Marsha Hunt and apologize profusely for cutting a large section of her performance.[31] Looking back, Christopher said: "For reasons of economic necessity and distribution concerns, we lost an entire story; we lost the sense of who Joe Bonham was before his injuries." (Christopher was not included in the editing decisions.)

The Investors ignored Trumbo's requests for more time to edit and preview the film. They told him that, under the terms of the original loan obtained to finance the movie, an answer print had to be previewed no later than January 15, 1971. The Investors also demanded that Trumbo show the print to the chief executives of Universal-International (on January 16) and Warner Bros. (on January 17). Those who viewed the print on January 15 and communicated directly with Trumbo agreed that the fantasy sequences did not work. In a telephone conversation, Michael Wilson told Trumbo that the fantasy sequences were "unnecessary, irrelevant or baffling." Zelma Wilson thought they did "not relate to [Joe] or his character. They are more sophisticated than he is." Adrian Scott agreed with Zelma, writing that too many of the fantasies departed from "a simple lad's capacity and imagination." Jean Butler thought the fantasies "tended to conflict with the picture's general feeling of truth." Freddie Fields simply said they did not work. Several viewers expressed the opinion that the movie was too long and its pace too slow.[32] The Warner executives said they didn't know whether the film could make any money, and Universal-International said it "wasn't their cup of tea."[33] But Trumbo no longer had the time or the money to make any additional changes. He did, however, take the time to respond to one criticism from an attendee at the sneak preview: that the movie did not show the gruesome details of Joe's condition. "I was," Trumbo replied, "far more interested in what was being done than to *whom* it was being done. . . . You want me to arouse emotional revulsion in the audience by showing it bloody stumps. Against whom should this revulsion be directed? The horror of his condition is sufficient to make my point."[34]

Then, as if Trumbo did not have enough to deal with, Alvah Bessie (one of the Hollywood Ten) did a peculiar thing that embarrassed the Trumbos and the film crew and possibly harmed the movie's distribution possibilities. The "dead Bavarian" incident began innocuously enough: Trumbo received a postcard from Bessie, requesting an audition for an actor friend named Jerry Zinnamon. Tony Monaco, the casting director, signed Zinnamon to play a dead Bavarian soldier whose sole function was to lie entangled in barbed wire during Joe's short scene in the trenches. Zinnamon worked for three days. At the end of his assignment, he wrote a highly exaggerated and critical letter to Bessie, describing the experience. Without asking Zinnamon's permission, and without consulting Trumbo, Bessie sent Zinnamon's letter to *Esquire*. In the accompanying note, Bessie wrote: "The enclosed letter was written by a friend. . . . It provides a somewhat different slant on Dalton" than the Trumbo-Allen correspondence the magazine had recently printed. Bessie described the letter as "one of the funniest pieces of exposition" he had read in years, and he was sure Trumbo would find it "hilarious."[35]

In his remarkably unfunny, mean-spirited letter, Zinnamon wrote that he had wandered around the set, eavesdropped on conversations, and heard various rumors:

> [That] the first week's shooting had to be redone; that the director had never directed a picture before; that his star [Timothy Bottoms] had never appeared in one . . . ; and the production manager comes from TV where they shoot fast, and he seems confused. The Great Man's son is behaving the way he has heard an assistant director should. They have worked sixteen- and twenty-hour days to catch up. They are weary and resent the fact there is little communication between the production end of the group and the crew, i.e., they are told the night before what the shooting will consist of the next day.[36]

When Zinnamon learned what Bessie had done, he confessed that he had only heard indirectly about one of the conversations he reported, that he had changed the identity of one of the participants, and that he had altered what had been told to him. But, he assured Bessie, the facts of the conversation were accurate.[37] Zinnamon then wrote to Don Erickson, an editor at *Esquire*, requesting five prepublication changes, including the deletion of several hearsay statements. Zinnamon was concerned that his statement about Trumbo having "obviously lost control" was not entirely fair. Zinnamon also realized that publishing the letter would violate Trumbo's wish to avoid all publicity about the shoot, and he hoped Erickson would delay publication until the film was released. Zinnamon, in a peculiar about-face, concluded by saying: "Believe it or not, I have much respect for Mr. Trumbo and this effort of his."[38] Erickson, however, made only a few of Zinnamon's requested changes; he did not send a copy to Trumbo for his comments, and he did not delay publication of the letter.

The December issue of *Esquire* actually appeared on newsstands in early November, and as soon as Trumbo read the letter, he went to Zinnamon's house and demanded that he write another letter to *Esquire* pointing out all the false parts. Zinnamon did so. He told Erickson in that letter: "I must admit that after much soul-searching, and more fact finding, that many of the statements I made were blatantly false, especially those concerning Mr. Trumbo's son, Chris; the reshooting of the first week's filming, disharmony of the crew, all of which I falsely believed to exist, and to have taken place."[39] However, Zinnamon also wrote an angry letter to Trumbo, accusing him of intimidation.[40] In his reply to Zinnamon, Trumbo challenged Zinnamon's interpretation of their conversation but conceded that, after rereading the original letter, he now saw it as a parody of a Hollywood motion picture company. As in all parodies, the "specific or factual truth must be ruthlessly sacrificed on the altar of that larger general truth which is the writer's goal." Although he remained "convinced" that Zinnamon's letter "was written with malice toward me and others, it was a private malice which could damage no one so long as it remained private."[41]

Trumbo then redirected his anger toward Bessie and Erickson: to Bessie for sending the letter to *Esquire* without obtaining Zinnamon's or Trumbo's consent, and to Erickson for not making Zinnamon's revisions, not heeding Zinnamon's warnings about the letter's potential damaging effects, and not checking his facts before publishing the letter.[42] Surprised and chagrined, Bessie wrote a contrite letter: "I am sure you know me well enough to know that I would never consciously have done anything to hurt you or yours, and the fact that you think I have grieves me enormously."[43] None of the Trumbos believed him, and none of them thought it was funny.[44] Erickson, for his part, professed dismay at Trumbo's angry letter, and he defended the editorial decisions he and his staff had made.[45]

After rereading the *Esquire* story, Mitzi said:

> All the memories came rushing back. We all thought it was a very hurtful piece, and I remember the sense of betrayal we felt. How could Alvah do that? We were always targets for that kind of stuff—attacks and lies were common, even expected, and we kids had been braced for them from an early age—but this one came from inside, from a "friend," and it felt very personal.
>
> The story was full not only of distortions but lies. There was no dissension on the set. The particular location where Zinnamon spent his days was hot and awful, and the shooting hours were protracted, but that is often the way it is on location; it is part of the process. Maybe Zinnamon was mad about being an "extra," with no speaking part. But why he transferred his anger to my father, calling him the "Great Man," I do not understand. My father was never like that with the crew; he was nice to everyone on the set; I never heard him raise his voice or get angry; everyone respected him and felt they were working on something special. Some of the crew even worshipped him. Yes, the film was behind schedule, but most films fall behind. Yes, the budget problems were intense, and most of the crew had deferred large parts of their salaries, but they were like a big family. They worked together well, and I did not witness anyone mistreating someone else.

In spite of all these frustrations and obstacles, and in spite of the grueling pace he had set for himself, Trumbo derived enormous pleasure from the experience of writing and directing this movie. Everyone associated with the production was gratified that, at last, a filmed version of *Johnny Got His Gun* had been made. But the process of arranging for the movie's distribution and exhibition brought a host of new difficulties and financial aggravations.

25

Johnny Got His Gun—The Movie

Distribution and Exhibition

> I knew that this was not going to be an immensely popular picture. An honest truck driver is not going to take his wife and children and spend twelve to fifteen dollars to see *Johnny*. It isn't what they want to see.
>
> —Dalton Trumbo

The distribution decision proved to be a contentious one, mainly because the Investors wanted to sign with a distributor that would pay enough money up front to allow them to recoup their investment immediately, while Trumbo and Campbell were more concerned with finding a distributor that would nurture the movie until it found its audience. Trumbo had outlined an approach in December 1970 and prepared a list of questions he wanted to discuss with the Investors: Should he take a copy of the print to Mexico City, show it to Luis Buñuel, and secure his endorsement? Should separate release agreements be negotiated for the United States–Canada and Europe? Should an independent distributor, such as Donald Rugoff (Cinema 5), be approached to handle the Western Hemisphere? In addition, Trumbo was against using a single negotiator and in favor of involving Bruce Campbell in all decisions related to presentation, advertisement, and distribution.[1] Last, he wanted the Investors to agree to more previews and further editing. (Probably because Trumbo felt he had already taken too much of Christopher's time, he did not include his son in the distribution discussions, and Christopher felt excluded.)

As indicated in the previous chapter, the Investors had refused to give Trumbo the time he requested, and they had demanded that the current print be shown to a select audience and to two sets of studio executives (Universal-International and Warner Bros.). During the third week in January 1971, the same print was shown in New York to the chief executives of Twentieth Century–Fox. According to Trumbo, Darryl F. Zanuck, the head of production, called the film "anti-American, anti-Army, and anti-patriotic." The other Fox executives said it was too long, but they expressed an interest in seeing a shorter, more polished final cut.[2] On January 27 Trumbo received a telephone call from Pete Myers, Fox's vice president in charge of domestic distribution. Myers informed Trumbo that because of Zanuck's negative response, Fox was not prepared to offer any substantial cash advance for distribution rights. However, if Zanuck's influence in the company should diminish in the future, Myers indicated that Fox might be able to make a better offer. He also suggested that Trumbo take *Johnny* to the Cannes Film Festival before committing to any distribution deal.[3] Trumbo provided a detailed report of this conversation to the Investors, and he recommended that they allow him to prepare a final cut and then show it to all the potential distributors.[4] Simon Lazarus and Harry Margolis disagreed, and at a meeting of the Investors on February 16, they appointed a committee of four, headed by Elaine B. Fischel, to make some kind of distribution deal.[5]

When this committee asked Trumbo to show the long version of *Johnny* to a select group of people, he refused, insisting that he had sole control over all previews. The Investors' distribution committee then tried to bypass Trumbo; they telephoned various studios, told whoever answered the phone that they were the official representatives of *Johnny*, and tried to arrange to show the movie to any studio executive who was willing to watch it. When Trumbo learned of these calls, he was horrified by the breach of protocol. He sent a letter to Fischel, asserting his contractual rights to negotiate distribution and ordering her to cease usurping those rights. He also told her that he and Campbell had shown the movie to the chairman of the Cannes Film Festival Committee, who had urged them to bring the final cut to Paris and show it to the full committee.[6] The Investors agreed to finance the Cannes trip, and they appointed Aubrey Finn and Ben Margolis to handle all distribution negotiations.

In mid-March Trumbo and Campbell exhibited the film not only at Cannes but also in Paris, London, Rome, New York City, and Mexico City. Trumbo claimed that Buñuel had attended the Mexico City showing and used his influence to convince the Cannes judges to accept *Johnny* for the upcoming festival.[7] An additional boost came from *New York Post* columnist Pete Hamill, who had attended the New York screening. He wrote perhaps the most glowing tribute the film would receive that year: "This was a work of art that tears, lifts, rips, and cuts; it is savage in its single-mindedness, but it is also most terribly human. . . . [T]he perfect place for a world premiere would be the next meeting of the National Security Council. Maybe it would even move those dusty little savages in the Brooks Brothers suits to examine the consequences of their deeds."[8] During their trip, Trumbo and Campbell also showed the movie to representatives from two independent companies—Cinema 5 and Cinemation[9]—both of which submitted bids to obtain the distribution rights.

Matters became more complicated on April 15 when Zanuck was forced out of Fox. As promised, Myers was willing to revisit the possibility of a distribution deal. The Investors, gratified by Myers's approach, decided that Trumbo, Campbell, and Lazarus should take the final cut to New York City, show it to Myers, and discuss possible contract terms. They were not, however, given the authority to make a final deal.[10] From Trumbo's point of view, the trip was an unmitigated disaster. Immediately after the screening, the four men met for dinner, and Lazarus, ignoring the instructions of the other Investors, launched into a unilateral negotiation with Myers. When Myers offered an $800,000 advance, Lazarus accepted the offer without consulting Trumbo and Campbell.[11] Shortly after he returned to Los Angeles, Trumbo met with the Investors and presented a list of fifteen reasons why they should reject the Fox offer; he also made a concerted effort to convince them to accept the offer from Cinema 5. When he reasserted his contractual right to control the distribution process, Ben Margolis told him, "Your contract isn't worth two cents." The papers Trumbo had signed, transferring ownership of the film rights to Aruba Bonaire Curacao, had invalidated his rights under the distribution clause, Margolis told him.[12] A few years later, Margolis stated: "I never said the agreement between Trumbo and the investors was not worth the paper it was printed on. I did say that Trumbo had breached the part of the agreement that stated he would bring the picture in for $600,000. He had been given the distribution power in exchange for that guarantee, thus his failure to perform wiped out his right to control the distribution." In addition, the contract Trumbo had signed with World Entertainers in May superseded the original March 1970 agreement between Trumbo and the Investors. However, according to Margolis, he advised the Investors that it would be "inequitable" to displace Trumbo completely from the distribution process.[13]

The Investors gave Margolis the authority to negotiate a distribution deal, no matter what Trumbo said. It finally dawned on Trumbo that Ben Margolis was not an impartial referee, as he regularly presented himself; he was, in fact, involved in a conflict of interest "which he himself would never tolerate in any legal matter."[14] As Trumbo wrote to Finn:

> [The Investors have] taken complete control of the film, and it is their exclusive interests that are now to be served. My greatest fear is that if the movie is not an instant success, they will declare it a failure, stop distribution, and declare it a loss on their books. . . . [I]t seems clear that from this day forward I must be prepared to fight the Investors and those Investors' representatives who have acted in a dual capacity as my attorneys and theirs. I have no choice but to fight, since if I do not fight, they have it in their power not only to destroy Bruce and me but, by serving their own exclusive interests, to deprive scores of artists and workers of their rightful rewards for days, weeks and even months of hard work honorably engaged upon and honorably completed. . . . If I begin the fight, I am inclined to carry it through to the end.[15]

Finn, however, told Trumbo that the distribution clause in the original March 1970 agreement was still valid and enforceable. If the matter came to court, Finn was certain Trumbo would prevail. Trumbo, however, feared that if he formally invoked that clause, the Investors might ask a court to issue an injunction to stop him from negotiating a distribution agreement. Even if the judge eventually decided in Trumbo's favor, *Johnny*'s release would have been delayed, at great cost to all concerned.[16]

Margolis immediately contacted Myers and secured slightly better terms than those offered to Lazarus. Trumbo and Campbell, however, remained adamantly opposed to the deal, and they hired agent Freddie Fields to negotiate with Cinema 5's Donald Rugoff. When Trumbo told the Investors about Fields on May 7, Lazarus stridently proclaimed that the Investors would refuse to accept any offer from Rugoff.[17] The next day Lazarus wrote to Trumbo: "I was never in my life so puzzled to understand your thinking with regards to the release of 'Johnny.'" Rather than being "proud of" the Fox deal negotiated by Margolis, "you come up with Rugoff." According to Lazarus, Rugoff distributed only movies that had been rejected by major studios, so they could never generate as much profit. In conclusion, Lazarus reasserted the dubious assumption that had motivated him from the beginning: "'Johnny' is a great picture that will play as many theaters as 'MASH' [*sic*]. And in my opinion will impress people more than 'MASH' did. . . . We have absolutely a sure success on our hands and all the credit goes to you, Dalton. For Heaven's sake don't let this opportunity slip under you."[18]

Trumbo rejected all of Lazarus's arguments. Yes, Trumbo acknowledged, Margolis had negotiated a better contract with Fox, but it still did not measure up to the contract *Johnny* deserved. "JOHNNY is a *special* film and it must be sold in a *special* way," Trumbo emphasized. It is "an uncompromising tragedy" and "an enormously depressing film," and many potential viewers will refuse to "submit themselves to what they know will be a painful, even devastating emotional experience." Rugoff, Trumbo continued, had achieved great success with "special" films such as *Z*, *Elvira Madigan*, and *Gimme Shelter*, and he had proved himself to be "a better distributor" than most of the major studios. Trumbo reminded Lazarus what he had told the Investors in March 1970: *Johnny* is not a comedy, like *M*A*S*H*; it will not be a major hit; and the Investors and producers will be fortunate if it grosses $8 million domestically and $4 million abroad.[19] He advised the Investors that he would do everything in his power to keep them from signing a distribution agreement with Fox.

Trumbo took *Johnny* to the Cannes Film Festival, accompanied by Cleo, Mitzi, Campbell, and Tim Bottoms. When they arrived, they learned that festival director Favre Le Bret had pulled the movie from the competition because he thought it was too grim; instead, he had scheduled it for an out-of-competition showing. But after receiving persuasive telegrams from Buñuel and other filmmakers, Le Bret moved *Johnny* to the critics' competition. The critics responded enthusiastically and voted unanimously to include *Johnny* in the main festival program. Le Bret grudgingly acceded and rescheduled the movie, but not for a fancy-dress evening showing. When asked to comment on that decision, Trumbo replied that it had apparently been made "to spare the sensibilities of people who dress in the evening. I don't know why they are being discriminated against." He had not questioned Le Bret about the decision because "when you're a guest you don't ask why you don't have a room with a bath."[20]

According to Trumbo's notes, "All we had going for us were 800 hand-out leaflets, six long-haired boys and girls carrying signs, a single

Trumbo giving an interview at Cannes, 1971. Photograph by Cleo Trumbo.

room on the wrong side of the Grand Hotel, and two tins of roasted Algerian ground-nuts. Once in a while when a certified journalistic swan swam close enough we stood him to a cup of instant coffee with real cream in it."[21] However, Mitzi recalled that they stayed at a very nice hotel (the Carlton) and that her father spent every day giving interviews to journalists on the room's balcony.

After its afternoon showing, *Johnny* was awarded three prizes. The one they most wanted—the International Critics Prize: Best of Festival—went to *Johnny* on the first ballot by the unanimous vote of critics from seventeen foreign countries. It also won the award given by the World Council of Churches, and it shared the Grand Prix Special de Jury (with Milos Forman's *Taking Off*). A few years later, when asked if there were any critics he respected, Trumbo replied, "Of *course* there are critics I respect!" and he specifically cited those seventeen.[22]

Two reviewers from Los Angeles who saw the *Johnny* screening sent back contrasting reports. The *Daily Variety* writer called it a "touching, moving film," neither "didactic nor preachy."[23] Charles Champlin, however, described it as "a passionate antiwar sermon" that went on too long. By the end of the movie, Champlin wrote, it had "lost much of its power to move us." Champlin also mentioned that the movie "was respectfully applauded," that Trumbo's press conference was both

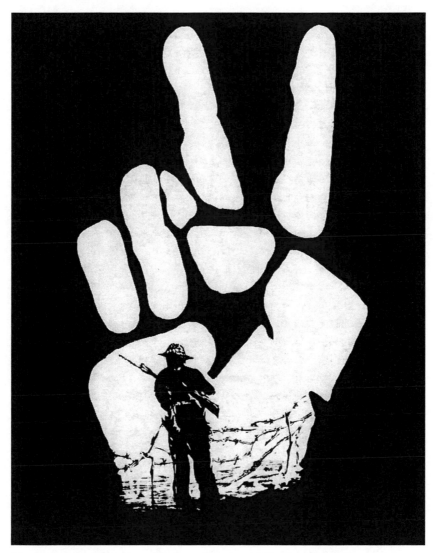

Cover of the *Johnny* press handout, Cannes, 1971. Courtesy of Trumbo family.

"crowded and enthusiastic," that most of the reviews were favorable, and that the chairperson of the festival jury, actress Michele Morgan, was "reportedly in tears when 'Johnny' ended."[24] Morgan later told *Los Angeles Times* columnist Linda Gross, "I was emotionally shattered" by the film.[25] Gossip columnist Joyce Haber reported that French film director Claude Lelouch was weeping when he told Trumbo and Campbell: "It's the greatest film I've ever seen."[26]

After the showing, representatives from Cinemation approached Trumbo and Campbell directly with an offer. Meanwhile, in Los Angeles, Fischel was attempting to regain control of the distribution impasse by engineering a coup against Trumbo and Campbell. She applied for and received authorization from Aruba Bonaire Curacao to take control of Robert Rich Productions. With that proxy in hand, she called a board meeting of the production company and announced that she was taking control of the company and the distribution rights to the film.[27] Finn categorically refused to turn over the firm's records, and he met with Ben Margolis to try to resolve, once and for all, the conflict between the producers and the Investors.

The Investors authorized Margolis and Finn to fly to Cannes, examine Cinemation's offer, and decide whether to accept it. Even though the advance was significantly lower than the one Fox had offered, Margolis and Finn approved the Cinemation deal. There are no records detailing what occurred, so it is not clear why Cinemation's offer of $450,000 was accepted. Whatever transpired in Cannes, Margolis drew up two contracts when he returned to the United States: one on behalf of Popularch Productions (a Harry Margolis company) for domestic rights, and one on behalf of Presentaciones Musicales, S.A. (one of Harry Margolis's offshore companies), for nondomestic rights. Those contracts were signed by Cinemation president Jerry Gross on June 12. The Investors immediately pocketed $300,000 of the advance, and it is not clear what they did with the remainder. Under the terms of the contracts, all additional payments from Cinemation were to be sent directly to Ben Margolis's law office. No allotment was made to the producers, the crew, or the creditors.

Trumbo, who had been repeatedly dunning the Investors to pay the crew and creditors, now sent letters to both groups, essentially telling them that no one (aside from the Investors) would be receiving any portion of the Cinemation advance payment. Nor did he have any money to pay them.[28] When script supervisor Marvin M. Weldon sent a letter to Trumbo inquiring about his money, Trumbo replied: "Because of a two-pronged legal coup brought off in October 1970, and May 1971, neither Bruce nor I presently exercise any control over money received or disbursed by the production, or over the production's account or accounting system. We have, indeed, been so thoroughly stripped of power that I'm not at all certain I am legally empowered even to write you this letter." But he assured Weldon he would make a concerted effort "to make certain that all who worked on deferments begin to receive regular reports from the production's management, dealing with the film's current economic state."[29] Trumbo sent a copy of Weldon's letter to Ben Margolis, and in his cover letter, Trumbo pointed out that the Investors had violated a long-standing industry tradition whereby creditors (not investors) always stand first in line for payments from advances:

> The management of this film absolutely *must* begin to conform with the professional and ethical standards of the motion picture industry of which it is temporarily a part. It absolutely *must* demonstrate, through regular and voluntary reports, that it regards a workman's skilled labor as no less sacred than the investors' dollar. When I say "must" I imply no threat, since you are in a better position than most to know that I am presently without a sufficient power to threaten even the housefly that lands on my nose. I mean only that it *should* be done, and that great harm will ensue to all of us if it is not done.[30]

The Investors ignored Trumbo's plea, and in November 1971 the crew members began to file claims with the State Division of Labor Law Enforcement for the overtime and deferral payments owed them.

While dealing with that problem, Trumbo was simultaneously working very hard to obtain as much publicity as possible for the film. At the end of June he took the film to the Fourth Atlanta International Film Festival, where it won the two top awards: the Golden Phoenix and the Golden Dove. In August *Johnny* was shown at a benefit screening for the National Peace Action Coalition, and in January 1972 it was exhibited at the Belgrade International Film Festival, where it won the Spectators Award and the Directors, Writers, and Technicians Award. Later that year, in December, it won the Grand Prix Award in the foreign film category at the Japanese Art Festival.

Trumbo was also giving dozens of interviews. In a radio interview in August, he expressed his hope that *Johnny*'s (and his) peace message would influence those who saw the movie and perhaps give them a different, more visceral perspective on war. To those who might compare *Johnny* with the movies he had written during World War II and conclude that the respective messages about war differed substantially, he would only say: "I am inconsistent."[31] He told another interviewer that he hoped the movie would contribute to the public's growing sentiment against war and its increasing predilection not to distinguish between "good and bad wars." The next war, he said, promised to be so horrible that "no cause" could possibly legitimate it. We must be prepared "to choose between refusing all war or total destruction."[32] That said, he hoped *Johnny* would not be viewed as simply an antiwar film, because "it is actually the struggle of a boy to come back to life. It is a struggle for discovery, the discovery of what he has lost." He also noted, wryly, that if Arthur Schlesinger Jr. liked it, "I have made a mistake."[33]

Johnny was previewed for some critics in early July. The *Hollywood Reporter* critic stated: "It is Trumbo's baby from start to finish. He wrote the novel, the screenplay and directed. He has done a fine job in all respects," but the critic warned readers that it is a "depressing" and "frightening" film.[34] And when it opened in New York on August 4, it received several positive reviews: "comes close to being the most devastating anti-war film ever made,"[35] "a true giant,"[36] "as deeply moving as I've ever known a film to be."[37] "Dalton Trumbo has with unerring aim moved steadily, heart-breakingly, to the climax he planned for this picture, that was in his novel."[38] Bruce Cook, Trumbo's future biographer, stated: "Most of what is wrong with *Johnny Got His Gun* can ultimately be attributed to the fact that this is the veteran screenwriter's first turn as a director. Yet all the many more things right with it are so because he has brought to his own material the sort of deeper understanding that no other director could have given."[39]

Most of the negative reviews offered a sharp contrast, finding no saving graces in the movie. Roger Greenspan wrote that the movie is "shrouded in virtue. But insistent virtue, without ideas, becomes demagoguery." He described all the dream sequences as "awkward, conventional in content, and grotesquely staged and photographed."[40] Rex Reed went even further, calling the movie "truly awful Trumbo . . . heavy-handed, mawkish, and revolting."[41] Two other reviewers were negative, but not as vituperative. Hollis Alpert called *Johnny* a "strangely old-fashioned work of moral outrage, replete with heavy symbolism, caricatures instead of characters, and a message that I, for one, hardly needed."[42] Jay Cocks noted Trumbo's tendency "to bear down so heavily that he often blunts the points he is laboring so hard to drive home."[43] Rather than actually reviewing the movie, Penelope Gilliatt concocted what she obviously thought was a witty conversation between a "friendly movie loon" who had seen *Johnny* and a "friendly doctor." The loon commented: it is "really more of an anti-amputation film than an anti-war film." The loon nearly passed out, but she could not "tell if it was because of the medical stuff or because Dalton Trumbo is like ether"; she looked away from the soppy and vulgar scenes so often she feared she might have developed a tic.[44]

Included in the film and video materials that Christopher deposited with the Academy Film Archives is an undated videotape of viewers' responses to a screening of *Johnny*. The most common descriptive terms were "powerful" and "hard-hitting." One person said it was "shocking"; another (a male) said it was "very scary. It could happen to me some day." A third said, "I feel absolutely limp." In terms of its message, one viewer called it "the antiwar film to end all antiwar films"; another said that "anyone who advocates war should see this film." One person thought it should be shown at every nuclear site in the country; another wanted it screened at the Pentagon. All the viewers who had read the book approved of its cinematic transition.[45]

Campbell later said that *Johnny* opened well, but word of mouth killed it. According to him, people responded with mixed emotions: "'I just saw this film and wow! It's fantastic but I threw up and I couldn't sleep since.' It was at the height of the Vietnam War. People just weren't ready for something like that."[46] But Donald Sutherland thought the movie's point of view was not strong enough. He later said: "The last four pages [of the book] put everything together, and they are very defiant and pure expressions of the position of the ordinary working person in a society. . . . Dalton did not include that in the film. He left the film open. And I thought it was incorrect, because the thrust of the whole book had been that men, in fact, could, once they recognized what the evil really was, join together and fight it."[47] I asked Sutherland if he had questioned Trumbo about the exclusion of those final words. He responded:

> I did speak with him about it, and he rambled for a while, his words muffled in his moustache. In the end, I came away with the impression that he believed those four pages amounted to a polemic and that polemics did not suit commercial film release. They'd never been in the script. The book was written in 1938. In 1940, Edmund Wilson published *To the Finland Station*. His prefaces in succeeding editions clearly show the move away from "socialism" and demonstrate why, by 1970, Dalton's film did not carry his power-to-the-people message of those last four pages.[48]

Trumbo, however, did not think he had deviated from that message in any meaningful way, and he responded in very strong terms when

left-wing critic Irwin Silber wrote in his review of the documentary
F.T.A. that Trumbo had "exercised considerable self-censorship on this
very same passage in his own film production of the novel." Trumbo
wrote:

> Do you think Donald Sutherland could have read the last chap-
> ter in *F.T.A.* without my consent? Do you think I would have
> given him permission to read it . . . if I had the slightest desire
> to suppress or censor it?
>   I gave permission for the speech in question to be used in
> *F.T.A.* because it was beautifully appropriate to the style, struc-
> ture and content of that particular film. I did not use the same
> speech in the film of *Johnny Got His Gun* . . . because it was
> grotesquely inappropriate to the style, structure and content of
> that particular film.

Then, in a burst of anger, Trumbo wrote: "If I tell you that the novel is
narrative in form while cinema is dramatic, or that *Johnny* as a novel
had two climaxes and one anti-climax, or that a film should have but
one climax and no anti-climax at all, you wouldn't know what I was
talking about."[49]

In August 1971 Trumbo, who was deeply worried about his financial
situation, asked Sol Scope a series of specific questions about his position with regard to *Johnny*. In effect, Scope replied that Trumbo had
no ownership rights in *Johnny* and no effective control over it. He was,
Scope said, merely a beneficiary of one of the trusts Harry Margolis
had set up in the Bahamas.[50] A few months later, Trumbo wryly told an
audience: "I didn't make *Johnny* to get rich. Nor actually did I make it
to get poor, but I shall more closely approach the second objective than
the first."[51]

Several months later, Campbell threatened to file a breach-of-
contract suit against Cinemation, charging the company with a series of
failures: to advertise adequately, to report earnings regularly, to book
the film into enough theaters, and to promote the movie for Academy
Awards.[52] When Cinemation officials did report the box-office receipts
for the period ending July 31, 1972, it did not make for pleasant reading: gross film rentals, $561,438; net received by Cinemation, $281,830;
balance due Cinemation before profits could be shared, $918,169.[53]
That same month, sixty-five members of *Johnny*'s production staff filed

to Dalton with all my love respect and hope for peace Donald

Donald Sutherland at an FTA performance, 1972. Photograph by Carolyn Mugar; courtesy of Donald Sutherland.

a class-action lawsuit against Robert Rich Productions, World Entertainers, Aruba Bonaire Curacao Trust Company Ltd., Cinemation, Ben Margolis, Harry Margolis, Dalton Trumbo, Bruce Campbell, and others. The plaintiffs alleged that they had not received their promised overtime payments or the 25 percent bonus on all accumulated overtime that was due once the picture was sold. They asked for $500,000 in punitive damages.[54] In September, Campbell filed for bankruptcy.[55]

But Campbell had not lost his belief in the movie. When Cinemation filed for Chapter 11 bankruptcy in July 1975, and a federal judge ordered that the company's film inventory be sold at auction, Campbell bought the rights to *Johnny* and ninety 35mm prints for the grand sum of $2,500. He planned to take *Johnny* on a national barnstorming tour—what he called a "cinematic Chautauqua." He intended to spend a week in each town, showing *Johnny* twice a day in a variety of churches and schools. Ben Margolis tried to stop him, but while he and Campbell's attorney were futilely trying to negotiate a settlement agreement, Campbell obtained a huge trailer and painted "Bruce Campbell Presents Johnny Got His Gun" on each side in huge letters, accompanied by a large picture of Jimmy Carter,[56] photographs of Timothy Bottoms, Jason Robards, Donald Sutherland, and Diane Varsi, and stills from the movie. Campbell embarked on a "sort of vendetta" to prove that the movie was commercially viable and capable of attracting an audience. The show, which Campbell described as "2½ hours of laughter and tears," typically opened with a Steve Martin movie, *The Funny Side of Eastern Canada*, that Campbell had made in 1974 for the Canadian government to promote tourism. The show also featured some live performers.[57] The tour did not attract large audiences, and Campbell ended it before the Investors' legal action against him came to court.[58] (Campbell died in 1996.)

Although Trumbo was confident that someday *Johnny* would be fully appreciated as the cinematic achievement he believed it to be, he acknowledged that, for the moment at least, it was the "one particular scab in my life and career that I simply can't avoid picking at, and the more I pick the worse it gets." He had never expected it to be a hit, but, he explained:

> What I *had* expected . . . was that at least one or two of that intolerable tribe called "top New York critics" would at least recognize what I had gone after, whether they liked it or not. I was wrong. I think I have never read worse reviews of a film than those by [that tribe]. I don't mean merely bad reviews, I mean vicious, angry, hateful, personally abusive reviews. . . . [I]t is a unique film which is uniquely mine, and did not deserve the contemptuous abuse it received in the most influential areas of American film criticism. Incidentally, its ownership reverts back in 1977, and then (if I'm alive) we'll have another fling at it.[59]

In December 1975 he was asked by *Esquire*: "If you owned a movie theatre, which five films would you show at least once a year?" He listed, in order, *Modern Times*, *Citizen Kane*, *Forbidden Games*, *Virgin Spring*, and *Johnny Got His Gun*. He explained why he included *Johnny* on the list:

1. It was miserably distributed when it was released.
2. I lost a fortune of my own money on it and would like to get some of it back.
3. It aroused such philosophers as [Penelope] Gilliatt, [Judith]

> Crist and [Howard] Greenspan to the point of absolute
> savagery, drew a gobbet of spittle from [Vincent] Canby, a
> Montenegran shepherd's curse from [John] Simon and three
> months of the worst billingsgate Rex Reed is capable of
> shrilling, which is very shrill indeed.
> 4. The picture has won ten international awards. . . .
> 5. If I have a horn that's worth blowing, and nobody else will blow
> it, I'm not at all averse to blowing it myself.[60]

As it turned out, *Johnny* (the film) did have a few more lives. In 1981 Cleo granted Bradley Rand Smith permission to adapt it into a one-man play. The following year, Jeff Daniels performed it in New York City at the Circle Repertory Company New.[61] In 1986 Fishbone, a ska band, wrote a song titled "Party at Ground Zero." The second verse began, "Johnny, go get your gun," and the third verse reiterated Johnny's (Joe's) last night with Sally (Kareen). In late 1988 the heavy-metal group Metallica made a music video titled "One," which included footage from *Johnny*. The video was ranked thirty-eighth on MTV's 2007 list of greatest music videos.

Perhaps the greatest tribute to the film, one that Trumbo would have embraced, came in 2004 by a British writer named John Patterson. Trumbo, Patterson wrote, "extended a hand of friendship from Old Left to New, and accordingly was well loved by both. In *Johnny* . . . , for all its flaws, he somehow links three great ages of the American left— 1917, 1939 and 1970—in a powerful statement emphasising the continuity between them. For that alone, it's more than worth one's time."[62]

26

The Final Years

After writing the *Johnny* chapter, follow with Pop's insane money management. Tell how he never really adjusted to having money or not having it, getting it, keeping it.

—Christopher Trumbo

I know how to make money and how to spend it, but know nothing about holding on to it. What does it mean when one says . . . "to husband one's resources"? Seems like marrying them. I husband a wife.

—Dalton Trumbo

Trumbo emerged from the *Johnny* production in dire financial straits. In August 1971 he turned to the King brothers for help. They arranged a $5,000 loan from Union Bank, for which Trumbo pledged 2,400 shares of King International Corporation.[1] Three months later he wrote to Frank King: "Right now, I can't even pay off the note you arranged for me at the Union Bank. I have sold off all but 250 shares of my King Brothers International stock, with the exception of four thousand shares which are in hock on a note at the Security Bank." Trumbo still had 3,000 shares of the company's stock in a pension fund, 2,400 of which he promised to deposit with King personally if he agreed to arrange for a ninety-day extension on the Union Bank loan. King agreed.[2] But that infusion of cash did not suffice. In December a Department of Water and Power employee came to the house to turn off the water. Payments on Trumbo's life insurance policies were due; he had to pawn about $14,000 worth of Cleo's jewelry, for which he received $1,500; and he asked his agent, George Litto, for a $6,500 advance on his monthly payments from World Entertainers (Litto advanced him only $3,000).[3]

On Thanksgiving Day 1971 Trumbo wrote a long letter to Christopher, explaining why he had been so grumpy the previous evening: "The two-year financial hiatus caused by *Johnny* has damned near done me in." He owed approximately $138,000; his largest life insurance policy was gone; he had to sell all but a few hundred shares of his King Brothers stock, at an average loss of $5 per share, and another huge block of stock had become worthless; his retirement trust fund had lost $70,000 of its value; the IRS had secured a lien against his WGAw retirement fund and against all payments from movie studios and television networks; the value of his real estate holdings had seriously shrunk; and his house was in foreclosure. After computing all the pluses and minuses, Trumbo estimated that the two years spent working on *Johnny* had cost him nearly $400,000. Although he had three or four movie projects in the works, Trumbo recognized and bemoaned an obvious fact: his days of receiving "$250,000, $325,000, or even the minimal $200,000 for a script" were over. But he believed that if he lowered his asking price too precipitously, he would find himself back where he had been during the black-market years, compensating for lower prices with a higher rate of production.

There were, however, some bright spots. *Additional Dialogue* "was perhaps the best-reviewed book of the year," and it was going to be published in Italy and the United Kingdom. In addition, three foreign editions of *Johnny* (the novel) were in the works (in Germany, France, and Finland), and 40,000 copies of the paperback edition were being sold each month in the United States. Further, Trumbo was being interviewed extensively, and he had been told he could earn $30,000 a year from lecturing. *Johnny* (the movie) had not done as well as he had hoped at the box office, but it had done wonders for his "reputation throughout the world." Nevertheless, Trumbo's financial troubles were unnerving him:

> I never did mind losing money, so it truly doesn't bother me. What *does* bother me is that I, who have never paid the slightest attention to accounts, must now spend as much time juggling one creditor against another, keeping my own books, calculating interest and penalties, as I spend in actual work. . . .
>
> And the frustrations naturally mount. Then along comes an overlooked item . . . and I could literally kick the walls in from rage. The point is that I am in one of those periodic crises of my life in which I must make new decisions about the patterns and direction of my professional life, and I am compelled to make

them in the midst of large distractions over matters which in the long run are essentially petty.[4]

It was not so much that Trumbo's big paydays were over; it was that they were fewer in number. As a consequence, he had to scramble to find projects to bridge the growing gaps in his cash flow. But none of his original ideas for scripts were garnering much interest. Perhaps his most grandiose idea was to write and direct two more movies to complete what he called the "pleasure" trilogy. It had begun with *Johnny* (the pleasures of war), would continue with "Morning Glory" (the pleasures of being black in the United States), and finish with "Post Meridian" (the pleasures of being poor in the United States).[5] Trumbo also sent Shirley Burke, his new literary agent, a collection of speeches, articles, and letters and asked her to find a publisher for them.[6] As it happened, she could not, but in the process of trying she piqued the interest of Hugh Van Dusen, an editor at Harper and Row, in undertaking a reprint of *The Time of the Toad*.[7]

Trumbo's financial condition steadily worsened. Sometime toward the end of 1971 his contract with World Entertainers was transferred to International Aesthetics Ltd., without his knowledge or consent. As a result, his monthly salary suddenly dropped from $4,000 to $2,600. This unexpected decrease in income had serious financial consequences for Trumbo and Cleo: two life insurance policies were forfeited, Cleo's car was seized by the Franchise Tax Board, their house was foreclosed twice, a valuable painting was returned to its seller at a cash loss of $3,000, and jewelry was pawned at spectacular interest rates.[8]

A very small break in the financial clouds occurred in November 1971, when Trumbo signed a contract with Eddie Lewis's production company (Millew Productions) to rewrite a script titled "Executive Action." The script was based on *Rush to Judgment*, Mark Lane's book about the assassination of President John F. Kennedy. Donald Sutherland purchased the rights to the book and commissioned Lane and Donald Freed to write the script. Their premise was that Lee Harvey Oswald had not acted alone, and they invented a group of conspirators who planned and carried out the assassination. Sutherland approved their premise, but he thought their script was so bad that it could not be shot. Nor was he satisfied with the revised script written by Walter Bernstein. So he sold the rights to Lewis's company for costs ($30,194) but kept a share (33.5 percent of the net profit).[9]

Lewis immediately contacted Trumbo, but, probably because he was operating on a shoestring budget, he offered what was, in effect, a black-market rate: Trumbo was to receive $5,000 for the first draft, $2,500 for any revisions, and 5 percent of the producer's profits. Along with Lane and Freed's script, Lewis provided Trumbo with fifty-two pages of documents compiled by Lane, Freed, and Steve Jaffe. Trumbo asked for more documentation to support the conspiracy thesis because, he said, "the conspiracy theory of history has always been a tough one" to swallow.[10] After reading fourteen other books on the subject and studying the film shot by Abraham Zapruder, Trumbo came to believe in the existence of a conspiracy to kill President Kennedy, but he had no idea who the conspirators might have been. When the time came to begin writing, he took a different perspective from Lane and Freed: whereas they had started with an incorrect assumption—that almost everyone in the United States believed in the conspiracy theory— Trumbo assumed the opposite—that almost everyone believed Oswald had acted alone. The movie would be much more effective, he decided, if the audience entered the theater believing that Oswald had been the lone gunman and exited it saying, "Now that you think of it, one man simply couldn't have killed him."[11]

Trumbo began work on a completely new script in December 1971, and he finished the second draft in February 1972. After reading it, Lane wrote to Lewis: "I believe that the work done by Dalton Trumbo has in many respects strengthened the film." Lane particularly liked Trumbo's idea of juxtaposing documentary footage of events leading up to the assassination with the conspirators' planning sessions.[12] Lewis and Sutherland both liked what Trumbo had written, but when Lewis tentatively assigned Trumbo sole credit, Freed and Lane requested an arbitration. In his explanation to the WGAw arbitration committee, Trumbo calculated that he had used only 19½ pages of Lane and Freed's 110-page script.[13] The arbitration committee members awarded Trumbo sole screen credit.

Lewis approached John Frankenheimer to direct, but he refused. Frankenheimer had been close friends with Robert F. Kennedy, and he could not be involved in a project that would, in all likelihood, offend the Kennedy family.[14] So Lewis turned to David Miller, who had directed *Lonely Are the Brave*. Miller enhanced Trumbo's conspiracy plot by employing a semidocumentary style and telling the actors to speak in a matter-of-fact, uninflected manner. Nora Sayre described the film as "a tasteful low-key blend of fact and invention,"[15] and Ralph J. Gleason wrote that it served "its purpose excellently."[16] Roger Ebert, in contrast, thought it was merely "a dramatized rewrite of all those old assassination conspiracy books,"[17] and Pauline Kael described the movie as "so graceless it's beyond even using as a demonstration of ineptitude. It's a dodo bird of a movie."[18]

While Trumbo was writing *Executive Action*, he authorized Burke to arrange a publishing deal for a novel he had been contemplating for more than a decade, titled *The Night of the Aurochs* (aka "Grieben"). She secured a contract with Bantam Books for $50,000: $4,000 on signing, $4,000 a month for four months, $5,000 a month for two months, and $20,000 on delivery and acceptance of the manuscript in March 1973. He thought he would be able to live on the monthly payments, allowing him to focus all his attention on the book.[19] This was a book, Mitzi stressed, that Trumbo "really wanted to write. He had amassed a vast collection of books about Germany and World War II; he read everything he could find on those subjects; he became an expert on the war and Nazi atrocities. He became so engrossed in the material that he would often bring books to the dinner table to read to us. The stories were so horrifying that meals were often left untouched."

To no one's surprise, Trumbo discovered that he was unable to live on the monthly payments from Bantam, so he made a deal with Warner Bros. in April 1972 to adapt Robert Ludlum's suspense novel *The Osterman Weekend*. It was a good deal, paying him $35,000 for the first draft, $25,000 for revisions, and an additional $25,000 if the movie were made and he received sole screenplay credit. Trumbo worked steadily on the script for four months. Just as he completed the first draft, however, the producers were fired and the project was canceled. (Ten years later, Twentieth Century–Fox made a film based on Ludlum's book, but using a different script.)

Just before the "Osterman" project fell through, Trumbo was given a chance to rewrite a script on a subject he knew better than anyone else. He was hired to revise portions of "The Way We Were," a script about the blacklist in Hollywood. The idea for the film had originated with Ray Stark, who commissioned Arthur Laurents to write an original script. Laurents, who had been blacklisted himself, said he based his script "on me, my life in college, during the war and during the Hollywood witch hunt." Laurents convinced Stark to hire Sydney Pollack to direct. Then, depending on whose story one believes, one or both of them fired Laurents, without telling him why.[20] Pollack later said that Laurents had patched together his characters from a diversity of actual people and constructed a romantic story line that was "too unbelievable by half." Pollack's major complaint, however, and the reason he turned to Trumbo, was that Laurents had failed to tell a believable political story; he had failed to "properly contextualize" the Committee on Un-American Activities and weave it into his script.[21]

Trumbo was hired specifically to rewrite the scenes involving the committee and to give them historical and political veracity. He was intrigued by the prospect of depicting on the screen his ideas about informing. He began by substituting characters based on witnesses he had known for Laurents's piecework ensembles. His major problem involved the main male character, Hubbell Gardner, a liberal (married to a Communist) who is subpoenaed by the committee. Although Trumbo did not know anyone who fit that description exactly, he was well acquainted with a liberal who approximated that character, and it is clear that a large portion of the dialogue Trumbo wrote for Hubbell's testimony was based on statements made by Edward G. Robinson during his third appearance before the committee.

As of August 13, Trumbo had submitted seventy-three revised pages and had completely rewritten the scenes of Hubbell's testimony before the committee. In Trumbo's script, Hubbell refuses to heed his attorney's advice and responds contentiously and carelessly to the committee's questions. He declares that he is not a member of the Communist Party and never attended a party meeting, but he refuses to answer any questions about his wife (Katie), who was named by previous witnesses. He states: "I won't take the First, Fifth, or any other constitutional amendment to cover my refusal: I'll simply refuse, and that's that." When he is asked to provide the names of people he thinks might be Communists, he again refuses. When he is asked if he has ever been a front for a blacklisted screenwriter, he replies in the negative.

During the lunch break, Hubbell's attorney informs him that the committee has evidence that he once attended an open party meeting and that, technically, he acted as a front. Fearing that he will be indicted for perjury, Hubbell crumbles and, on the advice of his attorney, returns to the witness stand, corrects his earlier statements, and provides the committee with the names of people he believes to be Communists. At the end of his testimony, Hubbell states: "I wish to thank the Committee for this opportunity to appear and clarify my position. I have been duped, I have been used, I have been lied to—but I acted from good motives. I have been slow to realize that persons I thought sincere were Communists. I am glad for the sake of myself and this nation that they have been exposed by this Committee."[22]

Pollack liked what Trumbo had written, telling him: "You really jumped in and produced an enormous amount of exciting work as well as stimulating and provoking the rest of us. How far I can go is the new problem to be dealt with. I begin to doubt the reality of getting poor old Hubbell to the stand. (One of your best scenes and damned exciting.) There seems to be strong resistance in all quarters. . . . People are sure afraid of Politics in movies. . . . It's not dead yet, but it doesn't look promising."[23]

Trumbo replied: "I was afraid all along that what probably *has* happened to the testimony scene *would* happen. They are, indeed, scared absolutely shitless of politics, which is the best reason why they shouldn't try to play in that particular arena."[24] As it happened, none of Trumbo's scenes were used, probably because Robert Redford refused to accept the part of Hubbell if he had to play an informer. Pollack later said the studio executives at Twentieth Century–Fox refused to accept a political movie, and Stark was not impressed with Trumbo's committee scenes. Redford, however, claimed that he and Barbra Streisand (Katie) would have "preferred a more political Dalton Trumbo–type script," but Pollack wanted the focus of the movie to be on the love story.[25]

According to Laurents, ten other writers worked on the script before he was finally called back by Stark and Pollack. None of them had kept track of the rewrites of the rewrites, there were holes in scenes, and the story had become "garbled."[26] At the behest of Redford, Laurents turned Hubbell into a do-good liberal who is not subpoenaed by the committee. Laurents received sole screen credit.

During the same period, Trumbo himself canceled an assignment that, at first blush, seemed to closely reflect his political outlook. Titled "The Walls of Jolo," it was a love story set in the midst of a Filipino tribe's freedom struggles. He had done some work on the script for Bryna and Seven Arts ten years earlier, and its new owner, MGM, asked him to complete it. But after working on the script for a few months, he told producer Roger Lewis that he was "passing through a *crise de coeur* in relation to *Jolo*." He had "been thinking a lot about violence in films," he said. He noted that some current violent films had some artful aspects (*The Wild Bunch* [Warner Bros., 1969] and *Straw Dogs* [ABC Pictures, 1971]), some were going to make a lot of money (*Dirty Harry* [Warner Bros., 1971] and *The Cowboys* [Warner Bros., 1972]), and one—*A Clockwork Orange* (Warner Bros., 1971)—was a technical marvel. Yet he was very happy he had not been connected with any of those films. He continued:

> I have slowly come to believe that films which focus on vio-
> lence—films which make men more violent than animals—
> films which make male human sexuality much less loving than
> male sexuality in the "lower orders"—are corrupt and corrupt-
> ing—that they *create* public taste rather than reflect or follow
> it—that they have a dehumanizing effect not just on the young
> but on all of us—and that one day, unless it stops, all of us will
> pay a fearful penalty for competing with each other to make
> the slaughter of man by man exciting and the rape of woman by
> man technically beautiful and emotionally desirable.

Because of these beliefs, he found himself consciously diminishing
both the physical and sexual violence implicit in the "Jolo" script, "not
because of what could or could not be filmed" but because he hated
writing violent scenes: "I realize that I can't do it, and that if I did do it
I would not be able to do it well. Forgive me for this late blooming of
self-realization and for the delay it has involved. You're *much* better off
without me."[27]

The screenwriter gods, however, had one more gift to bestow on
Trumbo. In October 1972 he was asked to rewrite the script for a movie
based on *Papillon*, Henri Charrière's memoir of his escapes from a variety of prisons in French Guiana. Trumbo was to be paid $20,000 up
front, $20,000 for four weeks, $10,000 on completion, and, if additional revisions were needed, $5,000 per week.[28] He hoped that money
would support him and Cleo long enough for him to concentrate solely
on *Aurochs* and finish it. He later remarked that the producers "were
so short of cash" that "they offered me a piece of the picture for my rescue operation, but the odds looked so crazy that I insisted not only on
cash but that my full fee be placed in a trust account before I tapped so
much as a key."[29]

Although Trumbo found the book dull, the assignment appealed
to him because it was more than an escape adventure story. Charrière
had crafted a sharp critique against injustice, and he portrayed himself as a man with an unshakable determination to resist the unjust,
unfair French criminal justice system and its brutal prisons. One trans-
lator of Charrière's memoir, Patrick O'Brien, called it "a furious protest against a society that can use human beings so, that can reduce
them to despair and that can for its own convenience shut them up" in
horrible prisons and prison cells. Toward the end of the book, as Papillon is contemplating the bench on which Alfred Dreyfus sat forty years

earlier when he was imprisoned on Devil's Island, he tells himself that this bench "must be an example to me. It must teach me not to give in." Dreyfus, Papillon reminds himself, "stuck it out," and he vows that he can do no less.[30]

By the time Trumbo was hired, the producers of the film possessed a glut of material: a treatment by David Newman and Robert Benton, three drafts of a screenplay by William Goldman, and three drafts of a screenplay by Lorenzo Semple Jr. In addition, the film's director, Franklin Schaffner, had thoroughly researched the subject of escapes from penal colonies, and he had his own ideas about how the film should be structured. If that were not enough, Dustin Hoffman had been hired to play Louis Dega, a role that was initially very small and needed to be vastly enlarged. Trumbo was given two-thirds of one of Semple's scripts, and he read several books on the subject. He then prepared a step outline (with questions), but when he met with Schaffner, he found they had a major disagreement over Papillon's obsession to escape. Schaffner saw it as a moral outcry against being imprisoned for something he did not do. Trumbo believed Papillon's outrage stemmed from the simple fact of being imprisoned at all: "His passion for escape springs from a passion for freedom, regardless of the morality of his conviction. Is not the rage which consumes him actually a rage for life in which life equates with freedom?" The director and writer also disagreed about how much the idea of revenge figured in Papillon's calculations. Schaffner thought the prison experience had dampened Papillon's desire for revenge against those who had framed him, but Trumbo, perhaps drawing on his own experience of unjust imprisonment, argued that Papillon had come to a rational decision to eschew revenge. Papillon had learned "that revenge is self-defeating, self-poisoning, obsessive to the exclusion of all other emotions, and, curiously, so ignoble that it is almost always the fantasy of the *weak*. The strong, after the first perfectly normal dreams of revenge, find stronger emotions and more powerful drives with which to govern and direct their lives."[31]

Schaffner, pressed for time, asked Trumbo to use as much of Semple's script as he could. Trumbo proceeded to write a new step outline that enlarged Dega's role and radically altered his character.[32] Trumbo also corrected or deleted the errors of historical fact committed by Semple,[33] but he added no political or historical comments of his own. Trumbo completed the revised script in mid-November, but he was not satisfied with it. He wrote to Schaffner: "We *do* have a problem"—namely, a 184-page script from which 45 pages should be cut and a further 101 pages should be completely rewritten "because they are *unsatisfactory*." Trumbo went on to express his frustration with the creative process, which must have reminded him of *Spartacus*. He expressly told Schaffner: "It may be, as you have said, that somebody, somewhere likes my script a little better than they liked its predecessors, but judging by what still remains to be done I'll be damned if I can figure out why they liked it better, or what there was in it they liked better, because practically nothing they read is going to remain in the next version." In other words, he wrote, "You are no better off than you were on the day you received Semple's final draft script, which, I begin to suspect you still like better than the one I've given you." Trumbo advised Schaffner: "You should either get a new writer who can do what you want done to the script, or, if you wish to continue with me, trust me a great deal more than you do now." Trumbo clarified that Schaffner should not assume he was reading a letter of resignation—quite the contrary, Trumbo emphasized: "I've never run out of a job when it's in trouble, and I won't on this one. I'm simply offering you the chance to get a better man for what you want, with no hard feelings here."[34]

Schaffner, who was facing a production deadline, did not want another screenwriter. After further discussions between the two, Trumbo completed a revised draft in January and a "final" draft in February, just before principal photography began. But it was clear to both Schaffner and Trumbo that the latter's "mouth-to-mouth resuscitation" of the script still required intensive care, especially with regard to continuity.[35] So Schaffner asked Trumbo to accompany the production crew to Spain and Jamaica for the principal photography. Trumbo agreed and spent every day rewriting, just barely managing to stay a few steps ahead of the shooting schedule. He was also recruited to play the role of the prison warden, and he delivered a forty-five-second speech welcoming the prisoners to French Guiana.

Just before he left for Spain, Trumbo underwent a physical examination, including a chest x-ray. At the end of March 1973, while he was in Jamaica, Trumbo learned that the x-ray had revealed a large shadow on one of his lungs. He immediately flew to Los Angeles, where his doctor told him that he had lung cancer. Trumbo, of course, found some humor in the experience:

> I saw it [the cancer] myself on a portable fluoroscope, which
> is rather like looking at tomorrow's rushes today and know-

Trumbo on the set of *Papillon*, 1973. Courtesy of Trumbo family.

ing there isn't a damned thing you can do about them. Frankly, I was surprised. I'd been a drinking man since my junior year in high school, and I knew that pickled meat keeps better than fresh. I'd been a three and four pack a day smoker for over forty years, and I knew that if you couldn't pickle meat you'd damned well better smoke it. I knew that nicotine narrows the arteries but I also knew that alcohol widens them, so what with

yin and yang and that sort of thing, I felt that therapy-wise I
had matters pretty well balanced out.[36]

On April 10 surgeons removed his entire left lung and many lymph
nodes. Three days later he suffered a massive myocardial infarction,
and on April 20 he emitted a massive belch that ripped out all the surgical stitches. In all, he spent thirty-two days in the hospital.

Meanwhile, Trumbo had left behind an unfinished script, and the
WGAw was on strike. Guild rules strictly prohibited members from
working on scripts of any kind, but Trumbo asked the strike committee to make an exception and allow his son, Christopher, to travel to
Jamaica to complete the script. His request was approved, and Christopher spent more than five weeks in Jamaica, writing constantly, as
his father had done. He rarely left his hotel room. In addition to completing the script, he altered (and improved) a few of his father's lines.
Among Christopher's changes was a conversation between Papillon and
Dega, after Papillon's release from several years of solitary confinement.
Papillon says to Dega: "You know something? I almost gave them your
name. I was really going to—I even called for the warden—and then,
when he came, I—well—I *didn't*." In Trumbo's version, Dega replies:
"Then you saved my life, too."[37] In Christopher's rewrite, Dega replies:
"Somebody once said that temptation resisted is the true meaning of
virtue."[38]

During his recovery, Trumbo learned that *Papillon*'s producer, Ted
Richmond, had tentatively assigned cowriting credits to Semple and
Trumbo. Before deciding whether arbitration was called for, Trumbo
asked to review all the treatments and scripts. It turned out that Benton, Newman, and Goldman had no interest in receiving a cocredit, but
Semple was certain that he merited one. After reading all the material
in his possession, Trumbo agreed with Semple.[39]

Papillon performed very well at the box office, but it was not as well
received by the critics. Vincent Canby wrote that the script, "like the
book, defines its characters less in terms of what they feel or think than
in terms of extravagant incidents and superhuman heroics."[40] Kevin
Thomas complimented the script's "sound construction, well-developed
relationships and smooth albeit slow movement," but overall he found
the movie "more depressing than involving." Thomas's final paragraph
could have been written about *Johnny Got His Gun*: "'Papillon' is an
eloquent tribute to the indomitability of the human spirit and a powerful indictment of those institutions dedicated only to breaking it. As

Trumbo in bed with his dogs, reading about Watergate, 1974. Photograph by
Cleo Trumbo.

such, it's lots easier to admire than enjoy."[41] Most critics legitimately
described the film as plodding or tedious. Pauline Kael, in a continuation of her ongoing antipathy toward Trumbo's scripts, wrote: "Solem-
nity is a crippling disease that strikes moviemakers when they're on top:
a few big hits and they hire Dalton Trumbo and go into their indomita-
ble-spirit-of-man lockstep."[42]

The script, however, was not *Papillon*'s main problem. Schaffner's direction—the lengthy, drawn-out scenes and excruciatingly slow

pace—was the film's biggest flaw. The second was Steve McQueen's portrayal of Papillon. McQueen's typical one-key, laconic performance obscures Papillon's motivations.

Trumbo's surgery and subsequent heart attack had a "brutal" effect on him, according to Mitzi:

> The radiation therapy that followed made him weak and sick, and recuperation was exhausting. After a few months he regained some strength, but he was never able to return to his usual lifestyle. Breathing was an effort for him, and an oxygen tank was installed at his bedside and in his office. Since our house was three levels, getting downstairs to his office was problematic, so he had three elevator chairs installed.
>
> We were told that he had to reduce his salt intake, and meal preparation changed so completely that, after a few months, we were told that perhaps a little more salt would be fine. He was nauseated much of the time, but he loved tapioca pudding, which we made fresh almost every day. Watching the Watergate hearings daily on television became his favorite activity, and Nixon's resignation brought him enormous satisfaction. It was, however, very difficult for him to give up smoking and drinking, but he had to—tobacco and alcohol nauseated him. He handled his illness with calm and strength, and he was rarely angry or impatient. He became a much gentler man, and with my young daughter, Sam [born in 1972], he was very sweet. She would sit on his bed, playing with her toys, or, when she got a bit older, they would lie back on the pillows, talking together very seriously. He was consumed by his newly established efforts to leave Cleo financially secure.

During his recuperation, Trumbo's financial situation worsened, and he wrote to Sol Scope in desperation, begging for information on his ties to International Aesthetics:

> I am confused, bewildered, and somewhat frightened by the nightmare quality of a relationship which on one side involves Cleo and me trying to discover what has happened to our affairs during the last eighteen months, and on the other side at least half a dozen attorneys, accountants, client representatives,

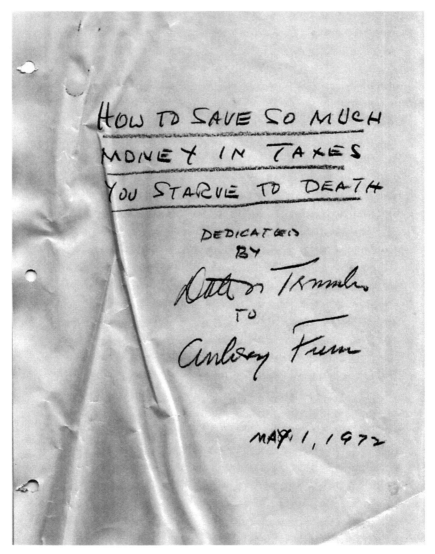

Note to Aubrey Finn accompanying Trumbo's correspondence with Harry
Margolis, 1972. Courtesy of Trumbo family.

or team secretaries, not one of whom seems willing or able to
take the responsibility of telling us what our situation really is.
. . . I swear to Christ, Sol, it's like something out of Kafka! In
fact it *is* Kafka—a pure Kafka dream in which things happen
to the protagonist for reasons that aren't explained at the hands
of people in the castle who have neither identities nor addresses

because the castle itself is only the imagined center of a land where everything moves with mysterious efficiency toward an end that is never revealed and doesn't exist. That's a hell of a dream to be trapped in, Sol. Wake me up, for God's sake, get me out of it and back into the world again.[43]

Scope, however, refused to accept responsibility for Trumbo's financial problems. Indeed, he exacerbated them by informing Trumbo that he still owed approximately $80,000 in legal fees to Harry and Ben Margolis. But they, out of the goodness of their lawyers' hearts, agreed to allow Trumbo to pay those debts as his cash flow permitted.[44]

A desperate Cleo wrote to Susanne Connell, who was handling their affairs at Harry Margolis's office: "I've been brooding of late about my chronic state of having no money." She hoped someone at the law firm might offer her a solution. A few weeks later Cleo wrote again, noting "her inability to meet her monthly payments" and asking for some sort of plan. In November she sent a third query: "How about a quick solution, before my gray hair turns snowy white?"[45]

Neither financial nor physical duress stayed Trumbo from his epistolary jousts, and he entered into battle with a former comrade (Albert Maltz) and a film historian (Richard Corliss)—the former reluctantly, the latter with relish. The exchange with Maltz was the most extensive and cut the deepest. Trumbo and Maltz had never been close friends, but they had been close allies during the Hollywood Ten's three-year struggle to stay out of prison and during the decade-long campaign to break the blacklist. During those years they had disagreed over a number of different matters, but in late 1972 something much bigger arose that irrevocably divided them.

Unbeknownst to Trumbo, Maltz had been stewing about Trumbo's Laurel Award speech but had not publicly criticized it. However, during the autumn of 1972, Maltz's ire was stoked by the confluence of three events, and he changed his mind: he received a copy of the Harper and Row reprint of *The Time of the Toad* (which he had praised highly), he read a newspaper story reporting Trumbo's appearance on the same film program with Michael Blankfort (whom Maltz classified as an informer), and he learned that Adrian Scott (the most well-loved member of the Ten) was dying. With regard to the second event, Maltz was further antagonized by the reporter's summary of Blankfort's remarks. Blankfort had quoted the "only victims" portion of Trumbo's Laurel

Award speech, as well as similar words used by Elia Kazan (another informer) in an interview about his new novel *The Assassins*.[46] The juxtaposition of the news about Scott, whose life and career had been seriously impacted by his blacklisting, and the words of the two informers, whose lives and careers had flourished during those years, ignited the smoldering embers of Maltz's resentment.

Maltz typed a two-page indictment of Trumbo that he considered running as a full-page ad in *Variety*. Shortly after he completed this statement, Victor S. Navasky arrived to interview Maltz for an article about the blacklist for *New York Times Magazine*. Navasky had barely sat down when Maltz handed him the statement and asked Navasky to print it exactly as written. "This is," Maltz informed him, "a subject of extreme importance." The gravamen of Maltz's case was stated succinctly in the opening sentences of his statement: "There is currently in vogue a thesis first pronounced by Dalton Trumbo which declares that everyone during the years of the blacklist was equally a 'victim.' This is factual nonsense and represents a bewildering moral position." When Navasky asked Maltz if he had ever told Trumbo how he felt about the speech, Maltz replied that he had, but he accused Trumbo of "double-talk. . . . I don't understand it, and I want to tell you, others don't understand it. Of course, because he has been a well-loved and properly admired man, nobody has spoken out before this. But my cup has run over and I'm speaking out."[47]

The next day, Navasky met with Trumbo and showed him what Maltz had written. According to Navasky, Trumbo's first response was to say (and "not unkindly"): "Fuck Albert Maltz." A few days later, Trumbo telephoned Navasky and requested that he omit from his article any personal references Trumbo had made about Maltz, because he thought it was unseemly for members of the Hollywood Ten to engage in a public quarrel.[48]

Maltz, however, chose not to leave his grievance in Navasky's hands, and he proceeded to express himself directly to Trumbo in a "blunt" letter. It began: "I cannot stomach your current behavior. It bewilders me, saddens me, outrages me. . . . How can you be so blind to what you are doing?" In effect, Maltz was castigating Trumbo for proffering an olive branch to informers (through his Laurel Award speech and his appearance with Blankfort). "When opportunities come," Maltz seemed to be threatening, "it will be a matter of conscience for me to make clear that you are speaking for yourself, but not for me."[49]

Trumbo did not rise to the bait, and he made an earnest attempt to mollify Maltz by outlining the circumstances that had brought Trumbo and Blankfort together on the same film program. Trumbo explained that he had acted courteously on that occasion because he had no desire to fan "the embers of justifiable hatred which had burned so brightly twenty-five years earlier." Trumbo then made two salient points: first, he should not be blamed when others used his words to advance "their various ideological precepts," and second, it would be best for all concerned if they let the matter rest. He wrote: "The idea of a public altercation, twenty-five years later and between two of the Ten's six surviving members [is] almost unbearable to me. It will pollute the memory of those who are dead and befoul the two who lived long enough to engage in it." But he could not resist warning Maltz what would happen if he decided to go public with his remarks: "I shall regret everything about it except that it was your hand and your reformer's rage that struck the first blow." Trumbo then accused Maltz of having done so already by speaking to Navasky.[50]

Maltz was not placated. His next letter was even more accusatory, charging that Trumbo had written his previous letter in a state of drunkenness. How else, Maltz asked, could one account for the "irrelevancies" and "excesses of statement" it contained? It was not Maltz's intention, he wrote (in the only conciliatory sentence in the letter), to make himself Trumbo's enemy. All Maltz wanted was for Trumbo to explain, if he could, why Maltz's interpretation of "the seemingly Christ-like statement" in Trumbo's Laurel speech was mistaken. Instead of doing that, Trumbo had evaded the issue, and he had done so bombastically, "with a roar of fury." (Actually, Trumbo had been dismayed, not furious. And if he had been drunk, he probably would have written a sentimental letter.) Maltz, continuing to ride his own hobbyhorse, then wrote: "What enrages you is not that I differ from you, but that I propose to do so *publicly*. You really do consider yourself to be royalty and you cannot conceive of engaging in a straightforward debate on matters of principle." Nor, Maltz concluded, could Trumbo—or anyone else, for that matter—offer a plausible defense of the "only victims" portion of the Laurel Award speech. After all, it had been written by the same person who had authored *The Time of the Toad*, which drew a sharp distinction between informers and blacklistees. "There *were*," Maltz declared, "villains and there *were* heroes in 'The Time of the Toad.'" But Trumbo's speech had obliterated that distinction by conjuring up "an abstract, evil time that made everyone 'victims,' that touched everyone with 'sins.' If that is the real truth, then what the hell was the fight of the Hollywood Ten, and the others who were blacklisted, all about?" Last, Maltz denied that he had gone public with his accusations against Trumbo, but he shaded the truth: he failed to acknowledge that he had asked Navasky to print his statement.[51]

After reading Maltz's letter, Trumbo immediately donned his battle gear and fired back a forty-one-page barrage. He began by announcing his casus belli: "The challenge of explaining *anything* in a way that can make sense to you, combined with the prospect of persuading you not to publish a critical word about a speech I delivered thirty-four months ago is much too exciting for a man of my diseased temperament to resist." But before addressing Maltz's accusations, Trumbo stepped back from the fray and offered one last bow to their friendship. In reference to Maltz's animus toward Blankfort, Trumbo wrote: "While I altogether reject your political reasons for condemning that Museum [film program] appearance, I respect your personal reasons, and wish I had understood them better at the time." Trumbo then went through Maltz's last letter section by section, challenging the basis of each. In particular, Trumbo denied saying that everyone was *equally* a victim. Rather, he had "used a number of phrases to denote the *inequalities* which characterized the situation" faced by blacklistees and informers. Unlike Maltz, who seemed to regard informers as the principal enemy, Trumbo had "always identified the main enemies as the Committee, the Cold War liberals, the producers, the Academy, and their various allies. I never really gave a damn about those who 'ate toadmeat' but didn't inform, and have devoted very little of my time or space to the informer on the theory that once he's informed he's about as dangerous as a de-fanged rattlesnake."

Trumbo then explained to Maltz the meaning and application of the words *hero* and *villain*. The Ten were not, according to Trumbo's definition, heroes, because they had not, on their own initiative, raised the banner of resistance: "The Ten did not volunteer to perform heroic deeds, they were subpoenaed like all other witnesses and compelled against their wills to take the stand and testify. The best evidence that they appeared unwillingly is provided by their motions to quash the subpoenas that finally delivered them into the Committee's hands." When they did decide to resist, they failed the second test of heroism; namely, their position was not "clear, decisive, noble, bold, intrepid, etc. Once summoned, the Ten *could* have invoked the First Amendment at the outset, and refused to give the Committee anything but their names. Had they done so, their position would have been much clearer than it was and their punishment would have been no greater." Objectively considered, the Ten "were, quite simply, ten men who chose in that particular moment and situation . . . to behave with honor; and who, in the face of enormous opposition, have had the courage to remain honorable in that aspect of their lives to this day. Isn't that enough?"

Just as the Ten did not merit the label "heroes," the informers did not merit the label "villains." There was very little evidence, if any, that they "*wanted* to become informers," Trumbo stated. "There is an abundance of evidence that they did *not* want to inform; that they did so with great reluctance; that they acted out of fear (not at all unfounded) and under great pressure." Trumbo then described the general nature of informer testimony: "Note how parsimonious most of the witnesses were when it came to giving names not previously on the record; how monotonously they repeated the names of those already doomed by others; how carelessly they searched their memories; how many lapses of memory they actually suffered. With the rarest exceptions, not one of them gave all of the names he could have given had he wanted to. I mention this not to excuse what they did, but to show how unwillingly they did it." In sum, "those sixty-odd unwilling witnesses were ordinarily decent people put to a test which you and I have declared to be immoral, illegal and impermissible. They failed the test and became informers. Had they not been put to the test, they would not have informed. They were, like us, victims of an ordeal that should not be imposed on anybody, and of the Committee which imposed it." The worst that could be said about them was that they chose "at that particular moment and situation to abandon honor and become informers." He observed, "They failed the test that should never have been imposed, and we did not. Their honor is compromised, and ours is not. Their lives were spoiled at the very core, and ours were not. They lost and we won, and if all of us had remained blacklisted to this day while all of them became millionaires, we would still be the winners, and they would still be the losers. What worse do you want done to them than they have already done to themselves?"

Trumbo resolutely refused to look at the situation in a Manichaean manner. In that regard, he pointedly asked Maltz: Was there not bad faith and good to be found on both sides? Honesty and dishonesty? Cowardice and courage? Selflessness and opportunism? Wisdom and stupidity?

Don't you believe that almost without exception each of us (on both sides, that is) felt compelled to say things he did not want to say, to do things he did not want to do, to deliver and receive wounds he truly did not want to exchange? I know that certainly *I* didn't want to make all of the speeches that my appearance before that Committee forced me to make. I didn't want to sell our ranch or accept bad assignments I'd formerly have turned down or write *Time of the Toad*—I was *compelled* to do those and a number of other things I'd never have thought of doing but for the House Committee on Un-American Activities. . . . I didn't want to wound Dore Schary, who had been my friend, by writing of him as I did in *Toad,* or to prove Emmet Lavery a liar before the membership of the Guild—I was *compelled* to deliver all of those wounds (and receive a few too) that I didn't want to deliver and didn't relish receiving.[52]

Maltz was not persuaded by Trumbo's explanation of what he had been trying to accomplish in the Laurel Award speech. But in his next letter he shifted to a challenge of Trumbo's comments on the motives of the Ten, which, according to Maltz, revised history. Trumbo responded (see chapter 9) and then left for Jamaica. During Trumbo's recuperation from surgery, Maltz sent him another letter, but Cleo returned it unopened.

When Navasky's article was printed, it included a short statement by Maltz containing two questionable accusations. The first—that Trumbo had not advanced his "only victims" doctrine while he was on the blacklist—ignored the fact that Trumbo could have changed his mind, for reasons he found persuasive. The second—that the "only victims" statement "has been ecstatically embraced" by informers—was irrelevant.[53] Simply put, Maltz's stated purpose of his correspondence with Trumbo simply does not square with the contents of the polemical letters he wrote or the comments he made afterward.

For example, in his oral history, Maltz claimed to be seeking a high-toned, philosophical discussion, but Trumbo had defeated that purpose by taking a tone "of bitter sarcasm with an underlying rage."[54] In an unpublished "Addenda on Trumbo," Maltz wrote: *"In order to defend his only victims thesis, he has to demean the reason why the Ten took the position it did."* And in an undated note titled "Why I Don't Want the Maltz-Trumbo Correspondence Published," Maltz impugned Trumbo's honesty, stating: "I was writing to a friend and a one-time comrade-in-arms, but Trumbo was writing for publication." But Maltz's self-righteousness had blinded him. No objective reader of Trumbo's forty-one-page letter can find credence in Maltz's statement that Trumbo's letters were "not always to the point or seriously enlightening or honest."[55]

Probably without realizing it, Maltz revealed the source of his animus in his second letter to Trumbo by characterizing the tone of Trumbo's first letter as "royal." Maltz apparently believed that Trumbo had appointed himself the official blacklist scribe whose imprimatur had to be stamped on all interpretations of events. Maltz had convinced himself that Trumbo, basking in his post-1960 success as a screenwriter, was speaking down to those (like Maltz) who had not enjoyed a similar breakthrough.

In the second, lesser joust, Trumbo sought to defend his reputation as a writer. In September 1971 film historian and critic Richard Corliss used his review of *Johnny Got His Gun* (the movie) to comment negatively on Trumbo's skills as a screenwriter: Trumbo "directs movies as he writes them, with every gesture underlined, every glance portentous, the camera catching his actors only when they 'act.'" In what would turn out to be an ironic conclusion, Corliss complimented Trumbo's letter-writing skills and then stated: "I could imagine no greater pleasure than joining the ranks of those FBI agents, passport officials, garage mechanics—and friends—who were the recipients of one of Dalton Trumbo's florid, cantankerous, incandescent salvos."[56]

The following year Corliss repeated many of the same negative comments in a chapter he contributed to *The Hollywood Screenwriters*. Although Corliss called Trumbo a "remarkable writer" and praised *Additional Dialogue*, he went on to state that Trumbo's "reputation as a top screenwriter is all but inexplicable. Those of his films that cannot be dismissed as sophisticated but uninspired hack work are inevitably cursed with either preachy self-importance or cheery (but still preachy) patriotism." Trumbo might have been able to accept those words as merely the opinion of another film critic, but Corliss then made a series of unfounded, untrue, and just plain silly generalizations about Trumbo: "His career virtually sets the mold for Hollywood's intellectual, left-wing screenwriters, who saw it as their mission to convert the very masses they despised writing down to. . . . Trumbo apotheosized the committed writer determined, in his own words, 'to use art as a weapon in the future of mankind, rather than as an adornment for the vanity of aesthetes and poseurs.' In Trumbo's hands, this weapon is a blunt, deadly instrument."[57] Corliss concluded with a series of insults about Trumbo's writing, his political courage, and his general credibility.

After writing several drafts expressing his cold rage, Trumbo finally sent Corliss a very long letter in which he listed the twenty-four "errors," five "absurdities," one "misquotation," two "deliberately false assumptions," and seven "forthright lies" in Corliss's commentary. In the preface to his very long response, Corliss wrote: "My own thoughts about you . . . are mixed and possibly complex. My sympathy and admiration for you and for much of your work (especially the *Johnny Got His Gun* novel and your collected letters) inform my article, and explain, I think, my disappointment that your screenplays didn't hit me the same way." Corliss then confessed to eleven of the "errors" and agreed to the "misquotation" charge. But he denied the validity of Trumbo's "absurdities" and "false assumptions" and rebutted all but one of the "lies."[58]

It is not clear whether Trumbo ever sent Corliss another letter, but he did write several partial drafts of an answer. In one, Trumbo wrote: "I'm sure you spent a great deal more time and engaged in a great deal more research in order to respond to my letter than you did in writing your essay. That's a healthy sign: had you reversed the process both of us would be happier today."[59]

Trumbo had one last battle to fight—against the inner nemesis that had perversely undermined his resolution to complete another novel. Trumbo had first started thinking about a book on the roots of Nazism in 1960. He wrote to his editor friend Angus Cameron: "About the novel, I want to call it Night of the Aurochs. Authorities differ as to whether the aurochs was a primitive European bison from which European cattle descended, or whether it was itself a primitive cow." Whatever its genus, "the zoological primitivity of the aurochs struck me as rather an apt corollary to the political primitives who called themselves Nazis. There is something dark and recessive in both."[60] He told Marc Jaffe, an editor at Bantam Books, that the book represented his attempt to more clearly understand the leitmotif of Nazism—namely, its homoeroticism, which he described as "the yearning for a leader who can be so absolutely obeyed that one is prepared to die at his command—a yearning strong in all of us but particularly strong among the Germans—what is it but a yearning for love, a yearning for someone, anyone in this meaningless world who can be loved so purely, so absolutely, that his wishes are more important than one's own life."[61]

In January 1974, in a thirty-eight-page handwritten letter to Michael Wilson, Trumbo stated that he intended to plumb the depths of "the male herd as tribal warriors." He was convinced that the seed of the Third Reich had been planted during the centuries when Germanic tribes had inhabited central Europe, and he shaped his central character, Grieben, to be the twentieth-century depiction of what was "inherent in the history of the German people." During the Nazi period, German tribalism took the form of a "sexual, political, and mystical fuck-up" and resulted in "the immolation of six-million Jews." This was, Trumbo asserted, "a God-like act. . . . It was so far beyond war and peace and human nature and natural evil as to become a spiritual event, a mystical event, a true 'act of God' which is to say the ultimate madness, the final insanity, apocalypse." But this "convinced and even fanatical Nazi" was a human being who "was fatally wounded by the atrocities he was obliged to commit which violated his humanity, yet were carried through manfully and resolutely in the course of duty to a holy cause." Caught up in "a cause he believed encompassed the salvation of mankind," Grieben did whatever he was told, and in doing so, he "destroyed his soul and spoiled his life and violated the essence, the spirit, the conscience, the very soul" of his young manhood.

It is clear from this letter and his copious notes that Trumbo intended to use Grieben's life and crimes as a template for a meditation on morality. And as Trumbo explored Grieben's rationales more extensively, he became increasingly aware of how suspicious he had become, in his "autumnal years," of the idea that morality could serve as a plausible basis for any cause or movement. And this realization strengthened his distrust of the word *hero*, as expressed in his correspondence with Maltz. Grieben was able to convince himself that although he had perpetrated "crimes" in his role as a Nazi, he had committed them "for a high purpose, a shining cause. He was, therefore, by definition, a hero. Even a moral hero if one wishes to put the matter in these terms. True he was the hero of a Satanic rather than a godly morality, but nonetheless the hero of a morality which was after all a morality of the *spirit*." Put somewhat differently, Grieben was victimized by a "false mysticism," and "nothing but mysticism can explain" the immolation of the Jews. In Trumbo's thinking, morality in the twentieth century had become a particularly "malignant form of mysticism." He explained to Wilson, "Since no person is uncertain in his own mind about what morality *is*, or that it is *good*, it follows that there can be no doubt or uncertainty about the wisdom—even the necessity—of imposing morality upon the rest of the world; and that in the cause of such imposition, such replacement of evil with good, no *necessary* act, however violent (Hiroshima) or cruel (Auschwitz), can be ruled out by truly believing moral men."[62]

This theme of mysticism runs parallel to Trumbo's use of the term *mystification* in his discussion of the reciprocal Cold War rhetoric and behavior of the United States and the Soviet Union. It is significant to note that in both instances, Trumbo was trying to understand how the notion of a higher good often obscures, deflects, and distorts moral-ity.[63] Of equal significance, though questioning the value of moral-ity, Trumbo continued to use a moral yardstick to evaluate Grieben and political leaders. For example, in his notes for "Grieben's Diary," Trumbo argued that the Holocaust could have been avoided if the West-ern democracies had behaved responsibly (morally) by helping the Jews leave Germany prior to the war and taking decisive steps to stop their slaughter.[64]

Had Trumbo lived longer (and completed the novel), he might have arrived at a more complex philosophical or intellectual basis for his concept of morality. But because of the intricacies of the thought pro-cesses he was creating for Grieben, his meticulous attention to detail, and his ongoing financial problems, the book progressed much more slowly than anticipated. He was, he admitted, finding it difficult to jus-tify this "detestable man." To do so, he had "to become this detestable Nazi," and he was "horrified" when he realized that this effort to get to the heart of Grieben was doing his (Trumbo's) "psyche no good."[65] He complained to Wilson in January 1974:

> I flounder toward the heart of this goddam book [*Aurochs*] I should never have started. And because of *Johnny* and the enor-mous (for me) sum I lost on it and the $100,000 I still owe, partly to the syndicate which financed it under Harry Margolis (and holds in trust everything we own—*everything*), and partly to the law firm of Margolis, McTernan, etc., I am driven by sheer economic necessity to scramble (at the age of 68) for every movie dollar that passes my door. Since the offers still come in (for reasons I can't explain) that alone represents a triumph of age over obsolescence which ordinarily would give me a certain amount of satisfaction. . . .
>
> What's really wrong is not the crappy money I should have and haven't, it's the fact that I'm actually not worth a shit physi-cally. . . .
>
> I suppose that I've got between 18 months and three years, and as far as I'm concerned that's fine because I don't *want* to live too long as I am (no pain mind you, nothing pitiable, noth-

ing but an incapacity that's unworthy of description)—but I *do* want to live long enough to leave Cleo without the debt I mentioned earlier, and to finish the novel.[66]

It turned out that he could do neither.

Trumbo continued to accept whatever script offers came along, each time reflecting on the dilemma that had plagued him his entire adult life: whether to stop working on a novel or play, however difficult the creative process, to accept a screenplay assignment that promised ready cash. When one producer approached him with an assignment while he was already writing a screenplay for another producer, he said: "If I finish the current job in good time and if my doctors then project six months of decent working health, I will be gravely torn between what, for want of better terms, I shall call the needs of the spirit or those of the flesh: i.e., between finishing a novel for Bantam which I truly think might have the impact and so-called 'significance' of *Johnny*, or doing another screenplay, a percentage of which might make me a lot of money. What my decision would be at that time I cannot even speculate."[67]

Trumbo died before finishing *Aurochs*. He had completed nine full chapters, which brought the story only to 1913. A few years later the incomplete novel and Trumbo's notes for the remainder were prepared for publication by Robert Kirsch. In her foreword, Cleo wrote:

Trumbo spent the early years of our marriage revealing [in *Johnny Got His Gun*] the ultimate pain of the *victim*. He would spend the last years of our marriage exploring the ultimate evil of the *oppressor*. . . .

He recognized the reality of evil in everyone and he was especially aware of the evil in himself. He could never accept the wholesale extermination of the Jews which took place during World War II. Neither could he ignore his human connection with it even though he was not a Jew. What he did, in fact, was to choose to take on what was not his by birth. It was his by history. It was his by a quality of conscience that would not permit him to disown it.

His purpose [in *Johnny Got His Gun*] was to tell a story that might challenge the concept of the glories of war. The story said: *This happens.* The story said: *This happens because of us.* . . . His purpose [in *Aurochs*] was to tell a story that might challenge the concept of evil as an external force. The story says: *This happens*. The story says: *This happens because of us.*[68]

Some people think that if Trumbo had lived to complete the novel, it would have been a masterpiece. Others find the chapters recounting Grieben's early love affair uncomfortably pornographic. It is unclear whether Trumbo could have made an effective case that childhood cruelty, German tribalism, and German socioeconomic conditions, in the form of Grieben, could adequately explain the Nazi phenomenon. He had set a difficult task for himself, but given his dazzling analytical mind and enormous rhetorical skills, it is possible that he could have met the challenge.

Realizing that news of his lung cancer could harm his screenwriting prospects, Trumbo devised a way to conceal it:

> There was smokescreen talk of pellagra, ptomaine poisoning, carbuncles, unsteady nerves, distemper and that sort of thing. However as recuperation began to take much longer than I'd expected, I examined the problem from a different point of view and realized that cancer, after all, is a holy disease—so holy, indeed, that people are afraid even to utter the word, with the result that I began chattering about cancer in almost every conversation and in reference to almost every subject. . . . At first people tried to deal with the thing by telling me how good I looked, what a blessing to lose all that weight. Slim as a boy. Lively as a cricket. How vigorous my voice sounded. And what good color I had. "Hell, his color's certainly good." "Did you ever see anybody with such good color?" The trouble with the color thing is that you begin to wonder what color you were before your color got so good.[69]

As with jail and the blacklist, Trumbo tried to find humor in his situation. His illness, he wrote to one of Christopher's friends, "was one of those things in which God said, 'I've had about enough from this man,' and set about the task of teaching me humility."[70] And when he received a note from Steve Allen wishing him a speedy recovery, Trumbo wrote a six-page response, expressing his astonishment that "a man of your wit and experience should have risked writing that very pleasant note. . . . Astounded not because of the grace which caused you to write it but because you should have known that any man who writes a letter which refers even fleetingly to any sort of operation recently undergone by his correspondent is bound to be rewarded with as long and detailed an account of the surgical event in question as its victim has strength for."[71] Six months before he died, Trumbo informed Michael Wilson that he was writing his own eulogy because "his estimate of himself was neither as awesome as that of his enemies nor as aweless as that of his friends, and he didn't trust some inarticulate and graceless sonofabitch like [Wilson] to strike a proper balance."[72]

Despite his poor health, Trumbo continued to receive screenwriting assignments, and he accepted as many as he could manage, hoping to provide Cleo with a more secure future. In the two years before his death, he took on four very different assignments—a spy thriller, a futuristic novel, an anthropological study, and an eighteenth-century novel—but he was able to complete only one of them. He revised two-thirds of another writer's adaptation of Robert Ludlum's espionage novel *The Scarlatti Inheritance* for Royal Productions; he wrote sixty-one pages of a script adapting Roberto Vacca's futuristic novel *La Morte di Megalopoli* for Paramount; and he finished one-third of a script for *Ishi: The Last of His Tribe*, which was to be produced by Eddie Lewis. (Christopher completed *Ishi* one year after his father's death. It aired on NBC-TV in December 1978.)

The one script Trumbo managed to complete, an adaptation of James Fenimore Cooper's *The Last of the Mohicans* for Dino De Laurentiis, caused him much stress and aggravation. De Laurentiis had agreed to pay Trumbo $75,000 for the first draft, $50,000 for the second draft, and a deferred payment of $25,000. The first draft was due in July 1974, but because his illness was slowing his writing pace, Trumbo asked for a four-month extension, which he claimed De Laurentiis verbally agreed to. Trumbo actually finished the first draft in August, but for reasons that are not clear, De Laurentiis refused to read it and filed a lawsuit in New York, charging that Trumbo had failed to deliver a timely first draft. Trumbo did not want to waste what little time he had left involved in litigation, so on September 23 he authorized his agent to settle the suit by paying De Laurentiis a $50,000 default fee. De Laurentiis was required to release Trumbo from all further obligations under the contract and return the script. But when Trumbo tried to sell the script to Columbia, De Laurentiis and Paramount Pictures claimed that Trumbo's title to the script was "encumbered" (meaning that De Laurentiis owned the proprietary rights). As expected, Columbia withdrew its offer, and Trumbo sued De Laurentiis, alleging that his claim to the

Walter Mirisch presents *The Brave One* Oscar to Trumbo, 1976. Photograph
by Sheedy & Long Photography.

script had been made "maliciously and without justification." Trumbo
contended that De Laurentiis had no interest whatsoever in the screenplay; he was merely trying to protect a different *Mohicans* screenplay to
be written by another writer.[73] Trumbo's deposition was scheduled for
March 3, 1976, but by then, he was too sick.

In the spring of 1975, motivated by Trumbo's deteriorating health,
Frank and Maury King finally did what they should have done years

earlier: they sent an affidavit to the Academy of Motion Picture Arts and Sciences certifying that Dalton Trumbo was Robert Rich. Spurred by Academy president Walter Mirisch, the Board of Governors voted to give Trumbo the Oscar. And so it was that on May 15, 1975, Mirisch went to St. Ives Drive to present Trumbo with the Oscar for *The Brave One*.[74]

The tardiness of that award and his own declining health piqued Trumbo's concern for Michael Wilson's reputation as a screenwriter and his friend's parlous health. Wilson had not had a screen credit since 1969 (for the unfortunate *Che!*) and had suffered a debilitating stroke in 1970. In January 1976 Trumbo wrote a letter to George Seaton in which he nominated Wilson for the Laurel Award. Trumbo lamented that his many afflictions, which had turned him into "a compulsive crotch-scratcher," would prevent him from attending the meeting of the awards committee. But he issued the committee a bulletin about his health: "My doctors are unanimously of the opinion that the slightest disappointment, the smallest frustration, the gentlest denial of my request or the most affectionate disagreement with my opinions is more than likely to topple me like a pole-axed steer and remove me from your midst forever."[75] The awards committee unanimously nominated Wilson, using parts of Trumbo's letter in its subsequent letter of recommendation to the guild's board.

Although Trumbo was too sick to attend the ceremony, Carl Foreman, who presented the award, quoted extensively from Trumbo's letter, and he told the audience that he had been "reliably informed . . . that somehow, in some fashion or other, he [Trumbo] is watching our every movement and listening to my every word." Wilson's speech surely gladdened Trumbo. After recounting his experience with the *Friendly Persuasion* credit, Wilson expressly warned his listeners: "I fear that unless you remember this dark epoch and understand it, you may be doomed to repeat it—not with the same cast of characters, of course, or the same issues." He concluded with the hope that should such a "gloomy scenario come to pass, . . . you younger men and women will shelter the mavericks and dissenters in your ranks and protect their right to work."[76]

Trumbo died from congestive heart failure on September 10, 1976. Six years earlier, he had said: "The blacklist has done more to make my name known than any work I have ever done."[77] The first lines of the obituaries that appeared in the *Los Angeles Times* and *New York Times* proved him correct: "Screenwriter Dalton Trumbo, who was blacklisted for more than a decade . . . died early Friday at his home in Hollywood."[78] "Dalton Trumbo, the Hollywood screen writer who was perhaps the most famous member of the blacklisted film industry authors called 'the Hollywood Ten,' died."[79]

Trumbo had decided to donate his body to science. He had written to the UCLA Medical Center, describing all the ways his smoking, drinking, operations, and so forth had taken their toll and offering his body so that students could learn about the nature of physical abuse and decline.

If Trumbo had been buried, the most appropriate epitaph for his gravestone would have been his own words describing the theme of his script based on *La Morte di Megalopoli*: "What I hope may come through in the simplest terms is [that] our characters, with all their weaknesses and fears, [were] striving to deal with a problem for which they were not prepared, and about which they actually haven't the slightest practical knowledge."[80] Etched in granite, these words would have preserved for future generations the theme of Trumbo's Laurel speech and his correspondence with Maltz: in times of moral crisis, look not for heroes or heroic behavior but for individuals with the courage to act in a virtuous manner, no matter the cost. The putative gravestone might have included, as a footnote, Trumbo's wry comment about his imprisonment and blacklisting: it was "a relatively gentle experience. However, when you've had a taste of it, you can easily imagine what a whole dose would be."[81]

27

Postmortem

If there is anything to be learned from the Hollywood blacklist, it is that it need not have happened at all.

—Cleo Trumbo

He's our author; he's our screenwriter; we have this regional ownership over him.

—Laurena Mayne Davis

Mitzi and her daughter, Samantha, had moved back to the St. Ives house in the spring of 1973. During the next three years, she recalled:

> My father talked to me about his assets, detailing them and reassuring himself and me that, after his death, Cleo would be financially secure. I knew he was fooling himself. No matter how hard he tried, there was simply no way for him to achieve financial stability at this point. When he died, there was no money and a great deal of debt. Cleo needed to take immediate action to pay the bills he left behind and unravel the complexities of her financial situation. The St. Ives house was put on the market, their pre-Columbian art collection [407 pieces] was auctioned at Sotheby's [for $35,000], and most of the furniture, jewelry, and paintings were sold. Trumbo's life insurance benefits were used to pay his debts. Cleo purchased a small house in the mid-Wilshire district and lived on her Social Security and a small pension from the WGAw. It took her eighteen years to pay the taxes, penalties, and loans incurred during Trumbo's last years. In the early 1980s, fearing that the Internal Revenue Service would put a lien on her house, she moved into a duplex

with me and my family. When we moved to Los Altos in 1994, Cleo came with us.

Even though she was a very private person, Cleo wrote a variety of speeches and letters, with Christopher's assistance, to remind people of the unjust, unfair, and sometimes illegal actions of the blacklisters and of the blacklist's deleterious effect on hundreds of people. She and the children were particularly sensitive about Trumbo's reputation as an honorable opponent of the blacklist and about his stature as a Hollywood screenwriter. They found unexpected support in the early 1980s when three books sympathetic to the blacklistees were published (*The Inquisition in Hollywood*, *Naming Names*, and *Hollywood Writers' Wars*). I was the only author to interview Christopher, who gave me good advice about how to approach the blacklist but did not indicate any interest in writing about it himself. But according to his wife, Nancy Escher, it was during this time that Christopher conceived the idea of writing a one-person play about his family's experience on the blacklist, using the letters his father had written between 1947 and 1960. His template was Hal Holbrook's personification of Mark Twain.

While Christopher was considering the play idea, he began to receive an increasing number of requests for information and interviews about both his father and the blacklist. As a result, he became more publicly involved in defending his father's actions and correcting those who had distorted or misrepresented them. His play, the movie based on it, and his plans for a biography transformed Christopher into a frontline combatant on behalf of his father's historical record. He was not, Mitzi recalled, "a natural fighter, like our father. Going on the offensive was not his style." But this fight, Nancy said, was one he willingly accepted. He campaigned mainly on two fronts: (1) refuting Kirk Douglas's claim that he "broke" the blacklist, and (2) getting Trumbo credit for the *Roman Holiday* screenplay.

Who "Broke" the Blacklist?

The Trumbo family has reluctantly, but consistently, challenged the recollections of Kirk Douglas, a man they admire but who, they believe, has distorted the historical record. In the early 1980s Douglas began to publicly and repeatedly claim, in a variety of venues, that he alone "broke" the blacklist.[1] His claim was seemingly legitimated in December 1988 when he was given the Bill of Rights Award of the ACLU of

Southern California "for having the courage and conviction to break the infamous Hollywood blacklist."[2]

It was only in 1991, and in private, that the Trumbos registered their first objection to Douglas's claim. The occasion was the WGAw's decision, coinciding with the release of a newly edited print of *Spartacus*, to resurrect its Robert Meltzer Award and bestow it on Douglas "for a singular act of courage in defense of freedom of expression and the rights of writers." The guild invited Cleo to appear onstage with Douglas. In a letter drafted by Christopher, Cleo informed the guild that the family would not attend the ceremony unless Otto Preminger (now deceased) were made a corecipient of that award. Cleo stated that this was a "matter of conscience" for her. "I will not," she continued, "be party to concealing the truth of matters when I know what the truth is. I will not lend my name, my husband's name, or my presence to any affair when I know that the truth will be subverted. This is the power I have, I have none other, and I have chosen to exercise that power by having dinner at home on March 20th."[3] Guild executives refused to include Preminger, and the Trumbos did not attend the ceremony.

In early 2002 the family first publicly objected to Douglas's claim. The occasion was a letter to the editor written by Jack Valenti, president of the Motion Picture Producers of America, concerning the *Los Angeles Times* story about a blacklist exhibit at the Academy of Motion Picture Arts and Sciences. Valenti informed the editors that their "engaging account" of the exhibit "had one large omission": the story of how the blacklist had been irretrievably broken by actor-producer Kirk Douglas.[4] Christopher and Cleo decided they had to respond. In their letter to the *Times*, which carried only Cleo's name, they wrote: "Unfortunately, Mr. Valenti's version of events contains its own 'large omission,' to wit, Otto Preminger was the first person to announce that Dalton Trumbo's name would appear on a film he had written. While it took men of principle and courage like Kirk Douglas and Otto Preminger to at long last defy the Hollywood studios, it is my unwavering conviction that it was primarily the efforts of blacklisted writers themselves that caused the blacklist to be broken."[5]

In his 2003 play *Trumbo: Red, White and Blacklisted*, Christopher wrote: "On January 20, 1960, the *NYT* carried the story that Otto Preminger had hired Dalton Trumbo to write the script for 'Exodus,' and that he would start shooting in April. On August 8, of the same year, Kirk Douglas announced in *Variety* that Trumbo had written the script for 'Spartacus.'" Douglas objected to the chronology.[6] A few years later Peter Askin, who had directed Christopher's play, began to conduct interviews for a documentary film based on the play. Douglas told Askin on film that he had broken the blacklist. Christopher and Mitzi vehemently objected to the inclusion of Douglas's claim in the documentary, and each wrote a letter to the producers saying it was inaccurate and unfair to many other people. Askin agreed, and that portion of the Douglas interview was eliminated from the final cut. In the film, Douglas states how proud he was to have signed Trumbo to write *Spartacus*. Douglas's clip is immediately followed by a clip of Otto Preminger discussing his decision to give Trumbo screen credit for *Exodus*.

Who Wrote *Roman Holiday*? A Drama in Four Acts

In act 1, one friend (Ian Hunter) agrees to front a script for another friend (Dalton Trumbo). The resulting film is a big hit and is much loved by audiences. Hunter receives an award for something he did not do (write an original story for the screen) and suffers for it. In act 2, Trumbo decides he wants credit for that film. Although honor and loyalty prevent him from asking for it openly, he drops a series of hints into the public record. In act 3, which takes place after Trumbo's death, Cleo contemplates making a public announcement that her husband wrote the original script, but she is dissuaded from doing so by a close friend of hers and the Hunters. In act 4, a WGAw committee appointed to restore credits to blacklisted writers is unable (or unwilling) to resolve the issue, leaving it to be decided by the writers' sons, Christopher Trumbo and Tim Hunter.

Act 1 opens in 1949, when the blacklisted Trumbo, on the eve of going to prison, is presented with an idea for a movie by his friend Ian Hunter. Trumbo writes an original screenplay based on that idea and asks Hunter, who possesses a similar style of wit, to be his front. Hunter is sympathetic to Trumbo's situation, but he is cognizant that if his role as a front becomes known, he will be facing the same predicament. So he agrees to be Trumbo's front but demands that the arrangement be kept strictly confidential. For this reason, the circle of people who know about Trumbo's relationship with Hunter is very small: the Trumbo family (Cleo and Trumbo were very open with their children about the blacklist), Ian and Alice Hunter (the Hunters were not as open with their son), George and Tiba Willner, and Ring and Frances Lardner. As it happens, Hunter is nominated for several awards: two Academy Award nominations—for best motion picture screenplay and best motion picture story—and a Screen Writers Guild nomination for best written comedy. In early 1954 Hunter wins the Oscar in the story category and the SWG award. Two years later, George Templeton, a movie and television producer who once purchased a black-market script from Trumbo, shares with an FBI agent his belief that Trumbo wrote *Roman Holiday*.[7]

The problem was, there was no original story for *Roman Holiday*, and it is baffling why Paramount executives and director William Wyler decided to assign Hunter an original story credit. (The more accurate credit, for best original story idea, was not an award category.) According to Cleo, Trumbo wrote only a script, and he told Christopher he destroyed all his copies of that script because he did not want there to be any evidence that might harm Hunter. In addition, Trumbo tried to help Hunter leverage *Roman Holiday*. In 1957 the mother of Margaret O'Brien asked Trumbo to write a *Roman Holiday*–type screenplay for her daughter, who had appeared a decade earlier in *Our Vines Have Tender Grapes*. Trumbo told her: "Well, these rumors do get around about a lot of pictures. Most of them are untrue, but I make it a point never to deny them. Why don't you go to the guy whose name is on it?"[8]

A few years later, Trumbo decided to use the success of *Roman Holiday* to persuade Kirk Douglas (unsuccessfully, as it turned out) to produce a comedy script, "Mr. Adam," Trumbo had written for the King brothers. In a draft of a 1959 letter, Trumbo wrote:

> About nine years ago an original screenplay was submitted to the Hollywood market. It was a comedy (always dangerous) about a love affair between a princess and a commoner (the hoariest old cliché in fiction). It received hearty curses from every story department in town, and swift rejection. Only a miracle of slick agenting saved it from a permanent place on the author's shelf. Thereafter Ben Hecht and Preston Sturges took a whack at rewriting it. After two years the studio finally came back to the script it originally had bought; Guild arbitration established that 75% of the filmed footage derived from the original screenplay as first purchased.[9]

A few months later, in the *New York Times* story reporting Preminger's announcement of the *Exodus* credit, A. H. Weiler mentioned that Trumbo had worked on *Roman Holiday*.[10] Weiler did not attribute the *Roman Holiday* statement specifically to Preminger, but in a follow-up story, Murray Schumach wrote, "There was general denial of Mr. Preminger's assertion that 'Roman Holiday' had been written by Mr. Trumbo."[11] Preminger was furious and threatened to sue the *Times*. Lardner talked to Trumbo and concluded that the source was "some previous rumor" in the newspaper's files. But here the plot thickens. Lardner thought that Hunter's son, Tim (who was almost thirteen), might be "disturbed" by the story. So when Tim asked Lardner if it were true, Lardner replied, "not to my certain knowledge." It might have been true, Lardner continued, that Tim's father "had consulted with Trumbo as we all did with each other about our scripts in those days, and, for all I know, being so appreciative of his counsel" Hunter had given Trumbo "a piece of the money, so that the phrase 'worked on' could conceivably be accurate." According to Lardner, Trumbo could not further allay Tim's suspicions by publicly denying the *Roman Holiday* rumor, because then he would be asked to confirm or deny the *Spartacus* rumor, both of which would be harmful to him. So Trumbo agreed to send Lardner "an imaginary telegram to the *Times* solely for Tim's benefit." Tim was apparently satisfied by both the explanation and the telegram.[12]

His son's sensibilities may be one reason why Hunter, who was uncomfortable with the story credit and the award (he kept the Oscar in the lower drawer of a file cabinet), did not make a public statement once the blacklist weakened. There are three other possible explanations: (1) he feared that doing so might lessen his employment opportunities (*Roman Holiday* was the most successful movie he had been associated with); (2) he feared that having acted as a front might also lessen his employment opportunities; and (3) he may have been harboring some latent animosity toward Trumbo. Evidence for the third explanation became apparent in May 1963, when Trumbo sent a short note to Hunter: "This being the year (in terms of real estate and snake venom) in which I will either be over the top of the hill or dead—and either way it's going to take all the money I can lay my hands on—I'm wondering if it will be possible for you to do anything soon in the cash department. If so, it would be quite helpful."[13] Since Trumbo rarely, if ever, dunned his friends, he must have been in dire straits. Hunter, however, was clearly offended; he indignantly pointed out the "vast gap" between their respective income brackets and informed Trumbo that he was mistaken if he thought Hunter "was rolling in dough." Trumbo wrote a five-page response, detailing his own money problems and discussing the etiquette of loan arrangements between blacklisted friends.

It was by no means an angry letter. Trumbo's primary concern was to make his position clear to Hunter while maintaining their friendship. At the end, he wrote: "I think the issue between us is 'Roman Holiday.' I think we shall never be friends as we were, as I want us to be again, until the cadaver is exposed of [*sic*]. Forget money, forget the loan, forget my request for its repayment, forget your reply, forget our recent conversations here [in Rome]. Think only of the possibility 'Roman Holiday' is our problem. Then tell me honestly as only a friend can (and must) your feelings about it, and all lesser troubles will be swept away from that bleak area which now separates us."[14] Trumbo did not send the letter, and it is unlikely that he ever broached the subject directly with Hunter, but Trumbo began to drop broad hints to others.

Four years later Bob Jennings, a close friend of Trumbo's, wrote: "One of his best scripts was Oscared in another man's name."[15] In 1970 Howard Suber, who was writing a doctoral dissertation on the Hollywood blacklist, claimed he had "tricked" Trumbo into admitting he wrote the story for *Roman Holiday*, but Trumbo had sworn him to secrecy until both he and Hunter had died. According to Suber, Trumbo and Hunter discussed the credit question after Trumbo returned from Mexico, and they decided that a public announcement could only hurt both of them; there was thus nothing to do "but let the false impression remain."[16] A few years later, however, Trumbo confessed to Bruce Cook that he had written the original screenplay for *Roman Holiday*.[17]

It is evident that Trumbo came to believe he deserved a cocredit (and wanted his name on the award plaque), but he also knew he could not publicly claim it. Perhaps his hints and revelations were part of a plan to goad Hunter into making the requisite announcement, or perhaps they were unplanned and spontaneous. Whatever his intent, the rumors did not work. Neither Ian nor Alice Hunter ever publicly admitted that Trumbo had written the original script, and Trumbo's public disclosures angered Ring Lardner Jr., a close friend to both Trumbo and Hunter. The Lardners felt they had been put in the middle. They told their daughter, Kate, many years after Trumbo's death: "Trumbo should have kept his big, fat mouth shut!"[18]

In 1977 Cleo gave serious thought to making a public announcement about her husband's authorship of *Roman Holiday*. Because she was a close friend of the Hunters and did not want to hurt or embarrass them, she sought Lardner's advice. According to Joe Lardner, his father tried to dissuade Cleo from making any kind of public announcement and cited several reasons. First, it would embarrass Hunter, who had already been embarrassed by the leaks on the subject; second, Hunter had agreed to the proposition only after receiving Trumbo's assurance of complete confidentiality; and third, Hunter had done a considerable amount of rewriting on the script. Lardner admitted he was not sure how much rewriting Hunter had done, but he was sure it was sufficient to merit a screenplay credit.[19] Apparently, Lardner made a compelling case, because Cleo remained silent. But Hunter did not. In December 1986 he told Bernard Dick that Trumbo had written the story but not the screenplay for *Roman Holiday*.[20]

Ian Hunter died in March 1991. By happenstance, two months later I wrote a letter to the board of the WGAw, stating that Albert Maltz deserved to share the SWG award for the *Broken Arrow* screenplay. (That award, for best written western movie, had been given to Michael Blankfort, Maltz's front.) I enclosed an article I had written about the making of *Broken Arrow* and a copy of the contract Maltz and Blankfort had signed.[21] When the guild's journal reprinted my article, a movie buff named Steven Barr contacted the guild and said, in effect: "I have heard that Dalton Trumbo wrote *Roman Holiday*, and I am not the only one who knows this."[22] When the guild's investigation of both these claims reached the newspapers, Howard Suber wrote an article for the *Los Angeles Times*, and one week later, Jan Herman (William Wyler's biographer) published an interview with Ian Hunter conducted shortly before his death. In that interview, Hunter told Herman: "My recollection is that Trumbo wrote an original story. . . . . [I]t was certainly Trumbo's story and mostly my screenplay with [John] Dighton."[23]

The following March, without any prompting by the Trumbos, the WGAw added Trumbo's name to its award plaque as a corecipient of the award for best written comedy for *Roman Holiday,* and it gave an award proclaiming that fact to Cleo Trumbo. (The guild did the same for Albert Maltz, naming him a corecipient of the award for best written western for *Broken Arrow* and presenting an award to Esther Maltz.) Ninth months later, the Academy's Board of Governors voted to award Trumbo a posthumous Oscar for his story for *Roman Holiday*. At a special ceremony held on May 12, 1993, at the Academy's Samuel Goldwyn Theater, Cleo spoke eloquently about her husband's two award-winning movies—*Roman Holiday* and *The Brave One*— the reality of the blacklist years, and the need for future vigilance:

> I don't want to leave you with the impression that living under the blacklist was a steady procession of motion picture assign-

ments and secret honors. It was not. Earning a living was a precarious business. The Hollywood blacklist put hundreds of people out of work, and, across the country, loyalty oaths forced thousands more out of their jobs in all walks of life, from the factory to the university. It was a time of fear and no one was exempt. Dalton called it "The Time of the Toad." . . .

This award makes the declaration that "The Time of the Toad" in our community has passed. But if we are not wise enough to learn the lessons of the blacklist, I am afraid that at some future time another generation will be faced with the same circumstance. Once again men and women will find themselves compelled to risk everything in a fight they did not choose, and stand up for the principles so eloquently stated in our Constitution.[24]

There matters stood until January 1996, when, at the urging of Paul Jarrico, the WGAw established a committee charged with investigating and restoring credits to writers who had written under pseudonyms or behind fronts.[25] When the committee contacted the families of all the potential candidates for credit restoration and the families of their fronts, the Trumbos decided to make a case for Trumbo's cocredit for the *Roman Holiday* screenplay. Christopher said to me:

I thought the idea of getting blacklisted writers credit for their uncredited screenplays was a worthy effort which was long overdue. . . . I should also add that as far as Cleo was concerned, and my sisters and I also, it was of no matter if Trumbo didn't receive any credits and/or awards for his uncredited blacklist work and we never lobbied for either. It was only when others began to address the problem and propose solutions that we—mostly through me, at Cleo's request—became involved. All of us, however, thought it was good that others, who hadn't achieved the kind of public recognition that Trumbo had, were at least being recognized for their work.

In June 1997 Cleo wrote to Lardner, expressing her dismay that at the time she accepted Trumbo's posthumous Oscar for *Roman Holiday*, none of those who knew the truth were "completely forthright concerning who did what. . . . I brought the matter up to Alice [Hunter] on her last visit to LA, but she became very angry and insisted Ian had written the script. So I backed off. But I remember that Trumbo wrote the screenplay of *Roman Holiday* . . . and that he wrote it as a screenplay rather than a story because he knew if it sold as a screenplay it would bring considerably more money than a story." She asked Lardner what he remembered and what he honestly thought about the situation.[26]

Lardner responded that Hunter had done "considerable work rewriting" Trumbo's screenplay, but he had no idea how much of the script Hunter had changed or how much Dighton had changed later. Lardner added: "I was quite aware of Ian's distress over the whole business, which was all the greater because the Oscar was for the one part (the original idea) in which he had no hand." Lardner concluded that the credit should read: "Screenplay by Dalton Trumbo, and Ian McLellan Hunter and John Dighton, from a story by Dalton Trumbo."[27]

A member of the guild kept Christopher apprised of the committee's progress and provided him with the documentary evidence it unearthed. At some point during the process, Christopher recounted:

> Paul [Jarrico] called me and said there was going to be a press conference later in the week and the final results of the [WGAw] committee's work was going to be announced. He told me what Trumbo's revised credits would be. *Roman Holiday* and *The Brave One* were the only credits that really interested me, and Paul said that Trumbo would receive a story credit for both. I objected, saying that Trumbo had written both projects as original screenplays, not stories. . . . Paul was adamant that the credits should stand as the committee had determined them. I was unyielding in my conviction. . . . I told Paul he could announce what he pleased, but if Trumbo received only story credit for *Roman Holiday* and *The Brave One* I would call Army Archerd [gossip columnist for *Daily Variety*]—and whomever else I could think of (I have a fertile imagination)—assert that Trumbo wrote the screenplays and blast the blacklist credit committee for incompetence. The procedures of the committee were wobbly—they knew it and so did I, so my threat carried some weight. Paul's eventual solution was to announce all the blacklist credits except Trumbo's. A reinvestigation of all of Trumbo's blacklisted scripts was made and a number of them changed from what the committee had previously determined.

In the fall of 1999 the committee members came to the following conclusions about Trumbo's blacklist work. They did not recommend correcting the screen credits for *The Abominable Snowman of the Himalayas* (1957), *The Beautiful Blonde from Bashful Bend* (1949), *Code Two* (1953), *The Brothers Rico* (1957), *The Deerslayer* (1957), *Enchanted Island* (1959), *From the Earth to the Moon* (1958), *Girl in the Woods* (1958), *Heaven Knows Mr. Allison* (1957), *Heaven with a Gun* (1958), *Last Train from Gun Hill* (1958), *Red Ball Express* (1952), and *Rocketship X-M* (1950). But they did recommend correcting, in Trumbo's favor, the screen credits for *The Boss* (1956), *The Brave One* (1956), *Cowboy* (1958), *The Green-Eyed Blonde* (1957), *He Ran All the Way* (1951), *The Prowler* (1951), and *Terror in a Texas Town* (1958).[28] Pending the receipt of additional information, the committee decided to table several other potential credits: *Carnival Story* (1954), *They Were So Young* (1955), *Wild Is the Wind* (1957), and *The Young Philadelphians* (1959). However, in the case of *Roman Holiday* (1953), the committee members accepted Christopher's statement that Trumbo had written the original screenplay, but because they did not have a copy of it, and because the Hunter family continued to deny that such a screenplay ever existed, they told Christopher they could not award Trumbo a cocredit.[29]

The Trumbos were not happy, but all avenues now seemed closed. One year later, however, Tim Hunter asked Lardner if Trumbo had in fact written a screenplay. Lardner confirmed that he had, but Hunter did nothing with that information. None of the Trumbos asked him to intervene, he recalled, and prior to Christopher's final illness, he did not discuss the matter with him.[30] In late December 2010, when Christopher knew he was dying, he said to his wife: "Since there is not a lot of time, you, Michael Butler, Jeff Freilich, and Larry could talk to him [Tim] and get him to agree to an official change in the credits. He's told the same story [as mine] to you and Michael, so you need to get him to the Guild [WGAw] and to the Academy and fix it. [It] will be a big send-off, a way to keep Ian's role positive to undertake what he did."[31]

Shortly after Christopher died, Tim Hunter wrote a letter to guild president John Wells, stating that Trumbo had written the original screenplay and merited a cocredit. The letter reflected Hunter's ambivalence on the subject. Leaving the original credits unchanged, he noted, "was tangible proof of a friendship, a symbol on celluloid of many friendships, and the manifestation of a pact between friends during a time of political persecution." He then said he did not know for sure who wrote the original script, but he had come to believe that Trumbo did.[32] It took eleven months for the guild to act. An announcement was finally made on December 19, 2011. Many of the stories that followed characterized it as "a death-bed promise between childhood friends."[33] But such bathetic comments overlook several facts—Christopher and Tim were not close friends, there was a seven-year difference in their ages, and they had grown up 3,000 miles apart.

Still, some reporters continued to get the facts wrong. For example, Richard Verrier wrote in the *Los Angeles Times*: "Hunter fronted for him [Trumbo] in selling the story [*sic*] for 'Roman Holiday.'"[34] But the *New York Times* got it right, heading its article: "Dalton Trumbo's Screenwriting Credit Restored to 'Roman Holiday.'"[35]

My Old Colorado Home

Trumbo returned to Colorado only once, in 1962, for Nikola's graduation from the University of Colorado. But after years of inattention, he was commemorated in Boulder and embraced in Grand Junction. In 1992 Kristina Baumli, a graduate student at the University of Colorado, launched a campaign to rename the fountain area outside the student union the "Dalton Trumbo Fountain Court." She garnered the support of thirty-six faculty members and received letters of support from Jane Fonda, Katharine Hepburn, Walter Matthau, Robert Redford, and Pete Seeger, among others. The following year the university's regents approved the proposal and designated the fountain's environs a "free-speech zone." The actual naming ceremony coincided with a Dalton Trumbo Memorial Conference that included a series of speeches and symposia examining the First Amendment, censorship, and, of course, Trumbo. Simultaneously, the Denver International Film Festival showed three of Trumbo's films—*Gun Crazy, Lonely Are the Brave,* and *Johnny Got His Gun*. Nikola did not attend the fountain's dedication ceremony because of the boycott protesting a recently passed anti-gay and anti-lesbian amendment to the state's constitution.[36] At the ceremony on October 17, Cleo said that Trumbo would have been dismayed by that amendment, which prohibited cities in Colorado from enacting antidiscrimination laws. "There is," she said, a "great need to protect minority groups against discrimination." She also said, "I can think of nothing Dalton would have liked better than to have a free-speech area dedicated to him. He would have been startled, but he would have been pleased. He was devoted to free speech—he wanted it

Trumbo fountain, Colorado University. Photograph by Mitzi Trumbo.

for everyone."[37] Christopher, Victor Navasky, Paul Jarrico, Ring Lardner Jr., and Kirk Douglas also spoke. Mitzi's daughters, Samantha and
Molly, cut the ribbon.

Of even greater significance was the Trumbo renaissance that
occurred in Grand Junction. When Bruce Cook visited the city in the
fall of 1973, he found a residue of hostility toward Trumbo. Just men-

tioning Trumbo's name, he said, elicited a negative response.[38] Astonishingly, that negative response stemmed from Trumbo's first novel, *Eclipse*, which had been published more than thirty-five years previously. But according to Ken Johnson, former publisher of the *Daily Sentinel*, Trumbo's name had been "mud" in Grand Junction since then.[39]

That "mud" slowly began to wash away a few years after Cook's visit. The rinsing process began in 1976 with an article by Richard Ott, editor of the *Grand Valley Gazette*. Ott planned to devote an upcoming issue of his newspaper to important events in the history of Grand Junction. He wrote to Trumbo and stated his intention to include the publication of *Eclipse*, which "had attained an almost mythical stature among the native population of the Grand Valley." Ott was convinced that any attempt "to discuss the significant events that have shaped the collective consciousness of the Valley would not be complete without mention of your lasting influence, and its origin." Ott also told Trumbo that the story of John Abbott had helped him better understand the Grand Valley and its people.[40] A few weeks later the *Gazette* printed a complimentary article, extolling Trumbo for highlighting the benevolence of W. J. Moyer, who had gone "largely unrewarded by the people in the Grand Valley." And yet, the author noted, "instead of enjoying the experience of having their lives presented in a unique perspective," the citizens of Grand Junction "chose to be insulted."[41]

The citizens of Grand Junction were not openly moved by this article. Fifteen years later, in 1991, Mesa County commissioner Mike Kelley made another attempt at resuscitation. He pushed through a resolution designating December 9 as "Dalton Trumbo Day." Kelley described Trumbo as "a local that never got enough recognition locally." About his resolution, Kelley said: "I'm not really sure what the day means, but I thought it would be good to give him some credit. . . . I don't want to upset any of the old-timers, but if it does stir up a little dust, it would be in the spirit in which Dalton left the county." Only fifty people attended the commemorative cocktail party Kelley arranged.[42]

Thirteen years later, Christopher's play about his father was staged in three Colorado cities: Beavercreek, Denver, and Grand Junction. In conjunction with the Grand Junction performance, Miffie Blozvich invited Christopher to read excerpts from his father's two Shale City books (*Eclipse* and *The Remarkable Andrew*) at the Mesa Public Library. Christopher's appearance, in November 2004, attracted the biggest audience the library had ever seen. After the event, Bernie Buescher and Ken Johnson asked Blozvich: "Do you think we should reprint *Eclipse* as a library fund-raiser?" A committee of ten was quickly formed, all of whom were fascinated by Trumbo, the book, and the history of its ostracism. In March 2005 Blozvich e-mailed Christopher about the committee and its plans.[43]

The Trumbos gave the library the copyright, and the committee arranged for 3,000 copies to be printed. The new edition included a foreword by Nikola, a roster of the novel's characters correlated with the people on whom they were based, excerpts from Trumbo's correspondence with Walter Walker, and numerous photographs contributed by Mitzi. To celebrate the publication, the "Dalton Gang" (now consisting of twenty-five members, including Christopher) organized a Dalton Trumbo tribute titled "Shale City Revisited." Sales of the book earned $65,000 for the library.[44] Ken Johnson, a member of the "Dalton Gang," said:

> *Eclipse* was his first novel and the start of his real career. It is a legacy the town's movers hated for years, and tried to ignore. It is always amazing how wounds, whether real or not, last so long. But seventy years later, and thirty years after his death, it seemed like we ought to get on with our lives.
>
> Trumbo gets extra points on my dance card for going to jail, too. At a time when there was a dirty rotten pinko Commie under every rock, Trumbo and nine others chose to say "Foul!" to the House Un-American Activities Committee.[45]

In January 2005 Laurena Mayne Davis, former managing editor of the *Daily Sentinel* and one of the leaders of the Trumbo renaissance, taught a course on Trumbo at Mesa State College (now Colorado Mesa University). The class met for eight days, eight hours a day. Davis assigned four books, showed ten of Trumbo's movies, and took the students on tours of Trumbo-related sites. Several months later, in September, *The Biggest Thief in Town* was performed on campus.

On December 9, 2005, the "Dalton Gang" organized a "Remembering Dalton Trumbo Birthday Bash" to celebrate his 100th birthday. Hundreds of people attended the main event, which was held at the Avalon Theatre. Christopher told the audience that if his father had lived to hear of the "Birthday Bash," he would have said: "That's nice, . . . and you gave them the copyright [to *Eclipse*]?" Kirk Douglas sent a letter to be read to the audience that evening, describing Trumbo as "a man that I love . . . one of the most interesting men I ever knew."[46] The

Rocky Mountain PBS station produced a documentary on Trumbo's Western Slope origins, the *Grand Junction Free Press* reprinted Nikola's foreword to *Eclipse*, 700 leather-bound special editions of *Eclipse* were put on sale, a Trumbo exhibit was mounted at the Museum of the West, three of his movies were shown, and historic walks and van tours of sites from his childhood and from *Eclipse* were conducted.

Davis told an interviewer: "*Eclipse* is our story. Not necessarily the story we might have chosen to be told," and one that might still hurt some people's feelings, but it is a story that contains "real clues about our community," and the community wanted to save it. She complimented Trumbo for his effective mimicking of the social realism of Sinclair Lewis.[47] Christopher later noted the irony of this situation—a book that had once driven a wedge between Trumbo and Grand Junction had now become a means of reuniting them. "Art," he commented wryly, "sometimes outlasts us."[48]

Flush with their success, the "Dalton Gang" did not want to stop, so they decided to commission a "Dalton Trumbo Historical Recognition Sculpture" to be placed on Main Street. After all, Trumbo was, in Johnson's words, "Grand Junction's most famous artistic export."[49] When the city council rejected the gang's request for funds, they raised $44,550 privately and commissioned a Utah artist, J. Michael Wilson, to sculpt it. During the fund-raising campaign, George Orbanek, publisher of the *Daily Sentinel*, wrote a scurrilous article about Trumbo—one that would not have looked out of place fifty years earlier. He called Trumbo an "unabashed admirer of Joseph Stalin," "an unrepentant apologist for Stalin," and a "commie b_____d." Orbanek then proceeded to distort the facts, calling Trumbo "a willing stooge of J. Edgar Hoover's FBI" and "a man capable of selling out some of his former compatriots on the left for remaining true to their anti-war principles of the late 1930s." Orbanek concluded that Trumbo deserved recognition for his screenplays, but not for being a decent human being or a champion of free speech.[50]

But his was an isolated voice, and during the second week of October 2007, the members of the Trumbo family (minus Cleo, who was ill) flew to Grand Junction to celebrate the unveiling of the sculpture. The sculpture, Mitzi said, was "inspired by a photograph I took of him in 1969. It depicts Trumbo in his bathtub, writing, coffee cup and cigarettes at hand. We were highly amused, since his physique had been enhanced with toned muscles, and our father in bronze was buff beyond his dreams." (The sculptor whimsically added swimming ducks, both

Trumbo's granddaughters (Mitzi's daughters), Samantha Campbell and Molly Gingras, and Samantha's daughter, Annabel Cleo Petersen, at the Trumbo sculpture in Grand Junction. Photograph by Mitzi Trumbo.

in the bathwater and in Trumbo's coffee cup.) The *Grand Junction Free Press* headed its story: "Honor Well Timed, but Long Overdue."[51] At the well-attended dedication, Ken Johnson asked: "Could the Trumbo caper trigger, maybe become a model for a SERIES of sculptures honoring those who pioneered the good things that make this such a special place to live?"[52] The response was positive, and the Legends Sculpture Project was born. To date, it has sponsored seven sculptures.

In October 2009 Cleo Trumbo died. Mitzi later wrote:

> I believe my mother was my father's greatest strength. He needed her stability, her steady and sunny personality, to anchor him. Trumbo was abrasive, argumentative, impetuous, and quick to act; Cleo was thoughtful, measured, and cautious. She slowed him down and saved him from making many mistakes, although he often barreled into situations without consulting her. She was his editor and his sounding board, and when he didn't heed her advice he got into the most trouble. And he was stubborn enough for that to be a fairly frequent occurrence.

Without her at his side, I often wondered if he would have had
the strength to continue once the blacklist became a reality.

As for Cleo, when I asked why she never remarried—and she
did not lack opportunities to do so—she replied that she would
never find another man as smart and interesting as Trumbo.

A Radical Like No Other

Two leitmotifs of this book are worth reemphasizing. First, Trumbo
thrice clawed his way to the top of the screenwriting profession. He
was one of the most consistently sought-after screenwriters during three
very different eras of moviemaking—the years of the studio system,
those of the black market, and those of independent production. Second, during those years he yearned to write novels, but the more success
he achieved as a screenwriter, the fewer novels he wrote: when he was
a bakery worker, he wrote seven; when he was a low-paid reader and
screenwriter, he wrote four; but when he was a highly paid screenwriter
(1940–1947 and 1960–1970), he completed none. He spent his screenwriting money faster than he earned it and could never wean himself
from the studio teat.

Some of his contemporaries thought he misused or failed to develop
what they considered a prodigious talent. Albert Maltz said Trumbo
"had enormous qualities as a man in terms of talent, in terms of a most
engaging personality, a brilliantly sharp mind and an offbeat, marvelous wit." But he had "one fatal flaw" that "interfered with the exercise
of his talent: he loved to live on a very grand scale."[53] Otto Preminger,
comparing Trumbo to legendary screenwriter and playwright Ben
Hecht, remarked: "I have the feeling that if pictures had not used the
talent of these people, then they would have become greater writers.
They got used to a higher life style, and they were spoiled for higher
ambitions as writers. . . . Both of them could have been, *should* have
been, more."[54]

More what? More successful? Than whom? Trumbo won a national
book award and two Academy Awards, had two plays produced on
Broadway, wrote five great political pamphlets, and composed one of
the best collections of letters of the twentieth century. As for his movie
work as a whole, Richard Corliss may have delivered an overall verdict
of mediocrity, but Peter Hanson concluded from his viewing of Trumbo's films: "While it is true that only a handful of great films appear on
his resumé, it is perhaps more significant to note the number of good

films Trumbo wrote. . . . If only for the sheer number of quality films to which he contributed, Trumbo's output is stunning."[55] I would add that few screenwriters of Trumbo's generation produced a more substantial body of work or a greater number of successful movies—*A Man to Remember, Kitty Foyle, Thirty Seconds over Tokyo*, three noir classics, *Roman Holiday, Spartacus, Lonely Are the Brave*, and *Executive Action* among them.

More integrated? Although Trumbo was conflicted about his two writing goals, he was neither torn nor divided. Similarly, he lived his life as though there were no contradictions among his success as a movie writer, his lifestyle, and his political radicalism. Indeed, he lived his life as if it were finely attuned in all its aspects. He did not ask whether he could be a Communist and a highly paid Hollywood screenwriter. He simply was both, comfortably. We cannot know if the fame, wealth, and family he had obtained by early 1947 would have satisfied him, whether that financial and emotional security would have allowed him the space to write the novels he had been contemplating for so many years. We do know that the destructive force of the domestic cold war, in the shape of the Committee on Un-American Activities, drove a wedge through his existence. For fourteen of his middle years, he had one goal—to destroy the blacklist. After achieving that goal, he could not seem to wind down from battle mode. Like Humpty-Dumpty, he could not reassemble the pieces of the life he had contemplated in 1946.

There was one exception: from the time of the blacklist until his death, he carefully and thoughtfully examined his political radicalism and tried to make it fit the changing circumstances of the world he lived in. He was aided in this endeavor by the slow maturing of his commitment to political activity. Since he never underwent a conversion experience, he did not become dogmatic, sectarian, rigid, or a devotee of any system. He was not a commitment junkie, jumping from one organization to another in what Leszek Kołakowski called "a never-ending search for a good, noble cause."[56] His main political goal was a united Left—united on behalf of freedom of expression, union organizing, social reform, and civil rights for minorities. Though he lashed out at those who were dividing the Left—particularly Cold War liberals—he was always willing to meet them on higher, less ideological ground. And, as evidenced by the Laurel speech, he was willing to drop old animosities and move forward.

I noted in the introduction that Trumbo's membership in the Communist Party was only one part of his life, that it did not define him.

But those who have written critically about him make that membership the centerpiece of his existence, and they are furious with him because, without humbly apologizing for "the crimes of Stalin," he became celebrated by a later generation. They conveniently ignore the fact that Trumbo never publicly extolled or defended Stalin or his "workers' paradise." He never deluded himself about Soviet communism. He never acted in bad faith. Some may ask why he did not publicly criticize Stalin and the Soviet Union, particularly after Khrushchev's 1956 speech. The answer is that he saw no need to join an anti-Communist chorus that, he believed, had done so much harm to the United States.

As his life reached its end, Trumbo seemed to regret only three things: the lack of success of the movie version of *Johnny Got His Gun*, his failure to complete *Night of the Aurochs*, and his inability to leave Cleo financially secure. Otherwise, he knew he had lived a fuller life than most. He might have said something similar to what Leon Trotsky wrote in his last will and testament: "If I had to begin all over again I would of course try to avoid this or that mistake but the main course of my life would remain unchanged."[57] Trumbo died as he had lived most of his adult life: a democratic socialist, an opponent of war and all forms of censorship, a believer in full freedom of opportunity for all, a successful writer, and a hopeless manager of money.

Acknowledgments

I owe debts of gratitude to a number of people. In Grand Junction, Laurena Mayne Davis provided me with much material on Trumbo's years there and showed me the highlights of her wonderful city. Miffie Blozvich and Ken Johnson were very informative about the activities of the Dalton Gang.

Donna Grafton, Peter Askin, and Peter Hanson sent me, respectively, her oral history with Christopher, his extensive interviews with Christopher, and his correspondence with Christopher.

Jules Brenner, Timothy Bottoms, Sherry Sonnett, Jeff Freilich, Michael Butler, Crawford Killian, Eddie Lewis, Donald Sutherland, Pepe Serna, Joe Lardner, and Kate Lardner shared their memories of Trumbo and Christopher with me. Michael Collins provided excerpts from his father's diary, and Jim Preminger spoke with me about his father (Ingo). Allison Anders and Bob Smith related information about Ashland, Kentucky.

The archivists at the Wisconsin Center for Film and Theater Research (notably Lee Grady), UCLA Special Collections, Warner Brothers Archives (University of Southern California), Writers Guild of America, West, library, and Margaret Herrick Library (Academy of Motion Picture Arts and Sciences) were courteous and helpful. Special thanks, and the award for most outstanding archivist, to Ned Comstock of the Cinematic Arts Library (University of Southern California); he so consistently goes above and beyond the expected that one must be careful not to take it for granted. A close second in the voting were Barbara Hall and Jenny Romero (Margaret Herrick), Julie Graham (UCLA), and May Haduong (Academy Film Archives). Extremely helpful were Sally Johnson (Montrose County Historical Museum), Aimee Brown (Mesa University Special Collections), Martin Gostanian (Paley Center), Michael Menard (Museum of Western Colorado), Ginny Kilander (American Heritage Center, University of Wyoming), Pamela Middlemas (Grand Junction High School), Katelynn Vance (Howard Gottlieb Research Center, Boston University), and Michele Welsing (Southern California Library for Social Studies and Research).

Anne Dean Dotson of the University Press of Kentucky sought the manuscript well before it was completed and backed it enthusiastically. Bailey Johnson, her assistant, tolerantly parried my occasionally impatient notes. Linda Lotz did an excellent job copyediting the manuscript.

Christine Holmgren provided her usual detailed and critical comments on form and content, as well as vital moral support. Steven Englund read and commented on some of the chapters.

I wish to pay special tribute to three of my predecessors in this field whose work has greatly facilitated my own: Howard Suber, Helen Manfull, and Bruce Cook. It is a shame and a crime that Suber's groundbreaking 1968 doctoral thesis on the blacklist was never published. In particular, I made frequent use of his meticulously and painstakingly arranged appendices listing all the Hollywood witnesses, their dates of appearance, their films, and the identities of those who named them. Manfull did a splendid job of selecting, editing, and annotating Trumbo's letters. Her volume, perched beside my computer, made my job of quoting Trumbo so much easier. Cook's interviews with Trumbo and his contemporaries, most of whom are now deceased, proved invaluable.

The Trumbo family has been incredibly supportive of this endeavor, even when, as frequently happened, they did not agree with my interpretations or choices. Molly Gingras (Trumbo's granddaughter) perused the MacKinlay Kantor papers, and Nikola Trumbo answered all my questions. But if Mitzi Trumbo and Nancy Escher had not existed, I would have had to summon a genie to create them. Their constant infusion of personal memories and anecdotes endowed my archival findings with flesh and spirit. They searched every nook and cranny in their respective homes for any bit of material that would assist me. Mitzi dug deep into her memory banks, even when it was not a pleasant task. She answered all my questions, critically read what I sent her, and helped me select and prepare the photographs. Richard Gingras (Mitzi's husband) provided his technical expertise on the sending of large data files.

My largest debt of gratitude is owed to Christopher, for his confident belief that I could complete what would have been his magnum opus in a satisfactory manner. I hope his faith in me has been rewarded.

Appendix

Black-Market Work

Deals

Gun Crazy: fronted by Millard Kaufman ($3,750), released in 1949.

"Fairview, U.S.A.": based on an original story by Danny Dare, 1949.

The Prowler: for Sam Spiegel, fronted by Hugo Butler, released in 1951.

Cowboy: 1950, for Sam Spiegel, fronted by Hugo Butler, slightly revised by Edmund North, released in 1958.

Original story about buffaloes: fronted by Millard Kaufman, sold to Twentieth Century–Fox for $40,000.

He Ran All the Way: for Bob Roberts, just before going to prison ($5,000 + 5 percent); fronted by Guy Endore; rewritten by Hugo Butler; released in 1951.

"The Butcher Bird": original script about a man unjustly convicted and executed for murder, fronted by Guy Endore, sold to Columbia for $40,000, not made.

Roman Holiday: fronted by Ian Hunter, sold to Paramount for $40,000, released in 1953.

"West from London": written in prison, sold to George Templeton ($2,500 or $3,500).

Original comedy about the girl who invented the Toni home permanent: suggested by Hugo Butler, fronted by Ian Hunter.

"Flight from Portabella": treatment, with Hugo Butler, started in 1948 and completed and sold in 1952 ($2,500).

"The Fair Young Maiden" (aka "The Love Maniac"): original story fronted by Ray Murphy and sold to Twentieth Century–Fox ($6,000).

Carnival Story: for the King brothers ($8,750), released in 1954.

The Brave One: for the King brothers ($10,000), released in 1956.

"Leap High My Love": for Henry Ehrlich, in Mexico.

"The Ring": story about a Mexican boxer, in collaboration with Hugo Butler, for the King brothers ($6,000).

They Were So Young: story of working-class women from Europe lured to Brazil and forced into prostitution, cowritten with Michael Wilson, released in 1954. (In their "Movie Worsts of 1955," the editors of *Harvard Lampoon* voted it the movie "with the most unattractive connotations" [February 1956, 10].)

Westerns (titles unknown): cowritten with Wilson ($5,000).

"Love Story" or "Love Song": revised version of "Remember, O Remember," fronted by Ben Perry ($3,750), ca. 1955.

"The Syndicate": for the King brothers (between $7,500 and $10,000).

"Mr. Adam": for the King brothers ($5,000 plus 7.5 percent), 1956.

Heaven with a Gun: for the King brothers, fronted by Robert Presnell Jr. ($10,000), rewritten by and credited to Richard Carr, released in 1969.

The Boss: for Walter Seltzer ($7,500), released in 1956.

"Bull Whip": for Walter Seltzer, about the mass slaughter of Mexican cattle during hoof-and-mouth disease scare.

Terror in a Texas Town: for Walter Seltzer, fronted by Ben Perry, released in 1958. (Trumbo had recommended Lawson and Lindemann, but when the backers rejected their script, Trumbo rewrote it in four days.)

"Cry of the Unborn": on illegal abortion rings, 1957, for George Bilson ($3,000).

"Citizen Soldier": television pilot for George Templeton ($1,250), about a military intelligence agent stationed in Germany. (Templeton had come into possession of classified documents, which he gave to Trumbo to read as background. Trumbo panicked when he realized what he had in his house, fearing he might be arrested as a spy.)

"Goat Song": based on a story by Jean Rouverol (Butler).

"Furia": first job for Eugene Frenke ($3,500), 1957; sold to Hal Wallis, rewritten and credited to Arnold Shulman, and released as *Wild Is the Wind*, 1957.

Heaven Knows Mr. Allison: polish for Eugene Frenke, released in 1957.

"Something for Nothing": for Sam Bischoff and David Diamond ($5,000).

The Cavern: for Edgar Ulmer and Michael Meshekoff ($5,000 or $7,500), rewritten and credited to Jack Davies, released in 1965. (Ingo Preminger had warned Ulmer not to use Trumbo's name.)

"Typee": done on speculation, bought by Ben Bogeaus ($10,000), rewritten and credited to James Leicester, released as *Enchanted Island* in 1958.

From the Earth to the Moon: for Ben Bogeaus ($10,000), rewritten and credited to Robert Blees, released in 1958.

"The Bridge of San Luis Rey": rewrite of script for Ben Bogeaus ($10,000).

"The Girl with the Green Eyes": for Sally Stubblefield ($12,000), released as *The Green-Eyed Blonde* in 1956.

Conspiracy of Hearts: adaptation of television show about Italian nuns rescuing Jews, for Adrian Scott, fronted by Robert Presnell Jr., made in the United Kingdom, 1960.

"Montezuma": for Eugene Frenke, sold to Bryna ($150,000).

"The Other Side of the Coin": as Peter Finch for Otto Preminger ($60,000).

"Girl of the Fifth Summer": detailed film story about the marriage between a black man and a white woman, based on idea by Alec March, fronted by Ben Perry, 1957. (In 1961 Trumbo paid March $4,000 and Perry $750 to surrender their respective rights. He then made an agreement with Bryna to write a screenplay for $40,000, but he never found the time to do so.)

"The Legionnaire": rewrite for Eugene Frenke.

"The Philadelphian": for Alec March, rewritten and credited to James Gunn, released as *The Young Philadelphians* in 1959.

"Will Adams": begun in mid-1950s and completed in mid-1960s.

"Sylva": for Universal Pictures.

Last Train from Gun Hill: for Bryna ($10,000), rewritten and credited to James Poe, released in 1959.

Spartacus: as Sam Jackson, for Bryna, released in 1960.

Exodus: for Otto Preminger, released in 1960.

"Bunny Lake": as Peter Finch, for Otto Preminger ($50,000), rewritten by John and Penelope Mortimer, released as *Bunny Lake Is Missing* in 1965.

Town without Pity: for Mirisch Brothers ($58,000), credited to Georg Hundalek and Sylvia Reinhardt, released in 1961.

The Last Sunset: for Bryna, released in 1961.

Lonely Are the Brave: for Bryna, released in 1962.

Consultations

The Red Pony (1949)
Heaven Knows, Mr. Allison (1957)
No Down Payment (1957)
Ten Days to Tulara (1958)
The Two-Headed Spy (1958)

Original Treatments and Unsold Scripts

"Conquest" (October 25, 1956)
"Spring and Summer" (ca. 1956)
"Cast the First Stone" (1958)
"Sword of Baristan" (July 11, 1961)
"The Flowers of Hiroshima" (ca. 1962)
"Small Town Girl" (no date, by Robert Rich)
"Professor and the Genie" (no date, by Robert Rich)
"Ordeal of Dr. Perez" (no date, by Robert Rich)

Chronology

December 9, 1905	James Dalton Trumbo born in Montrose, Colorado
1908	Trumbo family moves to Grand Junction, Colorado
1914–1918	First World War
1915	Maud Trumbo becomes a member of the First Church of the Christ, Scientist
1920–1924	Trumbo attends Grand Junction High School
1924–1925	Trumbo attends University of Colorado
1925	Trumbo family moves to Los Angeles
1925–1933	Trumbo works at Davis Perfection Bakery
1927	Orus Trumbo dies
October 1929	Great Depression begins
1929–1930	Trumbo takes courses at University of Southern California
January 31, 1931	Trumbo's first article published, in *Film Spectator*
June 1931	Trumbo hired as full-time writer for *Hollywood Spectator* but keeps his bakery job
November 1932	Franklin D. Roosevelt elected president
January 1933	Adolf Hitler becomes chancellor of Germany
June 1, 1934	Trumbo hired as reader by Warner Bros.
1935	Trumbo's first novel, *Eclipse*, published
September 16, 1935	Trumbo signs writer's contract with Warner Bros.
March 28, 1936	Trumbo receives his first screen credit, for *Road Gang*; joins Screen Writers Guild
April 1936	Trumbo fired by Warner Bros. for refusing to resign from Screen Writers Guild
June 1936	Trumbo hired by Columbia Pictures; *Washington Jitters* published by Knopf
July 1936	Spanish Civil War begins
April 1937	US Supreme Court upholds constitutionality of National Labor Relations Act, forcing

	studios to recognize and bargain with the guilds
October 1937–March 1938	Trumbo works at MGM
March 1938	Trumbo signs with RKO
March 31, 1938	Trumbo marries Cleo Beth Fincher
May 1938	Trumbos buy a ranch in Kern County, California; *Washington Jitters* has a short run in New York City
October 1938	*A Man to Remember* (RKO), Trumbo's first notable credit
January 26, 1939	Nikola Trumbo born
August 23, 1939	German-Soviet Nonaggression Treaty signed
September 1939	German armed forces invade Poland; Britain and France declare war on Germany
September 3, 1939	*Johnny Got His Gun* published by Lippincott
October 1939	Trumbo makes the first of a series of speeches opposing US entry into the war
February 1940	*Johnny Got His Gun* receives award as best original novel
June 1940	Alien Registration Act passed
September 25, 1940	Christopher Trumbo born
December 1940	*Kitty Foyle*, Trumbo's first A film, released
January 1941	Trumbo receives his only Academy Award nomination under his own name
February 1941	*The Remarkable Andrew* published by Lippincott
May 1941–May 1942	Trumbo under contract to Paramount Pictures
June 1941	German armed forces invade Soviet Union; United States begins sending military aid to Soviet Union
December 1941	Japanese forces attack Pearl Harbor; United States declares war on Japan; Germany declares war on United States
1942–1943	Trumbo becomes a supporter of the US war effort; joins Hollywood Writers' Mobilization, Hollywood Democratic Committee, and Sleepy Lagoon Defense Committee; writes scripts for *A Guy Named Joe* (MGM) and *Tender Comrade* (RKO)

October 19, 1942	Trumbo labeled a Communist fellow traveler by FBI
1943	Trumbo joins Communist Party
January 8, 1944	Trumbo meets with two FBI agents
1944	Trumbo writes scripts for *Thirty Seconds over Tokyo* and *Our Vines Have Tender Grapes* (MGM)
January 1945	House of Representatives votes to make Committee on Un-American Activities a permanent standing committee
April 1945	United Nations founding conference opens
May 1945	Germany surrenders
May–June 1945	Trumbo writes a speech for Secretary of State Edward R. Stettinius Jr. at UN Founding Conference
May 1945–November 1946	Trumbo serves as editor of *Screen Writer*
June–August 1945	Trumbo serves as war correspondent in the Pacific theater
August–September 1945	United States drops atomic bombs on two Japanese cities; Japan surrenders
October 4, 1945	Melissa (Mitzi) Trumbo born
1946	Trumbo serves as member of the executive board of Hollywood Independent Citizens Committee of the Arts, Sciences, and Professions
March 1947	President Harry S. Truman's loyalty order marks the beginning of the domestic cold war
May 1947	Subcommittee of Committee on Un-American Activities travels to Los Angeles to investigate "communist infiltration" of the motion picture industry; Truman Doctrine marks the beginning of the international Cold War
September 1947	Trumbo served with a subpoena to appear in Washington
October 28, 1947	Trumbo declines to answer the committee's questions about his political and guild affiliations
November 1947	Trumbo fired, blacklisted, and cited for contempt of Congress; he leaves the Communist Party

December 1947	Trumbo begins black-market scriptwriting with *Gun Crazy* for the King brothers; Trumbo indicted by a federal grand jury
May 1948	Trumbo tried, convicted, and sentenced to one year in prison
March 1949	*The Biggest Thief in Town* opens and quickly closes in New York City; Trumbo writes *The Time of the Toad*
June 1950	Korean War begins
1950–1951	Trumbo writes scripts for *The Prowler*, *He Ran All the Way*, and *Roman Holiday*
June 1950–April 1951	Trumbo incarcerated at Ashland (Ky.) Federal Correctional Institution
March 1951	Committee on Un-American Activities reopens its exposure of Communists in Hollywood; blacklist expands enormously
November 1951– January 1954	Trumbos move to Mexico; he begins work on *The Brave One*
September 1953	*Roman Holiday* opens; Ian Hunter receives credit for original story and cocredit for screenplay
July 1955	Geneva Conference offers promise of détente
February 1956	Nikita Khrushchev reveals some of Stalin's crimes
Spring 1956	Trumbo temporarily rejoins the Communist Party and writes *The Devil in the Book*
October 1956	*The Brave One* opens; the original story is credited to Robert Rich (Trumbo's pseudonym)
February 1957	Academy of Motion Picture Arts and Sciences enacts bylaw prohibiting blacklisted persons from being nominated for Academy Awards
March 1957	Robert Rich wins Academy Award for best screen story
January 1958	Trumbo signs his first contract with Eddie Lewis and Bryna Productions
March 1958	Screenplay for *The Bridge on the River Kwai*, written by two blacklistees, wins Academy Award
May 1958	Trumbo begins work on *Spartacus*

December 1958	Blacklisted Ned Young publicly announces that he cowrote the screenplay for *The Defiant Ones*
January 1959	Academy rescinds its anti-blacklist bylaw; Trumbo announces that he is Robert Rich
January 1960	Otto Preminger announces that Trumbo will receive screen credit for *Exodus*
August 1960	Universal Studios announces that Trumbo will receive screen credit for *Spartacus*
February 1960	Newly elected President John F. Kennedy leaves the White House to watch *Spartacus*
1961	Trumbo writes *The Last Sunset* (screen credit) and *Town without Pity* (uncredited)
1962	Trumbo writes *Lonely Are the Brave* (screen credit)
1964–1965	President Lyndon B. Johnson commits armed forces in Vietnam
1965	Trumbo writes *The Sandpiper* (cocredit)
1966	Trumbo writes *Hawaii* (cocredit)
Autumn 1967	Maud Trumbo dies
1968	Trumbo adapts *The Fixer*
1968–1971	Trumbo writes and directs *Johnny Got His Gun* (the movie)
January 1970	Trumbo's correspondence with Steve Allen printed in *Esquire*
March 1970	Trumbo receives Laurel Award of Writers Guild of America, for lifetime achievement
October 1970	*Additional Dialogue* published
1971	Trumbo writes *The Horsemen*
1973	Trumbo writes *Executive Action* and *Papillon* (cocredit)
May 1975	Trumbo receives Oscar for *The Brave One*
September 10, 1976	Trumbo dies
March 1992	Writers Guild of America adds Trumbo's name to best written comedy award for *Roman Holiday*
May 1993	Cleo Trumbo accepts posthumous Oscar for *Roman Holiday*
1999	Writers Guild of America officially credits Trumbo for nine of his black-market scripts

2003	Christopher Trumbo writes *Trumbo: Red, White and Blacklisted*
2005	*Eclipse* reprinted by a committee of Grand Junction citizens
2007	Peter Askin directs the documentary film *Trumbo*, based on Christopher's play; Trumbo sculpture unveiled in Grand Junction
October 2009	Cleo Trumbo dies
January 2011	Christopher Trumbo dies

Notes

Abbreviations

AHC	American Heritage Center, University of Wyoming
BCPM	Bruce Campbell Production Material, MHL
COMPIC	FBI, Communist Infiltration–Motion Picture Industry
CTP	Christopher Trumbo Papers, in the possession of Nancy Escher
DV	*Daily Variety*
FOIA	Freedom of Information Act
FOIA-DT	Dalton Trumbo FOIA file, CTP
HICCASP	Hollywood Independent Citizens Committee of the Arts, Sciences, and Professions
HR	*Hollywood Reporter*
KDP	Kirk Douglas Papers, WC
LAT	*Los Angeles Times*
MHL	Margaret Herrick Library, Academy of Motion Picture Arts and Sciences
MPPA	Motion Picture Producers Association
MWP	Michael Wilson Papers, UCLA
NYT	*New York Times*
PCA	Production Code Administration
SACLA	special agent in charge, Los Angeles FBI office
UCLA	Special Collections Library, UCLA
USC	Cinema and Television Library, University of Southern California
WC	Wisconsin Center for Film and Theater Research
WGAw	Writers Guild of America, West
WV	*Weekly Variety*

Introduction

The epigraph is from an untitled poem, November 15, 1953, Dalton Trumbo Papers, WC, 4/6.

1. See obituary, *LAT*, January 13, 2011, A8.

2. With apologies to Robert Graves and Alan Hodge, *The Reader over Your Shoulder* (London: Jonathan Cape, 1943). Unfortunately, Christopher's voice is least evident in the chapters covering events he knew better than anyone (23–25). When we arrived at that part of the oral history, he was fading. The transcript is available at http://bibpurl.oclc.org/web/43742.

3. The sculpture, created by Jenny Holzer, is located on the campus of the University of Southern California. See http://fisher.usc.edu/collections/blacklist.html. According to Jon Wiener, "there seems to be nowhere in America where a

history museum defends the blacklist or presents HUAC in a positive light." Jon Wiener, *How We Forgot the Cold War: A Historical Journey across America* (Berkeley and Los Angeles: University of California Press, 2012), 73, 79.

4. Christopher Trumbo, *Trumbo: Red, White and Blacklisted* (New York: Playscripts, 2007); *Trumbo* (Magnolia Home Entertainment, 2009), DVD.

5. More than thirty-five years ago, Bruce Cook wrote *Dalton Trumbo: A Biography of the Oscar-Winning Screenwriter Who Broke the Blacklist* (New York: Scribner's, 1977). Cook had Trumbo's full cooperation, and he was able to interview many more of Trumbo's contemporaries than I could, but he was not granted access to the letters Trumbo wrote after 1962.

6. *Playboy* interview, 1971, tape 4, Dalton Trumbo Papers, box 61, folder 9, UCLA. In late 1971 Larry Duboise of *Playboy* asked Trumbo to participate in a detailed interview. Trumbo worked on it for one year, and when it was not printed, he wrote an angry letter, accusing the magazine of stealing "not one but many hours of my life," a life already shortened by a lung operation and a heart attack (December 7, 1973, ibid., 56/10).

7. Contained in CTP.

8. MWP, 47/3.

9. Dalton Trumbo, *Additional Dialogue: Letters of Dalton Trumbo, 1942–1962*, ed. Helen Manfull (New York: M. Evans, 1970), 6 (subsequent cites are to this edition, unless otherwise noted). Manfull made her selection from the papers Trumbo sent to the Wisconsin Center in 1962. He was paid $40,000 for the consignment. In 1987 Cleo Trumbo sent the rest of his papers to the Special Collections Library at UCLA. She was not paid for them.

10. James Harrington, *A Discourse upon This Saying: The Spirit of the Nation Is Not Yet to Be Trusted with Liberty; Lest It Introduce Monarchy, or Invade the Liberty of Conscience* (1659), in *The Political Works of James Harrington*, ed. J. G. A. Pocock (Cambridge: Cambridge University Press, 1977), 744.

11. Rudolph von Jhering, *The Struggle for Law [Der Kampf ums Rechts]*, trans. John J. Labor (Chicago: Callaghan, 1879). The book obviously made a deep impression on Trumbo because he later used Jhering's name in his script revision for *Town without Pity* (United Artists, 1961). The main character, played by Kirk Douglas, is a lawyer trying to save four soldiers convicted of rape from the death penalty. To do so, he must destroy the testimony of the victim. Hating what he is about to do, he gets drunk and says to a bartender: "You know, there is another great German lawyer, Rudolph von Jhering. He said: 'The defense of man's rights is the poetry of law, the defense of man's rights,' or something like that. Do you remember how it goes?" The bartender replies: "I don't even know the gentleman." And Douglas says: "I hate to misquote a fellow like that. Anyway, he's dead." Cleo Trumbo also quoted Jhering in the peroration of the acceptance speech she delivered in May 1993, when she was presented with an Oscar for Trumbo's contribution to *Roman Holiday*. The award, for best story, had been given to Trumbo's front, Ian Hunter, in 1953 (see chapters 13 and 27).

12. Jhering, *Struggle for Law*, vii, 2, 26, 57, 59.

13. Quoted in Cook, *Dalton Trumbo*, 249.

14. Ibid., 19.

15. Quoted in Gregg Kilday, "To Each His Own: The Many Faces of Dalton Trumbo," *LAT*, September 19, 1976, Q34.

16. Quoted from *Trumbo* (2009 DVD). As will be seen, Trumbo had his fair share of detractors. Budd Schulberg, for example, once referred to him as a "Nazi posing as a libertarian." Victor S. Navasky, *Naming Names* (New York: Viking, 1980), 244.

17. E-mail, February 15, 2011.

18. For a comprehensive and thorough analysis of Trumbo's films and an excellent filmography, see Peter Hanson, *Dalton Trumbo, Hollywood Rebel: A Critical Survey and Filmography* (Jefferson, NC: McFarland, 2001).

19. I borrowed the "reservoir" idea from Arie M. Dubnov, who described it as a metaphor that "allows one to distinguish the context of *exposure* to ideas from a later *utilization* of those ideas, done in entirely different historical circumstances." Arie M. Dubnov, *Isaiah Berlin: The Journey of a Jewish Liberal* (New York: Palgrave Macmillan, 2012), 55.

20. Quoted in Nancy Lynn Schwartz, *The Hollywood Writers' Wars* (New York: Knopf, 1982), 185–87.

21. Ring Lardner Jr., "Tribute," *Scriptwriter*, October 1976, 4.

22. SACLA to director, FBI, April 12, 1943, FOIA-DT.

23. Letter to *NYT*, December 15, 1968, D21.

24. Albert Camus, *The Myth of Sisyphus and Other Essays*, trans. Justin O'Brien (New York: Vintage, 1955), 44.

25. Dalton Trumbo, talk at UCLA, May 17, 1972, UCLA Communications Studies Archives, www.youtube.com/watch?v=YhAXSDpvqVU.

26. Quoted in Cook, *Dalton Trumbo*, 92.

1. Under Western Skies

The second epigraph is from Phil Kerby, "The Dalton Trumbo Inquisition," *LAT*, September 16, 1976, II:1.

1. Trumbo's speech to the Committee for the Protection of the Foreign Born, San Francisco, April 14, 1956, WC, 40/5.

2. Biographical sketch for Lippincott, 1939, WC, 8/4. Unless otherwise noted, all Trumbo's memories of his youth come from four documents: the aforementioned Lippincott biography; "War in the West," n.d., CTP; "Notes" on his family, 1962, CTP; and notes for his letter to Guy Endore, n.d., UCLA, 80/7.

3. Conrad W. Feltner, *The Trumbo Family* (self-published, 1974).

4. Quoted in Laurena Mayne Davis, *125 People—125 Years: Grand Junction's Story* (Grand Junction: Museum of Western Colorado, 2007), xi.

5. Dalton Trumbo, *Eclipse* (London: Lovat Dickson and Thompson, 1935; reprint, Grand Junction, CO: Mesa County Public Library Foundation, 2005), 5. All page references are to the reprint edition.

6. Kathleen Underwood, *Town Building on the Colorado Frontier* (Albuquerque: University of New Mexico Press, 1987), 23–27, 31.

7. Leon W. Fuller, "Colorado's Revolt against Capitalism," *Mississippi Valley Historical Review* 21, no. 3 (December 1934): 343–60. There was apparently no significant militancy within labor unions in Grand Junction during Trumbo's years there. The violent strikes that occurred in Colorado, at Cripple Creek and Ludlow, involved miners in the southern portion of the state.

8. *San Juan Silver*, 1940, 192–93, Montrose County Historical Museum.

Millard Fillmore Tillery was named after the thirteenth president of the United States (1850–1853), who took office upon the death of Zachary Taylor. When Fillmore ran for president as the candidate of the pro-slavery, anti-immigrant American (Know-Nothing) Party in 1856, he carried Clinton County.

9. Dona Freeman, ed., *100 Years: Montrose County* (self-published, 1982), 31–35; *Montrose County Centennial, 1882–1982* (Greater Montrose Centennial Inc., 1982), 70–71.

10. Trumbo, *Eclipse*, iii.

11. Dave Fishell, "Dalton Trumbo Still Evokes Emotions," *Entertainer*, January 5, 1990, Dalton Trumbo clipping file, Loyd Files Research Library, Museum of Western Colorado. According to family legend, Tillery never handcuffed any of the bandits he captured. He reputedly told them that if they escaped, he would quickly recapture them.

12. None of the main edifices of Trumbo's early life are still extant. A different type of house now sits on the Gunnison lot; the grammar school has been razed; and the high school, *Sentinel* offices, and Christian Science church have been moved to different sites or rebuilt. Only Orus's workshop is still standing.

13. Dalton Trumbo, *Johnny Got His Gun* (1939; reprint, New York: Citadel Press, 2007), 107–8.

14. The store is still in business on Main Street. Its founder, B. M. Benge, was the inspiration for Harry Twinge in *Eclipse*, Trumbo's first published novel. He is characterized as someone who, when times get tough, acts like "a rabbit" and "a dirty little coward" (222).

15. Trumbo, *Johnny Got His Gun*, 21.

16. Harold Bell Wright was the best-selling US novelist during the first three decades of the twentieth century. Finley Peter Dunne was the chief editorial writer for the *Chicago Post*, where his creation, Mr. Dooley, regularly appeared, slyly and humorously commenting on politics in a thick Irish brogue. Dunne was one of the most popular authors of his time. His son, screenwriter Philip Dunne, was a contemporary of Trumbo's in Hollywood.

17. One assumes he was "sternly corrected" for the letter he wrote to his parents, reporting on a newspaper awards banquet in Boulder during his junior year in high school: "I just got back from the banquet at the Boulderado [Hotel]. Some keen affair—nigger waiters, orchestra and all that stuff" (letter dated February 26, 1923, CTP).

18. Trumbo to Herbert Biberman, April 26, 1952, UCLA, 57/13.

19. Trumbo, *Johnny Got His Gun*, 17.

20. Dedication in Trumbo's unfinished historical romance about the Spanish conquest of Peru, n.d. [ca. late 1920s], WC, 36/10; Trumbo to his mother, March 25, 1945, in the possession of Mitzi Trumbo.

21. Cook, *Dalton Trumbo*, 75.

22. Stephen Gottschalk, *The Emergence of Christian Science in American Religious Life* (Berkeley: University of California Press, 1973), 164.

23. Mary Baker Eddy, *Science and Health with Key to the Scriptures* (Boston: First Church of the Christ, Scientist, n.d. [ca. 1934]), xxiii.

24. Cook, *Dalton Trumbo*, 32–33.

25. Eddy, *Science and Health*, 410, 419.

26. *Playboy* interview, tape 1, UCLA, 61/2.

27. "Journal of Mesa County History," *Grand Valley Gazette* 4 (February–March 1976), CTP.

28. A very faded copy of the first and only issue of *Fax* is in the Dalton Trumbo Scrapbooks, reel 1, Division of Archives and Manuscripts, Wisconsin Historical Society; hereafter cited as "Scrapbooks."

29. *NYT,* June 28, 1970, 11.

30. Carl Abbott, *Colorado: A History of the Centennial State* (Boulder: Colorado Associated Press, 1976), 209, 212–14.

31. See www.lonchaney.org/filmography/102.html and youtube.com/watch?v= 4iFnce-4e74.

32. Walter Walker had invited the Klan to the city because he thought it was "merely a fine fraternal organization." However, when it captured the Republican Party and elected one of its members governor, Walker became an adamant opponent. See Alan J. Kania, *John Otto: Trials and Trails* (Niwot: University Press of Colorado, 1996), 225–26.

33. *Time,* January 26, 1961, 30.

34. Isabel Cunningham, "Dalton Trumbo Is in New York Working Hard on First Important Play," *Daily Sentinel,* n.d. [ca. 1949], Dalton Trumbo clipping file, Loyd Files Research Library, Museum of Western Colorado.

35. Teet Carle, MGM publicist, "Dalton Trumbo Has Had a Varied, Colorful Career since Boyhood Days Here," *Daily Sentinel,* October 10, 1937, ibid.

36. Davis, *125 People,* 84–85.

37. "Scrapbooks," reel 1.

38. Cook, *Dalton Trumbo,* 39.

39. *The Tiger* (Grand Junction High School yearbook), 1921.

40. WC, 41/1.

41. "Scrapbooks," reel 1.

42. *The Tiger,* 1922.

43. Ibid., 1923.

44. WC, 41/1.

45. "Scrapbooks," reel 1.

46. Cook, *Dalton Trumbo,* 43–44, 56–57, 85–86.

47. Trumbo to parents, September, 23, 1924, CTP.

48. Ibid., October 1, 1924.

49. Ibid., October 25 and November 4, 1924.

50. Cook, *Dalton Trumbo,* 47. Mildred Hart Shaw questioned the veracity of this story: "Junction Screenwriter Was Obsessed with His Hometown," *Daily Sentinel,* February 6, 1977, Dalton Trumbo File, Loyd Files Research Library, Museum of Western Colorado.

51. Trumbo to parents, October 25, 1924, CTP.

52. Ibid., November 11, 1924.

53. Ibid., December 3, 1924.

54. Statement for *Playboy* interview, 1971, UCLA 56/10.

55. Trumbo to parents, February 17, 1925, CTP.

56. *Trumbo: 100th Birthday* video, filmed at Avalon Theatre, Grand Junction, December 9, 2005. I am indebted to Ken Johnson for providing me with this DVD.

57. Undated note, CTP.

58. Trumbo to parents, June 1, 1925.

59. Dalton Trumbo, "Genius from Kingsley," typed manuscript (ca. 1927), 111, 121, WC, 36/2.

2. Baking Bread and Writing in Los Angeles

1. Trumbo, *Johnny Got His Gun*, 5.
2. Untitled, undated manuscript, WC, 35/3. Trumbo intended this to be part of a novel he later titled "The Gelding of the Unicorns." The nickname Shale City came into use during the 1920s, following the discovery of huge deposits of oil shale north of Grand Junction.
3. Ibid.
4. Trumbo, "Genius from Kingsley," 143–44, WC, 36/4.
5. Dalton Trumbo, "Bind the Unicorn," n.d., chap. 1, WC, 35/3. This later became chapter 10 of "The Gelding of the Unicorns."
6. Dalton Trumbo, "The Bakery Thing," n.d. [ca. 1956], CTP.
7. Trumbo, *Johnny Got His Gun*, 4.
8. Ibid., 67.
9. Trumbo, "Genius from Kingsley," 164.
10. Trumbo, *Johnny Got His Gun*, 6–7.
11. Dalton Trumbo, "A letter to his father, a sort of report to the dead on the state of the living, which will also inform his son, stimulated by his own reflections on fatherhood. A list of 291 memories, items to know, and comparisons," CTP.
12. WC, 34/1.
13. Trumbo, "Genius from Kingsley," 164, 215, 220, 242, 252.
14. Foreword to Trumbo, *Eclipse*, v–vi.
15. Trumbo, "The Bakery Thing."
16. Trumbo, "Genius from Kingsley," 165.
17. Foreword to *Eclipse*, vi.
18. J. Marks, "Dalton Trumbo," *Sundance*, November 12, 1972, 59.
19. Quoted in Navasky, *Naming Names*, 367.
20. *Playboy* interview, tapes 1 and 3, UCLA, 61/2. The Sacco and Vanzetti case was a cause célèbre of the Left. The two radical anarchists had been convicted of robbery and murder and sentenced to death. A conflict still rages among historians as to their guilt. Mencken was the most famous and highly regarded cultural critic of the 1920s.
21. Trumbo, "Genius from Kingsley," 259–63.
22. Marks, "Dalton Trumbo," 59; Kirk H. Porter and Donald Bruce Johnson, eds., *National Party Platforms, 1840–1964* (Urbana: University of Illinois Press, 1966), 250. The platform contained another statement about war that must have intrigued Trumbo: "Those who must furnish the blood and bear the burdens imposed by war should, whenever possible, be consulted before the supreme sacrifice is required of them."
23. Letters dated March 15, 1926, and January 11, 1927, WC, 1/2.
24. Holly to Trumbo, November 23, 1927, ibid.
25. Dalton Trumbo, "The Return," WC, 41/1.
26. Dalton Trumbo, "Bleak Street," WC, 33/8.
27. Charles A. Pearce to Dalton Trumbo, October 24, 1929, WC, 1/2.
28. Eugene F. Saxton to Dalton Trumbo, January 31, 1930, ibid.

29. D'Orsay to Trumbo, June 10, 1930, WC, 1/2.

30. Cook, *Dalton Trumbo*, 88.

31. Dalton Trumbo, "Carl Sandburg's *Good Morning America*," WC, 39/8.

32. Welford Beaton to Dalton Trumbo, December 17, 1930, WC, 1/2. Beaton was born in Canada in the early 1870s and later moved to Seattle, where he became a movie critic as well as the founder of *Pacific Ports*, a shipping magazine. He came to Hollywood during the 1920s to write stories for silent films, and he began publishing *Film Spectator* in 1927. A few years later he wrote a book, *Know Your Movies: The Theory and Practice of Motion Picture Production* (Hollywood, CA: Howard Hill, 1932). Director Cecil D. De Mille wrote in the foreword: "The film industry is under obligation to Welford Beaton. For years he has provided it with a mental stimulant. He thinks clearly, is a fluent and forceful writer, and in Hollywood enjoys a reputation for being absolutely honest in the expression of his opinions. The sturdy manner in which he has clung to his independence during the years he has been in Hollywood writing about its principal industry, has earned him the respect of those engaged in making motion pictures" (7–8).

33. James Dalton Trumbo, "An Appeal to George Jean," *Film Spectator*, January 31, 1931, 19–20.

34. Letter dated July 8, 1931, signature of writer unclear, "Scrapbooks," reel 1.

35. Dalton Trumbo, "Bootlegging for Junior," *Vanity Fair*, June 1932, 39, 66. Trumbo must have been asked to do several rewrites, because he received a letter from Clare Boothe Brokaw observing, "You have been such a good sport about rewriting it, and very persistent in your determination to do the piece well" (March 19, 1932, "Scrapbooks," reel 1).

36. Dalton Trumbo, "Crowding the Band Wagon," *Hollywood Spectator*, August 29, 1931, 20.

37. Dalton Trumbo, "Producers and Dumb Audiences," *Hollywood Spectator*, July 18, 1932, 17.

38. Dalton Trumbo, "A Puzzle," *Hollywood Spectator*, August 1, 1931, 18.

39. Dalton Trumbo, "I Fight the Jungle" [review of *East of Borneo*], *Hollywood Spectator*, September 26, 1931, 24.

40. James Dalton Trumbo, "Charlie Chaplin—An Appreciation," *Film Spectator*, February 28, 1931, 22, 23.

41. Dalton Trumbo, "Murnau's Parting Gift," *Hollywood Spectator*, August 1, 1931, 19.

42. Dalton Trumbo, "Sincere and Profound" [review of *An American Tragedy*], *Hollywood Spectator*, September 12, 1931, 22; "A Tribute" [review of *Street Scene*], *Hollywood Spectator*, September 26, 1931, 22.

43. Dalton Trumbo, "Story Value and Direction," *Hollywood Spectator*, September 26, 1931, 18–19.

44. Dalton Trumbo, "Frankenstein in Hollywood," *Forum*, March 1932, 142–46. For a tendentious and distorted analysis of Trumbo's political writing during this period, see Tim Palmer, "Side of the Angels: Dalton Trumbo, the Hollywood Trade Press, and the Blacklist," *Cinema Journal* 44, no. 4 (Summer 2005): 57–74.

45. Dalton Trumbo, "Producers and Dumb Audiences," *Welford Beaton's Hollywood Spectator*, July 18, 1932, 15.

46. Dalton Trumbo, "The Movie Colossus Stumbles," typescript, n.d., "Scrapbooks," reel 1.

47. Dalton Trumbo, "Hollywood Pays," *Forum*, February 1933, 118–19.

48. Dalton Trumbo, "All Hail, Collapse!" *Welford Beaton's Hollywood Spectator*, June 24, 1933, 12.

49. Dalton Trumbo, "The Fall of Hollywood," *North American Review* 236, no. 2 (August 1933): 140–47.

50. Dalton Trumbo, "Propaganda," *Welford Beaton's Hollywood Spectator*, September 26, 1931, 21. The first issue of *Experimental Cinema: A Monthly Projecting Important International Film Manifestations* was published on February 3, 1931, by Cinema Crafters of America, Philadelphia. The editors were David Platt, who would later become the film writer for the *Daily Worker*, and Lewis Jacobs, who wrote *The Rise of the American Film*, the first significant social history of the movies. The New York editor was Harry Alan Potamkin, the best Marxist film writer of his generation. On the inside front cover of the first issue, the editors announced: "*Experimental Cinema* as the advance guard of a new motion picture art believes it will be the nucleus of a profound and vital force toward the creation of a world-wide cinema ideology." Only five issues were published, the last one in 1934. The journal's main focus was the great Russian directors—Pudovkin, Dovzhenko, and Eisenstein.

51. Dalton Trumbo, "But It Ends with a Parade" [review of *The Patriots*], *Welford Beaton's Hollywood Spectator*, December 23, 1933, 8.

52. Dalton Trumbo, "Reports on Babylon," *Welford Beaton's Hollywood Spectator*, ca. February 1933, "Scrapbooks," reel 1.

53. Cook, *Dalton Trumbo*, 68.

54. Dalton Trumbo, "Kidnaped," *International Detective Magazine*, October 1933, 14–27; Cook, *Dalton Trumbo*, 69.

55. Cook, *Dalton Trumbo*, 71, 73.

56. Ibid., 72, 73, 75.

57. Dalton Trumbo, "Who Can Explain the Warners?" *Welford Beaton's Hollywood Spectator*, July 22, 1933, 11.

58. Dalton Trumbo, "More for Larry" [*Playboy* interview], ca. 1971, UCLA, 126/7.

3. Playing the Studio Game and Organizing Guilds

The epigraph is from Cook, *Dalton Trumbo*, 78.

1. Michael E. Birdwell, *Celluloid Soldiers: Warner Bros.'s Campaign against Nazism* (New York: New York University Press, 1999), 7, 17; Nick Roddick, *A New Deal in Entertainment: Warner Brothers in the 1930s* (London: British Film Institute, 1983), 20, 65.

2. Dalton Trumbo's payroll card, Warner Bros. Archive, USC.

3. Transcript of Edwin Martin radio show, KMTR, February 8, 1936, "Scrapbooks," reel 1.

4. Trumbo to Elsie McKeogh, February 12, 1936, WC, 1/2.

5. Cook, *Dalton Trumbo*, 91.

6. Trumbo to Mrs. R. L. Magill, July 5, 1936, Susan Rose Collection, Museum of Western Colorado.

7. Trumbo to George Bye, September 12, 1934, WC, 1/2.

8. McKeogh to Trumbo, October 4, 1934, ibid.

9. Trumbo to Terry Whalley, May 4, 1970, UCLA, 124/10.

10. Cook, *Dalton Trumbo*, 84. On Moyer's death in 1943, *Daily Sentinel* publisher Walter Walker wrote: "History will be kinder to W. J. Moyer than careless contemporaries have appeared to be." Quoted in Davis, *125 People*, 55–56.

11. Trumbo to Mrs. Magill, July 5, 1936.

12. Trumbo, *Eclipse*, 162.

13. See, for example, *Daily Sentinel*, April 21, 1935; unsourced, undated article, "Scrapbooks," reel 1.

14. Both letters are reprinted in *Eclipse*, xv. Walker continued to follow Trumbo's career, collecting clippings about the blacklisting and reviews of his movies. Walter Walker Papers, series I, Trumbo, Dalton, 1936–71, Special Collections, Tomlinson Library, Colorado Mesa University.

15. Alice Wright, "Who Was W. J. Moyer?" *Colorado West* (Sunday magazine of the *Daily Sentinel*), June 11, 1972, 15–18.

16. Morton Grant to Denny, n.d., WC, 1/2.

17. Trumbo to McKeogh, February 6, 1935, ibid.

18. McKeogh to Trumbo, February 13, 1935, ibid.

19. Dalton Trumbo, "Darling Bill," *Saturday Evening Post*, April 20, 1935, 8–9, 94–105. It was also included in the magazine's year-end anthology, *Post Stories*. Alfred Kazin called it "hilarious, a chortling satire on the New Deal and how dumb politicians really are" (*New York Herald-Tribune* clipping, "Scrapbooks," reel 1).

20. Dalton Trumbo, "Trouble in Horsefly," handwritten note on manuscript cover, WC, 39/6.

21. *Los Angeles Examiner*, April 26, 1935, 12.

22. Trumbo to McKeogh, February 12, 1935, WC, 1/2.

23. Ibid., April 22, 1935.

24. Ibid., October 10, 1935. Landau had opened one of the first talent agencies in Hollywood, and by the mid-1930s it was one of the largest. He represented, among others, Jean Harlow, Lionel Barrymore, and Marie Dressler.

25. Trumbo, interview by Jim Danelz, transcribed in a letter to Trumbo, January 8, 1973, CTP. In 1935 the major studios that owned theater chains inaugurated the double bill as a way to reverse falling attendance figures. To fill the bottom part of the bill, they established B film production units to make cheap movies.

26. Trumbo to McKeogh, October 10, 1935, WC, 1/2.

27. Dalton Trumbo, "Five C's for Fever the Fiver," *Saturday Evening Post*, November 30, 1935, 10–11, 36, 38–39. He also used "Five C's" as a coded come-back-to-me message to Sylvia, his former girlfriend. But after the story was published, Trumbo called Sylvia's mother to see if Sylvia had read it, and he learned that she had married her dancing partner a week earlier. Cook, *Dalton Trumbo*, 85–86.

28. Trumbo to McKeogh, February 12, 1936, WC, 1/2.

29. *Playboy* interview, tape 2, UCLA, 61/2.

30. *Road Gang* folder, Warner Bros. Archive, USC.

31. Untitled review of *Road Gang*, *Welford Beaton's Hollywood Spectator*, February 29, 1936, "Scrapbooks," reel 1.

32. *LAT*, March 21, 1936, 7.

33. William Boehnel, *New York World-Telegram*, February 24, 1936, clipping in *Road Gang* folder, Warner Bros. Archive, USC.

34. Reviews in *DV* and *HR* both printed on September 23, 1936, 3.

35. Clippings mentioned in this paragraph are in "Scrapbooks," reel 1.

36. Schwartz, *Hollywood Writers' Wars*, 36.

37. Dalton Trumbo, *Washington Jitters* (New York: Knopf, 1936), 184.

38. Dalton Trumbo, "Back to Smut," periodical not identified, March 31, 1936, 25, 86, CTP.

39. *Motion Picture Herald*, April 11, 1936, 7, and May 16, 1936, 68. Ramsaye referred to the journal carrying Trumbo's article as "a studio periodical. "

40. *Motion Picture Herald*, April 25, 1936, 21.

41. *HR*, April 27, 1936, 1, 2. There were two producers' associations: the Motion Picture Producers and Distributors of America, located in Washington, DC, which was concerned with public relations and self-regulation (it was renamed the Motion Picture Association of America in 1945); and the Association of Motion Picture Producers, located in Hollywood, which was exclusively concerned with labor relations.

42. Navasky, *Naming Names*, 175.

43. Trumbo quoted in Schwartz, *Hollywood Writers' Wars*, 68–69; also reported in *LAT*, August 23, 1939, 8, and *WV*, August 30, 1939, 5. I found neither a tape nor a transcript of this interview in the Nancy Lynn Schwartz Papers, AHC.

44. Schwartz, *Hollywood Writers' Wars*, 77.

45. *Playboy* interview, tape 3, UCLA, 61/2. There had been blacklists in Hollywood well before the most famous one in 1947. The previous blacklists had been the result of jurisdictional labor disputes. For a history of them, see Larry Ceplair, "Hollywood Unions and Hollywood Blacklists," in *The Wiley-Blackwell History of American Film*, ed. Cynthia Lucia, Roy Grundmann, and Art Simon (Malden, MA: Wiley-Blackwell, 2012), 2:445–64.

46. *HR*, February 11, 1937, 3; *LAT*, February 12, 1937, 23; *DV*, February 11, 1937, 3.

47. Lovat Dickson rejected the offer to publish it in the United Kingdom because a "satire on the New Deal will not be intelligible enough in England to make it popular." He also noted that his firm had lost money on *Eclipse* (March 20, 1936, WC, 1/2).

48. Trumbo to McKeogh, June 27, 1936, WC, 1/2.

49. Ibid.

50. Robert Riskin and Frank Capra used a similar framework for two of their films, *Meet John Doe* (1936) and *Mr. Smith Goes to Washington* (1939), both produced at Columbia.

51. Trumbo, *Washington Jitters*, 170.

52. Ibid., 237.

53. *NYT Book Review*, September 27, 1936, 21; Lisle Bell, *Books*, October 4, 1936, 16; *Boston Transcript*, September 26, 1935, 5; *LAT*, September 20, 1936, C9. According to gossip columnist Read Kendall, Trumbo had autographed a copy and sent it to Franklin D. Roosevelt (*LAT*, October 1, 1936, 11).

54. Trumbo to McKeogh, ca. September 1936, WC, 1/3.

55. Ibid., September 14, 1936.

56. Dalton Trumbo, "The World and All," *McCall's*, July 1937, 12, 57–58.

57. Trumbo to McKeogh, October 13, 1937, WC, 1/3.

58. *DV*, March 3, 1938, 7.

59. *N.L.R.B. v. Jones & Laughlin Steel Corporation*, 301 U.S. 1 (1937).

60. Schwartz, *Hollywood Writers' Wars*, 142. There is no citation for this quotation, and I did not find any documentation in the Schwartz Papers, AHC.

61. *DV*, June 29, 1938, 1.

62. Schwartz, *Hollywood Writers' Wars*, 123.

63. For the history of the Popular Front in Hollywood, see Larry Ceplair and Steven Englund, *The Inquisition in Hollywood: Politics in the Film Community, 1930–1960* (Garden City, NY: Anchor Press/Doubleday, 1980), 83–128; Thomas Patrick Doherty, *Hollywood and Hitler, 1933–1939* (New York: Columbia University Press, 2013), 96–173. Although the FBI reported that Trumbo was "active in the Hollywood Anti-Nazi League in 1939," I think it was misinformed. By that time, the activities of the league and the Motion Picture Democratic Committee, of which he was a member, were frequently coordinated. SACLA to director, January 7, 1942, FOIA-DT; *Hollywood Now*, June–November 1938.

64. Baron Friederich de Reichenberg, *Prince Metternich in Love and War* (London: Martin Secker, 1938), xiv.

65. Cook, *Dalton Trumbo*, 70.

66. Reichenberg, *Prince Metternich*, xv.

67. Trumbo to Ilse Lahn, January 8, 1958, WC, 5/9.

4. Marriage and *Johnny Got His Gun*

1. "Dalton Got His Gun," trans. into French by Rui Naguera, *Cinéma 71*, no. 58 (July–August 1971): 92.

2. Felton had begun his screenwriting career in 1936, worked for Warner Bros. for six years, became a freelancer, and amassed a long string of credits. But he drank excessively, spent extravagantly, and was prone to depression. He tried to commit suicide in 1949 and succeeded in 1972. Trumbo helped Felton out of some difficult situations but did not see much of him after being released from prison.

3. Unless otherwise noted, the biographical information about Cleo is based on transcripts of her own memories, scrapbooks in Mitzi's possession, and Mitzi's memories.

4. Virginia Wright's "Cine . . . Matters," "Scrapbooks," reel 1.

5. Cleo to Christopher, July 2002 and November 2005, CTP.

6. Ibid. Cook tells the story of the courtship very well (*Dalton Trumbo*, 105–18). It was the only chapter of his book that he submitted to the Trumbos for their approval.

7. Trumbo to McKeogh, May 5, 1938, WC, 1/3.

8. Cleo to Christopher, November 2005.

9. "Tattletale," *LAT*, August 27, 1939, E11.

10. SACLA to director, FBI, April 4, 1943, FOIA-DT.

11. Lippincott biography, WC, 8/4.

12. Jean Rouverol, *Refugees from Hollywood: A Journal of the Blacklist Years* (Albuquerque: University of New Mexico Press, 2000), 6. Rouverol was Butler's maiden name.

13. UCLA, 125/2. In the summer of 2012, Mitzi, Nancy Escher, and I visited the ranch. The main building is still there, sans furnishings, just as the Trumbos left it in 1951, as are most of the outbuildings. It is a rambling edifice, with rooms added onto rooms, some of them quite small. A fire had destroyed many of the surrounding trees, and the pond was dry. But it was still a relatively isolated and quiet place to live.

14. John Boruff and Walter Hart, *Washington Jitters: A Play in Two Acts* (New York: Samuel French, 1938). Miner does not mention the play in his oral history: *Worthington Miner: A Directors Guild of America Oral History*, interview by Franklin J. Schaffner (Metuchen, NJ: Directors Guild of America and Scarecrow Press, 1985).

15. *NYT*, May 3, 1938, 19.

16. *New Yorker*, May 14, 1938, 30.

17. *A Man to Remember* was a remake of a 1933 RKO film, *One Man's Journey*, which was based on Katherine L. Haviland-Taylor's 1932 story "Failure." It is possible that Trumbo read the story or saw the film while he was thinking about or working on *Eclipse*.

18. Kanin interview in Patrick McGilligan, ed., *Backstory: Interviews with Screenwriters of Hollywood's Golden Age* (Berkeley: University of California Press, 1986), 96–97.

19. Dalton Trumbo, script for *A Man to Remember*, 125, RKO Radio Pictures Collection, S-636, UCLA. I am indebted to Julie Graham for locating this script.

20. *LAT*, June 15, 1939, 8.

21. *NYT*, November 7, 1938, 23.

22. Bosley Crowther, "A Great Man to Keep an Eye Upon," *NYT*, July 2, 1939, 9:3.

23. Clipping in *A Man to Remember* production file, MHL.

24. Press release, ibid.

25. Lea Jacobs, "The B Film and the Problem of Cultural Distinction," *Screen* 33, no. 1 (Spring 1992): 9–10.

26. Lippincott biography, WC, 8/4.

27. Schwartz, *Hollywood Writers' Wars*, 185.

28. Salary information is from RKO Radio Pictures Collection, PRC 132, 182, and 209, UCLA. I am indebted to Julie Graham for her assistance in providing the payroll cards.

29. *Lexington Herald*, January 30, 1939, "Scrapbooks," reel 1.

30. Dalton Trumbo, untitled poem for Nikola, WC, 1/4.

31. Dalton Trumbo, script for *Five Came Back*, RKO Radio Pictures Collection, S-620, UCLA. When RKO remade this movie as *Back from Eternity* (1956), Trumbo did not receive credit. Howard Hughes, the studio owner and a vehement anti-Communist, did likewise with *The Girl Most Likely* (1957), a remake of *Tom, Dick and Harry*, for which Paul Jarrico wrote the original script.

32. *NYT*, July 5, 1939, 20.

33. Dalton Trumbo, script for *Heaven with a Barbed Wire Fence*, Twentieth Century–Fox Collection, USC.

34. *HR*, September 30, 1939, 3.

35. J. Marks, "Dalton Trumbo," *Sundance*, November 12, 1972, 58–59.

36. "Dalton Trumbo: An Interview," *Film Society Review* 7, no. 2 (October 1971): 25. I am indebted to Gary Crowdus for providing me with a copy of this interview.

37. Trumbo to Perry Gray, January 28, 1971, UCLA, 73/3.

38. Dalton Trumbo, undated interview, WC, 35/7.

39. Dalton Trumbo interview by Larry Bensky, Berkeley, CA, October 20, 1971, Paley Center for Media, Museum of Television and Radio, Beverly Hills, CA.

40. Trumbo to Linda Parenti, responding to an article by Irwin Silber and a review of *Johnny Got His Gun* (the film) in the *Guardian*, September 9, 1971, UCLA, 210/2.

41. Lippincott biography, WC, 8/4.

42. Trumbo to Barbara Silverman, August 20, 1959, CTP.

43. "Dalton Trumbo: First Production with 'Johnny Got His Gun,'" five-page typescript, n.d. [ca. summer 1971], UCLA, 50/7.

44. Between 1931 and 1939, six antiwar novels by US authors were published. For a list, see Philip E. Hager and Desmond Taylor, *The Novels of World War I: An Annotated Bibliography* (New York: Garland, 1981). For some reason, David Madden included an essay on *Johnny* in his anthology *Proletarian Writer of the Thirties* (Carbondale: Southern Illinois University Press, 1968). Leonard Kriegel, the author of that essay, cites Dos Passos, Hemingway, and James Joyce as Trumbo's main influences ("Dalton Trumbo's *Johnny Got His Gun*," 111).

45. *LAT*, December 3, 1939, C3.

46. Cleo Trumbo, foreword to Dalton Trumbo, *Night of the Aurochs*, ed. Robert Kirsch (New York: Viking, 1979), ix–x; emphasis in original.

47. Interview with Christopher Trumbo in *Dalton Trumbo: Rebel in Hollywood: The Story behind* Johnny Got His Gun, written, produced, and directed by Robert Fischer (Fiction Factory, 2006).

48. Trumbo to McKeogh, ca. January 1939, WC, 1/4.

49. Ibid., February 20, 1939.

50. McKeogh to Trumbo, February 27, 1939, WC, 1/4.

51. Lippincott to Trumbo, March 10, 1939, ibid.

52. The novel was serialized in the *Daily Worker* from March 17 to April 28, 1940, preceded by a two-thirds-page notice on March 13, 1940. Several months earlier, the newspaper had announced the Cagney radio performance of Trumbo's "stirring and bitter plea for peace" and noted the "immense strength" of the novel. *Daily Worker*, December 15, 1939, 7.

53. John Walcott to Elsie McKeogh, May 2, 1939, WC, 1/4.

54. *NYT*, February 14, 1940, 19. Reprints include Lippincott's seven between 1938 and 1941; Monogram Publishers, 1946; Liberty Book Club, 1952; Ace Books, 1960; Bantam Books, 1967 and 1970; Lyle Stuart, 1959 and 1970; and Citadel Press, 1991 and 2007. Trumbo earned $4,561.08 in royalties from Lippincott (J. B. Lippincott Collection, Historical Society of Pennsylvania). (I am grateful to Kaitlyn Pettengill for this information.) As of February 2014, the Citadel editions had sold 41,468 copies domestically. (I am grateful to Jackie Dinas, Kensington Publishing Corporation, for this information.)

55. *LAT*, December 3, 1939, C3.

56. *Atlantic*, November 1, 1940, n.p. [15].

57. Harold Strauss, "The Body Maimed," *NYT Book Review*, October 10, 1939, 7.

58. Luella Creighton, *Canadian Forum* 19 (December 1939): 294.

59. *New Republic*, October 11, 1939, 280.

60. *New Yorker*, September 9, 1939, 67.

61. Hilton to Trumbo, n.d., "Scrapbooks," reel 1.

62. *LAT*, September 30, 1939, A7.

63. SACLA to director, January 24, 1942, FOIA-DT.

64. Mrs. Richard Bagley to Trumbo, March 19, 1941, WC, 1/4.

65. Trumbo to Parenti, September 9, 1971.

66. A few years earlier, in his best-selling antiwar book *Cry Havoc!* (London: Jonathan Cape, 1933), British ultrapacifist Beverley Nichols had written: "I should like to see a model of a hideously wounded soldier on the respectable tables of disarmament conferences" (15).

67. SACLA to director, FBI, December 20, 1944, FOIA-DT.

68. Reprinted in the Citadel Press 2007 paperback edition, xvi–xvii.

69. Trumbo to Terry Whalley, May 4, 1970, UCLA, 124/10.

70. Trumbo to Parenti, September 9, 1971.

71. Dalton Trumbo, n.d. [ca. February 1973], UCLA, 211/2.

72. Trumbo to Richard Corliss, February 14, 1973, ibid.

73. Dalton Trumbo, talk at UCLA, May 17, 1972, UCLA Communications Studies Archives, www.youtube.com/watch?v=YhAXSDpvqVU.

74. Lippincott biography, WC, 8/4.

75. Raymond James Sontag and James Stuart Beddie, eds., *Nazi-Soviet Relations, 1939–1941* (Washington, DC: Department of State, 1948), 78.

76. Earl Browder, *The Second Imperialist War* (New York: International Publishers, 1940), 103–4; Maurice Isserman, *Which Side Were You On? The American Communist Party during the Second World War* (Middletown, CT: Wesleyan University Press, 1982), 39–43.

77. Sontag and Beddie, *Nazi-Soviet Relations*, 108.

78. *Public Opinion Quarterly*, March 1940, 94, 102, 111. One month earlier, non-Communist labor leader John L. Lewis had told the American Youth Congress he would not support a war "to suit the policies and requirements of imperialistic world governments." That speech was printed as a pamphlet and widely distributed by the CIO. *Jobs, Peace, Unity* (Washington, DC: Congress of Industrial Organizations, 1940), 6.

79. SACLA to director, October 10, 1939, and January 7, 1940, FOIA-DT. The United Studio Technicians Guild was organized by several members of the International Alliance of Theatrical Stage Employees to democratize the union. Some of the organizers were members of the Communist Party, but they did not have the party's support. Although they succeeded in getting a National Labor Relations Board representation election, they lost it, defeated by a campaign of red-baiting and thuggery. See Larry Ceplair, "A Communist Labor Organizer in Hollywood: Jeff Kibre Challenges the IATSE, 1937–1939," *Velvet Light Trap* 23 (Spring 1989): 64–74; Ceplair, "Hollywood Unions and Hollywood Blacklists," 445–64. A few years later, when the Conference of Studio Unions was organized to promote democratic unionism in Hollywood, Trumbo strongly supported it.

80. SACLA to director, February 18, 1943, COMPIC.

81. Dalton Trumbo, "Trumbo Hits War Makers: Screen Writer-Author Lists

Un-Neutral Acts," *Hollywood Now*, January 19, 1940, 1, 3. Prior to this issue, *Hollywood Now* had been advertised as a publication of the Hollywood Anti-Nazi League.

82. *LAT*, June 23, 1941, 6.

83. Dalton Trumbo radio interview by Fred Gale, "Something Special," WMCA-NY, August 26, 1971, Paley Center for Media, Museum of Television and Radio, Beverly Hill, CA.

5. From B Films to A Films

1. Dalton Trumbo, "To Own the World," October 18, 1939, Turner/MGM Collection, 3633/226, MHL.

2. John Beckett to Mr. McKenna, August 22, 1939, ibid.

3. Dalton Trumbo, *We Who Are Young*, script dated December 18, 1939, 8, 137–38, 150, ibid., 3634/227. In 1938 Albert Maltz had written a wonderful short story, "The Happiest Man in the World," on the same theme.

4. Joseph Breen to L. B. Mayer, March 12, 1940, MPPA/PCA Collection, MHL. The PCA was established in 1934 to enforce the industry's own set of rules: "A Code to Govern the Making of Motion and Talking Pictures" (1930). It was, in effect, an in-house censorship organization. All scripts and films made by members of the Motion Picture Producers and Distributors Association had to be submitted to the PCA, and no film could be released without a PCA-issued certificate of approval. From 1934 to 1954 the PCA was headed by Joseph I. Breen, a rigid conservative and a strict Catholic. See Thomas Patrick Doherty, *Pre-Code Hollywood: Sex, Immorality, and Insurrection in American Cinema, 1930–1934* (New York: Columbia University Press, 1999) and *Hollywood's Censor: Joseph I. Breen and the Production Code Administration* (New York: Columbia University Press, 2007).

5. Dorothy B. Jones alleged that Trumbo's script contained "identifiable Communist propaganda," although she did not specifically cite any of the lines in question. Dorothy B. Jones, "Communism and the Movies: A Study in Film Content," in *Report on Blacklisting*, vol. 1, *Movies*, ed. John Cogley (New York: Fund for the Republic, 1956), 201. Peter Hanson found what he called dialogue of "a vaguely Communist bent," but Trumbo did not write the lines Hanson cited. Hanson, *Dalton Trumbo, Hollywood Rebel*, 25. For Trumbo's original dialogue, see *We Who Are Young*, 151, Turner/MGM Collection, 3634/227, MHL. For the revisions made after he turned in his final script, see ibid., 3634/233.

6. *DV*, November 11, 1940, 3.

7. *HR*, November 11, 1940, 3.

8. *DV*, May 2, 1940, 1.

9. Trumbo to McKeogh, March 23, 1940, WC, 1/4.

10. According to Arlene Hawes Peterson, it was the best-selling novel for seven weeks and among the top six for another fifteen weeks. E-mail to author, March 22, 2012.

11. Cook, *Dalton Trumbo*, 141.

12. Report by Jay Sanford, September 13, 1939, RKO Radio Pictures Collection, S-719, UCLA.

13. Breen to J. R. McDonough, March 27, 1940, "Hollywood and the Production Code," reel 17, MHL.

14. Dalton Trumbo, *Kitty Foyle*, first draft continuity—incomplete, June 1, 1940, RKO Radio Pictures Collection, S-719, UCLA.

15. Ibid., second draft continuity—incomplete, June 28, 1940, 139.

16. Breen to Joseph J. Nolen, July 15, 1940, "Hollywood and the Production Code," reel 17, MHL.

17. Ibid., August 23, 1940.

18. *Kitty Foyle*, American Film Institute online catalog, www.afi.com/members/catalog.

19. *Motion Picture Herald*, December 21, 1940, clipping in *Kitty Foyle* production file, MHL; *Motion Picture Daily*, December 23, 1940, ibid. See also *New York Times*, January 12, 1941, 9:5; J. E. Smyth, "Hollywood as Historian, 1929–1945," in *The Wiley-Blackwell History of American Film, 1929–1945*, ed. Cynthia Lucia, Roy Grundmann, and Art Simon (Malden, MA: Wiley-Blackwell, 2012), 484.

20. *Saturday Evening Post*, August 5, 1946, 52.

21. Dalton Trumbo, *The Remarkable Andrew: Being the Chronicle of a Literal Man* (Philadelphia: Lippincott, 1941), 126–34.

22. Reprinted in Dalton Trumbo, "On Publishing a Book," *Clipper* 2, no. 1 (January 1941): 19–21.

23. Ibid.

24. Trumbo to McKeogh, late 1945 or early 1946, in Trumbo, *Additional Dialogue*, 39.

25. When Elsie asked Trumbo if she should try to sell the novel to a British publisher, he replied: "Cleo and I have been thinking about the morals of taking money out of England at a time when the English people are suffering so greatly. We have decided that we should like all of the royalties, including the advance, to be turned over to the British Red Cross." He added that although he and Cleo would like to contribute to the German Red Cross as well, they lacked the funds and feared that the money would "be diverted to other purposes." Trumbo to McKeogh, May 19, 1941, WC, 1/4.

26. *Times Literary Supplement*, October 18, 1941, 517.

27. *NYT Book Review*, February 2, 1941, 6.

28. *Saturday Review of Literature*, February 15, 1941, 10.

29. *Nation*, February 8, 1941, 164.

30. "Counsel from Hollywood," *Time*, February 3, 1941, 74–76.

31. *DV*, April 14, 1941, 2.

32. Dalton Trumbo, *The Remarkable Andrew*, Paramount Script Collection, B-7–B-9, MHL.

33. Memo from Charles R. Metzger, July 15, 1941; PCA to Luigi Luraschi, July 17, 1941, both in MPPA/PCA Collection, MHL.

34. *Film Daily*, January 19, 1942, 6.

35. *New Yorker*, March 14, 1942, 71.

36. "Dalton Got His Gun," *Cinéma* 71, no. 58 (July–August 1971): 93.

37. Dalton Trumbo, *Somewhere I'll Find You*, MGM Collection, USC.

6. Money, Politics, and War

1. Dalton Trumbo, "Command, Don't Beg!" *Black & White* 2 (1940): 3–4. Actually, Trumbo was incorrect: the Roosevelt administration had aided the Chinese in a variety of ways.

2. SACLA to director, January 7, 1942, FOIA-DT.

3. League of American Writers Archives, part 15, Bancroft Library, University of California–Berkeley.

4. *Daily Worker*, September 5, 1940, 7. When the *Daily Worker* reprinted this speech, the editors deemed it necessary to explain that the publication "does not necessarily agree with Mr. Trumbo's judgments on all the issues discussed." The Alien Registration Act was a collection of several anti-Communist measures that had been floating in and out of congressional committees for a number of years. Its main sponsor was Representative Howard W. Smith (D-Va.), and it consisted of three sections: subversive activities, deportation, and alien registration. The deportation section was expressly written to permit the attorney general to reopen the case against Harry Bridges (see note 7). Two months after the act became law, the attorney general did so.

5. US Congress, House of Representatives, Committee on Un-American Activities, *Hearings Regarding the Communist Infiltration of the Motion Picture Industry*, October 1947 (Washington, DC: Government Printing Office, 1947), 112; hereafter cited as 1947 Hearings. The American Peace Mobilization had been created in September 1940 to act as an umbrella for all the local "peace" front groups formed in the aftermath of the Nonaggression Treaty. The Lend-Lease Act (March 11, 1941) was designed to allow the president to circumvent a series of neutrality laws passed by an isolationist Congress. Labeled "An Act to Promote the Defense of the United States," it allowed the president to aid the Allies by lending, leasing, or selling defense articles to them. In the two years prior to passage of the Lend-Lease Act, Roosevelt had been sharply criticized by interventionists as an equivocator who was not doing enough to aid the United Kingdom or to prepare the United States for war. See Lynne Olson, *Those Angry Days: Roosevelt, Lindbergh, and America's Fight over World War II, 1939–1941* (New York: Random House, 2013). David Kaiser, however, has demonstrated that Roosevelt secretly started to prepare the country for war in late 1938. David Kaiser, *No End Save Victory: How FDR Led the Nation into War* (New York: Basic Books, 2014), 41–44.

6. SACLA to director, June 19, 1941, FOIA-DT. The North American strike was one of several in the defense industries during 1940 and 1941. All were blamed on "Communists."

7. Dalton Trumbo, *Harry Bridges: A Discussion of the Latest Effort to Deport Civil Liberties and the Rights of American Labor* (Hollywood Chapter of the League of American Writers, 1941), 2. One year later, Trumbo told his literary agent that he was interested in writing a biography of Bridges, which he intended to title "Harry Bridges: A Prejudiced Biography." Trumbo to McKeogh, ca. late 1942, WC, 1/4. However, when he learned a few months later that someone else had already embarked on such a project, he abandoned his own.

8. SACLA to director, October 19, 1942, FOIA-DT. See note 23.

9. William Z. Foster, *History of the Communist Party of the United States* (New York: International Publishers, 1952), 384.

10. Quoted in Cook, *Dalton Trumbo*, 137.

11. Trumbo, *Additional Dialogue*, 27–29.

12. Ibid. Wallace had declared that the United States had an obligation to contribute to the war and to the postwar settlement. He described a liberal

world system in which freedom, fairness, and opportunity would promote global peace. The Atlantic Charter was a statement of eight war aims agreed to by President Roosevelt and Prime Minister Winston Churchill on August 14, 1941. Number six stated: "after the final destruction of the Nazi tyranny, they hope to see established a peace which will afford to all nations the means of dwelling in safety within their own boundaries, and which will afford assurance that all the men in all the lands may live out their lives in freedom from fear and want." Henry Steele Commager, ed., *Documents of American History*, 8th ed. (New York: Appleton-Century-Crofts, 1968), 2:451.

13. Since June 1941, nearly 200 divisions of the German army had occupied the most populous, industrialized, and resource-rich region of the Soviet Union. Stalin's allies, however, regularly postponed the opening of this front (until the D-day landing in France in June 1944). Soviet and Communist Party leaders concluded that this delay was intentionally calculated to bleed the Soviet Union dry and leave it in a weakened condition at the end of the war. See Mark A. Stoler, *The Politics of the Second Front: American Military Planning and Diplomacy in Coalition Warfare* (Westport, CT: Greenwood Press, 1977).

14. SACLA to director, January 7, 1942, FOIA-DT. SACLA reported that the speech was printed and "widely distributed by Communists and given away in all their bookstores."

15. "Scrapbooks," reel 2.

16. [Dalton Trumbo], *The Sleepy Lagoon Case*, with a foreword by Orson Welles (Los Angeles: Sleepy Lagoon Defense Committee, 1943), 18–19, Sleepy Lagoon Defense Committee Records, 1942–1945, box 2, folder 3, UCLA. Though Trumbo's name does not appear on the pamphlet, it is clearly his style, and Nancy Lynn Schwartz credits it to him (*Hollywood Writers' Wars*, 198). Marian Bachrach, the Communist head of the Council for Pan-American Democracy, wrote the introduction. Guy Endore, another Hollywood writer, wrote a second pamphlet, *The Sleepy Lagoon Mystery*. Mark A. Weitz credits Endore with both pamphlets in *The Sleepy Lagoon Murder Case: Race Discrimination and Mexican-American Rights* (Lawrence: University Press of Kansas, 2010), but in his oral history, Endore states that he wrote only one pamphlet. See *Reflections of Guy Endore*, interview by Elizabeth I. Dixon, 1961–1962 (Los Angeles: UCLA Oral History Program, 1964).

17. *People v. Zamora*, 66 Cal. App. 2d, 166 (1944).

18. *Writers' Congress: The Proceeding of the Conference Held in October 1943, under the Sponsorship of the Hollywood Writers' Mobilization and the University of California* (Berkeley: University of California Press, 1944), 495–501. Although the Communist Party had been courting blacks for more than a decade, the party did not become an important political force in the Los Angeles black community until 1948. Josh Sides, *L.A. City Limits: African American Los Angeles from the Great Depression to the Present* (Berkeley: University of California Press, 2003), 139–40. In a report prepared for a party branch discussion sometime around 1950, the author calculated that fewer than 1 percent of those employed in the motion picture industry were black, and the vast majority of them were janitors. Anne Millar, "Negro Employment in the Motion Picture Industry," n.d., in the possession of Becca Wilson.

19. *Arts and Architecture* 61, no. 3 (February 1944): 16.

20. Trumbo to Andrew Sarris, August 4, 1960, UCLA, 120/11. One group

of left-wing writers at MGM pressured studio officials to eliminate some of the racist scenes and dialogue in *Tennessee Johnson*. Larry Ceplair, *The Marxist and the Movies: A Biography of Paul Jarrico* (Lexington: University Press of Kentucky, 2007), 59–60.

21. *Playboy* interview, tape 3, UCLA, 61/2.

22. SACLA to director, October 19, 1942, FOIA-DT. Biberman was a movie director who, like Trumbo, became one of the Hollywood Ten.

23. Director to SACLA, May 28, 1943, FOIA-DT. J. Edgar Hoover had created the Custodial Detention Program in December 1939. All FBI offices were ordered to identify persons of German, Italian, and Communist sympathies as candidates for detention during a "national security emergency." In addition, he wanted the names of all editors, publishers, and subscribers to German, Italian, and Communist newspapers and the membership lists of all suspect organizations. Agents were also instructed to cultivate informants and infiltrate these suspect organizations. Tim Weiner, *Enemies: A History of the FBI* (New York: Random House, 2012), 83–86.

24. Dalton Trumbo, 1959 preface to 2007 reprint *of Johnny Got His Gun*, xxvii; Trumbo, *Additional Dialogue*, 26. It is not clear how many letters Trumbo received. I found only two (WC 1/5). In one, Louise N. Wheelwright of Blowing Rock, North Carolina, wrote (on September 17, 1943) that she had acquired twenty-seven copies of *Johnny* and expressed her hope that Trumbo had "not gone over to the war-mongers' side." Another letter, from Annie Riley Hale of Altadena, California (October 25, 1943), inquired whether Trumbo had any copies of *Johnny* he wished to sell to her or to Ms. Wheelwright. She assured Trumbo that Wheelwright was "a dauntless *anti-war* crusader."

25. SACLA to director, December 20, 1944, FOIA-DT.

26. Undated note, CTP.

27. Dalton Trumbo to FBI, rough draft, ca. early 1944 [*sic*], in Trumbo, *Additional Dialogue*, 26–31. In the original typescript of *Additional Dialogue*, the dates in the author's introduction and the printed letter are ca. 1942, and Trumbo did not change either. When the book was printed, however, the date in the introduction remained ca. 1942 (22), but the letter was dated ca. 1944 (26). In both places, it is specifically referred to as a "rough draft." Trumbo later gave the date of the letter as December 1943; see Trumbo to Richard Corliss, February 14, 1973, UCLA, 211/2.

28. Richard Corliss, "Dalton Trumbo: The Pen Is Mightier than the Gun," *Village Voice*, September 2, 1971, 50.

29. Trumbo to Corliss, February 14, 1973, UCLA, 211/2.

30. Glenn Garvin, "Fools for Communism: Still Apologists after All These Years," reason.com/archives/2004/04/01/fools-for-communism/1.

31. Art Eckstein, "The Fountain of Lies," archive.frontpagemag.com/readArticle.aspx?ARTID=9274.

32. Dalton Trumbo, *A Guy Named Joe*, treatment, 93, MGM Collection, USC.

33. Breen to Mayer, October 21, 1942, and February 15, 1943, MPPA/PCA Collection, MHL.

34. *A Guy Named Joe*, American Film Institute online catalog, www.afi.com/members/catalog.

35. *Life*, January 17, 1944, 39.

36. *New Yorker*, January 1, 1944, 53.

37. *LAT*, March 17, 1944, II:10.

38. *HR*, December 24, 1943, 3.

39. *DV*, December 24, 1943, 3.

40. Trumbo to McKeogh, ca. October 1942, in Trumbo, *Additional Dialogue*, 24.

41. Trumbo to McKeogh, ca. late 1942, WC, 1/4.

42. Trumbo to McKeogh, January 23, 1943, WC, 1/5. "Fishermen" was a black comedy about the resistance movement in France (onionskin copy, 162 pp., WC, 16/5; paper copy, 135 pp., WC, 16/6). Alfred Lewis Levitt thought the script was "marvelous" because it was "so right about the war. It was so charming." Levitt UCLA Oral History, 1.15, tape 8, side 2, October 27, 1988.

43. Dalton Trumbo interview by Lawrence H. Suid, for his article "The Film Industry and the Military," April 10, 1974, UCLA, 171/3.

44. Dalton Trumbo, *Thirty Seconds over Tokyo*, May 8, 1943, 1–2, MGM Collection, USC.

45. Ibid.

46. Suid interview.

47. Breen to Mayer, September 9, 1943, MPPA/PCA Collection, MHL.

48. Clayton R. Koppes and Gregory D. Black, *Hollywood Goes to War: How Politics, Profits and Propaganda Shaped World War II Movies* (New York and London: Free Press/Collier Macmillan, 1987), 266–67.

49. *Thirty Seconds over Tokyo*, American Film Institute online catalog, www.afi.com/members/catalog.

50. "Dalton Got His Gun," *Cinéma* 71, no. 58 (July–August 1971): 95.

51. *NYT*, November 26, 1944, X1.

52. *Life*, November 13, 1944, 49.

53. *HR*, November 14, 1943, 3.

54. *DV*, November 14, 1943, 3, 14.

55. Robert Louis Stevenson, *Poems* (London: Heinemann, 1924), 1:148. Trumbo was able to sell original scripts to other studios because he had, from the beginning of his career, included in each contract a list of reserved titles and ideas for stories conceived prior to signing the contract.

56. Dalton Trumbo interview with Jim Danelz, transcribed in a letter to Trumbo, January 8, 1973, CTP.

57. *Tender Comrade* file, RKO Radio Pictures Collection, S-976, UCLA.

58. Dalton Trumbo, *Tender Comrade*, final draft, 64, S-977, ibid.

59. Three years later, Ginger's mother, Lela Rogers, misinformed a subcommittee of the Committee on Un-American Activities when she testified that Ginger had refused to say those lines. *LAT*, May 15, 1947, 5.

60. Letter to *HR*, November 10, 1970, 8.

61. "Dalton Got His Gun," 93–94.

62. Koppes and Black, *Hollywood Goes to War*, 165.

63. "Comrade Ginger," *New York Times*, June 2, 1944, 21.

64. *New York Critics' Reviews*, 1944, 350–51. I am indebted to Ned Comstock for sending me these reviews.

65. *DV*, December 29, 1943, 3.

66. *HR*, December 29, 1943, 3.

67. Jeff Smith, *Film Criticism, the Cold War, and the Blacklist: Reading the Hollywood Reds* (Berkeley: University of California Press, 2014), 293 n. 66.

68. Trumbo to Sisk, ca. August 1943, Robert Sisk Collection, 12/10, USC, courtesy of Ned Comstock.

69. Dalton Trumbo, *Our Vines Have Tender Grapes*, 161, MGM Collection, USC.

70. Cook, *Dalton Trumbo*, 159.

71. *New York Herald-Tribune*, September 7, 1945, 16.

72. *DV*, July 20, 1945, 3.

73. *HR*, July 19, 1945, 3.

74. *LAT*, September 29, 1945, A5.

75. *NYT*, September 7, 1945, 21.

76. Dalton Trumbo, "And Now Goodbye," sixth draft—estimating, January 15, 1945, 161, Milton E. Pickman Papers, 2/42, MHL.

77. Trumbo to McKeogh, July 3, 1944, WC, 1/5. The year 1943 was a lucrative one for Trumbo. His income from the studios totaled $136,360, and his expenses totaled $66,878 (Operating Statement, WC, 41/4).

78. WC, 41/5.

79. Trumbo to Maud Trumbo, March 25, 1945, in the possession of Mitzi Trumbo.

7. Into the Communist Party

1. Barbara Zheutlin and David Talbott, eds., *Creative Differences: Profiles of Hollywood Dissidents* (Boston: South End Press, 1978), 29.

2. Lardner had contributed to the screenplay adapted from Trumbo's story "Broadway Cavalier," released by Warner Bros. as *The Kid from Kokomo* (May 1939), but it is unlikely they met at that studio.

3. Schwartz, *Hollywood Writers' Wars*, 86.

4. Trumbo to Lardner, June 25, 1953, in Trumbo, *Additional Dialogue*, 276.

5. Ring Lardner Jr., *I'd Hate Myself in the Morning: A Memoir* (New York: Thunder's Mouth Press/Nation Books, 2000), 103.

6. Jean Butler, interview with the author, November 17, 1976.

7. E-mail from Michael Butler, August 22, 2012.

8. Lardner, *I'd Hate Myself*, 45.

9. Ring Lardner Jr., interview with the author, September 22, 1976.

10. Kate Lardner, *Shut up He Explained: The Memoir of a Blacklisted Kid* (New York: Ballantine, 2004), 31.

11. Lardner, *I'd Hate Myself*, 54. Hunter was one of the few Communists who managed to stay under the government's radar and serve in the Office of Strategic Services. He was also the only member of the group to have an award created in his name. In 1992, the year after he died, the Writers Guild of America, East, established the Ian McLellan Hunter award for lifetime achievement as a writer. Lardner was its first recipient. See also Tim Hunter, "The Senate Small Business Committee Pizza Parlor," *Cinema Journal* 44, no. 4 (Summer 2005): 112–15.

12. E-mail from Joe Lardner, August 22, 2012.

13. E-mail from Kate Lardner, September 3, 2012.

14. Lardner, *I'd Hate Myself*, 55–56.

15. Trumbo to McKeogh, ca. October 1942, in Trumbo, *Additional Dialogue*, 23.

16. Trumbo to Lardner, October 28, 1945, ibid., 31–35.

17. Herbert Biberman, *Salt of the Earth: The Story of a Film* (Sag Harbor, NY: Harbor Electronic Publishing, 2003), 46. For Wilson's Marxism, see Larry Ceplair, "The Base-Superstructure Debate in the Hollywood Communist Party," *Science and Society* 72, no. 3 (July 2008): 319–48; Larry Ceplair, "A Marxist in Hollywood: The Screenwriting Career of Michael Wilson (1914–1978)," *Historical Journal of Film, Radio and Television* 34, no. 2 (2014): 187–207.

18. Quoted by Carl Foreman in his speech at Wilson's Laurel Award ceremony, *WGAw News*, May 1976, 21.

19. Schwartz, *Hollywood Writers' Wars*, 185.

20. Lardner, *I'd Hate Myself*, 101; interview with Lardner, Nancy Lynn Schwartz Papers, box 28, AHC.

21. SACLA to director, October 19, 1942, and April 12, 1943, FOIA-DT.

22. SACLA to director, August 9, 1943, COMPIC. These records were given to the FBI by Elizabeth Benson (aka Leach), a party clerk.

23. Dalton Trumbo, "My Own View of the CP," WC, 40/7.

24. SACLA to director, December 20, 1944, FOIA-DT.

25. Trumbo, *Additional Dialogue*, 435 n. 16.

26. "Dalton Trumbo: An Interview," *Film Society Review* 7, no. 2 (October 1971): 28.

27. Cook, *Dalton Trumbo*, 146.

28. *Playboy* interview, tape 3, UCLA, 61/2. The founding convention of the Communist Political Association was held in late May 1944. It grew out of Browder's conviction that the wartime alliance between the United States and the Soviet Union would continue and that Communists in the United States would be more effective as "a non-party organization of Americans which, basing itself upon the working class, carries forward the tradition of Washington, Jefferson, Paine, Jackson, and Lincoln, under the changed conditions of modern industrial society." In other words, Browder wanted to situate his organization as a left-wing pressure group within the wartime and peacetime Popular Front. Maurice Isserman, *Which Side Are You On? The American Communist Party during the Second World War* (Middletown, CT: Wesleyan University Press, 1982), 1–2.

29. Richard Corliss, "Dalton Trumbo: The Pen Is Mightier than the Gun," *Village Voice*, September 2, 1971, 50; reprinted, with some alterations, in *The Hollywood Screenwriters: A Film Comment Book*, ed. Richard Corliss (New York: Avon, 1972), 169–79; *Talking Pictures: Screenwriters in the American Cinema, 1927–73* (Woodstock, NY: Overlook Press, 1974), 254–62.

30. Undated note, UCLA, 211/2.

31. Dalton Trumbo, *Additional Dialogue* (New York: Bantam Books, 1972), 459.

32. Corliss to Trumbo, March 10, 1973, UCLA, 211/2.

33. Cleo to Christopher, November 5, 1995, CTP. Trumbo loved his aunt, but he and Ted disagreed politically. According to Mitzi, Ted was "a conservative and a bigot. He hated Trumbo's politics."

34. Dalton Trumbo, "Ideas: Generally Politically," October 27, 1956, CTP.

35. Cook, *Dalton Trumbo*, 147–48.

36. Cleo to Christopher, November 5, 1995, CTP.

37. *Playboy* interview, tape 3, UCLA, 61/2.

38. Dalton Trumbo, "More for Larry," n.d., UCLA, 126/7.

39. Dalton Trumbo, "Notes Made after Interview for *Playboy*," UCLA, 127/8.

40. *Playboy* interview, tape 3, UCLA, 61/2.

41. Cleo to Christopher, November 5, 1995, CTP.

42. "Dalton Trumbo: An Interview," 28–29. Trumbo was not, contrary to John Joseph Gladchuk's ahistorical designation, a "moderate" Communist. John Joseph Gladchuk, *Hollywood and Anticommunism: HUAC and the Evolution of the Red Menace* (New York: Routledge, 2007).

43. Edward Dmytryk, *Odd Man Out: A Memoir of the Hollywood Ten* (Carbondale: Southern Illinois University Press, 1996), 61–62.

44. Patrick McGilligan and Paul Buhle, eds., *Tender Comrades: A Backstory of the Hollywood Blacklist* (New York: St. Martin's Press, 1997), 37–38.

45. SACLA to director, March 12, 1945, FOIA-DT.

46. Dalton Trumbo, "Secrecy and the Communist Party," n.d., [ca. 1957], WC, 40/7.

47. SACLA to director, December 20, 1944, FOIA-DT.

48. *LAT*, April 29, 1944, 1.

49. *Los Angeles Examiner*, May 10, 1944, 2:1.

50. *DV*, April 21, 1944, 4.

51. No title, n.d., WC, 40/7.

52. Nancy Lynn Schwartz Papers, box 29, AHC.

53. *DV*, July 5, 1944, 3.

54. Dalton Trumbo, "The Real Meaning of NCPAC," *Rob Wagner's Script*, February 3, 1945, 24.

55. Jacques Duclos, "A Propos de la Dissolution du Parti Communiste Américain," *Cahiers du communisme* 6 (April 1945): 21–38. In an interesting but not unusual twist, Duclos was later criticized at a meeting of European Communists for his "parliamentary illusions." Vojtech Mastny, *The Cold War and Soviet Insecurity: The Stalin Years* (Oxford: Oxford University Press, 1996), 6.

56. Quoted in Schwartz, *Hollywood Writers' Wars*, 225.

57. Quoted in McGilligan and Buhle, *Tender Comrades*, 36.

58. Letters dated May 8, 11, and 19, 1945, WC, 1/6.

59. Trumbo to Passport Division, [May 1945], FOIA-DT.

60. Hopper to Dorothy Thompson, January 12, 1948, Hedda Hopper Collection, folder 3424, MHL. As a result of his misreading of a letter in *Additional Dialogue* (392), Kenneth Lloyd Billingsley alleges that Alger Hiss was responsible for bringing Trumbo to San Francisco; see *Hollywood Party: How Communism Seduced the Film Industry in the 1930s and 1940s* (Rocklin, CA: Forum, 1998), 118. Neither the speech nor Trumbo are mentioned in *The Diaries of Edward R. Stettinius, Jr., 1943–1946*, ed. Thomas C. Campbell and George C. Herring (New York: New Viewpoints, 1973).

61. Stephen Schlesinger, *Act of Creation: The Founding of the United Nations* (Boulder, CO: Westview Press, 2003), 201.

62. Cook, *Dalton Trumbo*, 151.

63. Trumbo to Lynch, n.d., WC, 40/1.

64. Speech changes, WC, 40/2.

65. Trumbo to Lynch, n.d. [Sunday evening], WC, 40/1. In addition, Trumbo did not want the United Nations to allow its members to continue to dominate or control the colonies or territories they had occupied during the war.

66. Trumbo to Finletter, n.d., WC, 40/2, included in a selection of articles, speeches, and letters that he hoped might be published under the title "Not Making It at All," sent to Shirley Burke, November 12, 1971, UCLA, 159/8.

67. Speech of the Secretary of State, broadcast over the Mutual Broadcasting System and the Blue Network of the American Broadcasting Company, May 28, 1945, *Department of State Bulletin*, June 3, 1945, 1007–13.

68. WC, 40/1. Two years after Trumbo's testimony, in June 1949, Stettinius swore in an affidavit for Alger Hiss's first perjury trial that he was unaware of any questions about Hiss's loyalty. Schlesinger, *Act of Creation*, 107.

69. *Screen Writer*, June 1945, 36.

70. Trumbo to McKeogh, n.d. [late 1945], in Trumbo, *Additional Dialogue*, 37.

71. Dalton Trumbo, "Jerusalem Jerusalem!" n.d., 1–3, UCLA, 36/5.

72. All letters cited are in CTP.

73. Undated note, UCLA, 45/5.

74. Trumbo to Ray Blakerman, April 5, 1953, in Trumbo, *Additional Dialogue*, 263.

75. Ibid., 264–65.

76. Ibid., 265–66.

77. Dalton Trumbo, "Notes on a Summer Vacation," *Screen Writer*, September 1945, 17–41.

78. *LAT*, October 10, 1945, 1.

79. Brewer letter dated October 18, 1945, WC, 1/7. Trumbo wrote on this letter: "He was an incredible man with far too much power. Personally, he couldn't intimidate (or dare to try) a butterfly." In fact, during the early blacklist years, Brewer was one of the most powerful—and intimidating—individuals in Hollywood. For more on Brewer, see Ceplair, "Hollywood Unions and Hollywood Blacklists," 459–62.

80. Advertisement in *DV*, December 12, 1945, 11.

81. Dalton Trumbo, *The Real Facts behind the Motion Picture Lockout* (Los Angeles: United Labor and Citizens Committee, 1945), UCLA, 229/6.

82. Trumbo to McKeogh, n.d. [late 1945 or early 1946], in Trumbo, *Additional Dialogue*, 35–39.

83. Quoted in Christopher Trumbo, "Trumbo's One Man Band," speech delivered at Congreso Internacional 60 Aniversario HUAC, Universidad Complutense de Madrid, March 2008, CTP.

84. Trumbo interview with Danelz.

85. Jane Gottlieb to McKeogh, April 26, 1944, WC, 1/5. There is no script with that title at Wisconsin or UCLA. Actually, Trumbo did receive one credit while he was blacklisted: in November 1950 Columbia remade *You Belong to Me*, which was released as *Emergency Wedding*, starring Larry Parks; both were based on Trumbo's original story "The Doctor's Husband." The trade newspapers declared it a mildly amusing, lighthearted comedy. *HR*, November 10, 1950, 3; *DV*, November 10, 1950, 3. In the spring of 1944 Trumbo

adapted, for RKO, Philip Van Doren's short story "The Greatest Gift" (aka "The Man Who Was Never Born"). Trumbo enlarged the story, building it around his usual conceit of small towns, cynical politicians, and corrupt businessmen (WC, 18/1–3). The story was later rewritten by others and released as *It's a Wonderful Life* (1946).

8. Trumbo's Antifascist Persuasion

1. See, for example, Daniel J. Flynn, *A Conservative History of the American Left* (New York: Crown Forum, 2008), 211; Tony Judt, "The Last Romantic," *New York Review of Books*, November 20, 2003, 45.

2. Tony Judt with Timothy Snyder, *Thinking the Twentieth Century* (New York: Penguin, 2012), 189, 395.

3. Carey McWilliams, in a 1935 article and pamphlet, identified several such groups in Hollywood—namely, the Light Horse Cavalry, Hollywood Hussars, and California Esquadrille. Carey McWilliams, "Hollywood Plays with Fascism," *Nation*, May 29, 1935, 623. That same year, Sinclair Lewis's dystopian novel *It Can't Happen Here* was published, followed by the pamphlet *It Can Happen Here: Active Anti-Semitism in Los Angeles* (Los Angeles: American League against War and Fascism and Jewish Anti-Nazi League of Southern California, 1935). One year later, actress Paulette Goddard told a reporter that fascism was far outdistancing communism in Hollywood. John T. MacManus, "A Gamin Visits Gotham," *NYT*, October 18, 1936, 10:4. Finally, *Hollywood Now*, the journal of the Hollywood Anti-Nazi League, regularly reported on the activities of a variety of domestic fascist organizations and their periodic attempts to unite into national fronts. After listing a number of like quotations, Geoffrey S. Smith dismisses them as aspects of "a liberal crusade against American fascism" and asserts that they "helped create in the national mind a domestic threat where none in fact existed." Since it is difficult to prove a negative, Smith does not try. Geoffrey S. Smith, *To Save a Nation: American "Extremism," the New Deal, and the Coming of World War II*, rev. ed. (Chicago: Ivan Dee, 1992), 69. For a different view of this "threat," see Robert A. Rosenbaum, *Waking to Danger: Americans and Nazi Germany, 1933–1941* (Santa Barbara, CA: Praeger, 2010), 63; Francis MacDonnell, *Insidious Foes: The Axis Fifth Column and the American Home Front* (New York: Oxford University Press, 1995); Sander A. Diamond, *The Nazi Movement in the United States, 1924–1941* (Ithaca, NY: Cornell University Press, 1974).

4. Dalton Trumbo, "Morning Salute," n.d., WC, 45/4. For other examples of Communists' concerns about the postwar period, see Ceplair and Englund, *The Inquisition in Hollywood*, 193–95; Michael Wilson, "Come Away Home," *Yale Review* 34 (Winter 1945): 330–40. As for non-Communists, the participants at the Atlantic City Conference for Peaceworkers expressed their belief that US policies were "at least parallel [to those of the Soviet Union] if not actually provocative." Conservative cold warrior George Kennan believed that the Truman administration exaggerated and overreacted to Soviet "threats." And former president Herbert Hoover, in a radio address delivered in January 1952, accused the US government of propagandizing "war fears or psychosis." Lawrence S. Wittner, *Rebels against War: The American Peace Movement, 1933–1983* (Philadelphia: Temple University Press, 1984), 164; John Lewis Gaddis,

George F. Kennan: An American Life (New York: Penguin, 2011), 263, 391; Carl Marzani, *We Can Be Friends: The Origins of the Cold War* (New York: Topical Books, 1952), 20.

5. Dalton Trumbo, "The Russian Menace," *Rob Wagner's Script Magazine*, May 25, 1946, 10–12. Ring Lardner Jr. later expressed his thoughts about that period: "I was losing what remained of my illusions about Stalin and his 'socialist state,' yet it still seemed to me then that the Soviet leaders were more serious than ours about wanting peaceful relations. . . . I believed the need to avoid another war and abolish nuclear weapons transcended the type of political systems one embraced." Lardner, *I'd Hate Myself*, 113–14.

6. Undated speech, ca. late 1945–early 1946, WC, 40/7.

7. In March 1946 Communist Party leader Jack Stachel referred to "the struggle to forge a broad anti-fascist people's coalition." "Lessons of the Political Struggle," *Political Affairs* 25, no. 3 (March 1946): 208. But it was not until August that national chairman William Z. Foster announced that Communists must weaken and break the power of finance capital, "the breeder of economic chaos, fascism and war." "American Imperialism, Leader of World Reaction," *Political Affairs* 25, no. 8 (August 1946): 695.

8. Vice President Henry A. Wallace had begun to warn of postwar fascism a year before the war ended. In an article published in the *New York Times Sunday Magazine*, Wallace warned that the "world-wide, age-old struggle between fascism and democracy will not stop when the fighting ends"; postwar fascists "will inevitably push steadily for Anglo-Saxon imperialism and eventually for war with Russia." "Wallace Defines 'American Fascism,'" *NYT Sunday Magazine*, April 9, 1944, 7, 35.

9. WC, 40/7. McClanahan was antilabor and a zealous promoter of "Americanism." He attended several meeting of Smith's America First Party and, as a result, was recalled in March 1946.

10. No title, n.d., UCLA, 126/7.

11. Hollywood Fights Back national radio broadcast, reprinted in Gordon Kahn, *Hollywood on Trial: The Story of the 10 Who Were Indicted* (New York: Boni and Gaer, 1948; reprint, New York: Arno Press and the New York Times, 1972), v.

12. Trumbo to Executive Board, December 14, 1945, WC, 40/7.

13. *Screen Writer*, June 1946, 43. During Trumbo's tenure as editor, the Editorial Board fluctuated in number from six to ten but most commonly stood at eight or nine. During those months, two Communists were members: Ring Lardner Jr. and Paul Trivers. All articles submitted to *Screen Writer* were read and voted on by the entire Editorial Committee and then by the Editorial Board, and even some of Trumbo's editorials were revised. Memos from Salemson to Trumbo, June 12 and September 4, 1946, WC, 33/miscellaneous.

14. Dalton Trumbo, "Samuel Grosvenor Wood: A Footnote," *Screen Writer*, June 1945, 23–31.

15. *HR*, July 30, 1945, 28; *HR*, July 31, 1945, 6. On Wood's death in the autumn of 1949, Trumbo wrote "Elegy on the Death of Samuel Grosvenor Wood," which included these lines: "Gonna be lonesome / For him up there / Without any Communists / To get in his hair" (UCLA, 171/5). He later told an interviewer that Wood "was the grandfather of Hollywood reactionaries." "Dalton Got His Gun," *Cinéma* 71, no. 58 (July–August 1971): 93.

16. *Screen Writer*, August 1945, 39–40. For an examination of Wilkerson's anticommunism, see Daniel Miller and Gary Baum, "The Most Sinful Period in Hollywood History," *HR*, November 30, 2012, 48–57, 67.

17. *Screen Writer*, October 1945, 43. In 1941 *Life* magazine had labeled Dennis "America's No. 1 Intellectual Fascist." "The Ism of Appeasement," *Life*, January 20, 1941, 26. See also Gerald Horne, *The Color of Fascism: Lawrence Dennis, Racial Passing, and the Rise of Right-Wing Extremism in the United States* (New York: New York University Press, 2006).

18. *Screen Writer*, November 1945, 42, 43.

19. Ring Lardner Jr., "The Sign of the Boss," *Screen Writer*, November 1945, 1–12; critical letter from Lewis R. Foster, *Screen Writer*, December 1945, 38.

20. *Screen Writer*, December 1945, 39.

21. Alvah Bessie, "Blockade," *Screen Writer*, January 1946, 21–23.

22. Richard Macaulay, "Who Censors What?" typescript, WC, 33/ miscellaneous.

23. Trumbo to Macaulay, n.d., WC, 1/8; also reprinted in 1947 Hearings, 199–201.

24. Trumbo to Estabrook, rough draft, April 29, 1946, UCLA, 132/5.

25. "The Soviet Film Industry," *Screen Writer*, June 1946, 17–30.

26. *Screen Writer*, September 1946, 3, 5.

27. Hedda Hopper, "Looking at Hollywood," *LAT*, July 31, 1946, C3.

28. *HR*, August 20 and 22, 1946, 1. McCormick was a Communist and a labor organizer, and she had worked for the Sleepy Lagoon Defense Committee.

29. Trumbo, *Additional Dialogue*, 59–60. It is misdated by the editor.

30. Nancy Lynn Schwartz Papers, box 29, AHC.

31. Albert Maltz, "What Shall We Ask of Writers?" *New Masses*, February 12, 1946, 19–22.

32. Quoted in Bernard K. Johnpoll, ed., *A Documentary History of the CPUSA* (Westport, CT: Greenwood Press, 1994), 8:105.

33. Ibid., 133.

34. Joseph R. Starobin, *American Communism in Crisis, 1943–1957* (Berkeley: University of California Press, 1975), 121.

35. See Larry Ceplair, "Albert Maltz, Philip Stevenson, and 'Art Is a Weapon,'" *minnesota review* 69 (2007): 153–62.

36. Cook, *Dalton Trumbo*, 166.

37. US Congress, House of Representatives, Committee on Un-American Activities, *Investigation of Communist Activities in the Los Angeles Area 5*, March 12, 1953, 946.

38. Dalton Trumbo, "A Note to Myself at the Time," n.d., CTP.

39. Albert Maltz, "Moving Forward," *New Masses* 59 (March 1946): 8–22.

40. *Daily People's World*, April 10, 1946, 3.

41. William Z. Foster, "Elements of a People's Culture," *New Masses*, April 23, 1946, 9.

42. Trumbo to Sillen, [ca. April 1946], in Trumbo, *Additional Dialogue*, 42.

43. *Freedom Road* (1944) is a novel by Howard Fast about southern blacks during Reconstruction. Fast was a Communist Party member when he wrote it. *Deep Are the Roots* (1945) is a play about a black-white romance, written by Arnaud d'Usseau (a party member) and James Gow. All the other writers cited are anti-Communists of one form or another. Starting with the testimony

of John Charles Moffitt in October 1947 (see chapter 9), virtually every anti-Communist writer addressing this topic has distorted Trumbo's comment to mean that Hollywood Communists had, by dint of their collective power in the movie industry, blocked films like this from being made. As far as I can tell, only one of these writers, Kenneth Billingsley, actually read Trumbo's article (see Billingsley, *Hollywood Party*, 92); all the others quote or paraphrase him. See Terry Teachout, "The Odor of Sanctity," *Wall Street Journal*, November 5, 2003, W10; Robert Mayhew, *Ayn Rand and "The Song of Russia": Communism and Anti-Communism in 1940s Hollywood* (Lanham, MD: Scarecrow Press, 2005), 177; Daniel J. Flynn, *A Conservative History of the American Left* (New York: Crown Forum, 2008), 220; John V. Fleming, *The Anti-Communist Manifestos: Four Books that Shaped the Cold War* (New York: Norton, 2009), 159.

44. Dalton Trumbo, "Getting Hollywood into Focus," *Worker Magazine Section*, May 5, 1946, 1, 7.

45. In January 1943 a group of Communists and liberals established the Hollywood Democratic Committee. It worked with the National Citizens Political Action Committee and the Independent Voters Committee of Artists, Writers, and Scientists to reelect President Roosevelt and to elect progressives to Congress and the state legislature. In 1945 the Independent Voters changed its name to the Independent Citizens Committee of the Arts, Sciences, and Professions, and the Hollywood Democratic Committee changed its name to the Hollywood Independent Citizens Committee of the Arts, Sciences, and Professions. SACLA informed Director Hoover in December that HICCASP "is becoming the main pressure group [of the Hollywood Communist Party], taking the lead in all political action" (December 12, 1945, COMPIC).

46. Copies of speeches in WC, 1/10, 40/7.

47. Ronald Reagan, *An American Life* (New York: Simon and Schuster, 1990), 112–13; Seth Rosenfeld, *Subversives: The FBI's War on Student Radicals, and Reagan's Rise to Power* (New York: Farrar, Straus and Giroux, 2012), 123–24. See also Stephen Vaughn, *Ronald Reagan in Hollywood: Movies and Politics* (Cambridge: Cambridge University Press, 1994), 125.

48. De Havilland to Trumbo, June 27, 1946, WC, 1/10.

49. Revised speech, ibid.

50. Trumbo to Pascal, ca. June 1946, ibid.

51. Trumbo to HICCASP, undated draft, ibid.

52. Trumbo to Carey McWilliams, September 26, 1946, WC, 1/8. Rogers was not the preferred candidate of the Communists in HICCASP. After they overwhelmingly endorsed Ellis Patterson, the liberals who resigned from HICCASP formed a Democratic Victory Committee to support Rogers, who then won the Democratic primary. Records of the Independent Progressive Party and Californians for Liberal Representation, UCLA, 4/13; *HR*, May 21, 1946, 17. In radio speeches delivered in late October and early November, Roosevelt accused the Republicans of red-baiting and of raising "the shrill, hypocritical cry of 'communism.'" Speech of November 3, 1946, KHJ-Mutual, Robert Shaw Papers, 1/22, Southern California Library for Social Studies and Research.

53. Edward G. Robinson Collection, box 32, "Israel Speeches," USC.

54. Notes for Cook, UCLA, 125/2.

55. E-mail from Michael Butler, August 26, 2013.

56. March 12, 1947, WC, 40/4.

57. SACLA to director, September 15, 1947, FOIA-DT.

58. California Legislature, *Index: Un-American Activities in California, for Reports of 1943, 1945, 1947, 1948, 1949, 1951* (Sacramento: Senate of the State of California, [ca. 1951]).

9. The 1947 Hearings of the Committee on Un-American Activities

1. There were two exceptions: Karl E. Mundt (R-S.D.), who was elected to the Senate in 1948, and Richard M. Nixon (D-Calif.), who was elected to the Senate in 1950 and was subsequently elected vice president (1953–1961) and then president of the United States (1968–1974). They coauthored a bill that, under the guidance of Senator Pat McCarran (D-Nev.), became the Internal Security Act (enacted in September 1950), a cornerstone of the domestic cold war. Mundt did not attend a single session of the 1947 hearings.

2. *NYT*, February 11, 1947, 22.

3. US Congress, House of Representatives, Committee on Un-American Activities, *Investigation of Un-American Propaganda Activities in the United States of America, 80th Congress, First Session, March 24–27, 1947* (Washington, DC: Government Printing Office, 1947), 290–302; *DV*, April 10, 1947, 1, 15; *DV*, April 17, 1. For a sympathetic discussion of Johnston's position in 1947, see Jennifer Delton, "Rethinking Post–World War II Anticommunism," *Journal of the Historical Society* 10, no. 1 (March 2010): 34–37.

4. *LAT*, May 9, 1947, 1.

5. *LAT*, May 14, 1947, 1.

6. *LAT*, May 20, 1947, 1. The speech was reprinted in its entirety in a PCA pamphlet, Records of the Independent Progressive Party and Californians for Liberal Representation, UCLA, 6/1. According to Nancy Lynn Schwartz, Trumbo wrote Hepburn's speech (*Hollywood Writers' Wars*, 255–56), but I found neither the speech nor any reference to it in Trumbo's papers. Additional evidence of Trumbo's authorship came indirectly from Hepburn, who said that Edward G. Robinson had originally been scheduled to make the speech. William J. Mann, *Kate: The Woman Who Was Hepburn* (New York: Henry Holt, 2006), 347. As previously noted, Trumbo had written several speeches for Robinson.

7. The conference program is in Records of the Independent Progressive Party and Californians for Liberal Representation, UCLA, 4/13.

8. Nikola Trumbo, "A Different Kind of Childhood," *Cinema Journal* 44, no. 4 (Summer 2005): 96, 97.

9. WC, 40/7.

10. *DV*, September 22, 1947, 1, 9.

11. Alongside Trumbo in the Nineteen were Alvah Bessie, Herbert Biberman, Bertolt Brecht, Lester Cole, Richard Collins, Edward Dmytryk, Gordon Kahn, Howard Koch, Ring Lardner Jr., John Howard Lawson, Albert Maltz, Lewis Milestone, Samuel Ornitz, Larry Parks, Irving Pichel, Robert Rossen, Waldo Salt, and Adrian Scott. Twelve were writers, five were directors, one was a producer, and one was an actor. See Larry Ceplair, "The Unfriendly Hollywood Nineteen," in *The Political Companion to American Film*, ed. Gary Crowdus (Chicago: Lakeview Press, 1994), 437–40.

12. In fact, in May the committee's counsel, Robert Stripling, had asked SACLA for material on Bertolt Brecht, Edward Dmytryk, Hanns Eisler, Paul Henreid, Peter Lorre, Adrian Scott, and Salka Viertel, among others (SACLA to director, May 14, 1947, COMPIC). The list indicates that Stripling was focusing on German immigrants and the producer (Scott) and director (Dmytryk) of *Crossfire* (RKO, 1947), an anti–anti-Semitic movie.

13. *DV*, September 22, 1947, 1.

14. *HR*, September 30, 1947, 1.

15. Trumbo to Bob Coryell, Berg-Allenberg, December 4, 1947, WC, 2/2.

16. Albert Maltz, *The Citizen Writer in Retrospect* (Los Angeles: UCLA Oral History Program, 1983), 636–37; Howard Koch, affidavit, ca. early 1958, Howard Koch Papers, WC, 3/15; Edward Dmytryk, *It's a Hell of a Life but Not a Bad Living* (New York: Times Books, 1978), 95; Dmytryk, *Odd Man Out*, 36; Lester Cole, *Hollywood Red: The Autobiography of Lester Cole* (Palo Alto, CA: Ramparts Press, 1981), 266; Kahn, *Hollywood on Trial*, 1; Alvah Bessie, *Inquisition in Eden* (New York: Macmillan, 1965), 187; Patricia Bosworth, *Anything Your Little Heart Desires: An American Family Story* (New York: Simon and Schuster, 1997), 227–28. For more on the attorneys, see Erica Bose, "Three Brave Men: An Examination of Three Attorneys Who Represented the Hollywood Nineteen in the House Un-American Activities Committee Hearings in 1947 and the Consequences They Faced," *UCLA Entertainment Law Review* 6 (1998–1999): 321–65; Janet Stevenson, *The Undiminished Man: A Political Biography of Robert Walker Kenny* (Novato, CA: Chandler and Sharp, 1980); Ben Margolis, *Law and Social Conscience* (Los Angeles: UCLA Oral History Program, 1987).

17. Larry Parks, "Betty Darling . . . ," *Modern Screen*, March 1948, 93.

18. Bessie, *Inquisition in Eden*, 188; Ring Lardner Jr., *The Lardners: My Family Remembered* (New York: Harper and Row, 1976), 320; McGilligan and Buhle, *Tender Comrades*, 409; Lardner, *I'd Hate Myself*, 118–19; Dmytryk, *Odd Man Out*, 35, 53. Margolis later claimed he had offered advice only from "a technical legal standpoint." Margolis, *Law and Social Conscience*, 182.

19. Bessie, *Inquisition in Eden*, 189.

20. Margolis, *Law and Social Conscience*, 185.

21. Ibid., 183.

22. Charles Katz, interview with author, November 15, 1977; Trumbo to Eric Bentley, January 19, 1972, UCLA, 113/3; Lardner, *The Lardners*, 321; Lardner, *I'd Hate Myself*, 119.

23. Katz interview; Ceplair and Englund, *The Inquisition in Hollywood*, 269. The liberal justices were Hugo L. Black, William O. Douglas, Robert Jackson, Frank Murphy, and Wiley B. Rutledge. Murphy and Rutledge died before the Ten's appeal reached the Supreme Court.

24. Bosworth, *Anything Your Little Heart Desires*, 227–28.

25. Dmytryk, *It's a Hell of a Life*, 95; Dmytryk, *Odd Man Out*, 38.

26. Bosworth, *Anything Your Little Heart Desires*, 229.

27. Dmytryk, *It's a Hell of a Life*, 95.

28. Dmytryk, *Odd Man Out*, 36.

29. Bosworth, *Anything Your Little Heart Desires*, 227–28. Bosworth's case for her father is based solely on unconfirmed hearsay. Furthermore, both Dmytryk and Crum became informers (Dmytryk in 1951 to the committee, and

Crum in 1953 to the FBI), and it is likely that their post-informing states of mind affected their recall of previous events.

30. McGilligan and Buhle, *Tender Comrades*, 409–10.

31. Howard Koch Papers, box 3, folder 15, WC, 6–7.

32. Victor S. Navasky, *Naming Names* (New York: Viking, 1980), 393; Dalton Trumbo, undated transcript, in the possession of Mitzi Trumbo.

33. Dalton Trumbo, "Honor Bright and All that Jazz," *Nation*, 100th Anniversary Issue (1965), 183.

34. Joint Appendix, in *Dalton Trumbo, Appellant v. United States of America, Appellee*, US Court of Appeals for the District of Columbia, No. 9873 (1948), 581.

35. *LAT*, November 15, 1947, A18.

36. *DV*, October 16, 1947, 8–9; *HR*, October 16, 1947, 8–9.

37. Parks, "Betty Darling," 95.

38. Bosworth, *Anything Your Little Heart Desires*, 238.

39. Dmytryk, *Odd Man Out*, 53.

40. Howard Koch, *As Time Goes By: Memories of a Writer* (New York: Harcourt Brace Jovanovich, 1979), 167.

41. *Daily Worker*, October 20, 1947, 1. The *Daily Worker* followed the hearings closely, printing long, daily stories, an unsigned editorial, and several front-page banner headlines.

42. Bartley Crum affidavit, Bosworth Papers, Boston University; Schwartz, *Hollywood Writers' Wars*, 266–67.

43. 1947 Hearings, 58.

44. Ibid., 72.

45. Radio speech, October 20, 1947, CTP.

46. 1947 Hearings, 112–14.

47. Ibid., 199–201.

48. Ibid., 193, 194.

49. Ring Lardner Jr. Archive, interview 3, TV Legends, youtube.com/watch?v=qJmmS6rNVE &feature=relmfu. Two of the friendly witnesses went on to have very successful political careers: George Murphy was a one-term US senator (1965–1971), and Ronald Reagan was a two-term governor of California (1967–1975) and two-term president of the United States (1981–89).

50. *Daily Worker*, October 27, 1947, 1.

51. *New York Herald-Tribune*, October 22, 1947, 30; *NYT*, October 23, 1947, 24. The ad appeared in the October 22 editions of the *New York Herald-Tribune* (9), *NYT* (17), and *Los Angeles Examiner* (15), among others.

52. Sidney Olson, "The Movie Hearings," *Life*, November 24, 1947, 138. Olson was critical of the behavior of both the unfriendly witnesses and the committee, but he believed the latter had the right to ask the questions it did.

53. Reprinted in Kahn, *Hollywood on Trial*, 82–84; Trumbo, *Additional Dialogue*, 50–52. In fact, Hitler's appointment as chancellor and the Reichstag fire occurred in 1933. Hitler blamed the fire on the Communists and secured an emergency decree to suspend civil liberties.

54. 1947 Hearings, 330–41, reprinted in Trumbo, *Additional Dialogue*, 50–57. The fourth report of the California Senate's Fact-Finding Committee on Un-American Activities devoted nine pages to Trumbo's "Communist record" as detailed by Stripling, which "checks with the record of Dalton Trumbo in the

Senate Committee's file." California Legislature, *Fourth Report of the Senate Fact-Finding Committee on Un-American Activities, 1948: Communist Front Organizations* (Sacramento: California Senate, 1948), 132.

55. Dmytryk, *Odd Man Out*, 74. Dmytryk must have forgotten that, twenty years earlier, he told the makers of *Hollywood on Trial* (1976) that his feeling of dread had started after Lawson finished testifying.

56. *NYT*, October 29, 1947, 3.

57. *Los Angeles Examiner*, October 29, 1947, 1–2. The *Examiner* supported the hearings from beginning to end. And one week after they ended, it printed a three-part series on communism in Hollywood by friendly witness Rupert Hughes (November 3–5, 1947).

58. *LAT*, October 29, 1947, 2. This newspaper also supported the hearings.

59. *New York Herald-Tribune*, October 29, 1947, 26.

60. Bosworth, *Anything Your Little Heart Desires*, 244.

61. Martin Esslin, *Brecht: The Man and His Work*, rev. ed. (Garden City, NY: Anchor Books, 1971), 80. In his written statement, which he was not permitted to read, Brecht directly compared Nazi censorship of ideas with what was currently occurring in the United States. Reprinted in Kahn, *Hollywood on Trial*, 123–26; and in Eric Bentley, ed., *Thirty Years of Treason: Excerpts from Hearings before the House Committee on Un-American Activities, 1938–1968* (New York: Viking, 1971), 221–23.

62. Trumbo to Geoffrey Wolff, July 28, 1975, UCLA, 81/7.

63. 1947 Hearings, 522.

64. Robert Stripling, *The Red Plot against America* (Drexel Hill, PA: Bell, 1949), 75.

65. SACLA to director, December 7, 1947, FOIA-DT.

66. Nichols to Clyde Tolson, November 4, 1947, COMPIC.

67. Parks, "Betty Darling," 96.

68. For an analysis of the First Amendment's double edge during the Cold War, see Martin H. Redish, *The Logic of Persecution: Free Expression and the McCarthy Era* (Stanford, CA: Stanford University Press, 2005).

69. Dalton Trumbo, *The Time of the Toad: A Study of Inquisition in America, by One of the Hollywood Ten* (Hollywood: Hollywood Ten, 1949), 30.

70. Quoted in Navasky, *Naming Names*, 419.

71. No title, n.d., UCLA, 126/7.

72. Bentley, *Thirty Years of Treason*, 945.

73. No title, n.d., UCLA, 223/4.

74. Trumbo to Eric Bentley, January 19, 1972, UCLA, 113/3.

75. Notes re Corliss, ca. September 1971, UCLA, 211/2.

76. Notes to letter to Corliss, ca. February 1973, ibid.

77. Arthur Schlesinger Jr., "The Life of the Party," *Saturday Review of Literature*, July 16, 1949, 6–7, 34–36.

78. Trumbo to the editor, *Saturday Review of Literature*, August 20, 1949, 21. For my analysis of anti-Communist liberalism, see Larry Ceplair, *Anti-Communism in Twentieth-Century America: A Critical History* (Santa Barbara, CA: Praeger, 2011).

79. Schlesinger's reply, *Saturday Review of Literature*, August 20, 1949, 21.

80. Trumbo to Schlesinger, n.d. [ca. autumn 1949], in Trumbo, *Additional Dialogue*, 135–36.

81. Trumbo to Emil Freed, November 13, 1961, UCLA, 221/3.

82. See chapter 22. In an undated note to himself, written in 1967, Trumbo compared Schlesinger's non-Communist Left to "a Communist network subverting from within. . . . Its philosophy of non-subversion was especially contrived to support and encourage the beleaguered non-totalitarian mind in its lonely struggle to save the non-slave world—non-black as well as non-white non-poor as well as non-rich—from the non-truth of the non-free world, where non-democracy prowled the street, non-safe, as a non-fed, non-tame beast. The scheme was such a non-miss that it spawned the non-hot war, the non-totalitarian ADA [Americans for Democratic Action], and the non-self-corrupting Congress for Intellectual [Cultural] Freedom" (UCLA, 211/2).

83. Murray Kempton, *Part of Our Time: Some Ruins and Monuments of the Thirties* (New York: Simon and Schuster, 1955), 182–83, 204.

84. Kempton to Trumbo, ca. September 1957, WC, 5/7. Christopher sent this correspondence to the *Nation*. See "Part of Our Time, Too," *Nation*, April 5, 1999, 60–64.

85. Murray Kempton, "The Limits of Irony" [review of Walter Goodman, *The Committee*], *New Republic*, April 13, 1968, 34.

86. No title, n.d., WC, 40/7. In retrospect, it is unclear why the lawyers were so confident that a First Amendment stance would resonate with the Supreme Court. In fact, in none of the previous congressional contempt cases had the Court granted certiorari on the grounds that the right to free speech implied the right to remain silent when asked about one's political opinions and affiliations. Carl Beck, *Contempt of Congress: A Study of the Prosecutions Initiated by the Committee on Un-American Activities, 1945–1957* (New Orleans: Hauser Press, 1959), 50.

87. No title, n.d., UCLA, 126/7.

88. Ibid.

89. Trumbo to Maltz, January 12, 1973, CTP.

90. Maltz to Trumbo, January 16, 1973, CTP.

91. Photocopies in Nancy Lynn Schwartz Papers, box 29, AHC.

92. No title, n.d., UCLA, 81/7.

10. Blacklisted, Indicted, Convicted

The first epigraph is from Lillian Ross, "Come in, Lassie!" *New Yorker*, February 21, 1948, 32. In the second epigraph, Christopher is alluding to the months between the British and French declarations of war against Germany (September 1939) and the actual commencement of combat (April 1940).

1. Trumbo to Adrian Scott, September 4, 1956, WC, 5/4. Before he began his prison sentence, Trumbo wrote to Robinson (ca. spring 1950): "Before taking off for my year's vacation, I would be sadly remiss if I did not tell you how very much you helped me in a time of great need, and how deeply I appreciate it." Edward G. Robinson Collection, USC Film and Television Center, 30/14E. I am indebted to Ned Comstock for sending this letter to me.

2. Affidavit of Floyd L. Hendrickson, MGM contract department, *Trumbo v. Loew's*, February 19, 1948, Biberman-Sondergaard Papers, WC, 56/8.

3. Trumbo to Martin Gang, February 1, 1948, WC, 2/3.

4. Speech in CTP.

5. Affidavit of Howard Strickling, *Trumbo v. Loew's*, April 23, 1948, Biberman-Sondergaard Papers, WC, 56/8.

6. Lavery to Screen Writers Guild, n.d., Nancy Lynn Schwartz Papers, box 29, AHC. Lavery told me that his goal was to keep the guild from being rent by its two extremes. He believed the guild had nothing to hide and that a confrontation with the committee would be fatal to it. Finally, he said: "My notion of due process was not Trumbo's." Interview with author, September 25, 1976.

7. Report by Cole, Collins, Kahn, and Lardner, n.d., ibid.

8. *HR*, November 20, 1947, 1.

9. Interview (ca. 1955), in Elizabeth Poe Kerby Collection, 3/45, MHL. Trumbo later wrote about the Committee for the First Amendment: "They had sensed the House Committee's purpose more accurately than the rest of the country, and were willing, at that time and in those circumstances, to stake their reputation in a fight against it." Dalton Trumbo, "Honor Bright and All that Jazz," *Nation*, 100th Anniversary Issue (1965), 184. For more on the Committee for the First Amendment, see Ceplair and Englund, *The Inquisition in Hollywood*, 275–90; Philip Dunne, *Take Two* (New York: McGraw-Hill, 1980).

10. *DV*, November 26, 1947, 13; *HR*, November 26, 1947, 15.

11. Ceplair and Englund, *The Inquisition in Hollywood*, 344–45. Pauline Finn was one of the unsung organizers of left-wing organizations in Hollywood, including the Hollywood Writers' Mobilization. Her husband, Aubrey Finn, was a lawyer who worked for labor unions and defended civil liberties cases. After the Trumbos returned from Mexico, Aubrey Finn became Trumbo's personal attorney.

12. Interview (ca. 1955) in Elizabeth Poe Kerby Collection, 1/6, MHL.

13. Ceplair and Englund, *The Inquisition in Hollywood*, 325.

14. SACLA to director, November 17, 1947, COMPIC. Another source claimed that patrons had thrown stones at the screen. The link between this "incident" and the hearings is not evident. None of the eighteen had worked on this movie (based on the life of composer Robert Schumann), and Hepburn had not spoken publicly since her speech at Gilmore Stadium in May. William J. Mann thinks the theater owners may have been seeking a handy excuse to stop showing a movie that was not drawing an audience. Mann, *Kate*, 360, 577.

15. *WV*, November 12, 1947, 3, 18.

16. Eric Johnston deposition, *Screen Writers Guild, et al. v. MPAA, et al.*, SDNY, April 28, 1952, 69–70, Biberman-Sondergaard Papers, WC, 56/5.

17. *HR*, November 26, 1947, 1, 7, reprinted in Ceplair and Englund, *The Inquisition in Hollywood*, 445.

18. Eric Johnston deposition, *Trumbo v. Loew's*, April 22, 1948, 7–8, 12, Biberman-Sondergaard Papers, WC, 56/8.

19. *Congressional Record*, 80th Congress, 1st session, 93:9, November 24, 1947, 10770–97.

20. Trumbo to Bob Coryell, Berg-Allenberg, December 4, 1947, WC, 2/2. His suspension continued until his contract expired in March 1950. Eddie Mannix to Hedda Hopper, April 25, 1950, Hedda Hopper Papers, 69/2210, MHL.

21. Trumbo to Pomerance, December 27, 1947, WC, 2/2; other portions of this letter are in Trumbo, *Additional Dialogue*, 67.

22. Dore Schary deposition, *Independent Productions Corporation v. Loew's*, March 13–20, 1964, 76, Biberman-Sondergaard Papers, WC, 43/1; Dore Schary Papers, WC, 101/5–6.

23. Jarrico conversation with the author, ca. 1976.

24. SACLA to director, March 10, 1948, FOIA-DT.

25. Bessie, *Inquisition in Eden*, 226.

26. SACLA to director, December 19, 1947, COMPIC.

27. Executive Board to Screen Writers Guild members, May 27, 1948, MWP, 45/10a. The suit languished in the courts for five years. On February 5, 1953, the members voted overwhelmingly to drop it, in exchange for a statement from the Motion Picture Producers Association that there had never been a blacklist. Robert Ardrey recalled that "only three or four of the original plaintiffs spoke in favor of pursuing the suit." "Hollywood: The Toll of the Frenzied Forties," *Reporter*, March 21, 1957, 31.

28. Scott to Cerf with "Outline of Book on Hearings," 1, 20, Adrian Scott Papers, box 4, folder 23, AHC. Dmytryk swore under oath that "not long after our return to Hollywood, Mr. Crum disassociated himself from any active participation with the Hollywood Ten." Affidavit in support of Crum, April 5, 1953, Patricia Bosworth Papers, box 2, Boston University.

29. Cerf to Scott, December 8, 1947, Scott Papers, 4/23.

30. Ibid., December 15, 1947.

31. Ibid., February 21, 1948.

32. Trumbo to McKeogh, December 4, 1947, in Trumbo, *Additional Dialogue*, 62.

33. Gang to Loew's, December 15, 1947, WC, 2/2. It was not until January 1952 that Loew's settled the suits of Cole and Trumbo. According to a report in the *LAT* (January 5, 1952, A5), the plaintiffs received $107,500, but Trumbo told Helen Manfull they received $250,000 (Trumbo, *Additional Dialogue*, 193 n. 40). In either case, after giving sums of money to those of the Ten who needed it, Trumbo netted $28,000. Lardner finally settled his suit with Twentieth Century–Fox in 1955 for $10,000, and he gave $380.95 to Trumbo. Ring Lardner Jr. Papers, 25/329, MHL.

34. Trumbo to Pomerance, December 27, 1947, in Trumbo, *Additional Dialogue*, 67.

35. See classiclit.about.com/library/bl-etexts/wwhitman/bl-ww-pent.htm.

36. Trumbo to McKeogh, January 12, 1948, in Trumbo, *Additional Dialogue*, 70–71. One year earlier, McKeogh had received a letter from Lee Sabinson, a Broadway producer, offering to pay Trumbo an advance for any play on any topic. McKeogh to Trumbo, December 29, 1946, WC, 2/2.

37. *Playboy* interview, tape 3, UCLA, 61/2.

38. Cook, *Dalton Trumbo*, 199.

39. *Mainstream: A Literary Quarterly* 1, no. 1 (Winter 1947): 16–22.

40. Trumbo to Tugend, February 18, 1948, in Trumbo, *Additional Dialogue*, 82.

41. Trumbo to Lewis Meltzer, draft, April 7, 1959, UCLA, 123/4.

42. Trumbo to Zimbalist, February 5, 1948, in Trumbo, *Additional Dialogue*, 77–78. On learning of Zimbalist's death in 1961, Trumbo wrote to Joe Cohn of MGM, telling him that Zimbalist had, on two occasions, loaned him "substantial sums of money" and had never asked for repayment. Trumbo

wanted to contact his widow and arrange a repayment schedule (June 27, 1961, UCLA, 114/3).

43. Trumbo to Katz, March 29, 1948, in Trumbo, *Additional Dialogue*, 90.

44. WC, 2/1.

45. Trumbo's 1948 income tax return, WC, 41/6.

46. Milestone could not make the loan because his production company was losing money and his bank would not accept a note signed by Trumbo. To compensate, Milestone offered Trumbo a polish job on his next picture (probably *The Red Pony*), and Trumbo was paid $5,000 by Lewis Milestone Productions in 1949. Rex Cole to Trumbo, October 12, 1948, WC, 41/6, 41/7.

47. Trumbo to Rex Cole, October 29, 1948, WC, 41/6.

48. Ibid., June 8, 1949, WC, 41/7.

49. Trumbo's 1949 income tax return, ibid.

50. Joint Appendix, in *Dalton Trumbo, Appellant v. United States of America, Appellee*, US Court of Appeals for the District of Columbia, No. 9873 (1948), 9–10.

51. *The New Hampshire*, April 25, 1948, "Scrapbooks," reel 2.

52. *Barsky et al. v. United States*, 165 F. 2d 241, 247–50 (1948).

53. *LAT*, March 11, 1948, 1.

54. Dunne, *Take Two*, 200.

55. Joint Appendix, 234.

56. Ibid., 446.

57. Ibid., 530.

58. Ibid., 543–44.

59. Ibid., 546–47.

60. Ibid., 549.

61. Interview notes by Nancy Lynn Schwartz, Nancy Lynn Schwartz Papers, box 28, AHC.

62. Statement, ca. June 1950, CTP.

63. Trumbo to Cleo, May 7, 1948, in Trumbo, *Additional Dialogue*, 82–83.

64. *Daily Worker*, May 6, 1948, 3.

65. *PM*, May 16, 1948, CTP. The twelve leaders of the Communist Party were indicted on July 20, 1948. Eleven were tried and convicted of conspiracy to advocate the overthrow of the government. Their convictions were upheld by the US Supreme Court in *Dennis v. United States*, 341 U.S. 494 (1951).

66. Records of the Independent Progressive Party and Californians for Liberal Representation, UCLA, 6/1.

67. Maltz note, n.d., UCLA, 3/10.

68. Trumbo to Beanie Baldwin, July 17, 1948, WC, 2/6.

69. Trumbo to Literature Division, National Council of the Arts, Sciences, and Professions, October 2, 1948, ibid.

70. Trumbo to Maltz, ca. late 1961–early 1962, in Trumbo, *Additional Dialogue*, 560.

11. *The Time of the Toad*

1. Trumbo to Katz, May 29, 1948, in Trumbo, *Additional Dialogue*, 93–94.

2. Trumbo to Daniel Sacks, October 12, 1956, WC, 5/5.

3. Dalton Trumbo, *The Biggest Thief in Town* (New York: Dramatists Play Service, 1949), 73.

4. Trumbo to Lee Sabinson, July 1, 1948, in Trumbo, *Additional Dialogue*, 96. Kraft, a stage and screen writer, was blacklisted in 1951.

5. Trumbo to Sabinson, August 27, 1948, WC, 2/4.

6. Trumbo to Mary, January 19, 1949, Biberman-Sondergaard Papers, WC, 1/7.

7. "Scrapbooks," reel 2.

8. Dalton Trumbo, "About the Play," *Theatre Arts*, January 1950, 58.

9. *NYT*, March 30, 1949, 31.

10. *NYT*, March 31, 1949, 31.

11. *New York Herald-Tribune*, March 31, 1949, "Scrapbooks," reel 2.

12. *New Yorker*, April 9, 1949, 55–56.

13. *Daily Worker*, April 5, 1949, "Scrapbooks," reel 2.

14. Trumbo to Sally Deutsch, October 8, 1949, WC, 3/1.

15. Trumbo to Coryell, July 17, 1948, in Trumbo, *Additional Dialogue*, 102.

16. Trumbo to Willner, July 17, 1948, ibid., 103. Willner was a partner of Nat Goldstone. Three years later, Willner was named as a Communist by Meta Reis, and when he appeared before the committee on April 24, 1951, he invoked the Fifth Amendment. He was blacklisted and could no longer function as an agent in Hollywood. Reis, who worked for Berg-Allenberg, had secured that job partly as a result of what she termed a "sensationally generous" letter of recommendation from Trumbo, whom she had met through Alice (Goldberg) Hunter. At the bottom of his copy of the letter, Trumbo wrote: "She turned informer! I had signed an agency contract with Berg-Allenberg because they had hired her." Reis to Trumbo, October 12, 1945, WC, 1/7. Reis, who appeared before the committee on April 13, 1951, named twenty people, but perhaps out of gratitude, she did not name Trumbo.

17. SACLA to director, February 14, 1950, FOIA-DT.

18. Trumbo to McKeogh, September 6, 1948, WC, 2/5.

19. Note attached to script dated May 24, 1947, MacKinlay Kantor Collection, box 72, Library of Congress. I am indebted to Molly Gingras, Mitzi Trumbo's daughter, for mining this material.

20. WGAw news release, October 27, 1992, in *Gun Crazy* production clipping file, MHL. See also Rebecca Mead, "First at Ninety," *New Yorker*, September 17, 2007, 36. Kaufman was never named, subpoenaed, or blacklisted.

21. Note attached to script dated June 25, 1948, Kantor Collection, box 73.

22. Trumbo to Willner, October 2, 1948, in Trumbo, *Additional Dialogue*, 104.

23. Trumbo to Sabinson, October 9, 1948, ibid., 108.

24. *DV*, October 31, 1949, 3.

25. *Motion Picture Daily*, November 11, 1949, clipping in *Gun Crazy* production file, MHL.

26. *HR*, October 31, 1949, 3, 9.

27. See Stanley Kauffmann, "Not So Crazy," *New Republic*, June 24, 1991, 26; Nicholas Christopher, *Somewhere in the Night: Film Noir and the American City* (New York: Free Press, 1997), 193.

28. Trumbo to Elsie and Ted Riner, September 20, 1948, WC, 2/5.

29. Gang to Trumbo, September 28, 1948, and Katz to Trumbo, September 30, 1948, ibid.

30. Trumbo to McKeogh, October 11, 1948, ibid.

31. Trumbo to Willner, October 11, 1948, ibid.

32. Kaufman to Trumbo, August 25, 1948, WC, 41/6.

33. Trumbo to McKeogh, November 8, 1948, in Trumbo, *Additional Dialogue*, 110.

34. "Remember, O Remember" script, WC, 23/5.

35. Trumbo to Willner, April 18, 1949, WC, 2/9.

36. Willner to Trumbo, June 10, 1949, WC, 3/1.

37. Quoted in McGilligan and Buhle, *Tender Comrades*, 165. Joseph Losey, the film's director, recalled that he and Spiegel had to drive to the ranch to discuss the script with Trumbo: "The car had a blowout in the wilderness, we didn't get to Trumbo's place till one or two in the morning, the conversation went on all night, and we left at dawn." Quoted in Tom Milne, ed., *Losey on Losey* (Garden City, NY: Doubleday, 1968), 93. During that time, Butler and Hunter cowrote the script for *A Woman of Distinction*. "They were both not working, both depressed, and they thrashed it out, just a film by two men desperate for money" (*Tender Comrades*, 165).

38. *WV*, April 25, 1951, 6.

39. *LAT*, June 4, 1951, B9.

40. Trumbo to Katz, April 28, 1952, WC, 4/5.

41. Trumbo's dispute with Losey occurred seventeen years later when Losey, in a published interview, complained that Trumbo's script had indicated all the camera angles—a practice Losey never again tolerated. Trumbo responded: "I not only handed Losey a first and second draft of the script, but also, under the pseudonym of John Abbott, dubbed the voice of the cuckolded husband. . . . Not once did Mr. Losey complain about the script's objectionable shots and 'camera angles' or the fruity quality of my voice on the sound track." Letter to *NYT*, December 15, 1968, D21, responding to Andrew Sarris, " . . . And the Man Who Made It," *NYT*, November 17, 1968, II:23. Trumbo also criticized Losey for failing to give any credit to Hugo Butler, who had fronted the script for *The Prowler*, revised it, and later wrote two other uncredited scripts for Losey: *Cost of Living* (United Artists, 1950) and *The Big Night* (United Artists, 1951). And he stated that, in his opinion, *The Prowler* was "rather poor." Losey responded with letters to both the newspaper and Trumbo, but the former was not printed. To Trumbo he wrote: "I was astonished and distressed to read your letter to the Editor. . . . Why didn't you write *me*? What are you so angry about? Something has set you off into a totally irrelevant rage." Losey professed to be at a loss as to why Trumbo thought he was being attacked or Butler derogated: "Do you really think I tried to hold you up as a horrific example?" (UCLA, 131/4). "Are you truly naive enough to believe," Trumbo replied, "that you can derogate men's work in the most public fashion possible without some sort of public, rather than private, response. You chose the method of communication, not I. I have nothing at all against your work, Joe, so long as you do not make lofty public pronunciamientos about the elements in my work which you would not now accept." Finally, Trumbo scored Losey for his lack of "kindliness to others" when he was being interviewed (January 20, 1969, UCLA, 131/4). Losey's biographer called this letter "strikingly perceptive," and screenwriter Daniel Mainwaring, who had written the screenplay for the Losey-directed *The Lawless* (Pine-Thomas, 1950), fully agreed with

Trumbo's assessment. See David Caute, *Joseph Losey: A Revenge on Life* (New York: Oxford University Press, 1994), 241; Mainwaring to Trumbo, n.d. [ca. late 1968], UCLA, 116/14.

42. Trumbo to Willner, August 6, 1949, WC, 3/2.

43. Katz to Cleo and Butler, October 20, 1950, WC, 41/8. During this time, Spiegel had an argument with Columbia Pictures boss Harry Cohn and stopped making movies at the studio for five years. When he returned in 1954, he was no longer interested in *My Reminiscences*. Three years later, Cohn gave the script to Julian Blaustein, another independent producer under contract to the studio. Cohn, however, had removed the title page with Butler's name on it, and he referred to it as the "Huston script." Blaustein gave it to Edmund North to revise. When the studio gave North sole screenplay credit, he balked and asked the WGAw to arbitrate. North was told that the original script had been written by a blacklisted writer, and Columbia was exercising its privilege, under the producer-guild collective-bargaining agreement, to refuse to give that writer credit. North learned of Butler's involvement only years later. According to Trumbo, he "privately expressed to Hugo his repugnance at receiving sole screenplay credit in this fashion." Edmund Hall North, *Studio System to the Television Era* (Los Angeles: UCLA Oral History Program, 1986), 71; interview with Susan North Meadow, October 11, 2009; Cook, *Dalton Trumbo*, 206.

44. Trumbo to Albert Maltz, August 6, 1949, in Trumbo, *Additional Dialogue*, 125.

45. Trumbo to Willner, April 21, 1950, ibid., 140–41.

46. Trumbo to Biberman, April 26, 1950, ibid., 143.

47. Dalton Trumbo, "Postmeridian," ca. early 1950, UCLA, 36/1.

48. *Lawson v. United States* and *Trumbo v. United States*, 126 F. 2d 52 (1949).

49. Trumbo to Maud Trumbo, November 1, 1949, in Trumbo, *Additional Dialogue*, 132. Trumbo also contemplated writing a play with the same title, and he composed a seven-page summary of it. The protagonist was a university professor who is subpoenaed by a state un-American activities committee and fired when he refuses to reveal his affiliations (WC, 32/6a).

50. Biberman to Trumbo, n.d., WC, 32/6a.

51. Trumbo, *Time of the Toad*, 5. See Émile Zola, "Le Crapaud," *Le Figaro*, February 28, 1896, in *Oeuvres Complètes*, ed. Henri Mitterand (Paris: Cercle du Livre Précieux, 1969), 14:729–35.

52. Biberman to Trumbo, October 6, 1949, WC, 3/1.

53. Maltz to Trumbo, October 11, 1949, ibid.

54. Townsends to Trumbo, November 16, 1949, ibid.

55. Interview in *Dalton Trumbo: Rebel in Hollywood: The Story behind Johnny Got His Gun*, written, produced, and directed by Robert Fischer (Fiction Factory, 2006).

56. Trumbo to Morton, November 8, 1949, WC, 3/1.

57. "Important Confidential Bulletin," n.d., Paul Jarrico Collection, Rare Books and Manuscripts Library, Columbia University.

58. Trumbo to Belfrage, October 14, 1968, UCLA, 144/2.

59. Meeting speech, May 17, 1949, CTP.

60. *The Hollywood Ten*, Film Division of the Southern California Chapter, National Council of the Arts, Sciences, and Professions, 1950.

61. Untitled, n.d., WC, 40/7.

62. Trumbo to Ted Riner, ca. November 1, 1949, in Trumbo, *Additional Dialogue*, 130.

63. *LAT*, October 20, 1949, 5.

64. Trumbo to Riner, 131.

65. *LAT*, October 21, 1949, A2.

66. Trumbo to Riner, 131.

67. Ian Hunter, draft of eulogy, Ian Hunter Collection, box 4, MHL.

68. *Daily Worker*, April 4, 1950, 8. One of the *Barsky* defendants was Howard Fast, who, after being released from prison, wrote a novel titled *Spartacus* (see chapter 18).

69. Willner to Trumbo, May 17, 1950, WC, 3/4.

70. Trumbo to Roberts, April 1, 1952, UCLA, 135/1. One of the reasons Trumbo agreed to do this script was that he owed Roberts $5,000, which was to be repaid from Trumbo's share of the profits. Roberts had loaned Trumbo the money to purchase stock in Xanadu Film Corporation, which Roberts had founded in late 1946. Ring Lardner Jr., Allan Scott, Richard Collins, Hugo Butler, and John Garfield also purchased stock. When Xanadu folded the following year, Roberts and Garfield established Roberts Pictures, which was financed by Garfield.

71. Larry Swindell, *Body and Soul: The Story of John Garfield* (New York: Morrow, 1975), 233.

72. US Congress, House of Representatives, Committee on Un-American Activities, *Communist Infiltration of Hollywood Motion-Picture Industry—Part 2* (Washington, DC: Government Printing Office, 1951), 328–64.

73. Swindell, *Body and Soul*, 240.

74. *DV*, May 23, 1951, 4.

75. Swindell, *Body and Soul*, 254, 261–66; *Life*, June 4, 1951, 129. A few years later, Trumbo considered writing a movie based on Garfield's life.

76. Cleo to WGAw, ca. May 1997, in the possession of Mitzi Trumbo.

77. Quoted in McGilligan and Buhle, *Tender Comrades*, 73–74.

78. *DV*, June 21, 1951, 1.

79. *LAT*, June 22, 1951, B6.

80. *NYT*, June 21, 1951, 24.

81. *Nation*, July 16, 1951, 23.

82. *He Ran All the Way* production file, MHL.

83. Trumbo to Willner, March 29 and April 10, 1950, WC, 3/4; Trumbo to Frank and Maury King, April 23, 1950, ibid.

84. Diary entry, May 2, 1950, courtesy of Michael Collins.

12. Incarceration and Drift

The epigraph is from Dalton Trumbo, "For a Convict's Wife," UCLA, 122/13.

1. Trumbo to Cleo and children, June 11, 1950, in Trumbo, *Additional Dialogue*, 151.

2. Ibid.

3. Undated, handwritten notes on Thomas Committee, UCLA, 81/7.

4. Director to SACLA, July 26, 1950, and January 24, 1951, FOIA-DT.

5. Trumbo to Cleo, June 21, 1950, in Trumbo, *Additional Dialogue*, 155.

6. E-mail to the author, April 28, 2014. Anders is currently working on a television show situated in 1950 Ashland.

7. E-mail from Bob Dolan Smith, May 3, 2014.

8. Trumbo to Cleo, June 22, 1950, in Trumbo, *Additional Dialogue*, 157.

9. Trumbo, *Additional Dialogue*, 155 n. 11.

10. Burt Prelutsky, draft of "Alias Dalton Trumbo," November–December 1961, CTP.

11. Ibid.

12. Trumbo to Cleo, August 13, 1950, in Trumbo, *Additional Dialogue*, 174.

13. Trumbo to Cleo, August 18, 1950, WC, 4/1.

14. See the list in WC, 4/1.

15. Popper to Cleo, November 11, 1950, CTP.

16. Trumbo to Margolis, November 13, 1950, WC, 4/2.

17. Margolis to the eight prisoners, November 22, 1950, and Trumbo to Margolis, November 26, 1950, WC, 4/2. Biberman and Dmytryk had already been released.

18. Trumbo to Cleo, December 8, 1950, WC, 3/3.

19. Trumbo to Cleo, January 1, 1951, in Trumbo, *Additional Dialogue*, 197.

20. Ibid. The Trumbos reported income of $47,667.57 in 1950, but between October 1950 and March 1951, their receipts totaled $7,300, all remittances from Hugo Butler's fronting.

21. Dalton Trumbo, talk at UCLA, May 27, 1972, UCLA Communications Studies Archives, www.youtube.com/watch?v=YhAXSDpvqVU.

22. Trumbo to Cleo, February 14, 1951, in the possession of Mitzi Trumbo.

23. Trumbo to Cleo, February 26, 1951, ibid.

24. The stories are in WC, 39/7; the scripts are in WC, 32/1. Trumbo's former agent, Arthur Landau, brokered the sale of the "London" script.

25. According to Parks's wife, Betty Garrett, he was given a list of names and merely indicated which ones were party members. Thus, in her words: "He was not volunteering. He was reading." Betty Garrett with Ron Rapoport, *Betty Garrett and Other Songs: A Life on Stage and Screen* (Lanham, MD: Madison Books, 1998), 137.

26. Cook, *Dalton Trumbo*, 10–11.

27. Dalton Trumbo, "Final Notes," April 4, 1951, CTP. One fragment of this unfinished novel was published: "Babylon Descendant," *California Quarterly* 4, no. 1 (1956): 3–9.

28. Quoted in Ceplair, *The Marxist and the Movies*, 124–25. Five months later, Trumbo's political mentor, Dashiell Hammett, entered Ashland to finish serving a six-month sentence for contempt of court. He had refused to tell a federal district court judge anything about himself or the bail funds he administered on behalf of the Civil Rights Congress.

29. Trumbo to Adrian Scott, September 4, 1956, WC, 5/4.

30. In his autobiography, Robinson mistakenly claimed that Trumbo had written to him from prison, asking for $2,500. Edward G. Robinson with Leonard Spigelgass, *All My Yesterdays: An Autobiography* (New York: Hawthorn Books, 1973), 255–56. In fact, Trumbo wrote to Robinson from the Washington, DC, jail on June 14, 1950, saying he would start repaying the loan as soon as he was released from prison (Trumbo, *Additional Dialogue*,

153). When Robinson appeared before the committee for a third time in April 1952, he confessed to having been "duped and used" by Albert Maltz, Dalton Trumbo, and John Howard Lawson. He also told the committee about the loan he had made to Trumbo. US Congress, *Communist Infiltration of Hollywood Motion-Picture Industry—Part 7*, April 30, 1952, 2421, 2427.

31. Speech in WC, 40/7.

32. SACLA to director, September 5, 1951, FOIA-DT. The Bureau also decided to retain Trumbo's Security Index Card in its active file.

33. Statements of account from Equitable Investment Corporation, UCLA, 134/4.

34. Trumbo to Jane Lynch, WGAw, March 21, 1960, UCLA, 123/4.

35. Draft of letter to Lewis Meltzer, April 7, 1959, UCLA, 123/4; the clause after the semicolon was crossed out. In 1954 the Screen Writers Guild merged with the Radio Writers Guild and the Television Writers Guild to form the Writers Guild of America, West, and the Writers Guild of America, East. Movie writers were assigned to the western guild. For a discussion of the guild's capitulation on this important point, see Ceplair and Englund, *The Inquisition in Hollywood*, 411; Ceplair, *The Marxist and the Movies*, 126–28.

36. Trumbo to Algren, June 15, 1951, in Trumbo, *Additional Dialogue*, 213–14. For more on Algren, see Bettina Drew, *Nelson Algren: A Life on the Wild Side* (New York: Putnam's, 1989), 211.

37. Algren to Trumbo, June 19, 1951, WC, 4/3.

38. Trumbo to Murphy, August 8, 1951, WC, 4/4.

39. Trumbo to King Brothers, May 28, 1951, in Trumbo, *Additional Dialogue*, 209–10.

40. Trumbo to Frank King, July 18, 1951, King Brothers Collection, box 47, MHL.

41. Maltz to Trumbo, June 14, 1951, WC, 4/3.

42. Trumbo to Butler, June 25, 1951, in Trumbo, *Additional Dialogue*, 216–17.

43. Butler to Trumbo, ca. late June, WC, 4/4.

44. Trumbo to Biberman, July 16, 1951, ibid.

45. Trumbo to Shipley, September 24, 1951, FOIA-DT. Kingsley Martin wrote in the *New Statesman and Nation* that *The Biggest Thief in Town* "is extremely funny and excellently acted." Harold Conway in the *Evening Standard* called it "a highly delectable theatrical dish. . . . [T]he author, Dalton Trumbo, outrages taste with the best-humored gusto" (both clippings in CTP). The play was performed in the United Kingdom several times, and Cleo periodically received small royalty checks.

46. Young to Trumbo, October 26, 1951, FOIA-DT. It is clear that passport policy during the Cold War was intended as a form of punishment and debasement of "subversives." Certainly, it could not prevent their ideas being circulated overseas via publications; nor could they effectively undermine national security from Denmark.

47. Trumbo to Butler, August 6, 1950, in Trumbo, *Additional Dialogue*, 223–24.

48. *LAT*, December 14, 1950, 18; *LAT*, January 13, 1951, 16; Jean Field Committee Records, mss. 71, Southern California Library for Social Studies and Research.

49. Biberman to Trumbo, June 12, 1951, WC, 4/3.

50. Biberman to Trumbo, July 19, 1951, WC, 4/4.

51. Trumbo to Biberman, ca. August 1951, in Trumbo, *Additional Dialogue*, 228–29.

13. Oh, Oh, Mexico

The first epigraph is from Dalton Trumbo, interview by Keith Berwick, "Speculation," November 17, 1970, UCLA Film and Television Archive.

1. Rouverol, *Refugees from Hollywood*, 6–8. On an undated index card, Trumbo had written: "They're taking names and they're making lists. And when they open up the [detention] camps [which had been established by the Internal Security Act of September 1950]—they'll look at the lists and those are the people who've got reservations in Camp America" (CTP).

2. Pepper, who had headed the key Hollywood Popular Front political committees, had moved to Mexico and teamed with Henry Ehrlich, who was interested in making movies with blacklisted people and willing to act as a front for them. Pepper secured the services of director Luis Buñuel, and he convinced a group of blacklisted musicians to invest in *Robinson Crusoe*. Jeannette Bello quoted in Diana Anhalt, *A Gathering of Fugitives: American Political Expatriates in Mexico, 1948–1965* (Santa Maria, CA: Archer Books, 2001), 60–61, 73. Trumbo and Buñuel later tried to make *Johnny Got His Gun* (see chapter 23). For another take on the Mexican exile experience, see Rebecca Mina Schreiber, *Cold War Exiles in Mexico: U.S. Dissidents and the Culture of Critical Resistance* (Minneapolis: University of Minnesota Press, 2008). For the European exiles, see Rebecca Prime, *Hollywood Exiles in Europe: The Blacklist and Cold War Film Culture* (New Brunswick, NJ: Rutgers University Press, 2014).

3. Trumbo to Rex Cole, January 15, 1952, WC, 41/8.

4. Rouverol, *Refugees from Hollywood*, 17–19. According to Mitzi, Cleo's brother-in-law Harry Baskerville was a professional photographer and taught her about cameras and darkroom techniques; Cleo, in turn, taught Mitzi.

5. Ibid., 36, 38.

6. E-mail to the author, November 2, 2011.

7. UCLA, 125/2.

8. *Playboy* interview, tape 4, UCLA, 61/2.

9. Nikola Trumbo, "A Different Kind of Childhood," *Cinema Journal* 44, no. 4 (Summer 2005): 99.

10. Director to legal attaché, February 26, 1952, FOIA-DT.

11. Richard English, "Mexico Clamps down on Stalin," *Saturday Evening Post*, August 30, 1952, 16–17, 41, 44. English had been instrumental in Edward Dmytryk's rehabilitation program, penning for him a mea culpa in the *Saturday Evening Post* ("What Makes a Hollywood Communist?" May 19, 1951, 30–31, 147–50). It was published shortly after Dmytryk reappeared before the Committee on Un-American Activities on April 25, 1951, and answered all its questions, including the one asking for the names of Communists in the industry (he did not name Trumbo). Dmytryk was immediately hired by the King brothers and then signed a deal with Columbia. He worked steadily thereafter.

12. Rouverol, *Refugees from Hollywood*, 35–36. The Hunters told Cook

that George Pepper got Trumbo interested in collecting (Cook, *Dalton Trumbo*, 233).

13. Biberman to Trumbo, February 10 and 23, 1952, WC, 4/4.

14. Trumbo to Biberman, February 26, 1952, UCLA, 57/13.

15. Ibid., n.d. [ca. March 1952].

16. Biberman-Sondergaard Papers, WC, 21/5.

17. Biberman, "On the Theory . . . ," WC, 1/9.

18. Trumbo to Biberman, April 7, 1952, UCLA, 57/13.

19. Biberman to Trumbo, April 10, 1952, ibid.

20. Trumbo to Biberman, April 26, 1952, 28–30, ibid.

21. Trumbo's letter discussing Wilson's script has not come to light, but Biberman wrote in response to it: "I received your carefully estimated appraisal on Mike's story—and I have sent it on to Mike. It will be discussed by all of us after it has been circulated." Trumbo's critique apparently focused on the central relationship (between Ramon and Esperanza), and as a result of those comments, Wilson arranged a meeting with Mexican Americans in Los Angeles and made another trip to Bayard, New Mexico, to speak with the principals there (letter dated June 6, 1952, MWP, 45/12).

22. Trumbo to Biberman, November 13, 1952, UCLA, 57/13.

23. Trumbo to Sam Sillen, December 5, 1953, in Trumbo, *Additional Dialogue*, 282–83.

24. Trumbo to Lawson, December 6, 1953, WC, 4/7.

25. Lardner, *I'd Hate Myself*, 140.

26. Acceptance speech to Academy of Motion Picture Arts and Sciences on receiving a posthumous Oscar for best motion picture story, May 1993, in the possession of Mitzi Trumbo. That script no longer exists. According to Christopher, his father destroyed the entire *Roman Holiday* file because he did not want to leave any evidence that might discredit Ian Hunter, who had acted as his front.

27. Bernard Smith to Sidney Justin, October 4, 1949, *Roman Holiday* Correspondence and Memoranda, 1949–1950, box 34, Unrealized Projects Series, Frank Capra Papers, Wesleyan University Cinema Archives, Middletown, CT.

28. Ibid., January 10 and 25, 1950.

29. Jan Herman, *A Talent for Trouble: The Life of Hollywood's Most Acclaimed Director, William Wyler* (New York: Putnam's, 1995), 347; Joseph McBride, *Frank Capra: The Catastrophe of Success* (New York: Simon and Schuster, 1992), 553, 585.

30. Paramount Collection, Scripts, MHL.

31. Lardner to Cleo, June 22, 1997, CTP.

32. The reader's reports and screen credit information are in the Frank Capra Papers. Koenig had been subpoenaed by the Committee on Un-American Activities, and when he testified on September 24, 1951, he invoked the Fifth Amendment. Although Paramount executives allowed Wyler to continue to employ Koenig, they refused to give him an associate producer screen credit for *Roman Holiday*. Gabriel Miller, *William Wyler: The Life and Films of Hollywood's Most Celebrated Director* (Lexington: University Press of Kentucky, 2013), 315, 318–19.

33. Lardner to Trumbo, March 17, 1954, WC, 5/1. Gardner was an entertainment reporter for the *New York Herald-Tribune*.

34. Rouverol, *Refugees from Hollywood*, 75.

35. Trumbo to King Brothers, March 30, 1953, WC, 4/5.

36. Trumbo to Kraft, April 6, 1953, in Trumbo, *Additional Dialogue*, 268.

37. Conversation with Christopher Trumbo.

38. Trumbo to Wilson, November 15, 1953, in Trumbo, *Additional Dialogue*, 277–78.

39. Wilson to Trumbo, December 17, 1953, WC, 4/6.

40. Rouverol, *Refugees from Hollywood*, 91.

41. Trumbo to Butlers and Peppers, ca. February 1954, in Trumbo, *Additional Dialogue*, 286–90. I could not discover what happened to the Packard. Perhaps Trumbo sold it in Mexico City or left it in Matamoros.

42. The political atmosphere in John Howard Lawson's home was markedly different. See Jeff Lawson, "An Ordinary Life," in *Red Diapers: Growing up in the Communist Left*, ed. Judy Kaplan and Linn Shapiro (Urbana: University of Illinois Press, 1998), 57. For memories of other children of the blacklisted, see *Cinema Journal* 44, no. 4 (Summer 2005); Dan Bessie, *Rare Birds: An American Family* (Lexington: University Press of Kentucky, 2001); Lardner, *Shut up He Explained*.

43. Trumbo to Wheeler, May 18, 1956, in Trumbo, *Additional Dialogue*, 332–42. See also Trumbo's letter excoriating the Camp Fire Girls for their treatment of Cleo. Cleo [*sic*] to Mrs. Williams, February 23, 1956, in Trumbo, *Additional Dialogue*, 328–32.

44. Trumbo, "A Different Kind of Childhood," 99.

45. Trumbo to Hugo Butler, ca. 1956, in Trumbo, *Additional Dialogue*, 305–6.

46. Trumbo, "A Different Kind of Childhood," 100.

47. Trumbo to Christopher, September 1, 1956, in Trumbo, *Additional Dialogue*, 344–46.

48. Trumbo to Nikola, September 3, 1956, ibid., 346–52.

49. Trumbo to Christopher, November 8, 1958, ibid., 443–51.

50. E-mail from Michael Butler, December 13, 2011.

51. For Peter Askin's comments on Christopher, see www.pbs.org/wnet/americanmasters/episodes/dalton-trumbo/interview-with-director-peter-askin/1167, August 11, 2009.

14. Negotiating the Black Market, Working with the King Brothers

The epigraph is from Trumbo to Maltz, March 10, 1954, WC, 5/1.

1. For the founding of the Independent Productions Corporation, see Ceplair, *The Marxist and the Movies*, 128–35.

2. Trumbo to Bogeaus, ca. 1957, WC, 5/7.

3. Steve Martin, *Born Standing Up: A Comic's Life* (New York: Scribner, 2007), 90. Many of the pseudonyms were derived from family names: Sam Jackson, James Bonham, Elizabeth B. Weston, Peter Flint, Robert Rich, C. F. Demaine, James Evelyn Bonham, Theodore Flexman, Beth Fincher, Orville McElliott, and Millard Tillery. His favorite pseudonym for correspondence was Doc Abbott, the protagonist of his first published novel (*Eclipse*) and his favorite script (*A Man to Remember*).

4. Untitled note, n.d., UCLA, 122/5.

5. Zelma Wilson, *Rebel and Architect* (Los Angeles: UCLA Oral History Program, 1994), 234.

6. "Cleo" to Seltzer, May 23, 1955, in the possession of Mitzi Trumbo. In the correspondence between Trumbo and Seltzer, Trumbo was "Sam" and Seltzer was "Bromo."

7. *Los Angeles Examiner*, October 11, 1956, 4:10.

8. *DV*, August 20, 1956, 3; *HR*, August 20, 1956, 3.

9. Paul Mavis, posted July 4, 2011.

10. SACLA to director, March 27, 1956, COMPIC. In 1952 the Bureau of German Affairs (US Department of State) had appointed Templeton chief of the motion picture program in the Federal Republic of Germany. His task was to oversee the making and distributing of documentary short-subject films.

11. All biographical data on the Kings are from Perry Lieber, RKO, press release, n.d. [ca. 1951], King International Corporation file, MHL; Robert Lewin, "The King Brothers," *Life*, November 22, 1948, 118–26.

12. Quoted in Patrick McGilligan, ed., *Backstory 2: Interviews with Screenwriters of the 1940s and 1950s* (Berkeley: University of California Press, 1991), 346–49.

13. Lewin, "King Brothers."

14. Quoted in Howard Suber, "The Anti-Communist Blacklist in the Hollywood Motion Picture Industry" (PhD diss., UCLA, 1968), 81.

15. Dmytryk, *Odd Man Out*, 174.

16. Levitt Oral History, 1.4, tape 2, side 2, April 15, 1988.

17. King Brothers Collection, box 48, MHL. The script was sold to Bryna Productions and was produced in 1955. Ben Kadish (pseudonym of blacklisted Robert L. Richards) received story credit; Frank Davis received script credit.

18. Ibid., box 60.

19. Ibid. This script had a long, sorry history. Guy Endore had started work on it two years earlier. For fifteen years the Kings tried to sell Trumbo's version, without success.

20. Ibid., box 48. After numerous rewrites, it was finally produced by MGM in 1969. Trumbo and Presnell declined any credit. Presnell was married to Marsha Hunt, who had been blacklisted owing to her support of the Hollywood Ten. She would later appear in the film version of *Johnny Got His Gun*.

21. King Brothers Collection, box 44, MHL. This script was rewritten many times—the last time by Christopher and Sherry Sonnett. The film was never made.

22. Trumbo to Frank King et al., September 13, 1952, King Brothers Collection, box 47, MHL.

23. In his oral history, Ostrow said he had loaned Trumbo money on two previous occasions. The first time, in about 1949, Trumbo had used his house as collateral and repaid the loan. The second loan, for several thousand dollars, had come in response to a telegram from Trumbo stating that six blacklisted families "were working on this script and they got it in the hands of somebody in New York, and they expect money out of it very quickly." Ostrow claimed that Trumbo never fully repaid the second loan. Ostrow is very fuzzy on the details of this project, and there is no mention of it in the Trumbo papers. Seniel Ostrow, *A Passion for Justice* (Los Angeles: UCLA Oral History Program, 1987), 166–67, 389–90.

24. Trumbo to Kings, April 10, 1953, in Trumbo, *Additional Dialogue*, 270–73.

25. Undated note, ca. March 1973, UCLA, 211/2.

26. *DV*, May 16, 1975, 17.

27. *LAT*, November 4, 1956, F3.

28. Trumbo to Frank King, December 29, 1956, King Brothers Collection, box 61, MHL.

29. Trumbo to Kings, April 19, 1957, in Trumbo, *Additional Dialogue*, 394–95.

30. Trumbo to Frenke, n.d., UCLA, 134/5.

31. Seltzer to Trumbo, December 30, 1955, in the possession of Mitzi Trumbo.

32. Elizabeth Poe Kerby, "The Hollywood Story," *Frontier*, May 1954, 6–25; John Cogley, *Report on Blacklisting* (New York: Fund for the Republic, 1956). Kerby was a first-rate investigative reporter. For the story of her life, see Larry Ceplair, "Reporting the Blacklist: Anti-Communist Challenges to Elizabeth Poe Kerby," *Historical Journal of Film, Radio and Television* 28, no. 2 (June 2008): 135–52.

33. For the story of Foreman's testimony and blacklisting while he was working on *High Noon*, see Larry Ceplair, "Shedding Light on *Darkness at High Noon*," *Cineaste* 27, no. 4 (Fall 2002): 20–22; Prime, *Hollywood Exiles in Europe*, 69–72.

34. Paul Jacobs, "Good Guys, Bad Guys, and Congressman Walter," *Reporter*, May 15, 1958, 29–31. See also John Cogley, "A Matter of Ritual," *Commonweal*, May 10, 1957, 149. As an unexpected consequence of Foreman's new job, he could not complete the script he had been adapting from the novel *The Bridge on the River Kwai*. He was replaced by Michael Wilson. See chapter 17.

35. *LAT*, January 14, 1956, 4.

36. Quoted in Navasky, *Naming Names*, 393. Kerby, who dug deeply for her groundbreaking article, was convinced that clearances were being purchased, but she could not prove it; nor could she convince Cogley. Drafts of her proposed chapter on that subject are in the Elizabeth Poe Kerby Papers, 2/24, 3/42, MHL. Two other likely recipients of this largesse were writer Sidney Buchman and actress Judy Holliday, both prized employees of Columbia Pictures.

15. From the Communist Party to the New Left

The epigraph is from Dalton Trumbo, "Secrecy and the Communist Party [1]," n.d., 6, WC, 40/9.

1. *Playboy* interview, tape 1, UCLA, 61/2.

2. *Bridges v. United States*, 346 U.S. 209 (1953).

3. [Dalton Trumbo], "The Everlasting Bridges Case," in *The ILWU Story* (San Francisco: International Longshoremen's and Warehousemen's Union, 1955), 51, 62–63. I am indebted to Robin Walker, librarian and archivist of the ILWU, for sending me a copy of this article.

4. Trumbo to Newman, March 19, 1955, UCLA, 160/6.

5. Trumbo's research material is in WC, 32/12. For the espionage activities of CPUSA members, see Harvey Klehr, John Earl Haynes, and Fridrikh

Igorevitch Firsov, *The Secret World of American Communism* (New Haven, CT: Yale University Press, 1995). For Sobell's spying, see *NYT*, September 12, 2008, A1; Ronald Radosh and Steven T. Usdin, "The Sobell Confession: Four Men with Leica Cameras, 1,885 Pages of Documents; the Other Secrets Passed to Stalin by the Rosenberg Ring," *Weekly Standard*, March 28, 2011, www.weeklystandard.com/articles/sobell-confesssion_554817.html.

6. See Dorothy Healey and Maurice Isserman, *Dorothy Healey Remembers: A Life in the American Communist Party* (New York: Oxford University Press, 1990), 133–46.

7. Dalton Trumbo, "My Own View of the CP," n.d., 22, WC, 40/9.

8. Dalton Trumbo, *The Devil in the Book* (Los Angeles: California Emergency Defense Committee, May 1956), 6, reprinted in Dalton Trumbo, *The Time of the Toad: A Study of Inquisition in America, and Two Related Pamphlets* (New York: Harper and Row, 1972).

9. *LAT*, May 7, 1957, B7.

10. *Yates v. United States*, 354 U.S. 298 (1957).

11. Trumbo, "My Own View of the CP," 22.

12. Trumbo to Lawson, n.d., WC, 5/5.

13. Trumbo, "My Own View of the CP," 22–23. For a different reading of this document, see Ronald Radosh and Allis Radosh, *Red Star over Hollywood: The Film Colony's Long Romance with the Left* (San Francisco: Encounter Books, 2005), 207–33.

14. Trumbo, "Secrecy and the Communist Party," n.d. Both versions are in WC, 4/9.

15. "Tract for the Times," *Liberation*, March 1956, 3; "Shall We Vote?" *Liberation*, October 1956, 6.

16. "The New Left: What Should It Look Like?" *National Guardian*, October 29, 1956, 8.

17. Dalton Trumbo, "The New American Left," *National Guardian*, November 26, 1956, 10.

16. Blacklist and Black-Market Politics

The epigraph is from Trumbo to John Wexley, April 3, 1958, WC, 6/1.

1. Endore, *Reflections of Guy Endore*, 192–95. For more on Endore, see Joseph G. Ramsey, "Guy Endore and the Ironies of Political Repression," *minnesota review* 70 (Spring–Summer 2008): 141–51.

2. Trumbo to Endore, unsent draft, n.d., WC, 5/5.

3. Trumbo to Endore, December 30, 1956, in Trumbo, *Additional Dialogue*, 363–76. We know today that rape is used as a political weapon to destroy the social fabric of a rival tribe or religion.

4. Endore to Trumbo, January 4, 1957, WC, 5/5.

5. Endore, *Reflections*, 230–31.

6. Ibid., 233–34. One year after receiving Trumbo's letter, on the day after the Supreme Court refused to review the dismissal of *Wilson v. Loew's* (the blacklistees' class-action lawsuit), Endore notified Trumbo that he had written a letter to Francis Walter, chairman of the Committee on Un-American Activities, stating: "I am voluntarily submitting herewith my affidavit in triplicate outlining my relationship with the Communist Party as I view it in light of

today." Endore to Trumbo, March 11, 1958, WC, 5/9. The letter did not seem to work. In subsequent years, Endore did not have a screen credit under his own name. When King Brothers released *Captain Sindbad* (1963), which Endore had cowritten with Ian Hunter, the script was credited to their pseudonyms (Harry Relis and Samuel B. West).

7. John Bright to "My dear friends," May 28, 1957, WC, 5/9. Bright later told Trumbo that he had discussed his response with a few close friends but had not circulated copies of it. Bright to Trumbo, September 22, 1958, WC, 6/2. But these words are belied by statements in the original letter and its salutation: "My dear friends."

8. Trumbo to Bright, June 3, 1957, WC, 5/8.

9. Trumbo to Bright, draft, n.d., WC, 5/9.

10. Trumbo to Bright, August 12, 1957, WC, 5/9. When I interviewed Bright in 1991 for the UCLA Oral History Program, I did not know of this exchange, and he did not mention it. Pat McGilligan and Ken Mate had interviewed him eight years earlier, but the portion of that interview published in 1997 does not mention this exchange either. See McGilligan and Buhle, *Tender Comrades*, 130–54.

11. Dalton Trumbo, "Present State of the Blacklist," WC, 40/9.

12. Ibid. Two blacklistees, Ben Maddow and Cy Endfield, did appear before a subcommittee of the Committee on Un-American Activities in an effort to get off the blacklist. For the story behind Endfield's appearance in March 1960, see Prime, *Hollywood Exiles in Europe*, 163–68. For Maddow's explanation of his appearance, see McGilligan, *Backstory 2*, 185–87.

13. Trumbo, "Present State of the Blacklist."

14. *Wilson et al. v. Loew's et al.*, 355 U.S. 597 (1958).

15. WC, 40/7. A few years later, when Michael Wilson consulted him about filing a suit regarding the credit on *Friendly Persuasion* (see chapter 17), Trumbo advised against it. Ben Margolis to Michael Wilson, April 17, 1957, MWP, 10/11.

16. Trumbo to Eddie Lewis, August 20, 1958, WC, 6/3.

17. Trumbo to Wexley, April 3, 1958, WC, 6/1. There is no response from Wexley in the collection.

17. Using and Revealing Robert Rich

1. *Playboy* interview, tape 4, UCLA, 61/2.

2. Trumbo's letters to the writers are in Trumbo, *Additional Dialogue*, 382–84; Morgan to Trumbo, February 5, 1957, WC, 5/7. One year later, when Trumbo heard that Kirk Douglas was planning to meet Vice President Richard Nixon, he proposed a series of talking points about the blacklist "in a style, which I hope is cool and detached enough that they might be left in the possession of Mr. N without compromising the person who turned them over to him." Trumbo's notes, titled "The Effect in Other Nations," discussed the successes of some of the blacklistees working abroad, the ridicule currently being heaped on the Academy, and the harm being done to Hollywood's world market. A note in *Additional Dialogue* states that the meeting occurred, but Nixon refused to make a statement about the blacklist (425). Douglas, however, claims the meeting was postponed and he did not meet

Nixon until many years later. See Douglas, *I Am Spartacus!* 82; Douglas, *Ragman's Son*, 431.

3. *Playboy* interview, tape 4, UCLA, 61/2.

4. In terms of undesirables winning awards, Wilson was the major thorn in the Academy's side during those years. On September 20, 1951 (just three weeks after Wilson invoked the Fifth Amendment at a committee hearing), *A Place in the Sun* (Paramount) opened. Several months later, Wilson and his cowriter won the Academy Award for best screenplay. The next year, the Wilson-scripted *Five Fingers* (Twentieth Century–Fox) opened, and he received another nomination for best screenplay.

5. Minutes, Board of Governors, February 6, 1957, provided by Executive Director Bruce Davis, for use in an exhibit I curated for the Academy: "The Reds and the Blacklist," February 2002.

6. *DV*, March 8, 1957, 4.

7. Interview with Jim Danelz, transcribed in a letter to Trumbo, January 8, 1973, CTP.

8. Undated note, ca. March 1973, UCLA, 211/2.

9. Cook, *Dalton Trumbo*, 260.

10. *DV*, April 2, 1957, 1, 4.

11. *DV*, April 8, 1957, 1.

12. *DV*, April 2, 1957, 6; *NYT*, April 9, 1957, 40.

13. Undated note, ca. March 1973, UCLA, 211/2.

14. Excerpted in *Hollywood on Trial* (Cinema Associates, 1976).

15. "Hollywood Whodunit: An Oscar, Whowunit?" *Life*, April 15, 1957, 162. The poem had four more lines, which were printed ten years later in C. Robert Jennings, "The Hollywood Ten, Plus Twenty," *LAT*, September 3, 1967, A17.

16. "Hollywood Whodunit," 161.

17. Lahn to Trumbo, March 29, 1957, WC, 5/7. The story was Ed Lacy's "The Paradise Package," *Esquire*, June 1956, 60, 120, 123–24.

18. WC, 33/1.

19. Dalton Trumbo, "Blacklist = Black Market," *Nation*, May 4, 1957, 383–87.

20. Bright to editor, *Nation*, August 17, 1957, 60.

21. Trumbo to Bright, September 15, 1958, WC, 6/2. On his copy of the letter, Trumbo wrote: "John came to L.A. & wanted to see me. (We are more or less cordial to each other, for I respect him despite differences.)" In the following years, Trumbo tried to get Bright writing jobs. Bright, for his part, brought *Johnny Got His Gun* to the attention of Bruce Campbell, who would eventually produce the movie version. Trumbo then hired Bright as an adviser on *Johnny*.

22. Trumbo to Bessie, May 23, 1957, WC, 5/7.

23. Maltz to Trumbo, May 20, 1957, ibid.

24. Dalton Trumbo, "Movie Mystery: Who Is Robert Rich?" *Frontier*, June 1957, 12–13.

25. Speech, September 20, 1957, WC, 40/6. Trumbo probably borrowed the term "the Quiet American" from the title of Graham Greene's 1955 novel.

26. *WV*, September 25, 1957, 46.

27. SACLA to director, October 25, 1957, FOIA-DT.

28. Bilson to Finn, December 8, 1957, WC, 6/2.

29. Interview with Jim Preminger, January 23, 2012.

30. Joshua Samuel Smith, "The Hollywood Black List 1957/58," typescript in the author's possession.

31. *HR*, August 4, 1958, 1.

32. Ilse Lahn to Michael Wilson, March 21, 1958, MWP, 48/1.

33. Aware Inc. had been established in 1953 as a smear-and-clear agency by a group of New York City actors and Vincent Hartnett. Its exposé bulletin was titled *Confidential Notebooks*. For the story of the Faulk suit, see John Henry Faulk, *Fear on Trial* (New York: Simon and Schuster, 1964).

34. King Brothers Collection, box 45, MHL; *DV*, May 16, 1957, 17. In all, five plagiarism suits were filed, and two were settled out of court.

35. Undated note, WC, 10; Trumbo to Frank King, April 28, 1962, in Trumbo, *Additional Dialogue*, 562–63.

36. WC, 6/4; Cook, *Dalton Trumbo*, 263–64.

37. Trumbo to Seaton, January 11, 1958, WC, 5/9. It is possible that Trumbo and Seaton met at MGM during the late 1930s. Seaton had been president of the SWG (1948–1949), and he served as Academy president for three years (1955–1958).

38. *LAT*, March 27, 1958, 1, 2. In December 1984 the Board of Governors presented posthumous Oscars to the widows of Foreman and Wilson.

39. Trumbo to Wilson, March 30, 1958, in Trumbo, *Additional Dialogue*, 414–16. Wilson responded that because of his distance from Hollywood, he found himself "at a loss to account for and comprehend the depth of [Trumbo's] anger," nor could he "honestly imagine" what Trumbo had in mind to break the blacklist. April 28, 1958, MWP, 48/4.

40. Trumbo to Butler, ca. early 1956, in Trumbo, *Additional Dialogue*, 302–4. Helen Manfull dated this letter January 1955, but it was more likely written in early 1956.

41. Two blacklisted writers worked on *High Noon*: Ben Maddow wrote an early, "very rough, tentative version," and Carl Foreman wrote the script that was filmed. For years it was taken as gospel that Maddow had written *Johnny Guitar*, but the writer who received the credit, Philip Yordan, called that story "a total fabrication." Maddow told an interviewer: "I can't tell you if I wrote it or not. . . . I can't remember working on it." Maddow and Yordan interviews in McGilligan, *Backstory 2*, 178, 183, 359.

42. UCLA, 156/4.

43. Trumbo to Landau, July 18, 1956, WC, 5/6.

44. Trumbo to Butler, December 15, 1957, in Trumbo, *Additional Dialogue*, 409–10.

45. Trumbo to Bob Roberts, January 8, 1958, UCLA, 135/1.

46. Trumbo to James Selig, January 4, 1961, UCLA, 158/5.

47. Trumbo to March, n.d., WC, 22/8.

48. UCLA, 122/5.

49. Contracts are in UCLA, 58/1.

50. Trumbo to Finn, May 21, 1956, WC, 5/3.

51. Lewis to Jackson, January 14, 1958, WC, 5/9.

52. UCLA, 158/5.

53. Dalton Trumbo, "Reconstruction of Events," October 5, 1960, UCLA, 71/7.

54. Trumbo to Abowitz, October 11, 1958, WC, 6/3. Five years later, Trumbo learned he had been misdiagnosed.

55. Trumbo to Walter Mirisch, October 12, 1958, WC, 6/3.

56. Trumbo to Maltz and Wilson, January 9, 1959, in Trumbo, *Additional Dialogue*, 471–74.

57. *NYT*, January 1, 1959, 38.

58. Trumbo to Maltz, January 9, 1959, in Trumbo, *Additional Dialogue*, 472.

59. Videotapes of the broadcast in the author's possession; transcript of January 9 broadcast in Nedrick Young Papers, WC, 9/3.

60. Trumbo to Maltz and Wilson, January 9, 1959, in Trumbo, *Additional Dialogue*, 472.

61. Trumbo to Wilson, January 10, 1959, MWP, 48/4.

62. *LAT*, January 15, 1959, B1.

63. King Brothers Collection, box 61, MHL.

64. *Time*, January 26, 1959, 77.

65. Trumbo to Stout, January 16, 1959, in Trumbo, *Additional Dialogue*, 475–76.

66. Videotapes of the broadcasts in the author's possession.

67. Interview transcript, King Brothers Collection, box 61, MHL.

68. Trumbo to Seaton, January 20, 1959, in Trumbo, *Additional Dialogue*, 477.

69. *HR*, January 19, 1959, 1.

70. *LAT*, January 20, 1959, 1, 8.

71. *Newsweek*, January 26, 1959, 25; *Time*, January 26, 1959, 77.

72. Cook, *Dalton Trumbo*, 247.

73. Trumbo to Wilson, February 24, 1959, in Trumbo, *Additional Dialogue*, 480–83. Many years later, Trumbo said Wilson had accomplished more by the sheer excellence of his work than did Trumbo's speeches and pamphlets and Smith and Douglas's script for *The Defiant Ones*. The nominations and awards for *Friendly Persuasion* (1956) and *The Bridge on the River Kwai* (1957) did much more to expose the blacklist's faulty structure. Trumbo to Maltz, January 12, 1972, CTP.

74. *HR*, March 2, 1959, 1.

75. *DV*, March 31, 1959, 1.

76. Trumbo to Finn, August 4, 1959, in Trumbo, *Additional Dialogue*, 506.

77. Dalton Trumbo, "Hail, Blithe Spirit!" *Nation*, October 24, 1959, 243–46.

78. Trumbo to Wilson, February 24, 1959, in Trumbo, *Additional Dialogue*, 484.

79. Trumbo to Kings, 1958, in Trumbo, *Additional Dialogue*, 464–65.

18. *Spartacus*

1. KDP, 40/26. One month later, Lewis signed a contract with Bryna in which he agreed to deliver the "Brave Cowboy" screenplay for the same financial considerations stated in his agreement with Trumbo, except that Lewis was to receive $2,500 upon commencement of principal photography (Karl Price to Jeff Asher, May 27, 1959, KDP, 40/26). The following year, Trumbo inscribed

a copy of *Johnny Got His Gun*: "To Eddie Lewis—who risked his name to help a man who'd lost his name. Words simply cannot say it, and I shan't try to force them. But you understand, as does your friend, Dalton Trumbo (June 2, 1959)."

2. Howard Fast's "Commentary" for the DVD version of *Spartacus* (The Criterion Collection, 2001).

3. Gerald Sorin, *Howard Fast: Life and Literature in the Left Lane* (Bloomington: Indiana University Press, 2012), 235–40. Fast claimed, in his "Commentary" for the *Spartacus* DVD, that when his novel was originally published, it "was severely attacked by the left wing, by the Communist Party. The two who joined most viciously in the attack on the book were Dalton Trumbo and John Howard Lawson. These were the two most important people in the left Communist cultural apparatus on the coast." There is, however, one difficulty with this accusation: *Spartacus* was printed in December 1951, when Trumbo was already living in Mexico. There is no mention of this book in his correspondence; nor are there any articles in his papers criticizing it. In fact, Fast wrote in his memoirs that Lawson alone had "attacked it bitterly." See Howard Fast, *The Naked God: The Writer and the Communist Party* (New York: Praeger, 1957), 147–48; Howard Fast, *Being Red* (Boston: Houghton Mifflin, 1990), 299. Further, the novel received a generally glowing review in the *Daily Worker*, May 17, 1952, 7–8.

4. Abraham Polonsky Papers, WC, 12/42.

5. Trumbo to Maltz, January 21, 1958, in Trumbo, *Additional Dialogue*, 413–14.

6. Kirk Douglas, *I Am Spartacus! Making a Film, Breaking the Blacklist* (New York: Open Road, 2012), 48. Douglas's book must be used very carefully and regularly cross-referenced with his previous account of the making of *Spartacus* in *The Ragman's Son: An Autobiography* (New York: Simon and Schuster, 1988). Some parts are frankly dubious. See my review, "Kirk Douglas, *Spartacus*, and the Blacklist," *Cineaste* 38, no. 1 (Winter 2012): 11–13.

7. Howard Fast, Spartacus outline, KDP, 38/10.

8. Transcript of Tucker interview, July 8, 1960, 4–5, KDP, 38/6.

9. Douglas, *Ragman's Son*, 307; Douglas, *I Am Spartacus!* 49.

10. *Spartacus* DVD "Commentary." See also Douglas, *Ragman's Son*, 307.

11. Interview with Lewis, August 9, 2012. See also my oral history interview with him, http://oralhistory.library.ucla.edu/Browse.do?descCvPk=479210.

12. March 11, 1958, KDP, 4/1.

13. Quoted in Cook, *Dalton Trumbo*, 103.

14. Margolis, *Law and Social Conscience*, 306–7.

15. Douglas, *Ragman's Son*, 308. According to Lewis, Trumbo made that remark to him (interview, August 9, 2012).

16. "Notes for U-I Research (based on preceding material)," KDP, 38/11.

17. Trumbo to Lewis, n.d., CTP.

18. "Suggested Step Outline," 12–13, KDP, 38/11.

19. Ibid., 21, 33, 51.

20. "Afterthoughts," 3, KDP, 38/11.

21. "Suggested Step Outline," 13, KDP, 38/11.

22. Douglas, *Ragman's Son*, 309.

23. Trumbo to Lewis, April 29, 1958, CTP.

24. Jefferson W. Asher Jr. to Eddie Lewis, June 22, 1960, KDP, 33/19.

25. Transcript of Tucker interview, 13.

26. Douglas, *Ragman's Son*, 311.

27. Kathleen Sharp, *Mr. and Mrs. Hollywood: Edie and Lew Wasserman and Their Entertainment Empire* (New York: Carroll and Graf, 2003), 149.

28. Copies of Trumbo's first draft are in WC, 26, and UCLA, 160/5; Fast's draft is in WC, 26/4.

29. Stan Margulies to Douglas, July 9, 1958, KDP, 34/3.

30. Douglas, *Ragman's Son*, 310.

31. Trumbo to Lewis, July 24, 1958, WC, 6/2. Helen Manfull did not include this portion of the letter in Trumbo, *Additional Dialogue*, 436–37. I have not found a copy of a contract agreeing to pay Trumbo that much money. The only two contracts in the Kirk Douglas Papers are the one between "Sam Jackson" and Lewis, dated June 1, 1958, and a loan-out agreement between Springfield and Bryna, dated December 1, 1958. In the Trumbo Papers there is another loan-out agreement between Springfield and Bryna, dated November 2, 1959. Trumbo was probably paid, in total, $65,000.

32. Trumbo to Lewis, July 24, 1958, WC, 6/2.

33. Trumbo to Lewis, July 24, 1958, in Trumbo, *Additional Dialogue*, 438–39.

34. Douglas, *Ragman's Son*, 309.

35. Transcript of conversation between Douglas and Fast, KDP, 38/7.

36. Douglas to Fast, November 7, 1958, KDP, 34/4; also in Howard Fast Papers, Rare Books and Manuscripts Department, University of Pennsylvania, courtesy of Nancy Shawcross.

37. *Spartacus* DVD "Commentary."

38. Dalton Trumbo, "Spartacus," n.d., WC, 27/5.

39. Peter Ustinov, *Dear Me* (Boston: Little Brown, 1977), 299.

40. Interview with Jim Danelz, transcribed in a letter to Trumbo, January 8, 1973, CTP.

41. Trumbo to Wilson, February 24, 1959, in Trumbo, *Additional Dialogue*, 484.

42. For the various versions, see Mann interview in *Framework* 15–17 (1981): 19; Lewis in *Spartacus* DVD "Commentary"; Douglas, *Ragman's Son*, 316; Douglas, *I Am Spartacus!* 99–101; transcript of interview with Robert Forrest, July 8, 1960, KDP, 38/6; interview with Ustinov, "1992 Interviews," *Spartacus* DVD.

43. Cook, *Dalton Trumbo*, 271–72.

44. Jefferson Asher Jr. to George Chasin, July 7, 1960, KDP, 35/4.

45. Interview with Harris, June 30, 2013.

46. Douglas, *Ragman's Son*, 273–75, 332.

47. Trumbo to Douglas, February 24, 1959, WC, 6/4.

48. Dalton Trumbo, talk at UCLA, May 17, 1972, UCLA Communications Studies Archives, www.youtube.com/watch?v=YhAXSDpvqVU. For other commentaries on Trumbo and Kubrick, see Alison Futrell, "Seeing Red: Spartacus as Domestic Economist," in *Imperial Projections: Ancient Rome in Modern Popular Culture*, ed. Sandra R. Joshel, Margaret Malamud, and Donald T. McGuire (Baltimore: Johns Hopkins University Press, 2001), 77–118; Natalie Zemon Davis, "Trumbo and Kubrick Argue History," *Raritan* 22, no.

1 (Summer 2002): 173–90; Martin M. Winkler, ed., *Spartacus: Film and History* (Malden, MA: Blackwell, 2007).

49. Fast to Douglas, n.d., KDP, 34/5.

50. Gary to Douglas, March 8, 1959, ibid.

51. Trumbo to Douglas, February 24, 1959, WC, 6/4.

52. Trumbo to Douglas, March 30, 1959, WC, 24/8, and KDP, 24/6.

53. Trumbo to Lewis, n.d., WC, 24/8.

54. Ibid., n.d., KDP, 24/6.

55. Douglas to Kubrick, ibid. Douglas included this memo in *I Am Spartacus!* (120) but omitted the opening paragraph: "This scene, based on an idea that existed in one of the earlier versions. . . . "

56. Trumbo to Lewis, n.d., KDP, 24/6.

57. Dalton Trumbo, "General Broadcast," May 16, 1959, KDP, 24/6.

58. Douglas to Fast, May 26, 1959, Fast Papers.

59. Jefferson W. Asher Jr. to Nat Goldstone, June 29, 1959, KDP, 34/7.

60. Jefferson W. Asher Jr. to Eddie Lewis, June 22, 1960, KDP, 33/1.

61. Quoted in Sorin, *Howard Fast*, 341.

62. Ustinov, *Dear Me*, 302; Douglas, *I Am Spartacus!* 111.

63. Trumbo to Kubrick, n.d., WC, 24/8.

64. Trumbo to Lewis, May 31, 1959, KDP, 24/6.

65. Douglas, *I Am Spartacus!* 124–27.

66. Interview with Lewis, August 9, 2012.

67. N.d., WC, 24/8.

68. Douglas, *Ragman's Son*, 325; Douglas, *I Am Spartacus!* 137.

69. Quoted in Cook, *Dalton Trumbo*, 272.

70. Winston Churchill, speech delivered at Harrow School, October 29, 1941, www.winstonchurchill.org/learn/speeches-of-winston-churchill/103-never-give-in.

71. Dalton Trumbo, "Report on *Spartacus*: The Two Conflicting Points of View," n.d., KDP, 24/6.

72. Dalton Trumbo, "Report on *Spartacus*: Scene-by-Scene Run-through," ibid.

73. Dalton Trumbo, notes, August 23, 1959, WC, 24/8. Ironically, Kubrick agreed with Trumbo, but when he tried to cut the crucifixion scene, Douglas erupted violently, and the scene was reinstated. Douglas, *I Am Spartacus!* 141–42.

74. N.d., WC, 25/6.

75. Dalton Trumbo, "A Last General Note on *Spartacus*," KDP, 24/8.

76. Ibid.

77. Lewis to WGAw, re drafts of *Spartacus*, June 23, 1960, UCLA, 123/4. In this document, Lewis noted: "It is almost impossible to submit what you would consider a 'Final Shooting Script.'" After the fourth "revised final draft" was completed and mimeographed for distribution in late January, all subsequent revisions were distributed to all concerned. "[S]ince they were so numerous and practically concurrent with the shooting schedule, [they] were never at any time frozen into a 'Final Screenplay.'" Spartacus: *The Illustrated History*, a copublication of Bryna and Universal that came out in 1960, stated: "He [Trumbo] did seven versions of the script, totaling 1,534 pages and over 250,000 words" [5].

78. Both notes, undated, are in CTP.

79. Dalton Trumbo, "Note: The Mass-Marriage," n.d., WC, 24/8. In other

undated notes, Trumbo referred to the director as "young director Kildare" and "Stanley P. Kestler Kubrick" (ibid.).

80. N.d., WC, 24/8.

81. Dalton Trumbo, "The Sequence on Vesuvius: Notes," WC, 24/8.

82. *Los Angeles Mirror*, September 21, 1960, Stanley Kubrick biography file, MHL.

83. Trumbo to Lewis, September 21, 1960, UCLA, 131/4.

84. *LAT*, September 29, 1960, C9.

85. *Limelight*, October 27, 1960, Kubrick biography file, MHL.

86. Transcript of Lerner interview, June 1960, KDP, 38/6.

87. *NYT*, October 2, 1960, X9.

88. *DV*, October 7, 1960, 3.

89. *Time*, October 24, 1960, 102.

90. *LAT*, October 16, 1960, B3.

91. *NYT*, October 7, 1960, 28.

92. Harry C. Schnurr, "In the Entertainment World: *Spartacus*," *Classical World* 54, no. 3 (December 1960): 103.

93. René Chateau, "Entretien avec Michael Wilson and Dalton Trumbo," *Positif* 64–65 (August–September 1964): 101; transcript of interview, n.d., UCLA, 230/12.

94. *Chicago Daily News*, September 4–5, 1971, UCLA, 50/7.

95. Trumbo to Wilson, July 8, 1961, MWP, 48/1.

96. Quoted in Joseph Gelmis, *The Film Director as Superstar* (Garden City, NY: Doubleday, 1970), 314.

97. Quoted in Michel Ciment, *Kubrick*, trans. Gilbert Adair (New York: Holt, Rinehart and Winston, 1982), 151.

98. Interview with Harris, June 30, 2013.

99. Mary Beard, for example, used that phrase three times in her article, twice in one paragraph. Mary Beard, "Pinning down Spartacus," *New York Review of Books*, May 9, 2013, 19–20.

100. Interview with David Chandler, August 2, 1960, reprinted in Martin M. Winkler, ed., Spartacus: *Film and History* (Malden, MA: Blackwell, 2007), 22, 25.

101. Dalton Trumbo, first draft screenplay, July 15, 1958, 49, 108–9, UCLA, 160/5.

102. Trumbo to Picasso, undated draft, WC, 25/7.

19. *Exodus* and the Credit Announcements

The epigraph is quoted in Tom Ryan, *Otto Preminger Films* Exodus (New York: Random House, 1960), 10.

1. WC, 22/6. Boulle's novel is about a conflict between the owner of a rubber plantation and Communist guerrillas in Malaya. Pierro's novel tells the story of a group of Italian soldiers transporting prostitutes to Albania during World War II. The latter was made into a movie by an Italian company in 1965.

2. Maltz, *Citizen Writer in Retrospect*, 2:912–13.

3. Burt Prelutsky, draft of "Alias Dalton Trumbo," November–December 1961, CTP.

4. Trumbo to Jane Lynch, March 21, 1960, UCLA, 123/4.

5. Ryan, *Otto Preminger*, 10–11.

6. In fact, the copy of Maltz's script (dated November 6, 1959) in the Trumbo Papers (WC, 14/5) is 280 pages. It contains a list of scene summaries with Trumbo's handwritten marginal notes: "kept," "out," "kept—rewritten," and "from book—completely changed."

7. "Dalton Got His Gun," trans. into French by Rui Naguera, *Cinéma 71*, no. 58 (July–August 1971): 101.

8. Trumbo to Ingo Preminger, January 14, 1960, WC, 6/7.

9. Maltz, *Citizen Writer in Retrospect*, 944–48. In the Maltz Papers at Wisconsin, there is a complete, very long script carrying Maltz's name as author.

10. Trumbo to Maltz, January 4, 1960, and Maltz to Trumbo, January 16, 1960, WC, 6/7.

11. Trumbo to Ingo Preminger, April 8, 1961, UCLA, 131/11.

12. Trumbo interview with Roger Ebert, n.d., www.rogerebert.com/interviews/interview-with-dalton-trumbo.

13. Quoted in *Hollywood on Trial* (Cinema Associates, 1976).

14. "Dalton Trumbo: First Production with 'Johnny Got His Gun,'" five-page typescript, n.d. [ca. summer 1971], UCLA, 50/7.

15. *Hollywood on Trial*.

16. Dalton Trumbo, "Exodus" script, Eva Marie Saint Papers, 2/10, MHL.

17. *HR*, December 14, 1960, 3.

18. *Film Daily*, December 15, 1960, 5.

19. *DV*, December 14, 1960, 3.

20. *New Republic*, December 19, 1960, 21–22.

21. Trumbo to Michael Wilson, July 8, 1961, MWP, 48/1.

22. Interview with Jim Danelz, transcribed in a letter to Trumbo, January 8, 1973, CTP.

23. Interview in McGilligan and Buhle, *Tender Comrades*, 219. For an argument that the "economics of runaway productions," in the form of films directed by Joseph Losey and Jules Dassin, was eroding the blacklist, see Prime, *Hollywood Exiles in Europe*, 59–82.

24. Jon Lewis, "'We Do Not Ask You to Condone This': How the Blacklist Saved Hollywood," *Cinema Journal* 39, no. 2 (Winter 2000): 4; *Hollywood v. Hard Core: How the Struggle over Censorship Saved the Modern Film Industry*, paperback ed. (New York: NYU Press, 2002), 12.

25. *Minneapolis Tribune*, August 22, 1959. The story was picked up by *WV*, August 26, 1959, 1, and *DV*, August 27, 1959, 1. On August 22 Arnaud d'Usseau wrote to Michael Wilson to tell him that Carl Foreman was "having a rough time because of the Legion's activities" (MWP, 48/4).

26. Trumbo to Kahane, September 27, 1959, UCLA, 80/8. John Howard, chairman of the Counter Subversive Commission of the California American Legion, also accused Kahane of lying. He told Elizabeth Kerby that "Ben was lying through his teeth, and he knew it." Howard, however, was referring to Kahane's statement that 220 Communists were no longer working in the industry. Interview, October 28, 1960, Elizabeth Poe Kerby Collection, 1/2, MHL.

27. Trumbo to Aubrey Finn, October 2, 1959, WC, 6/6.

28. Silberberg to Finn, October 22, 1959, and Trumbo to Finn, November 3, 1959, WC, 6/4.

29. Jeff Smith has argued that "Trumbo's efforts alone could not have suc-

ceeded in ending the blacklist," but he was the first to realize that "he would receive screen credit only after Hollywood had solved the public relations problems presented by the blacklist. Thus, Trumbo worked with, instead of against, Hollywood to solve these problems." Jeffrey P. Smith, "'A Good Business Proposition': Dalton Trumbo, *Spartacus*, and the End of the Blacklist," *Velvet Light Trap* 23 (Spring 1989): 75–100.

30. Douglas, *I Am Spartacus!* 146–47.

31. Douglas, *Ragman's Son*, 323.

32. Douglas, *I Am Spartacus!* 147.

33. Interview with Lewis, August 9, 2012. Kubrick never told his associate, James B. Harris, that he wanted the writer's screen credit (Harris interview, June 30, 2013).

34. Lewis interview.

35. WC, 24/2.

36. *Hollywood Citizen-News*, December 28, 1959, 10.

37. *NYT*, January 20, 1960, 1, 8.

38. "Scrapbooks," reel 2; see also Ryan, *Otto Preminger*, 10–11. Later that year, Preminger announced that he had hired Ring Lardner Jr. to adapt Patrick Dennis's novel *The Genius*. When he was criticized for so doing by Daniel O'Connor, chairman of the American Legion's Americanism Commission, he gave virtually the same response he had given Duggan. Murray Schumach, *The Face on the Cutting-Room Floor: The Story of Movie and Television Censorship* (New York: Morrow, 1964), 130.

39. Otto Preminger, *Preminger: An Autobiography* (Garden City, NY: Doubleday, 1977), 118.

40. *HR*, January 21, 1960, 1.

41. Lewis interview.

42. Frederick Banker to Al Baer, January 25, 1960, KDP, 34/12.

43. Trumbo, *Additional Dialogue*, 494 n. 21.

44. Douglas, *Ragman's Son*, 323. Douglas disliked Preminger's bullying and dictatorial directing methods. They tangled a few years later on the set of *In Harm's Way* (Sigma Productions, 1965). Ibid., 380–81.

45. Douglas, *I Am Spartacus!* 150–51. I searched every issue of *Daily Variety* and *Hollywood Reporter* from December 1, 1959, to January 20, 1960, and I found no reference to Douglas's "now-widely-talked-about lunch with Trumbo in the Universal commissary" (150). The *Reporter*'s Mike Connolly, who reported every blacklist rumor that floated through Hollywood, mentioned *Spartacus* on a few occasions but wrote nothing about the lunch. Nor did Hedda Hopper. Likewise, there are no clippings referring to the lunch in the Douglas biography file at the Margaret Herrick Library or in the Douglas Papers at Wisconsin.

46. *LAT*, January 20, 1960, 2, 7.

47. *HR*, January 21, 1960, 1.

48. Hy Hollinger, "Preminger's Private Hornet: Trumbo," *WV*, January 27, 1960, 5.

49. Press release in Nedrick Young Papers, WC, 9/3.

50. *WV*, January 27, 1960, 18.

51. Scott to Preminger, January 26, 1960, Adrian Scott Papers, 5/42, AHC.

52. Trumbo, *Additional Dialogue*, 493–94, n. 21.

53. N.d., CTP.

54. Schumach, *Face on the Cutting-Room Floor*, 124.

55. *Los Angeles Examiner*, January 26, 1960, "Scrapbooks," reel 2.

56. "Tom Duggan Show," January 29, 1960, typed transcript, sent by Bob Rains to Stan Margulies, February 5, 1960, KDP, 34/12. In March the American Legion contributed to Frank Sinatra's decision to renege on his announcement that he had hired Albert Maltz to adapt William Bradford Huie's *The Execution of Private Slovik*. The April edition of *American Legion Magazine* carried a story titled "Will the Public Support Re-entry of Reds in Films?" (29–32). For the full Sinatra-Maltz story, see Jack Salzman, *Albert Maltz* (Boston: Twayne, 1978), 129–31; Michael Freedland, *All the Way: A Biography of Frank Sinatra* (London: Weidenfeld and Nicolson, 1997), 275; and J. Randy Taraborrelli, *Sinatra: Behind the Legend* (Secaucus, NJ: Birch Lane Press, 1997), 230.

57. Trumbo to Lewis, n.d. [ca. January 1960], in Trumbo, *Additional Dialogue*, 534–35.

58. *NYT*, February 22, 1960, 12. One year later, Schumach credited Preminger as the first person to openly use a blacklisted writer (*NYT*, June 9, 1961, 27). But three years later, in his book about censorship, he credited Douglas with being the first person to defy the blacklist: "Douglas wanted to say so openly but, though a courageous man, he encountered resistance" from Universal executives. "Even after the *New York Times* said flatly that Trumbo had written the script, no one of importance connected with the movie would admit it" (Schumach, *Face on the Cutting-Room Floor*, 132).

59. *NYT*, May 31, 1960, 27.

60. *NYT*, May 12, 1960, 42. In October, Dassin's *Never on Sunday* was released in the United States, carrying his name on the screen, and he was interviewed extensively. See, for example, Murray Schumach's article in *NYT*, October 16, 1960, X9. However, it would be another two years before he was signed by a US company (Filmways for *Topkapi*, 1964). Dassin had written a clearance letter in early 1959. See Prime, *Hollywood Exiles in Europe*, 168.

61. *DV*, June 20, 1960, 5. Spiegel reneged on this agreement.

62. *WV*, June 29, 1960, 3.

63. *DV*, June 20, 1960, 1, 4.

64. Harry Niemeyer to David A. Lipton, June 20, 1960, KDP, 34/13.

65. KDP, 34/19.

66. MPPA/PCA file on *Spartacus*, MHL.

67. Trumbo to Frances G. Knight, August 28, 1956, UCLA, 80/7. A test oath is a tool of government to determine one's "fitness" to exercise a right (e.g., voting, running for office). It was first used in England in 1661 to exclude Catholics from public office. The "test" was their willingness to reject, under oath, the doctrine of transubstantiation.

68. *Kent v. Dulles*, 357 U.S. 116 (1958); letters dated May 21 and July 1, 1958, UCLA, 80/7. The July 1 letter is reprinted in Trumbo, *Additional Dialogue*, 429–34.

69. Trumbo to Finn, ca. June 28, 1960, KDP, 33/20.

70. Announcement of credit, August 3, 1960, UCLA, 123/4.

71. Trumbo to George Roy Hill, December 4, 1965, UCLA, 2/2.

72. Bob Rains to David Lipton and Stan Margulies, August 2, 1960, KDP, 33/21.

73. *NYT*, August 8, 1960, 25.

74. Interview with Jim Danelz, transcribed in a letter to Trumbo, January 8, 1973, CTP.

75. Stan Margulies to Douglas, August 8, 1960, KDP, 33/21.

76. Trumbo to Lardner, August 17, 1961, Ring Lardner Jr. Collection, folder 196, MHL.

77. *NYT*, February 5, 1961, 39.

78. *NYT*, September 5, 1960, 11.

79. Johnston to members, November 4, 1960, Nedrick Young Collection, WC, 8/6.

80. Scott to Jarrico, February 9, 1961, Paul Jarrico Papers, Rare Books and Manuscripts Library, Columbia University.

20. Back on the Screen

1. Trumbo to Wilson, December 9, 1960, in Trumbo, *Additional Dialogue*, 536.

2. Trumbo to Bessie, January 3, 1961, ibid., 540.

3. Trumbo to Wilson, December 9, 1960, ibid., 536.

4. Wilson to Trumbo, December 12, 1960, WC, 6/8. Two months earlier, Lardner told Hunter he had discussed "the letter-writing clearance bit" with Trumbo and Ingo Preminger and added: "I have heard that you are very much involved with this problem." Lardner to Hunter, October 25, 1960, Ian McLellan Hunter Papers, 4/15, MHL. When Trumbo was in London in August 1960, Joseph Losey told him that he was in the process of writing a letter to Columbia Pictures in which he planned to deny that he was a Communist and disavow his previous political associations. For a copy of the letter, dated September 26, 1960, see Caute, *Joseph Losey*, 135. Losey sent copies to Trumbo and Adrian Scott, among others, and Scott replied that neither he nor Trumbo were "at all critical of what circumstances compelled you to do" (ibid., 136).

5. Cole to Paul Jarrico, November 21, 1960, Paul Jarrico Papers, Rare Books and Manuscripts Library, Columbia University. Shapiro based his strategy on *Klor's v. Broadway-Hale*, 395 U.S. 207 (1959), in which the Supreme Court had ruled that a group boycott violates sections 1 and 2 of the Sherman Antitrust Act, even when the victim is a single small merchant.

6. Trumbo to Wilson, July 8, 1961, MWP, 48/1.

7. Trumbo to Margolis, December 27, 1960, UCLA, 131/5.

8. Margolis to Trumbo, January 3, 1961, ibid. In his oral history, Margolis credited Trumbo's brilliant handling of the strategy to break the blacklist, but he also acknowledged that "there was a good deal of criticism of the fact that he was doing [it] through the back door. In effect that he was—what he was doing was saying, 'Okay, I want to go back to work,' by saying, 'Well, so I was a commu—' without saying it, saying 'I was a communist, and I'm sorry.' Trumbo, of course, denied always that that was his intent, or the effect of what he said." Margolis, *Law and Social Conscience*, 266–67. In effect, Margolis seemed to be implying, unfairly, that Trumbo's critics may have been right.

9. Trumbo to Wilson, July 8, 1961, MWP, 48/1. Coincidentally or not, Young did not have another movie credit.

10. Ultimately, the request for an injunction was denied, six of the plaintiffs

dropped out, and support from the blacklisted community diminished sharply. In June 1965 the remaining defendants settled the suit for $80,000.

11. *NYT,* January 8, 1961, X7.

12. Trumbo to Jennings, December 21, 1960, in Trumbo, *Additional Dialogue,* 538–39.

13. *Time,* January 26, 1961, 30.

14. Trumbo to *Saturday Evening Post* editors, September 14, 1961, UCLA, 221/5.

15. Ring Lardner Jr., "My Life on the Blacklist," *Saturday Evening Post,* October 14, 1961, 40, 44.

16. Ibid., 38.

17. Trumbo to Lardner, August 7, 1961, UCLA, 221/3.

18. Trumbo to Maltz, n.d. [ca. late 1961 or early 1962], in Trumbo, *Additional Dialogue,* 556–57.

19. Trumbo to Lawford, February 2, 1962, UCLA, 221/3. Several months earlier, Hopper had written to a friend that her anti-Communist tirades had long ago become unpopular with her readers and the syndicate that distributed her column. She added: "I am glad that I am nearing the end and won't be around when the Scummies [Communists] walk in." Hopper to Eleanor Nash, June 14, 1961, Hedda Hopper Papers, 6/129, MHL.

20. Butler to Ring Lardner Jr., December 20, 1961, Ring Lardner Jr. Papers, 22/268, MHL.

21. Trumbo to Wilson, October 2, 1961, Ian Hunter Collection, 4/4, MHL.

22. Maltz to Trumbo, October 21, 1961, UCLA, 221/4.

23. Vechel Howard, *Sundown at Crazy Horse* (Greenwich, CT: Gold Medal Book, 1957).

24. Trumbo to Eugene Frenke, November 3, 1959, WC, 27/9.

25. Aldrich memos, ibid.

26. Douglas, *Ragman's Son,* 328.

27. Trumbo to Lewis, June 28, 1961, WC, 6/10.

28. Trumbo to Wilson, July 8, 1861, MWP 48/1.

29. René Chateau, "Entretien avec Michael Wilson and Dalton Trumbo," *Positif* 64–65 (August–September 1964): 101.

30. Interview in *Cinema* 2, no. 6 (July–August 1965): 16.

31. "Dalton Trumbo: First Production with 'Johnny Got His Gun,'" five-page typescript, n.d. [ca. summer 1971], UCLA, 50/7.

32. *LAT,* May 14, 1961, B3.

33. *DV,* May 24, 1961, 3.

34. *HR,* May 24, 1961, 3.

35. *Limelight,* May 25, 1961, 4.

36. Memos from Werner F. Wolfen, Irell & Manello, reporting two conversations with Trumbo, May 7 and 10, 1965, UCLA, 132/3. Douglas does not mention these problems in his autobiography.

37. Interview by Keith Berwick, "Speculation," November 17, 1970, UCLA Film and Television Archive.

38. Wolfen memo.

39. Reinhardt to Trumbo, November 3, 1960, UCLA, 119/27.

40. Ibid., November 10, 1960, UCLA, 132/2.

41. Note, November 13, 1960, UCLA, 119/27.

42. Undated note, UCLA, 122/5.

43. Trumbo to Frenke, January 7, 1961, UCLA, 158/11.

44. Trumbo to Mirisch Brothers Productions, May 4, 1961, UCLA, 221/4. Trumbo later told Wilson that the movie, "which is two-thirds mine" and "offers an absolutely stunning performance by Kirk," did not carry his name because "I thought I was only going to doctor" it and "my name was excluded originally by *me!*" (Trumbo to Wilson, July 8, 1961, MWP, 48/1). However, in 1999, when a WGAw committee was investigating blacklist credits, Cleo told the members that Trumbo's work on *Town without Pity* consisted of a minor rewrite, and she requested that he not receive credit for it (Blacklist Credits Committee: Dalton Trumbo Considerations, n.d., CTP).

45. Mirisch to Trumbo, May 5, 1961, UCLA 221/4. In his memoir, Walter Mirisch states that the WGAw ruled against Trumbo's credit, but Mirisch disagreed with that ruling because Trumbo had "accomplished a great deal in improving the script." Walter Mirisch, *We Thought We Were Making Movies* (Madison: University of Wisconsin Press, 2008), 199. In fact, the matter had not been submitted to the guild.

46. Trumbo to Eddie Lewis, June 28, 1961, WC, 6/10. Lewis was not involved with the making of this film.

47. Trumbo to Mirisch and Trumbo to Lewis, June 28, 1961, UCLA, 221/4.

48. Reinhardt to Trumbo and Trumbo to Mirisch, August 15, 1961, ibid.

49. *LAT*, November 20, 1961, C17.

50. *Newsweek*, October 30, 1961, 77.

51. *New Yorker*, October 14, 1961, 178–79; *NYT*, October 11, 1961, 53.

52. *NYT*, June 9, 1961, 27.

53. Trumbo to Lewis, June 28, 1961, WC, 6/10.

54. Trumbo to Ingo Preminger, April 8, 1961, UCLA, 131/11.

55. Douglas interview in "Trumbo Remembered," KCET, 1983.

56. Abbey to Miller, March 17, 1961, KDP, 40/26.

57. The scripts are in WC, 20.

58. Trumbo to Biberman, January 28, 1964, CTP.

59. Chateau, "Entretien," 102.

60. Douglas, *Ragman's Son*, 338.

61. Dalton Trumbo, talk at UCLA, UCLA Communications Studies Archives, www.youtube.com/watch?v=YhAXSDpvqVU.

62. Interview with Jim Danelz, transcribed in a letter to Trumbo, January 8, 1973, CTP.

63. Abbey to Miller, March 17, 1961, KDP, 40/26.

64. Douglas, *Ragman's Son*, 338.

65. Trumbo to Wilson, July 8, 1961, MWP, 48/1.

66. *NYT*, August 19, 1962, X7; Douglas, *Ragman's Son*, 341.

67. *Saturday Review*, July 21, 1962, *Lonely Are the Brave* clipping file, MHL.

68. *New Yorker*, July 14, 1962, 61.

69. Trumbo to Gill, July 31, 1962, WC, 7/2. Douglas told Trumbo that Gill's review was "a very odd one" (August 27, 1962, WC, 7/1). Pauline Kael, who commented on the movie five years later, had not read the novel either. She wrote: "The Dalton Trumbo script gives the film that awful messagey self-righteousness of *High Noon* and *The Gunfighter* and a fake ironic tragedy, an

O. Henry finish—the 'last' cowboy is run down by a truck loaded with toilets" ("Saddle Sore," *New Republic*, August 5, 1967, 38–41).

70. Trumbo to Douglas, October 1961, UCLA, 221/3.

71. Douglas to Trumbo, October 20, 1961, ibid.

72. Douglas, *Ragman's Son*, 337.

73. Trumbo to Ingo Preminger, n.d., UCLA, 221/4.

74. Ibid., April 8, 1961, UCLA, 131/11.

75. Trumbo to Otto Preminger, May 7, 1961, in Trumbo, *Additional Dialogue*, 545–46.

76. Wilson to Trumbo, May 25, 1961, UCLA, 221/4.

77. Trumbo to Ingo Preminger, May 26, 1961, ibid.

78. Chris Fujiwara, *The World and Its Double: The Life and Work of Otto Preminger* (New York: Faber and Faber, 2008), 331.

79. SACLA to director, September 13, 1956, FOIA-DT.

80. Ibid., November 10, 1958, and March 28, 1960.

81. Director to SACLA, April 14, 1960, FOIA-DT.

82. Director to A. H. Belmont, April 14, 1960, ibid. COINTELPRO was designed to infiltrate and disrupt the organizations Hoover disliked, including black civil rights groups and, a few years later, the New Left.

83. Director to SACLA, April 26, 1960, ibid.

84. Ibid., January 6 and February 27, 1961.

85. M. D. Fraiden to Trumbo, March 2, 1961, UCLA, 158/5.

86. *Playboy* interview, tape 1, UCLA, 61/2. For more on the income tax investigation, see Trumbo, *Additional Dialogue*, 542–43.

21. *Hawaii* and *The Sandpiper*

1. Trumbo to Wilson, July 8, 1961, MWP, 48/1.

2. *An Oral History with Daniel Taradash*, interview by Barbara Hall (Oral History Program, MHL, 2001), 384.

3. Taradash to Zinnemann, June 2, 1961, Daniel Taradash Papers, 44/1, AHC. Taradash and Trumbo had never met, but Taradash admired Trumbo's adaptations of *Spartacus* and *Exodus*. A copy of Taradash's treatment is in UCLA, 18/4.

4. Taradash to Harold Mirisch and Fred Zinnemann, September 29, 1961, and Taradash to Michener, October 1, 1961, ibid.

5. "Hawaii" Arbitration: Trumbo Statement, 1966, 3–4, UCLA, 5/2.

6. *DV*, November 30, 1961, 1, 4.

7. Trumbo to Mirisch, January 26, 1964, UCLA, 116/25.

8. Andrew Horton, *The Films of George Roy Hill* (New York: Columbia University Press, 1984), 54.

9. Trumbo to Taradash, November 3, 1964, Taradash Papers, 44/1.

10. *LAT*, October 23, 1966, W28.

11. Hill to Trumbo, ca. December 1965, UCLA, 2/2.

12. Mirisch, *We Thought We Were Making Movies*, 219–31.

13. Dalton Trumbo, drafts of response to second "Hawaii" arbitration, UCLA, 1/6.

14. Michener to Trumbo, August 28, 1965, photocopy attached to letter from Trumbo to Kathleen Winsor, September 11, 1965, UCLA, 69/1. In Trum-

bo's annotated copy of the novel, he underlined a portion of one of Jerusha's conversations with Abner: "You . . . must . . . preach . . . love" (p. 338, UCLA, 18/2).

15. *NYT*, October 11, 1966, 54.

16. *Oral History with Taradash*, 403.

17. *DV*, June 9, 1967, 2.

18. Quoted in *NYT*, December 11, 1966, D13.

19. Kagan to WGAw, December 8, 1965, UCLA, 2/2; Hill to Trumbo, ca. December 1965, ibid.

20. "Hawaii" Arbitration, 21.

21. Daniel Taradash statement, "Hawaii" arbitration, Taradash Papers, 44/5.

22. Dorfman to Trumbo, ca. January 1966, UCLA, 2/2.

23. Hill to Trumbo, January 28, 1966, UCLA, 2/2. It should be noted that Hill and Walter Mirisch had another falling out at the end of the movie, so it is possible that Hill saw Mirisch's "evil" hand in the credit decision.

24. Finn to Trumbo, February 2, 1966, UCLA, 2/2.

25. *Oral History with Taradash*, 400–401.

26. Taradash statement, Taradash Papers, 48/6.

27. Trumbo statement, UCLA, 32/2.

28. Trumbo to Mirisch, September 17, 1968, UCLA, 131/5.

29. Ingo to Trumbo, October 11, 1962, UCLA, 114/14. In October 1963 Trumbo chose Ingo Preminger as his sole representative. Up until that time, he had employed several agents.

30. Trumbo to Ingo, October 22, 1962, UCLA, 81/1.

31. Quoted in McGilligan and Buhle, *Tender Comrades*, 173–74.

32. At the end of his life, Trumbo, Preminger, and Robert Aldrich were the only ones who "stood by Hugo, fed and housed him, defraying the Butler family expenses" (e-mail from Michael Butler, December 24, 2011). Mitzi recalled that Hugo came to stay with her parents in 1967, the year before he died. "It was terrible to see him so diminished and so sad. My father was so gentle with him."

33. Trumbo to Christopher, August 6, 1962, in the possession of Mitzi Trumbo.

34. Trumbo to Frenke, March 7, 1963, UCLA, 58/1.

35. Ibid., May 28, 1963, UCLA, 133/13.

36. Interview in *Cinema* 2, no. 6 (July–August 1965): 14.

37. Trumbo to Frenke, January 24, 1964, UCLA, 58/1.

38. Ingo to Trumbo, August 15, 1963, UCLA, 129/3; Ingo to Wilson, July 9, 1963, MWP, 48/2. The script Wilson wrote for Ransohoff, "The Light of Day," was not made into a movie.

39. Trumbo to Burton and Taylor, May 25, 1964, UCLA, 144/2.

40. Quoted in Dirk Sheppard, *Elizabeth: The Life and Career of Elizabeth Taylor* (Garden City, NY: Doubleday, 1974), 381.

41. Trumbo to Wilson, November 7, 1964, MWP, 48/5.

42. Wilson to Trumbo, November 10, 1964, UCLA, 125/2.

43. Wilson to Ransohoff, November 13, 1964, MWP, 48/2.

44. Trumbo to Ransohoff, November 16, 1964, MWP, 48/5.

45. Trumbo to Wilson, November 30, 1964, ibid.

46. Wilson to Trumbo, December 2, 1964, UCLA, 125/2.

47. Trumbo to Ransohoff, n.d., MWP, 48/2.

48. Wilson to Ransohoff, December 8, 1964, ibid.

49. Copy of Wilson to Ransohoff, December 8, 1964, UCLA, 122/9.

50. Notification of credit, UCLA, 123/6.

51. Trumbo to Ransohoff, January 27, 1965, UCLA, 81/4.

52. Trumbo to Ransohoff, February 18, 1965, UCLA, 80/5.

53. Ransohoff to Trumbo, February 24, 1965, UCLA, 132/5. An article published in *Newsweek* reported that Minnelli "is only lukewarm about the script" (December 21, 1964, 73), and Minnelli stated in his autobiography that he hated the script and was continually plotting ways to improve it. Vincente Minnelli with Hector Arce, *I Remember It Well* (Garden City, NY: Doubleday, 1974), 356. Two of Taylor's biographers assert that Minnelli deliberately reshaped the script to reflect the Taylor-Burton love affair. Alexander Walker, *Elizabeth: The Life of Elizabeth Taylor* (New York: Grove Weidenfeld, 1990), 276; Willliam J. Mann, *How to Be a Movie Star: Elizabeth Taylor in Hollywood* (New York: Houghton Mifflin Harcourt, 2009), 341.

54. Trumbo to Ransohoff, March 25, 1965, UCLA, 81/4. Wilson remained on good terms with Ransohoff. The following year, Ransohoff hired Wilson to revise a screenplay titled "Castle Keep," written by Daniel Taradash. Ransohoff, however, did not use Wilson's revised script.

55. Michael Wilson, "The Sandpiper," treatment dated October 12, 1963, Turner/MGM Collection, S-128, F-126, MHL.

56. *LAT*, July 16, 1965, C10.

57. *Life*, July 16, 1965, 22.

58. *Saturday Review*, July 24, 1965, 51.

59. Jennings to Trumbo, September 10, 1965, and Trumbo to Jennings, September 16, 1965, UCLA, 221/5.

60. Quoted in *The Richard Burton Diaries*, ed. Chris Williams (New Haven, CT: Yale University Press, 2012), 80 (entry dated May 16, 1965).

61. Trumbo to Jennings, August 6, 1965, UCLA, 81/4.

62. Undated note, UCLA, 223/1.

63. Undated note, UCLA, 127/8.

64. "Dalton Got His Gun," *Cinéma 71*, no. 58 (July–August 1971): 103.

65. *NYT*, June 28, 1970, 11.

66. Trumbo to Gregory, July 13, 1965, UCLA, 130/5.

67. Trumbo to Ingo Preminger, December 18, 1963, UCLA, 129/3.

68. Preminger to Ulmer and Reggiani, December 26, 1963, UCLA, 129/3. The film was made in Italy, released in West Germany in June 1964, and released in the United States in December 1965. The screenplay was credited to Jack Davies and Michael Pertwee. It was Ulmer's last movie.

69. *HR*, November 8, 1966, 2; *DV*, November 8, 1966, 1.

70. Finn to Bischoff, November 9, 1966, and Bischoff to Finn, November 18, 1966, UCLA, 114/19.

22. *The Fixer* and the Laurel Award

The epigraph is quoted in C. Robert Jennings, "Hollywood Ten, Plus Twenty," *LAT*, September 3, 1967, A17.

1. Jennings, "Hollywood Ten."

2. Martin, *Born Standing Up*, 91–92.

3. *Playboy* interview, tape 7, UCLA, 61/2. Two other blacklisted screenwriters, Ian Hunter and Waldo Salt, successfully substituted marijuana for alcohol late in their lives. Lardner, *I'd Hate Myself*, 55.

4. Peter O'Toole, after reading the "Will Adams" script, telegrammed Trumbo: "the language is bloody marvelous." Several months later he told an interviewer that it was "the finest script that ever breathed." O'Toole to Trumbo, January 20, 1965, in the possession of Mitzi Trumbo; *Playboy*, September 1965, 96.

5. Trumbo to Winsor, August 6, 1965, UCLA, 69/1.

6. Winsor to Trumbo, August 15, 1965, ibid.

7. Trumbo to Winsor, August 27, 1965, ibid.

8. Winsor to Trumbo, September 3, 1965, ibid.

9. Trumbo to Winsor, September 11, 1965, ibid.

10. Undated series of drafts, UCLA, 223/1.

11. Bernard Malamud, "Source of *The Fixer*," in *Talking Horse: Bernard Malamud on Life and Work*, ed. Alan Cheuse and Nicholas Delbanco (New York: Columbia University Press, 1996), 88.

12. "Dalton Trumbo Discusses Screenwriter's Task," *Los Angeles Herald-Examiner*, December 2, 1968, D7.

13. Jenna Malamud Smith, *My Father Is a Book* (Boston: Houghton Mifflin, 2006), 213.

14. Trumbo to Lewis and Frankenheimer, August 25, 1967, Turner/MGM Collection, 932967, MHL.

15. Trumbo to Malamud, February 28, 1967, UCLA, 92/5.

16. Ibid., March 14, 1967.

17. Malamud to Trumbo, March 16, 1967, UCLA, 92/5.

18. Trumbo to Malamud, March 21, 1967, ibid.

19. Malamud to Trumbo, March 23, 1967, ibid.

20. Trumbo to Malamud, August 5, 1968, ibid. Later that year, Trumbo made a similar statement to an interviewer in "Dalton Trumbo Discusses Screenwriter's Task."

21. "Dalton Trumbo Discusses Screenwriter's Task." While he was writing, Lewis and Frankenheimer were negotiating with Alan Arkin to play the role of Yakov. A conference was arranged with Arkin's agent, Meta Reis Rosenberg. Rosenberg, fearing that Trumbo would say something to Arkin about her informing, asked George Willner to intercede and convince Trumbo to play nice. Willner called Trumbo, who, "after cursing her out," said: "'You tell Meta if I see her at a business meeting I'll say hello but if I see her socially I'll kick her ass'" (quoted in Navasky, *Naming Names*, 174). Ultimately, Alan Bates was cast as Yakov.

22. Transcript of Frankenheimer interview by Charles Champlin for the Directors Guild of America, May 1992, Charles Champlin Collection, folder 263a, tape 6/50, MHL; for the edited version, see *John Frankenheimer: A Conversation with Charles Champlin* (Burbank, CA: Directors Guild of America, 1995), 112.

23. Trumbo to Frankenheimer, March 26, 1968, UCLA, 114/12.

24. Trumbo to Lewis, August 13, 1968, UCLA, 116/10.

25. Ibid., n.d., UCLA, 131/4. On one of the ads, Trumbo wrote: "I'll know better next time" (UCLA, 121/1). The ads appeared in *HR*, July 31, 1967, 6–7, and *DV*, August 1, 1967, 6–7.

26. Trumbo to Frankenheimer, March 26, 1968, UCLA, 114/12.

27. Alex Madsen, "Onward and Upward with Dalton Trumbo," *Sight and Sound*, Summer 1971, 156.

28. Interview with Jim Danelz, transcribed in a letter to Trumbo, January 8, 1973, CTP.

29. Transcript of Frankenheimer interview by Champlin, tape 6/40–41; *John Frankenheimer: A Conversation*, 107.

30. *The Films of John Frankenheimer—Forty Years in Film: John Franken-heimer Talks about His Life in the Cinema to Gerald Pratley* (Bethlehem, PA: Lehigh University Press; London: Cygnus Arts, 1998), 80–81.

31. *LAT*, December 11, 1968, A8.

32. *NYT*, December 9, 1968, 59.

33. Trumbo to Adler, December 16, 1968, UCLA, 80/5.

34. UCLA, 235/15. Kessel's novel was first published in France under the title *Les Cavaliers* (Paris: Gallimard, 1967); it was translated into English by Patrick O'Brian (New York: Farrar, Straus and Giroux, 1968). The title refers to *buzkashi* riders, who engage in a sport similar to polo; it is played by opposing teams on horseback using a dead, headless goat rather than a ball. It is extremely violent.

35. Kessel to Lewis, November 21, 1968, UCLA, 131/1.

36. Notes from conference with Eddie Lewis, February 27, 1969, UCLA 213/6.

37. Ibid.

38. UCLA, 213/7.

39. Transcript of Frankenheimer interview by Champlin, tape 8/4–5; *John Frankenheimer: A Conversation*, 129; *Films of John Frankenheimer*, 111. In a 1971 interview, Frankenheimer called Trumbo "the best screenwriter we've got," and he spoke highly of *The Horsemen*. *LAT*, July 18, 1971, C17.

40. *DV*, June 23, 1971, 3.

41. *LAT*, September 23, 1971.

42. *HR*, June 28, 1971, 3.

43. E-mail from Manfull to the author, May 22, 2011.

44. Trumbo, *Additional Dialogue*, 10.

45. Ibid., 11.

46. UCLA, 187/4, 187/5.

47. *NYT Book Review*, November 1, 1970, 6.

48. *Sight and Sound*, Summer 1971, 157.

49. *Harper's*, March 1971, 24.

50. *Saturday Review of Literature*, October 31, 1970, 29.

51. Dalton Trumbo, "En Garde, Foolish World!" *Esquire*, July 1970, 87–89, 127–32; Cole to Trumbo, June 22, 1970, and Trumbo to Cole, June 24, 1970, UCLA, 114/3.

52. Lardner to Trumbo, July 22, 1970, Ring Lardner Jr. Papers, 37/477, MHL.

53. "Honor Bright, and All that Jazz," *Nation*, 100th Anniversary Edition, 1965, 183–90; reprinted in Trumbo, *Time of the Toad* (1972 reprint). Drafts of the article are in UCLA, 153/3 and 153/4.

54. Peter Bart, "The Highly Unlikely Dalton Trumbo," *NYT*, December 11, 1966, D13.

55. Trumbo to Morse, ca. 1965, UCLA, 223/1.

56. *NYT*, June 28, 1970, 11.

57. *DV*, March 8, 1971, 3.

58. Trumbo, *Johnny Got His Gun*, xxix.

59. Interview with Jane Fonda, Docudrama DVD, 2008; Jane Fonda, *My Life So Far* (New York: Random House, 2005), 272–73. See also "The Show the Pentagon Couldn't Stop," *Ramparts*, September 1972, 29–32. A ninety-four-minute documentary film titled *F.T.A.* was released by American-International in July 1972.

60. Program for a special showing of the documentary, *F.T.A.* clipping file, MHL. One reviewer of the film wrote: "Sutherland delivers a moving and impassioned bit of antiwar oratory penned by Dalton Trumbo" (*HR*, July 11, 1972, 3). And Jay Cocks stated in *Time*: "At one point, reading a passage from Dalton Trumbo's antiwar novel *Johnny Got His Gun*, Sutherland seems paralyzed by moral fervor" (September 4, 1972, 68). For more on the FTA, see Mark Shiel, "Hollywood, the New Left, and FTA," in *Un-American Hollywood: Politics and Film in the Blacklist Era*, ed. Frank Krutnik, Steve Neale, Brian Neve, and Peter Steinfeld (New Brunswick, NJ: Rutgers University Press, 2007), 210–24.

61. E-mail from Sutherland, August 16, 2012. In Joe's last oration to himself, he states: "If you make a war if there are guns to be aimed if there are bullets to be fired if there are men to be killed they will not be us." Among those guys are those "who string the long moaning high tension wires" (Trumbo, *Johnny Got His Gun*, 250). In his 1990 introduction to the 2007 Citadel Press reprint of *Johnny*, Kovic wrote: "Trumbo's word moved me so much that day [spring 1971] I wanted to speak out, and I was able to. I went up to the stage, and made my very first speech as a political activist." The book became "the cornerstone in a great monument of protest and dissent that my life would become—it was the anchor, the key foundation" (xiv).

62. Trumbo to Wolper, March 12, 1968, UCLA, 117/12. According to Alexandra Styron, the adaptation project "was derailed by an organization calling itself the Black Anti-Defamation Association, created by Ossie Davis and Ruby Dee." Alexandra Styron, *Reading My Father: A Memoir* (New York: Scribner, 2011), 25.

63. *LAT*, February 24, 1970, II:6.

64. UCLA, 113/9.

65. Patricia Bosworth, *Jane Fonda: The Private Life of a Public Woman* (Boston: Houghton Mifflin Harcourt, 2011), 291, 293.

66. Dalton Trumbo, statements written to add to *Playboy* interview, n.d., [ca. 1972], UCLA, 56/10.

67. April 3, 1968, UCLA, 58/15. In a letter to Soviet writer Konstantin Simonov, Trumbo had written that the Soviet decision to resume nuclear testing "has brought the world a step closer to the irreversible genetic deterioration of the human race, or its practical annihilation. I am bewildered by the Soviet Peace Committee's approval of Soviet nuclear testing as the necessary handmaiden to world peace, and appalled by a statement of the Organization of Soviet Biologists that 'renewal of explosions of nuclear weapons under the

present conditions is in the interests of . . . the whole progress of mankind'"
(September 5, 1961, UCLA, 221/5).

68. UCLA, 80/8.

69. November 1968, CTP.

70. All the quoted letters are from "The Happy Jack Fish Hatchery Papers:
In Which the Messrs. Steve Allen, Dalton Trumbo and Arthur Schlesinger, Jr.
Debate the True Meaning of Liberalism," *Esquire*, January 1970, 73–77, 166–
74; reprinted in *Esquire*, 40th Anniversary Issue, October 1973, and in Steve
Allen, *But Seriously: Steve Allen Speaks His Mind* (Amherst, NY: Prometheus
Books, 1996), 152–90. Allen's syllogism is valid only if one accepts his premise
that there is only one type of liberal. Trumbo referred to Schlesinger's liberalism as "a refined version of what you get in the Hearst press" (*Playboy* interview, tape 3, UCLA, 61/2). The Happy Jack Fish Farm was located in Azusa,
and the *Esquire* title might be alluding to Mel Blanc's oft-repeated background
announcement on the Jack Benny radio show: "All aboard for Anaheim, Azusa,
and Cu-ca-monga." Several writers of Trumbo's generation thought this line
was hilarious.

71. Trumbo to Erickson, n.d., UCLA, 58/14.

72. *DV*, March 16, 1970, 1.

73. UCLA, 60/8.

74. Ibid.

75. *DV*, March 16, 1970, 32.

76. WGAw *Newsletter*, April 1970, 10; Trumbo, *Additional Dialogue*, 569–
70. The Meltzer Award was given for the writing of a feature film that, "in
addition to its value as entertainment, most effectively contributes to a better understanding of the problems of our times" (Screen Writers Guild press
release, July 1947, UCLA, 60/8). I have been unable to find any reference to
Meltzer in the indices of the committee's hearings transcripts. However, an FBI
report had identified him as a Communist (SACLA to director, August 9, 1943,
COMPIC). Michael Wilson, who was a close friend of Meltzer's, said that
Meltzer was a party member. Michael Wilson, *I Am the Sum of My Actions*
(Los Angeles: UCLA Oral History Program, 1982), 121.

77. *DV*, March 16, 1970, 32.

78. Primo Levi, *The Drowned and the Saved*, trans. Raymond Rosenthal
(New York: Summit Books, 1988), 36–69.

79. Trumbo, draft of letter to Huebsch, April 28, 1970, UCLA, 124/3.

80. Lester Cole, *Hollywood Red: The Autobiography of Lester Cole* (Palo
Alto, CA: Ramparts Press, 1981), 396.

81. Maltz, *Citizen Writer in Retrospect*, 1008; for more on Maltz and the
speech, see chapter 26.

82. Quoted in McGilligan, *Backstory*, 143.

83. E-mail from Becca Wilson to the author, December 10, 2011. Wilson
was "unforgiving" in his attitude toward informers (Navasky, *Naming Names*,
379). A mea culpa is in order here: Thirty-some years ago, Steven Englund and
I earnestly, but now I think wrongly, criticized the "only victims" phrase in *The
Inquisition in Hollywood*, 420–21.

84. Cleo to Christopher, November 5, 2005, CTP. Richard Collins, another
informer, told his son that he agreed with Trumbo: "they were all victims."
E-mail from Michael Collins to the author, September 5, 2013.

85. In January 1999 the Board of Governors of the Academy of Motion Picture Arts and Sciences voted to present Elia Kazan an Oscar for lifetime achievement. Kazan was one of the most notorious and disliked informers, and the announcement of this award provoked a significant public protest in Hollywood. Schlesinger favored the award, attacked the protesters, and devoted three paragraphs to the Laurel speech. "Hollywood Hypocrisy," *NYT*, February 28, 1999, IV:9.

23. *Johnny Got His Gun*—The Movie: Preproduction

The epigraph is from Dalton Trumbo, *Hollywood Spectator*, August 1, 1931, 16–17.

1. Trumbo to Cameron and Kahn, March 15, 1954, WC, 5/1.

2. Roberts to Trumbo, October 22, 1957, and Trumbo to Roberts, January 8, 1958, UCLA, 135/1.

3. Krassner to Trumbo, January 21, 1958, WC, 6/1.

4. Trumbo, *Johnny Got His Gun*, xxviii.

5. Trumbo to Eric Glass, December 18, 1962, UCLA, 221/3.

6. Trumbo interview with Roger Ebert, n.d., www.rogerebert.com/interviews/interview-with-dalton-trumbo; "Dalton Trumbo: First Production with 'Johnny Got His Gun,'" five-page typescript, n.d. [ca. summer 1971], UCLA, 50/7; *LAT*, November 26, 1967, D12. Buñuel had been living in Mexico since 1946. Among the many films he directed, wrote, and cowrote were two with Hugo Butler: *The Adventures of Robinson Crusoe* (1953) and *The Young One* (1961).

7. Quoted in John Baxter, *Buñuel* (New York: Carroll and Graf, 1994), 272.

8. Letters of September 16, 1965, UCLA, 221/5. For a Spanish version of their script, see Dalton Trumbo and Luis Buñuel, *Johnny Got His Gun (Johnny cogio su fusil): Guión cinematográfica, basado en la novella homónima de Dalton Trumbo* (Teruel, Spain: Instituto de Estudios Turalenses, 1993).

9. UCLA, 44/6, 15–16.

10. Ibid., 106.

11. UCLA, 39/2, 102.

12. "Dalton Got His Gun," trans. into French by Rui Naguera, *Cinéma 71*, no. 58 (July–August 1971): 105.

13. Trumbo to Maltz, January 26, 1968, UCLA, 113/11.

14. Campbell had owned a production company in San Francisco that went broke. He moved to Los Angeles, where he met Roy Silver, comedian Bill Cosby's manager. Silver convinced Cosby to establish a production partnership with Campbell (whose name came first in the company name because it sounded better than any of the other configurations). Campbell and Silver had grand dreams for expanding the company's income beyond Cosby's concert dates, records, and television specials. They formed a record company (Tetragrammaton) and made a movie (never released): *Picasso Summer*, with Yvette Mimieux and Albert Finney.

15. Trumbo to Bright, March 7, 1968, ibid.

16. Campbell deposition in *Kaleidoscope Productions, Inc. v. Robert Rich Productions, Inc. et al.*, January 12, 1972, Margolis-McTernan Papers, series 5, box 3, 5–6, Southern California Library for Social Studies and Research.

17. "Trumbo-CSC Joint Venture," UCLA, 115/5.

18. Transcript of meeting, in BCPM, box 2, book 13.

19. William Wolf, "Moviemaker with Conviction," *Cue*, April 22, 1968, 16.

20. *HR*, June 26, 1968, 5.

21. Trumbo to Marceau, August 26, 1968, UCLA, 113/11; Trumbo to Silver, August 28, 1968, BCPM.

22. Haggiag to Campbell, July 26, 1968, Dalton Trumbo Memos, box 1, book 1, BCPM. Haggiag was born in 1913 in Tripoli, Libya. He began making films in Italy during the 1940s. He also founded Dear Films, which distributed movies for some of the major Hollywood studios. He coproduced *The Barefoot Contessa* (1954) and produced *Candy* (1968).

23. Maltz to Trumbo, August 12, 1968, UCLA, 131/5.

24. Trumbo to Maltz, August 16, 1968, ibid.

25. BCPM, box 2, book 13.

26. Conversation with the author, December 23, 2011.

27. UCLA, 114/11. Always on the lookout for some quick money, Trumbo pitched a television western to CSC. Titled "Refugio," it would star Bill Cosby as the leader of a singular community—"no paradise, nor are its citizens by any means saints. Its mores are those of any other western community. . . . Their only flat prohibition is the gun—that instrument of capital crime and racial or national persecution of which they are heartily sick." They are classic Robin Hood–type bandits who rob banks and rustle cattle, but they "are not against *all* bankers, *all* sheriffs, *all* cattle barons, *all* Army commanders. They are only against those who oppress, swindle, dispossess, steal from, swindle or persecute others for their own benefit—those, in short, who themselves act in violation of Federal or Territorial law" (UCLA, 119/2).

28. Trumbo to Matthau, September 26, 1968, UCLA, 116/20.

29. Trumbo to Campbell and Silver, February 4, 1969, UCLA, 114/10.

30. Trumbo to Haggiag, October 1, 1968, BCPM, box 1, book 3.

31. Trumbo to Bright, October 14, 1968, UCLA, 113/11.

32. "Conversations on Film: With Dalton Trumbo," *Cinema Canada*, January–February 1969, 13.

33. Trumbo to Rivkin, December 19, 1968, UCLA, 119/30.

34. Trumbo to Campbell, February 18, 1969, UCLA, 114/10; BCPM, box 1, book 5.

35. *DV*, May 13, 1969, 1, 8.

36. "Dalton Trumbo: An Interview," *Film Society Review* 7, no. 2 (October 1971): 26.

37. Trumbo to Peter E. Strauss, August 29, 1969, UCLA, 117/13.

38. Dodd to Trumbo, February 10, 1970, UCLA, 57/8.

39. Undated note, CTP. Lazarus had been subpoenaed by the Committee on Un-American Activities in March 1953, to be questioned about *Salt*. He proved to be a very contentious witness (*Investigation of Communist Activities in the Los Angeles Area*, pt. 2, 478–98).

40. Trumbo to Elaine B. Fischel, March 3, 1971, UCLA, 64/3.

41. Undated note, UCLA, 69/5; Trumbo to Jarrico, November 26, 1973, UCLA, 208/5.

42. Memorandum of Agreement between Dalton Trumbo as Author and Owner of Script and Director of Motion Picture with Simon M. Lazarus, Harry

Margolis, and Margolis, McTernan, Smith, Scope and Herring on Behalf of Investors, UCLA, 71/10.

43. Trumbo to Ben Margolis, April 26, 1974, UCLA, 63/5.

44. Margolis deposition in *Kaleidoscope v. Robert Rich*, July 3, 1974, 6–8, 14–15, Margolis-McTernan Papers, box 2. Margolis made no mention of *Johnny Got His Gun* in his oral history.

45. As noted in chapter 17, Trumbo had created Robert Rich Productions in 1958, but it quickly dissolved. To make way for this new company, Frenke and Trumbo dissolved Springfield at the end of May, although Trumbo's relationship with Springfield continued to haunt him with regard to the IRS and the WGAw.

46. UCLA, 71/5.

47. World Entertainers was a business-management and accounting firm; it held contracts, received payments, and disbursed expenses. In their later depositions, both Ben Margolis and Campbell claimed they were unaware of the role World Entertainers played in the making and financing of *Johnny*.

48. Campbell deposition in *Kaleidoscope v. Robert Rich*, 9–28. Harry Margolis was known as "the father of the foreign trust." He did not invent these tax-saving devices, but after he began to use them in the early 1960s, they became very popular, especially among entertainers and physicians in Southern California. Because he charged a high fee for his services, and because the litigation costs could be substantial if the government challenged these trusts, only the very rich could afford them (*LAT*, April 17, 1978, A3, 24–25). He was later indicted for tax fraud; see chapter 25, n. 50.

49. Trumbo to Mark Peterson, April 6, 1970, BCPM, box 2, book 7.

50. Trumbo to colleagues, April 1, 1970, UCLA, 67/1.

51. Campbell deposition in *Kaleidoscope v. Robert Rich*, 72; Trumbo to Mark Peterson, April 6, 1970, BCPM, box 2, book 7.

52. Trumbo to Campbell, May 13, 1970, UCLA, 67/1.

53. Trumbo to Margolis, March 26, 1970, UCLA, 63/8.

54. Trumbo to Sutherland, March 26, 1970, UCLA, 73/10. At some point, Trumbo had added a Christ scene that was not in the book. Christ is fashioning crosses for graves, and Joe is telling him about his problems communicating. Each suggestion Christ offers is met by Joe's statement, "I cannot, because I am missing" this or that body part. Christ finally says, "You need a miracle." This scene indicates Trumbo's belief that many human afflictions are beyond the power of religious belief to alleviate.

55. Interview by Fred Gale, "Something Special," WMCA-NY, August 26, 1971, Paley Center, courtesy of Martin Gostanian.

56. Bottoms, interview with the author, March 7, 2012.

57. E-mail from Jules Brenner to the author, January 26, 2012.

58. Trumbo diary, UCLA, 210/6; Trumbo to Matthau, June 9, 1970, BCPM, box 2, book 8. Matthau, who had suffered a heart attack in 1966, had just completed three movies and was about to start a fourth. The doctor feared the intense shooting schedule and outdoor scenes in *Johnny* would undermine his patient's health.

59. UCLA, 71/10. Frenke bowed out on June 23 because of his ongoing differences with Campbell and because Trumbo was clearly favoring Campbell. Though he was paid in full, Frenke remained embittered about the experi-

ence and angry at Trumbo. Given Kathy Fields's meager acting experience and skills, her casting in the movie (and her pay) is perplexing. It is possible that Trumbo hoped to win future favors from her father, superagent Freddie Fields.

60. Trumbo to Jules Brenner, July 9, 1970, UCLA, 44/2.

24. *Johnny Got His Gun*—The Movie: Principal Photography and Editing

1. *American Cinematographer*, August 1971, 814.
2. Buñuel to Trumbo, July 5, 1970, BCPM, box 2, book 8.
3. Trumbo to Buñuel, n.d., UCLA, 38/1.
4. Interview with Bottoms, March 7, 2012.
5. Interview with Fielding, April 5, 2011.
6. *American Cinematographer*, August 1971, 763.
7. E-mail from Brenner, January 26, 2012.
8. Interview with Serna, April 3, 2012.
9. *American Cinematographer*, August 1971, 814, 822.
10. E-mail from Brenner, January 26, 2012.
11. Trumbo diary, August 22, 1970, UCLA, 210/6.
12. Trumbo to Finn, n.d., UCLA, 69/5.
13. Trumbo diary, August 23, 1970, UCLA, 210/6.
14. Campbell deposition in *Kaleidoscope v. Robert Rich*, 42–44, 47, 82. Ben Margolis later said that his function became keeping down costs and seeing that the picture was completed (deposition in ibid., 21–22).
15. Trumbo to Sol Scope et al., November 1, 1970, UCLA, 71/9.
16. Interview with Bottoms, March 7, 2012.
17. E-mail from Brenner, March 8, 2012.
18. Margolis to Trumbo, October 17, 1970, UCLA, 63/8.
19. Trumbo to Campbell, Finn, Ben and Harry Margolis, Simon Lazarus, Ronald Adolphson, Elaine Fischel, Quentin Breen, Michael Donner, Sol Scope, September 12, 1970, UCLA, 65/2.
20. Ibid.
21. Brenner to Trumbo, September 25, 1970, UCLA, 113/3.
22. Lardner to Trumbo, September 22, 1970, ibid.
23. Trumbo to editors, n.d., BCPM, box 2, book 9.
24. Dornisch to Trumbo, n.d., UCLA, 114/9.
25. Minutes of meeting, November 16, 1970, UCLA, 116/24.
26. Fischel to Trumbo and Campbell, December 24, 1970, BCPM, box 2, book 10. Apparently, Popularch Productions was an investment consortium formed by Harry Margolis, but I was unable to discover when he did so. In their respective depositions for the *Kaleidoscope* lawsuit, Ben Margolis and Campbell claimed they knew nothing about it. In his response to interrogatories in that suit, Harry Margolis stated that Popularch had borrowed $350,000 from the Anglo Dutch Capital Company in July 1970, giving as security the personal guarantees of the individual Popularch partners. It was a demand-type obligation at 10 percent interest per annum, with the interest payable monthly. The loan was assumed by ALMS, N.V., in November. Popularch then borrowed more than $2 million from ALMS between November 1970 and November

1971, which was fully repaid in 1972 (response to second set of interrogatories, *Kaleidoscope v. Robert Rich*, June 28, 1974).

27. A copy of this print is at the Academy Film Archive (4319-4). I am deeply grateful to May Haduong for arranging my viewing of it.

28. Trumbo to Bottoms, February 8, 1971, UCLA, 113/3.

29. Trumbo to Campbell et al., BCPM, box 2, book 12.

30. Notes for a letter to Perry Gray, January 28, 1971, UCLA, 73/3; Trumbo to Bottoms, February 8, 1971, UCLA, 113/3.

31. Interview in *Dalton Trumbo: Rebel in Hollywood: The Story behind Johnny Got His Gun*, written, produced, and directed by Robert Fischer (Fiction Factory, 2006).

32. UCLA, 43/4.

33. Trumbo to Elaine B. Fischel, March 7, 1971, UCLA, 64/3.

34. Notes for a letter to Perry Gray, January 28, 1971, UCLA, 73/3.

35. Bessie to Harold Hays, August 6, 1970, UCLA, 128/1. Bessie was referring to "The Happy Jack Fish Hatchery Papers," *Esquire*, January 1970, 73–77, 166–74.

36. Jerry Zinnamon, "Diary of a Dead Bavarian," *Esquire*, December 1970, 72.

37. Zinnamon to Bessie, August 17, 1970, UCLA, 128/1.

38. Zinnamon to Erickson, September 9, 1970, ibid.

39. Ibid., November 6, 1970, UCLA, 114/2.

40. Zinnamon to Trumbo, November 6, 1970, UCLA, 128/1.

41. Trumbo to Zinnamon, November 17, 1970, ibid.

42. Trumbo to Erickson, November 17, 1970, ibid.

43. Bessie to Trumbo, November 6, 1970, UCLA, 114/2.

44. Cleo to Alvah and Sylviane Bessie, November 11, 1970, UCLA, 114/2. For Bessie's account of the incident, see Cook, *Dalton Trumbo*, 297.

45. Erickson to Trumbo, November 24, 1970, UCLA, 114/2.

25. *Johnny Got His Gun*—The Movie: Distribution and Exhibition

The epigraph is from Cook, *Dalton Trumbo*, 303–4.

1. Trumbo to Investors, December 21, 1970, UCLA, 44/2. Rugoff's family owned a chain of theaters, and he had established his distribution company in 1963.

2. Trumbo to Elaine B. Fischel, March 7, 1971, UCLA, 64/3.

3. Trumbo to Lazarus, April 23, 1971, UCLA, 63/6.

4. Trumbo to Investors, January 27, 1971, UCLA, 65/2.

5. UCLA, 64/2.

6. Trumbo to Fischel, March 3, 1971, ibid.

7. UCLA, 69/5. In fact, Buñuel had not seen the film prior to communicating with the Cannes officials. Trumbo had sent him a telegram, asking Buñuel to find "an honorable way" to approach festival officials "about accepting the film before you have seen it. I am told it will help us greatly. If not I understand." John Baxter, *Buñuel* (New York: Carroll and Graf, 1994), 298. According to Baxter, when Buñuel finally did see the film, he thought it was "too academic." However, the Trumbo Papers contain an excerpt from an undated letter from Buñuel in which the director stated: "I liked *Johnny* enormously. The film has

the power of the novel, as well as its devastating impact and the moments of very great and high emotion. . . . The impression delivered by the film is one of the strongest I have felt" (UCLA, 50/7).

8. Pete Hamill, "Dalton Gets His Gun," *New York Post*, April 6, 1971, clipping in UCLA, 50/7. Almost four months later, Trumbo wrote to Hamill and thanked him profusely. Trumbo to Hamill, July 30, 1971, UCLA, 73/5.

9. Cinemation had been founded in 1966. Its early releases were "shock dramas": *Girl on a Chain Gang, Teenage Mother, I Drink Your Blood, I Eat Your Skin, Mondo Cane, Africa Blood and Guts*, and *The Man from O.R.G.Y.* But it also distributed two highly regarded foreign films: *Juliet of the Spirits* and *Red Desert*.

10. Trumbo to Lazarus, April 23, 1971, UCLA, 63/6; Fox offer, UCLA, 116/7.

11. UCLA, 58/3.

12. Trumbo to Finn, May 3, 1971, UCLA, 64/1.

13. Margolis deposition, *Kaleidoscope v. Robert Rich*, 59–60. Two years later, Trumbo wrote to Margolis: "*Johnny* placed both of us in an absolutely impossible relationship of conflicting interests, experience, responsibility, and professional understanding. Since neither of us is tolerant to the point of self-abnegation nor humble to the point of sainthood, the wonder is not that we merely wounded, but that we didn't kill each other. . . . [N]ever—not even in the bitterest of our disagreements—have I doubted your word or your good faith" (July 3, 1973, UCLA, 208/5).

14. Trumbo to Sol Scope, n.d., UCLA, 63/4. Indeed, at this point, one needed a scorecard to keep track of the attorney lineup. Robert Rich Productions (Trumbo and Campbell) was represented by Aubrey Finn. The Investors were represented by Ben and Harry Margolis and Sol Scope. World Entertainers and the other foreign corporations were represented by Harry Margolis and Sol Scope. Trumbo was represented, in financial matters, by Harry Margolis and Sol Scope.

15. Trumbo to Finn, May 3, 1971, UCLA, 64/1.

16. Trumbo to Freddie Fields, May 6, 1971, ibid.

17. UCLA, 69/5.

18. Lazarus to Trumbo, May 8, 1971, UCLA 116/7.

19. Trumbo to Lazarus, May 10, 1971, UCLA, 63/6.

20. *NYT*, May 15, 1971, 20; *LAT*, May 17, 1971, E1.

21. Untitled, undated, UCLA, 81/5.

22. Untitled, undated, ibid.

23. *DV*, May 18, 1971, 3.

24. *LAT*, May 17, 1971, E1, 12.

25. *LAT*, July 19, 1971, A6.

26. *LAT*, June 1, 1971, F15.

27. UCLA, 73/4.

28. Trumbo to creditors, July 15, 1971, UCLA, 119/2.

29. Trumbo to Weldon, August 30, 1971, ibid.

30. Trumbo to Margolis, August 30, 1971, UCLA, 119/30. Margolis later claimed he had no idea how the Cinemation money was distributed (deposition for *Kaleidoscope v. Robert Rich*, 61).

31. Interview by Fred Gale, "Something Special," WMCA-NY, August 26, 1971, Paley Center.

32. "Par de la l'inhuman," *Jeune Cinéma* 55 (May 1971): 104–5.

33. Interview by Larry Bensky, October 20, 1971, Paley Center.

34. *HR*, July 15, 1971, 3.

35. *New York Daily News*, August 5, 1971, clipping in UCLA, 50/7.

36. John Schubeck, WABC-TV, August 4, 1971, ibid.

37. *Newsday*, August 5, 1971, ibid.

38. *New York Post*, August 5, 1971, ibid.

39. *National Observer*, August 23, 1971, ibid.

40. *NYT*, August 5, 1971, 25.

41. *New York Daily News*, August 6, 1971, 57.

42. *Saturday Review*, August 28, 1971, 48.

43. *Time*, August 30, 1971, 52.

44. *New Yorker*, August 7, 1971, 65–66. A few years later, contemplating the negative reviews, Trumbo wrote: "I feel about critics the same way I feel about proctologists" (undated, handwritten note, ca. December 1974, UCLA, 208/8).

45. *"Johnny Got His Gun* comments from public after screening of film," 9362-1, Academy Film Archive.

46. *Sacramento Bee*, March 26, 1980, F1.

47. "Trumbo Remembered," KCET, 1983.

48. E-mail from Sutherland, August 16, 2012. Edmund Wilson, *To the Finland Station: A Study in the Writing and Acting of History* (New York: Harcourt, Brace, 1940), was republished by Doubleday in 1947 (hardcover) and again in 1953 and 1955 (paperback). It was republished by Farrar, Straus and Giroux in 1972, with a new introduction by Wilson that was, in effect, an apologia of his "too hopeful bias" toward, and idealized view of, the Russian Revolution (v–vi).

49. Irwin Silber, "Two Good Antiwar Movies," *Guardian*, August 16, 1972, 14; Trumbo to Silber, draft, ca. September 1972, UCLA, 210/2.

50. Trumbo to Scope, August 27, 1971, and Scope to Trumbo, September 9, 1971, UCLA, 64/3. In 1975 Harry Margolis, two of his associates, and Banco Popular Antilliano (Netherlands Antilles) were indicted on twenty-four counts of tax fraud. Government prosecutors alleged that the offshore trusts created by Margolis were shams. At a preliminary hearing, the judge threw out eighteen of the counts, and at his trial, Margolis was acquitted of the other six. However, when Elaine Fischel refused a court order to produce some documents, claiming that they were protected by the attorney-client and work-product privileges, the judge cited her for contempt. Her conviction and sentence were upheld by the court of appeals. *LAT*, October 1, 1977, A28; *LAT*, October 4, 1977, D8; *LAT*, April 17, 1978, A3, 24–25; *In the Matter of Elaine B. Fischel, Contemner-Appellant. United States of America v. Harry Margolis, et al.*, USCA, 9th District, June 13, 1977.

51. Dalton Trumbo, talk at UCLA, May 17, 1972, UCLA Communications Studies Archives, www.youtube.com/watch?v=YhAXSDpvqVU.

52. *HR*, January 13, 1972, 1, 12.

53. UCLA, 69/Margolis folder.

54. *HR*, July 21, 1972, 16. The suit was settled, two years later, for $60,000.

55. As a result of Campbell's increasingly erratic behavior, Mitzi separated from him in the spring of 1973 and subsequently filed for divorce. They had one daughter, Samantha, who was born in April 1972.

56. Carter, who was then governor of Georgia, had seen the movie at the Atlanta Film Festival. Afterward, he said the novel should be sent to every member of the government, military, and United Nations and should be read by every American.

57. *Sacramento Bee*, March 26, 1980, F1; *WV*, November 29, 1978; Dave Barry, "'Johnny' . . . A Second Coming," *LAT Calendar*, March 5, 1978, 35. See Campbell interviews at College of Marin, ca. March 1980; KMTF-TV, Fresno, April 11, 1980; KJEO-TV, Fresno, April 10, 1980; KCRA-TV, Sacramento, March 23, 1980; and KAIL-TV, Fresno, April 11, 1980. All the television interviews are held at the Academy Film Archive. Campbell had hoped the Martin film would serve as a pilot for a television series of half-hour films about different cities, but he could not find a buyer: those who saw the film did not find Martin very funny.

58. After years of uncertainty about who held the title to the movie, it was acquired from World Entertainers by Kirk Hallam of Roxbury Entertainment and issued in DVD format by Shout Factory (2009), accompanied by a very good documentary.

59. Trumbo to Cook, February 18, 1976, UCLA, 81/7.

60. *Esquire*, April 1976, 77, UCLA, 56/4.

61. A filmed version of the play, with a different cast, was issued on DVD in 2008 by Greenwood Hill Productions.

62. John Patterson, "Boys from the Blacklist," June 11, 2004,

26. The Final Years

The second epigraph is from *Chicago Daily News*, September 2, 1971, UCLA, 50/7.

1. Correspondence in King Brothers Collection, box 57, MHL.

2. Trumbo to King, November 11, 1971, UCLA, 116/4.

3. UCLA, 119/3.

4. Trumbo to Christopher, Thanksgiving Day 1971, CTP.

5. *Newsweek*, August 9, 1971, 70–71.

6. Trumbo to Burke, November 12, 1971, UCLA, 159/8.

7. Van Dusen to Trumbo, January 3, 1972, UCLA, 124/3. The volume also included "The Devil in the Book" and "Honor Bright and All that Jazz."

8. Trumbo to Ben Margolis, ca. October or November 1973, UCLA, 64/7.

9. Eddie Lewis Papers, box 4, AHC.

10. Trumbo to Lewis, July 24, 1972, ibid.

11. Ibid.

12. Lane to Lewis, July 6, 1972, ibid.

13. Trumbo to Huguette Kline, October 5, 1973, UCLA, 192/3.

14. Frankenheimer interview with Champlin, May 1992, tape 7/21, MHL; *John Frankenheimer: A Conversation*, 185.

15. *NYT*, November 8, 1973, 60.

16. *Rolling Stone*, December 20, 1973, 13.

17. *Chicago Sun-Times*, November 20, 1973, www.rogerebert.com/apps/pbcs.dll/article?AID=/19731120/REVIEWS/311200301/1023.

18. *New Yorker*, November 19, 1973, 236.

19. Correspondence in UCLA, 113/5.

20. Arthur Laurents, *Original Story By: A Memoir of Broadway and Hollywood* (New York: Knopf, 2000), 263–64.

21. Michael Feeley Callan, *Robert Redford: The Biography* (New York: Knopf, 2011), 192–94.

22. "The Way We Were" notes, August 12, 1972, UCLA, 180/1, 179/2.

23. Pollack to Trumbo, August 25, 1972, UCLA, 123/25.

24. Trumbo to Pollack, September 22, 1972, ibid.

25. Callan, *Robert Redford*, 194.

26. Laurents, *Original Story By*, 272–73.

27. Trumbo to Roger Lewis, October 10, 1972, UCLA, 116/15. On the cover of the envelope containing a copy of this script, Trumbo wrote: "Written in anger and under pressure. . . . Never made because script no good" (UCLA, 157/2). A few months earlier, Pauline Kael, Trumbo's nemesis, had negatively reviewed four of those films, condemning their exploitative use of violence. Ben Yagoda, *About Town: The New Yorker and the World It Made* (New York: Scribner, 2000), 354.

28. Financial records, UCLA, 56/12.

29. Undated note, UCLA, 58/12.

30. Henri Charrière, *Papillon*, trans. Patrick O'Brien (London: Granada Paperback, 1970), vi, 431.

31. Notes on meeting with Schaffner, October 16, 1972, UCLA, 87/4.

32. Notes, October 20, 1972, UCLA, 87/4.

33. UCLA, 92/3.

34. Trumbo to Schaffner, December 1972, ibid.

35. Trumbo to David Wardlow, July 20, 1973, UCLA, 208/5.

36. Note, UCLA, 58/12.

37. Dalton Trumbo, "Papillon," December 31, 1972, UCLA, 92/3.

38. Christopher Trumbo, "Revisions," April 10, 1973, UCLA, 92/1.

39. Semple to Trumbo, September 24, 1973, and Trumbo to Semple, September 26, 1973, ibid.

40. *NYT*, December 17, 1973, 59.

41. *LAT*, December 19, 1973, E1.

42. *New Yorker*, December 24, 1973, 72.

43. Trumbo to Scope, August 27, 1973, UCLA, 64/7.

44. Scope to Trumbo, November 9, 1973, UCLA, 63/1.

45. Cleo to Connell, ca. July 1973, July 30, 1973, and ca. November 1973, UCLA, 213/3. Two years later, a very ill Trumbo signed a conditional sales agreement with Presentaciones Musicales, S.A. The latter agreed to pay the Trumbos $400,000 for their house, lot, furniture, paintings, and artifacts. The Trumbos received an immediate cash payment of $80,000 and the remainder in the form of interest-bearing (6.6 percent) bonds, payable in ten years. The company held a note receivable for the value of the assets purchased.

46. Kazan said: "I didn't find any heroes or villains in life, so I didn't write any. We're all victims" (*Tuscaloosa News*, March 5, 1972, 14B). During the 1930s and 1940s Maltz and Blankfort were the closest of friends. After Maltz was blacklisted, Blankfort fronted for him on *Broken Arrow* (Twentieth Century–Fox, 1950). However, Maltz cut off all relations when Blankfort appeared before the Committee on Un-American Activities (January 28, 1952), named his cousin and ex-wife, and congratulated the committee on the work it was

doing. Kazan was a notorious figure among the blacklistees. He and Edward Dmytryk were the most universally loathed of the informers. At the time of his testimony in 1952, he was the most famous and well-paid director in Hollywood and on Broadway. He named names and then took out an advertisement in the *New York Times* defending that act.

47. Navasky, *Naming Names*, 389.

48. Ibid., 392–94.

49. Maltz to Trumbo, December 23, 1972. All the originals of this correspondence are in CTP; selections are reprinted in Navasky, *Naming Names*, 394–99, and Cook, *Dalton Trumbo*, 310–17.

50. Trumbo to Maltz, December 29, 1972, CTP. Scott had died on Christmas Day, and five days later, both Trumbo and Maltz spoke at his memorial.

51. Maltz to Trumbo, January 3, 1973, CTP.

52. Trumbo to Maltz, January 12, 1973, CTP.

53. Victor Navasky, "To Name or Not to Name," *NYT Magazine*, March 25, 1973, 111.

54. Maltz, *Citizen Writer in Retrospect*, 1008.

55. Albert Maltz Collection, 17/8, WC.

56. Richard Corliss, "The Pen Is Mightier than the 'Gun,'" *Village Voice*, September 2, 1971, 49–50.

57. Richard Corliss, "Trials and Traumas: Dalton Trumbo," in *The Hollywood Screenwriters: A Film Comment Book*, ed. Richard Corliss (New York: Avon Books, 1972), 169–70; reprinted in Richard Corliss, *Talking Pictures: Screenwriters in the American Cinema, 1927–1973* (Woodstock, NY: Overlook Press, 1974).

58. Trumbo to Corliss, February 14, 1973, and Corliss to Trumbo, March 10, 1973, UCLA, 211/2.

59. UCLA, 211/2.

60. Trumbo to Cameron, April 17, 1961, UCLA, 127/4. There is an eighteen-page typescript titled "Grieben" and dated November 28, 1960, in the Ian McLellan Hunter Papers, 4/4, MHL.

61. Trumbo to Jaffe, June 6, 1972, UCLA, 159/8. At the time of this letter, Trumbo had renegotiated his contract with Bantam, which gave him a $10,000 advance to be followed by payments totaling another $40,000.

62. Trumbo to Wilson, January 11 or 12, 1974, MWP, 47/3.

63. Since then, many thinkers on the subject of morality have raised the same doubts Trumbo expressed. Steven Pinker, for example, recently wrote: "The human moral sense can excuse any atrocity in the minds of those who commit it, and it furnishes them with motives for acts of violence that brings them no tangible benefit." Pinker concludes that people motivated by a moral cause have visited "incalculable suffering" on the world. Steven Pinker, *The Better Angels of Our Nature: Why Violence Has Declined* (New York: Viking, 2011), 622.

64. Dalton Trumbo, *Night of the Aurochs*, ed. Robert Kirsch (New York: Viking, 1979), 109–10, 126.

65. Dalton Trumbo, talk at UCLA, May 17, 1972, UCLA Communications Studies Archives, www.youtube.com/watch?v=YhAXSDpvqVU.

66. Trumbo to Wilson, January 11 or 12, 1974, MWP, 47/3.

67. Trumbo to Robert S. Muehlenbeck, October 19, 1974, UCLA, 58/5.

68. Trumbo, *Night of the Aurochs*, ix, x.

69. Note, UCLA, 58/12.

70. Trumbo to Tracey Olsen, ca. July 1973, UCLA, 208/5.

71. Trumbo to Allen, August 19, 1975, in the possession of Mitzi Trumbo.

72. MWP, 47/3.

73. *EST International Limited and Dalton Trumbo v. Dino De Laurentiis Corp., et al.*, Superior Court for County of Los Angeles, No. C127076.

74. *DV*, May 16, 1975, 1; *HR*, May 16, 1975, 3.

75. Trumbo to Seaton, January 19, 1976, UCLA, 81/7.

76. *WGAw News*, May 1976, 21, 23; MWP, 10/9A.

77. "A Conversation with Dalton Trumbo," Keith Berwick's "Speculation," November 17, 1970, UCLA Film and Television Archives.

78. *LAT*, September 11, 1976, 1.

79. *NYT*, September 11, 1976, 17. For similar opening sentences, see *Time*, September 20, 1976, 69, and *Newsweek*, September 20, 1976, 65.

80. Note for Fernando Ghia, December 28, 1975, UCLA, 195/5.

81. "Dalton Trumbo Discusses Screenwriter's Task," *Los Angeles Herald-Examiner*, December 22, 1968, D7.

27. Postmortem

The epigraphs are from speech of March 22, 1992, accepting the WGAw's posthumous award for Trumbo's contribution to *Roman Holiday*, in the possession of Mitzi Trumbo; and interview in "Trumbo: 100th Birthday Video," Avalon Theatre, Grand Junction, CO, December 9, 2005, courtesy of Ken Johnson.

1. According to Bill Nichols, who interviewed him between 1980 and 1982, Douglas "was eager to take credit for 'breaking the blacklist,' but much less eager to describe how much aid he offer [*sic*] or advantage he took . . . of blacklisted writers" in those years. Letter to the editor, *Cineaste* 38, no. 2 (Spring 2013): 41; e-mail to the author, March 26, 2013.

2. *DV*, December 5, 1988, 2, 4.

3. Cleo to WGAw, ca. March 1991, CTP. Preminger's widow told her husband's biographer, Chris Fujiwara, that the guild gave Douglas "a great award for being the first person to break the blacklist, when in fact he hadn't been." E-mail, August 21, 2011. Victoria Preminger, the director's daughter, told me that her family remains "very strongly" opposed to Douglas's claim. E-mail, August 31, 2011.

4. *LAT*, February 9, 2002, B23. I was the curator of that exhibit.

5. *LAT*, February 16, 2002, B22. One week later, Douglas wrote to Cleo: "Your letter to the L.A. Times made me very sad. . . . I'm very proud of the fact that I was the first one to break the blacklist" (February 26, 2002, CTP).

6. Christopher Trumbo, *Trumbo: Red, White and Blacklisted* (New York: Playscripts, 2007), 41; Douglas to Christopher, November 11, 2003, CTP.

7. SACLA to director, March 27, 1956, COMPIC. Prime incorrectly states that there were rumors floating around the production that Trumbo had written the script (*Hollywood Exiles in Europe*, 69).

8. Cook, *Dalton Trumbo*, 243–44.

9. Trumbo to Douglas, n.d. [ca. 1959], Ian McLellan Hunter Collection, 4/4, MHL.

10. *NYT*, January 20, 1960, 8.

11. *NYT*, January 21, 1960, 26.

12. Lardner to Hunter, January 22, 1960, Hunter Collection, 4/5, MHL.

13. Trumbo to Hunter, May 24, 1963, ibid., 4/4. In October 1962 Trumbo had unexpectedly received a $500 loan repayment from Paul Jarrico. Trumbo noted in his reply that nonpayment of the thousands of dollars he had loaned over the years "has been the foundation stone of my life. To see it nudged aside, and my rule even threatened with subversion, is a bit traumatic." Trumbo to Jarrico, October 17, 1962, UCLA, 221/3.

14. Trumbo to Hunter, August 28, 1963, in the possession of Mitzi Trumbo.

15. C. Robert Jennings, "The Hollywood Ten, Plus Twenty," *LAT*, September 3, 1967, A14.

16. Howard Suber, "Dalton Trumbo's Real Role in 'Roman Holiday,'" *LAT*, August 19, 1991, F3.

17. Cook, *Dalton Trumbo*, 225, 295–96.

18. Conversation with Kate Lardner, July 30, 2012.

19. E-mails from Joe Lardner, August 16 and 17, 2012.

20. Bernard Dick, *Radical Innocence: A Critical Study of the Hollywood Ten* (Lexington: University Press of Kentucky, 1989), 203.

21. Larry Ceplair, "Who Wrote What? A Tale of a Blacklisted Writer and His Front," *Cineaste* 18, no. 2 (1991): 18–21.

22. Conversation with Steven Barr, August 21, 2012. Barr told me he may have cited Dick's book as corroborating evidence.

23. Suber, "Dalton Trumbo's Real Role"; "Dalton Trumbo Asked Me to Front for Him," *LAT Calendar*, August 25, 1991, 19, 85.

24. Speech in the possession of Mitzi Trumbo.

25. See Ceplair, *The Marxist and the Movies*, 237–42.

26. Cleo to Lardner, June 1997, CTP.

27. Lardner to Cleo, June 22, 1997, in the possession of Mitzi Trumbo. In his memoir *I'd Hate Myself in the Morning*, published in 2000, Lardner states that Trumbo wrote the first draft of the screenplay (140).

28. WGAw printout, in the author's possession.

29. Blacklist Credits Committee: Dalton Trumbo Considerations, n.d. [ca. September 1999], CTP.

30. E-mail from Tim Hunter, November 25, 2012.

31. Notes, December 21, 2010, CTP.

32. Reprinted in *Written By*, January 2012, 38.

33. Mike Fleming, "WGA Restores Blacklisted Writer Dalton Trumbo's Screen Credit on 'Roman Holiday,'" www.deadline.com/2011/12/wga-restores-blacklisted-writer-dalton-trumbo's-screen-credit-on-roman-holiday.

34. *LAT*, December 20, 2011, D2.

35. *NYT*, December 21, 2011, C3.

36. Amendment 2 prohibited Colorado governments and municipalities from specifically protecting the rights of people of "homosexual, lesbian or bisexual orientation, conduct, practices or relationships." It was later ruled unconstitutional by the US Supreme Court in *Romer v. Evans*, 517 U. S., 620 (1996).

37. Speech in the possession of Mitzi Trumbo. See also www.dailycamera.com/features/cd_20341226/dalton-trumbo-fountain-free-speech-cu.

38. Cook, *Dalton Trumbo*, 40.

39. E-mail from Ken Johnson, May 4, 2013.

40. Richard Ott to Trumbo, February 17, 1976, UCLA, 171/15.

41. "Dalton Trumbo: Writer, Myth-Maker, Radical Blacklist-Breaker," *Grand Valley Gazette*, February–March 1976, 15.

42. *Daily Sentinel*, December 8, 1991, 1, 9.

43. E-mail from Blozvich to Christopher, March 4, 2005, courtesy of Ken Johnson; e-mail from Johnson, May 4, 2013.

44. Interview with Blozvich, September 18, 2012.

45. Quoted in Davis, *125 People*, 57–58.

46. *Daily Sentinel*, December 8, 2005, B1.

47. Interview by Ryan Warner, *Colorado Matters*, KCFR, December 27, 2005.

48. *Grand Junction Free Press*, October 15, 2007, 2.

49. Ken Johnson, "Trumbo Talk," DVD, n.d.

50. George Orbanek, "Dalton Trumbo Represents Lousy 'Martyr' for Freedom," *Daily Sentinel*, October 7, 2007, 3B. He was referring to the letters Trumbo gave to the FBI during World War II.

51. *Grand Junction Free Press*, October 5, 2007, A12.

52. Johnson, "Trumbo Talk. "

53. Maltz, *Citizen Writer in Retrospect*, 692.

54. Quoted in Cook, *Dalton Trumbo*, 276.

55. Hanson, *Dalton Trumbo, Hollywood Rebel*, 205.

56. Leszek Kołakowski, "The History of the Left," in *Is God Happy? Selected Essays* (New York: Basic Books, 2013), 44.

57. See www.trotsky.net/trotsky_year/trotsky_testament.html.

Index

John Gilbert: The Last of the Silent Film Stars
Eve Golden

Saul Bass: Anatomy of Film Design
Jan-Christopher Horak

Pola Negri: Hollywood's First Femme Fatale
Mariusz Kotowski

Mamoulian: Life on Stage and Screen
David Luhrssen

Maureen O'Hara: The Biography
Aubrey Malone

My Life as a Mankiewicz: An Insider's Journey through Hollywood
Tom Mankiewicz and Robert Crane

Hawks on Hawks
Joseph McBride

William Wyler: The Life and Films of Hollywood's Most Celebrated Director
Gabriel Miller

Raoul Walsh: The True Adventures of Hollywood's Legendary Director
Marilyn Ann Moss

Charles Walters: The Director Who Made Hollywood Dance
Brent Phillips

Some Like It Wilder: The Life and Controversial Films of Billy Wilder
Gene D. Phillips

Ann Dvorak: Hollywood's Forgotten Rebel
Christina Rice

Arthur Penn: American Director
Nat Segaloff

Claude Rains: An Actor's Voice
David J. Skal with Jessica Rains

Buzz: The Life and Art of Busby Berkeley
Jeffrey Spivak

Victor Fleming: An American Movie Master
Michael Sragow

Thomas Ince: Hollywood's Independent Pioneer
Brian Taves

Carl Theodor Dreyer and Ordet: *My Summer with the Danish Filmmaker*
Jan Wahl

CPSIA information can be obtained at www.ICGtesting.com
Printed in the USA
BVOW04*0340021214

377178BV00001B/1/P